THE FIRST KINGDOM

MIGRATION

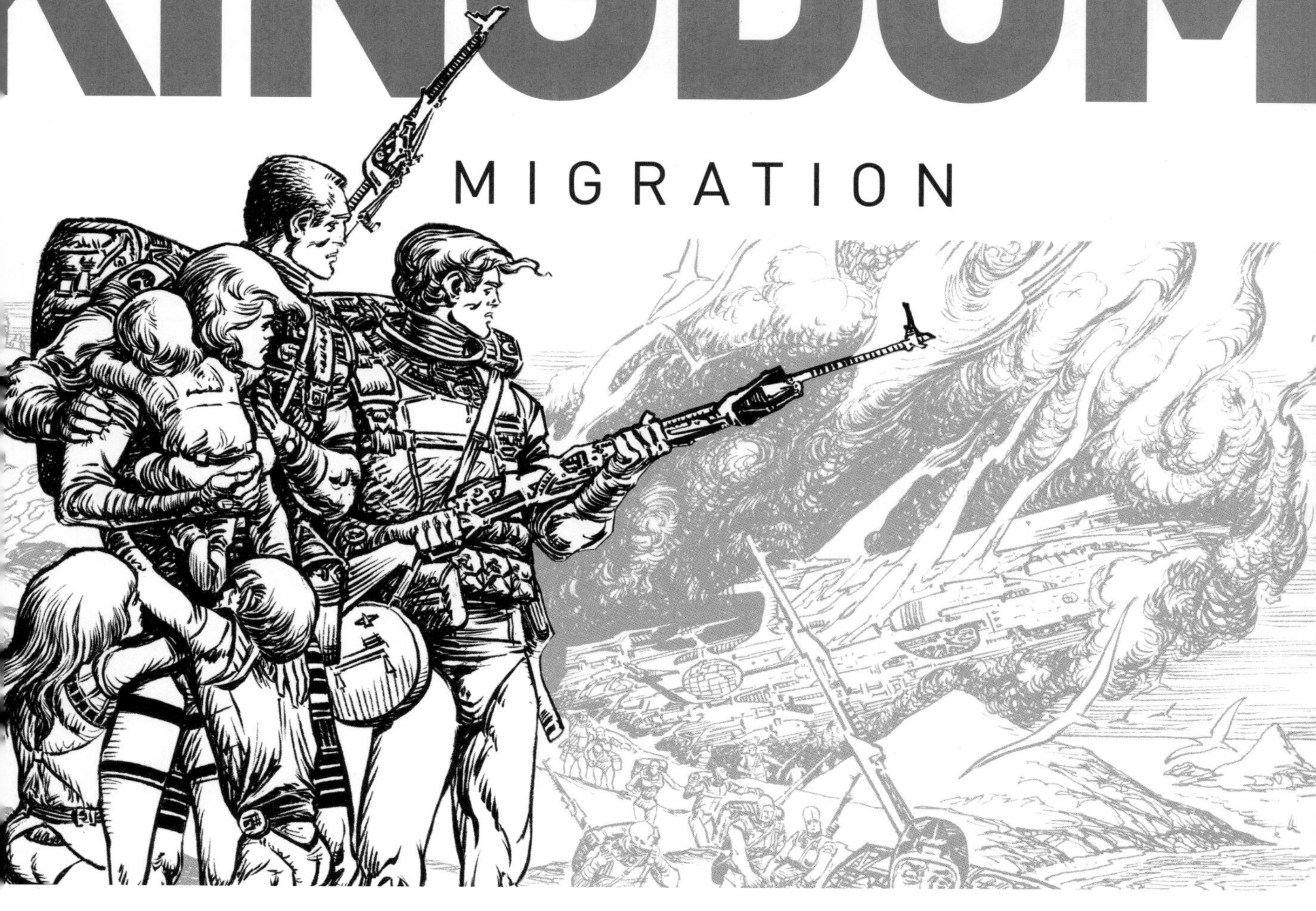

Written and Illustrated by

Jack Katz

TITAN COMICS

ACKNOWLEDGMENTS

Jack Katz: First and foremost, I would like to thank Caroline Gold for her steadfast friendship and support and for helping me through the difficult years that it took me to put together *The First Kingdom*. Thanks also to my friends and former students Bob Gill, Brian Miller and Darren Kessler for their extraordinary encouragement and support. A special thanks to my long-time friend, Harvey Myman, and to my always-resourceful agent, Peter Beren. I am especially grateful to the talented crew at Titan Comics for their hard work and belief in Trilogy now being published in complete form for the first time anywhere, including Nick Landau, Chris Teather, Steve White and the whole Titan gang.

Titan Comics would like to thank Peter Beren, Paula Burns and Brian Miller for their help in the making of this volume.

Read the entire **six-book saga**, now complete for the first time.

Volume 1: The Birth of Tundran
Available Now

Volume 2: The Galaxy Hunters
Available Now

Volume 3: Vengeance
Available Now

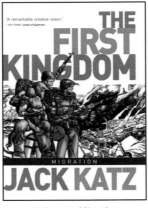

Volume 4: Migration
Available Now

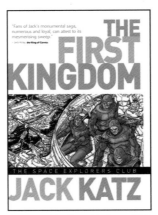

Volume 5: The Space Explorers Club
On Sale Sept. 2014

Volume 6: Destiny
On Sale Dec. 2014

THE FIRST KINGDOM

THE FIRST KINGDOM
VOLUME 4
MIGRATION
ISBN: 9781782760139

Published by Titan Comics
A division of Titan Publishing Group Ltd.
144 Southwark St., London. SE1 0UP

A CIP catalogue record for this title is available from the British Library.
First edition: July 2014.
10 9 8 7 6 5 4 3 2 1

Printed in China.
Titan Comics. TC0032

TITAN COMICS

COLLECTION EDITOR STEVE WHITE
ART EDITOR ANDREW JAMES
COLLECTION DESIGNER DAN BURA

REMASTERED EDITION
Artwork Scans:
Howard Brainen & Two Cat Digital
Artwork Restoration:
Peter James
Remastered Lettering:
Gabriela Houston

INTRO-DUCTION

by **WILL EISNER** 1986

At a time in the development of comics book, when the form seems to be approaching a rendezvous with respectability, *The First Kingdom* series is nearing completion. In total it will comprise 24 volumes of complex and stunning art.

As far as I know there is nothing quite like this effort around and its creator, Jack Katz, deserves applause and congratulations. This work represents one of the most awesome undertakings in modern comic book history. Think of it! For about 11 years one of the field's more competent draftsmen has devoted himself to the creation of one huge tapestry. Here is a work filled with science-fiction imagery, built around a philosophical chronicle and told with the scope and fervor of a medieval religious mural.

Years ago Jack showed me the first pages – the original art boards. He was just starting on the project and I commented admiringly on the great rendering of his always-classic anatomy. I was, I confess, more impressed then with the fact that

a well-regarded professional had the courage to leave the security of the establishment comic book marketplace and strike out for a financially uncertain independence. To me this was very important because he was, by example, helping to establish a beachhead for the 'free agent' comic book artist and writer who happily populates the field today. Certainly he carved a position for the graphic novel concept and helped establish a category for work produced with a literary intent.

In the years that followed, Jack fulfilled the promise he made himself and showed that a devotion to an inner vision can surely pay off. His books are collected by a substantial core of followers and his art has improved to a point where they can be 'study pieces' in my classroom. The marvellous thing is that Jack is still 'growing' and I look forward to his next undertaking.

Previously printed in *The First Kingdom* #23

FORE-WORD

by Alex Toth 1983

Jack's drawings of his youth, while we were students at New York City's High School of Industrial Art, forecast the mythic work I address here – his long running series, *The First Kingdom* – a work apart, its own, in and of its own world; one requiring and given single-minded dedication, and also requiring the denial of other, perhaps more commercially profitable work along the way.

Thus, to do such a work over so long a period excludes access to the steady flow of needed dollars from shorter 'outside' comics accounts to sustain oneself over the long haul. For many, there simply isn't the time, energy, concentration, nor (perhaps) the desire to do so; I, for one, could not and would not resist the

" I tip my hat to Jack for, first, conceiving of so immense a creation and, second, for sticking to it, no matter how tough a grind it is. "

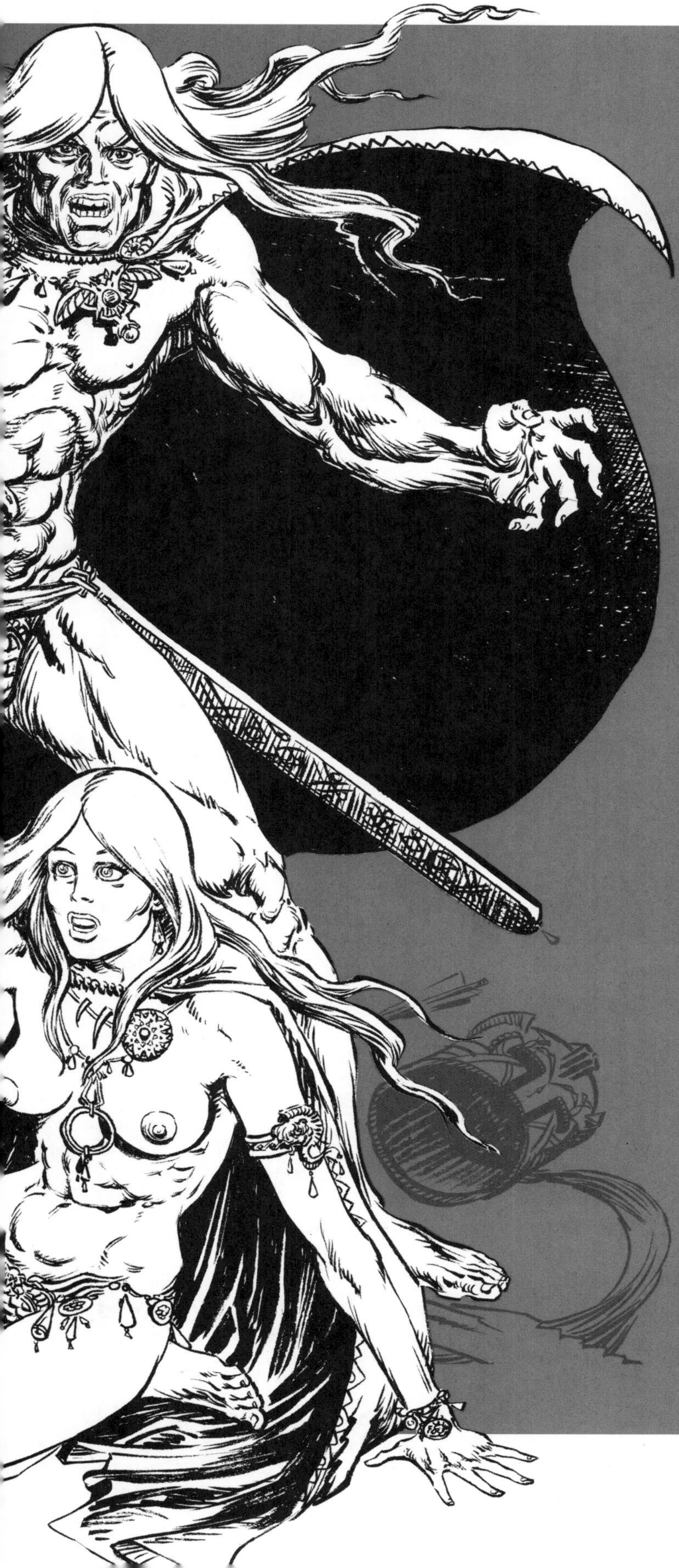

seductive respite to another, shorter strip/story assignment of a different hue to refresh myself en route to that too-far-off twenty-fourth episode finale. That 'change', helpful in preserving a modicum of sanity, health and fresh viewpoint (sez me!)…

So, I tip my hat to Jack for, first, conceiving of so immense a creation and, second, for sticking to it, no matter how tough a grind it is; grind on he does – to the inevitable finish of issue #24. Ah, but then what, I wonder? Will he launch another multiple-episode venture? Or can/will he scale down his stories to one-shots or anthologies?

Whatever he chooses to do, he will no doubt enjoy the (hopefully considerable) royalties from the constantly repeated body of work of this series for the rest of his years – a worthy investment , then, for all his damned hard work, to be sure! The prospect of future color editions should increase *Kingdom*'s attractiveness in the marketplace and prolong its lifespan.

All the while, I'm certain Jack will be planning/plotting new vehicles for our tarnished medium – after a much-needed rest, that is – and his reassessment of comics' ever-changing present and future directions – though I suspect he will always go his own way, no matter prognostications. He has thus far, has he not? I applaud that – it may well be, aside from being S.I.A. alumni, our only common trait, a trait we admired in our personal artist heroes. Neither of us have ever run with the herd, causing more problems than profit – more pain than popular support. Right or wrong (in others' eyes), it's the only way we know to go! So – for my own series: *Bravo For Adventure*!

Originally printed in *The First Kingdom* #19

THE FIRST KINGDOM
CHARACTERS

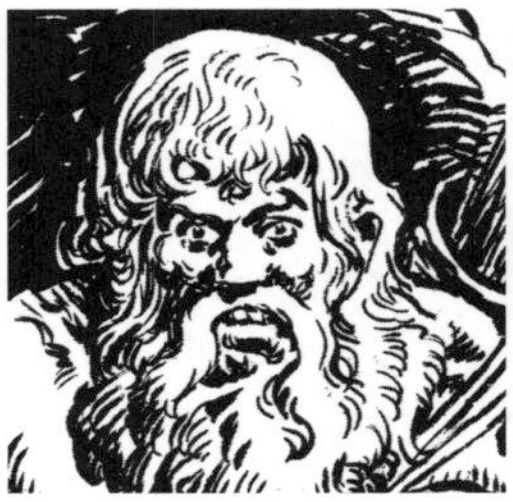
ACCROMOS

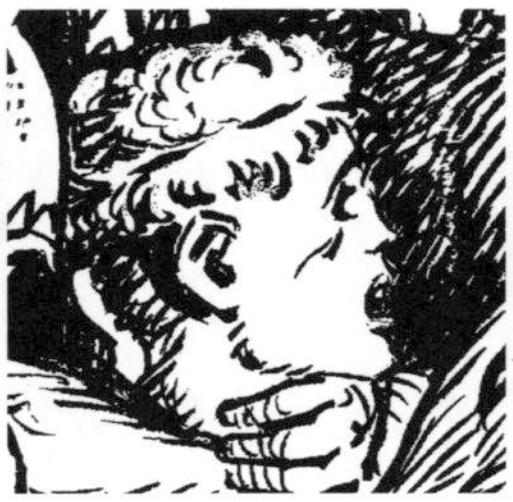
ALANDON

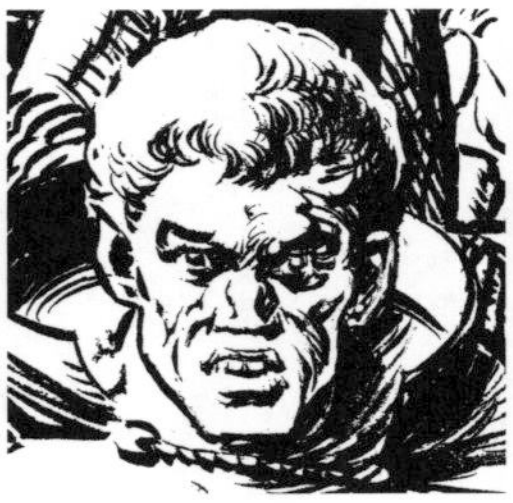
CATARA

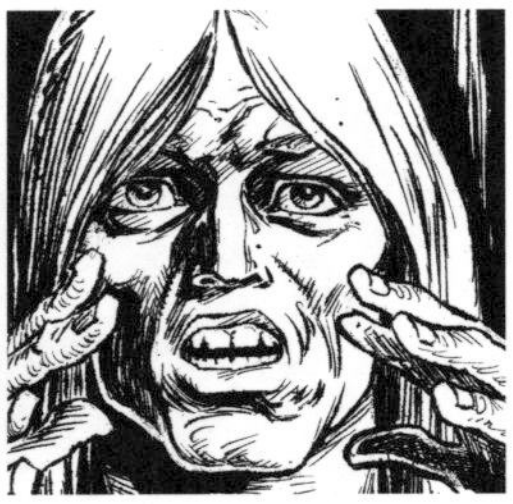
DARKENMOOR

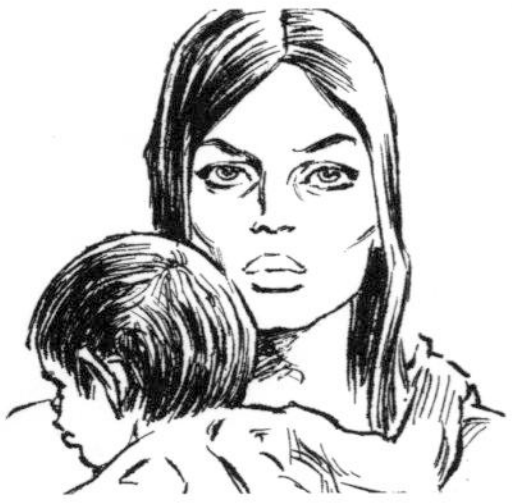
NEDLAYA

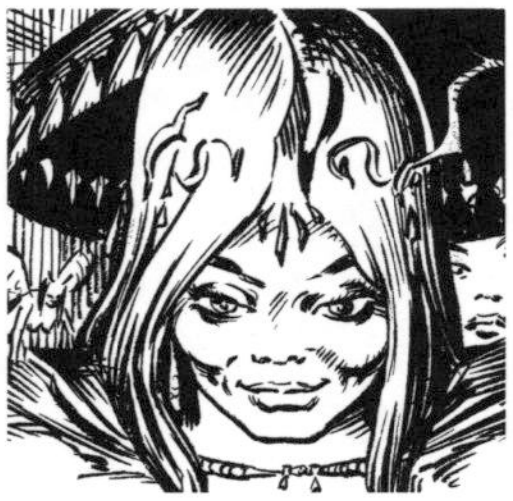
CILEDA

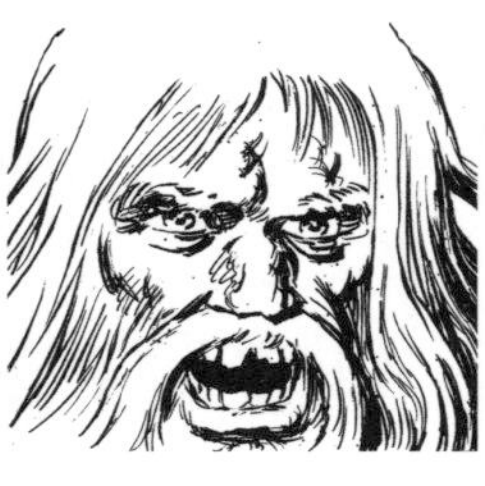
KENARG

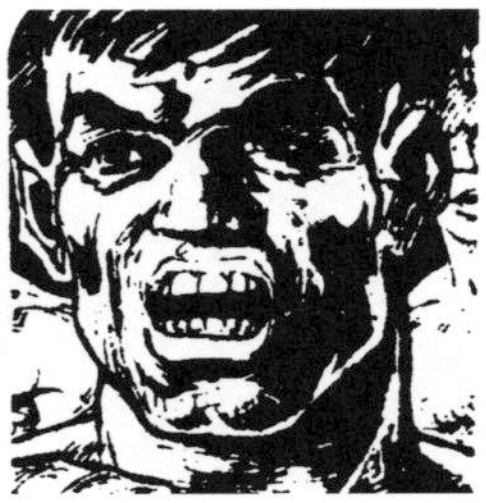
ACCAR

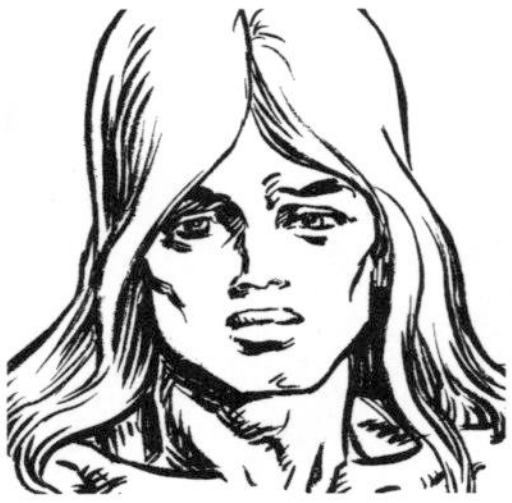
TUNDRAN

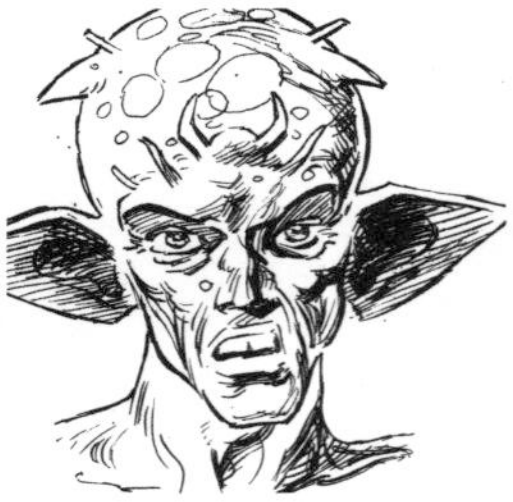
TEROG

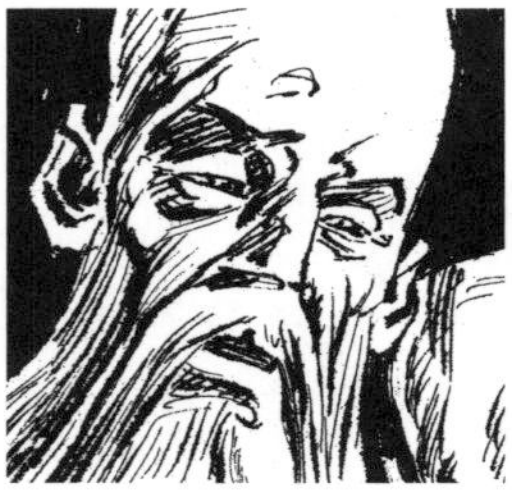
IGRAN

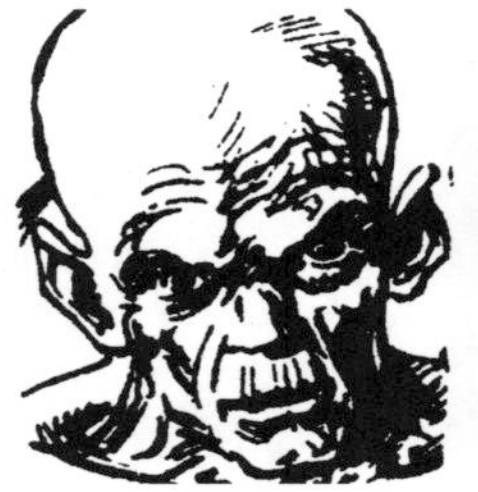
NATOR

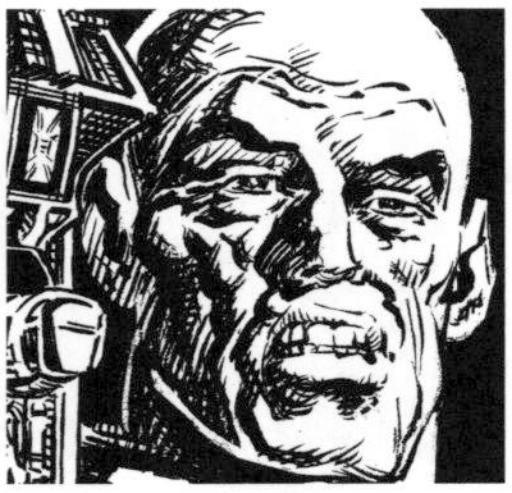
CYBRICK

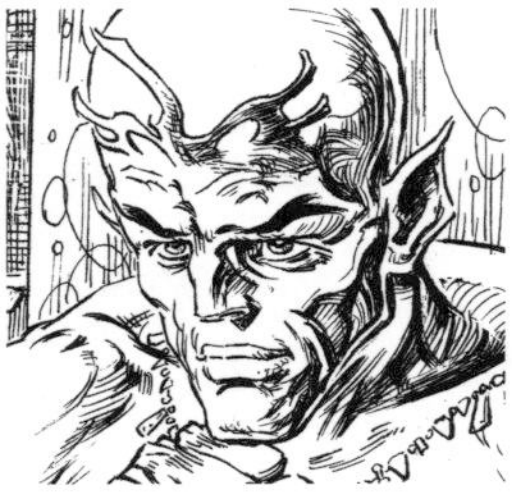
OMROCK ORAM

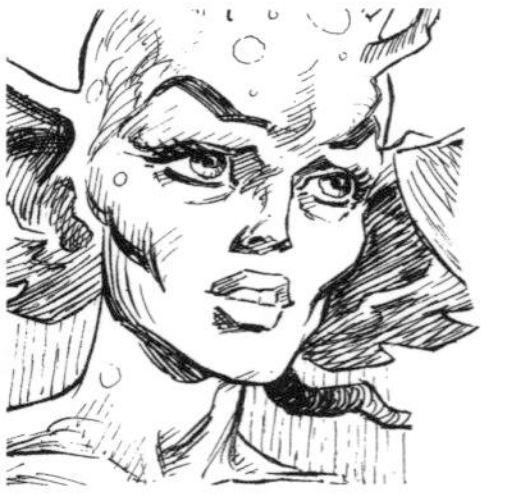
HIMEMET

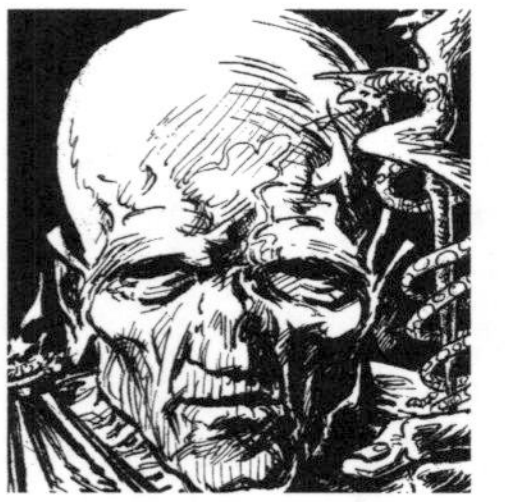
CEER

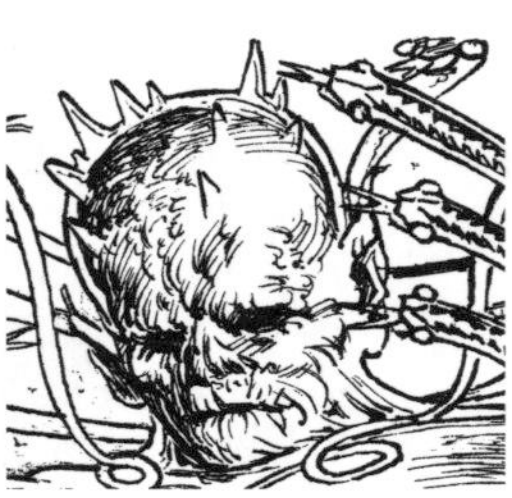
ZAKARRA

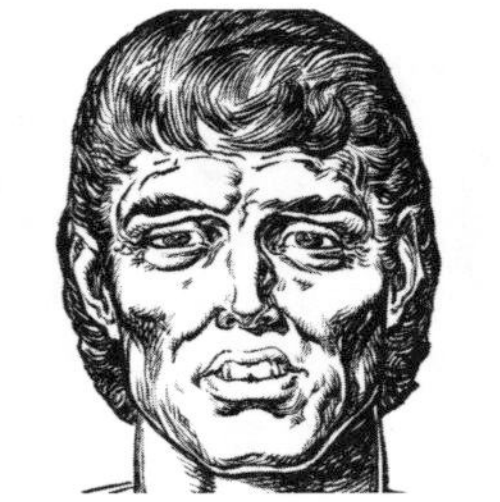
ATTAR

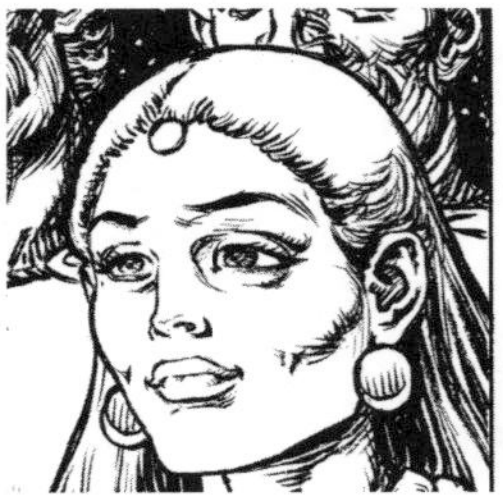
CALTEYOL

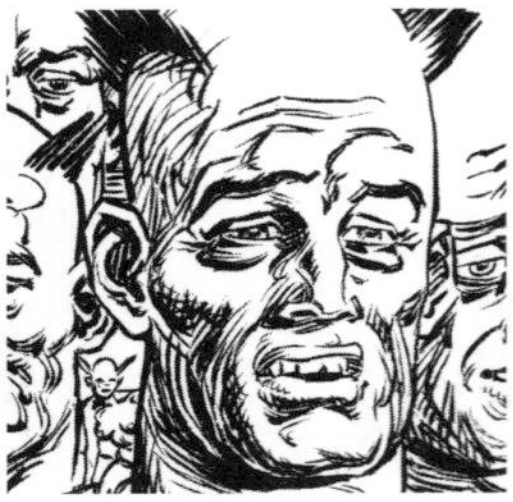
CASTO

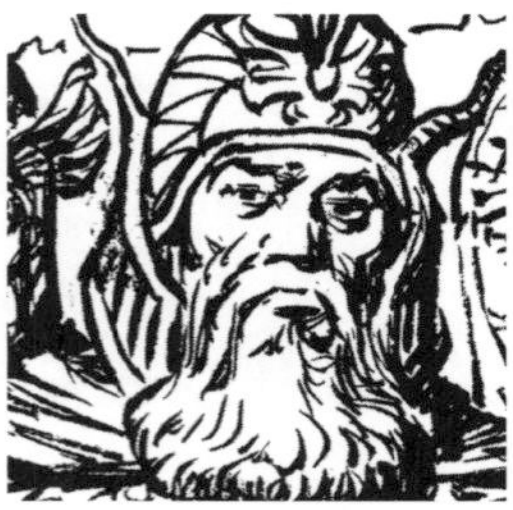
CATARA

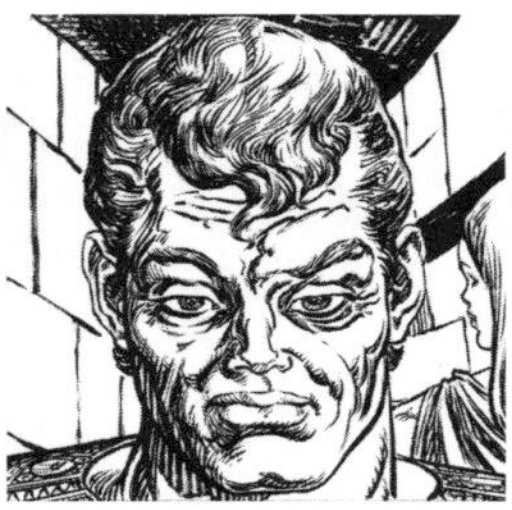
CETRAY

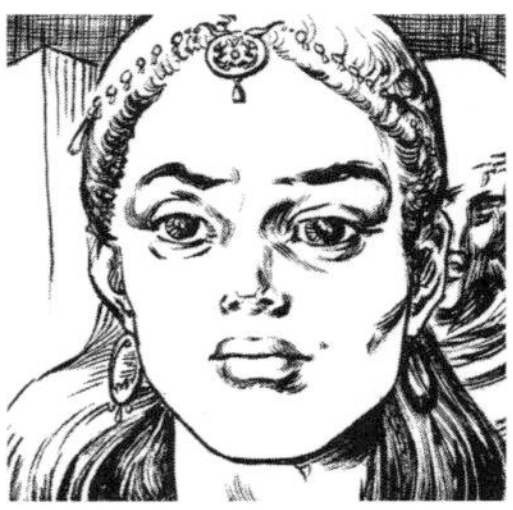
CLEAD

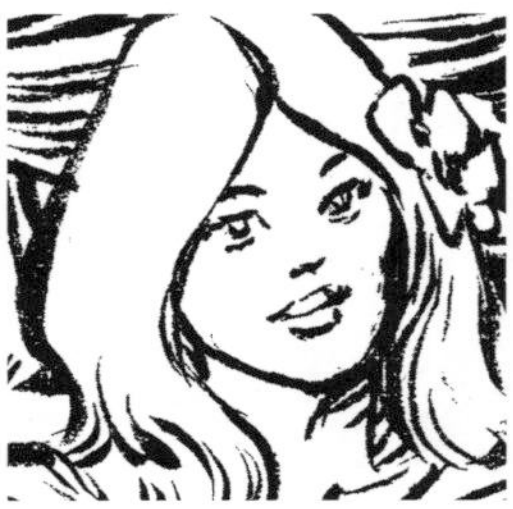
EVIRE

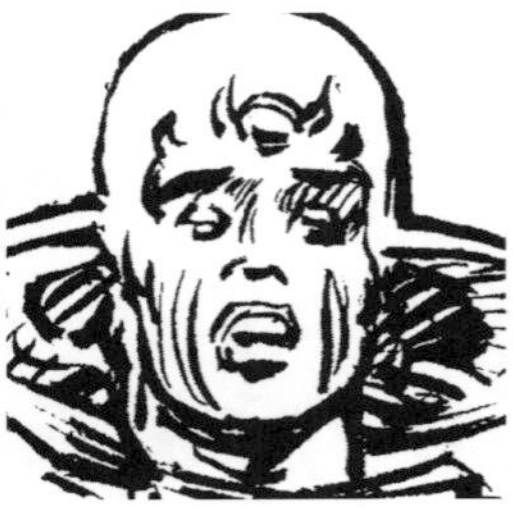
GORET

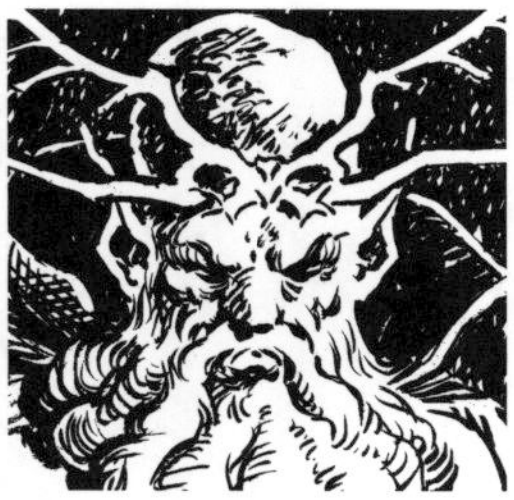

DRANOK

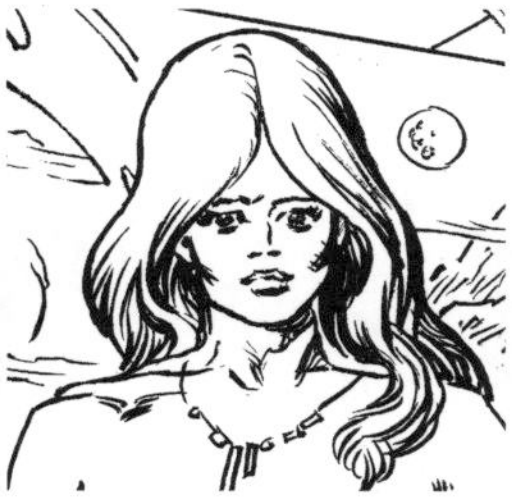

ERAD

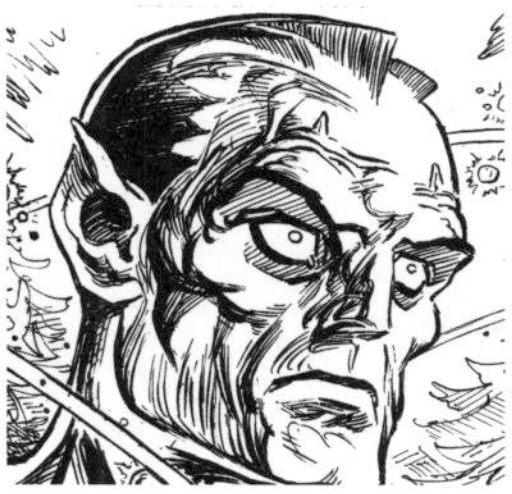

ADIEAUM

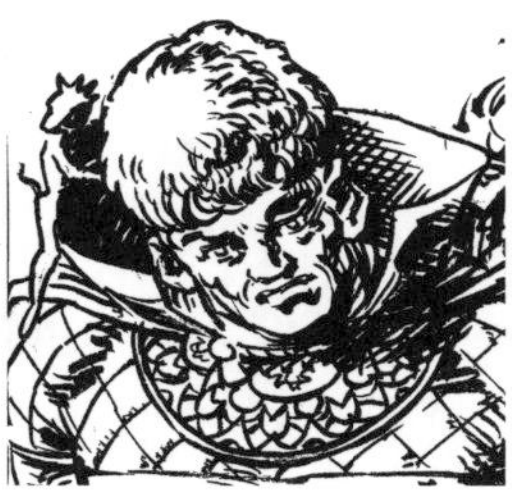

VOLARG

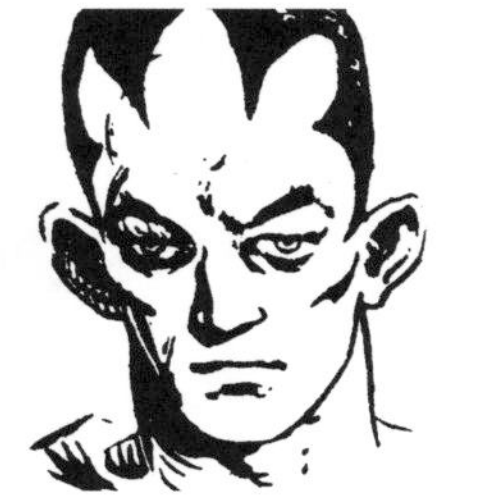

KARNORE

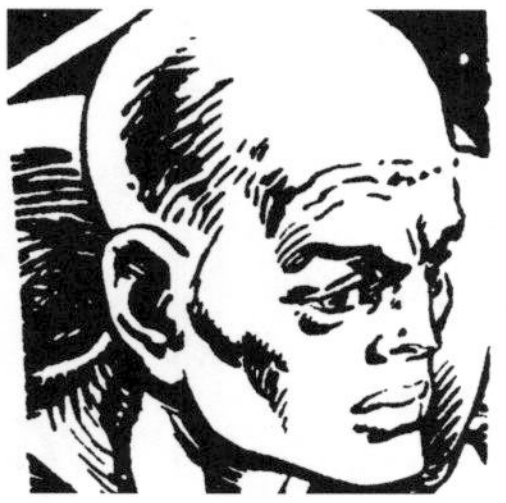

THE ENTITY

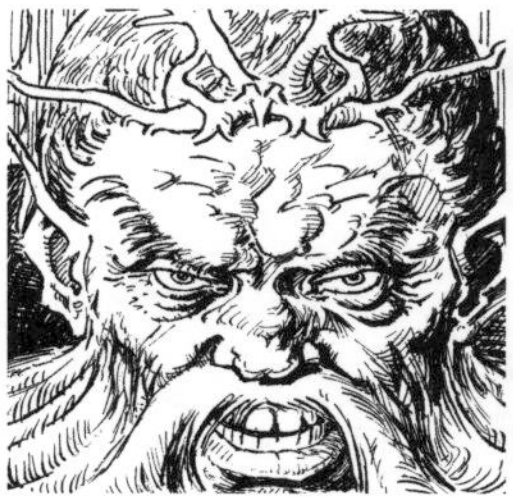

DRANOK

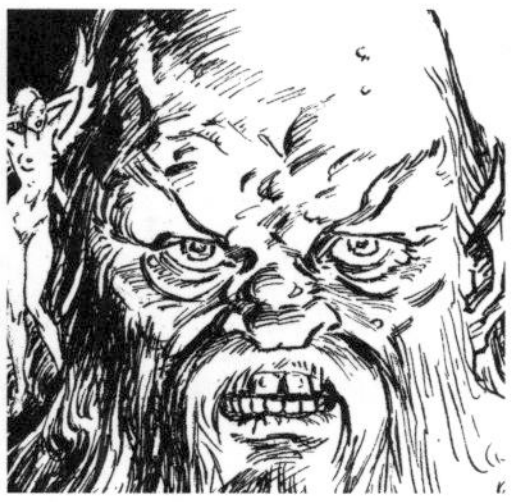

LAXTON

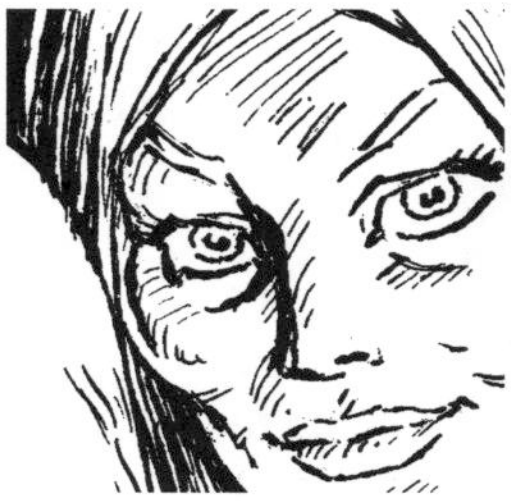

SKYREE

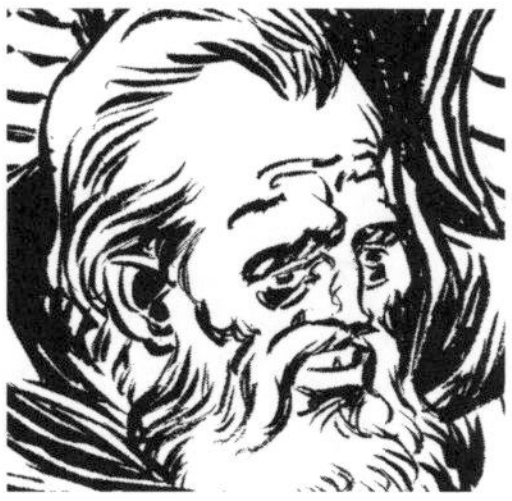

NOVECO

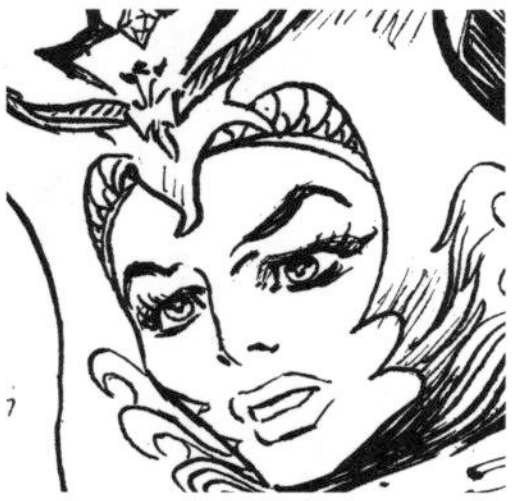

ADONIEDE

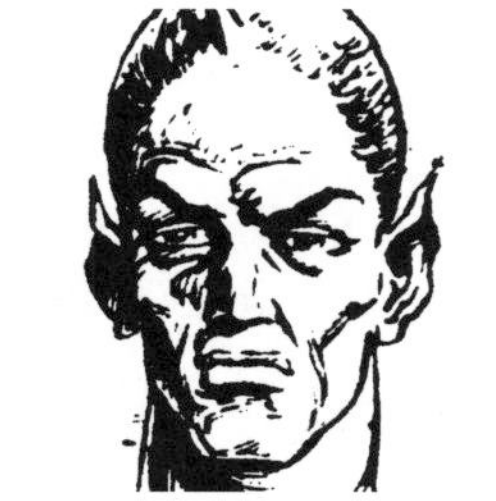

ADRELAR

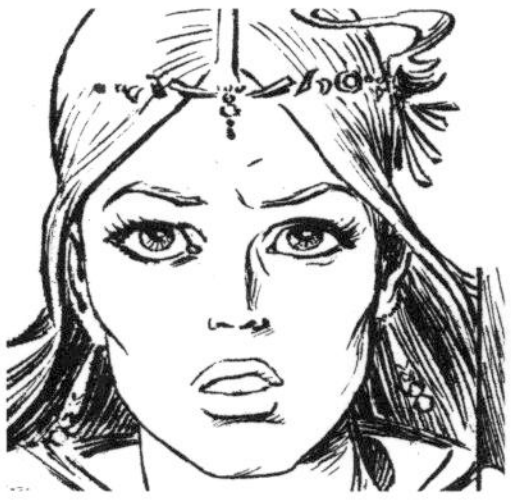

SELOWAN

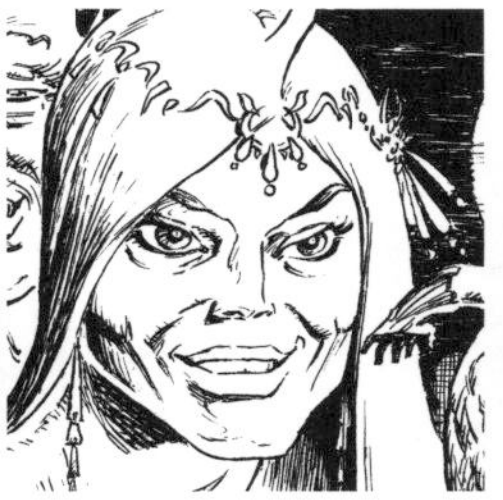

TEDRA

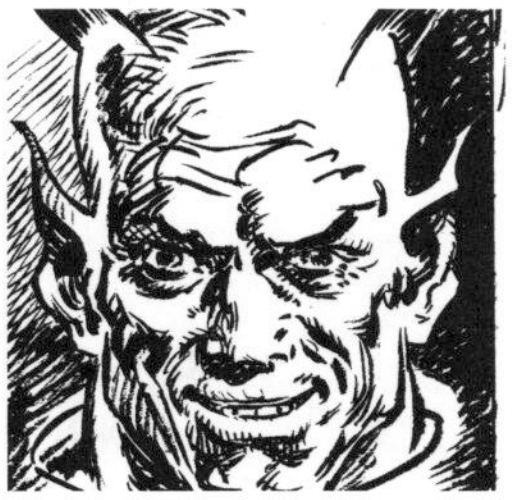

NADAN

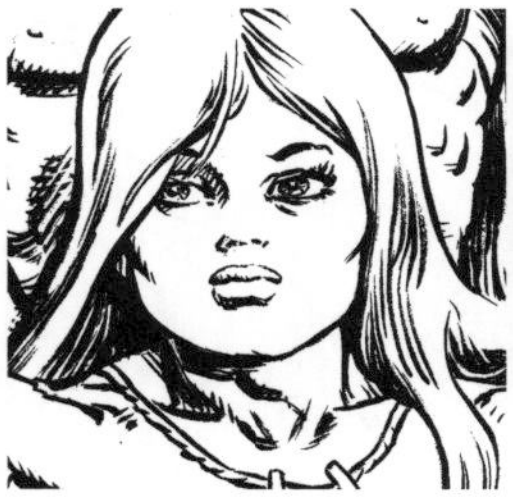

FARA

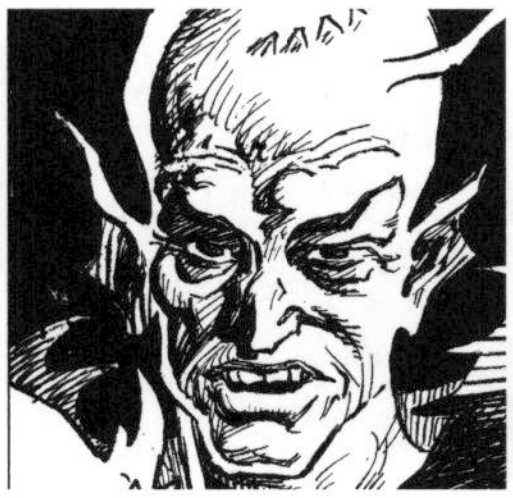

AQUARE

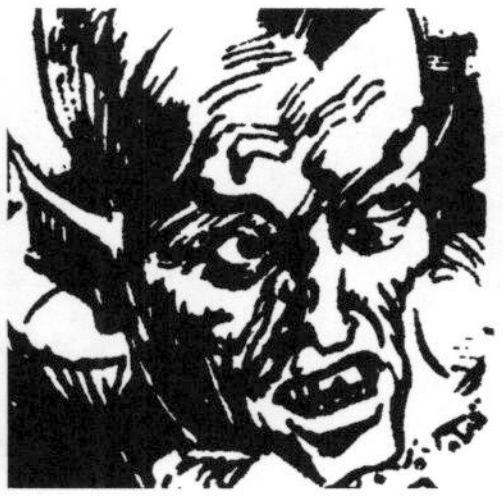

OLED

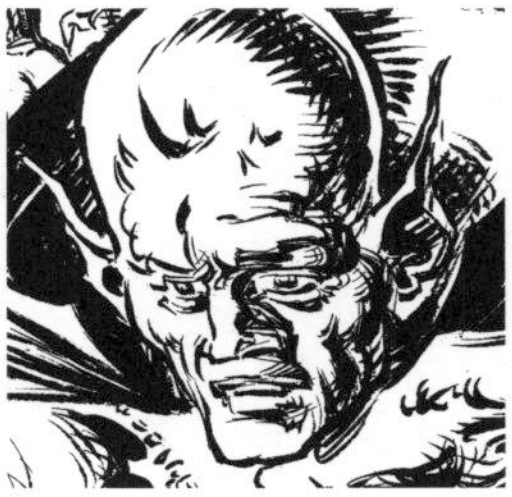

LAXTON

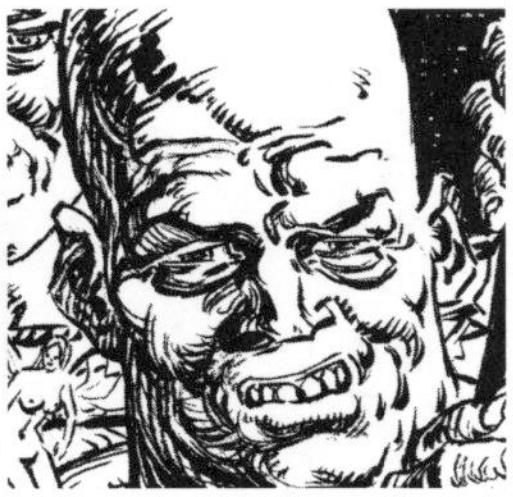

ROMEC

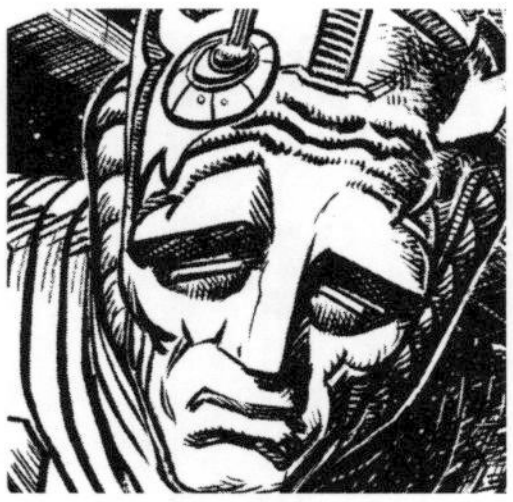

THE EYETELECT

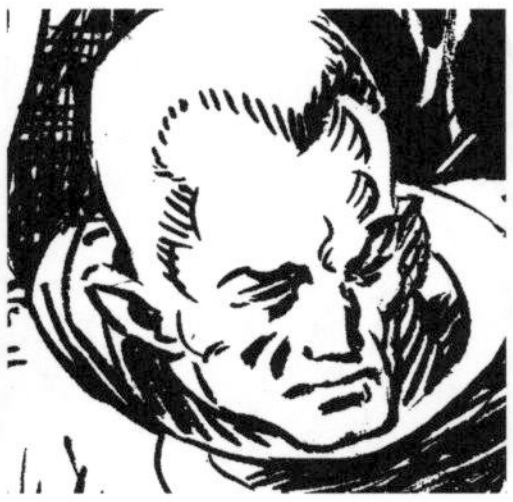

MANOG

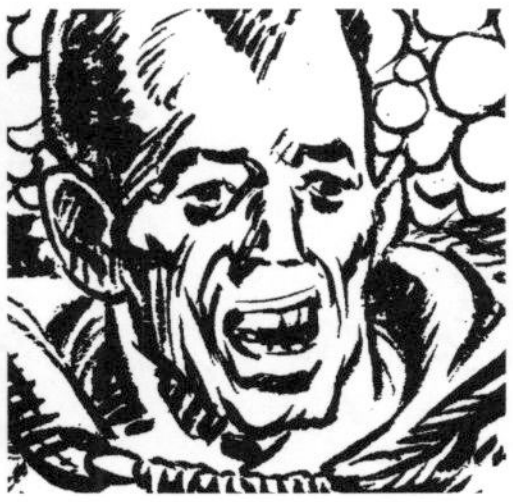

VARGRAN

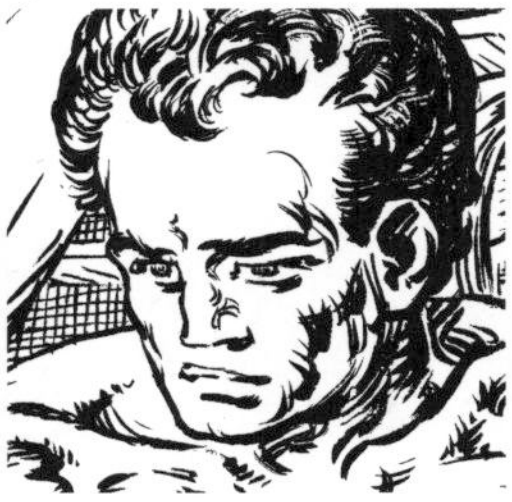

VARO

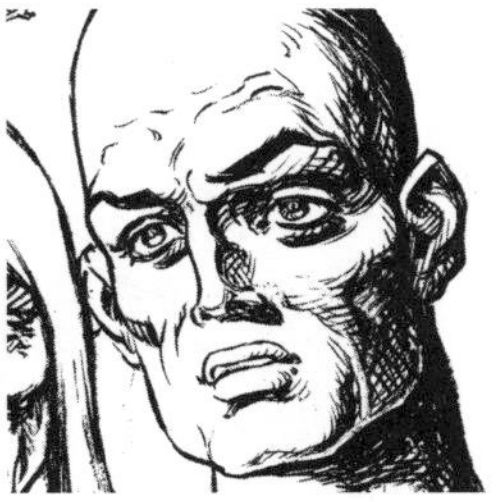

QUETTAR

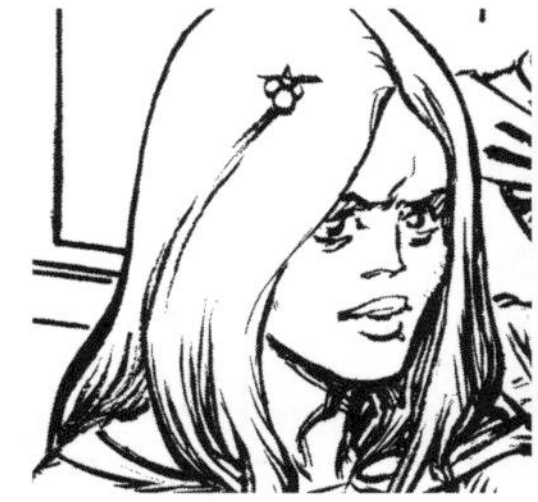

YERLEA

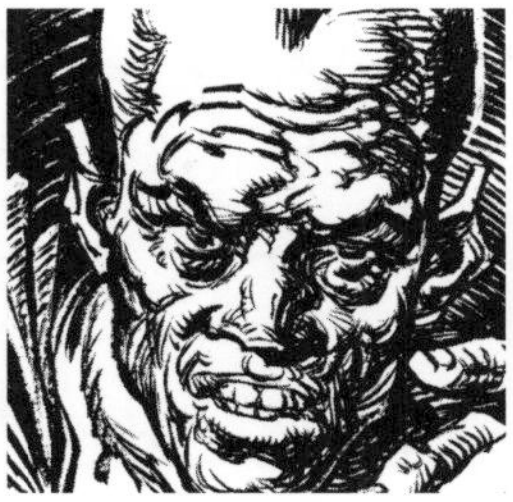

VORGAN

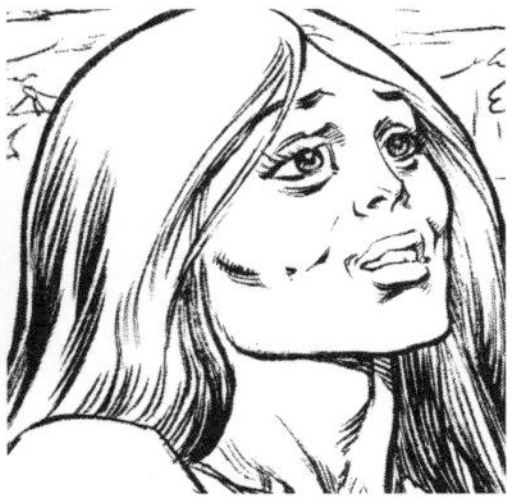

TAPLEY

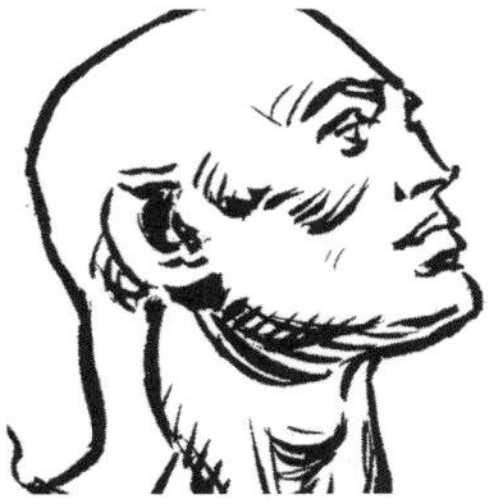

OVAR

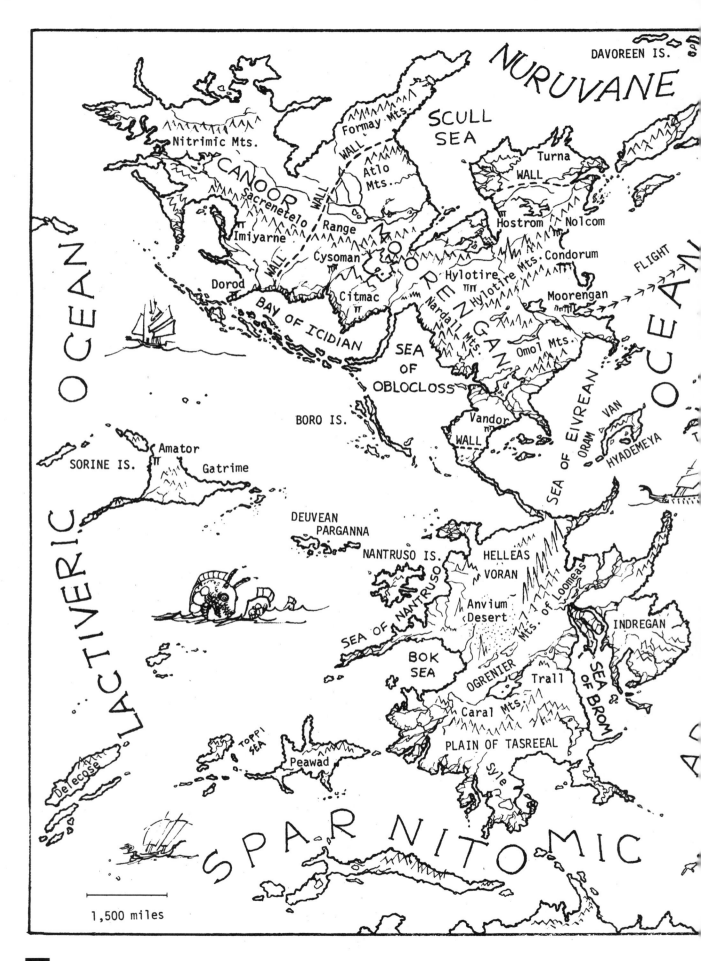

DAVOREEN IS.

NURUVANE

SCULL SEA

Formay Mts.

WALL

Atlo Mts.

Turna

WALL

Nitrimic Mts.

CANOOR

Sacrenetelo Range

WALL

Imiyarne

Hostrom   Nolcom

Cysoman

Condorum

Hylotire   Hylotire Mts.

Dorod

Citmac

Nardall Mts.

Moorengan

FLIGHT

BAY OF ICIDIAN

RENGAN

Omol Mts.

OCEAN

SEA OF OBLOCLOSS

BORO IS.

Vandor

WALL

VAN

ORAM

HYADEMEYA

SEA OF EIVREAN

LACTIVERIC

SORINE IS.   Amator

Gatrime

DEUVEAN PARGANNA

NANTRUSO IS.

HELLEAS

VORAN

Anvium Desert

Mts. of Loomeas

INDREGAN

SEA OF BROM

OCEAN

SEA OF NANTRUSO

BOK SEA

OGRENIER

Trall

Caral Mts.

Delecose

TOPPI SEA

Peawad

PLAIN OF TASREEAL

Syle

AD

SPARNITOMIC

1,500 miles

8

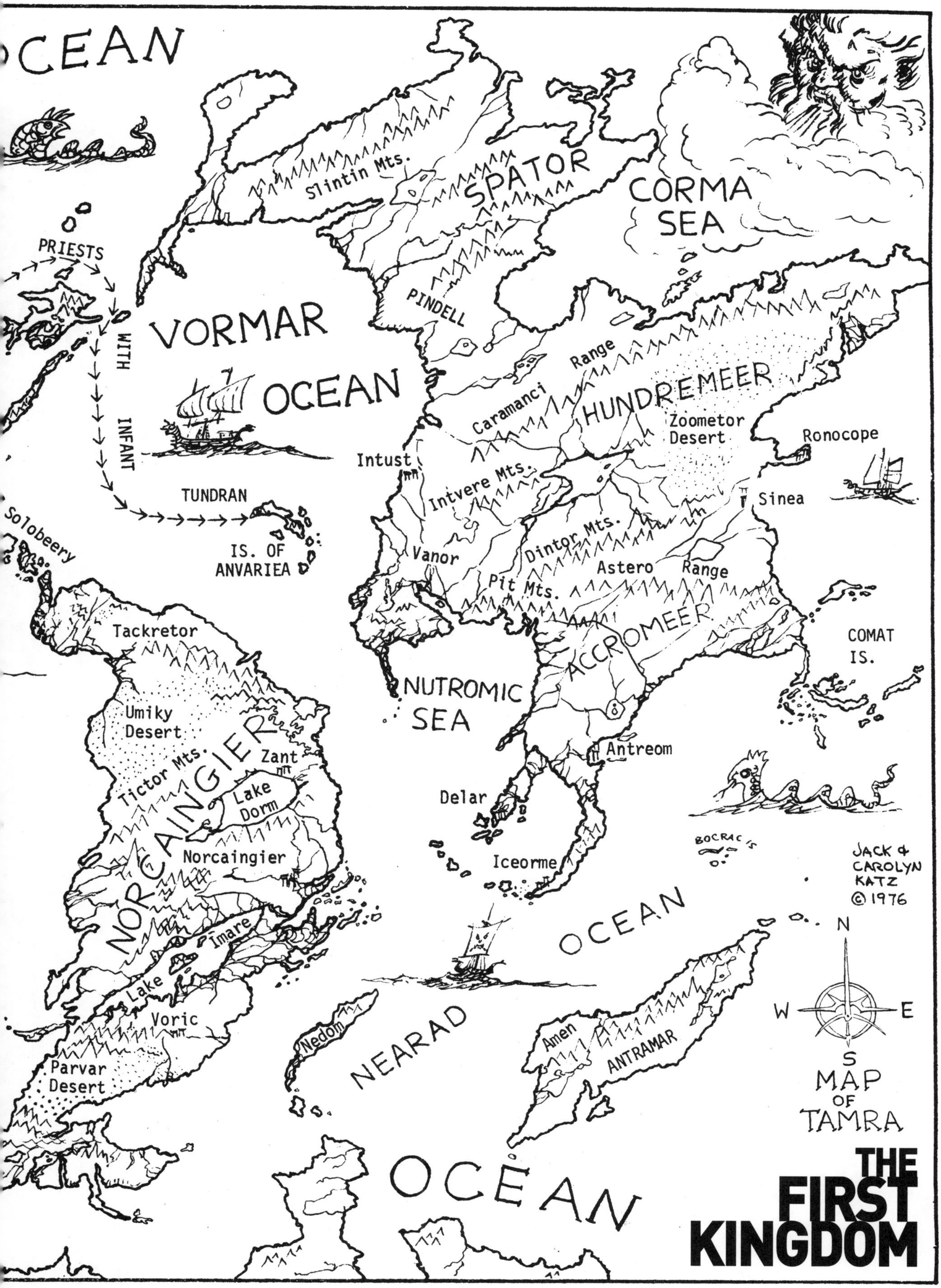
OCEAN
Slintin Mts.
SPATOR
CORMA SEA
PRIESTS
WITH
INFANT
VORMAR OCEAN
PINDELL
Range
Caramanci
HUNDREMEER
Zoometor Desert
Ronocope
Intust
Intvere Mts.
Sinea
TUNDRAN
Solobeery
IS. OF ANVARIEA
Vanor
Dintor Mts.
Astero
Range
Pit Mts.
ACCROMEER
COMAT IS.
Tackretor
NUTROMIC SEA
Umiky Desert
Tictor Mts.
NORCAINGIER
Zant
Lake Dorm
Antreom
Delar
Norcaingier
Iceorme
BOCRAC IS
JACK & CAROLYN KATZ © 1976
OCEAN
Imare
Lake
Voric
Nedom
NEARAD
Amen
ANTRAMAR
N
W
E
S
MAP OF TAMRA
Parvar Desert
OCEAN
THE FIRST KINGDOM

STORY SO FAR

A global apocalypse has catastrophically reshaped Earth into the Tamra. The few human survivors have been helped in their struggle to rebuild their world by a pantheon of new deities – the Transgods.

Leaders of these new tribes are Darkenmoor and Nedlaya, lovers risen from the savagery of the Tamra to build the first great city of the new Earth, Moonrengan. But their peaceful reign is dashed by Nedlaya's twisted brother, Vargran, who betrays and kills Darkenmoor.

The royal couple's young son, Tundran, and his love, Fara, strike out for the city, intent on rightfully reclaiming the throne, while allies stay behind to form an army of rebels. But their journey is interrupted by Omrock Oram, a god who warns them that the course they are taking could threaten all life.

Meanwhile, intrigue ravages Helleas Voran, the home of the Transgods. Their laws forbid interactions between god and human, but more and more are influencing the lives of the people of the Tamra. For her love of Darkenmoor, goddess Selowan is banished as a spirit into the unborn Fara by her father and Helleas Voran's ruler, Dranok. And in act of petty vengeance, Laxton, bitter ex-ruler of Helleas, makes Selowan's sister Tedra, mortal.

More significantly, the enigmatic Aquare is actively meddling in human affairs. It is he who knows and understands the origins of the Transgods; that they are the offspring of cyborg experiments begun aboard a Galactic Hunter, a giant spaceship whose crew were tasked with interceding in potentially devastating planetary conflicts. It had arrived over Earth intent on stopping the nuclear war that devastated the planet but failed after the crew were injected with a serum that destroyed their memories and mutated the ship's officers, Terog and Himmemet. Aquare also knows that one of the gods, Ogsoltoman, is a survivor from the Galactic Hunter's mission; as Admiral Manog, it was he who initiated the program that led to the cyborg experiment.

Dranok orders Ogsoltoman to reveal the past but to do so would reveal that Helleas Voran's leader is the sole survivor of a failed cyborg experiment so Ogsoltoman obscures the truth with a false history. However, he meets with another survivor of the ship, Ceer, an oracle imbued with vast knowledge by an entity dedicated to the protection of humanity. Ceer has been monitoring both Darkenmoor and his son, but Ogsoltoman reveals that some of the oracle's memories have been wiped clean. It is the former's 'brother', Tintrim, who unveils the truth about the Ultranoids, multi-dimensional beings who gave birth to humanity. The Ultranoids were almost destroyed in an intergalactic war by a race even more powerful than themselves, leaving the survivors to flee into space. This revelation transforms Aquare's perception of humanity, whom he saw as primitive and unworthy of his attentions.

Back on the Tamra, Tundran has entered his stolen capital city, taking the guise of a blind slave. But the mutants and friends of Tundran, Terog and Himemet, have been forced to betray him…

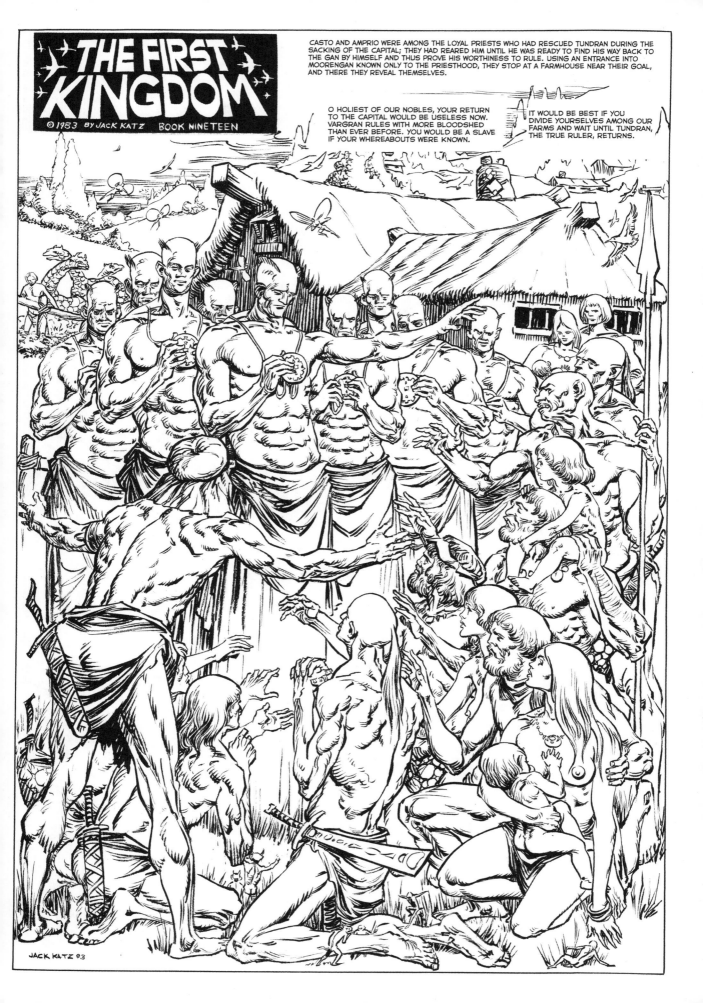

THE FIRST KINGDOM

© 1983 BY JACK KATZ   BOOK NINETEEN

CASTO AND AMPRIO WERE AMONG THE LOYAL PRIESTS WHO HAD RESCUED TUNDRAN DURING THE SACKING OF THE CAPITAL; THEY HAD REARED HIM UNTIL HE WAS READY TO FIND HIS WAY BACK TO THE GAN BY HIMSELF AND THUS PROVE HIS WORTHINESS TO RULE. USING AN ENTRANCE INTO MOORENGAN KNOWN ONLY TO THE PRIESTHOOD, THEY STOP AT A FARMHOUSE NEAR THEIR GOAL, AND THERE THEY REVEAL THEMSELVES.

O HOLIEST OF OUR NOBLES, YOUR RETURN TO THE CAPITAL WOULD BE USELESS NOW. VARGRAN RULES WITH MORE BLOODSHED THAN EVER BEFORE. YOU WOULD BE A SLAVE IF YOUR WHEREABOUTS WERE KNOWN.

IT WOULD BE BEST IF YOU DIVIDE YOURSELVES AMONG OUR FARMS AND WAIT UNTIL TUNDRAN, THE TRUE RULER, RETURNS.

JACK KATZ 83

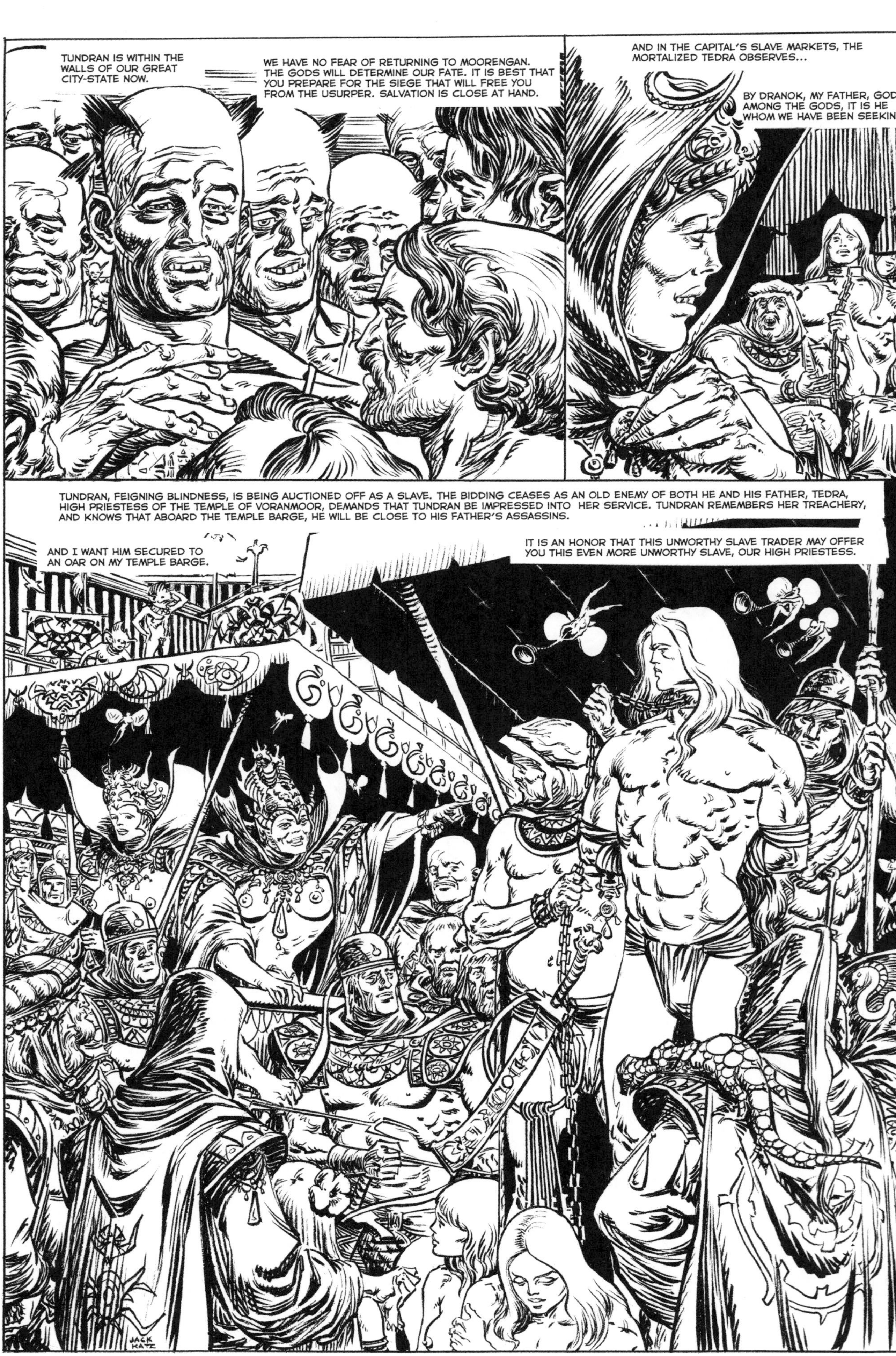
TUNDRAN IS WITHIN THE WALLS OF OUR GREAT CITY-STATE NOW.
WE HAVE NO FEAR OF RETURNING TO MOORENGAN. THE GODS WILL DETERMINE OUR FATE. IT IS BEST THAT YOU PREPARE FOR THE SIEGE THAT WILL FREE YOU FROM THE USURPER. SALVATION IS CLOSE AT HAND.
AND IN THE CAPITAL'S SLAVE MARKETS, THE MORTALIZED TEDRA OBSERVES...
BY DRANOK, MY FATHER, GOD AMONG THE GODS, IT IS HE WHOM WE HAVE BEEN SEEKING!
TUNDRAN, FEIGNING BLINDNESS, IS BEING AUCTIONED OFF AS A SLAVE. THE BIDDING CEASES AS AN OLD ENEMY OF BOTH HE AND HIS FATHER, TEDRA, HIGH PRIESTESS OF THE TEMPLE OF VORANMOOR, DEMANDS THAT TUNDRAN BE IMPRESSED INTO HER SERVICE. TUNDRAN REMEMBERS HER TREACHERY, AND KNOWS THAT ABOARD THE TEMPLE BARGE, HE WILL BE CLOSE TO HIS FATHER'S ASSASSINS.
IT IS AN HONOR THAT THIS UNWORTHY SLAVE TRADER MAY OFFER YOU THIS EVEN MORE UNWORTHY SLAVE, OUR HIGH PRIESTESS.
AND I WANT HIM SECURED TO AN OAR ON MY TEMPLE BARGE.
JACK KATZ

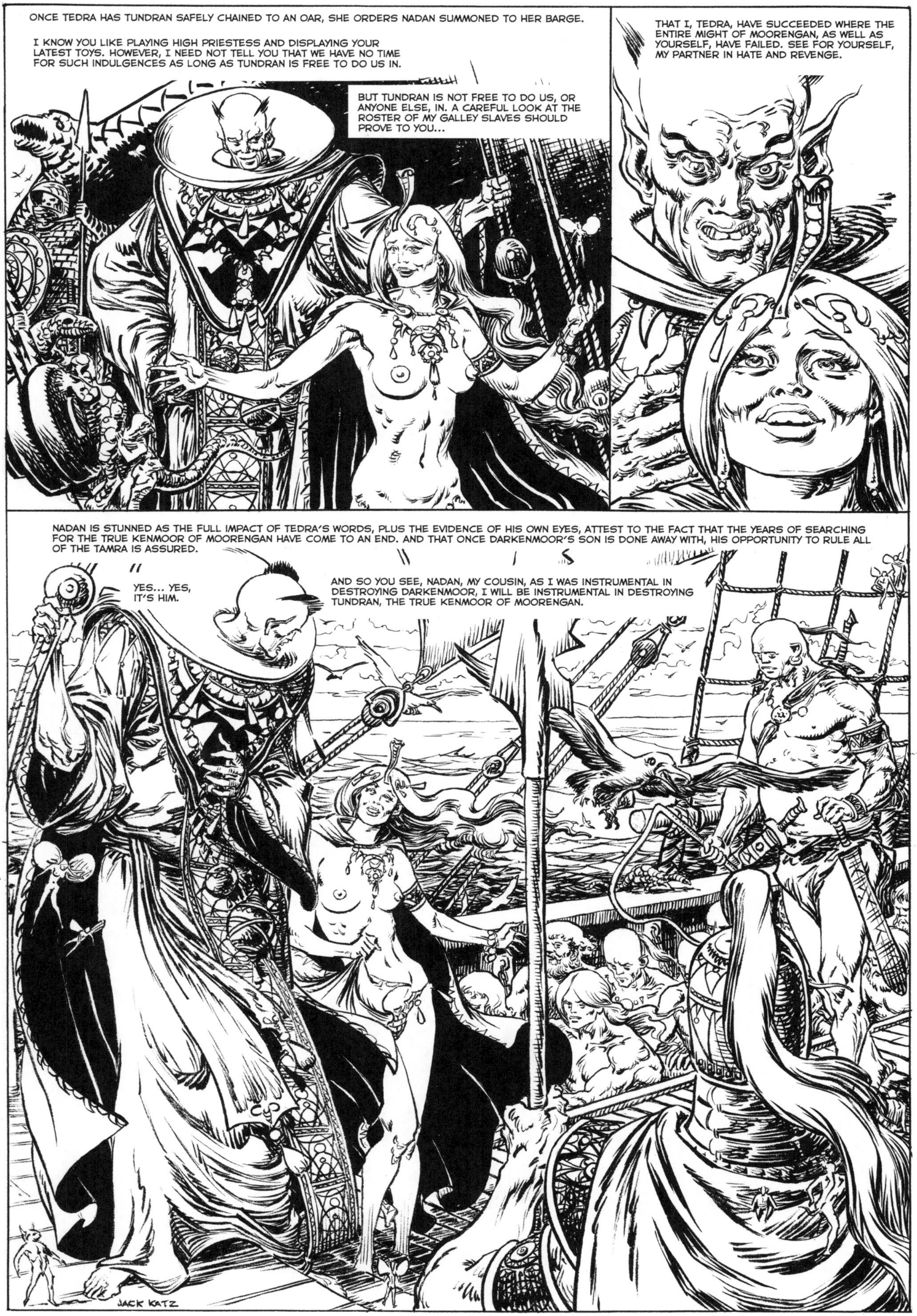
ONCE TEDRA HAS TUNDRAN SAFELY CHAINED TO AN OAR, SHE ORDERS NADAN SUMMONED TO HER BARGE.
I KNOW YOU LIKE PLAYING HIGH PRIESTESS AND DISPLAYING YOUR LATEST TOYS. HOWEVER, I NEED NOT TELL YOU THAT WE HAVE NO TIME FOR SUCH INDULGENCES AS LONG AS TUNDRAN IS FREE TO DO US IN.
BUT TUNDRAN IS NOT FREE TO DO US, OR ANYONE ELSE, IN. A CAREFUL LOOK AT THE ROSTER OF MY GALLEY SLAVES SHOULD PROVE TO YOU...
THAT I, TEDRA, HAVE SUCCEEDED WHERE THE ENTIRE MIGHT OF MOORENGAN, AS WELL AS YOURSELF, HAVE FAILED. SEE FOR YOURSELF, MY PARTNER IN HATE AND REVENGE.
NADAN IS STUNNED AS THE FULL IMPACT OF TEDRA'S WORDS, PLUS THE EVIDENCE OF HIS OWN EYES, ATTEST TO THE FACT THAT THE YEARS OF SEARCHING FOR THE TRUE KENMOOR OF MOORENGAN HAVE COME TO AN END. AND THAT ONCE DARKENMOOR'S SON IS DONE AWAY WITH, HIS OPPORTUNITY TO RULE ALL OF THE TAMRA IS ASSURED.
YES... YES, IT'S HIM.
AND SO YOU SEE, NADAN, MY COUSIN, AS I WAS INSTRUMENTAL IN DESTROYING DARKENMOOR, I WILL BE INSTRUMENTAL IN DESTROYING TUNDRAN, THE TRUE KENMOOR OF MOORENGAN.
JACK KATZ

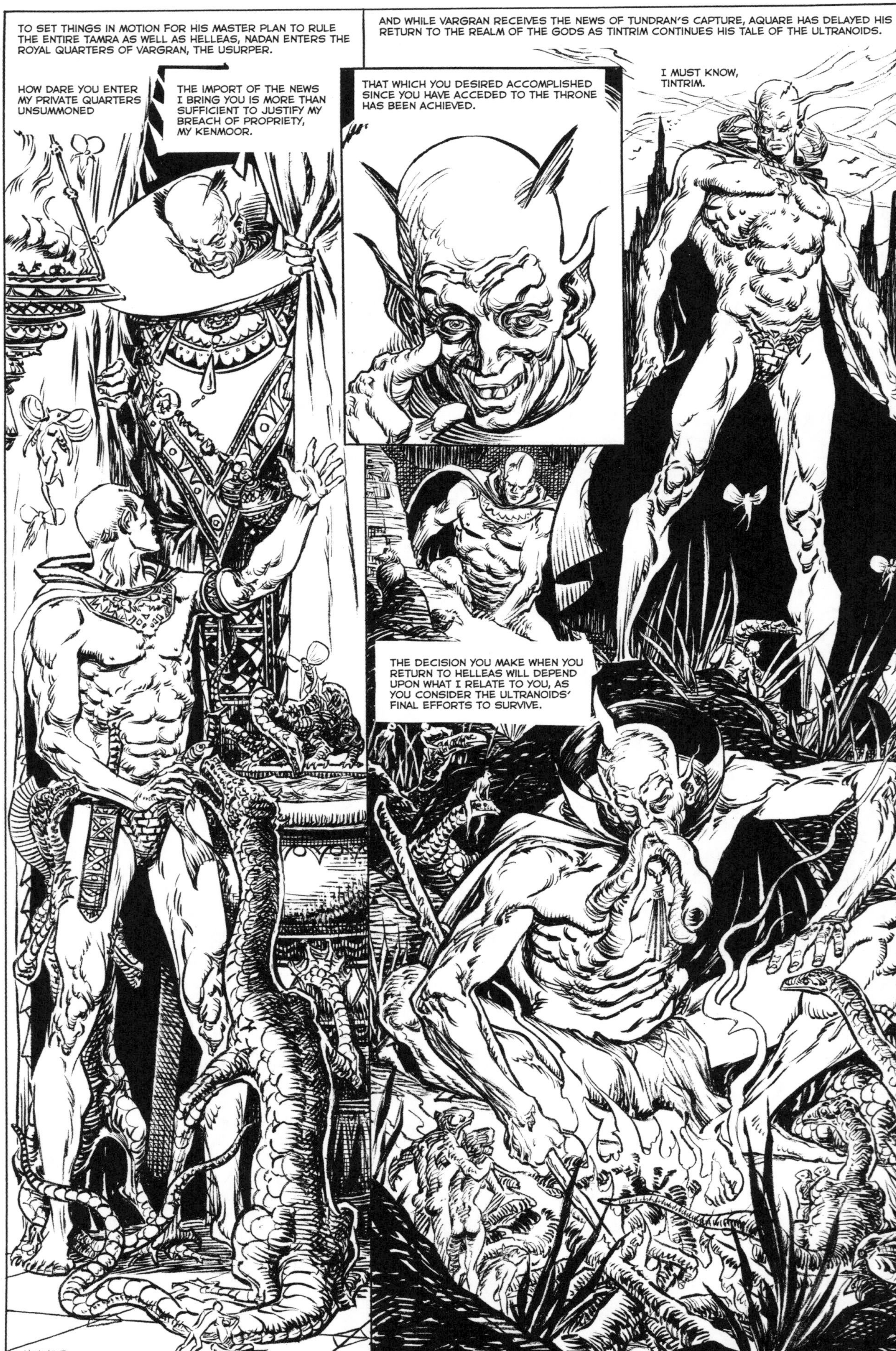
TO SET THINGS IN MOTION FOR HIS MASTER PLAN TO RULE THE ENTIRE TAMRA AS WELL AS HELLEAS, NADAN ENTERS THE ROYAL QUARTERS OF VARGRAN, THE USURPER.
HOW DARE YOU ENTER MY PRIVATE QUARTERS UNSUMMONED
THE IMPORT OF THE NEWS I BRING YOU IS MORE THAN SUFFICIENT TO JUSTIFY MY BREACH OF PROPRIETY, MY KENMOOR.
THAT WHICH YOU DESIRED ACCOMPLISHED SINCE YOU HAVE ACCEDED TO THE THRONE HAS BEEN ACHIEVED.
AND WHILE VARGRAN RECEIVES THE NEWS OF TUNDRAN'S CAPTURE, AQUARE HAS DELAYED HIS RETURN TO THE REALM OF THE GODS AS TINTRIM CONTINUES HIS TALE OF THE ULTRANOIDS.
I MUST KNOW, TINTRIM.
THE DECISION YOU MAKE WHEN YOU RETURN TO HELLEAS WILL DEPEND UPON WHAT I RELATE TO YOU, AS YOU CONSIDER THE ULTRANOIDS' FINAL EFFORTS TO SURVIVE.
JACK KATZ

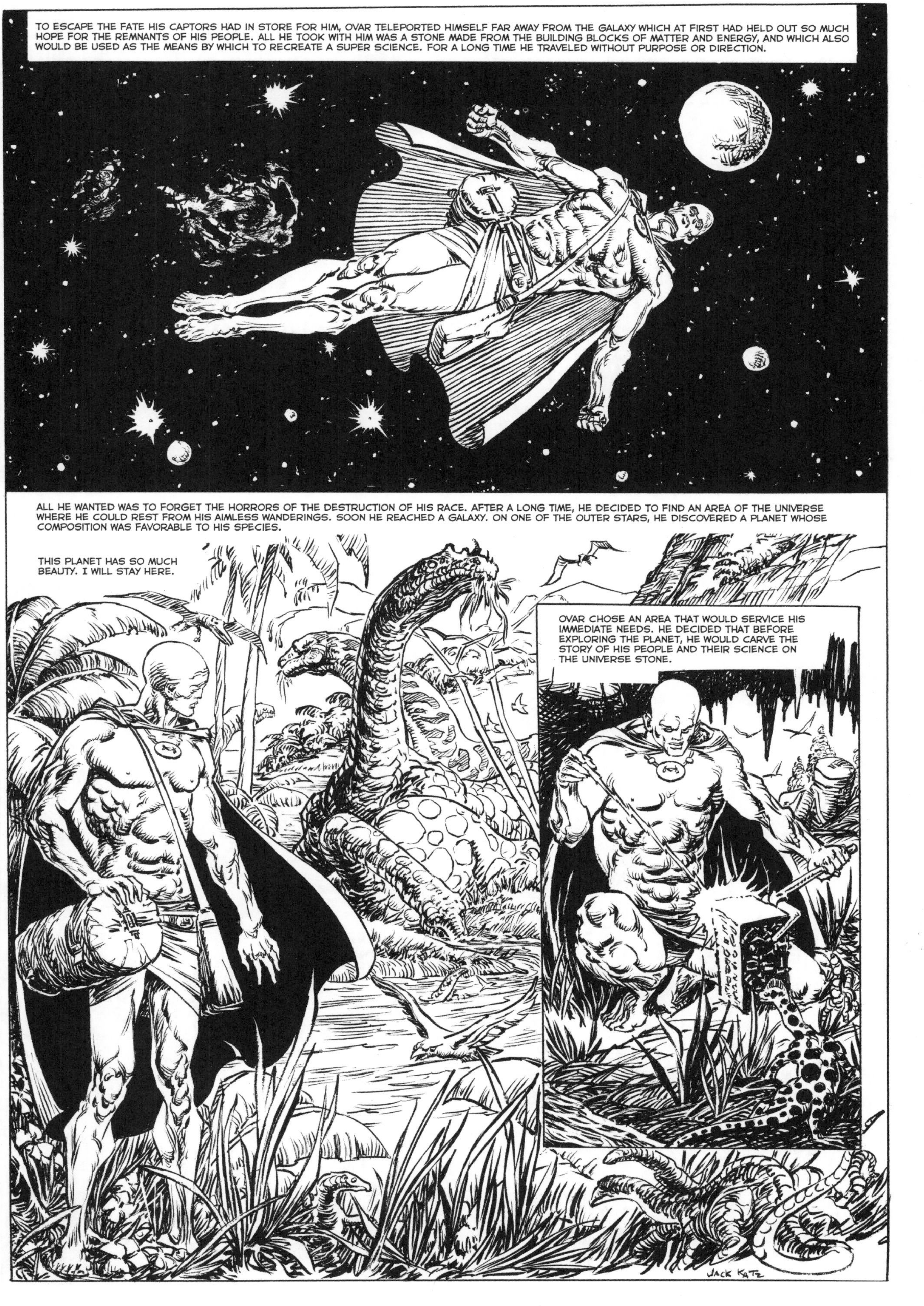
TO ESCAPE THE FATE HIS CAPTORS HAD IN STORE FOR HIM, OVAR TELEPORTED HIMSELF FAR AWAY FROM THE GALAXY WHICH AT FIRST HAD HELD OUT SO MUCH HOPE FOR THE REMNANTS OF HIS PEOPLE. ALL HE TOOK WITH HIM WAS A STONE MADE FROM THE BUILDING BLOCKS OF MATTER AND ENERGY, AND WHICH ALSO WOULD BE USED AS THE MEANS BY WHICH TO RECREATE A SUPER SCIENCE. FOR A LONG TIME HE TRAVELED WITHOUT PURPOSE OR DIRECTION.
ALL HE WANTED WAS TO FORGET THE HORRORS OF THE DESTRUCTION OF HIS RACE. AFTER A LONG TIME, HE DECIDED TO FIND AN AREA OF THE UNIVERSE WHERE HE COULD REST FROM HIS AIMLESS WANDERINGS. SOON HE REACHED A GALAXY. ON ONE OF THE OUTER STARS, HE DISCOVERED A PLANET WHOSE COMPOSITION WAS FAVORABLE TO HIS SPECIES.
THIS PLANET HAS SO MUCH BEAUTY. I WILL STAY HERE.
OVAR CHOSE AN AREA THAT WOULD SERVICE HIS IMMEDIATE NEEDS. HE DECIDED THAT BEFORE EXPLORING THE PLANET, HE WOULD CARVE THE STORY OF HIS PEOPLE AND THEIR SCIENCE ON THE UNIVERSE STONE.
JACK KATZ

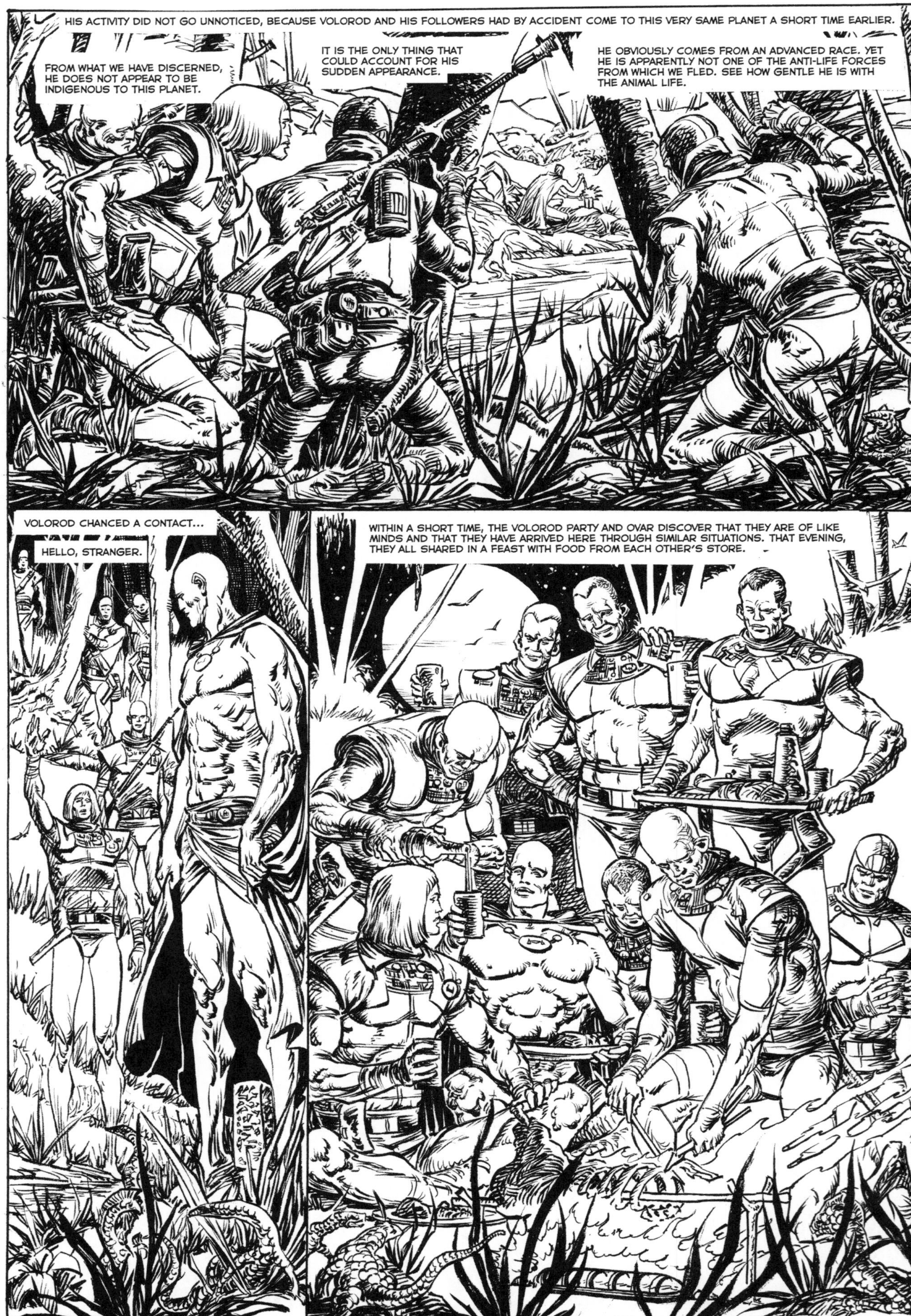
HIS ACTIVITY DID NOT GO UNNOTICED, BECAUSE VOLOROD AND HIS FOLLOWERS HAD BY ACCIDENT COME TO THIS VERY SAME PLANET A SHORT TIME EARLIER.
FROM WHAT WE HAVE DISCERNED, HE DOES NOT APPEAR TO BE INDIGENOUS TO THIS PLANET.
IT IS THE ONLY THING THAT COULD ACCOUNT FOR HIS SUDDEN APPEARANCE.
HE OBVIOUSLY COMES FROM AN ADVANCED RACE. YET HE IS APPARENTLY NOT ONE OF THE ANTI-LIFE FORCES FROM WHICH WE FLED. SEE HOW GENTLE HE IS WITH THE ANIMAL LIFE.
VOLOROD CHANCED A CONTACT...
HELLO, STRANGER.
WITHIN A SHORT TIME, THE VOLOROD PARTY AND OVAR DISCOVER THAT THEY ARE OF LIKE MINDS AND THAT THEY HAVE ARRIVED HERE THROUGH SIMILAR SITUATIONS. THAT EVENING, THEY ALL SHARED IN A FEAST WITH FOOD FROM EACH OTHER'S STORE.
JACK KATZ

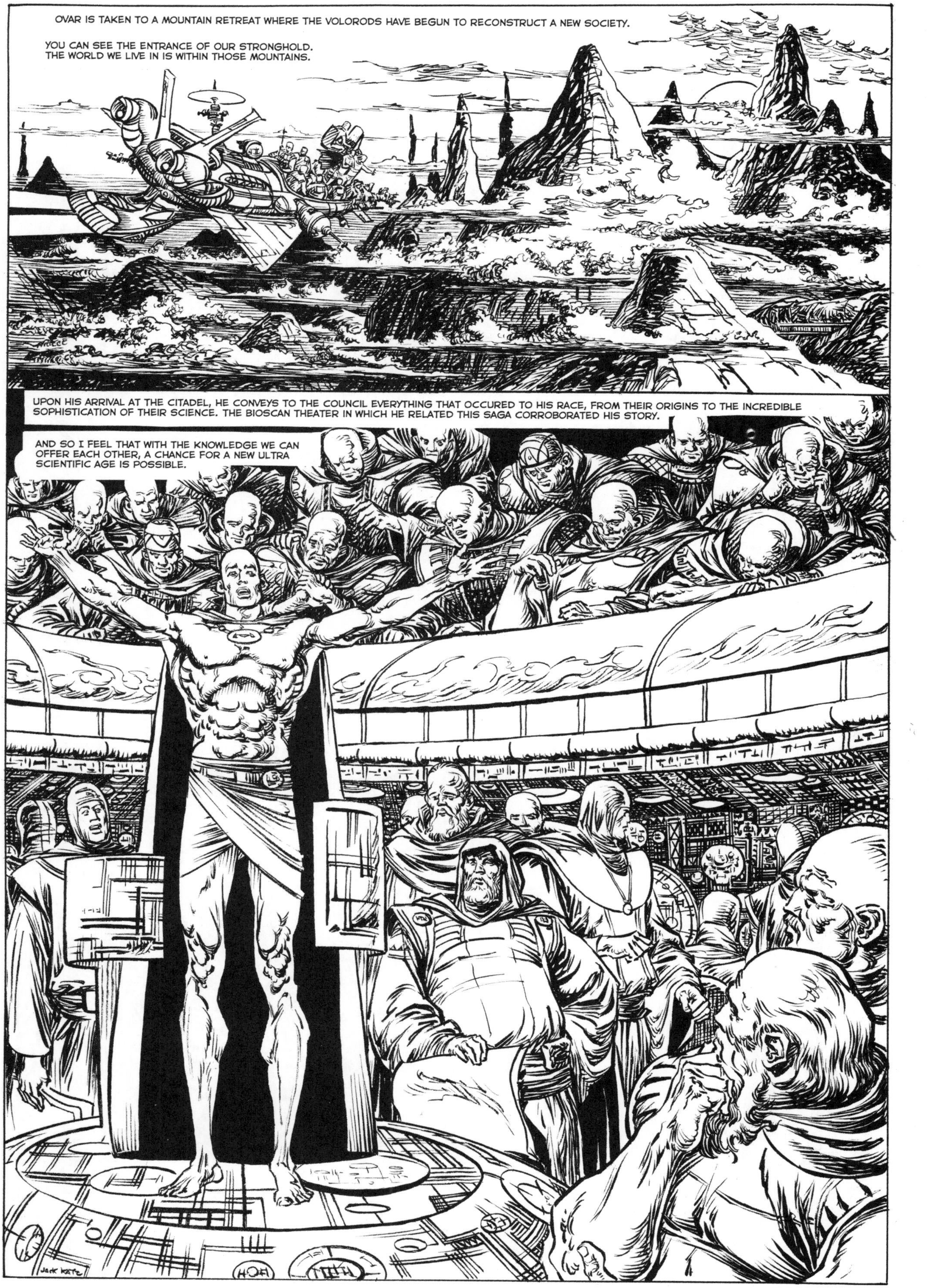
OVAR IS TAKEN TO A MOUNTAIN RETREAT WHERE THE VOLORODS HAVE BEGUN TO RECONSTRUCT A NEW SOCIETY.
YOU CAN SEE THE ENTRANCE OF OUR STRONGHOLD. THE WORLD WE LIVE IN IS WITHIN THOSE MOUNTAINS.
UPON HIS ARRIVAL AT THE CITADEL, HE CONVEYS TO THE COUNCIL EVERYTHING THAT OCCURED TO HIS RACE, FROM THEIR ORIGINS TO THE INCREDIBLE SOPHISTICATION OF THEIR SCIENCE. THE BIOSCAN THEATER IN WHICH HE RELATED THIS SAGA CORROBORATED HIS STORY.
AND SO I FEEL THAT WITH THE KNOWLEDGE WE CAN OFFER EACH OTHER, A CHANCE FOR A NEW ULTRA SCIENTIFIC AGE IS POSSIBLE.
JACK KATZ

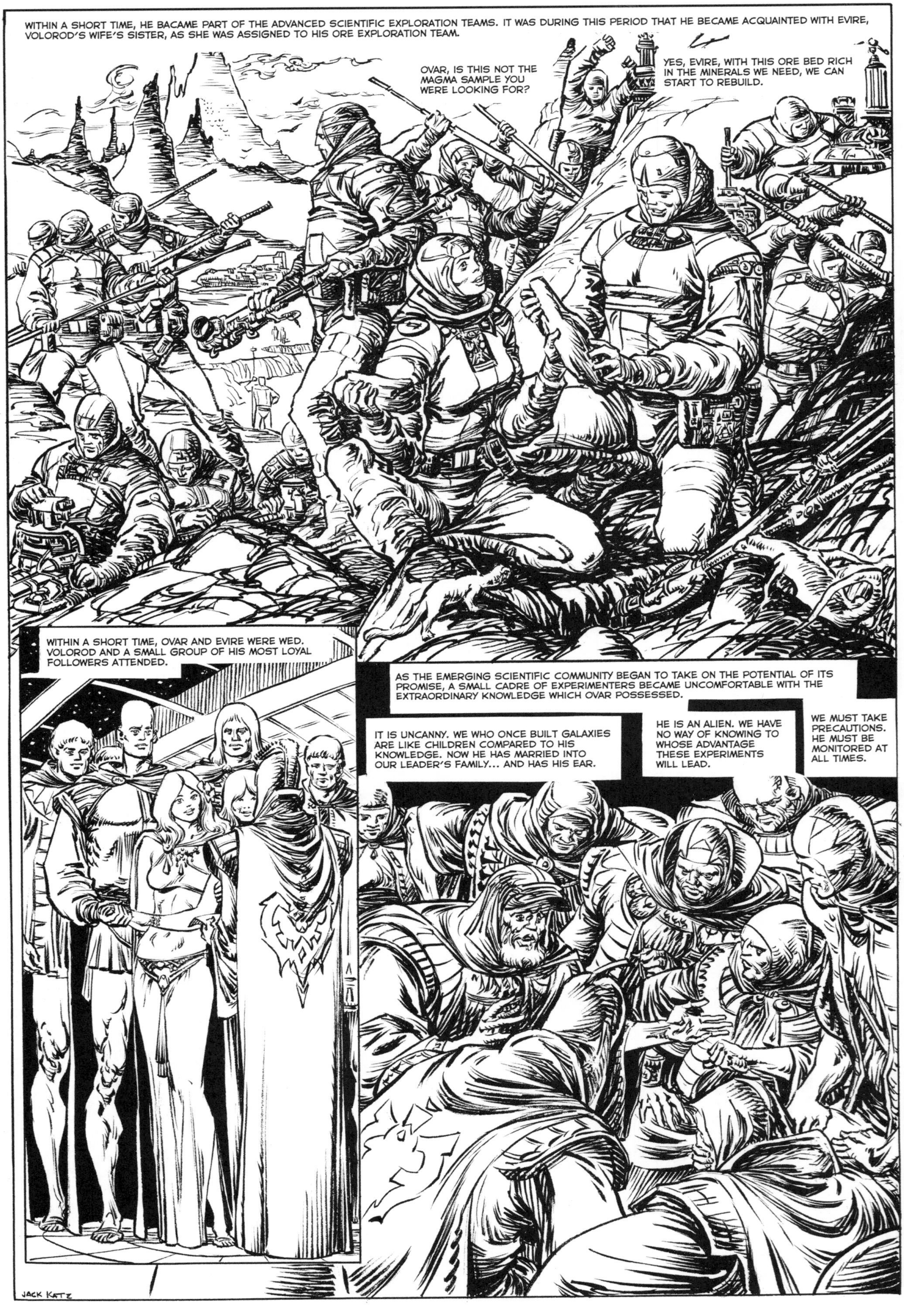
WITHIN A SHORT TIME, HE BACAME PART OF THE ADVANCED SCIENTIFIC EXPLORATION TEAMS. IT WAS DURING THIS PERIOD THAT HE BECAME ACQUAINTED WITH EVIRE, VOLOROD'S WIFE'S SISTER, AS SHE WAS ASSIGNED TO HIS ORE EXPLORATION TEAM.
OVAR, IS THIS NOT THE MAGMA SAMPLE YOU WERE LOOKING FOR?
YES, EVIRE, WITH THIS ORE BED RICH IN THE MINERALS WE NEED, WE CAN START TO REBUILD.
WITHIN A SHORT TIME, OVAR AND EVIRE WERE WED. VOLOROD AND A SMALL GROUP OF HIS MOST LOYAL FOLLOWERS ATTENDED.
AS THE EMERGING SCIENTIFIC COMMUNITY BEGAN TO TAKE ON THE POTENTIAL OF ITS PROMISE, A SMALL CADRE OF EXPERIMENTERS BECAME UNCOMFORTABLE WITH THE EXTRAORDINARY KNOWLEDGE WHICH OVAR POSSESSED.
IT IS UNCANNY. WE WHO ONCE BUILT GALAXIES ARE LIKE CHILDREN COMPARED TO HIS KNOWLEDGE. NOW HE HAS MARRIED INTO OUR LEADER'S FAMILY... AND HAS HIS EAR.
HE IS AN ALIEN. WE HAVE NO WAY OF KNOWING TO WHOSE ADVANTAGE THESE EXPERIMENTS WILL LEAD.
WE MUST TAKE PRECAUTIONS. HE MUST BE MONITORED AT ALL TIMES.
JACK KATZ

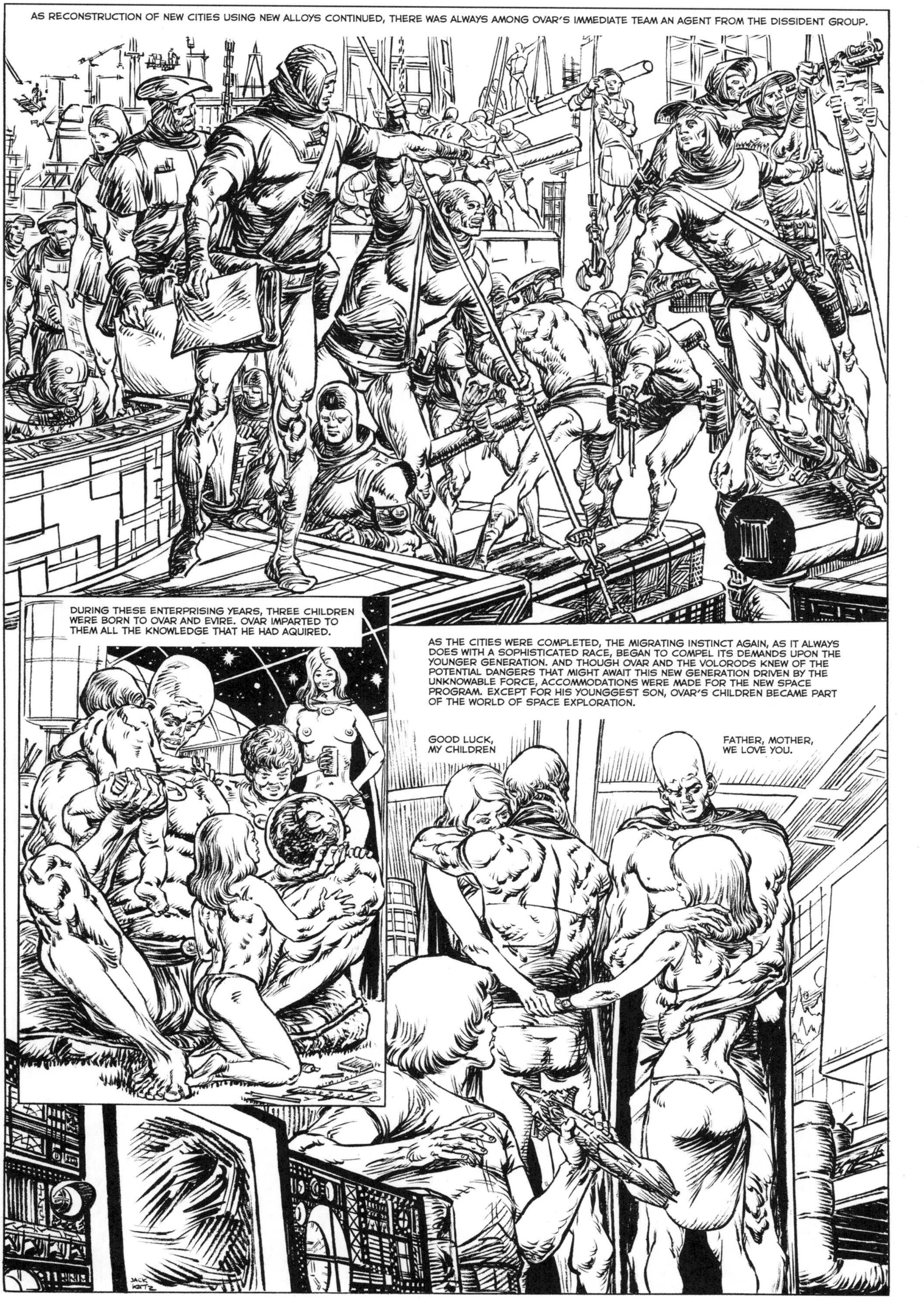
AS RECONSTRUCTION OF NEW CITIES USING NEW ALLOYS CONTINUED, THERE WAS ALWAYS AMONG OVAR'S IMMEDIATE TEAM AN AGENT FROM THE DISSIDENT GROUP.
DURING THESE ENTERPRISING YEARS, THREE CHILDREN WERE BORN TO OVAR AND EVIRE. OVAR IMPARTED TO THEM ALL THE KNOWLEDGE THAT HE HAD AQUIRED.
AS THE CITIES WERE COMPLETED, THE MIGRATING INSTINCT AGAIN, AS IT ALWAYS DOES WITH A SOPHISTICATED RACE, BEGAN TO COMPEL ITS DEMANDS UPON THE YOUNGER GENERATION. AND THOUGH OVAR AND THE VOLORODS KNEW OF THE POTENTIAL DANGERS THAT MIGHT AWAIT THIS NEW GENERATION DRIVEN BY THE UNKNOWABLE FORCE, ACCOMMODATIONS WERE MADE FOR THE NEW SPACE PROGRAM. EXCEPT FOR HIS YOUNGGEST SON, OVAR'S CHILDREN BECAME PART OF THE WORLD OF SPACE EXPLORATION.
GOOD LUCK, MY CHILDREN
FATHER, MOTHER, WE LOVE YOU.
JACK KATZ

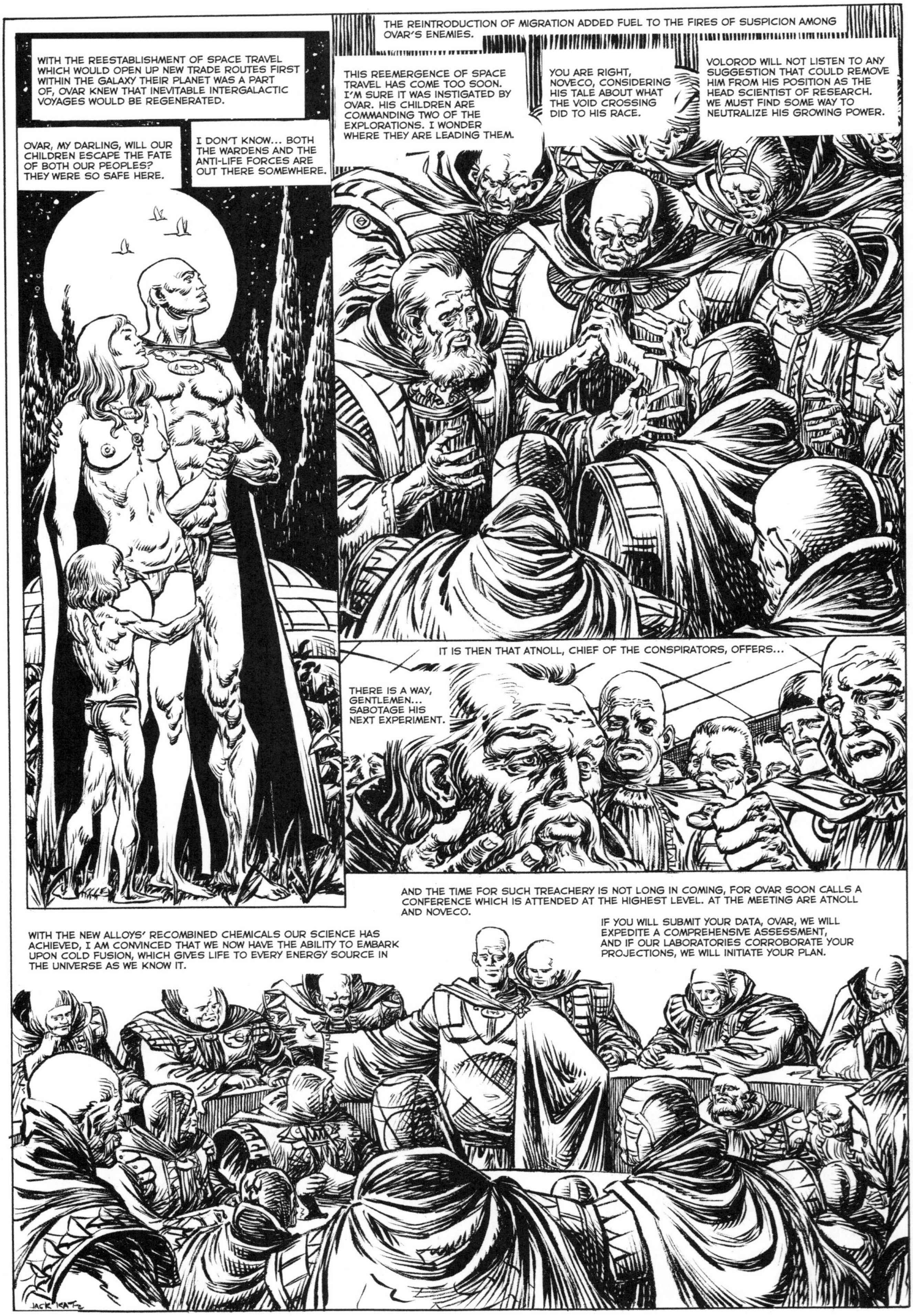
WITH THE REESTABLISHMENT OF SPACE TRAVEL WHICH WOULD OPEN UP NEW TRADE ROUTES FIRST WITHIN THE GALAXY THEIR PLANET WAS A PART OF, OVAR KNEW THAT INEVITABLE INTERGALACTIC VOYAGES WOULD BE REGENERATED.
OVAR, MY DARLING, WILL OUR CHILDREN ESCAPE THE FATE OF BOTH OUR PEOPLES? THEY WERE SO SAFE HERE.
I DON'T KNOW... BOTH THE WARDENS AND THE ANTI-LIFE FORCES ARE OUT THERE SOMEWHERE.
THE REINTRODUCTION OF MIGRATION ADDED FUEL TO THE FIRES OF SUSPICION AMONG OVAR'S ENEMIES.
THIS REEMERGENCE OF SPACE TRAVEL HAS COME TOO SOON. I'M SURE IT WAS INSTIGATED BY OVAR. HIS CHILDREN ARE COMMANDING TWO OF THE EXPLORATIONS. I WONDER WHERE THEY ARE LEADING THEM.
YOU ARE RIGHT, NOVECO, CONSIDERING HIS TALE ABOUT WHAT THE VOID CROSSING DID TO HIS RACE.
VOLOROD WILL NOT LISTEN TO ANY SUGGESTION THAT COULD REMOVE HIM FROM HIS POSITION AS THE HEAD SCIENTIST OF RESEARCH. WE MUST FIND SOME WAY TO NEUTRALIZE HIS GROWING POWER.
IT IS THEN THAT ATNOLL, CHIEF OF THE CONSPIRATORS, OFFERS...
THERE IS A WAY, GENTLEMEN... SABOTAGE HIS NEXT EXPERIMENT.
AND THE TIME FOR SUCH TREACHERY IS NOT LONG IN COMING, FOR OVAR SOON CALLS A CONFERENCE WHICH IS ATTENDED AT THE HIGHEST LEVEL. AT THE MEETING ARE ATNOLL AND NOVECO.
WITH THE NEW ALLOYS' RECOMBINED CHEMICALS OUR SCIENCE HAS ACHIEVED, I AM CONVINCED THAT WE NOW HAVE THE ABILITY TO EMBARK UPON COLD FUSION, WHICH GIVES LIFE TO EVERY ENERGY SOURCE IN THE UNIVERSE AS WE KNOW IT.
IF YOU WILL SUBMIT YOUR DATA, OVAR, WE WILL EXPEDITE A COMPREHENSIVE ASSESSMENT, AND IF OUR LABORATORIES CORROBORATE YOUR PROJECTIONS, WE WILL INITIATE YOUR PLAN.
JACK KATZ

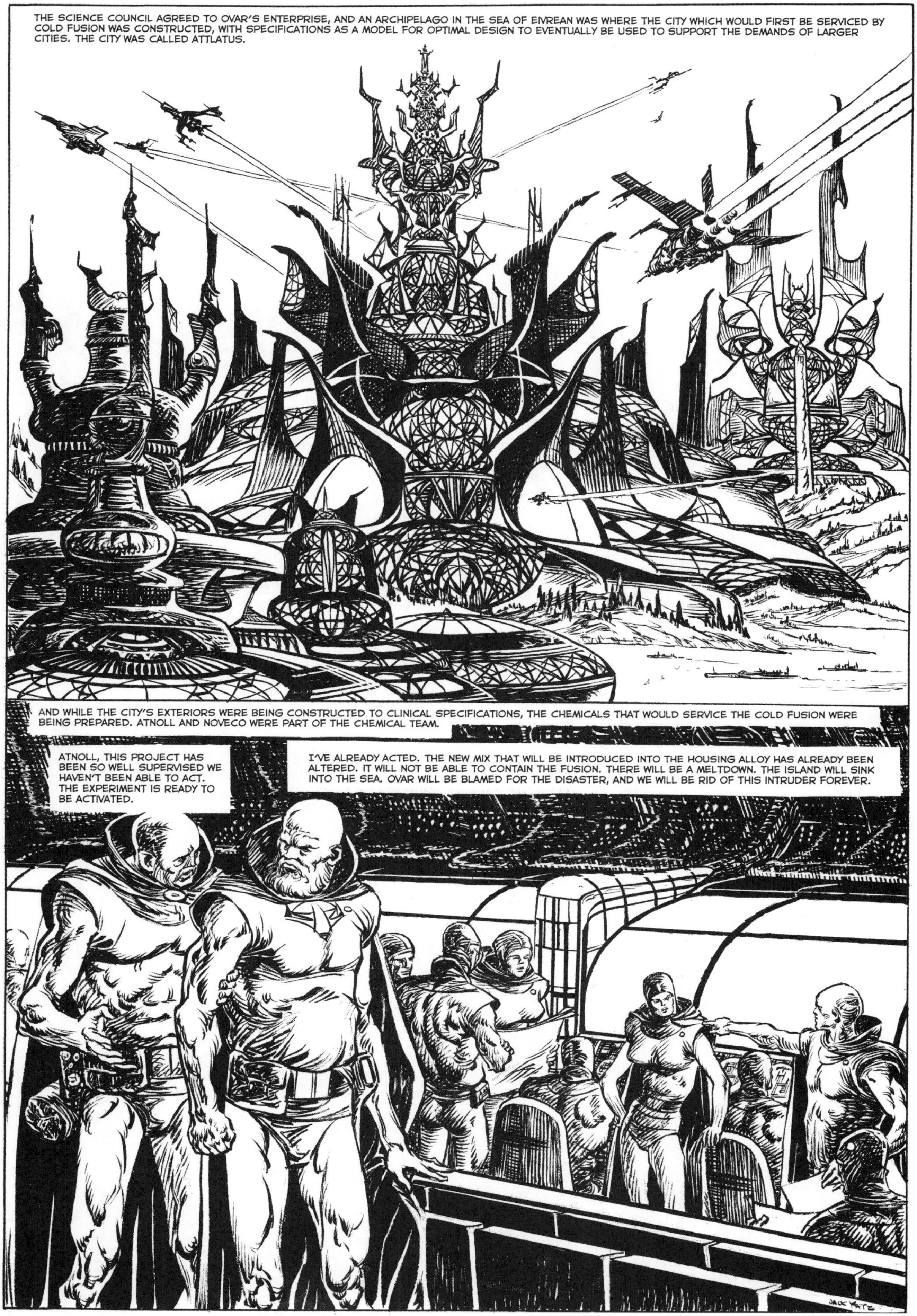
THE SCIENCE COUNCIL AGREED TO OVAR'S ENTERPRISE, AND AN ARCHIPELAGO IN THE SEA OF EIVREAN WAS WHERE THE CITY WHICH WOULD FIRST BE SERVICED BY COLD FUSION WAS CONSTRUCTED, WITH SPECIFICATIONS AS A MODEL FOR OPTIMAL DESIGN TO EVENTUALLY BE USED TO SUPPORT THE DEMANDS OF LARGER CITIES. THE CITY WAS CALLED ATTLATUS.
AND WHILE THE CITY'S EXTERIORS WERE BEING CONSTRUCTED TO CLINICAL SPECIFICATIONS, THE CHEMICALS THAT WOULD SERVICE THE COLD FUSION WERE BEING PREPARED. ATNOLL AND NOVECO WERE PART OF THE CHEMICAL TEAM.
ATNOLL, THIS PROJECT HAS BEEN SO WELL SUPERVISED WE HAVEN'T BEEN ABLE TO ACT. THE EXPERIMENT IS READY TO BE ACTIVATED.
I'VE ALREADY ACTED. THE NEW MIX THAT WILL BE INTRODUCED INTO THE HOUSING ALLOY HAS ALREADY BEEN ALTERED. IT WILL NOT BE ABLE TO CONTAIN THE FUSION. THERE WILL BE A MELTDOWN. THE ISLAND WILL SINK INTO THE SEA. OVAR WILL BE BLAMED FOR THE DISASTER, AND WE WILL BE RID OF THIS INTRUDER FOREVER.

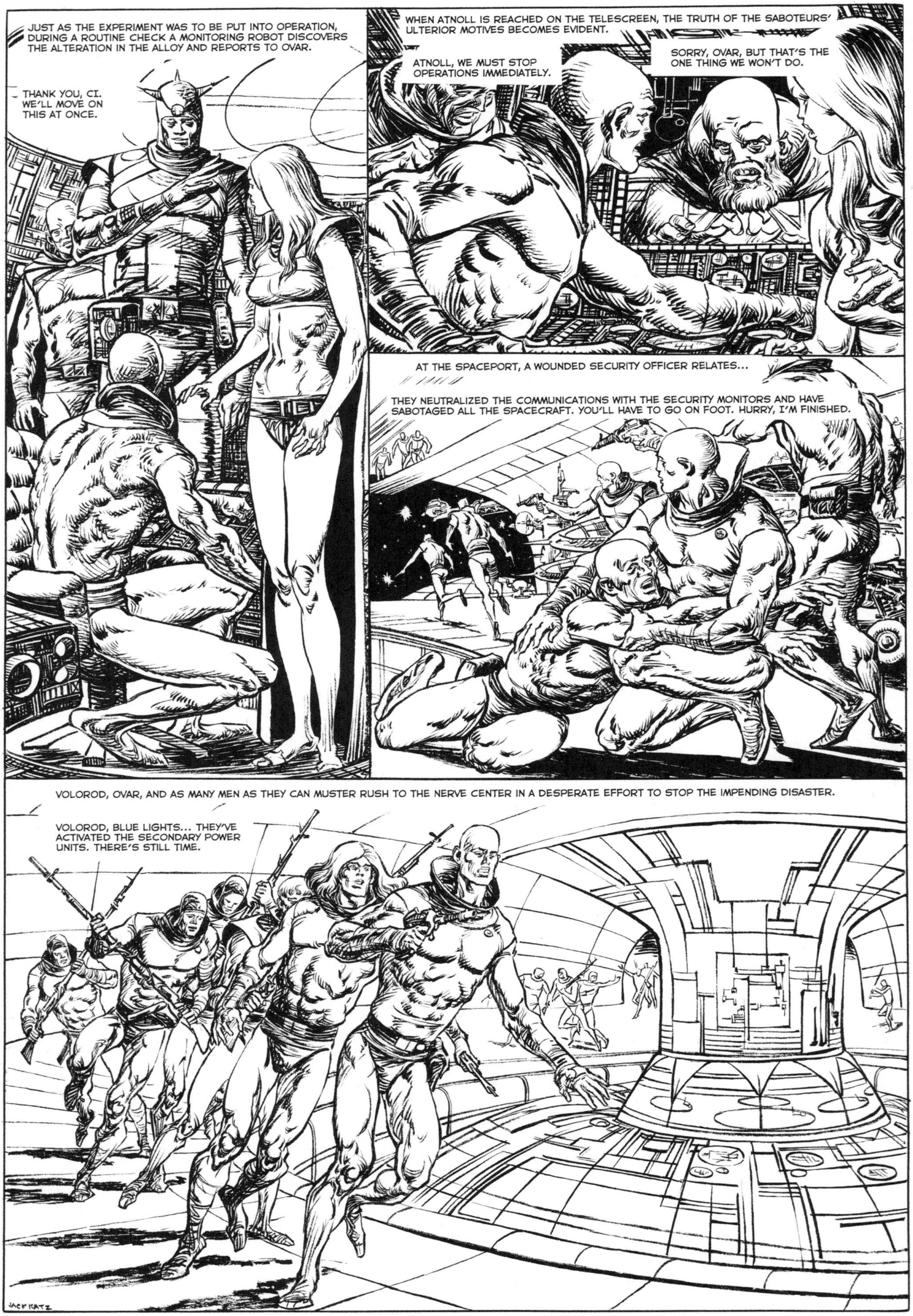
JUST AS THE EXPERIMENT WAS TO BE PUT INTO OPERATION, DURING A ROUTINE CHECK A MONITORING ROBOT DISCOVERS THE ALTERATION IN THE ALLOY AND REPORTS TO OVAR.
THANK YOU, CI. WE'LL MOVE ON THIS AT ONCE.
WHEN ATNOLL IS REACHED ON THE TELESCREEN, THE TRUTH OF THE SABOTEURS' ULTERIOR MOTIVES BECOMES EVIDENT.
ATNOLL, WE MUST STOP OPERATIONS IMMEDIATELY.
SORRY, OVAR, BUT THAT'S THE ONE THING WE WON'T DO.
AT THE SPACEPORT, A WOUNDED SECURITY OFFICER RELATES...
THEY NEUTRALIZED THE COMMUNICATIONS WITH THE SECURITY MONITORS AND HAVE SABOTAGED ALL THE SPACECRAFT. YOU'LL HAVE TO GO ON FOOT. HURRY, I'M FINISHED.
VOLOROD, OVAR, AND AS MANY MEN AS THEY CAN MUSTER RUSH TO THE NERVE CENTER IN A DESPERATE EFFORT TO STOP THE IMPENDING DISASTER.
VOLOROD, BLUE LIGHTS... THEY'VE ACTIVATED THE SECONDARY POWER UNITS. THERE'S STILL TIME.
JACK KATZ

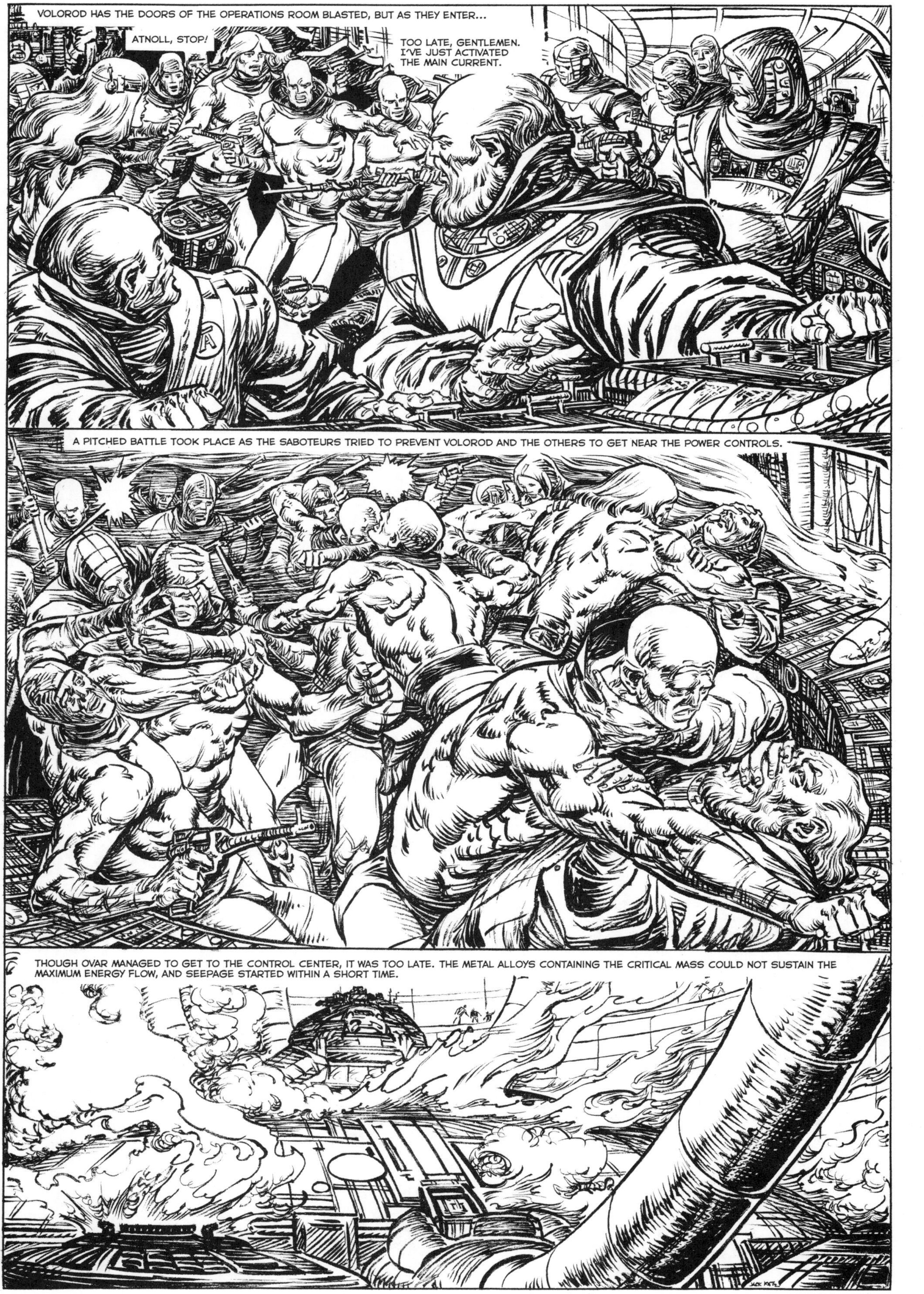

VOLOROD HAS THE DOORS OF THE OPERATIONS ROOM BLASTED, BUT AS THEY ENTER...
ATNOLL, STOP!
TOO LATE, GENTLEMEN. I'VE JUST ACTIVATED THE MAIN CURRENT.
A PITCHED BATTLE TOOK PLACE AS THE SABOTEURS TRIED TO PREVENT VOLOROD AND THE OTHERS TO GET NEAR THE POWER CONTROLS.
THOUGH OVAR MANAGED TO GET TO THE CONTROL CENTER, IT WAS TOO LATE. THE METAL ALLOYS CONTAINING THE CRITICAL MASS COULD NOT SUSTAIN THE MAXIMUM ENERGY FLOW, AND SEEPAGE STARTED WITHIN A SHORT TIME.

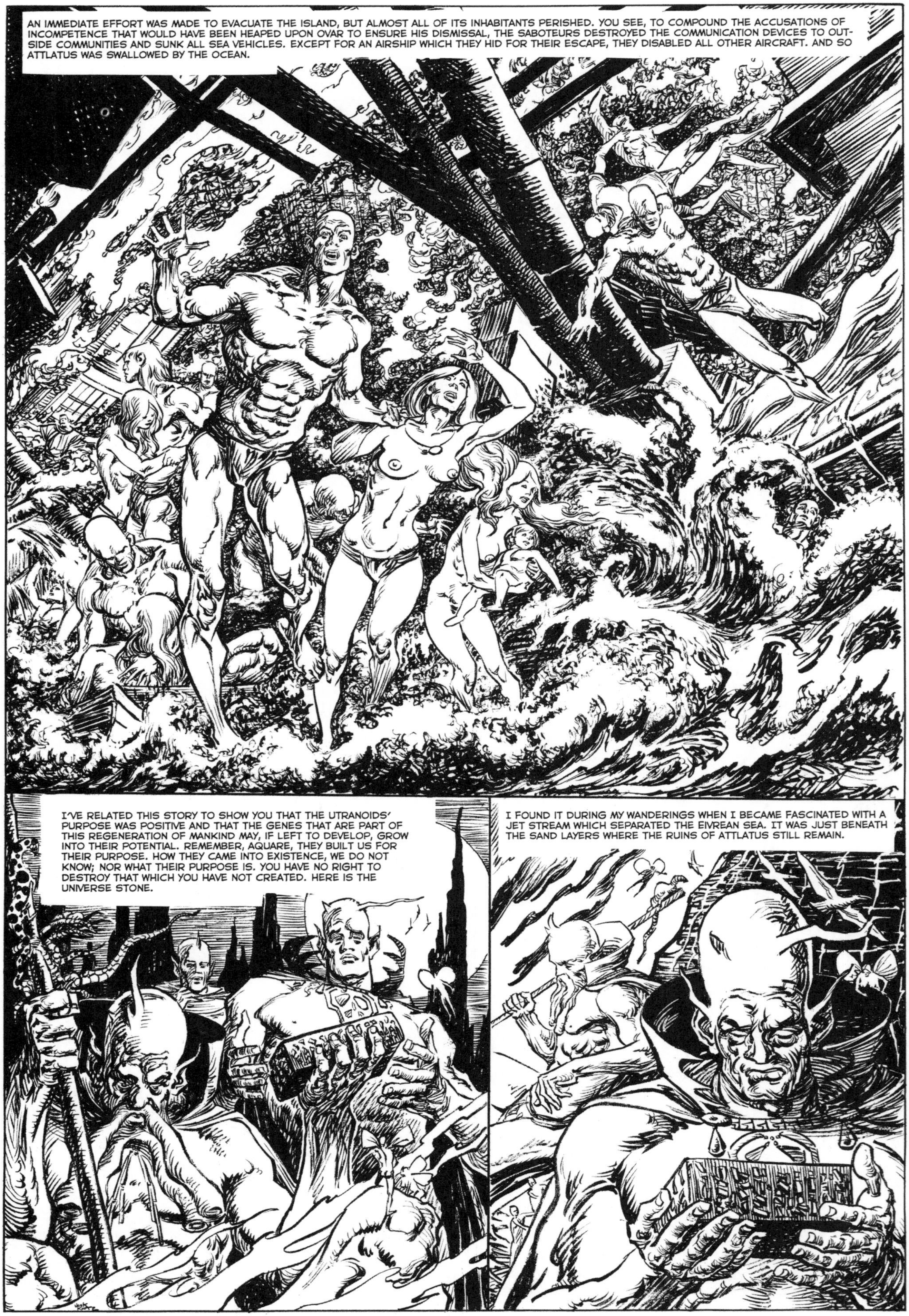
AN IMMEDIATE EFFORT WAS MADE TO EVACUATE THE ISLAND, BUT ALMOST ALL OF ITS INHABITANTS PERISHED. YOU SEE, TO COMPOUND THE ACCUSATIONS OF INCOMPETENCE THAT WOULD HAVE BEEN HEAPED UPON OVAR TO ENSURE HIS DISMISSAL, THE SABOTEURS DESTROYED THE COMMUNICATION DEVICES TO OUTSIDE COMMUNITIES AND SUNK ALL SEA VEHICLES. EXCEPT FOR AN AIRSHIP WHICH THEY HID FOR THEIR ESCAPE, THEY DISABLED ALL OTHER AIRCRAFT. AND SO ATTLATUS WAS SWALLOWED BY THE OCEAN.
I'VE RELATED THIS STORY TO SHOW YOU THAT THE UTRANOIDS' PURPOSE WAS POSITIVE AND THAT THE GENES THAT ARE PART OF THIS REGENERATION OF MANKIND MAY, IF LEFT TO DEVELOP, GROW INTO THEIR POTENTIAL. REMEMBER, AQUARE, THEY BUILT US FOR THEIR PURPOSE. HOW THEY CAME INTO EXISTENCE, WE DO NOT KNOW; NOR WHAT THEIR PURPOSE IS. YOU HAVE NO RIGHT TO DESTROY THAT WHICH YOU HAVE NOT CREATED. HERE IS THE UNIVERSE STONE.
I FOUND IT DURING MY WANDERINGS WHEN I BECAME FASCINATED WITH A JET STREAM WHICH SEPARATED THE EIVREAN SEA. IT WAS JUST BENEATH THE SAND LAYERS WHERE THE RUINS OF ATTLATUS STILL REMAIN.

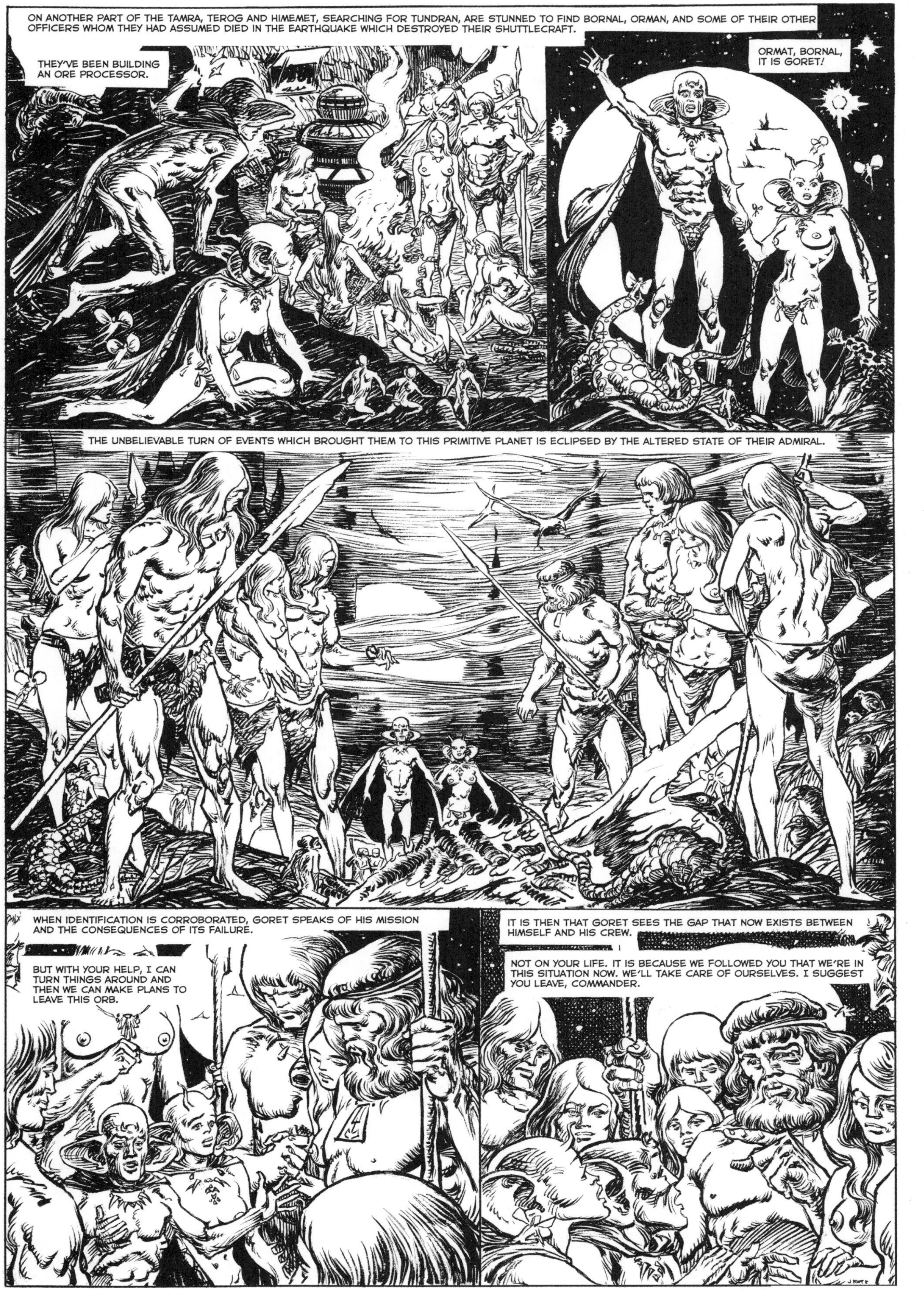
ON ANOTHER PART OF THE TAMRA, TEROG AND HIMEMET, SEARCHING FOR TUNDRAN, ARE STUNNED TO FIND BORNAL, ORMAN, AND SOME OF THEIR OTHER OFFICERS WHOM THEY HAD ASSUMED DIED IN THE EARTHQUAKE WHICH DESTROYED THEIR SHUTTLECRAFT.
THEY'VE BEEN BUILDING AN ORE PROCESSOR.
ORMAT, BORNAL, IT IS GORET!
THE UNBELIEVABLE TURN OF EVENTS WHICH BROUGHT THEM TO THIS PRIMITIVE PLANET IS ECLIPSED BY THE ALTERED STATE OF THEIR ADMIRAL.
WHEN IDENTIFICATION IS CORROBORATED, GORET SPEAKS OF HIS MISSION AND THE CONSEQUENCES OF ITS FAILURE.
BUT WITH YOUR HELP, I CAN TURN THINGS AROUND AND THEN WE CAN MAKE PLANS TO LEAVE THIS ORB.
IT IS THEN THAT GORET SEES THE GAP THAT NOW EXISTS BETWEEN HIMSELF AND HIS CREW.
NOT ON YOUR LIFE. IT IS BECAUSE WE FOLLOWED YOU THAT WE'RE IN THIS SITUATION NOW. WE'LL TAKE CARE OF OURSELVES. I SUGGEST YOU LEAVE, COMMANDER.

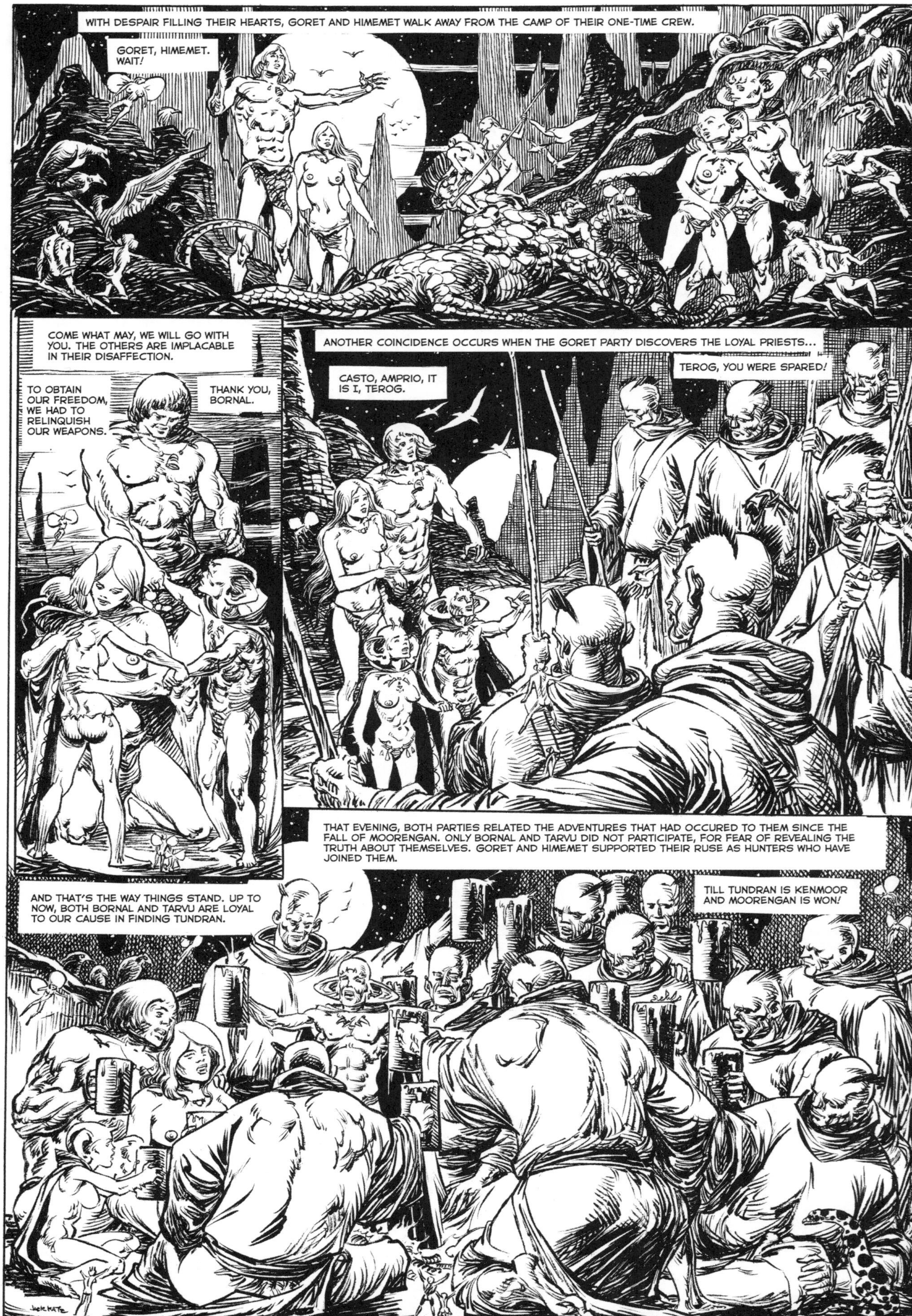
WITH DESPAIR FILLING THEIR HEARTS, GORET AND HIMEMET WALK AWAY FROM THE CAMP OF THEIR ONE-TIME CREW.
GORET, HIMEMET. WAIT!
COME WHAT MAY, WE WILL GO WITH YOU. THE OTHERS ARE IMPLACABLE IN THEIR DISAFFECTION.
TO OBTAIN OUR FREEDOM, WE HAD TO RELINQUISH OUR WEAPONS.
THANK YOU, BORNAL.
ANOTHER COINCIDENCE OCCURS WHEN THE GORET PARTY DISCOVERS THE LOYAL PRIESTS...
CASTO, AMPRIO, IT IS I, TEROG.
TEROG, YOU WERE SPARED!
THAT EVENING, BOTH PARTIES RELATED THE ADVENTURES THAT HAD OCCURED TO THEM SINCE THE FALL OF MOORENGAN. ONLY BORNAL AND TARVU DID NOT PARTICIPATE, FOR FEAR OF REVEALING THE TRUTH ABOUT THEMSELVES. GORET AND HIMEMET SUPPORTED THEIR RUSE AS HUNTERS WHO HAVE JOINED THEM.
AND THAT'S THE WAY THINGS STAND. UP TO NOW, BOTH BORNAL AND TARVU ARE LOYAL TO OUR CAUSE IN FINDING TUNDRAN.
TILL TUNDRAN IS KENMOOR AND MOORENGAN IS WON!

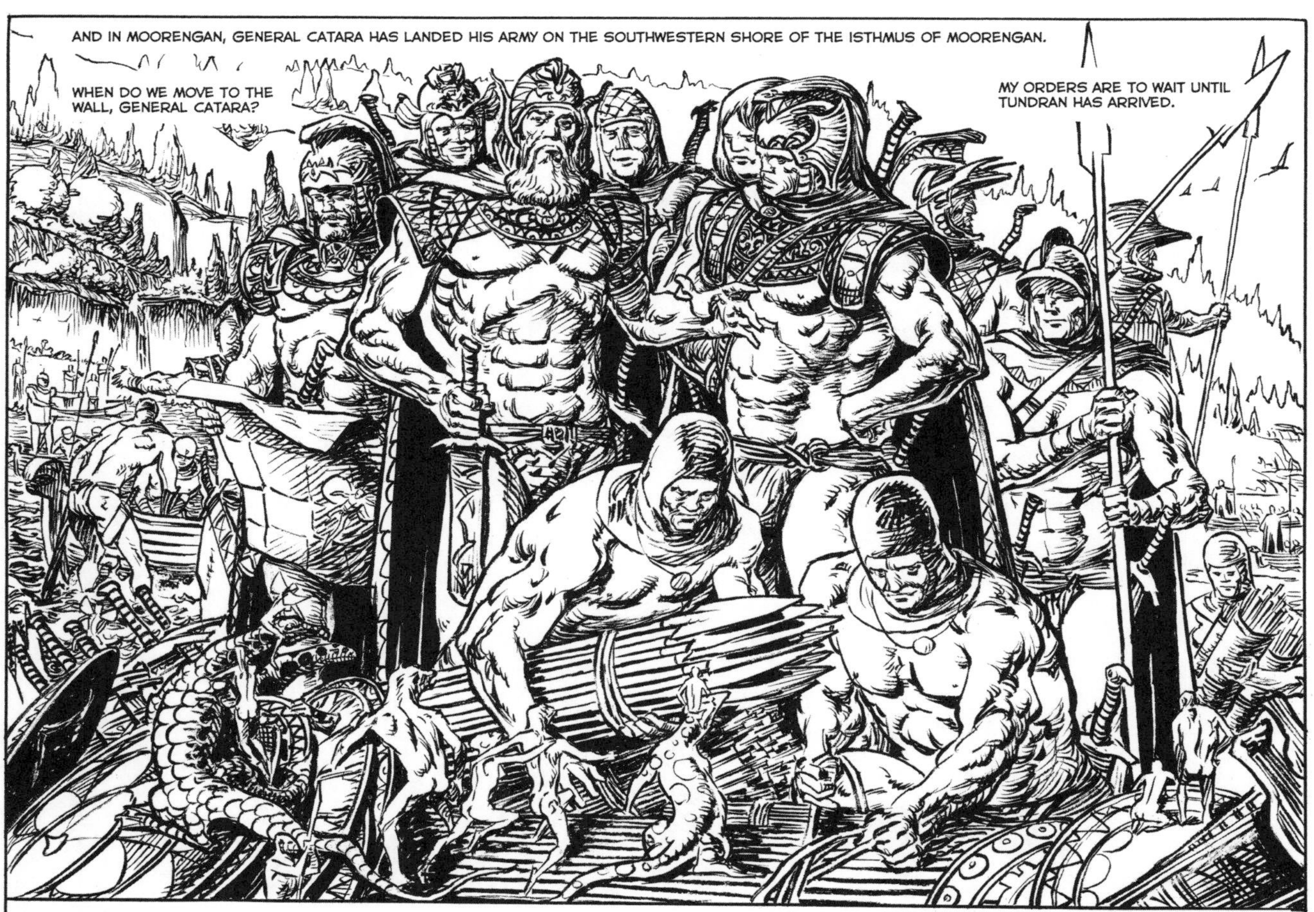
AND IN MOORENGAN, GENERAL CATARA HAS LANDED HIS ARMY ON THE SOUTHWESTERN SHORE OF THE ISTHMUS OF MOORENGAN.
WHEN DO WE MOVE TO THE WALL, GENERAL CATARA?
MY ORDERS ARE TO WAIT UNTIL TUNDRAN HAS ARRIVED.

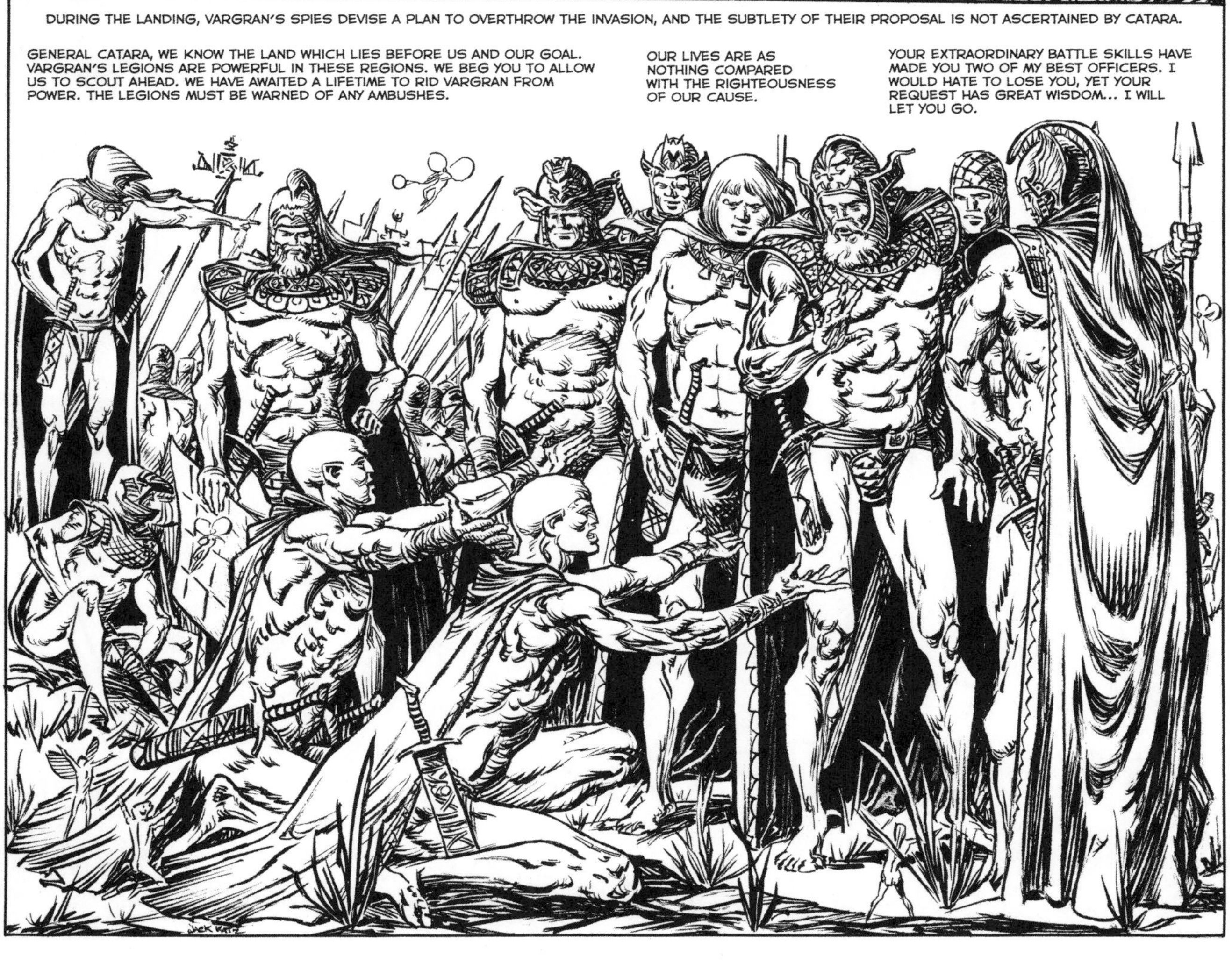
DURING THE LANDING, VARGRAN'S SPIES DEVISE A PLAN TO OVERTHROW THE INVASION, AND THE SUBTLETY OF THEIR PROPOSAL IS NOT ASCERTAINED BY CATARA.
GENERAL CATARA, WE KNOW THE LAND WHICH LIES BEFORE US AND OUR GOAL. VARGRAN'S LEGIONS ARE POWERFUL IN THESE REGIONS. WE BEG YOU TO ALLOW US TO SCOUT AHEAD. WE HAVE AWAITED A LIFETIME TO RID VARGRAN FROM POWER. THE LEGIONS MUST BE WARNED OF ANY AMBUSHES.
OUR LIVES ARE AS NOTHING COMPARED WITH THE RIGHTEOUSNESS OF OUR CAUSE.
YOUR EXTRAORDINARY BATTLE SKILLS HAVE MADE YOU TWO OF MY BEST OFFICERS. I WOULD HATE TO LOSE YOU, YET YOUR REQUEST HAS GREAT WISDOM... I WILL LET YOU GO.
JACK KATZ

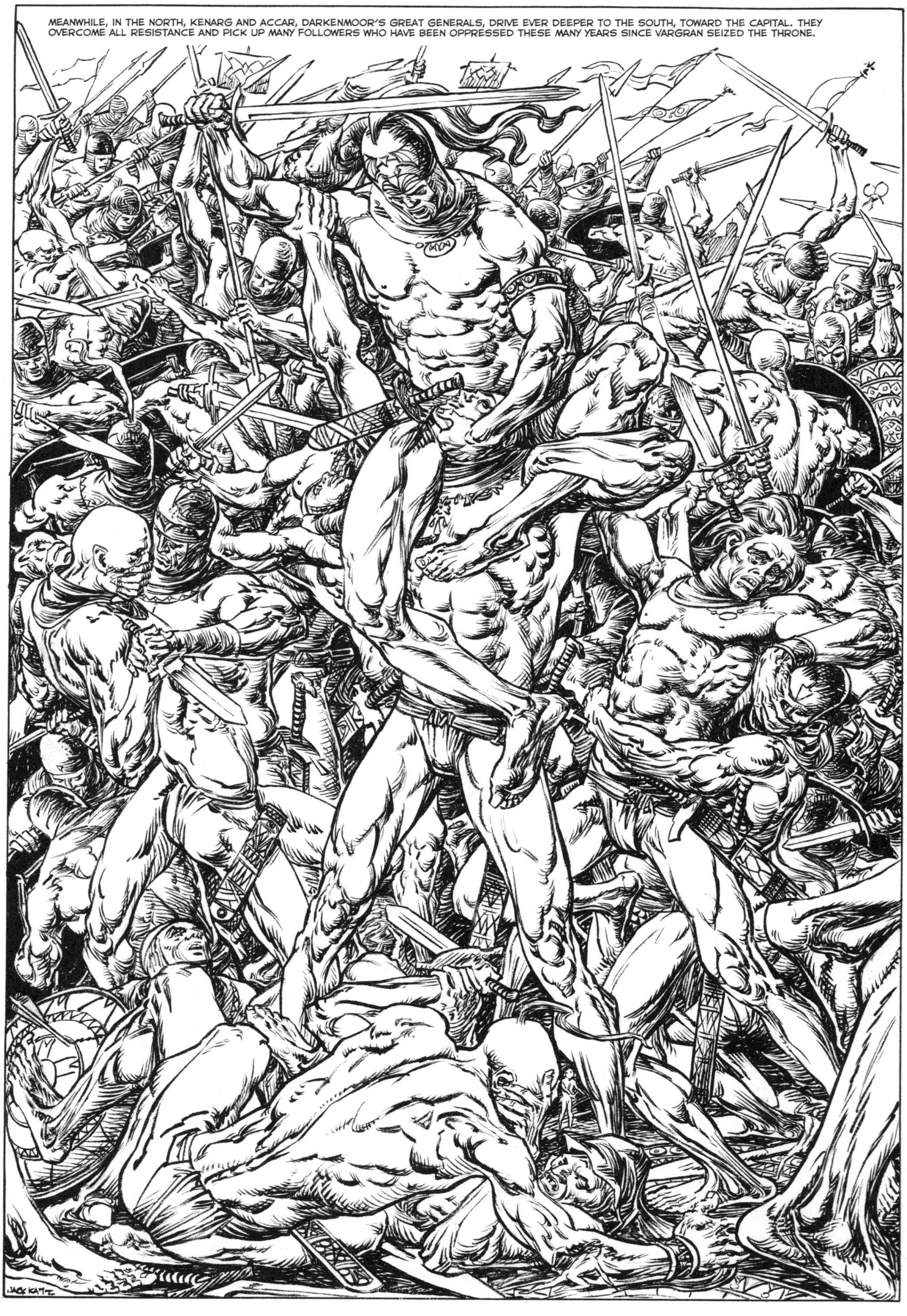
MEANWHILE, IN THE NORTH, KENARG AND ACCAR, DARKENMOOR'S GREAT GENERALS, DRIVE EVER DEEPER TO THE SOUTH, TOWARD THE CAPITAL. THEY OVERCOME ALL RESISTANCE AND PICK UP MANY FOLLOWERS WHO HAVE BEEN OPPRESSED THESE MANY YEARS SINCE VARGRAN SEIZED THE THRONE.
JACK KATZ

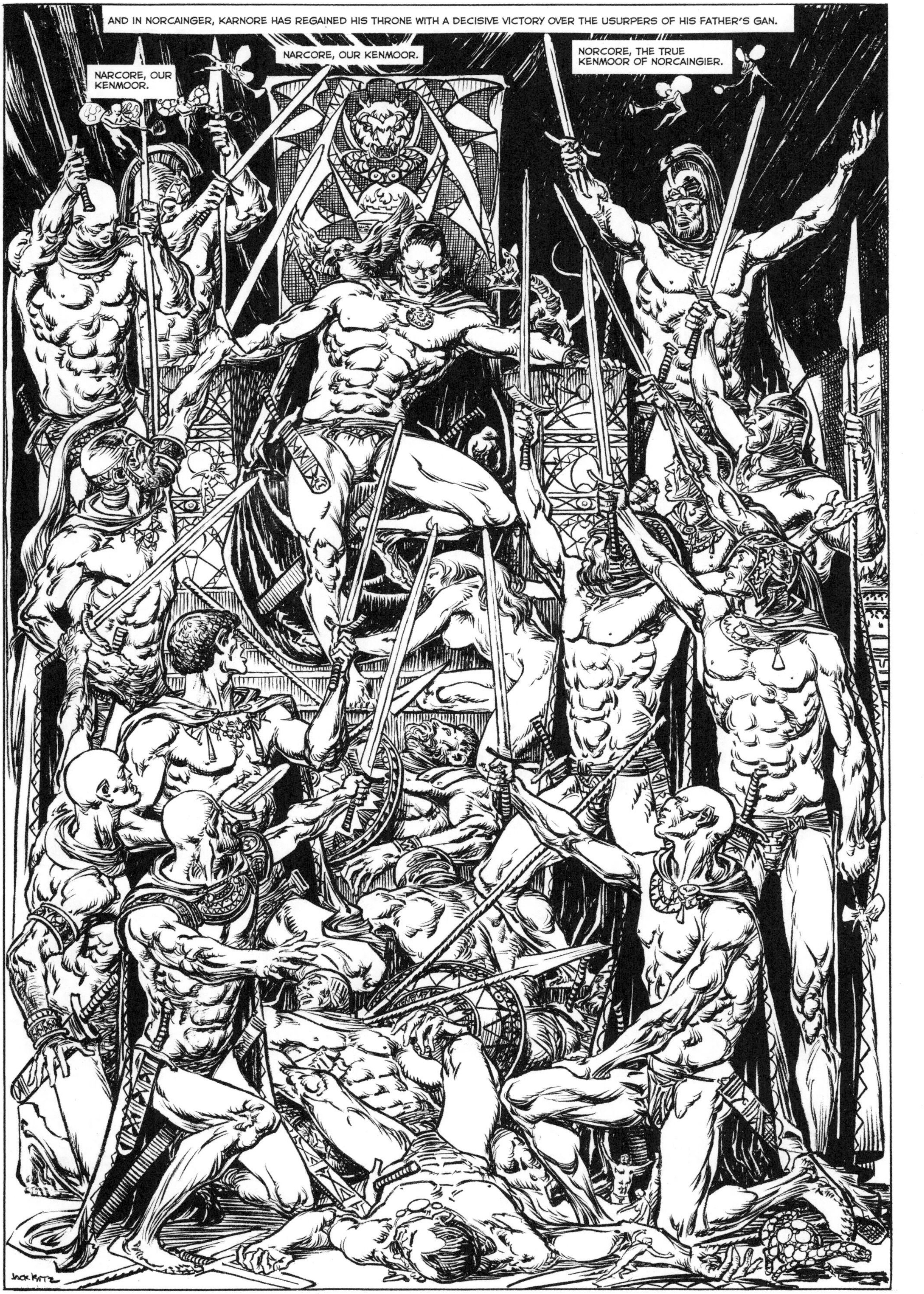
AND IN NORCAINGER, KARNORE HAS REGAINED HIS THRONE WITH A DECISIVE VICTORY OVER THE USURPERS OF HIS FATHER'S GAN.
NARCORE, OUR KENMOOR.
NARCORE, OUR KENMOOR.
NORCORE, THE TRUE KENMOOR OF NORCAINGIER.
JACK KATZ

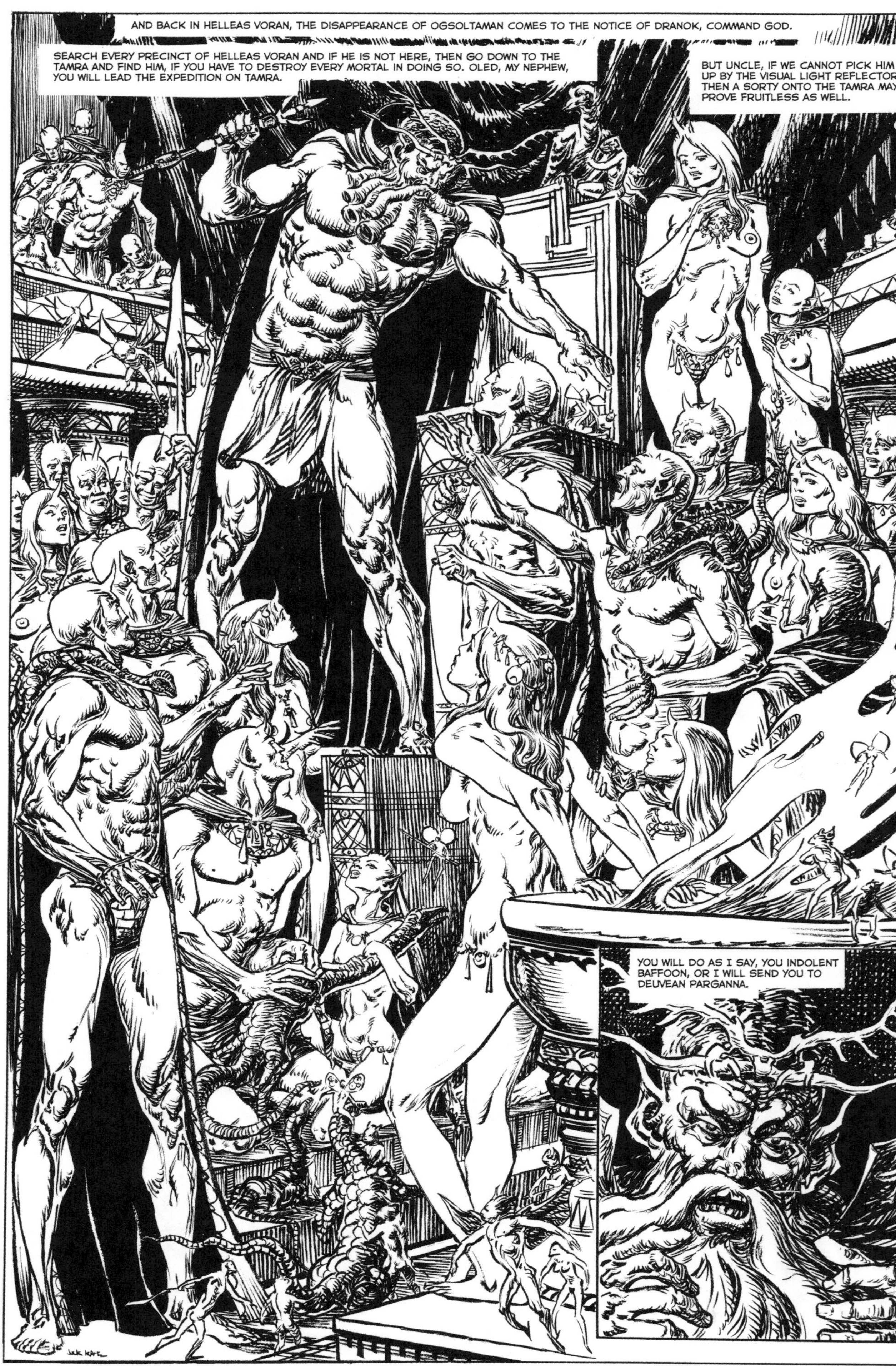
AND BACK IN HELLEAS VORAN, THE DISAPPEARANCE OF OGSOLTAMAN COMES TO THE NOTICE OF DRANOK, COMMAND GOD.
SEARCH EVERY PRECINCT OF HELLEAS VORAN AND IF HE IS NOT HERE, THEN GO DOWN TO THE TAMRA AND FIND HIM, IF YOU HAVE TO DESTROY EVERY MORTAL IN DOING SO. OLED, MY NEPHEW, YOU WILL LEAD THE EXPEDITION ON TAMRA.
BUT UNCLE, IF WE CANNOT PICK HIM UP BY THE VISUAL LIGHT REFLECTOR, THEN A SORTY ONTO THE TAMRA MAY PROVE FRUITLESS AS WELL.
YOU WILL DO AS I SAY, YOU INDOLENT BAFFOON, OR I WILL SEND YOU TO DEUVEAN PARGANNA.

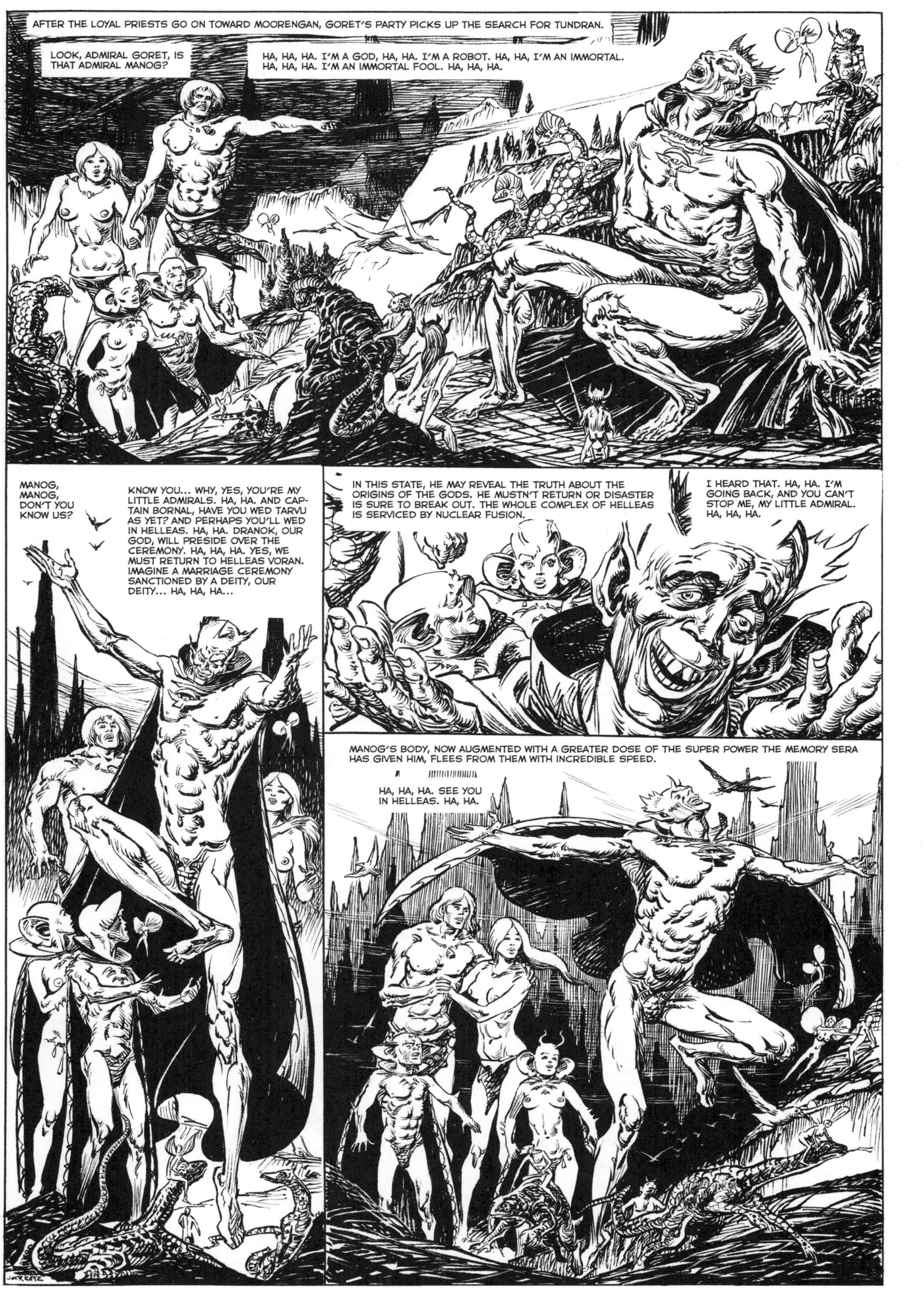
AFTER THE LOYAL PRIESTS GO ON TOWARD MOORENGAN, GORET'S PARTY PICKS UP THE SEARCH FOR TUNDRAN.
LOOK, ADMIRAL GORET, IS THAT ADMIRAL MANOG?
HA, HA, HA. I'M A GOD, HA, HA. I'M A ROBOT. HA, HA, I'M AN IMMORTAL. HA, HA, HA. I'M AN IMMORTAL FOOL. HA, HA, HA.
MANOG, MANOG, DON'T YOU KNOW US?
KNOW YOU... WHY, YES, YOU'RE MY LITTLE ADMIRALS. HA, HA. AND CAPTAIN BORNAL, HAVE YOU WED TARVU AS YET? AND PERHAPS YOU'LL WED IN HELLEAS. HA, HA. DRANOK, OUR GOD, WILL PRESIDE OVER THE CEREMONY. HA, HA, HA. YES, WE MUST RETURN TO HELLEAS VORAN. IMAGINE A MARRIAGE CEREMONY SANCTIONED BY A DEITY, OUR DEITY... HA, HA, HA...
IN THIS STATE, HE MAY REVEAL THE TRUTH ABOUT THE ORIGINS OF THE GODS. HE MUSTN'T RETURN OR DISASTER IS SURE TO BREAK OUT. THE WHOLE COMPLEX OF HELLEAS IS SERVICED BY NUCLEAR FUSION.
I HEARD THAT. HA, HA. I'M GOING BACK, AND YOU CAN'T STOP ME, MY LITTLE ADMIRAL. HA, HA, HA.
MANOG'S BODY, NOW AUGMENTED WITH A GREATER DOSE OF THE SUPER POWER THE MEMORY SERA HAS GIVEN HIM, FLEES FROM THEM WITH INCREDIBLE SPEED.
HA, HA, HA. SEE YOU IN HELLEAS. HA, HA.

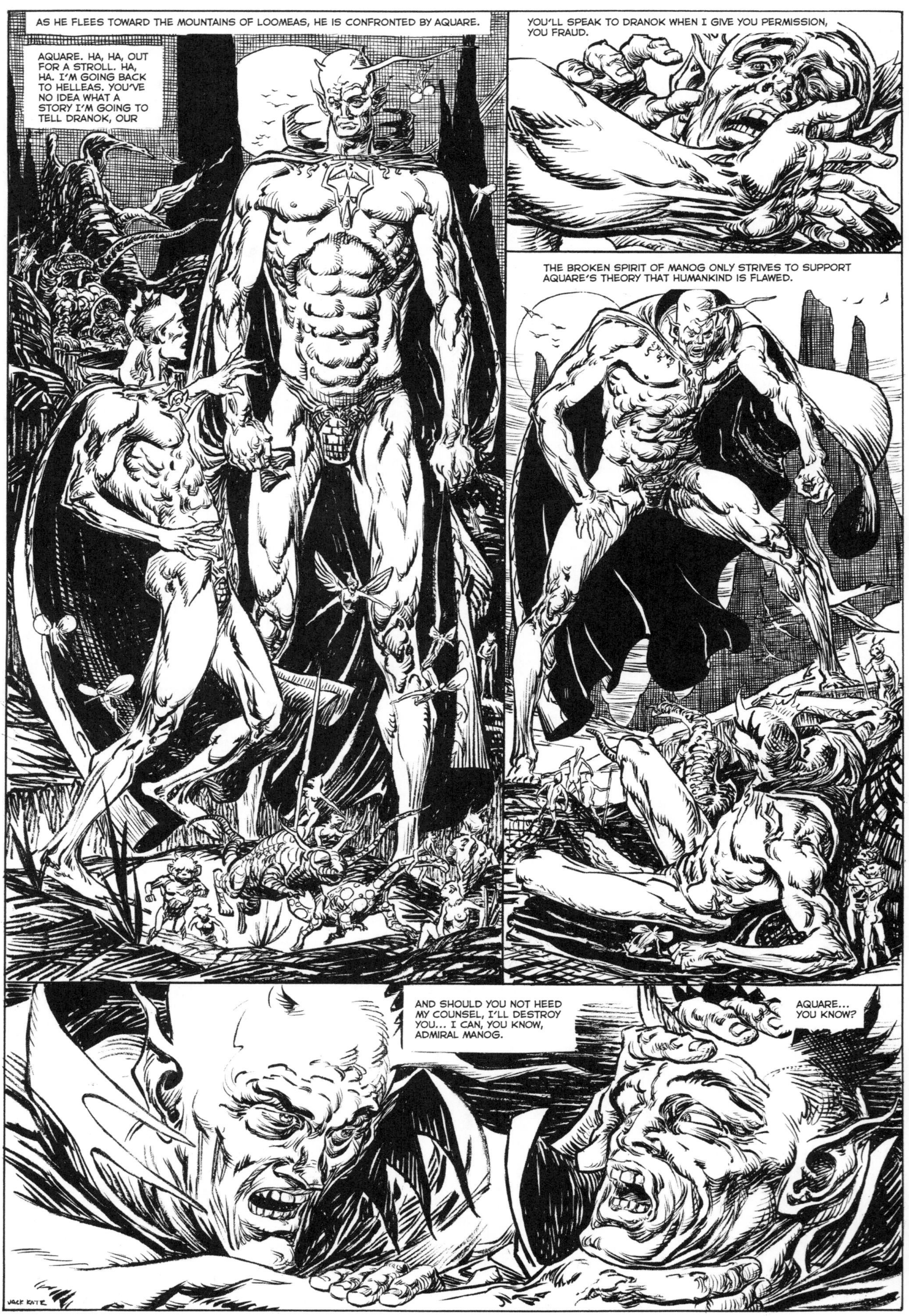
AS HE FLEES TOWARD THE MOUNTAINS OF LOOMEAS, HE IS CONFRONTED BY AQUARE.
AQUARE. HA, HA, OUT FOR A STROLL. HA, HA. I'M GOING BACK TO HELLEAS. YOU'VE NO IDEA WHAT A STORY I'M GOING TO TELL DRANOK, OUR
YOU'LL SPEAK TO DRANOK WHEN I GIVE YOU PERMISSION, YOU FRAUD.
THE BROKEN SPIRIT OF MANOG ONLY STRIVES TO SUPPORT AQUARE'S THEORY THAT HUMANKIND IS FLAWED.
AND SHOULD YOU NOT HEED MY COUNSEL, I'LL DESTROY YOU... I CAN, YOU KNOW, ADMIRAL MANOG.
AQUARE... YOU KNOW?
JACK KATZ

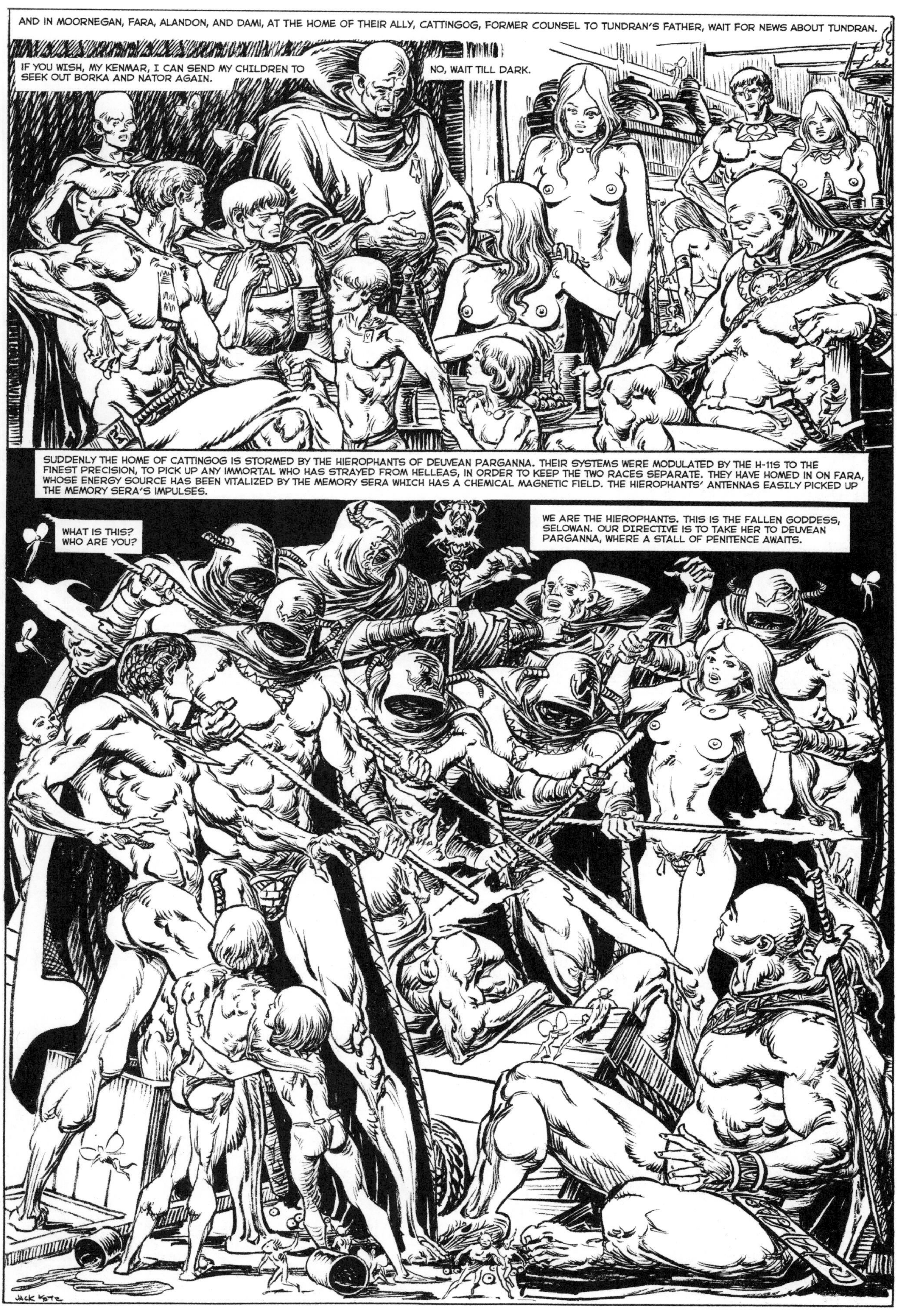
AND IN MOORNEGAN, FARA, ALANDON, AND DAMI, AT THE HOME OF THEIR ALLY, CATTINGOG, FORMER COUNSEL TO TUNDRAN'S FATHER, WAIT FOR NEWS ABOUT TUNDRAN.
IF YOU WISH, MY KENMAR, I CAN SEND MY CHILDREN TO SEEK OUT BORKA AND NATOR AGAIN.
NO, WAIT TILL DARK.
SUDDENLY THE HOME OF CATTINGOG IS STORMED BY THE HIEROPHANTS OF DEUVEAN PARGANNA. THEIR SYSTEMS WERE MODULATED BY THE H-11S TO THE FINEST PRECISION, TO PICK UP ANY IMMORTAL WHO HAS STRAYED FROM HELLEAS, IN ORDER TO KEEP THE TWO RACES SEPARATE. THEY HAVE HOMED IN ON FARA, WHOSE ENERGY SOURCE HAS BEEN VITALIZED BY THE MEMORY SERA WHICH HAS A CHEMICAL MAGNETIC FIELD. THE HIEROPHANTS' ANTENNAS EASILY PICKED UP THE MEMORY SERA'S IMPULSES.
WHAT IS THIS? WHO ARE YOU?
WE ARE THE HIEROPHANTS. THIS IS THE FALLEN GODDESS, SELOWAN. OUR DIRECTIVE IS TO TAKE HER TO DEUVEAN PARGANNA, WHERE A STALL OF PENITENCE AWAITS.
JACK KATZ

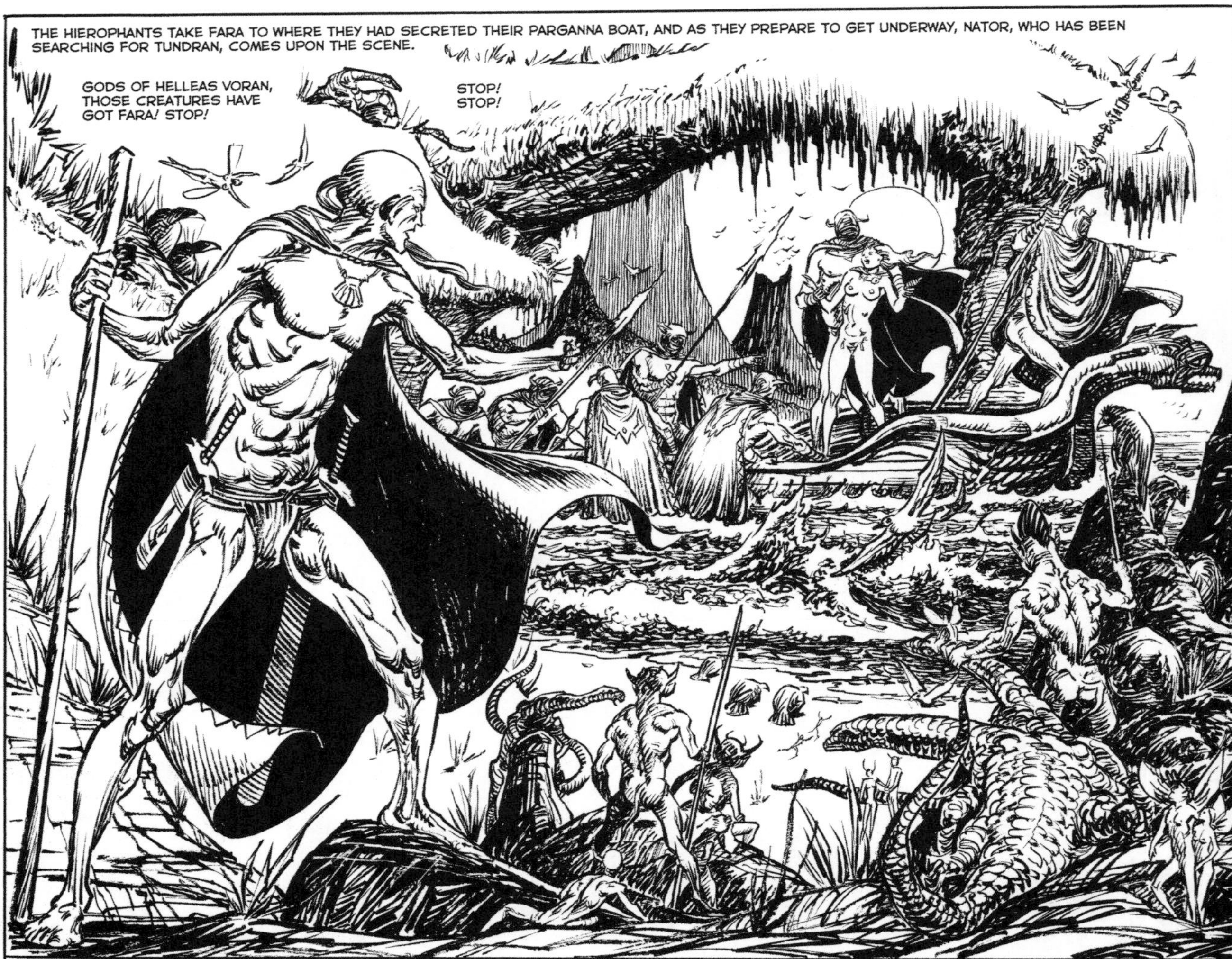
THE HIEROPHANTS TAKE FARA TO WHERE THEY HAD SECRETED THEIR PARGANNA BOAT, AND AS THEY PREPARE TO GET UNDERWAY, NATOR, WHO HAS BEEN SEARCHING FOR TUNDRAN, COMES UPON THE SCENE.
GODS OF HELLEAS VORAN, THOSE CREATURES HAVE GOT FARA! STOP!
STOP! STOP!

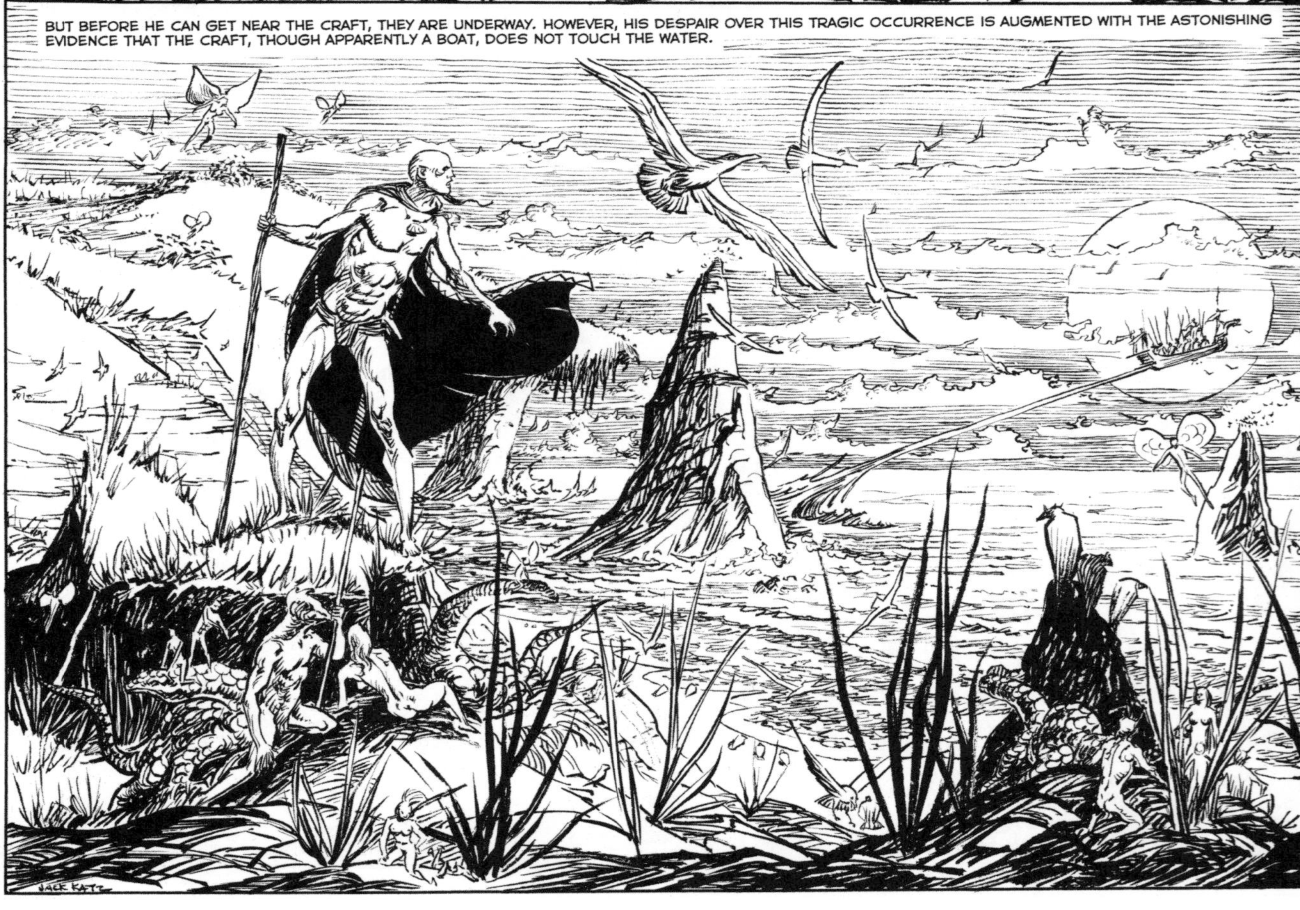
BUT BEFORE HE CAN GET NEAR THE CRAFT, THEY ARE UNDERWAY. HOWEVER, HIS DESPAIR OVER THIS TRAGIC OCCURRENCE IS AUGMENTED WITH THE ASTONISHING EVIDENCE THAT THE CRAFT, THOUGH APPARENTLY A BOAT, DOES NOT TOUCH THE WATER.
JACK KATZ

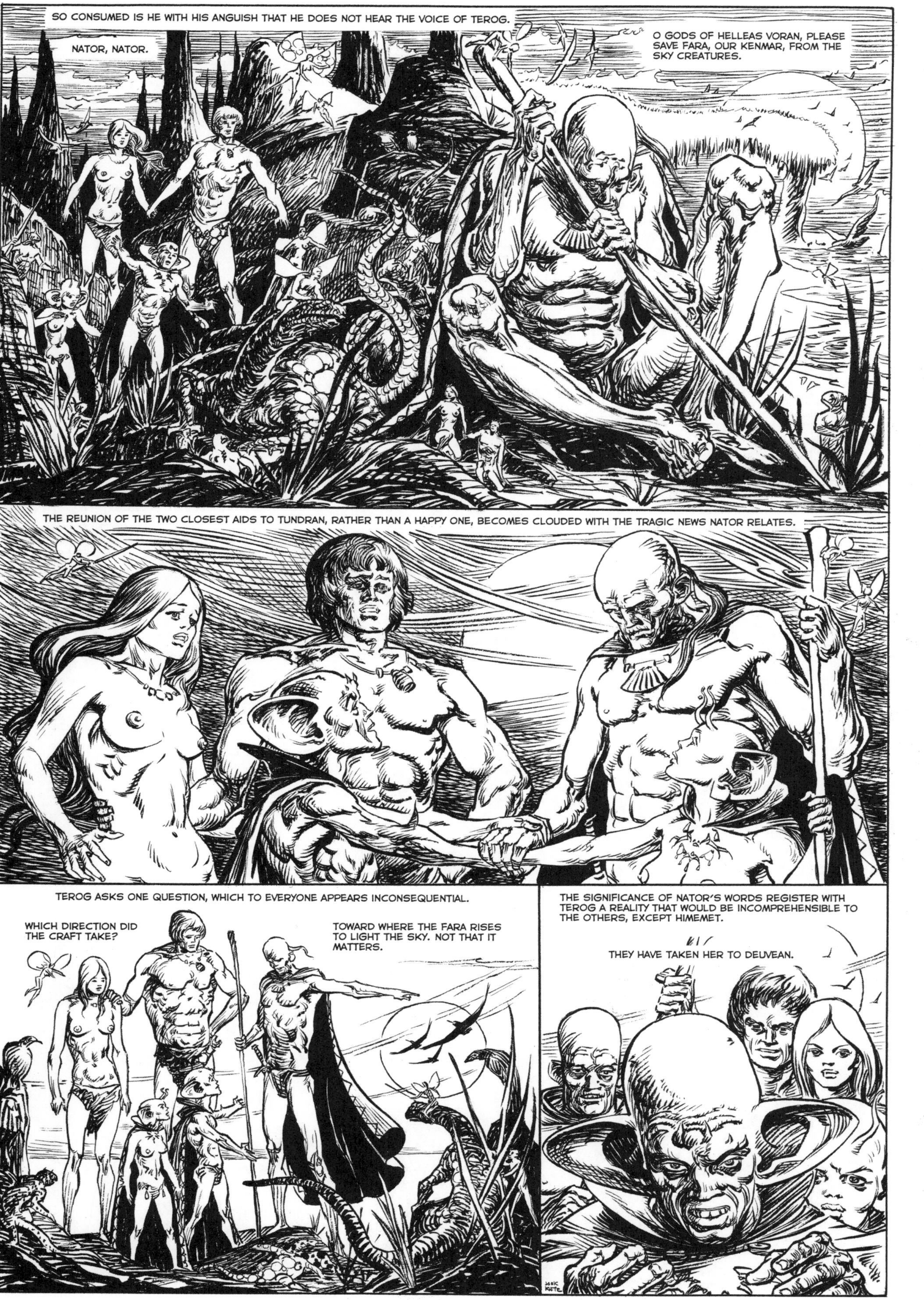
SO CONSUMED IS HE WITH HIS ANGUISH THAT HE DOES NOT HEAR THE VOICE OF TEROG.
NATOR, NATOR.
O GODS OF HELLEAS VORAN, PLEASE SAVE FARA, OUR KENMAR, FROM THE SKY CREATURES.
THE REUNION OF THE TWO CLOSEST AIDS TO TUNDRAN, RATHER THAN A HAPPY ONE, BECOMES CLOUDED WITH THE TRAGIC NEWS NATOR RELATES.
TEROG ASKS ONE QUESTION, WHICH TO EVERYONE APPEARS INCONSEQUENTIAL.
WHICH DIRECTION DID THE CRAFT TAKE?
TOWARD WHERE THE FARA RISES TO LIGHT THE SKY. NOT THAT IT MATTERS.
THE SIGNIFICANCE OF NATOR'S WORDS REGISTER WITH TEROG A REALITY THAT WOULD BE INCOMPREHENSIBLE TO THE OTHERS, EXCEPT HIMEMET.
THEY HAVE TAKEN HER TO DEUVEAN.

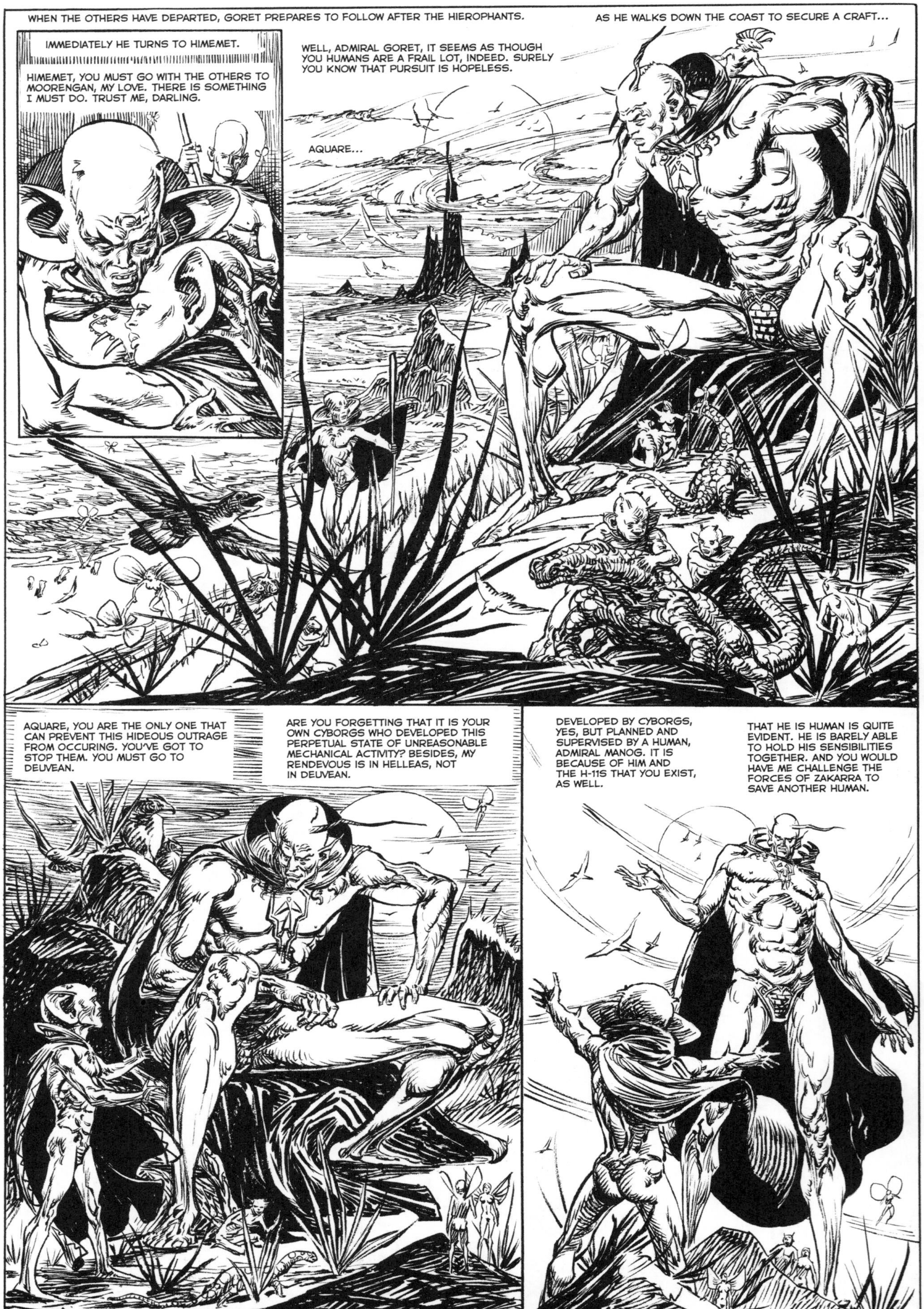

WHEN THE OTHERS HAVE DEPARTED, GORET PREPARES TO FOLLOW AFTER THE HIEROPHANTS.
IMMEDIATELY HE TURNS TO HIMEMET.
HIMEMET, YOU MUST GO WITH THE OTHERS TO MOORENGAN, MY LOVE. THERE IS SOMETHING I MUST DO. TRUST ME, DARLING.
AS HE WALKS DOWN THE COAST TO SECURE A CRAFT...
WELL, ADMIRAL GORET, IT SEEMS AS THOUGH YOU HUMANS ARE A FRAIL LOT, INDEED. SURELY YOU KNOW THAT PURSUIT IS HOPELESS.
AQUARE...
AQUARE, YOU ARE THE ONLY ONE THAT CAN PREVENT THIS HIDEOUS OUTRAGE FROM OCCURING. YOU'VE GOT TO STOP THEM. YOU MUST GO TO DEUVEAN.
ARE YOU FORGETTING THAT IT IS YOUR OWN CYBORGS WHO DEVELOPED THIS PERPETUAL STATE OF UNREASONABLE MECHANICAL ACTIVITY? BESIDES, MY RENDEVOUS IS IN HELLEAS, NOT IN DEUVEAN.
DEVELOPED BY CYBORGS, YES, BUT PLANNED AND SUPERVISED BY A HUMAN, ADMIRAL MANOG. IT IS BECAUSE OF HIM AND THE H-11S THAT YOU EXIST, AS WELL.
THAT HE IS HUMAN IS QUITE EVIDENT. HE IS BARELY ABLE TO HOLD HIS SENSIBILITIES TOGETHER. AND YOU WOULD HAVE ME CHALLENGE THE FORCES OF ZAKARRA TO SAVE ANOTHER HUMAN.
JACK KATZ

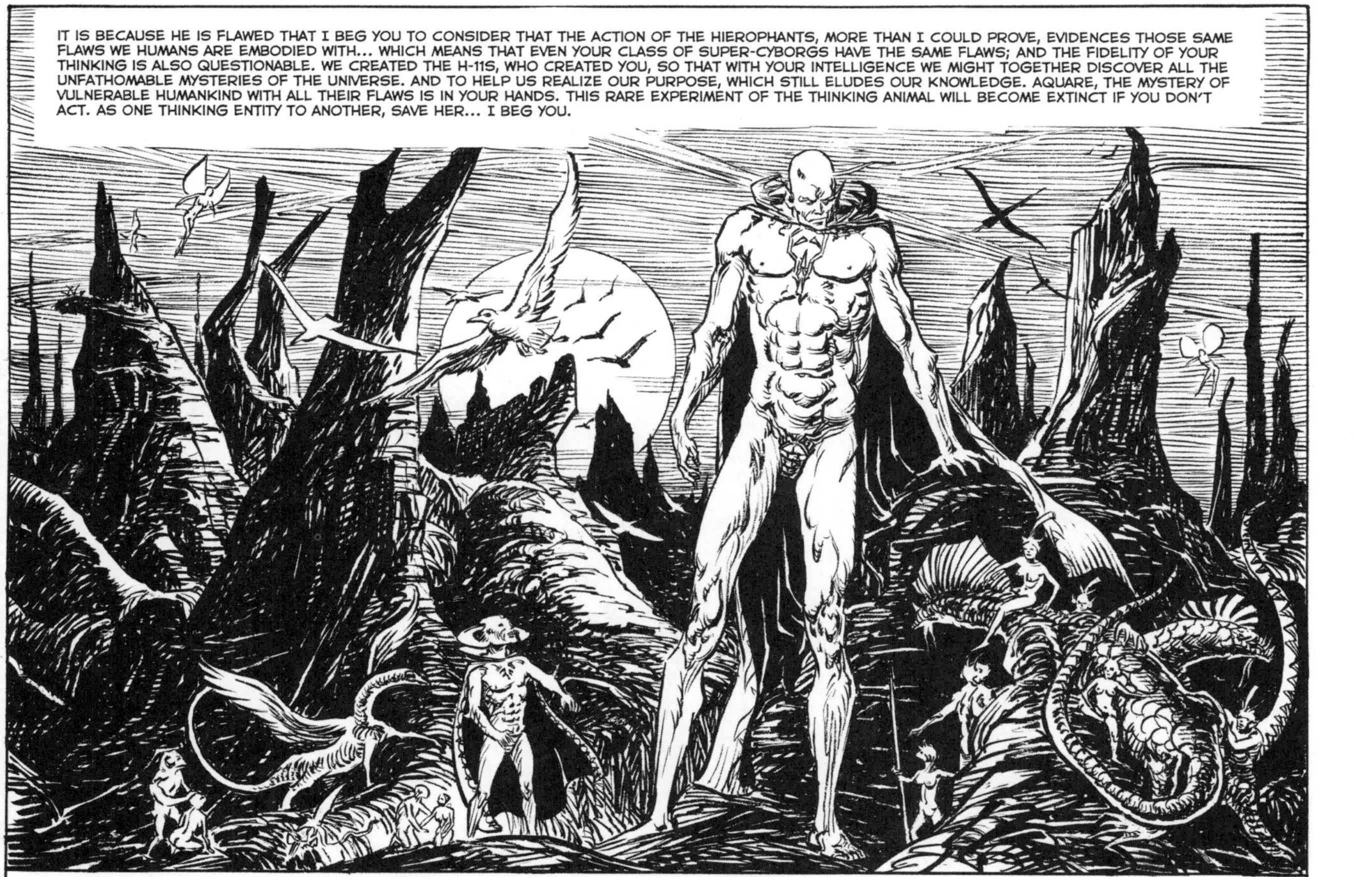
IT IS BECAUSE HE IS FLAWED THAT I BEG YOU TO CONSIDER THAT THE ACTION OF THE HIEROPHANTS, MORE THAN I COULD PROVE, EVIDENCES THOSE SAME FLAWS WE HUMANS ARE EMBODIED WITH... WHICH MEANS THAT EVEN YOUR CLASS OF SUPER-CYBORGS HAVE THE SAME FLAWS; AND THE FIDELITY OF YOUR THINKING IS ALSO QUESTIONABLE. WE CREATED THE H-11S, WHO CREATED YOU, SO THAT WITH YOUR INTELLIGENCE WE MIGHT TOGETHER DISCOVER ALL THE UNFATHOMABLE MYSTERIES OF THE UNIVERSE. AND TO HELP US REALIZE OUR PURPOSE, WHICH STILL ELUDES OUR KNOWLEDGE. AQUARE, THE MYSTERY OF VULNERABLE HUMANKIND WITH ALL THEIR FLAWS IS IN YOUR HANDS. THIS RARE EXPERIMENT OF THE THINKING ANIMAL WILL BECOME EXTINCT IF YOU DON'T ACT. AS ONE THINKING ENTITY TO ANOTHER, SAVE HER... I BEG YOU.

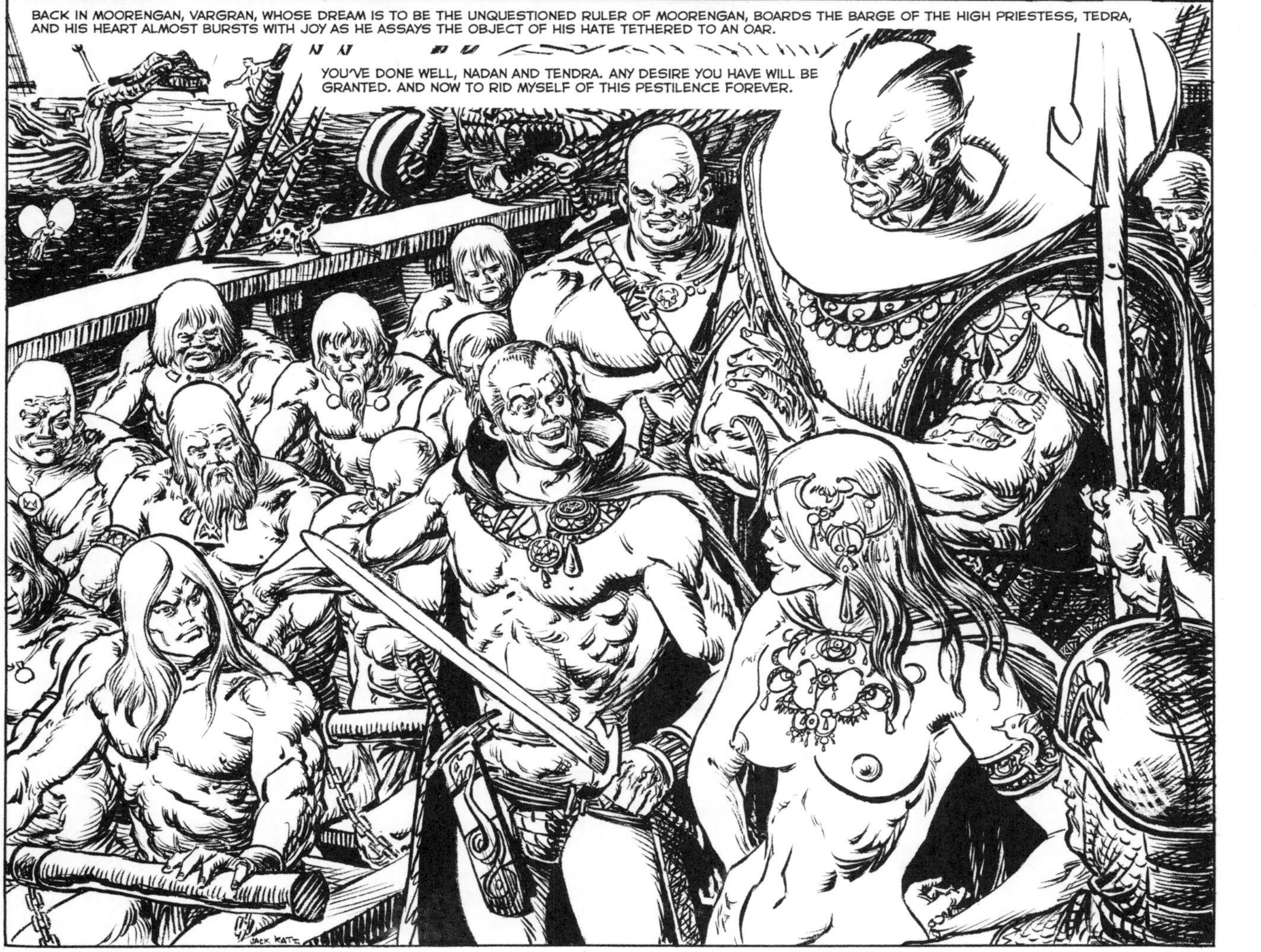
BACK IN MOORENGAN, VARGRAN, WHOSE DREAM IS TO BE THE UNQUESTIONED RULER OF MOORENGAN, BOARDS THE BARGE OF THE HIGH PRIESTESS, TEDRA, AND HIS HEART ALMOST BURSTS WITH JOY AS HE ASSAYS THE OBJECT OF HIS HATE TETHERED TO AN OAR.
YOU'VE DONE WELL, NADAN AND TENDRA. ANY DESIRE YOU HAVE WILL BE GRANTED. AND NOW TO RID MYSELF OF THIS PESTILENCE FOREVER.
JACK KATZ

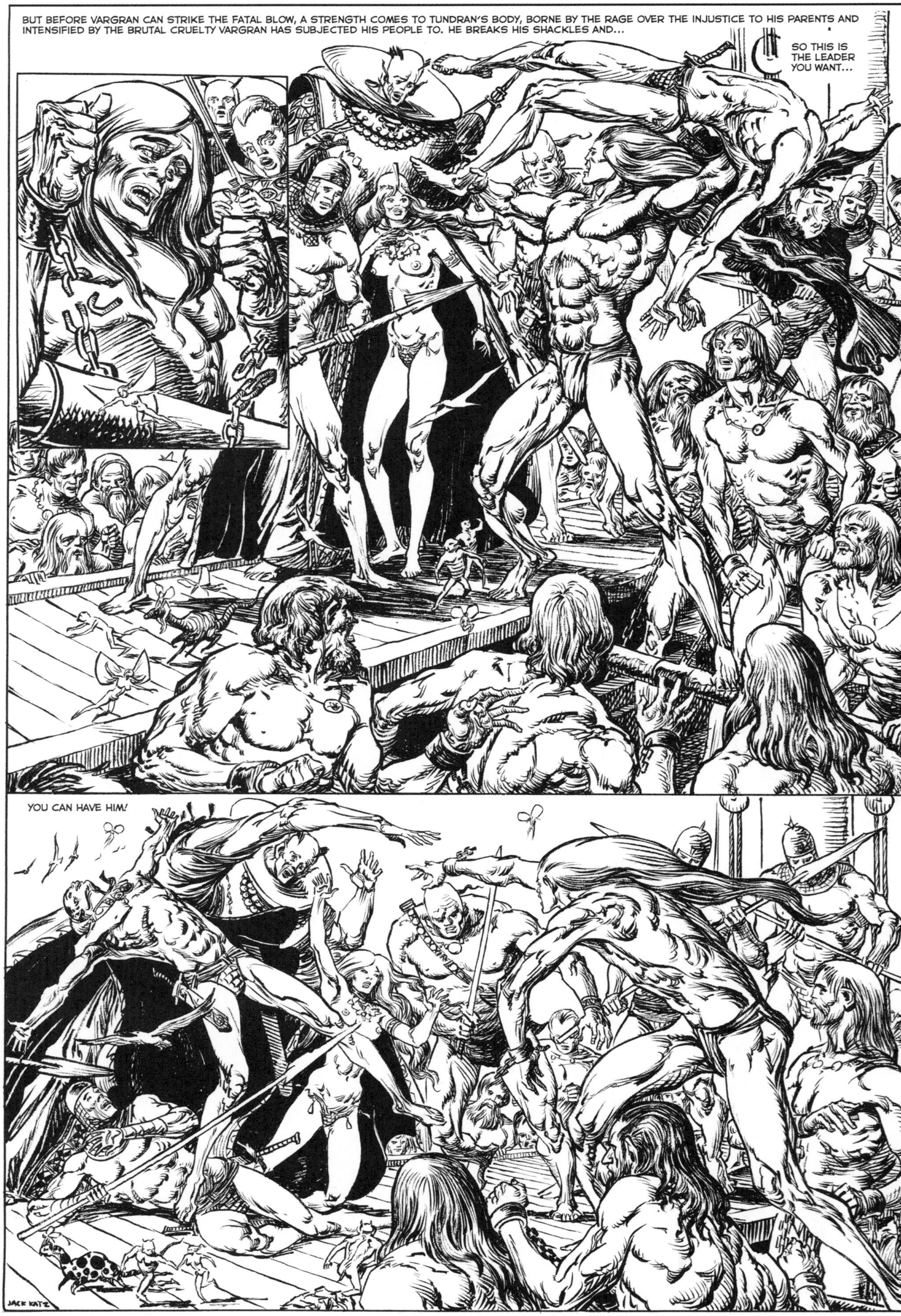
BUT BEFORE VARGRAN CAN STRIKE THE FATAL BLOW, A STRENGTH COMES TO TUNDRAN'S BODY, BORNE BY THE RAGE OVER THE INJUSTICE TO HIS PARENTS AND INTENSIFIED BY THE BRUTAL CRUELTY VARGRAN HAS SUBJECTED HIS PEOPLE TO. HE BREAKS HIS SHACKLES AND...
SO THIS IS THE LEADER YOU WANT...
YOU CAN HAVE HIM!
JACK KATZ

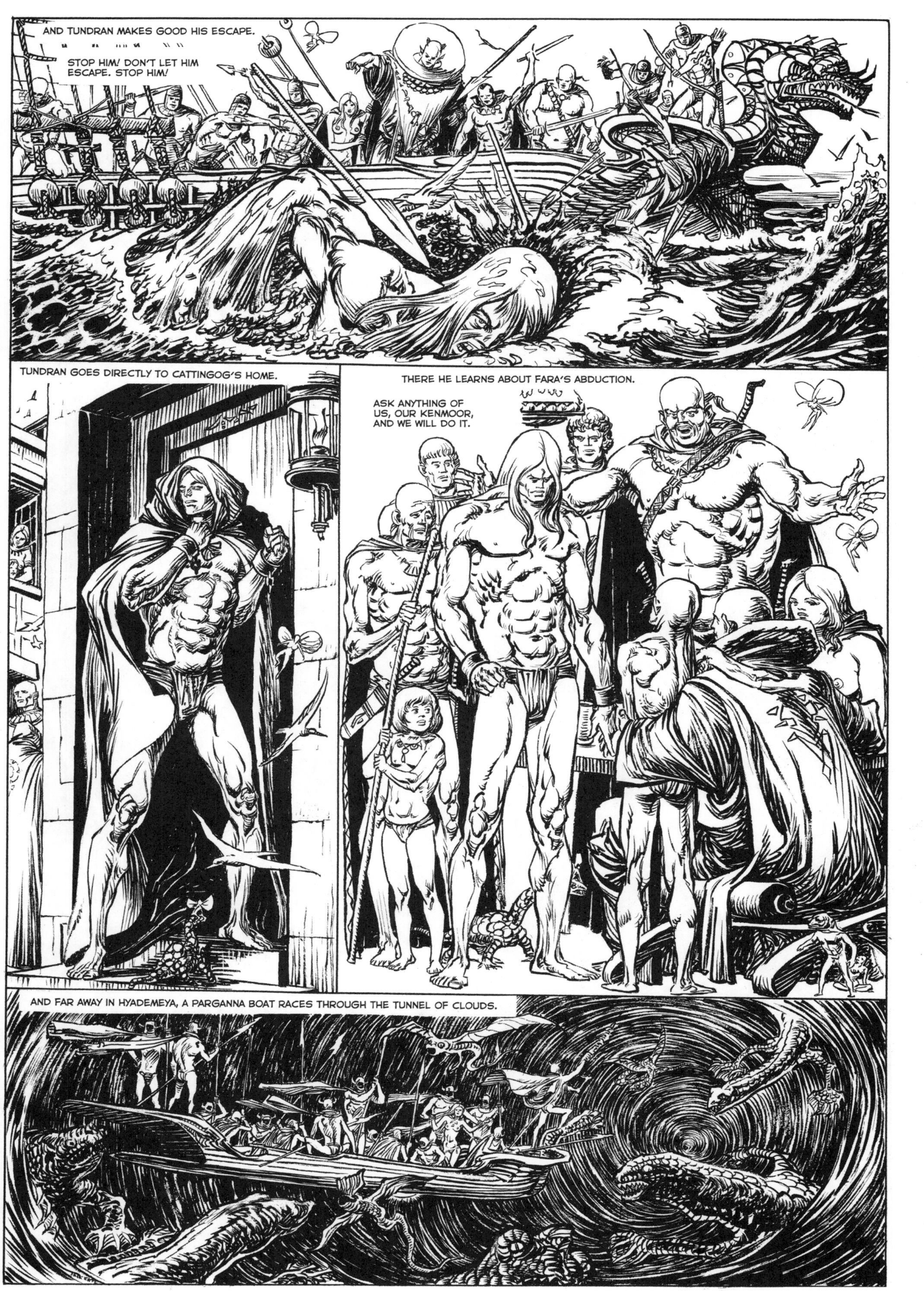
AND TUNDRAN MAKES GOOD HIS ESCAPE.
STOP HIM! DON'T LET HIM ESCAPE. STOP HIM!
TUNDRAN GOES DIRECTLY TO CATTINGOG'S HOME.
THERE HE LEARNS ABOUT FARA'S ABDUCTION.
ASK ANYTHING OF US, OUR KENMOOR, AND WE WILL DO IT.
AND FAR AWAY IN HYADEMEYA, A PARGANNA BOAT RACES THROUGH THE TUNNEL OF CLOUDS.

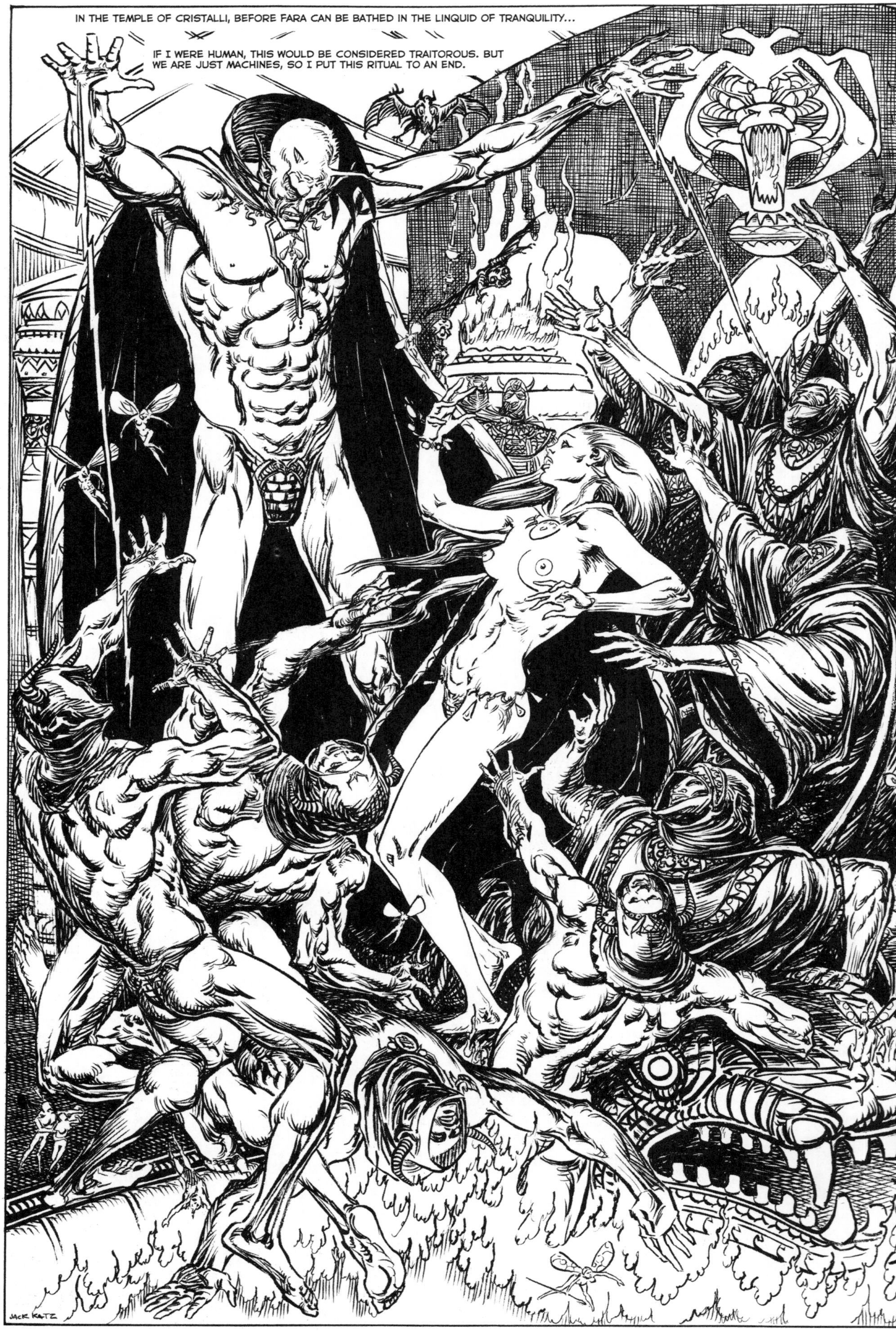
IN THE TEMPLE OF CRISTALLI, BEFORE FARA CAN BE BATHED IN THE LINQUID OF TRANQUILITY...
IF I WERE HUMAN, THIS WOULD BE CONSIDERED TRAITOROUS. BUT WE ARE JUST MACHINES, SO I PUT THIS RITUAL TO AN END.
JACK KATZ

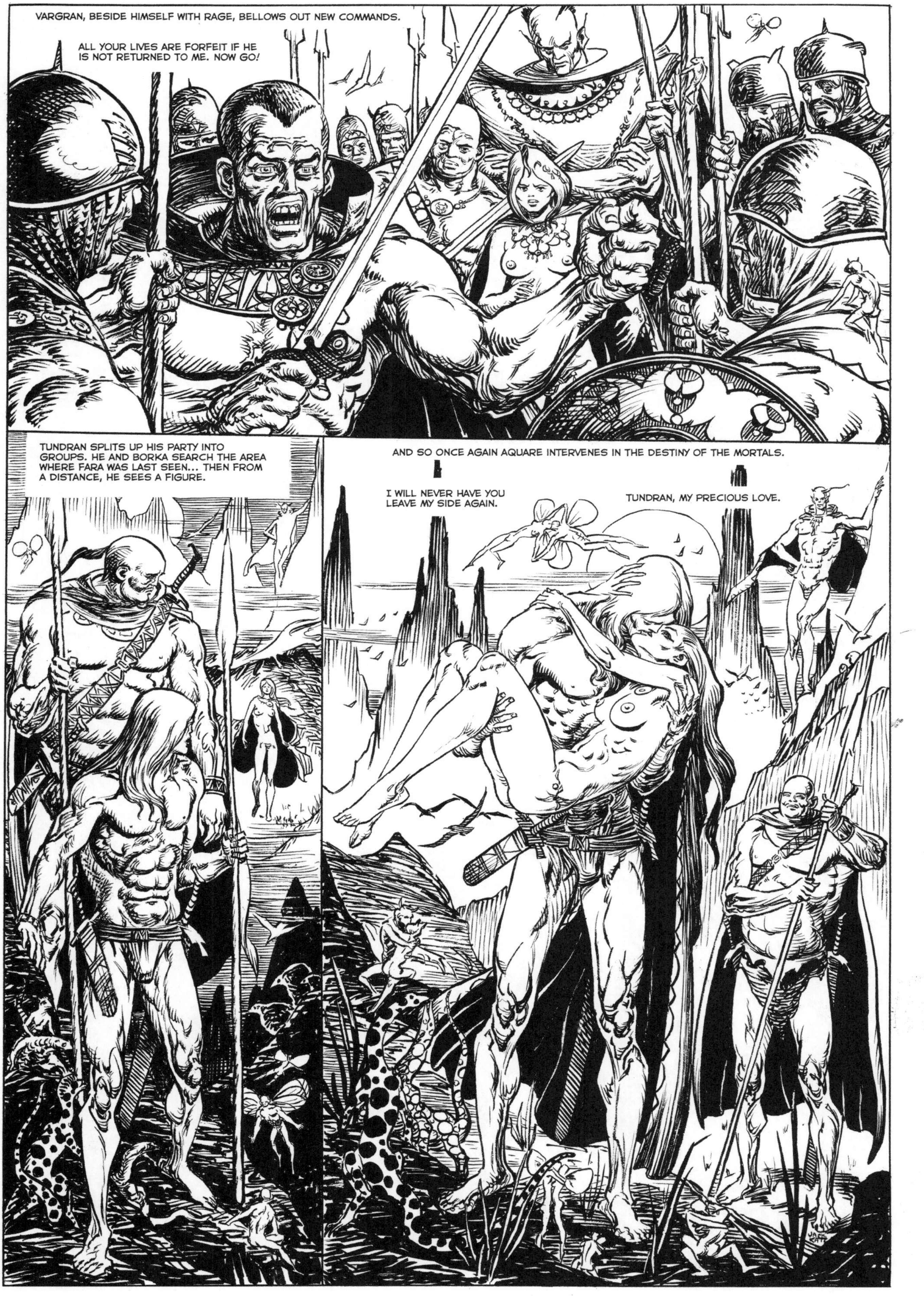
VARGRAN, BESIDE HIMSELF WITH RAGE, BELLOWS OUT NEW COMMANDS.
ALL YOUR LIVES ARE FORFEIT IF HE IS NOT RETURNED TO ME. NOW GO!
TUNDRAN SPLITS UP HIS PARTY INTO GROUPS. HE AND BORKA SEARCH THE AREA WHERE FARA WAS LAST SEEN... THEN FROM A DISTANCE, HE SEES A FIGURE.
AND SO ONCE AGAIN AQUARE INTERVENES IN THE DESTINY OF THE MORTALS.
I WILL NEVER HAVE YOU LEAVE MY SIDE AGAIN.
TUNDRAN, MY PRECIOUS LOVE.

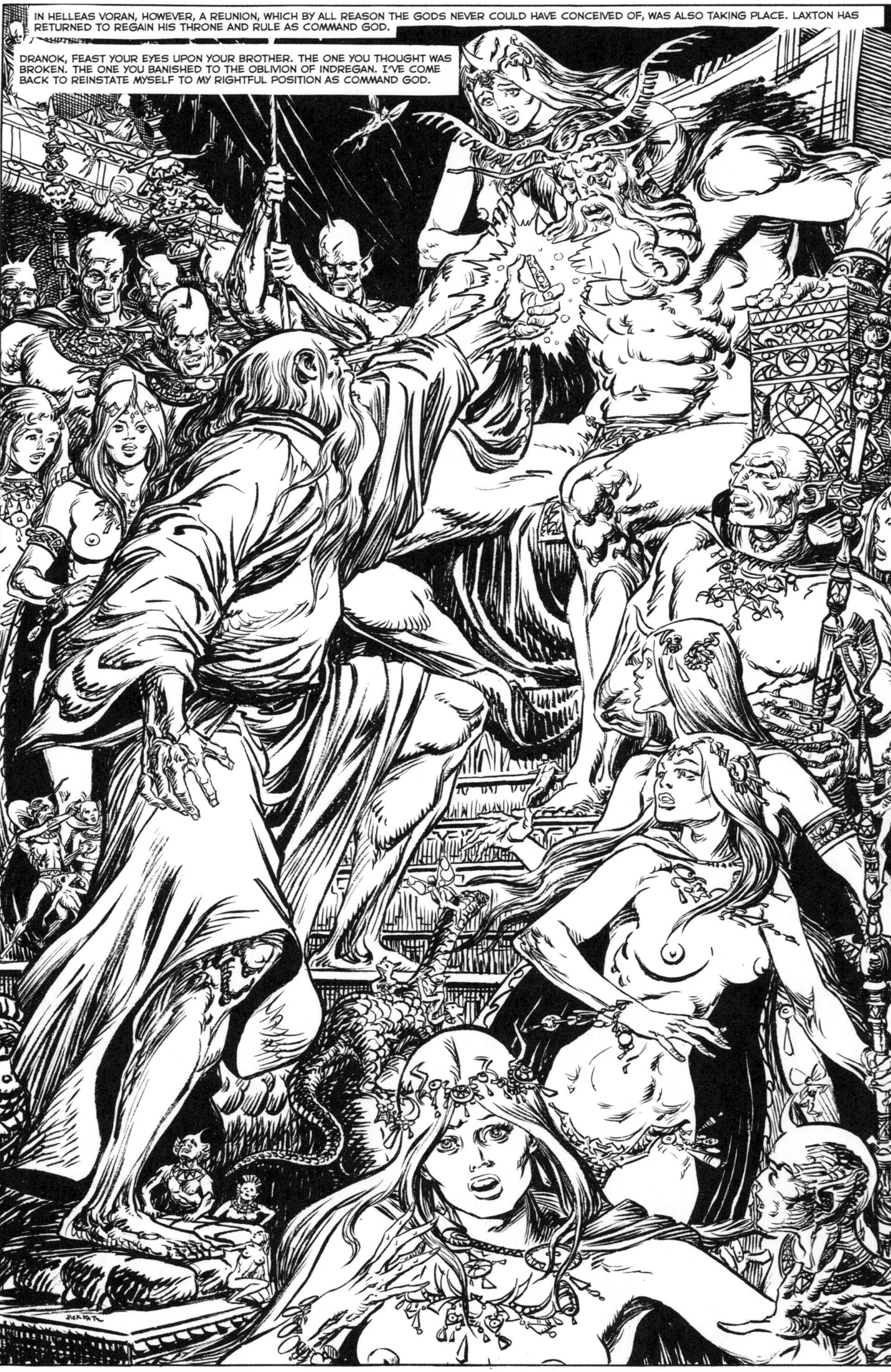
IN HELLEAS VORAN, HOWEVER, A REUNION, WHICH BY ALL REASON THE GODS NEVER COULD HAVE CONCEIVED OF, WAS ALSO TAKING PLACE. LAXTON HAS RETURNED TO REGAIN HIS THRONE AND RULE AS COMMAND GOD.
DRANOK, FEAST YOUR EYES UPON YOUR BROTHER. THE ONE YOU THOUGHT WAS BROKEN. THE ONE YOU BANISHED TO THE OBLIVION OF INDREGAN. I'VE COME BACK TO REINSTATE MYSELF TO MY RIGHTFUL POSITION AS COMMAND GOD.

TO BE CONTINUED

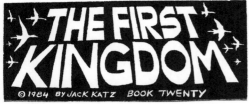

THE FIRST KINGDOM

© 1984 BY JACK KATZ BOOK TWENTY

FROM DIFFERENT PARTS OF MOORENGAN, ARMIES DETERMINED TO OVERTHROW THE WILLFUL REGENCY OF VARGRAN THE USURPER BEGIN THEIR MOVE TOWARD THE CAPITAL. THE BATTLE THAT WILL DECIDE THE FATE OF MOORENGAN IS SOON IN COMING, AND FOR TUNDRAN AND FARA THE TEST OF THEIR METTLE AND WORTHINESS TO ACCEDE TO THE THRONE IS AT HAND.

SO THE FATE OF TUNDRAN AND FARA SEEMS TO BE MOVING TOWARD WHAT APPEARS TO BE AN INEVITABLE OUTCOME. I WILL LET YOU KNOW THAT THROUGH TUNDRAN AND FARA WILL WIN EVERY TEST LAID BEFORE THEM TO ACHIEVE VICTORY, THEY WILL NEVER SIT UPON THE THRONE OF MOORENGAN. YOU SEE, THERE ARE THINGS THAT ARE GREATER THAN VICTORY, MORE REWARDING THAN RULERSHIP... THINGS WHICH WE ARE ALL THE INGERITORS OF. AH, BUT I'M GETTING AHEAD OF MYSELF. BACK TO OUR STORY...

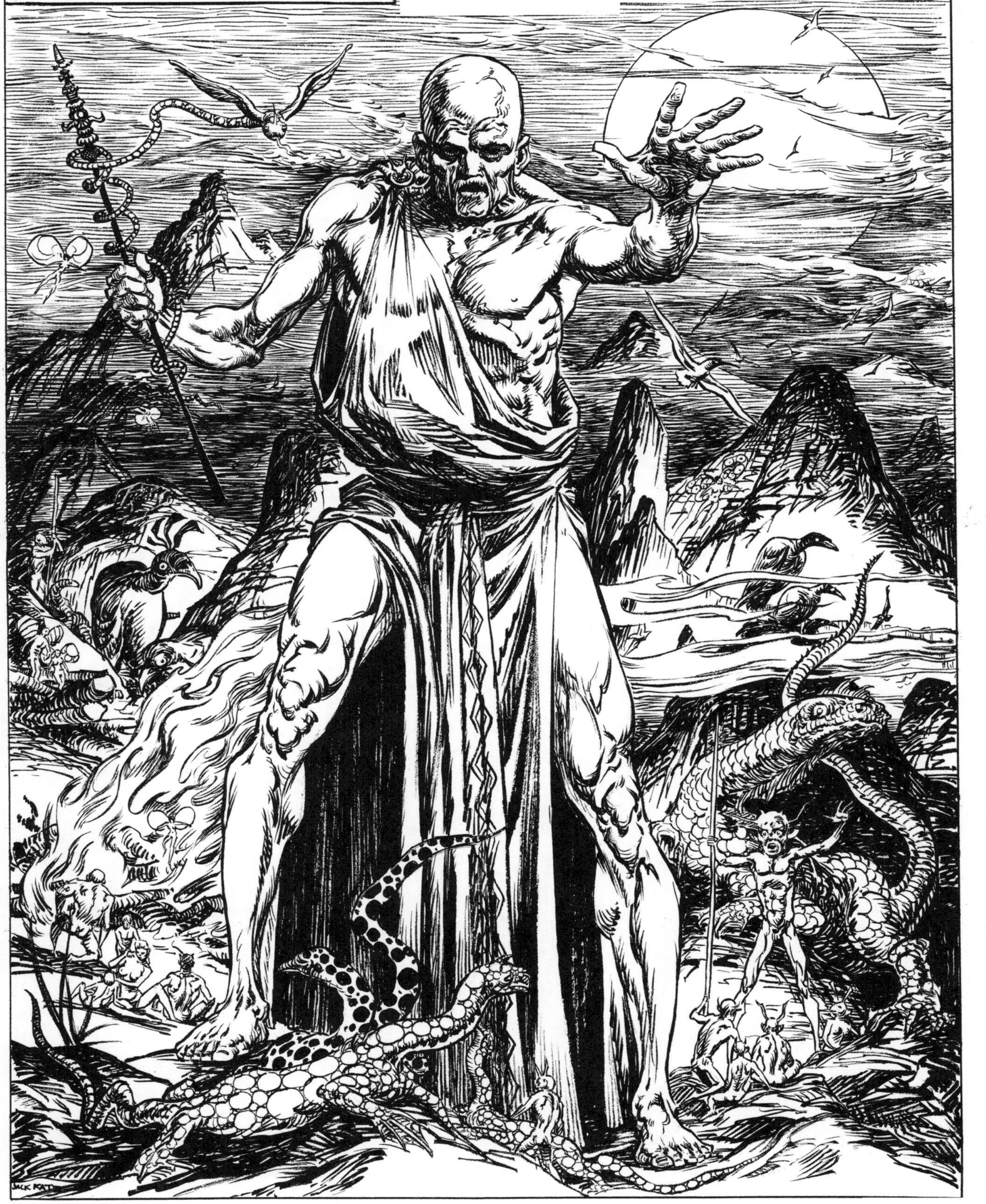

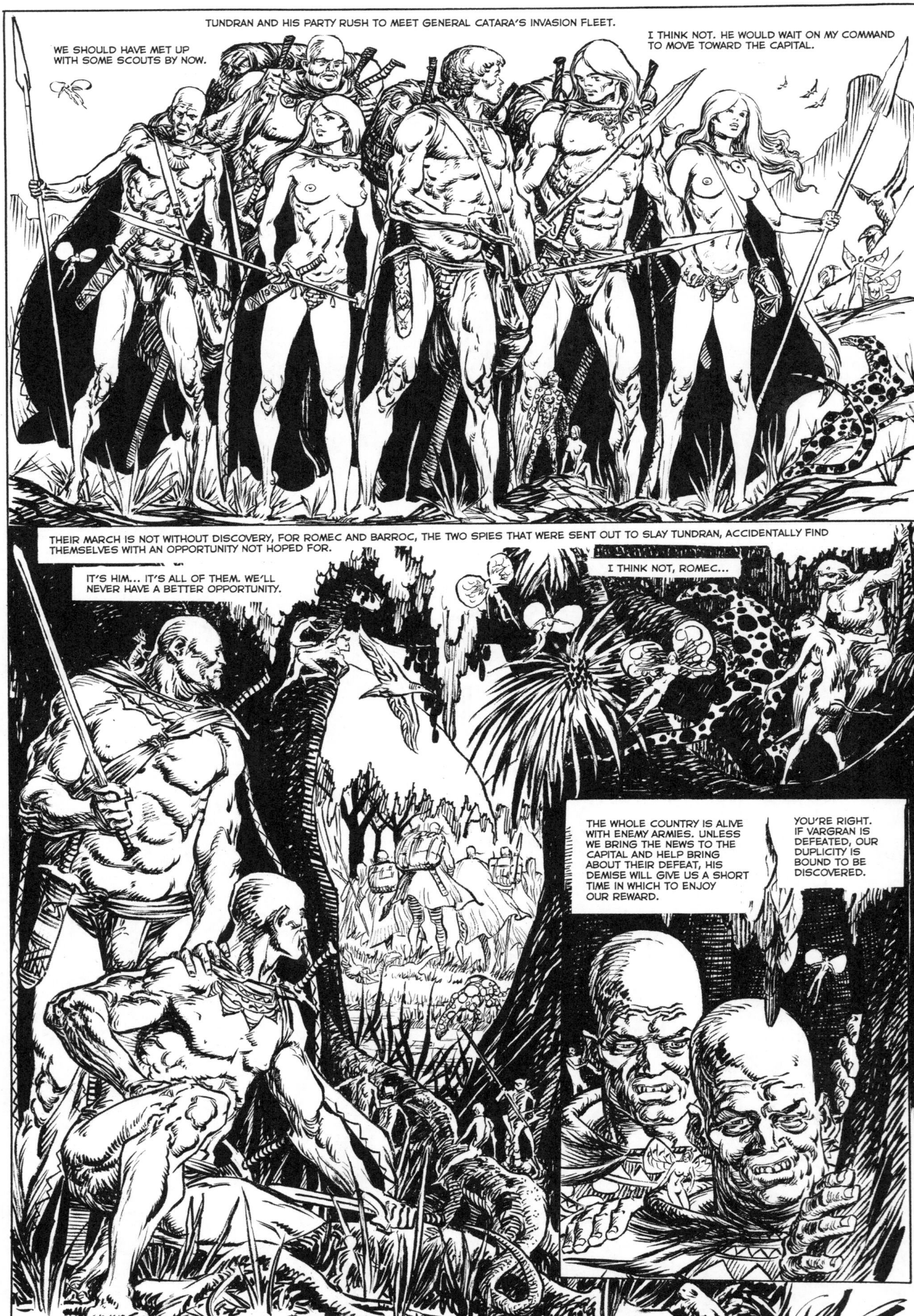
TUNDRAN AND HIS PARTY RUSH TO MEET GENERAL CATARA'S INVASION FLEET.
WE SHOULD HAVE MET UP WITH SOME SCOUTS BY NOW.
I THINK NOT. HE WOULD WAIT ON MY COMMAND TO MOVE TOWARD THE CAPITAL.
THEIR MARCH IS NOT WITHOUT DISCOVERY, FOR ROMEC AND BARROC, THE TWO SPIES THAT WERE SENT OUT TO SLAY TUNDRAN, ACCIDENTALLY FIND THEMSELVES WITH AN OPPORTUNITY NOT HOPED FOR.
IT'S HIM... IT'S ALL OF THEM. WE'LL NEVER HAVE A BETTER OPPORTUNITY.
I THINK NOT, ROMEC...
THE WHOLE COUNTRY IS ALIVE WITH ENEMY ARMIES. UNLESS WE BRING THE NEWS TO THE CAPITAL AND HELP BRING ABOUT THEIR DEFEAT, HIS DEMISE WILL GIVE US A SHORT TIME IN WHICH TO ENJOY OUR REWARD.
YOU'RE RIGHT. IF VARGRAN IS DEFEATED, OUR DUPLICITY IS BOUND TO BE DISCOVERED.
JACK KATZ

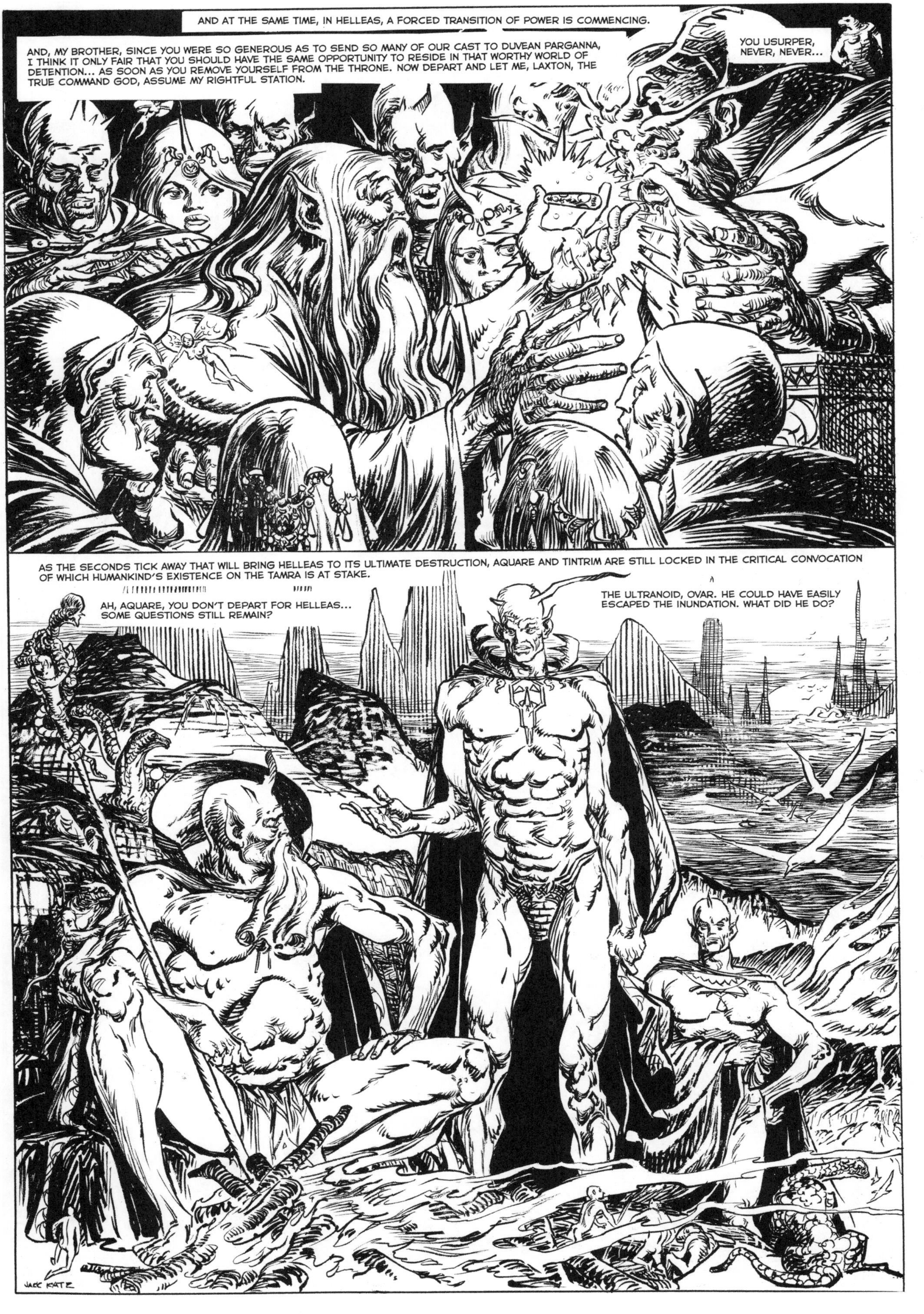
AND AT THE SAME TIME, IN HELLEAS, A FORCED TRANSITION OF POWER IS COMMENCING.
AND, MY BROTHER, SINCE YOU WERE SO GENEROUS AS TO SEND SO MANY OF OUR CAST TO DUVEAN PARGANNA, I THINK IT ONLY FAIR THAT YOU SHOULD HAVE THE SAME OPPORTUNITY TO RESIDE IN THAT WORTHY WORLD OF DETENTION... AS SOON AS YOU REMOVE YOURSELF FROM THE THRONE. NOW DEPART AND LET ME, LAXTON, THE TRUE COMMAND GOD, ASSUME MY RIGHTFUL STATION.
YOU USURPER, NEVER, NEVER...
AS THE SECONDS TICK AWAY THAT WILL BRING HELLEAS TO ITS ULTIMATE DESTRUCTION, AQUARE AND TINTRIM ARE STILL LOCKED IN THE CRITICAL CONVOCATION OF WHICH HUMANKIND'S EXISTENCE ON THE TAMRA IS AT STAKE.
AH, AQUARE, YOU DON'T DEPART FOR HELLEAS... SOME QUESTIONS STILL REMAIN?
THE ULTRANOID, OVAR. HE COULD HAVE EASILY ESCAPED THE INUNDATION. WHAT DID HE DO?
JACK KATZ

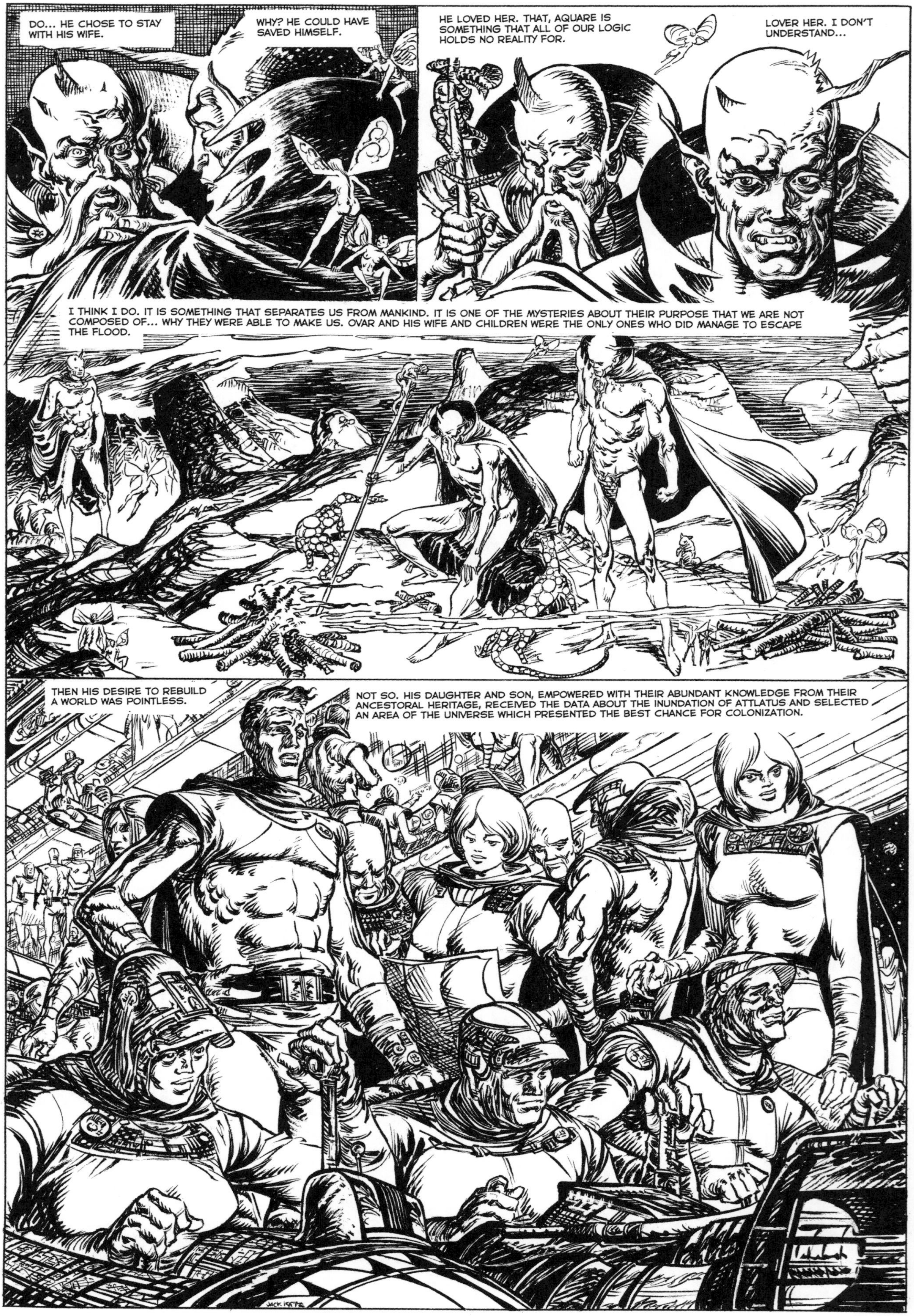
DO... HE CHOSE TO STAY WITH HIS WIFE.
WHY? HE COULD HAVE SAVED HIMSELF.
HE LOVED HER. THAT, AQUARE IS SOMETHING THAT ALL OF OUR LOGIC HOLDS NO REALITY FOR.
LOVER HER. I DON'T UNDERSTAND...
I THINK I DO. IT IS SOMETHING THAT SEPARATES US FROM MANKIND. IT IS ONE OF THE MYSTERIES ABOUT THEIR PURPOSE THAT WE ARE NOT COMPOSED OF... WHY THEY WERE ABLE TO MAKE US. OVAR AND HIS WIFE AND CHILDREN WERE THE ONLY ONES WHO DID MANAGE TO ESCAPE THE FLOOD.
THEN HIS DESIRE TO REBUILD A WORLD WAS POINTLESS.
NOT SO. HIS DAUGHTER AND SON, EMPOWERED WITH THEIR ABUNDANT KNOWLEDGE FROM THEIR ANCESTORAL HERITAGE, RECEIVED THE DATA ABOUT THE INUNDATION OF ATTLATUS AND SELECTED AN AREA OF THE UNIVERSE WHICH PRESENTED THE BEST CHANCE FOR COLONIZATION.
JACK KATZ

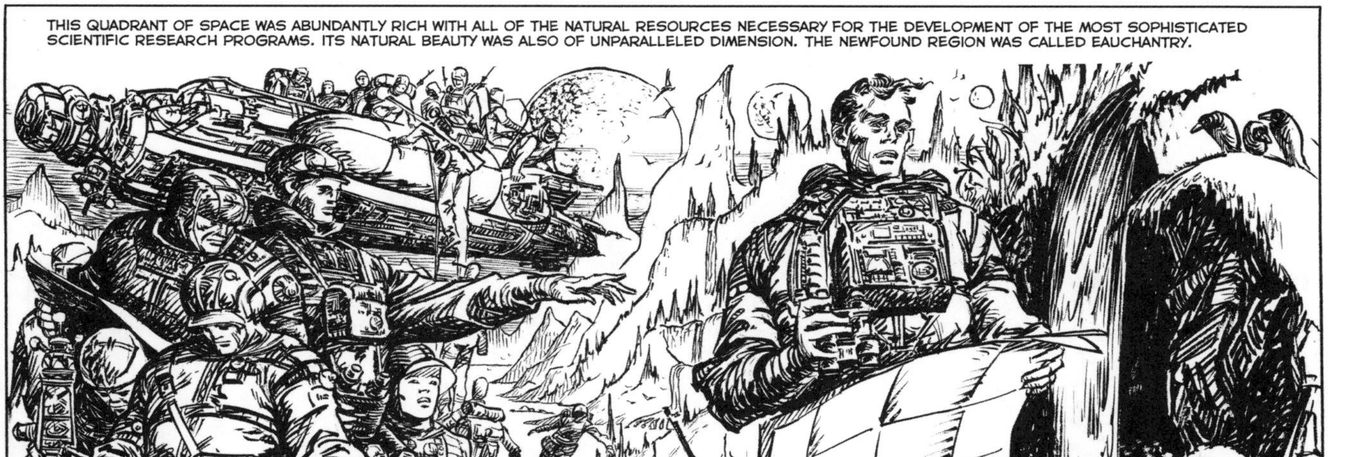
THIS QUADRANT OF SPACE WAS ABUNDANTLY RICH WITH ALL OF THE NATURAL RESOURCES NECESSARY FOR THE DEVELOPMENT OF THE MOST SOPHISTICATED SCIENTIFIC RESEARCH PROGRAMS. ITS NATURAL BEAUTY WAS ALSO OF UNPARALLELED DIMENSION. THE NEWFOUND REGION WAS CALLED EAUCHANTRY.

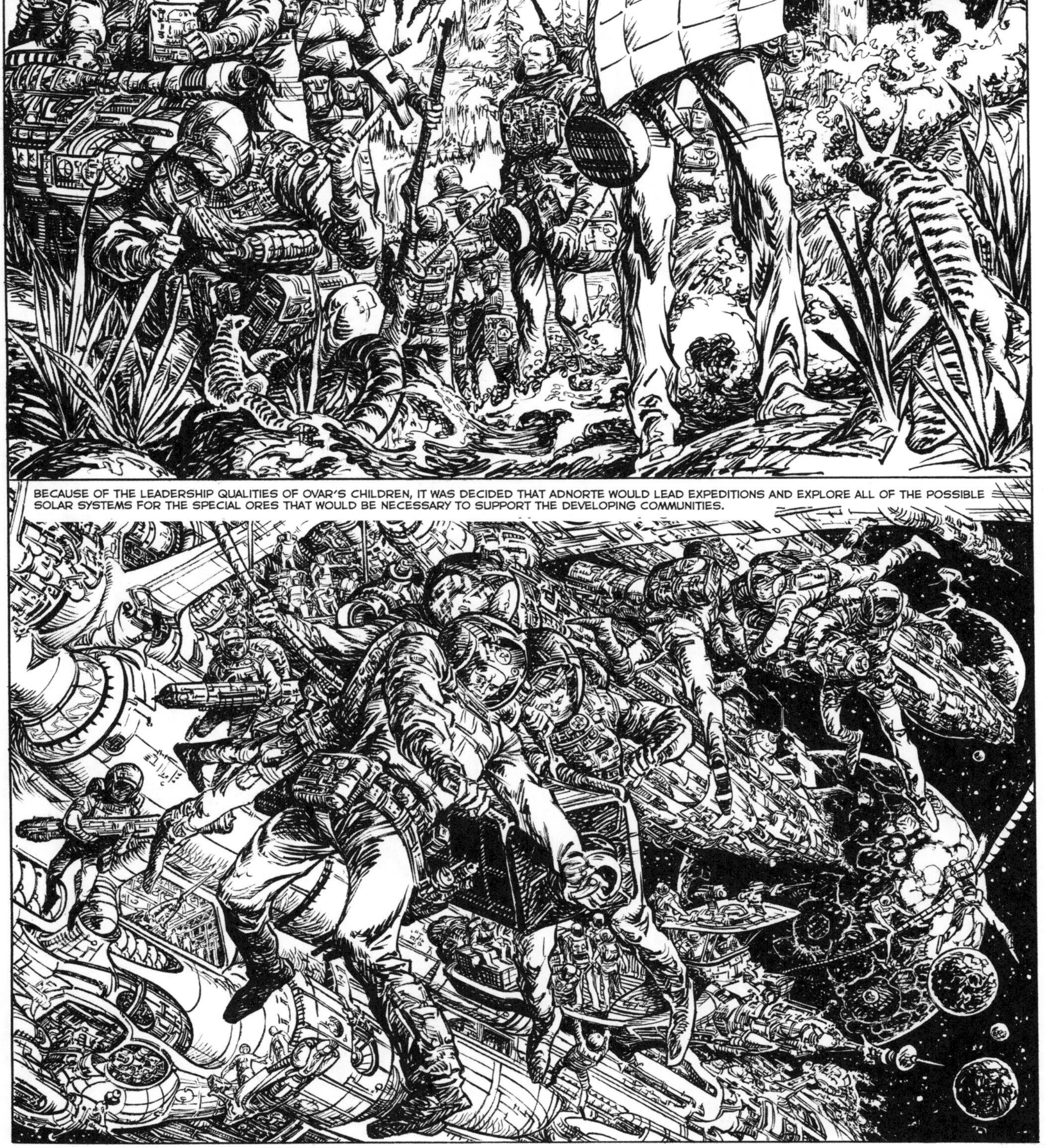
BECAUSE OF THE LEADERSHIP QUALITIES OF OVAR'S CHILDREN, IT WAS DECIDED THAT ADNORTE WOULD LEAD EXPEDITIONS AND EXPLORE ALL OF THE POSSIBLE SOLAR SYSTEMS FOR THE SPECIAL ORES THAT WOULD BE NECESSARY TO SUPPORT THE DEVELOPING COMMUNITIES.

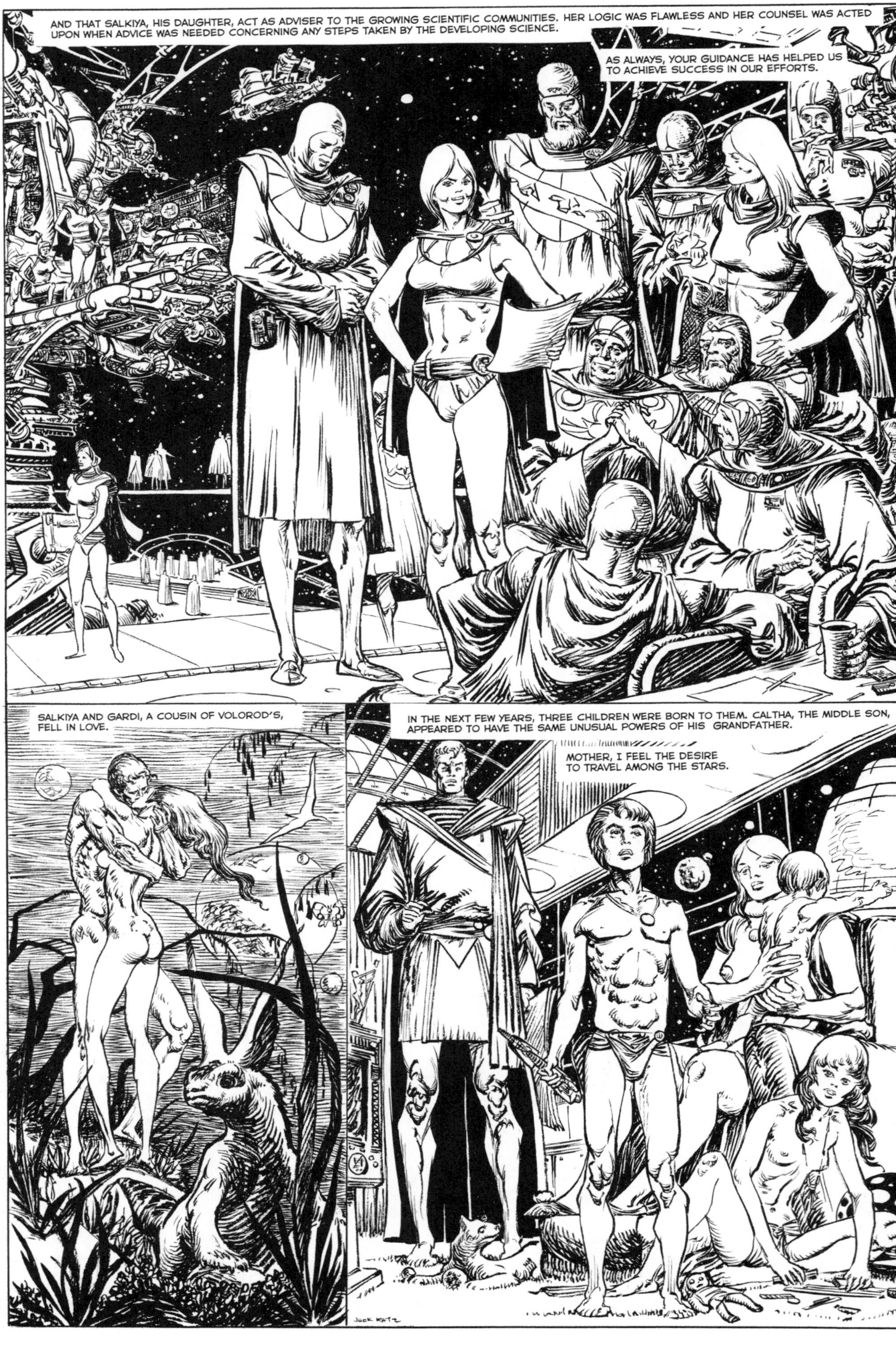
AND THAT SALKIYA, HIS DAUGHTER, ACT AS ADVISER TO THE GROWING SCIENTIFIC COMMUNITIES. HER LOGIC WAS FLAWLESS AND HER COUNSEL WAS ACTED UPON WHEN ADVICE WAS NEEDED CONCERNING ANY STEPS TAKEN BY THE DEVELOPING SCIENCE.
AS ALWAYS, YOUR GUIDANCE HAS HELPED US TO ACHIEVE SUCCESS IN OUR EFFORTS.
SALKIYA AND GARDI, A COUSIN OF VOLOROD'S, FELL IN LOVE.
IN THE NEXT FEW YEARS, THREE CHILDREN WERE BORN TO THEM. CALTHA, THE MIDDLE SON, APPEARED TO HAVE THE SAME UNUSUAL POWERS OF HIS GRANDFATHER.
MOTHER, I FEEL THE DESIRE TO TRAVEL AMONG THE STARS.
JACK KATZ

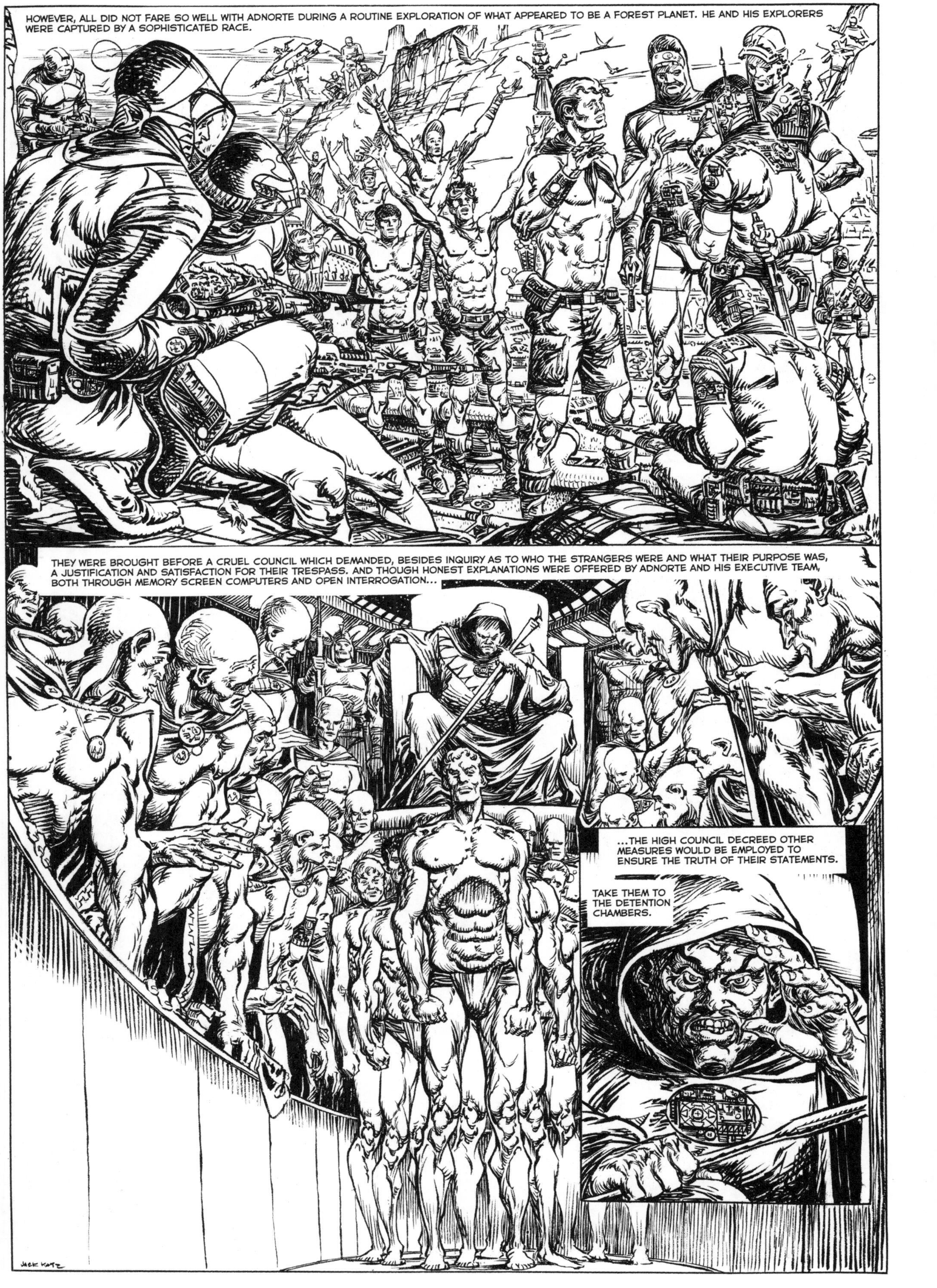
HOWEVER, ALL DID NOT FARE SO WELL WITH ADNORTE DURING A ROUTINE EXPLORATION OF WHAT APPEARED TO BE A FOREST PLANET. HE AND HIS EXPLORERS WERE CAPTURED BY A SOPHISTICATED RACE.
THEY WERE BROUGHT BEFORE A CRUEL COUNCIL WHICH DEMANDED, BESIDES INQUIRY AS TO WHO THE STRANGERS WERE AND WHAT THEIR PURPOSE WAS, A JUSTIFICATION AND SATISFACTION FOR THEIR TRESPASS. AND THOUGH HONEST EXPLANATIONS WERE OFFERED BY ADNORTE AND HIS EXECUTIVE TEAM, BOTH THROUGH MEMORY SCREEN COMPUTERS AND OPEN INTERROGATION...
...THE HIGH COUNCIL DECREED OTHER MEASURES WOULD BE EMPLOYED TO ENSURE THE TRUTH OF THEIR STATEMENTS.
TAKE THEM TO THE DETENTION CHAMBERS.
JACK KATZ

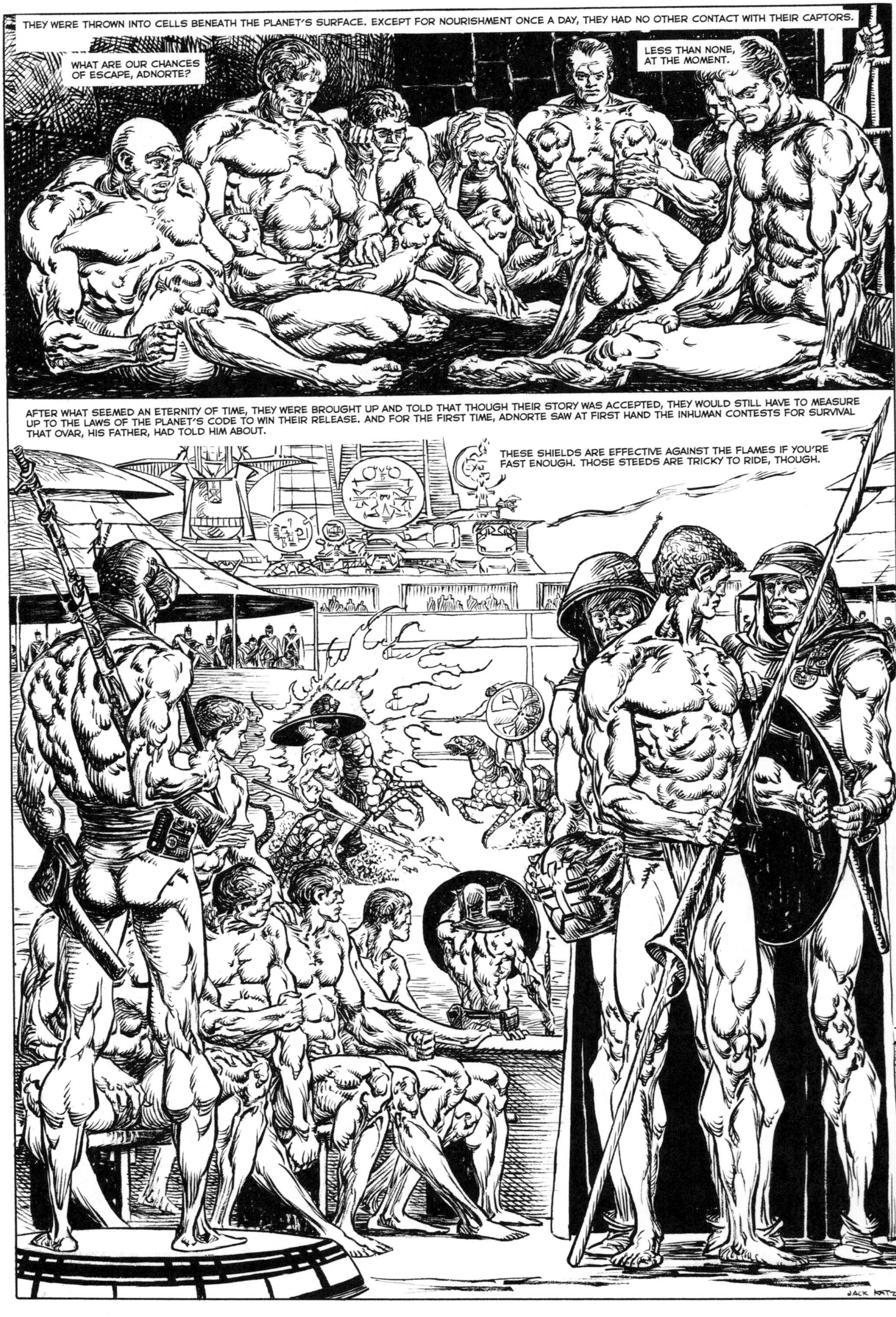
THEY WERE THROWN INTO CELLS BENEATH THE PLANET'S SURFACE. EXCEPT FOR NOURISHMENT ONCE A DAY, THEY HAD NO OTHER CONTACT WITH THEIR CAPTORS.
WHAT ARE OUR CHANCES OF ESCAPE, ADNORTE?
LESS THAN NONE, AT THE MOMENT.
AFTER WHAT SEEMED AN ETERNITY OF TIME, THEY WERE BROUGHT UP AND TOLD THAT THOUGH THEIR STORY WAS ACCEPTED, THEY WOULD STILL HAVE TO MEASURE UP TO THE LAWS OF THE PLANET'S CODE TO WIN THEIR RELEASE. AND FOR THE FIRST TIME, ADNORTE SAW AT FIRST HAND THE INHUMAN CONTESTS FOR SURVIVAL THAT OVAR, HIS FATHER, HAD TOLD HIM ABOUT.
THESE SHIELDS ARE EFFECTIVE AGAINST THE FLAMES IF YOU'RE FAST ENOUGH. THOSE STEEDS ARE TRICKY TO RIDE, THOUGH.
JACK KATZ

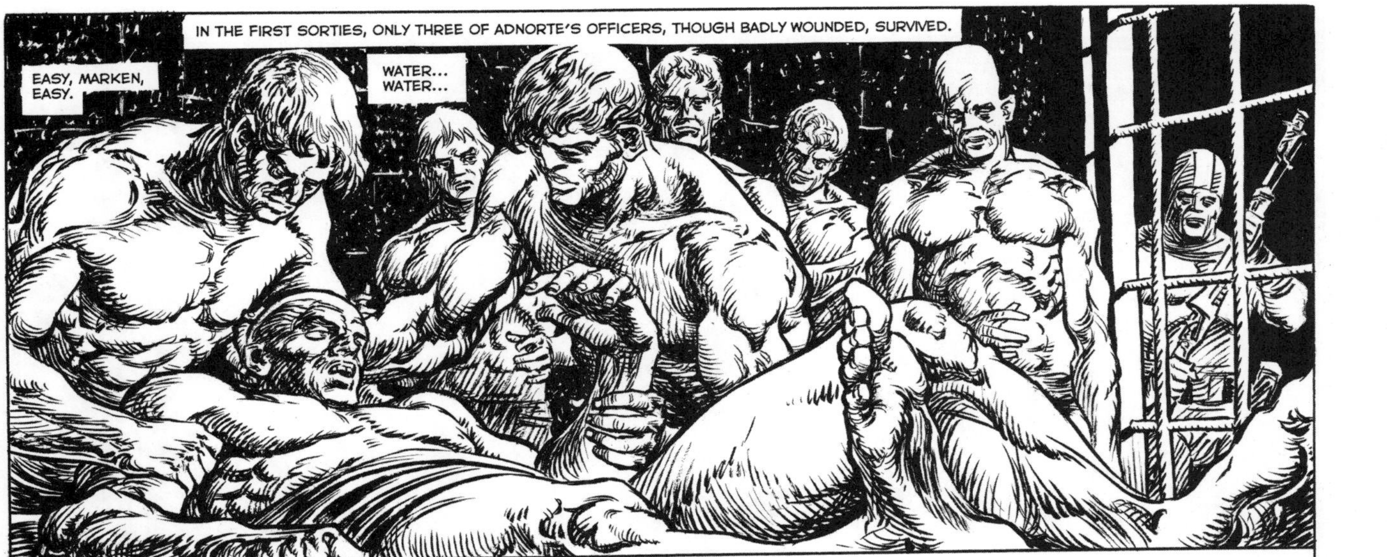
IN THE FIRST SORTIES, ONLY THREE OF ADNORTE'S OFFICERS, THOUGH BADLY WOUNDED, SURVIVED.
EASY, MARKEN, EASY.
WATER... WATER...

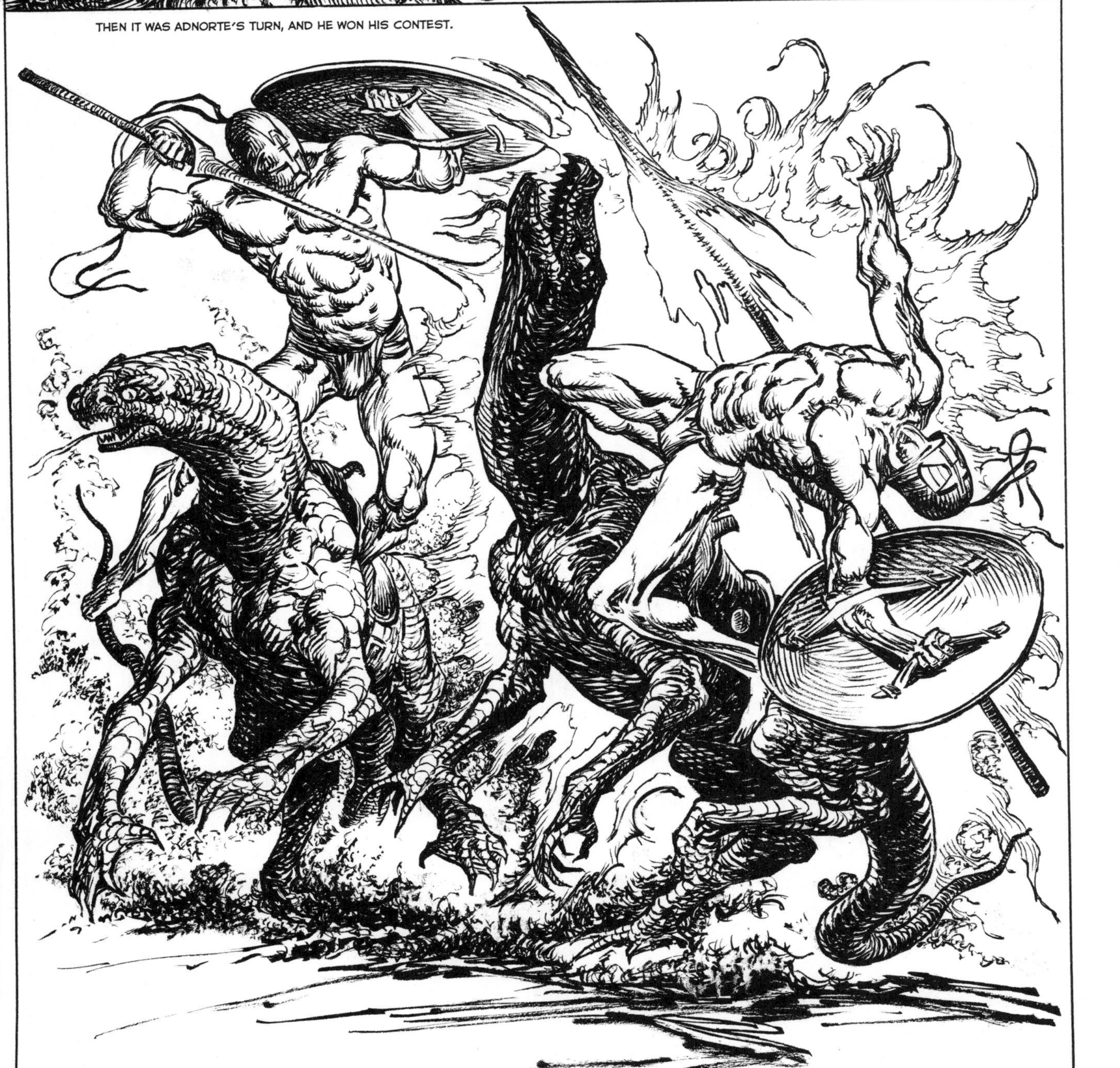
THEN IT WAS ADNORTE'S TURN, AND HE WON HIS CONTEST.
JACK KATZ

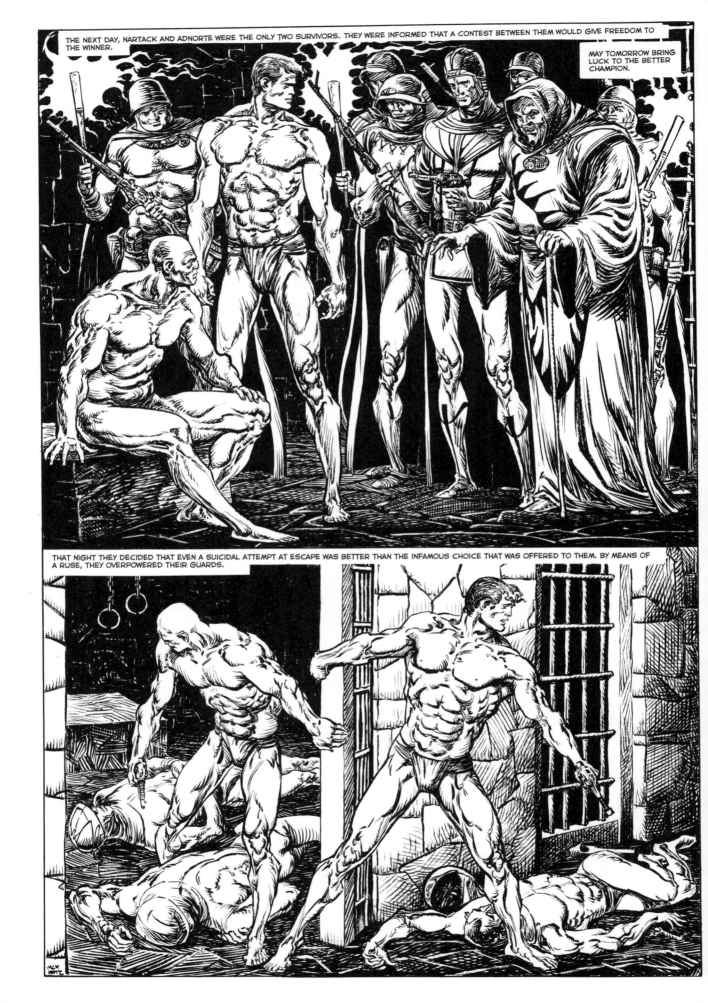

THE NEXT DAY, NARTACK AND ADNORTE WERE THE ONLY TWO SURVIVORS. THEY WERE INFORMED THAT A CONTEST BETWEEN THEM WOULD GIVE FREEDOM TO THE WINNER.

MAY TOMORROW BRING LUCK TO THE BETTER CHAMPION.

THAT NIGHT THEY DECIDED THAT EVEN A SUICIDAL ATTEMPT AT ESCAPE WAS BETTER THAN THE INFAMOUS CHOICE THAT WAS OFFERED TO THEM. BY MEANS OF A RUSE, THEY OVERPOWERED THEIR GUARDS.

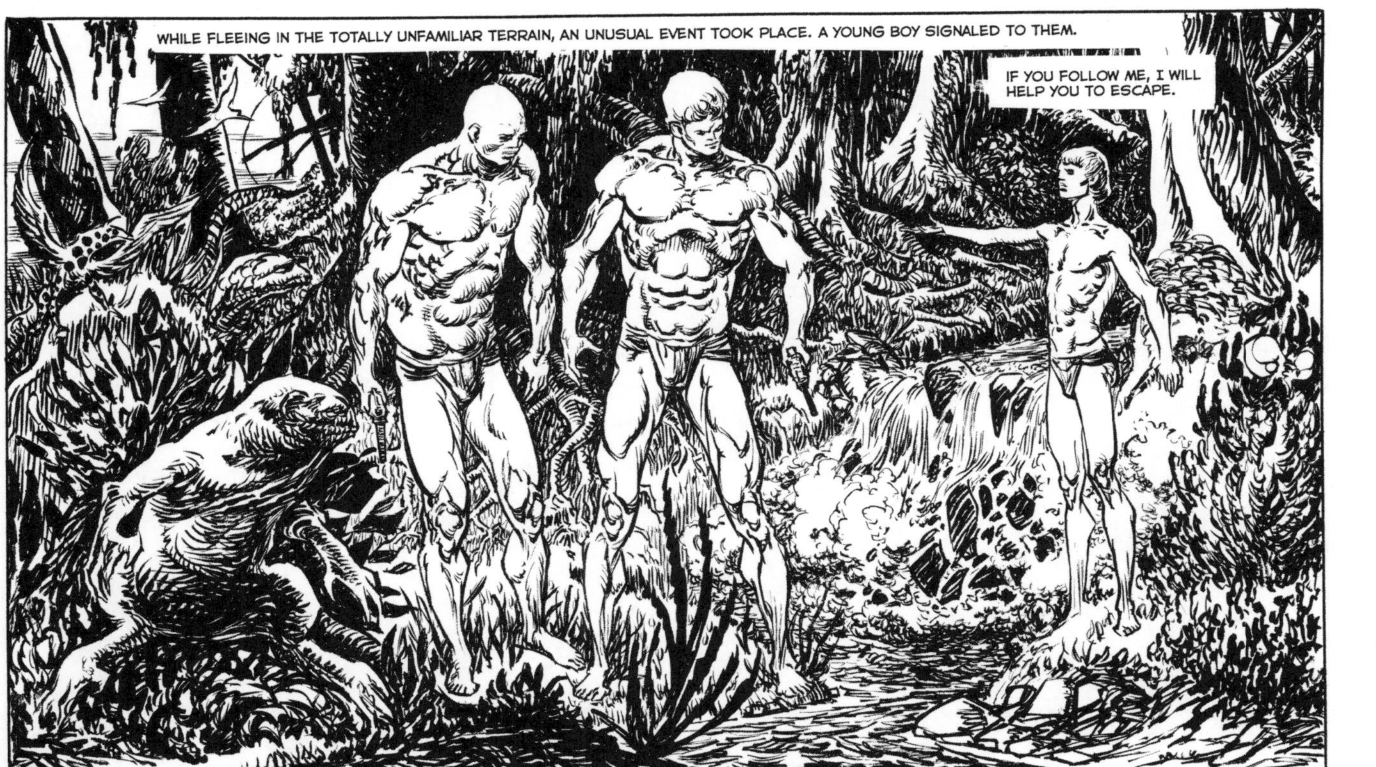
WHILE FLEEING IN THE TOTALLY UNFAMILIAR TERRAIN, AN UNUSUAL EVENT TOOK PLACE. A YOUNG BOY SIGNALED TO THEM.
IF YOU FOLLOW ME, I WILL HELP YOU TO ESCAPE.

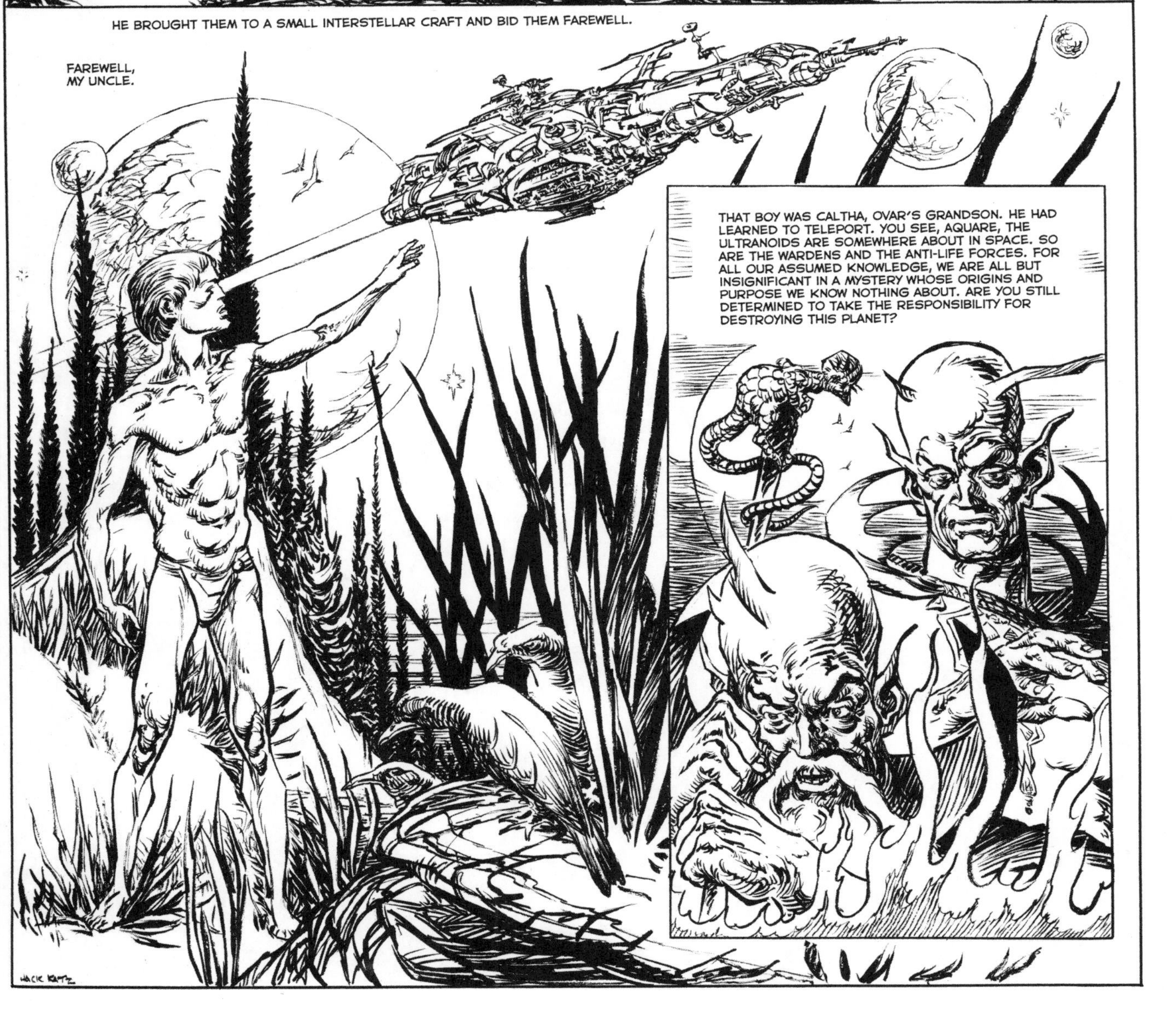
HE BROUGHT THEM TO A SMALL INTERSTELLAR CRAFT AND BID THEM FAREWELL.
FAREWELL, MY UNCLE.
THAT BOY WAS CALTHA, OVAR'S GRANDSON. HE HAD LEARNED TO TELEPORT. YOU SEE, AQUARE, THE ULTRANOIDS ARE SOMEWHERE ABOUT IN SPACE. SO ARE THE WARDENS AND THE ANTI-LIFE FORCES. FOR ALL OUR ASSUMED KNOWLEDGE, WE ARE ALL BUT INSIGNIFICANT IN A MYSTERY WHOSE ORIGINS AND PURPOSE WE KNOW NOTHING ABOUT. ARE YOU STILL DETERMINED TO TAKE THE RESPONSIBILITY FOR DESTROYING THIS PLANET?
JACK KATZ

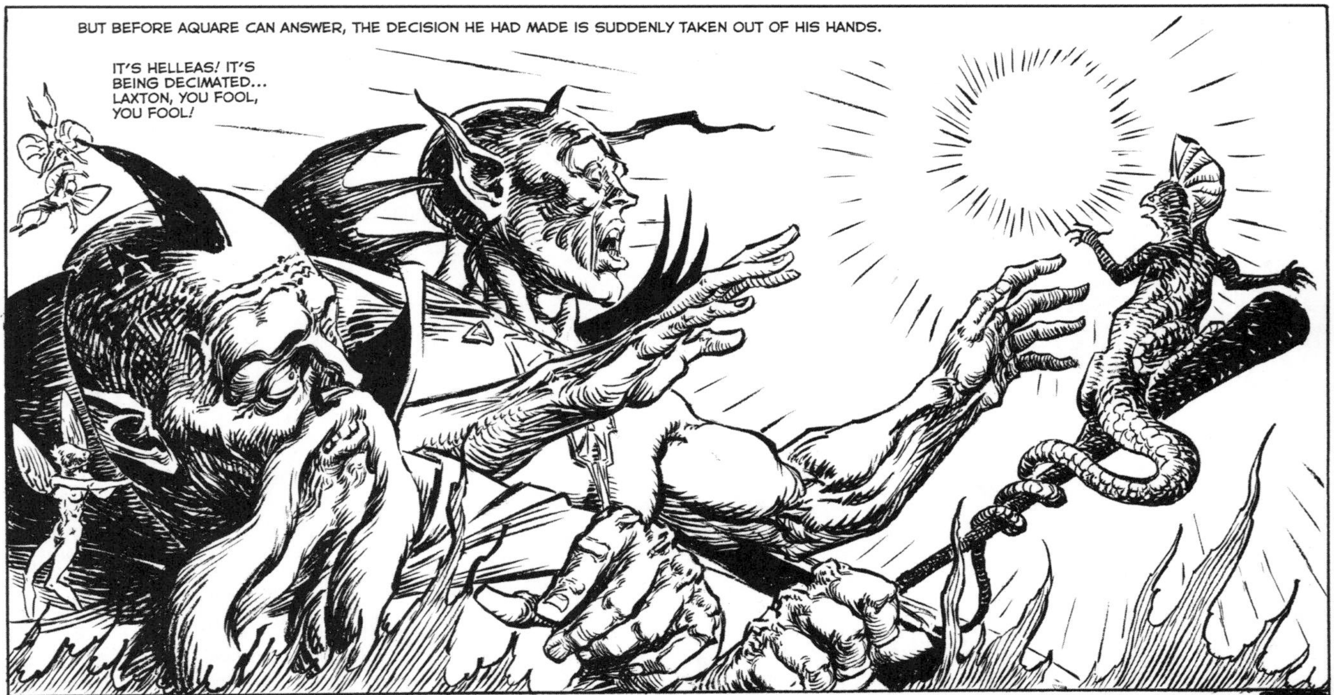
BUT BEFORE AQUARE CAN ANSWER, THE DECISION HE HAD MADE IS SUDDENLY TAKEN OUT OF HIS HANDS.
IT'S HELLEAS! IT'S BEING DECIMATED... LAXTON, YOU FOOL, YOU FOOL!

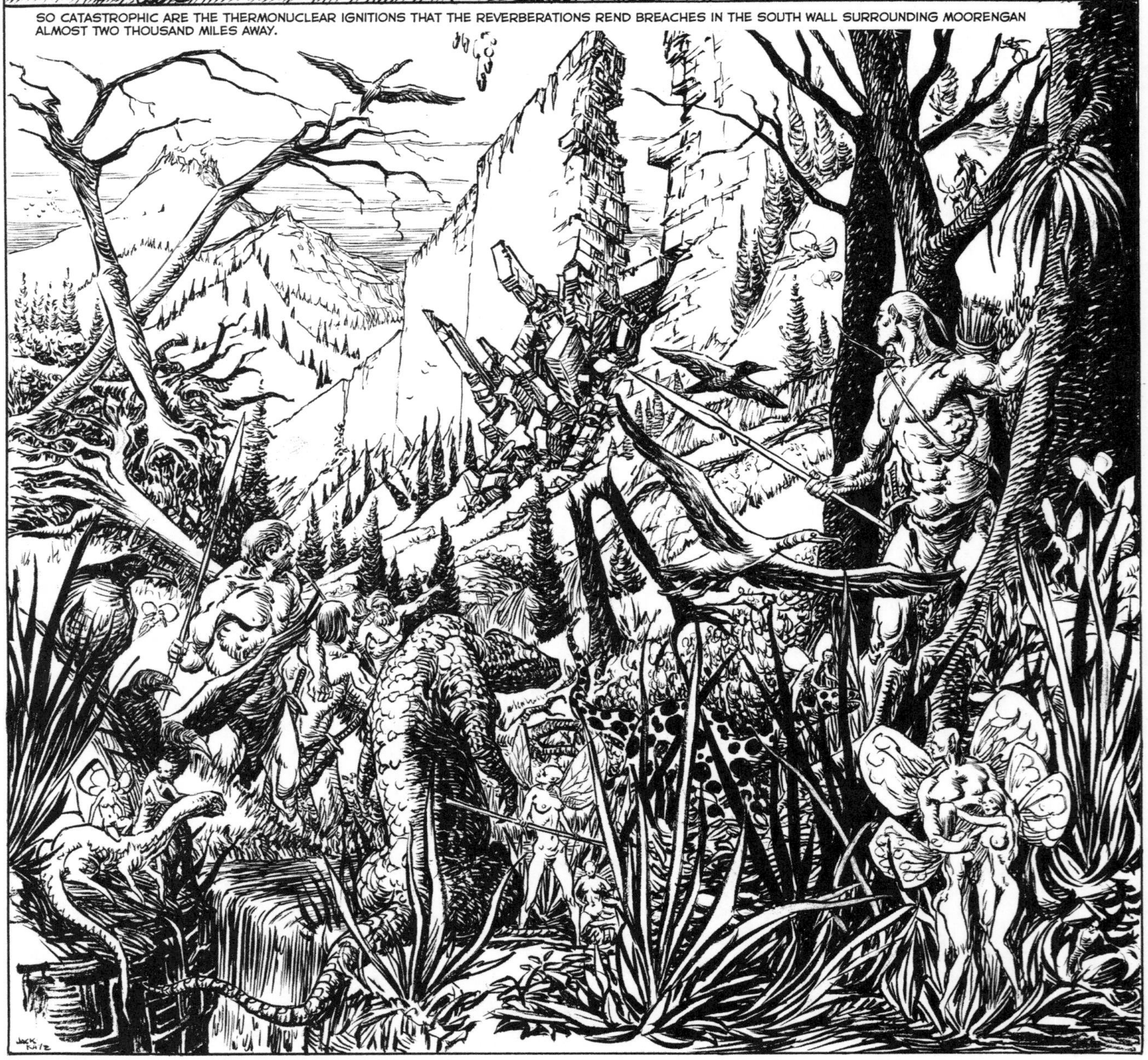
SO CATASTROPHIC ARE THE THERMONUCLEAR IGNITIONS THAT THE REVERBERATIONS REND BREACHES IN THE SOUTH WALL SURROUNDING MOORENGAN ALMOST TWO THOUSAND MILES AWAY.

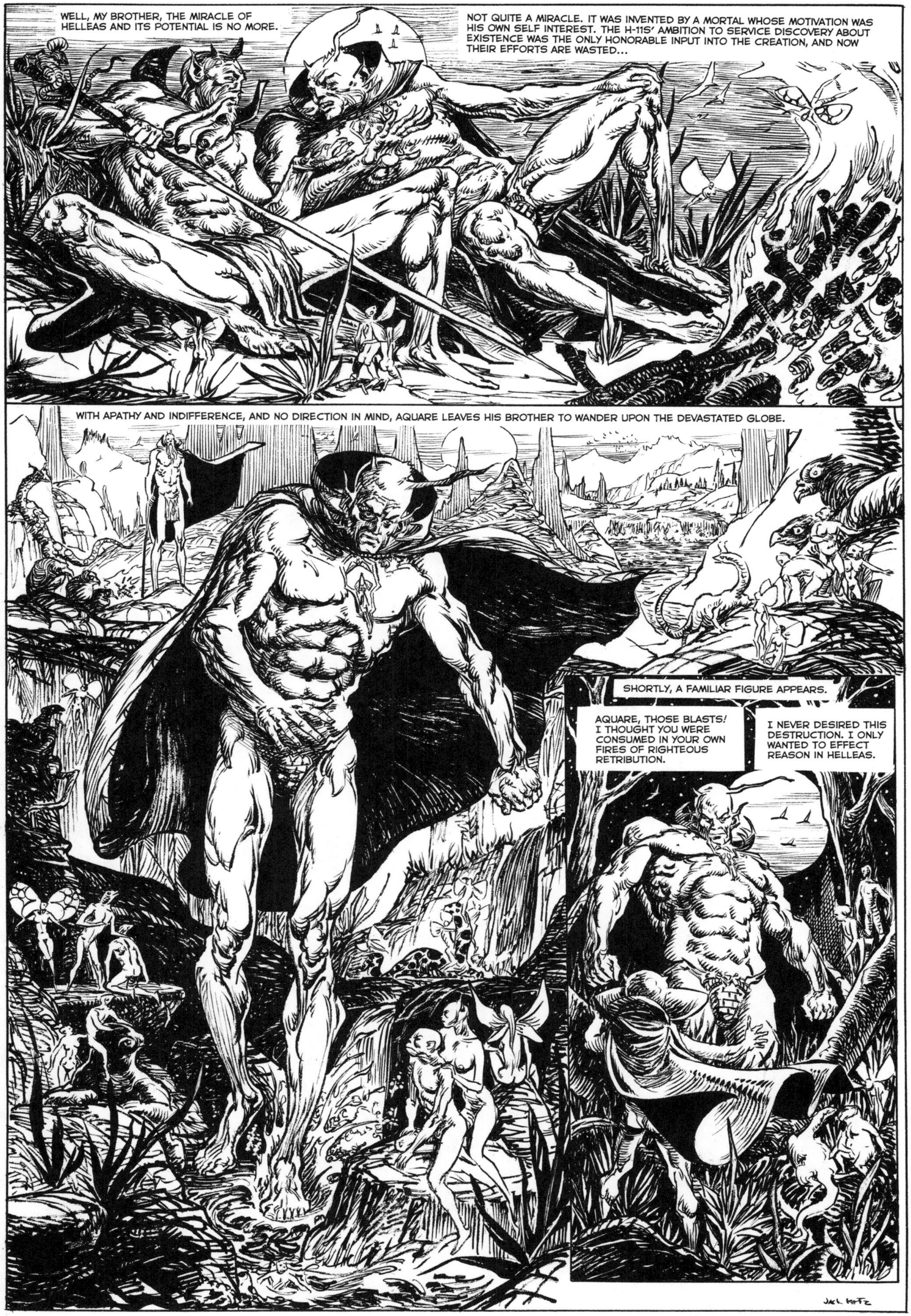
WELL, MY BROTHER, THE MIRACLE OF HELLEAS AND ITS POTENTIAL IS NO MORE.
NOT QUITE A MIRACLE. IT WAS INVENTED BY A MORTAL WHOSE MOTIVATION WAS HIS OWN SELF INTEREST. THE H-11S' AMBITION TO SERVICE DISCOVERY ABOUT EXISTENCE WAS THE ONLY HONORABLE INPUT INTO THE CREATION, AND NOW THEIR EFFORTS ARE WASTED...
WITH APATHY AND INDIFFERENCE, AND NO DIRECTION IN MIND, AQUARE LEAVES HIS BROTHER TO WANDER UPON THE DEVASTATED GLOBE.
SHORTLY, A FAMILIAR FIGURE APPEARS.
AQUARE, THOSE BLASTS! I THOUGHT YOU WERE CONSUMED IN YOUR OWN FIRES OF RIGHTEOUS RETRIBUTION.
I NEVER DESIRED THIS DESTRUCTION. I ONLY WANTED TO EFFECT REASON IN HELLEAS.

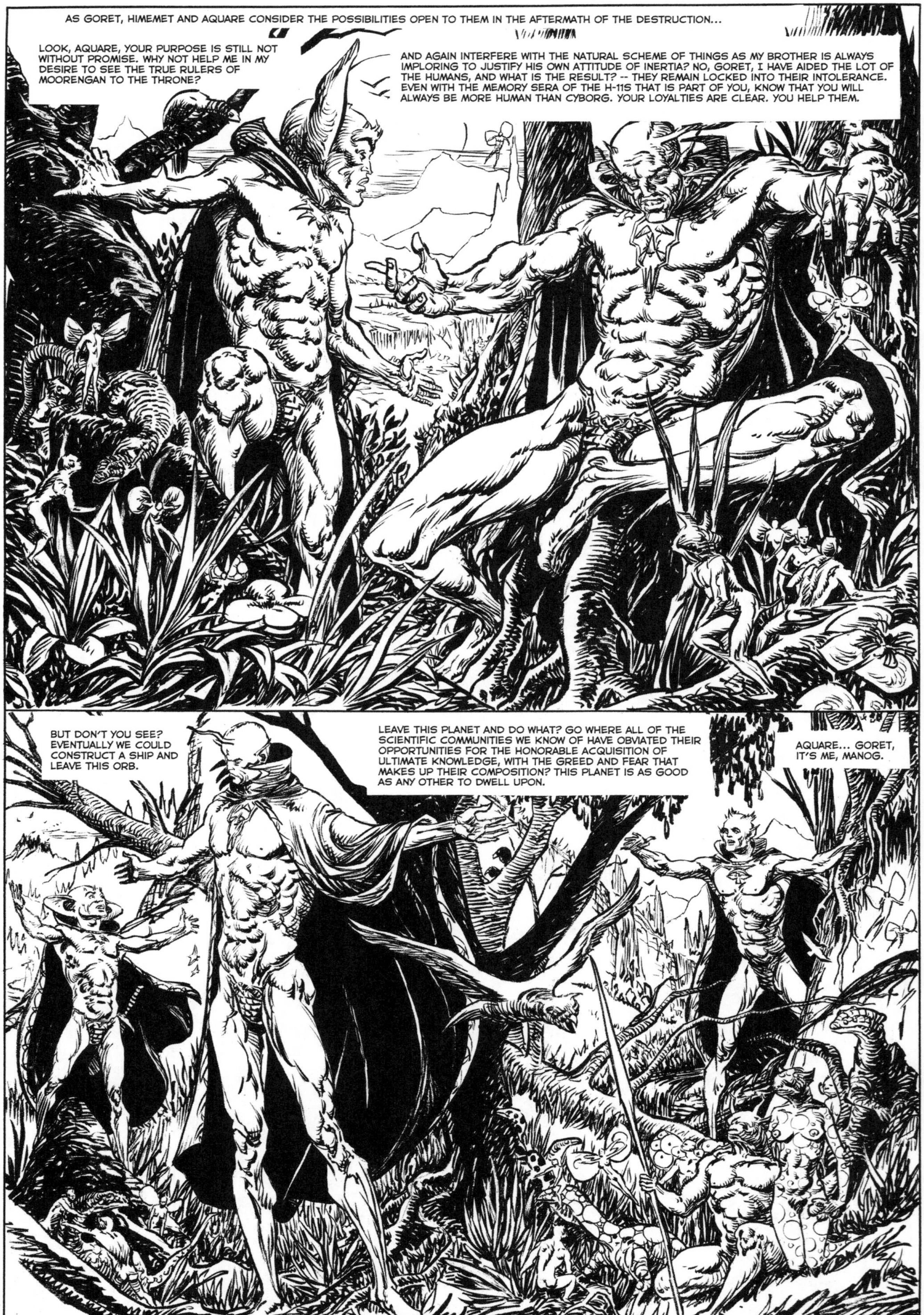
AS GORET, HIMEMET AND AQUARE CONSIDER THE POSSIBILITIES OPEN TO THEM IN THE AFTERMATH OF THE DESTRUCTION...
LOOK, AQUARE, YOUR PURPOSE IS STILL NOT WITHOUT PROMISE. WHY NOT HELP ME IN MY DESIRE TO SEE THE TRUE RULERS OF MOORENGAN TO THE THRONE?
AND AGAIN INTERFERE WITH THE NATURAL SCHEME OF THINGS AS MY BROTHER IS ALWAYS IMPLORING TO JUSTIFY HIS OWN ATTITUDE OF INERTIA? NO, GORET, I HAVE AIDED THE LOT OF THE HUMANS, AND WHAT IS THE RESULT? -- THEY REMAIN LOCKED INTO THEIR INTOLERANCE. EVEN WITH THE MEMORY SERA OF THE H-11S THAT IS PART OF YOU, KNOW THAT YOU WILL ALWAYS BE MORE HUMAN THAN CYBORG. YOUR LOYALTIES ARE CLEAR. YOU HELP THEM.
BUT DON'T YOU SEE? EVENTUALLY WE COULD CONSTRUCT A SHIP AND LEAVE THIS ORB.
LEAVE THIS PLANET AND DO WHAT? GO WHERE ALL OF THE SCIENTIFIC COMMUNITIES WE KNOW OF HAVE OBVIATED THEIR OPPORTUNITIES FOR THE HONORABLE ACQUISITION OF ULTIMATE KNOWLEDGE, WITH THE GREED AND FEAR THAT MAKES UP THEIR COMPOSITION? THIS PLANET IS AS GOOD AS ANY OTHER TO DWELL UPON.
AQUARE... GORET, IT'S ME, MANOG.
JACK KATZ

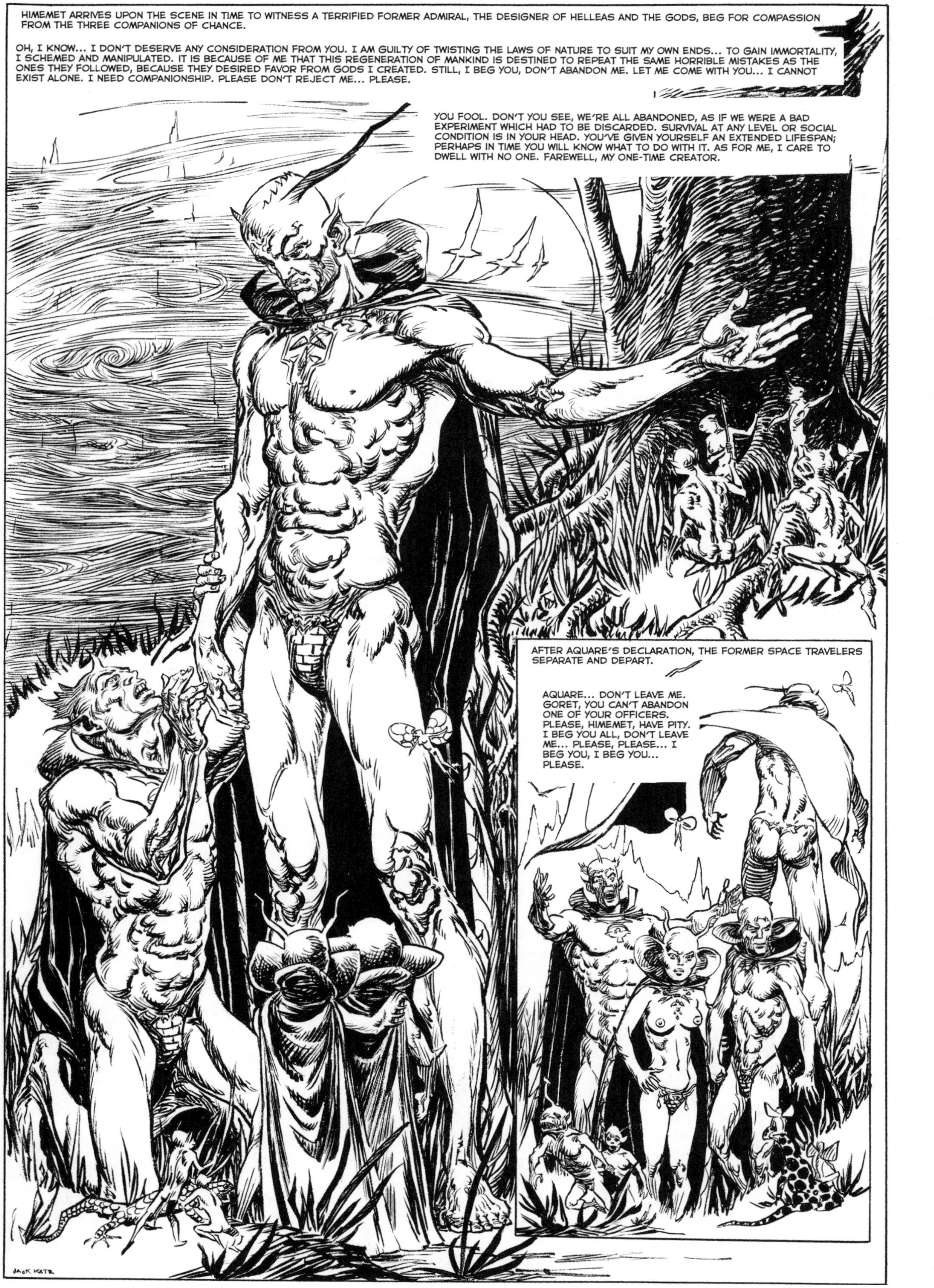
HIMEMET ARRIVES UPON THE SCENE IN TIME TO WITNESS A TERRIFIED FORMER ADMIRAL, THE DESIGNER OF HELLEAS AND THE GODS, BEG FOR COMPASSION FROM THE THREE COMPANIONS OF CHANCE.
OH, I KNOW... I DON'T DESERVE ANY CONSIDERATION FROM YOU. I AM GUILTY OF TWISTING THE LAWS OF NATURE TO SUIT MY OWN ENDS... TO GAIN IMMORTALITY, I SCHEMED AND MANIPULATED. IT IS BECAUSE OF ME THAT THIS REGENERATION OF MANKIND IS DESTINED TO REPEAT THE SAME HORRIBLE MISTAKES AS THE ONES THEY FOLLOWED, BECAUSE THEY DESIRED FAVOR FROM GODS I CREATED. STILL, I BEG YOU, DON'T ABANDON ME. LET ME COME WITH YOU... I CANNOT EXIST ALONE. I NEED COMPANIONSHIP. PLEASE DON'T REJECT ME... PLEASE.
YOU FOOL. DON'T YOU SEE, WE'RE ALL ABANDONED, AS IF WE WERE A BAD EXPERIMENT WHICH HAD TO BE DISCARDED. SURVIVAL AT ANY LEVEL OR SOCIAL CONDITION IS IN YOUR HEAD. YOU'VE GIVEN YOURSELF AN EXTENDED LIFESPAN; PERHAPS IN TIME YOU WILL KNOW WHAT TO DO WITH IT. AS FOR ME, I CARE TO DWELL WITH NO ONE. FAREWELL, MY ONE-TIME CREATOR.
AFTER AQUARE'S DECLARATION, THE FORMER SPACE TRAVELERS SEPARATE AND DEPART.
AQUARE... DON'T LEAVE ME. GORET, YOU CAN'T ABANDON ONE OF YOUR OFFICERS. PLEASE, HIMEMET, HAVE PITY. I BEG YOU ALL, DON'T LEAVE ME... PLEASE, PLEASE... I BEG YOU, I BEG YOU... PLEASE.
JACK KATZ

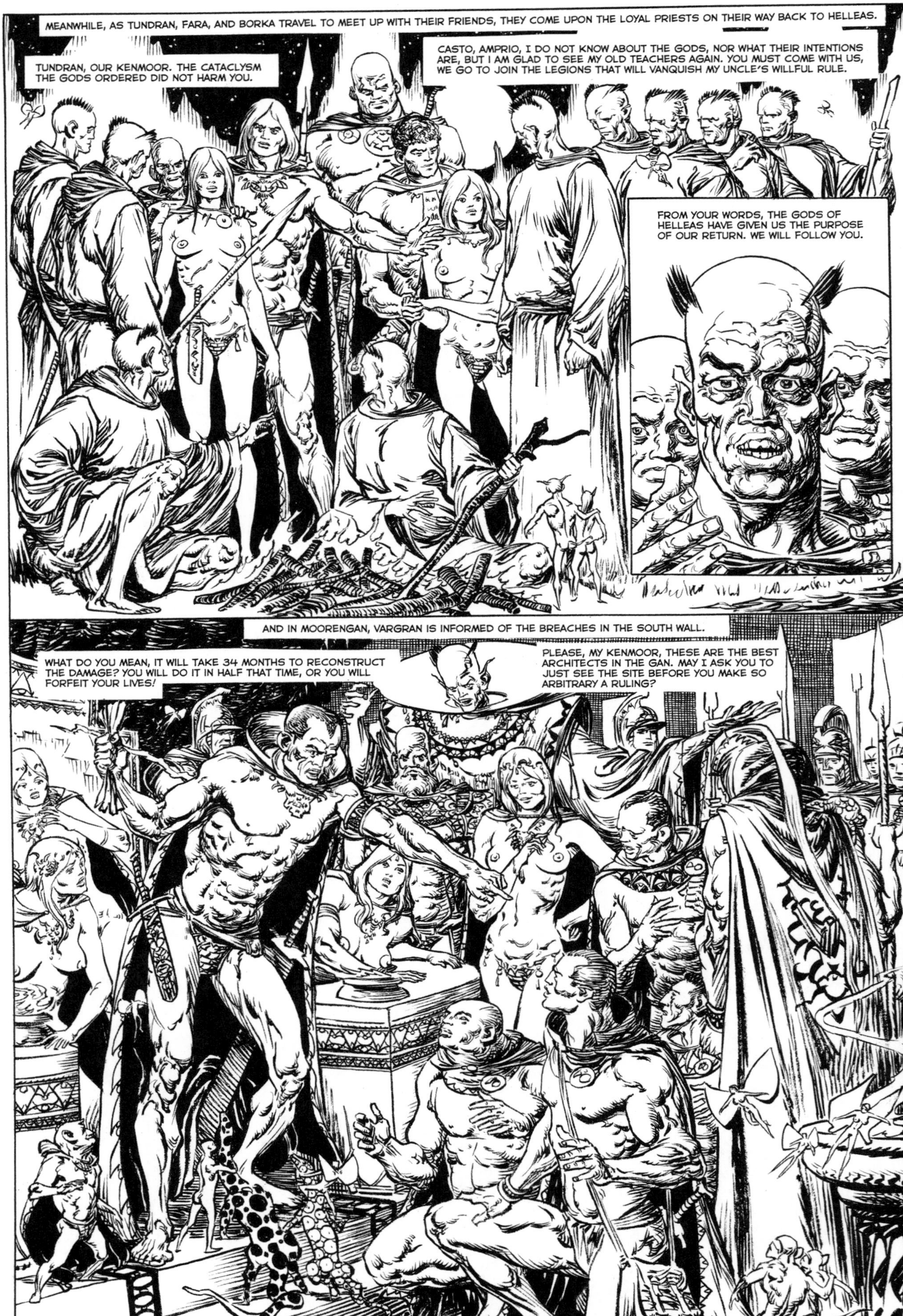
MEANWHILE, AS TUNDRAN, FARA, AND BORKA TRAVEL TO MEET UP WITH THEIR FRIENDS, THEY COME UPON THE LOYAL PRIESTS ON THEIR WAY BACK TO HELLEAS.
TUNDRAN, OUR KENMOOR. THE CATACLYSM THE GODS ORDERED DID NOT HARM YOU.
CASTO, AMPRIO, I DO NOT KNOW ABOUT THE GODS, NOR WHAT THEIR INTENTIONS ARE, BUT I AM GLAD TO SEE MY OLD TEACHERS AGAIN. YOU MUST COME WITH US, WE GO TO JOIN THE LEGIONS THAT WILL VANQUISH MY UNCLE'S WILLFUL RULE.
FROM YOUR WORDS, THE GODS OF HELLEAS HAVE GIVEN US THE PURPOSE OF OUR RETURN. WE WILL FOLLOW YOU.
AND IN MOORENGAN, VARGRAN IS INFORMED OF THE BREACHES IN THE SOUTH WALL.
WHAT DO YOU MEAN, IT WILL TAKE 34 MONTHS TO RECONSTRUCT THE DAMAGE? YOU WILL DO IT IN HALF THAT TIME, OR YOU WILL FORFEIT YOUR LIVES!
PLEASE, MY KENMOOR, THESE ARE THE BEST ARCHITECTS IN THE GAN. MAY I ASK YOU TO JUST SEE THE SITE BEFORE YOU MAKE SO ARBITRARY A RULING?
JACK KATZ

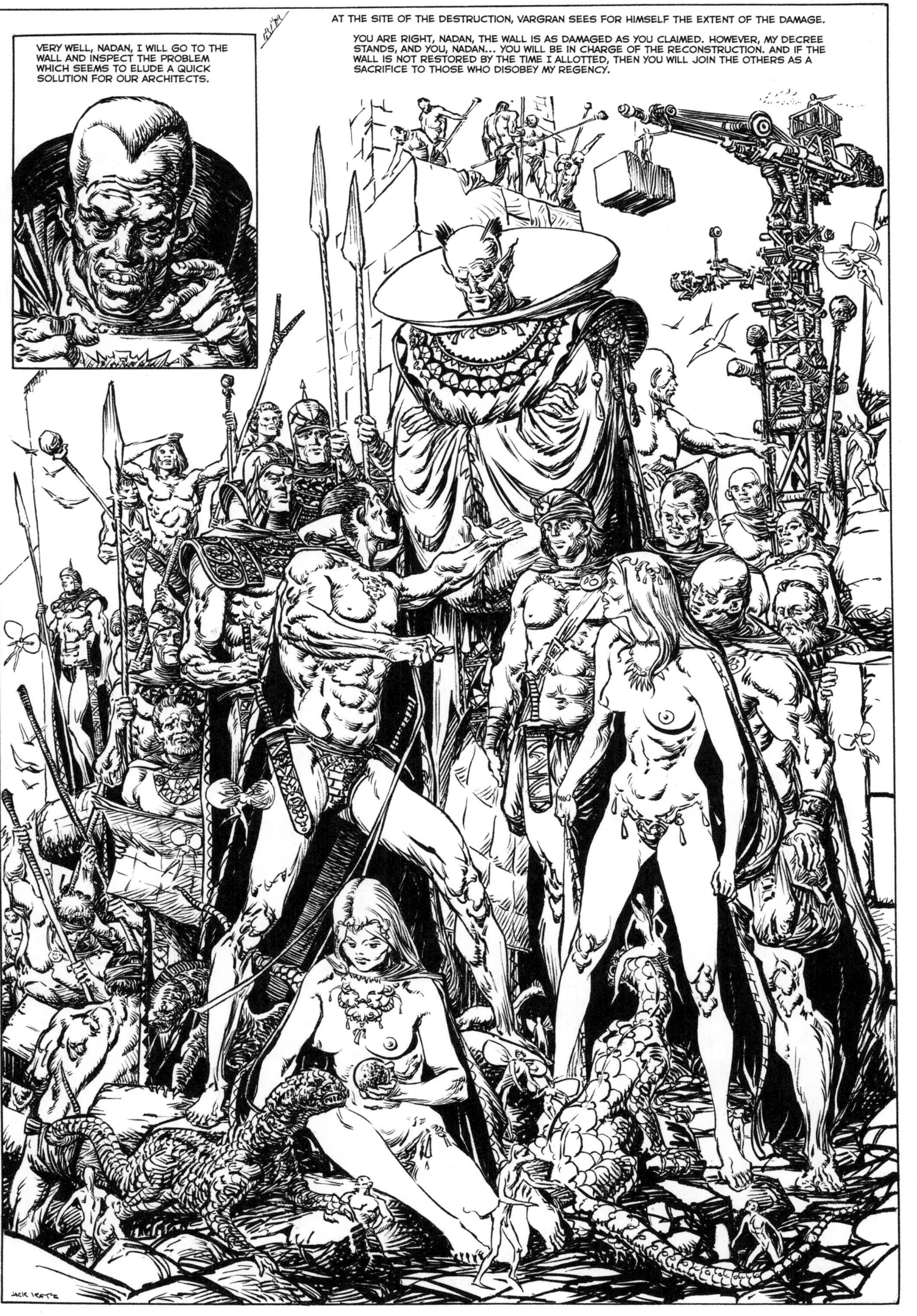
VERY WELL, NADAN, I WILL GO TO THE WALL AND INSPECT THE PROBLEM WHICH SEEMS TO ELUDE A QUICK SOLUTION FOR OUR ARCHITECTS.
AT THE SITE OF THE DESTRUCTION, VARGRAN SEES FOR HIMSELF THE EXTENT OF THE DAMAGE.
YOU ARE RIGHT, NADAN, THE WALL IS AS DAMAGED AS YOU CLAIMED. HOWEVER, MY DECREE STANDS, AND YOU, NADAN... YOU WILL BE IN CHARGE OF THE RECONSTRUCTION. AND IF THE WALL IS NOT RESTORED BY THE TIME I ALLOTTED, THEN YOU WILL JOIN THE OTHERS AS A SACRIFICE TO THOSE WHO DISOBEY MY REGENCY.
JACK KATZ

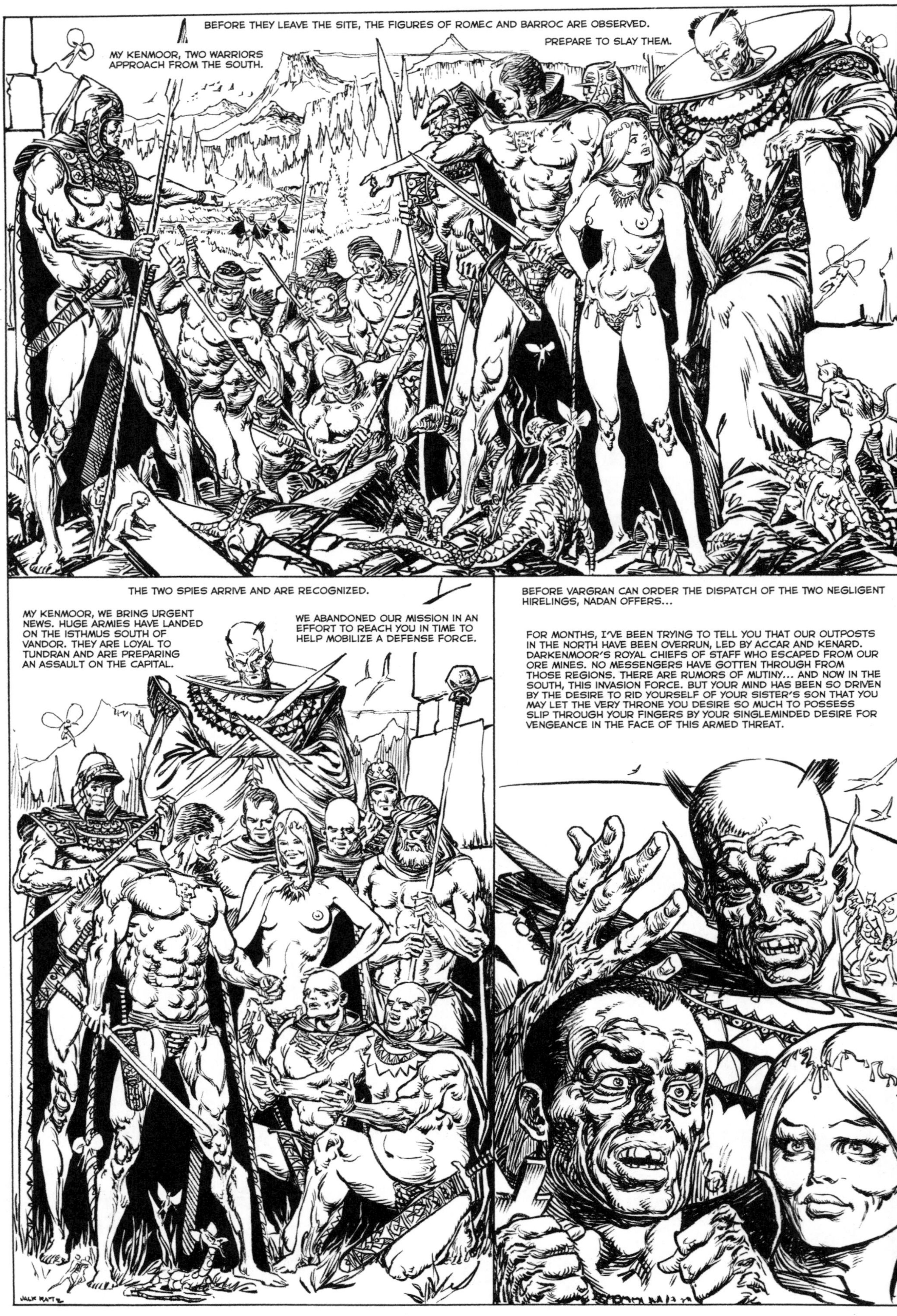
BEFORE THEY LEAVE THE SITE, THE FIGURES OF ROMEC AND BARROC ARE OBSERVED.
MY KENMOOR, TWO WARRIORS APPROACH FROM THE SOUTH.
PREPARE TO SLAY THEM.
THE TWO SPIES ARRIVE AND ARE RECOGNIZED.
MY KENMOOR, WE BRING URGENT NEWS. HUGE ARMIES HAVE LANDED ON THE ISTHMUS SOUTH OF VANDOR. THEY ARE LOYAL TO TUNDRAN AND ARE PREPARING AN ASSAULT ON THE CAPITAL.
WE ABANDONED OUR MISSION IN AN EFFORT TO REACH YOU IN TIME TO HELP MOBILIZE A DEFENSE FORCE.
BEFORE VARGRAN CAN ORDER THE DISPATCH OF THE TWO NEGLIGENT HIRELINGS, NADAN OFFERS...
FOR MONTHS, I'VE BEEN TRYING TO TELL YOU THAT OUR OUTPOSTS IN THE NORTH HAVE BEEN OVERRUN, LED BY ACCAR AND KENARD. DARKENMOOR'S ROYAL CHIEFS OF STAFF WHO ESCAPED FROM OUR ORE MINES. NO MESSENGERS HAVE GOTTEN THROUGH FROM THOSE REGIONS. THERE ARE RUMORS OF MUTINY... AND NOW IN THE SOUTH, THIS INVASION FORCE. BUT YOUR MIND HAS BEEN SO DRIVEN BY THE DESIRE TO RID YOURSELF OF YOUR SISTER'S SON THAT YOU MAY LET THE VERY THRONE YOU DESIRE SO MUCH TO POSSESS SLIP THROUGH YOUR FINGERS BY YOUR SINGLEMINDED DESIRE FOR VENGEANCE IN THE FACE OF THIS ARMED THREAT.

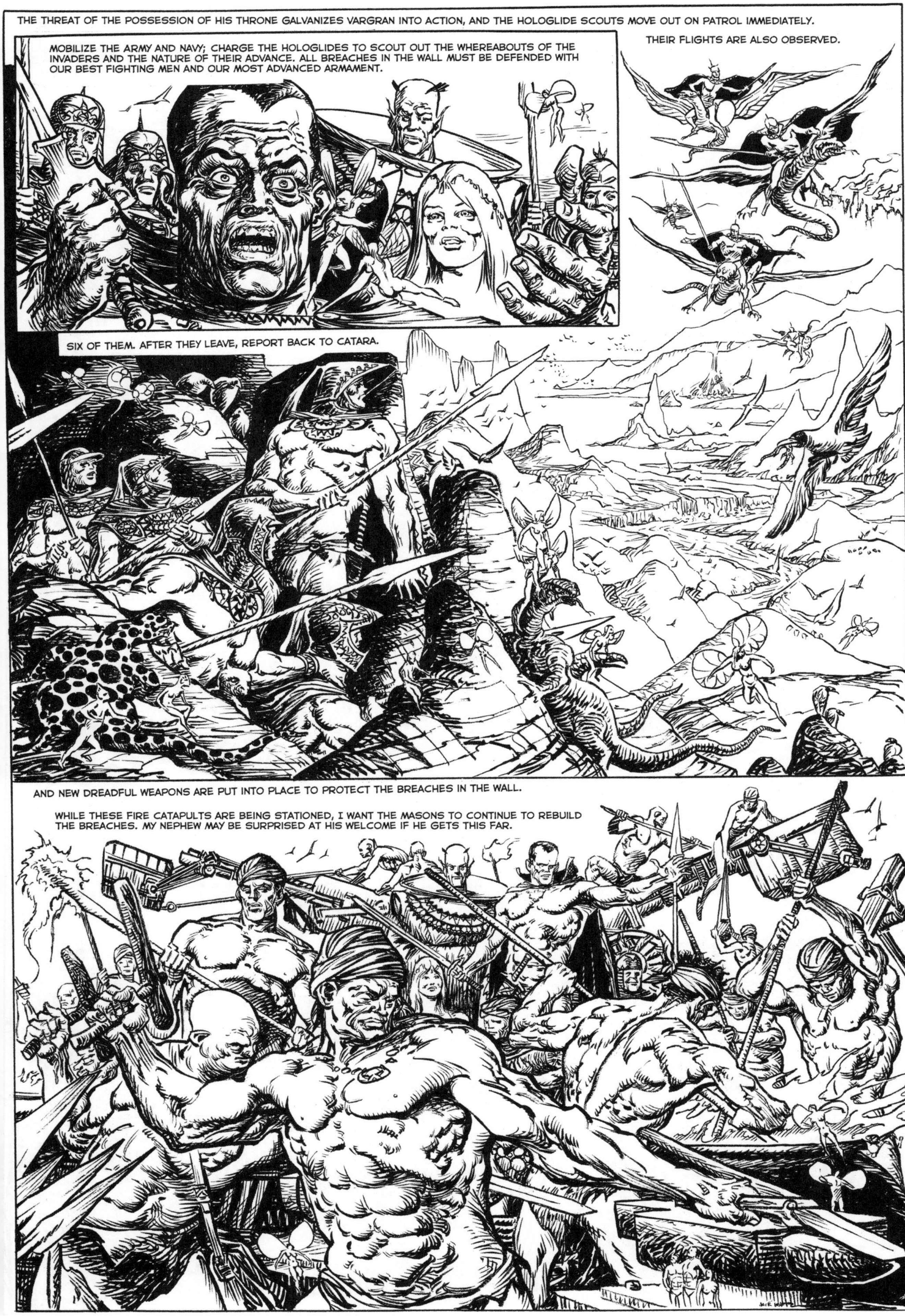
THE THREAT OF THE POSSESSION OF HIS THRONE GALVANIZES VARGRAN INTO ACTION, AND THE HOLOGLIDE SCOUTS MOVE OUT ON PATROL IMMEDIATELY.
MOBILIZE THE ARMY AND NAVY; CHARGE THE HOLOGLIDES TO SCOUT OUT THE WHEREABOUTS OF THE INVADERS AND THE NATURE OF THEIR ADVANCE. ALL BREACHES IN THE WALL MUST BE DEFENDED WITH OUR BEST FIGHTING MEN AND OUR MOST ADVANCED ARMAMENT.
THEIR FLIGHTS ARE ALSO OBSERVED.
SIX OF THEM. AFTER THEY LEAVE, REPORT BACK TO CATARA.
AND NEW DREADFUL WEAPONS ARE PUT INTO PLACE TO PROTECT THE BREACHES IN THE WALL.
WHILE THESE FIRE CATAPULTS ARE BEING STATIONED, I WANT THE MASONS TO CONTINUE TO REBUILD THE BREACHES. MY NEPHEW MAY BE SURPRISED AT HIS WELCOME IF HE GETS THIS FAR.

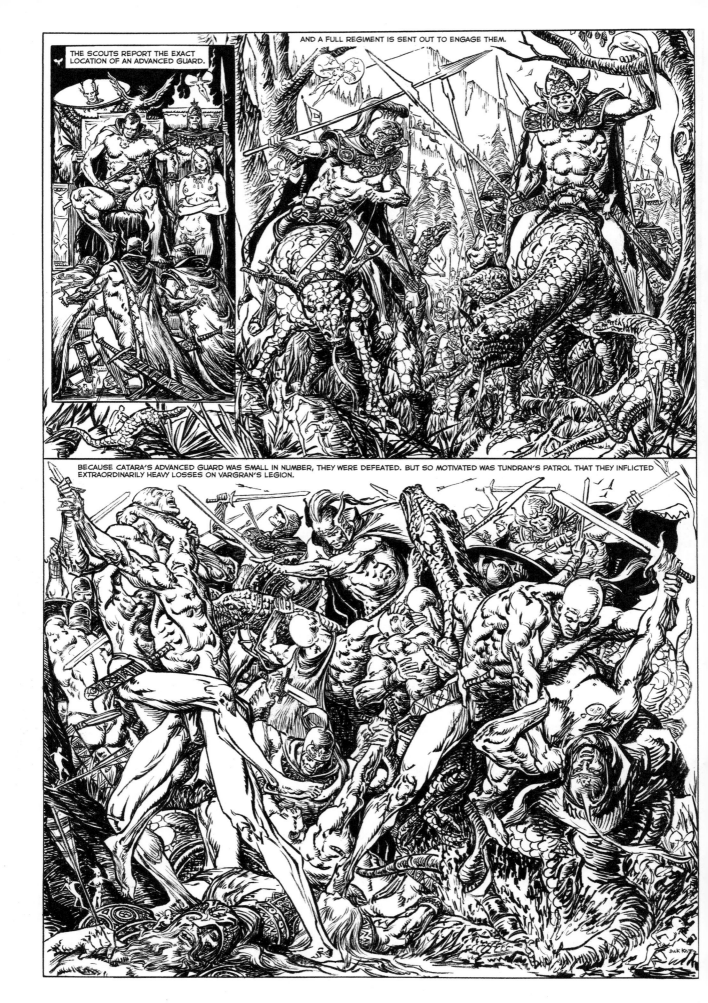

THE SCOUTS REPORT THE EXACT LOCATION OF AN ADVANCED GUARD.

AND A FULL REGIMENT IS SENT OUT TO ENGAGE THEM.

BECAUSE CATARA'S ADVANCED GUARD WAS SMALL IN NUMBER, THEY WERE DEFEATED. BUT SO MOTIVATED WAS TUNDRAN'S PATROL THAT THEY INFLICTED EXTRAORDINARILY HEAVY LOSSES ON VARGRAN'S LEGION.

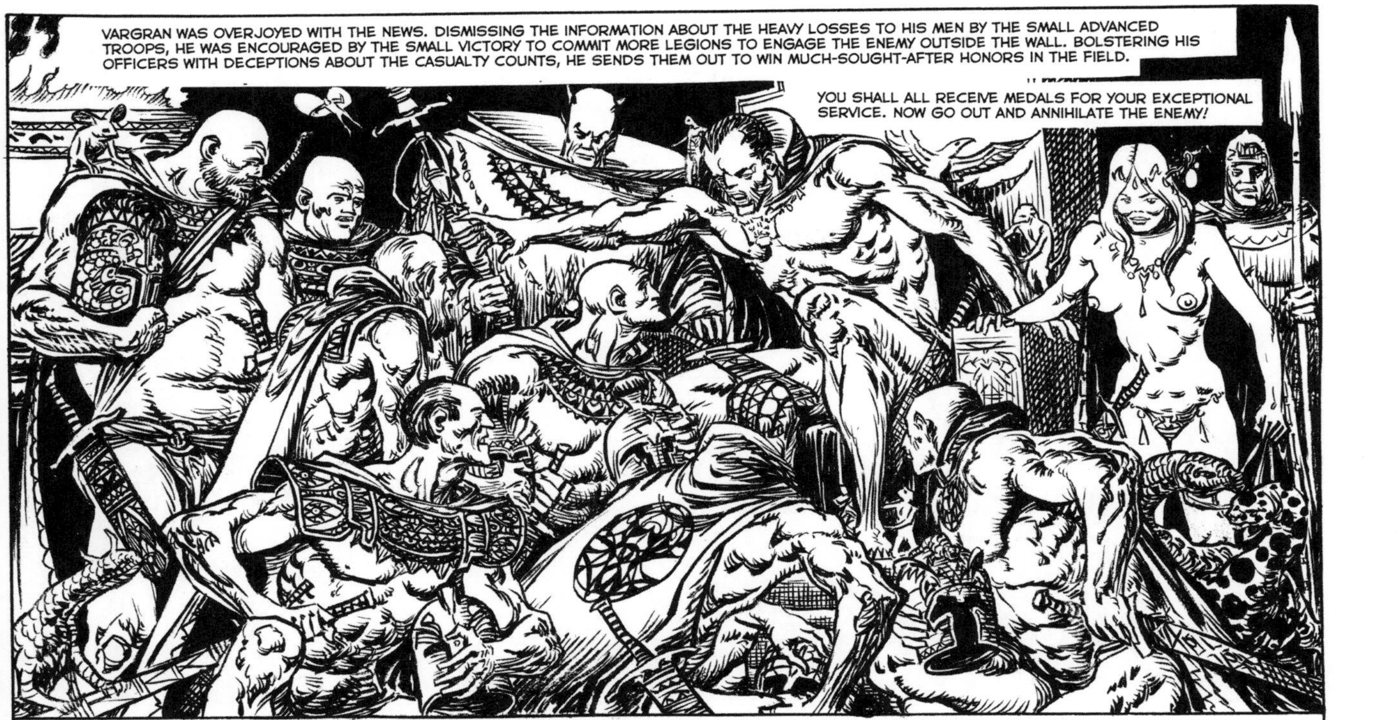
VARGRAN WAS OVERJOYED WITH THE NEWS. DISMISSING THE INFORMATION ABOUT THE HEAVY LOSSES TO HIS MEN BY THE SMALL ADVANCED TROOPS, HE WAS ENCOURAGED BY THE SMALL VICTORY TO COMMIT MORE LEGIONS TO ENGAGE THE ENEMY OUTSIDE THE WALL. BOLSTERING HIS OFFICERS WITH DECEPTIONS ABOUT THE CASUALTY COUNTS, HE SENDS THEM OUT TO WIN MUCH-SOUGHT-AFTER HONORS IN THE FIELD.
YOU SHALL ALL RECEIVE MEDALS FOR YOUR EXCEPTIONAL SERVICE. NOW GO OUT AND ANNIHILATE THE ENEMY!

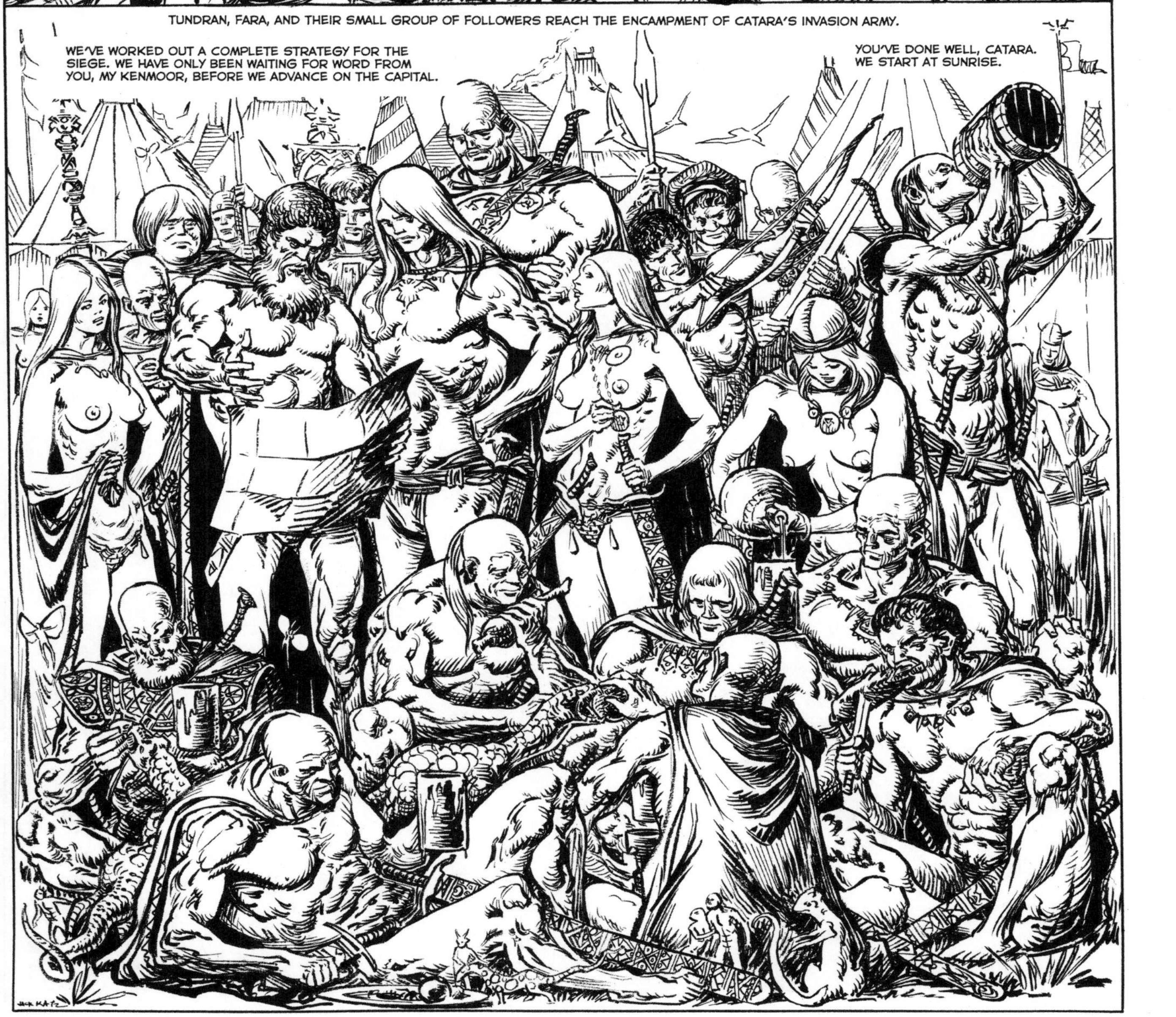
TUNDRAN, FARA, AND THEIR SMALL GROUP OF FOLLOWERS REACH THE ENCAMPMENT OF CATARA'S INVASION ARMY.
WE'VE WORKED OUT A COMPLETE STRATEGY FOR THE SIEGE. WE HAVE ONLY BEEN WAITING FOR WORD FROM YOU, MY KENMOOR, BEFORE WE ADVANCE ON THE CAPITAL.
YOU'VE DONE WELL, CATARA. WE START AT SUNRISE.

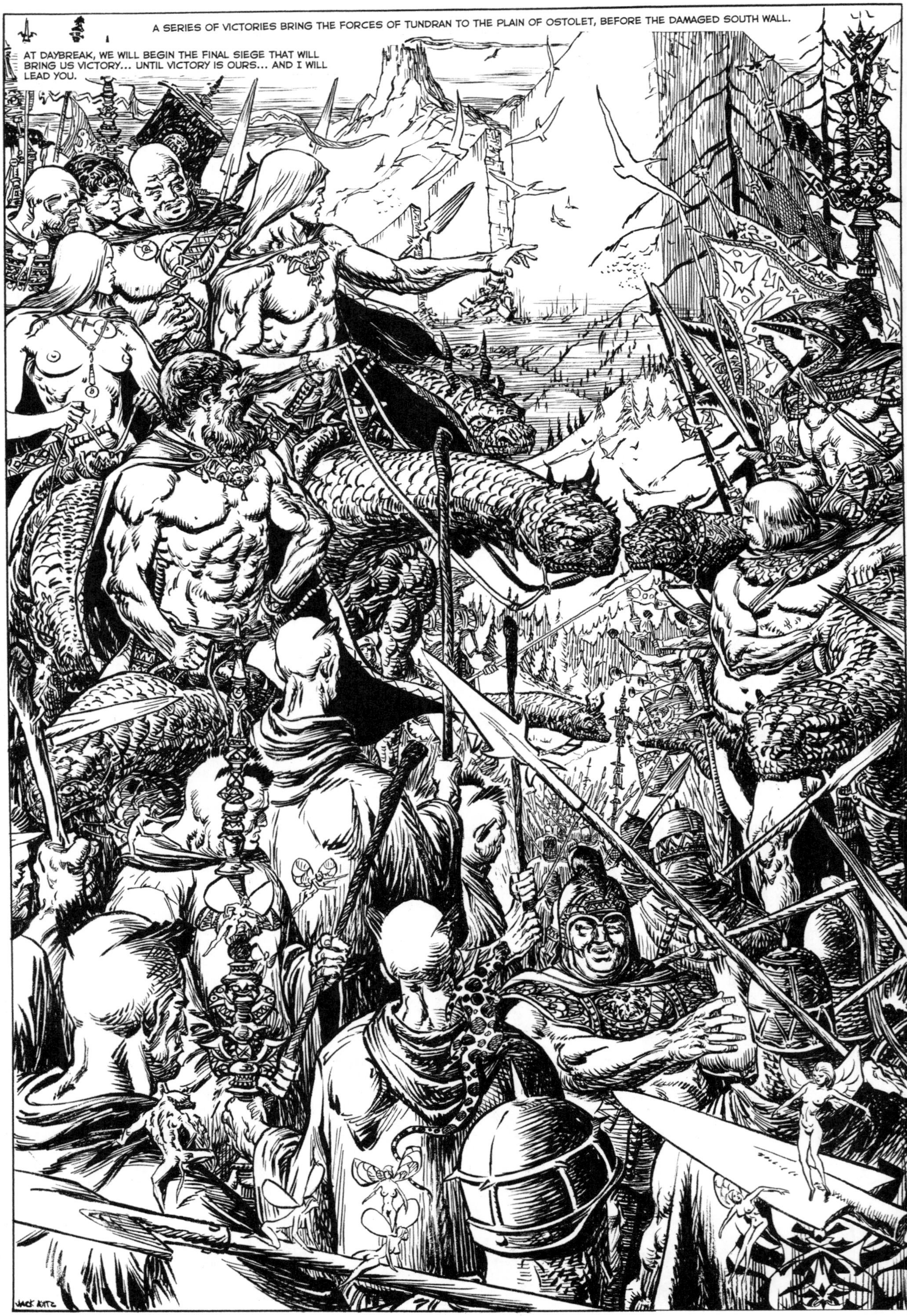
A SERIES OF VICTORIES BRING THE FORCES OF TUNDRAN TO THE PLAIN OF OSTOLET, BEFORE THE DAMAGED SOUTH WALL.
AT DAYBREAK, WE WILL BEGIN THE FINAL SIEGE THAT WILL BRING US VICTORY... UNTIL VICTORY IS OURS... AND I WILL LEAD YOU.
JACK KATZ

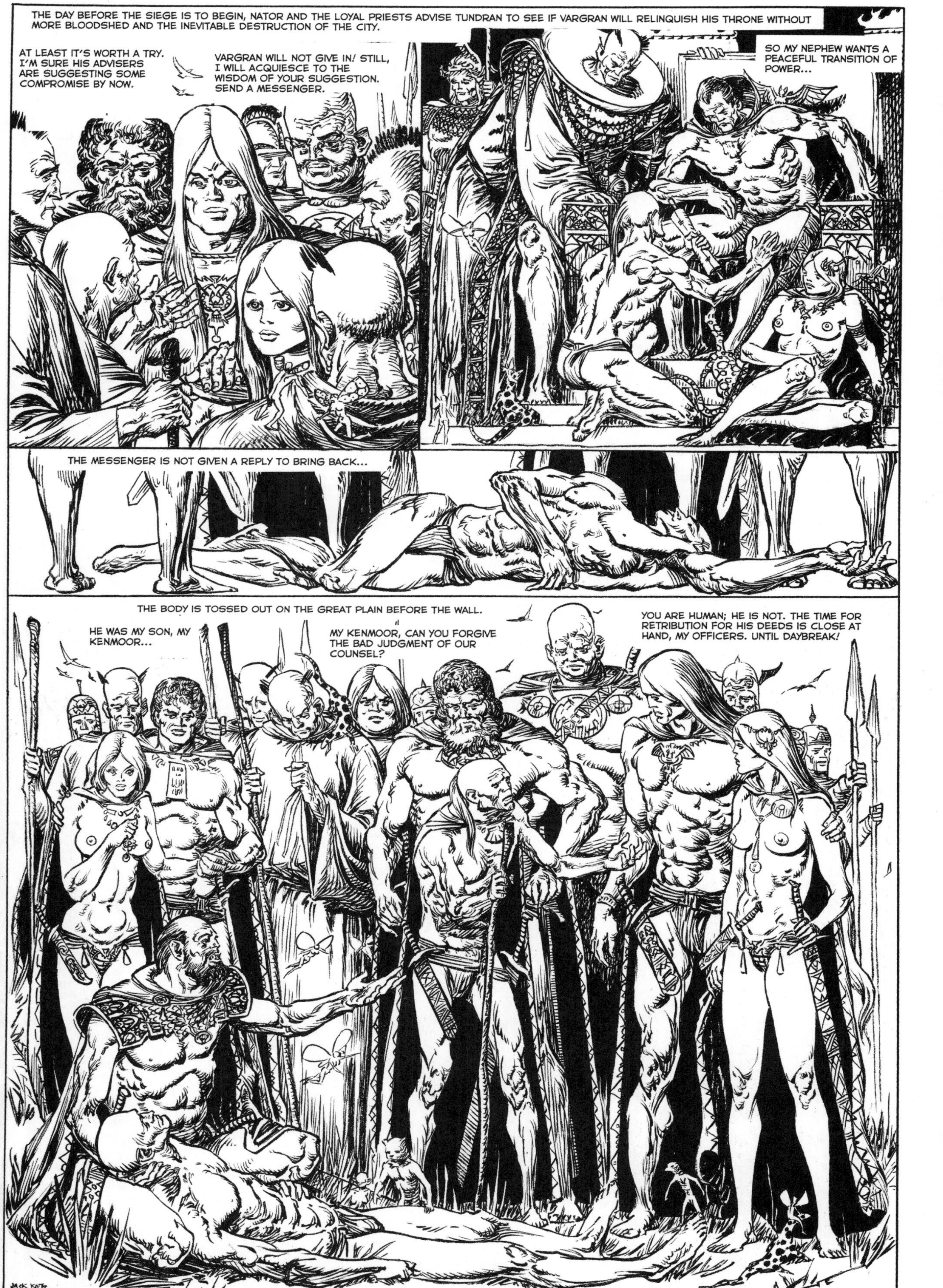
THE DAY BEFORE THE SIEGE IS TO BEGIN, NATOR AND THE LOYAL PRIESTS ADVISE TUNDRAN TO SEE IF VARGRAN WILL RELINQUISH HIS THRONE WITHOUT MORE BLOODSHED AND THE INEVITABLE DESTRUCTION OF THE CITY.
AT LEAST IT'S WORTH A TRY. I'M SURE HIS ADVISERS ARE SUGGESTING SOME COMPROMISE BY NOW.
VARGRAN WILL NOT GIVE IN! STILL, I WILL ACQUIESCE TO THE WISDOM OF YOUR SUGGESTION. SEND A MESSENGER.
SO MY NEPHEW WANTS A PEACEFUL TRANSITION OF POWER...
THE MESSENGER IS NOT GIVEN A REPLY TO BRING BACK...
THE BODY IS TOSSED OUT ON THE GREAT PLAIN BEFORE THE WALL.
HE WAS MY SON, MY KENMOOR...
MY KENMOOR, CAN YOU FORGIVE THE BAD JUDGMENT OF OUR COUNSEL?
YOU ARE HUMAN; HE IS NOT. THE TIME FOR RETRIBUTION FOR HIS DEEDS IS CLOSE AT HAND, MY OFFICERS. UNTIL DAYBREAK!
JACK KATZ

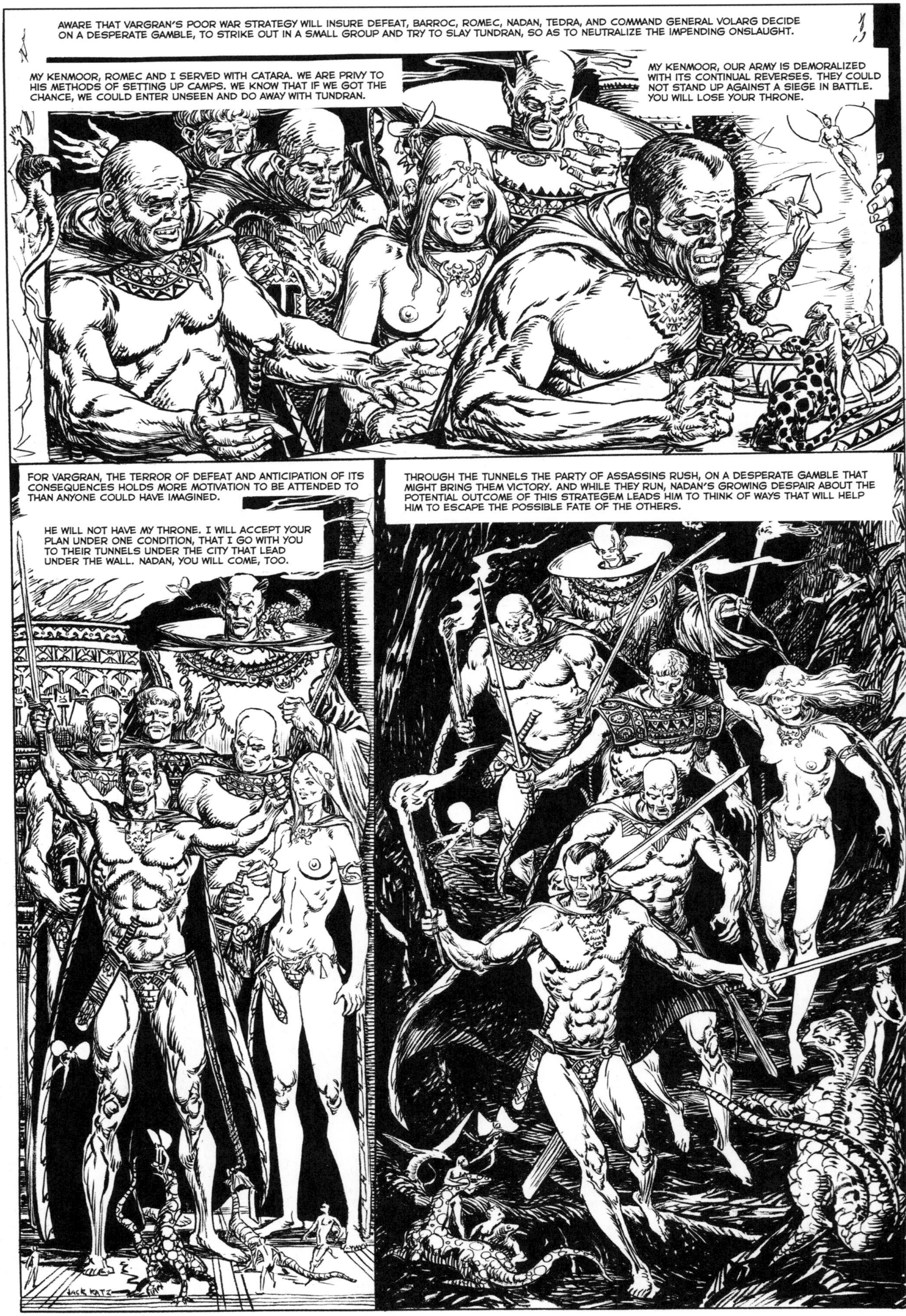
AWARE THAT VARGRAN'S POOR WAR STRATEGY WILL INSURE DEFEAT, BARROC, ROMEC, NADAN, TEDRA, AND COMMAND GENERAL VOLARG DECIDE ON A DESPERATE GAMBLE, TO STRIKE OUT IN A SMALL GROUP AND TRY TO SLAY TUNDRAN, SO AS TO NEUTRALIZE THE IMPENDING ONSLAUGHT.
MY KENMOOR, ROMEC AND I SERVED WITH CATARA. WE ARE PRIVY TO HIS METHODS OF SETTING UP CAMPS. WE KNOW THAT IF WE GOT THE CHANCE, WE COULD ENTER UNSEEN AND DO AWAY WITH TUNDRAN.
MY KENMOOR, OUR ARMY IS DEMORALIZED WITH ITS CONTINUAL REVERSES. THEY COULD NOT STAND UP AGAINST A SIEGE IN BATTLE. YOU WILL LOSE YOUR THRONE.
FOR VARGRAN, THE TERROR OF DEFEAT AND ANTICIPATION OF ITS CONSEQUENCES HOLDS MORE MOTIVATION TO BE ATTENDED TO THAN ANYONE COULD HAVE IMAGINED.
HE WILL NOT HAVE MY THRONE. I WILL ACCEPT YOUR PLAN UNDER ONE CONDITION, THAT I GO WITH YOU TO THEIR TUNNELS UNDER THE CITY THAT LEAD UNDER THE WALL. NADAN, YOU WILL COME, TOO.
JACK KATZ
THROUGH THE TUNNELS THE PARTY OF ASSASSINS RUSH, ON A DESPERATE GAMBLE THAT MIGHT BRING THEM VICTORY. AND WHILE THEY RUN, NADAN'S GROWING DESPAIR ABOUT THE POTENTIAL OUTCOME OF THIS STRATEGEM LEADS HIM TO THINK OF WAYS THAT WILL HELP HIM TO ESCAPE THE POSSIBLE FATE OF THE OTHERS.

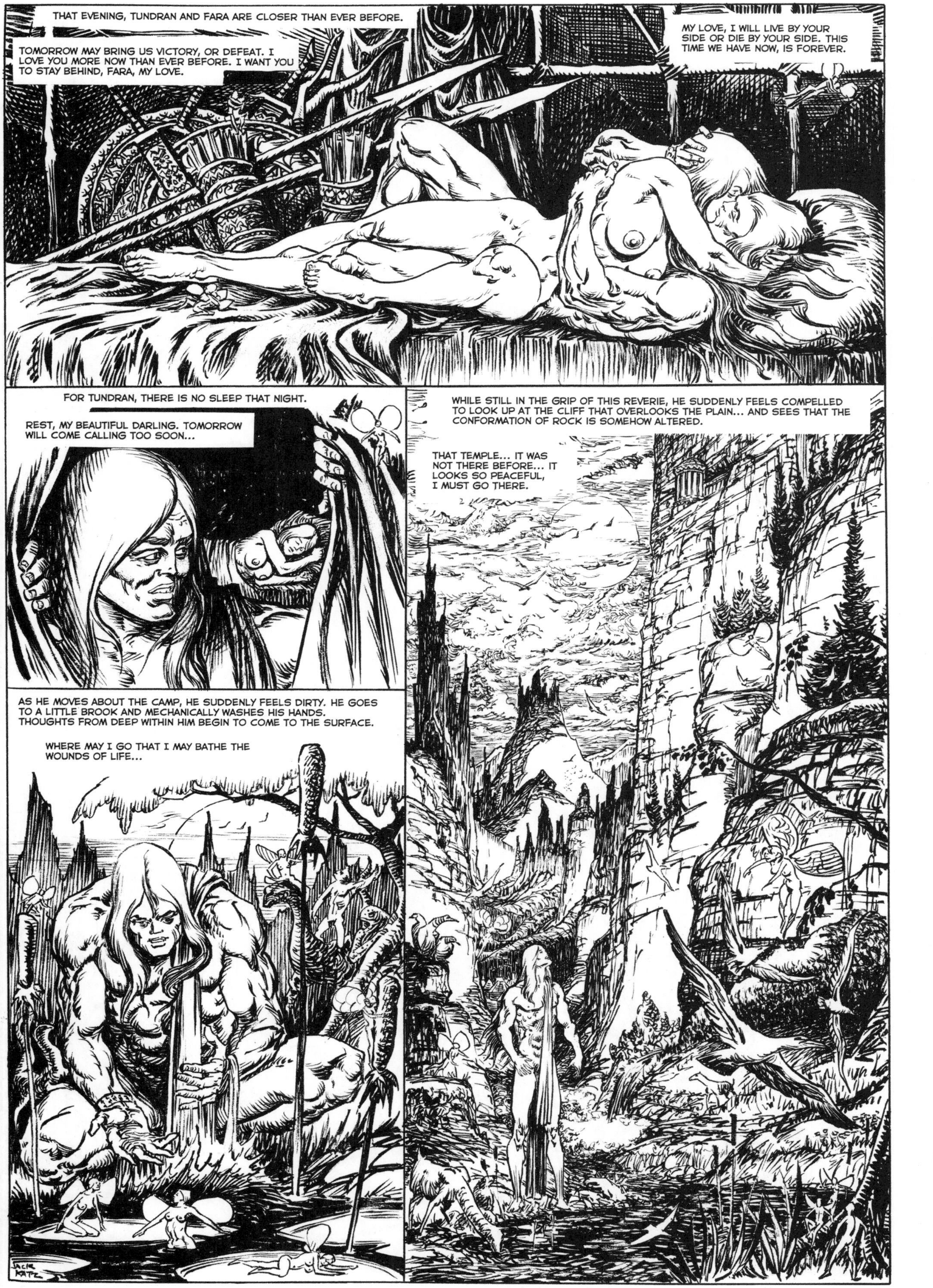
THAT EVENING, TUNDRAN AND FARA ARE CLOSER THAN EVER BEFORE.
TOMORROW MAY BRING US VICTORY, OR DEFEAT. I LOVE YOU MORE NOW THAN EVER BEFORE. I WANT YOU TO STAY BEHIND, FARA, MY LOVE.
MY LOVE, I WILL LIVE BY YOUR SIDE OR DIE BY YOUR SIDE. THIS TIME WE HAVE NOW, IS FOREVER.
FOR TUNDRAN, THERE IS NO SLEEP THAT NIGHT.
REST, MY BEAUTIFUL DARLING. TOMORROW WILL COME CALLING TOO SOON...
AS HE MOVES ABOUT THE CAMP, HE SUDDENLY FEELS DIRTY. HE GOES TO A LITTLE BROOK AND MECHANICALLY WASHES HIS HANDS. THOUGHTS FROM DEEP WITHIN HIM BEGIN TO COME TO THE SURFACE.
WHERE MAY I GO THAT I MAY BATHE THE WOUNDS OF LIFE...
WHILE STILL IN THE GRIP OF THIS REVERIE, HE SUDDENLY FEELS COMPELLED TO LOOK UP AT THE CLIFF THAT OVERLOOKS THE PLAIN... AND SEES THAT THE CONFORMATION OF ROCK IS SOMEHOW ALTERED.
THAT TEMPLE... IT WAS NOT THERE BEFORE... IT LOOKS SO PEACEFUL, I MUST GO THERE.
JACK KATZ

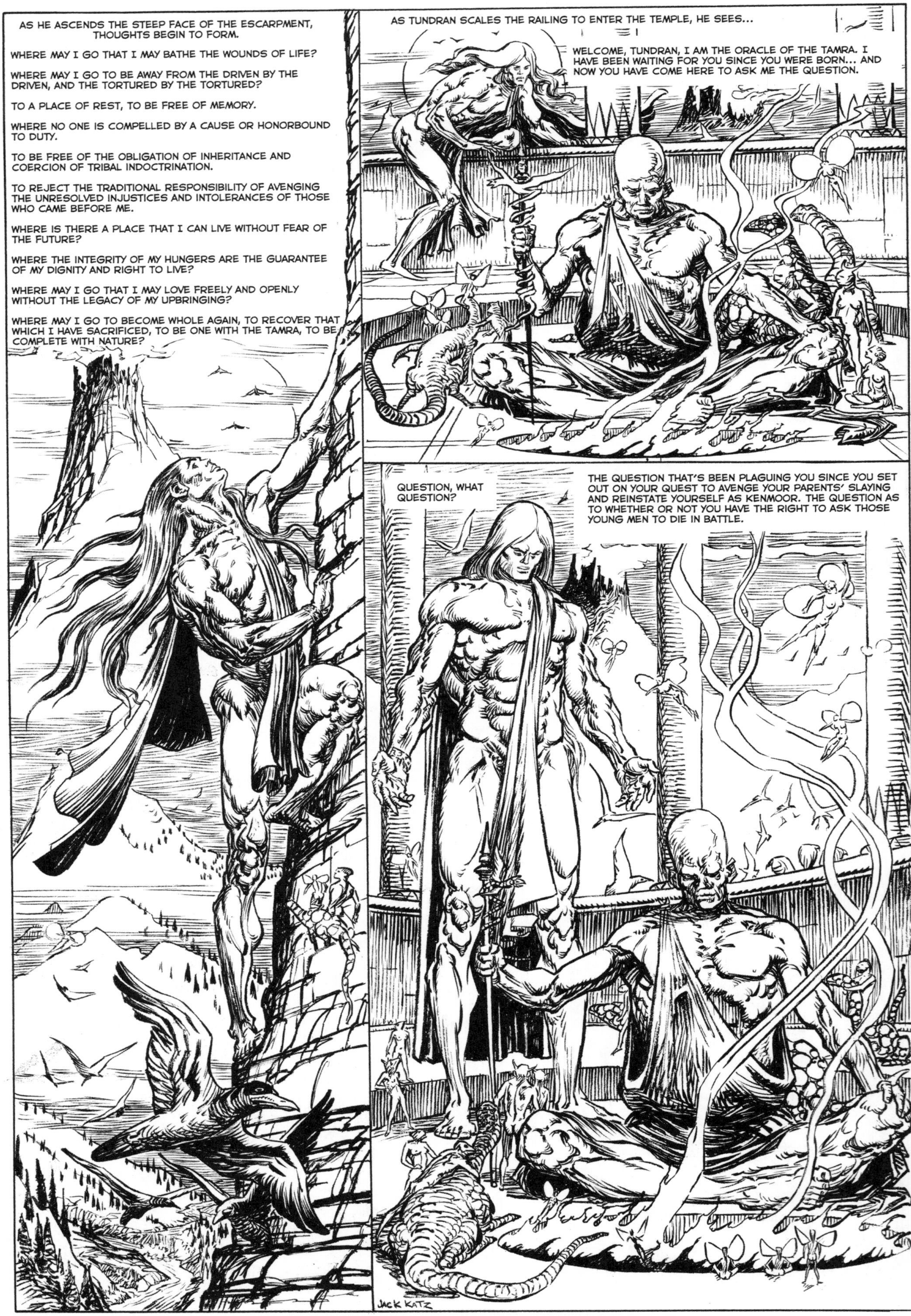
AS HE ASCENDS THE STEEP FACE OF THE ESCARPMENT, THOUGHTS BEGIN TO FORM.
WHERE MAY I GO THAT I MAY BATHE THE WOUNDS OF LIFE?
WHERE MAY I GO TO BE AWAY FROM THE DRIVEN BY THE DRIVEN, AND THE TORTURED BY THE TORTURED?
TO A PLACE OF REST, TO BE FREE OF MEMORY.
WHERE NO ONE IS COMPELLED BY A CAUSE OR HONORBOUND TO DUTY.
TO BE FREE OF THE OBLIGATION OF INHERITANCE AND COERCION OF TRIBAL INDOCTRINATION.
TO REJECT THE TRADITIONAL RESPONSIBILITY OF AVENGING THE UNRESOLVED INJUSTICES AND INTOLERANCES OF THOSE WHO CAME BEFORE ME.
WHERE IS THERE A PLACE THAT I CAN LIVE WITHOUT FEAR OF THE FUTURE?
WHERE THE INTEGRITY OF MY HUNGERS ARE THE GUARANTEE OF MY DIGNITY AND RIGHT TO LIVE?
WHERE MAY I GO THAT I MAY LOVE FREELY AND OPENLY WITHOUT THE LEGACY OF MY UPBRINGING?
WHERE MAY I GO TO BECOME WHOLE AGAIN, TO RECOVER THAT WHICH I HAVE SACRIFICED, TO BE ONE WITH THE TAMRA, TO BE COMPLETE WITH NATURE?
AS TUNDRAN SCALES THE RAILING TO ENTER THE TEMPLE, HE SEES...
WELCOME, TUNDRAN, I AM THE ORACLE OF THE TAMRA. I HAVE BEEN WAITING FOR YOU SINCE YOU WERE BORN... AND NOW YOU HAVE COME HERE TO ASK ME THE QUESTION.
QUESTION, WHAT QUESTION?
THE QUESTION THAT'S BEEN PLAGUING YOU SINCE YOU SET OUT ON YOUR QUEST TO AVENGE YOUR PARENTS' SLAYING AND REINSTATE YOURSELF AS KENMOOR. THE QUESTION AS TO WHETHER OR NOT YOU HAVE THE RIGHT TO ASK THOSE YOUNG MEN TO DIE IN BATTLE.
JACK KATZ

SHOULD YOU DECIDE ON REVENGE, YOU WILL BE VICTORIOUS IN YOUR SIEGE. BUT KNOW THIS, THAT ALL THOSE YOUNG MEN WILL HAVE GIVEN THEIR LIVES FOR NOTHING. YOU CAN'T CHANGE MANKIND. THEIR FEAR OF MORTALITY AND THEIR INABILITY TO NEGOTIATE THE HOSTILITY OF NATURE EMBITTERS THEM AND JUSTIFIES THEIR DUPLICITY, GREED, AND BRUTALITY. AND AFTER YOUR REIGN, CAN YOU GUARANTEE THAT THOSE WHO COME AFTER YOU WILL STILL UNDERSTAND WHY FREEDOM IS SO PRECIOUS, WITHOUT THE HISTORICITY OF YOUR OWN PUNISHING EDUCATION? AND WHO ARE YOU TO LAY DOWN LAWS OF HOW PEOPLE SHOULD LEAD THEIR LIVES? AND OF ALL THE PEOPLE YOU KNOW, HOW MANY COULD NOT BE CORRUPTED? NOW ALL THEY WANT TO DO IS THROW OFF THE YOKE OF THIS TYRANT, AND SO MEN WITH DIFFERENT GRIEVANCES HAVE GATHERED FROM ALL PARTS OF THE TAMRA FOR THE PURPOSE OF DESTRUCTION. AND YOU WILL LEAD THEM. IS THIS THE LEGACY YOU WANT TO LEAVE? HOW MANY YOUNG MEN WILL DIE ON BOTH SIDES, WHOSE LIVES ARE JUST BEGINNING? HAVE YOU THE RIGHT TO TAKE THOSE LIVES? HAVE YOU THE RIGHT TO ORDER THE DESTRUCTION OF LIFE... THAT WHICH YOU CANNOT CREATE...

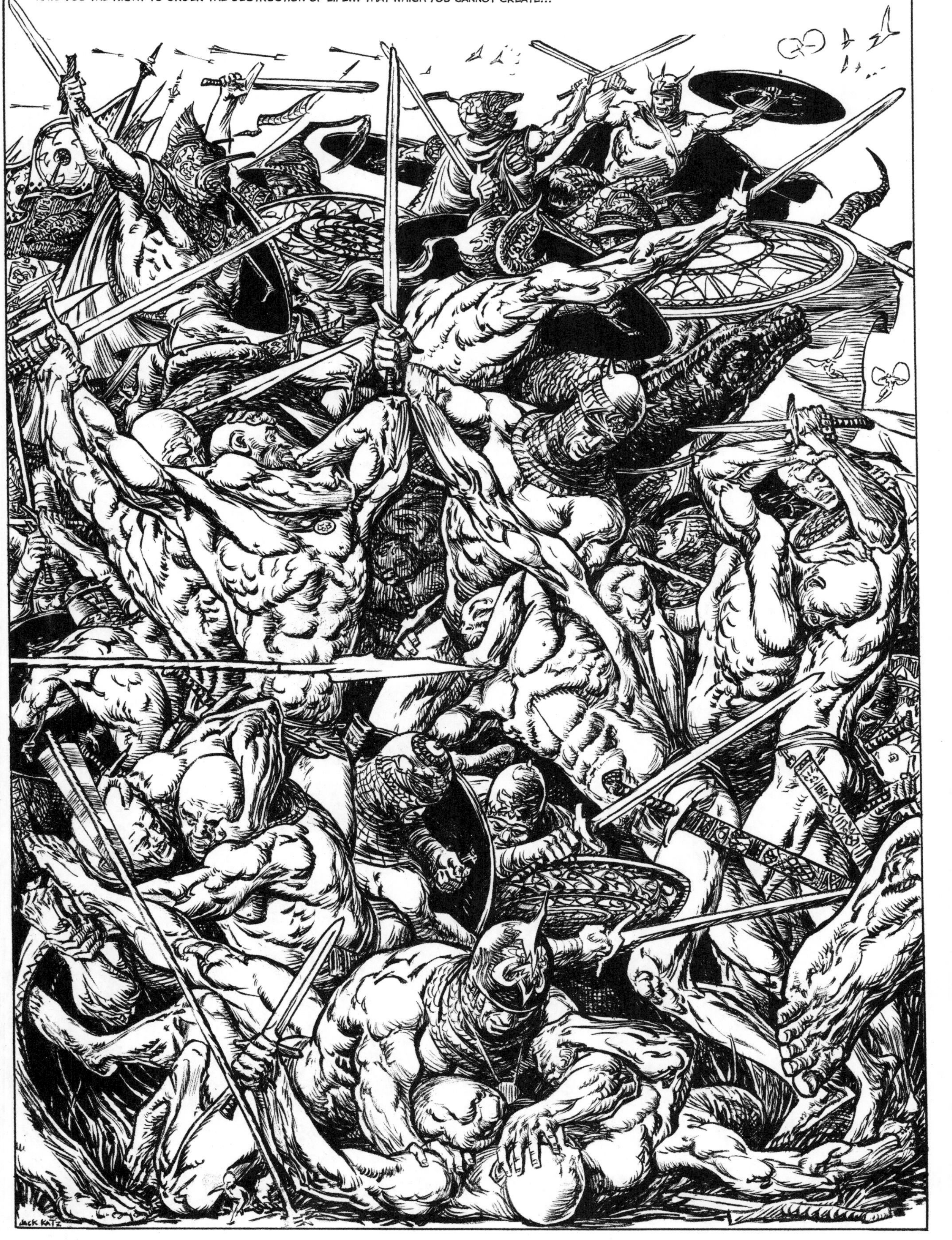
JACK KATZ

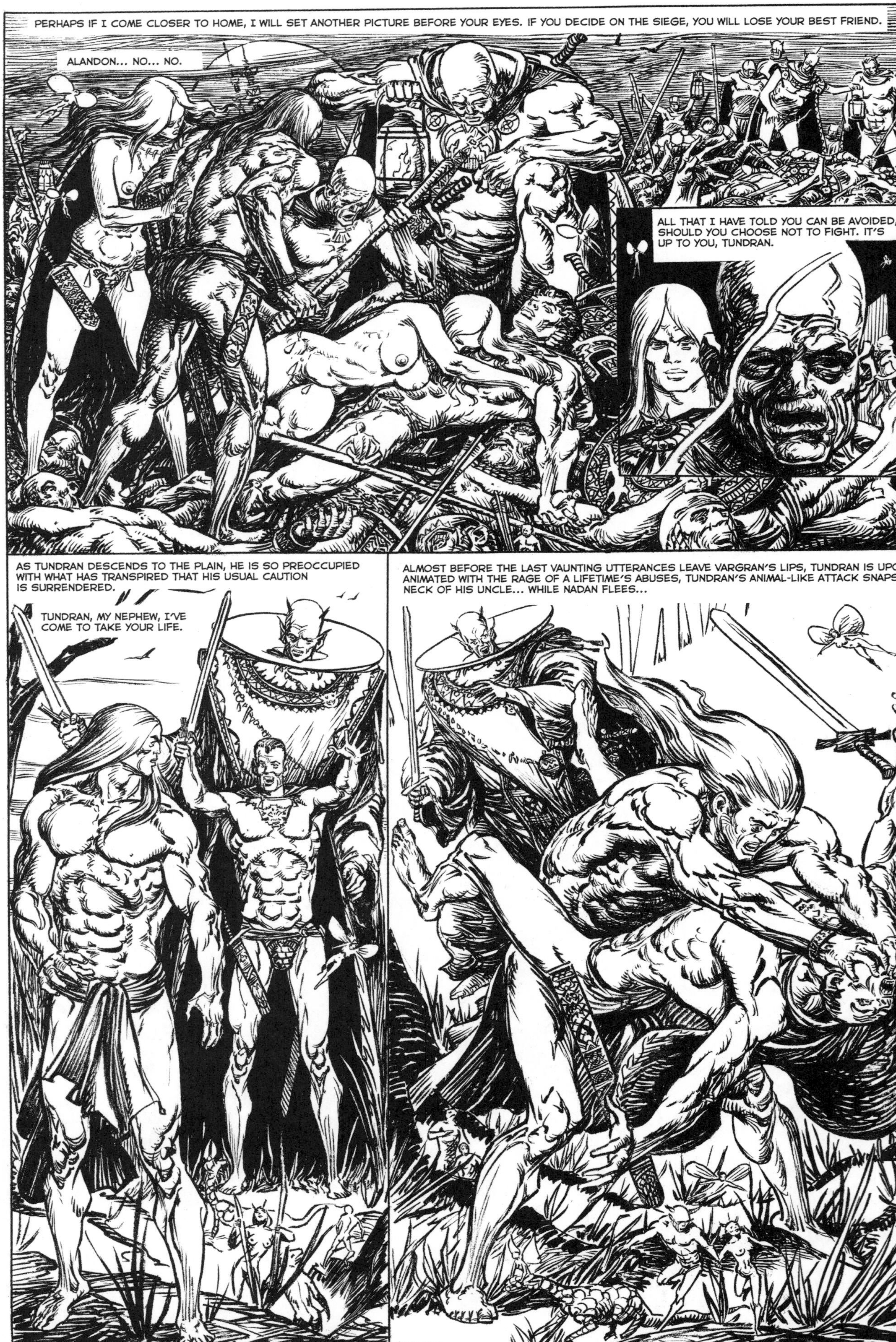
PERHAPS IF I COME CLOSER TO HOME, I WILL SET ANOTHER PICTURE BEFORE YOUR EYES. IF YOU DECIDE ON THE SIEGE, YOU WILL LOSE YOUR BEST FRIEND.
ALANDON... NO... NO.
ALL THAT I HAVE TOLD YOU CAN BE AVOIDED, SHOULD YOU CHOOSE NOT TO FIGHT. IT'S UP TO YOU, TUNDRAN.
AS TUNDRAN DESCENDS TO THE PLAIN, HE IS SO PREOCCUPIED WITH WHAT HAS TRANSPIRED THAT HIS USUAL CAUTION IS SURRENDERED.
TUNDRAN, MY NEPHEW, I'VE COME TO TAKE YOUR LIFE.
ALMOST BEFORE THE LAST VAUNTING UTTERANCES LEAVE VARGRAN'S LIPS, TUNDRAN IS UPON HIM. ANIMATED WITH THE RAGE OF A LIFETIME'S ABUSES, TUNDRAN'S ANIMAL-LIKE ATTACK SNAPS THE NECK OF HIS UNCLE... WHILE NADAN FLEES...
JACK KATZ

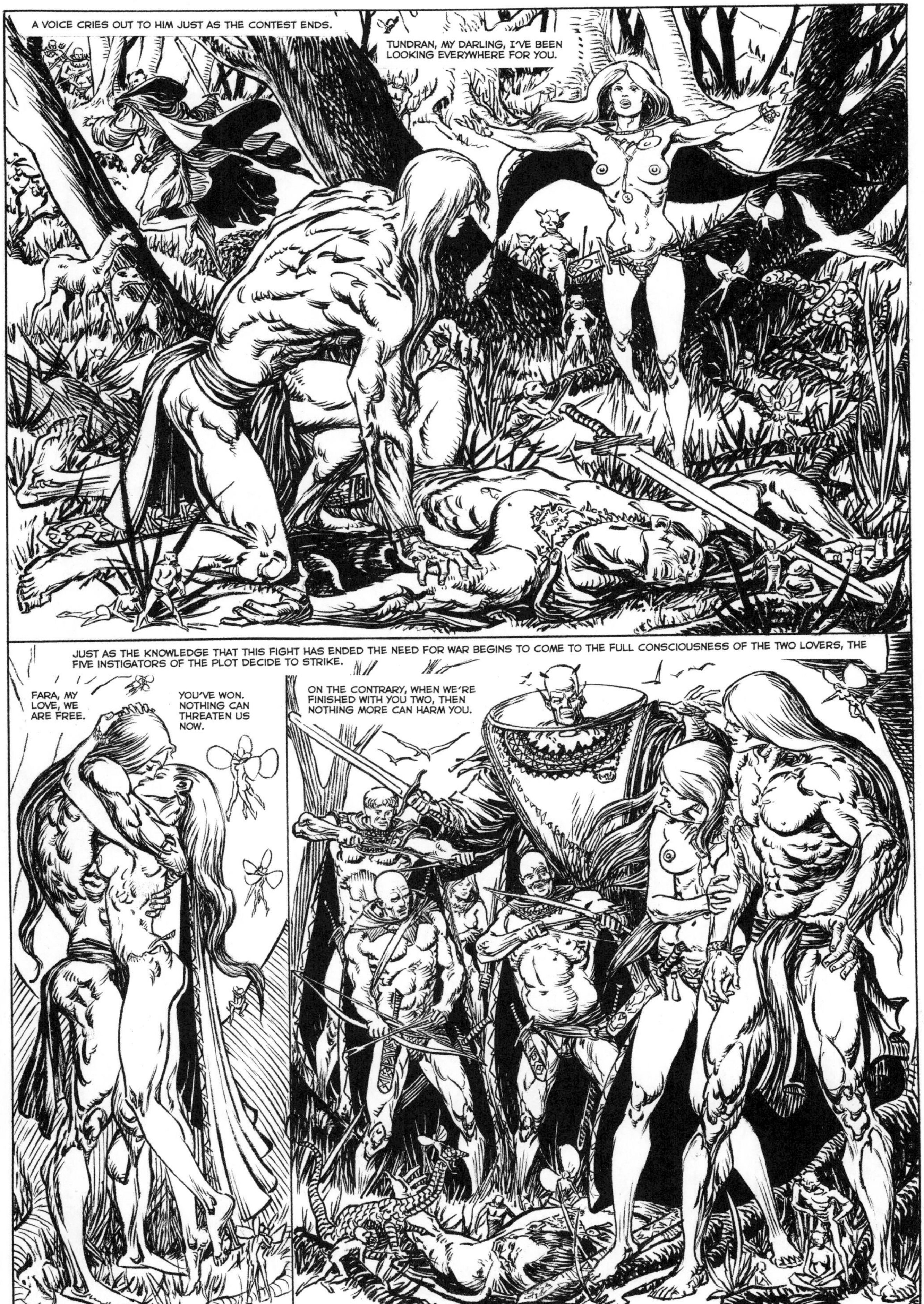
A VOICE CRIES OUT TO HIM JUST AS THE CONTEST ENDS.
TUNDRAN, MY DARLING, I'VE BEEN LOOKING EVERYWHERE FOR YOU.
JUST AS THE KNOWLEDGE THAT THIS FIGHT HAS ENDED THE NEED FOR WAR BEGINS TO COME TO THE FULL CONSCIOUSNESS OF THE TWO LOVERS, THE FIVE INSTIGATORS OF THE PLOT DECIDE TO STRIKE.
FARA, MY LOVE, WE ARE FREE.
YOU'VE WON. NOTHING CAN THREATEN US NOW.
ON THE CONTRARY, WHEN WE'RE FINISHED WITH YOU TWO, THEN NOTHING MORE CAN HARM YOU.
JACK KATZ

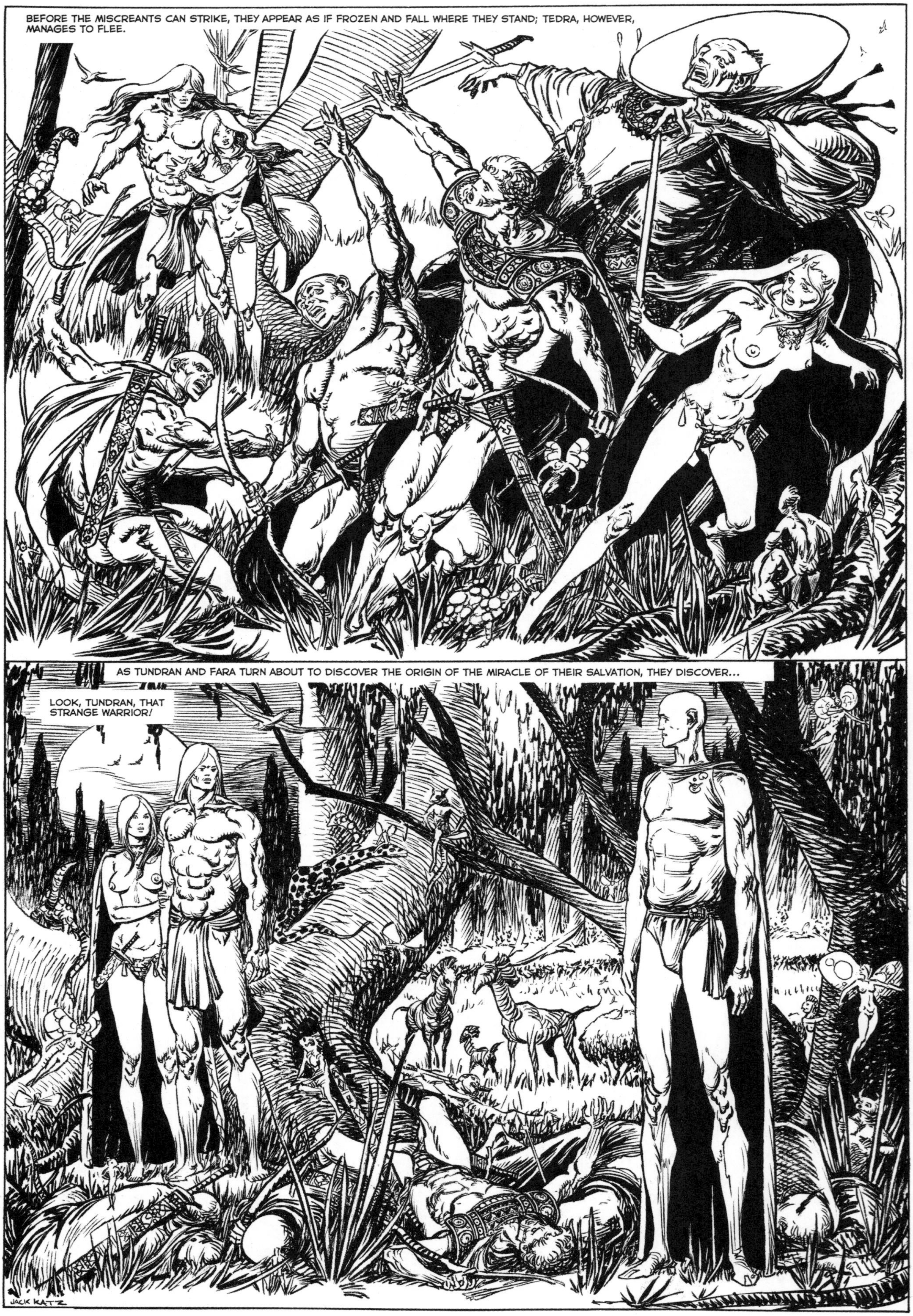
BEFORE THE MISCREANTS CAN STRIKE, THEY APPEAR AS IF FROZEN AND FALL WHERE THEY STAND; TEDRA, HOWEVER, MANAGES TO FLEE.
AS TUNDRAN AND FARA TURN ABOUT TO DISCOVER THE ORIGIN OF THE MIRACLE OF THEIR SALVATION, THEY DISCOVER...
LOOK, TUNDRAN, THAT STRANGE WARRIOR!
JACK KATZ

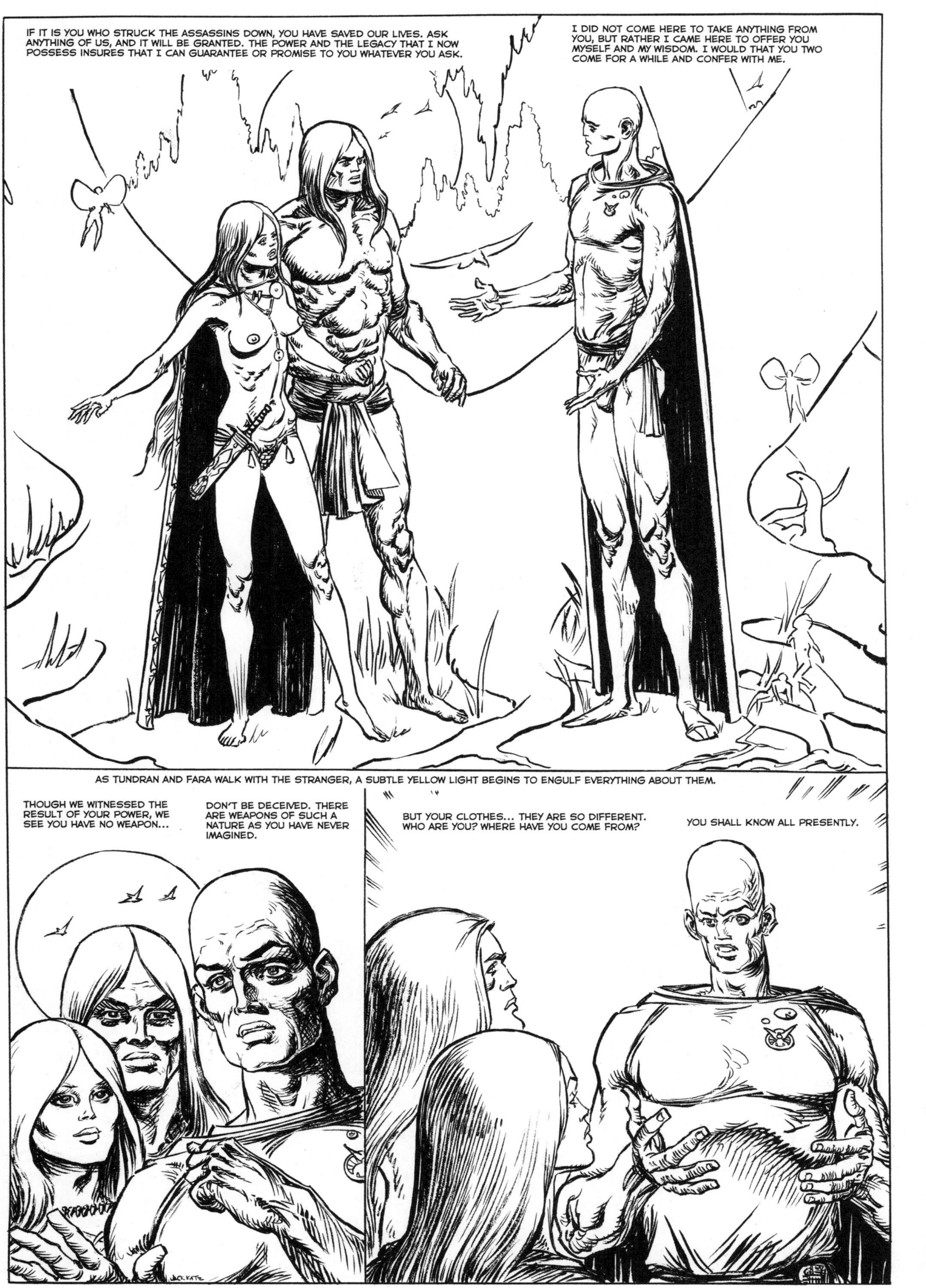
IF IT IS YOU WHO STRUCK THE ASSASSINS DOWN, YOU HAVE SAVED OUR LIVES. ASK ANYTHING OF US, AND IT WILL BE GRANTED. THE POWER AND THE LEGACY THAT I NOW POSSESS INSURES THAT I CAN GUARANTEE OR PROMISE TO YOU WHATEVER YOU ASK.
I DID NOT COME HERE TO TAKE ANYTHING FROM YOU, BUT RATHER I CAME HERE TO OFFER YOU MYSELF AND MY WISDOM. I WOULD THAT YOU TWO COME FOR A WHILE AND CONFER WITH ME.
AS TUNDRAN AND FARA WALK WITH THE STRANGER, A SUBTLE YELLOW LIGHT BEGINS TO ENGULF EVERYTHING ABOUT THEM.
THOUGH WE WITNESSED THE RESULT OF YOUR POWER, WE SEE YOU HAVE NO WEAPON...
DON'T BE DECEIVED. THERE ARE WEAPONS OF SUCH A NATURE AS YOU HAVE NEVER IMAGINED.
BUT YOUR CLOTHES... THEY ARE SO DIFFERENT. WHO ARE YOU? WHERE HAVE YOU COME FROM?
YOU SHALL KNOW ALL PRESENTLY.

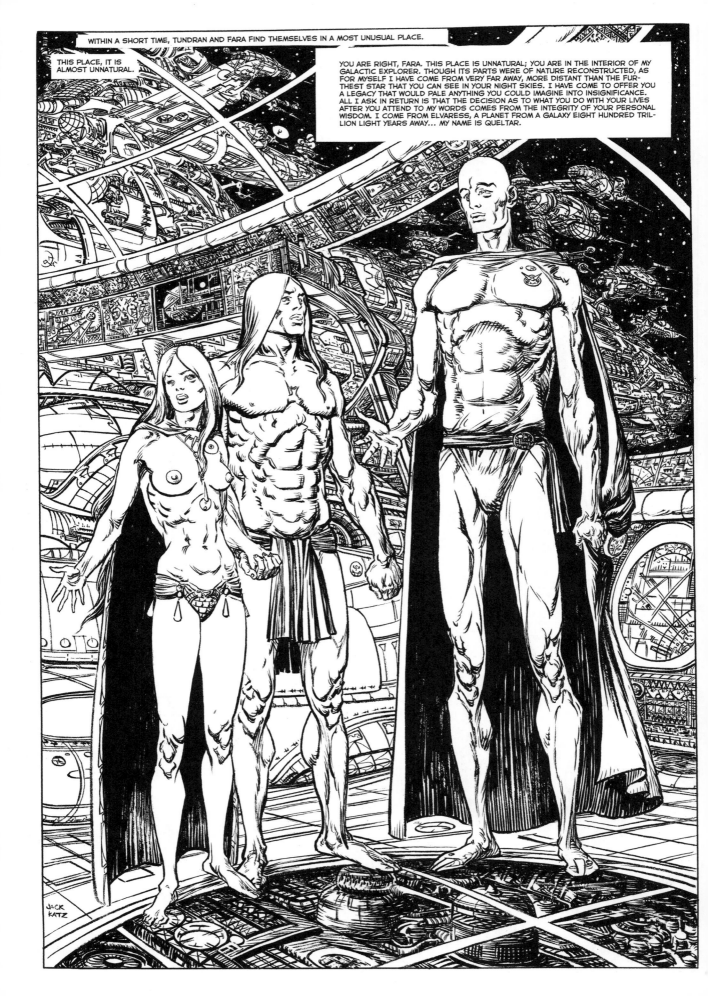

WITHIN A SHORT TIME, TUNDRAN AND FARA FIND THEMSELVES IN A MOST UNUSUAL PLACE.

THIS PLACE, IT IS ALMOST UNNATURAL.

YOU ARE RIGHT, FARA. THIS PLACE IS UNNATURAL; YOU ARE IN THE INTERIOR OF MY GALACTIC EXPLORER. THOUGH ITS PARTS WERE OF NATURE RECONSTRUCTED, AS FOR MYSELF I HAVE COME FROM VERY FAR AWAY, MORE DISTANT THAN THE FURTHEST STAR THAT YOU CAN SEE IN YOUR NIGHT SKIES. I HAVE COME TO OFFER YOU A LEGACY THAT WOULD PALE ANYTHING YOU COULD IMAGINE INTO INSIGNIFICANCE. ALL I ASK IN RETURN IS THAT THE DECISION AS TO WHAT YOU DO WITH YOUR LIVES AFTER YOU ATTEND TO MY WORDS COMES FROM THE INTEGRITY OF YOUR PERSONAL WISDOM. I COME FROM ELVARESS, A PLANET FROM A GALAXY EIGHT HUNDRED TRILLION LIGHT YEARS AWAY... MY NAME IS QUELTAR.

JACK KATZ

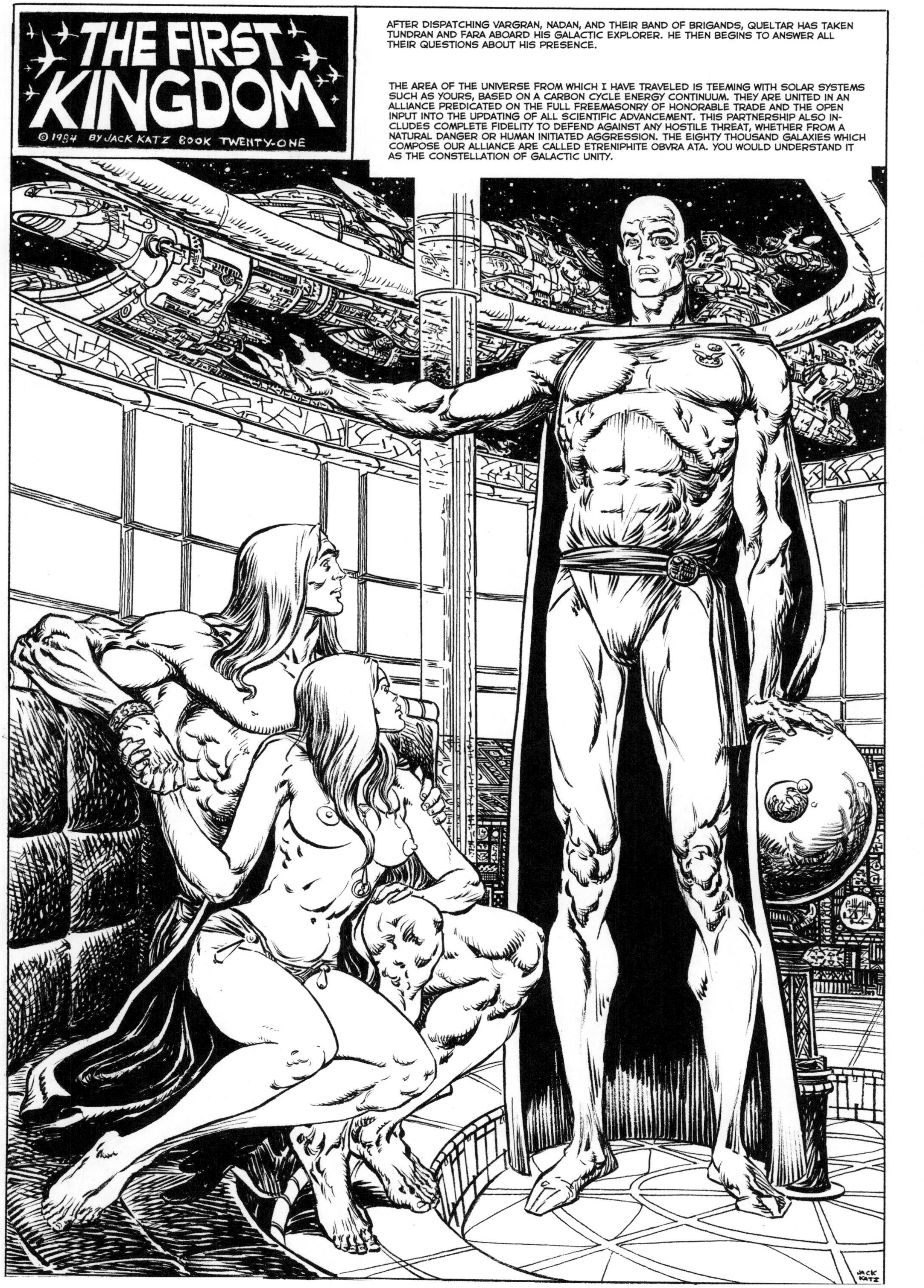
THE FIRST KINGDOM
©1984 BY JACK KATZ BOOK TWENTY-ONE
AFTER DISPATCHING VARGRAN, NADAN, AND THEIR BAND OF BRIGANDS, QUELTAR HAS TAKEN TUNDRAN AND FARA ABOARD HIS GALACTIC EXPLORER. HE THEN BEGINS TO ANSWER ALL THEIR QUESTIONS ABOUT HIS PRESENCE.
THE AREA OF THE UNIVERSE FROM WHICH I HAVE TRAVELED IS TEEMING WITH SOLAR SYSTEMS SUCH AS YOURS, BASED ON A CARBON CYCLE ENERGY CONTINUUM. THEY ARE UNITED IN AN ALLIANCE PREDICATED ON THE FULL FREEMASONRY OF HONORABLE TRADE AND THE OPEN INPUT INTO THE UPDATING OF ALL SCIENTIFIC ADVANCEMENT. THIS PARTNERSHIP ALSO INCLUDES COMPLETE FIDELITY TO DEFEND AGAINST ANY HOSTILE THREAT, WHETHER FROM A NATURAL DANGER OR HUMAN INITIATED AGGRESSION. THE EIGHTY THOUSAND GALAXIES WHICH COMPOSE OUR ALLIANCE ARE CALLED ETRENIPHITE OBVRA ATA. YOU WOULD UNDERSTAND IT AS THE CONSTELLATION OF GALACTIC UNITY.
JACK KATZ

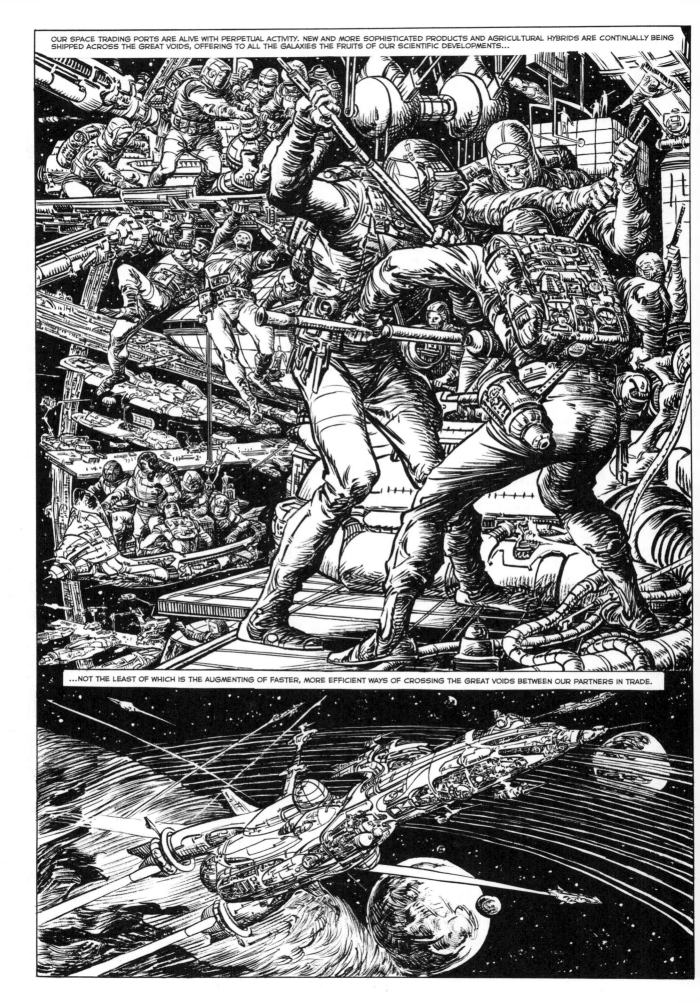

OUR SPACE TRADING PORTS ARE ALIVE WITH PERPETUAL ACTIVITY. NEW AND MORE SOPHISTICATED PRODUCTS AND AGRICULTURAL HYBRIDS ARE CONTINUALLY BEING SHIPPED ACROSS THE GREAT VOIDS, OFFERING TO ALL THE GALAXIES THE FRUITS OF OUR SCIENTIFIC DEVELOPMENTS...

...NOT THE LEAST OF WHICH IS THE AUGMENTING OF FASTER, MORE EFFICIENT WAYS OF CROSSING THE GREAT VOIDS BETWEEN OUR PARTNERS IN TRADE.

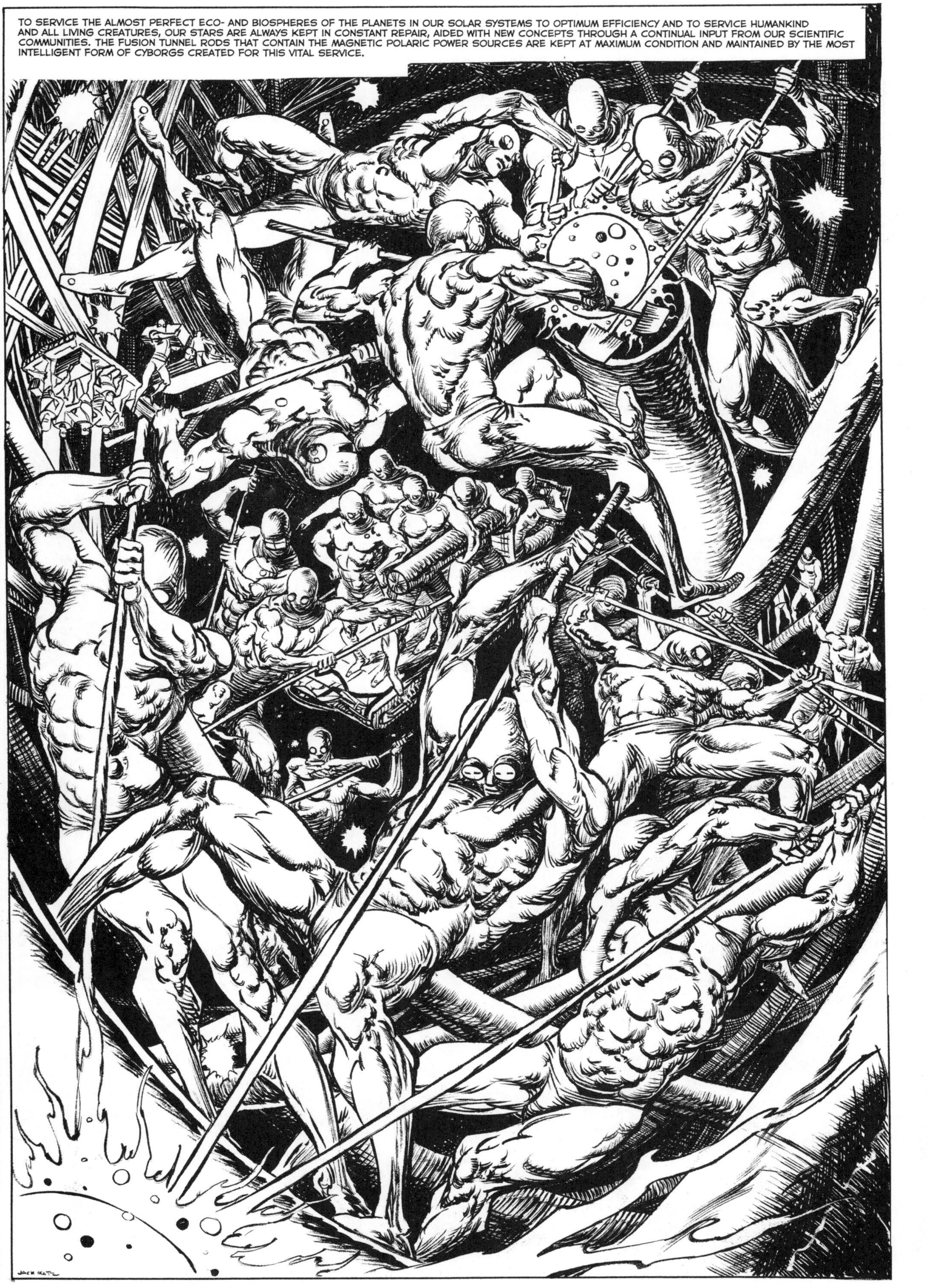
TO SERVICE THE ALMOST PERFECT ECO- AND BIOSPHERES OF THE PLANETS IN OUR SOLAR SYSTEMS TO OPTIMUM EFFICIENCY AND TO SERVICE HUMANKIND AND ALL LIVING CREATURES, OUR STARS ARE ALWAYS KEPT IN CONSTANT REPAIR, AIDED WITH NEW CONCEPTS THROUGH A CONTINUAL INPUT FROM OUR SCIENTIFIC COMMUNITIES. THE FUSION TUNNEL RODS THAT CONTAIN THE MAGNETIC POLARIC POWER SOURCES ARE KEPT AT MAXIMUM CONDITION AND MAINTAINED BY THE MOST INTELLIGENT FORM OF CYBORGS CREATED FOR THIS VITAL SERVICE.

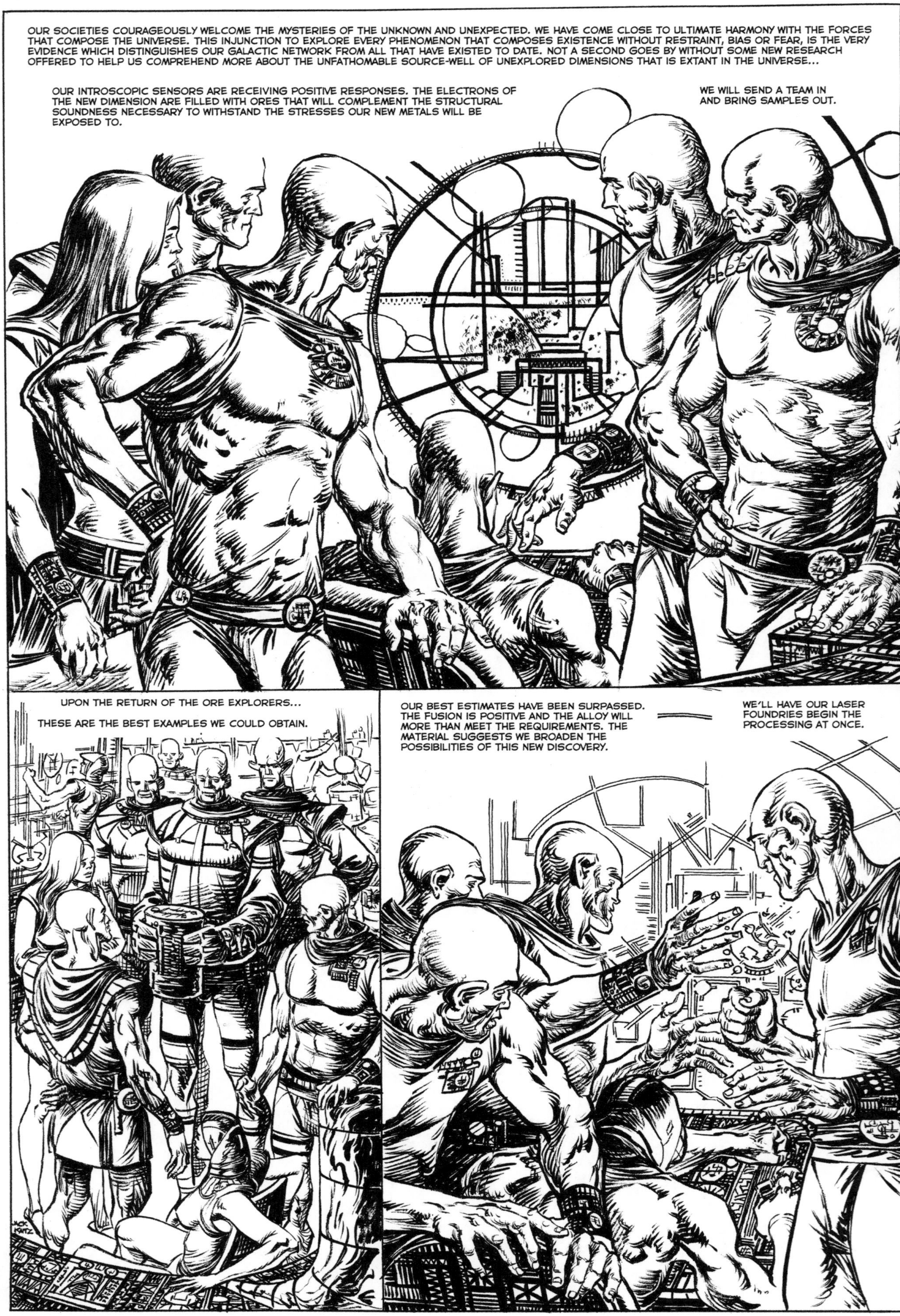

OUR SOCIETIES COURAGEOUSLY WELCOME THE MYSTERIES OF THE UNKNOWN AND UNEXPECTED. WE HAVE COME CLOSE TO ULTIMATE HARMONY WITH THE FORCES THAT COMPOSE THE UNIVERSE. THIS INJUNCTION TO EXPLORE EVERY PHENOMENON THAT COMPOSES EXISTENCE WITHOUT RESTRAINT, BIAS OR FEAR, IS THE VERY EVIDENCE WHICH DISTINGUISHES OUR GALACTIC NETWORK FROM ALL THAT HAVE EXISTED TO DATE. NOT A SECOND GOES BY WITHOUT SOME NEW RESEARCH OFFERED TO HELP US COMPREHEND MORE ABOUT THE UNFATHOMABLE SOURCE-WELL OF UNEXPLORED DIMENSIONS THAT IS EXTANT IN THE UNIVERSE...
OUR INTROSCOPIC SENSORS ARE RECEIVING POSITIVE RESPONSES. THE ELECTRONS OF THE NEW DIMENSION ARE FILLED WITH ORES THAT WILL COMPLEMENT THE STRUCTURAL SOUNDNESS NECESSARY TO WITHSTAND THE STRESSES OUR NEW METALS WILL BE EXPOSED TO.
WE WILL SEND A TEAM IN AND BRING SAMPLES OUT.
UPON THE RETURN OF THE ORE EXPLORERS...
THESE ARE THE BEST EXAMPLES WE COULD OBTAIN.
OUR BEST ESTIMATES HAVE BEEN SURPASSED. THE FUSION IS POSITIVE AND THE ALLOY WILL MORE THAN MEET THE REQUIREMENTS. THE MATERIAL SUGGESTS WE BROADEN THE POSSIBILITIES OF THIS NEW DISCOVERY.
WE'LL HAVE OUR LASER FOUNDRIES BEGIN THE PROCESSING AT ONCE.

BY THE DISCOVERY AND THE PROTECTION OF MANY LIFE FORMS, FROM THE INFINITESIMAL PARTICLES OF STELLAR DUST, TO THE STUDY OF THE IMMENSITY OF SPACE ITSELF, THE TREASURE OF LIFE WITHOUT THREAT HAS GIVEN US A CHANCE TO COMPREHEND THE UNKNOWN. OUR YOUNG ARE INTRODUCED TO ALL THE PHENOMENA AND ARE GIVEN ACCESS TO ALL THE KNOWLEDGE ABOUT EXISTENCE. OUR LIBRARIES HOLD GREAT STOREHOUSES OF DATA, AND ARE CONTINUALLY BEING TAPPED BY YOUNG AND OLD. AND IT IS BY GENTLE TEACHING METHODS THAT WE MANAGE NOT TO DEFEAT THE CURIOSITY OF THE YOUNG. BY AWAKENING AND STIMULATING THEIR IMAGINATION, WE INTRODUCE OUR CHILDREN INTO THE WORLD OF KNOWLEDGE. THESE FERTILE OPPORTUNITIES FOR BOTH EDUCATIONAL AND PERSONAL DEVELOPMENT BY OUR ENCOURAGING ATMOSPHERE IS REWARDED MANY TIMES OVER, FOR OUR SOCIETY KNOWS THAT ANY ADVANCEMENT IN ANY AREA OF IDEAS, BE IT THE ARTS, SERVICES, OR DISCIPLINES, BENEFITS ALL.

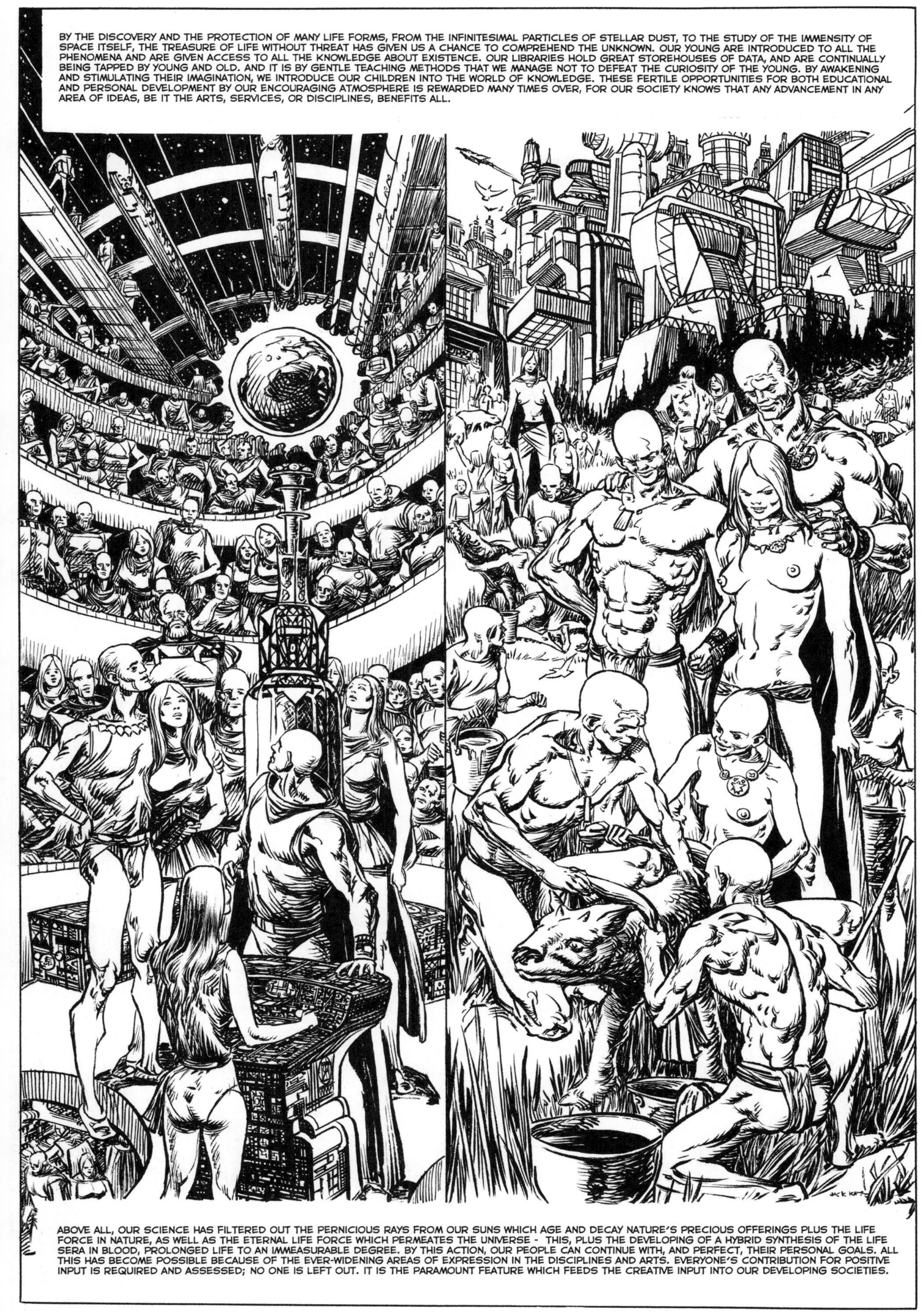

ABOVE ALL, OUR SCIENCE HAS FILTERED OUT THE PERNICIOUS RAYS FROM OUR SUNS WHICH AGE AND DECAY NATURE'S PRECIOUS OFFERINGS PLUS THE LIFE FORCE IN NATURE, AS WELL AS THE ETERNAL LIFE FORCE WHICH PERMEATES THE UNIVERSE - THIS, PLUS THE DEVELOPING OF A HYBRID SYNTHESIS OF THE LIFE SERA IN BLOOD, PROLONGED LIFE TO AN IMMEASURABLE DEGREE. BY THIS ACTION, OUR PEOPLE CAN CONTINUE WITH, AND PERFECT, THEIR PERSONAL GOALS. ALL THIS HAS BECOME POSSIBLE BECAUSE OF THE EVER-WIDENING AREAS OF EXPRESSION IN THE DISCIPLINES AND ARTS. EVERYONE'S CONTRIBUTION FOR POSITIVE INPUT IS REQUIRED AND ASSESSED; NO ONE IS LEFT OUT. IT IS THE PARAMOUNT FEATURE WHICH FEEDS THE CREATIVE INPUT INTO OUR DEVELOPING SOCIETIES.

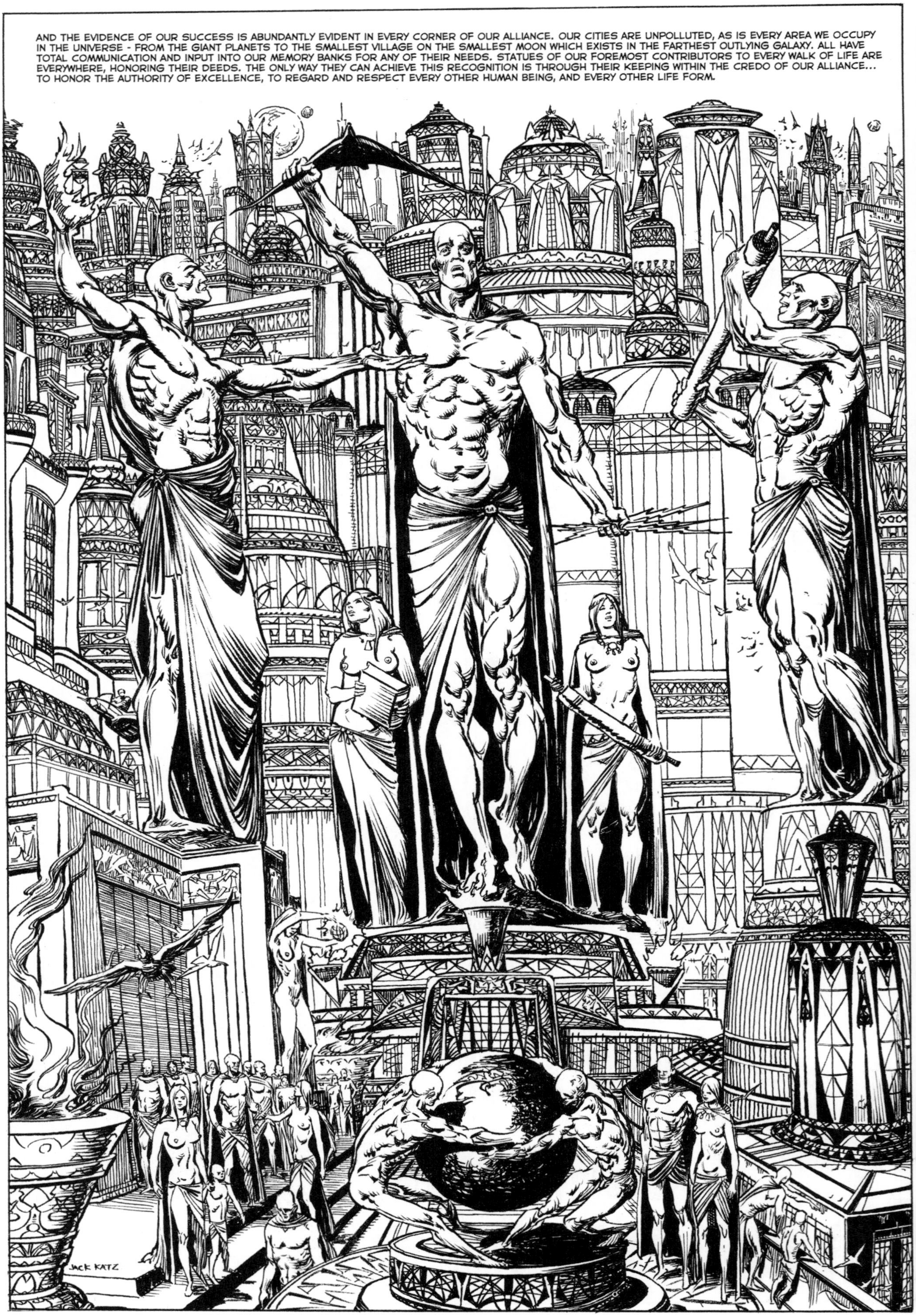
AND THE EVIDENCE OF OUR SUCCESS IS ABUNDANTLY EVIDENT IN EVERY CORNER OF OUR ALLIANCE. OUR CITIES ARE UNPOLLUTED, AS IS EVERY AREA WE OCCUPY IN THE UNIVERSE - FROM THE GIANT PLANETS TO THE SMALLEST VILLAGE ON THE SMALLEST MOON WHICH EXISTS IN THE FARTHEST OUTLYING GALAXY. ALL HAVE TOTAL COMMUNICATION AND INPUT INTO OUR MEMORY BANKS FOR ANY OF THEIR NEEDS. STATUES OF OUR FOREMOST CONTRIBUTORS TO EVERY WALK OF LIFE ARE EVERYWHERE, HONORING THEIR DEEDS. THE ONLY WAY THEY CAN ACHIEVE THIS RECOGNITION IS THROUGH THEIR KEEPING WITHIN THE CREDO OF OUR ALLIANCE... TO HONOR THE AUTHORITY OF EXCELLENCE, TO REGARD AND RESPECT EVERY OTHER HUMAN BEING, AND EVERY OTHER LIFE FORM.
JACK KATZ

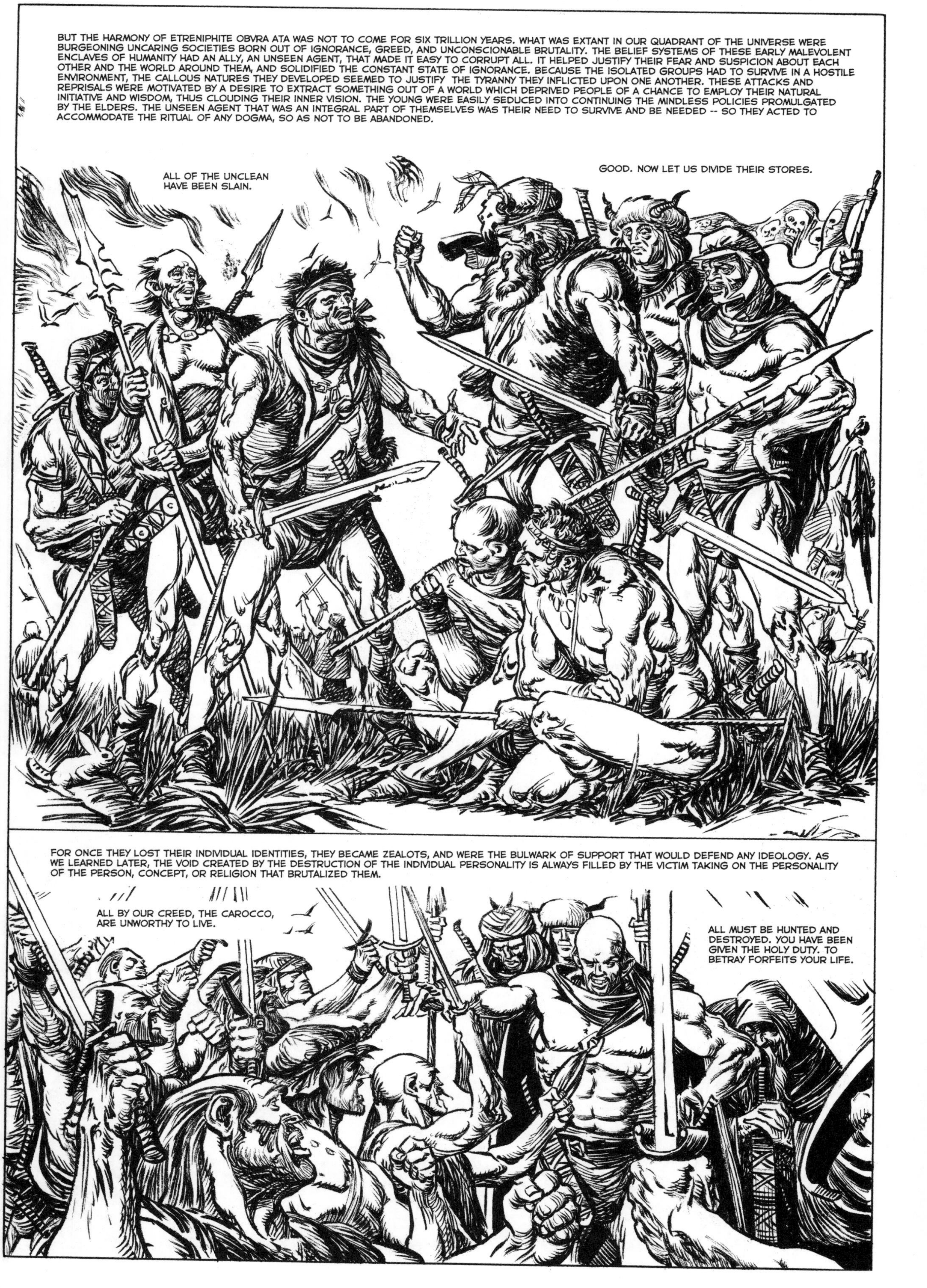
BUT THE HARMONY OF ETRENIPHITE OBVRA ATA WAS NOT TO COME FOR SIX TRILLION YEARS. WHAT WAS EXTANT IN OUR QUADRANT OF THE UNIVERSE WERE BURGEONING UNCARING SOCIETIES BORN OUT OF IGNORANCE, GREED, AND UNCONSCIONABLE BRUTALITY. THE BELIEF SYSTEMS OF THESE EARLY MALEVOLENT ENCLAVES OF HUMANITY HAD AN ALLY, AN UNSEEN AGENT, THAT MADE IT EASY TO CORRUPT ALL. IT HELPED JUSTIFY THEIR FEAR AND SUSPICION ABOUT EACH OTHER AND THE WORLD AROUND THEM, AND SOLIDIFIED THE CONSTANT STATE OF IGNORANCE. BECAUSE THE ISOLATED GROUPS HAD TO SURVIVE IN A HOSTILE ENVIRONMENT, THE CALLOUS NATURES THEY DEVELOPED SEEMED TO JUSTIFY THE TYRANNY THEY INFLICTED UPON ONE ANOTHER. THESE ATTACKS AND REPRISALS WERE MOTIVATED BY A DESIRE TO EXTRACT SOMETHING OUT OF A WORLD WHICH DEPRIVED PEOPLE OF A CHANCE TO EMPLOY THEIR NATURAL INITIATIVE AND WISDOM, THUS CLOUDING THEIR INNER VISION. THE YOUNG WERE EASILY SEDUCED INTO CONTINUING THE MINDLESS POLICIES PROMULGATED BY THE ELDERS. THE UNSEEN AGENT THAT WAS AN INTEGRAL PART OF THEMSELVES WAS THEIR NEED TO SURVIVE AND BE NEEDED -- SO THEY ACTED TO ACCOMMODATE THE RITUAL OF ANY DOGMA, SO AS NOT TO BE ABANDONED.
ALL OF THE UNCLEAN HAVE BEEN SLAIN.
GOOD. NOW LET US DIVIDE THEIR STORES.
FOR ONCE THEY LOST THEIR INDIVIDUAL IDENTITIES, THEY BECAME ZEALOTS, AND WERE THE BULWARK OF SUPPORT THAT WOULD DEFEND ANY IDEOLOGY. AS WE LEARNED LATER, THE VOID CREATED BY THE DESTRUCTION OF THE INDIVIDUAL PERSONALITY IS ALWAYS FILLED BY THE VICTIM TAKING ON THE PERSONALITY OF THE PERSON, CONCEPT, OR RELIGION THAT BRUTALIZED THEM.
ALL BY OUR CREED, THE CAROCCO, ARE UNWORTHY TO LIVE.
ALL MUST BE HUNTED AND DESTROYED. YOU HAVE BEEN GIVEN THE HOLY DUTY. TO BETRAY FORFEITS YOUR LIFE.

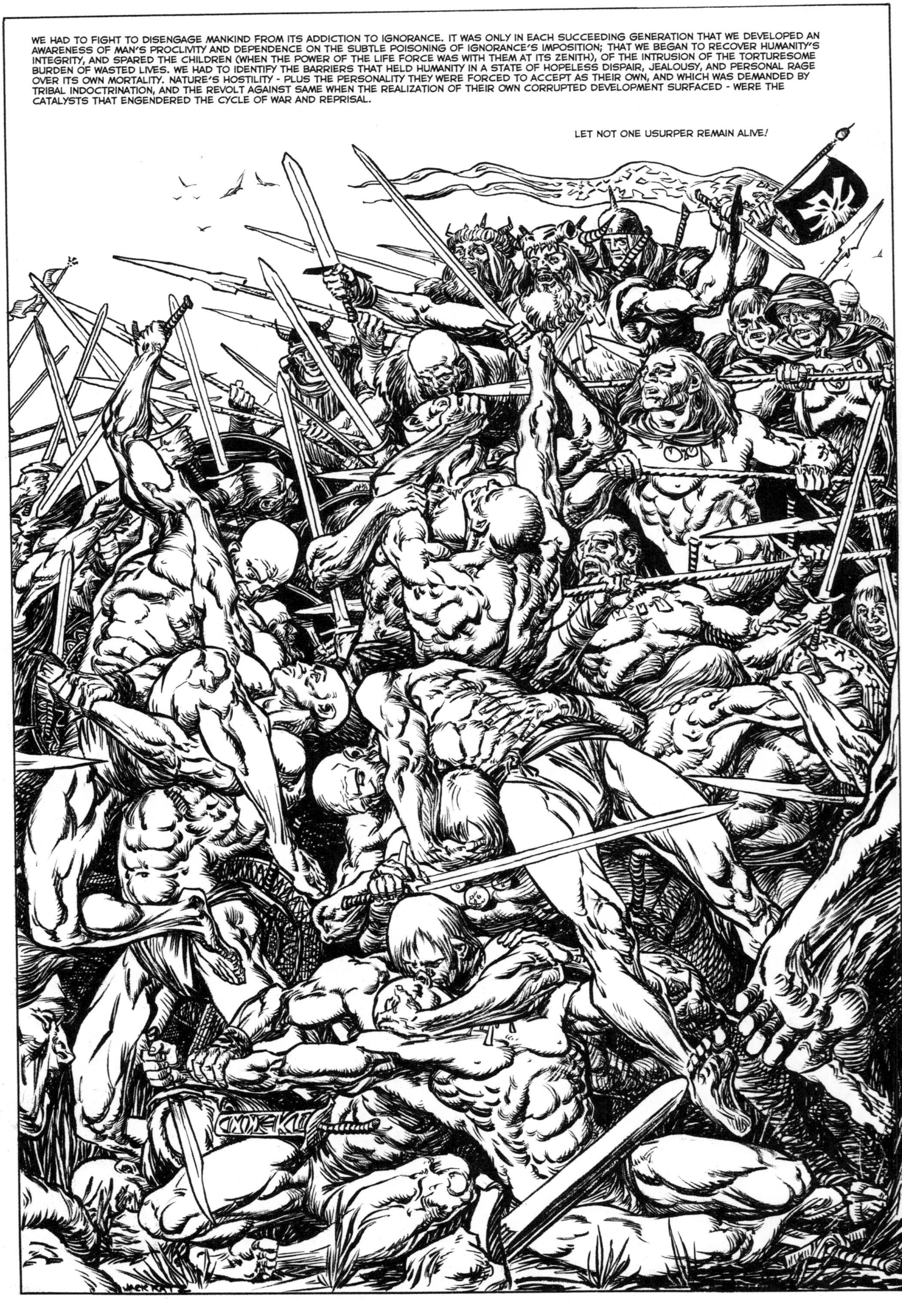
WE HAD TO FIGHT TO DISENGAGE MANKIND FROM ITS ADDICTION TO IGNORANCE. IT WAS ONLY IN EACH SUCCEEDING GENERATION THAT WE DEVELOPED AN AWARENESS OF MAN'S PROCLIVITY AND DEPENDENCE ON THE SUBTLE POISONING OF IGNORANCE'S IMPOSITION; THAT WE BEGAN TO RECOVER HUMANITY'S INTEGRITY, AND SPARED THE CHILDREN (WHEN THE POWER OF THE LIFE FORCE WAS WITH THEM AT ITS ZENITH), OF THE INTRUSION OF THE TORTURESOME BURDEN OF WASTED LIVES. WE HAD TO IDENTIFY THE BARRIERS THAT HELD HUMANITY IN A STATE OF HOPELESS DISPAIR, JEALOUSY, AND PERSONAL RAGE OVER ITS OWN MORTALITY. NATURE'S HOSTILITY - PLUS THE PERSONALITY THEY WERE FORCED TO ACCEPT AS THEIR OWN, AND WHICH WAS DEMANDED BY TRIBAL INDOCTRINATION, AND THE REVOLT AGAINST SAME WHEN THE REALIZATION OF THEIR OWN CORRUPTED DEVELOPMENT SURFACED - WERE THE CATALYSTS THAT ENGENDERED THE CYCLE OF WAR AND REPRISAL.
LET NOT ONE USURPER REMAIN ALIVE!

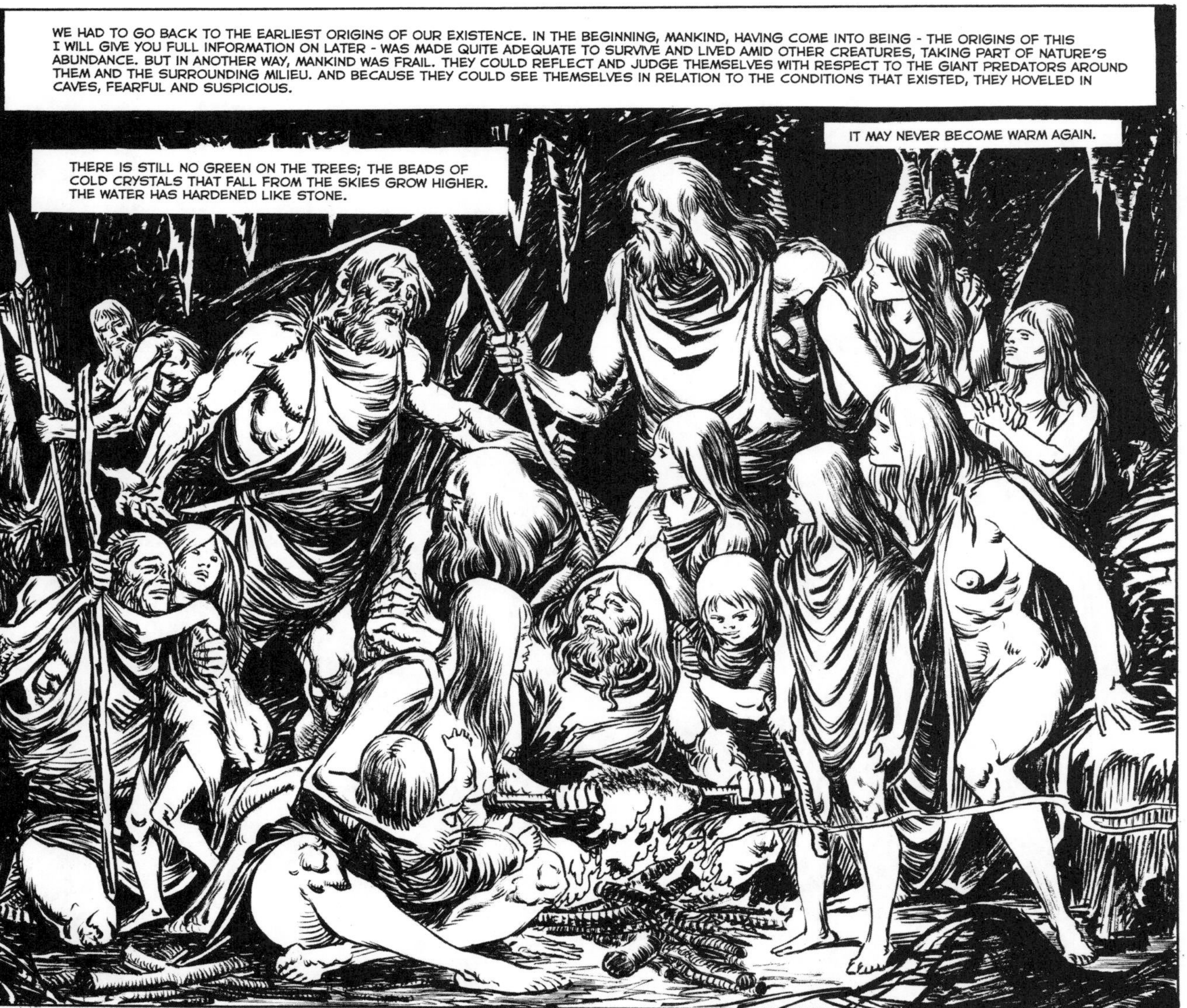
WE HAD TO GO BACK TO THE EARLIEST ORIGINS OF OUR EXISTENCE. IN THE BEGINNING, MANKIND, HAVING COME INTO BEING - THE ORIGINS OF THIS I WILL GIVE YOU FULL INFORMATION ON LATER - WAS MADE QUITE ADEQUATE TO SURVIVE AND LIVED AMID OTHER CREATURES, TAKING PART OF NATURE'S ABUNDANCE. BUT IN ANOTHER WAY, MANKIND WAS FRAIL. THEY COULD REFLECT AND JUDGE THEMSELVES WITH RESPECT TO THE GIANT PREDATORS AROUND THEM AND THE SURROUNDING MILIEU. AND BECAUSE THEY COULD SEE THEMSELVES IN RELATION TO THE CONDITIONS THAT EXISTED, THEY HOVELED IN CAVES, FEARFUL AND SUSPICIOUS.
THERE IS STILL NO GREEN ON THE TREES; THE BEADS OF COLD CRYSTALS THAT FALL FROM THE SKIES GROW HIGHER. THE WATER HAS HARDENED LIKE STONE.
IT MAY NEVER BECOME WARM AGAIN.

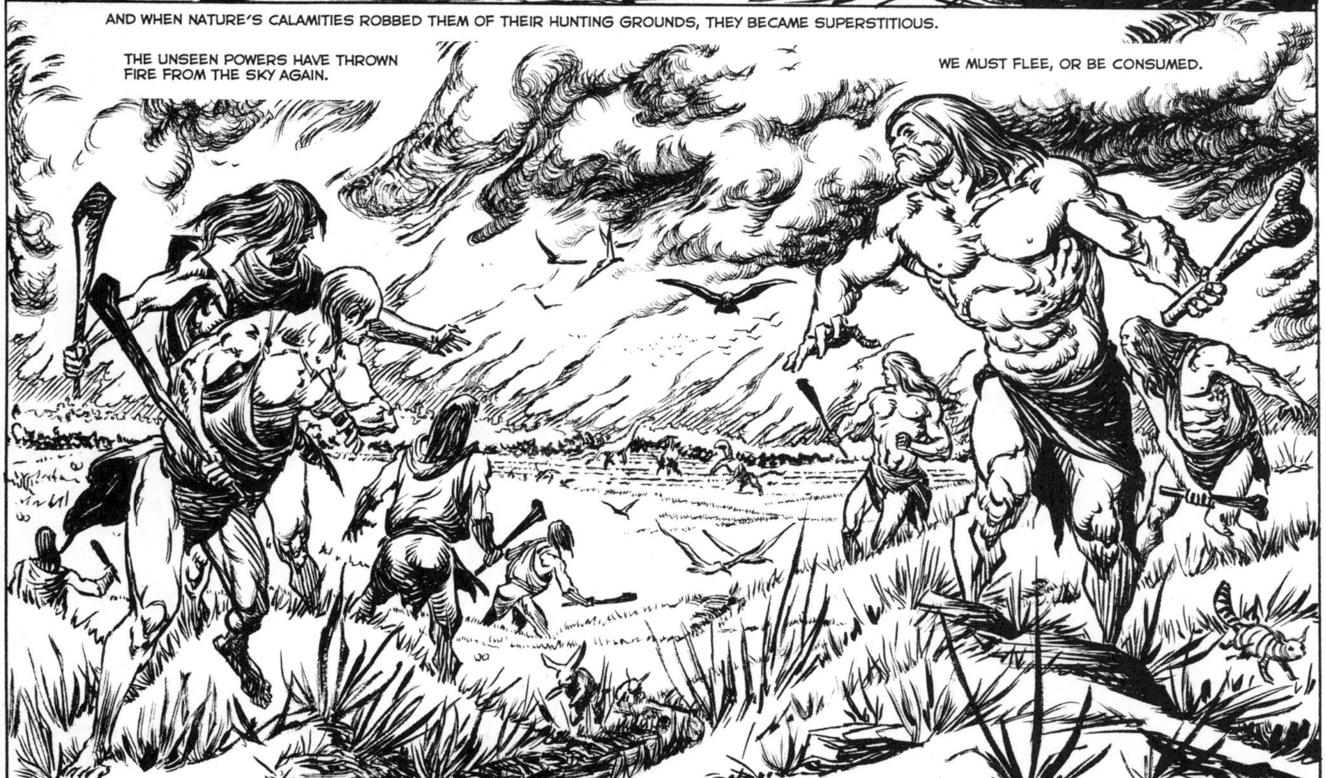
AND WHEN NATURE'S CALAMITIES ROBBED THEM OF THEIR HUNTING GROUNDS, THEY BECAME SUPERSTITIOUS.
THE UNSEEN POWERS HAVE THROWN FIRE FROM THE SKY AGAIN.
WE MUST FLEE, OR BE CONSUMED.
JACK KATZ

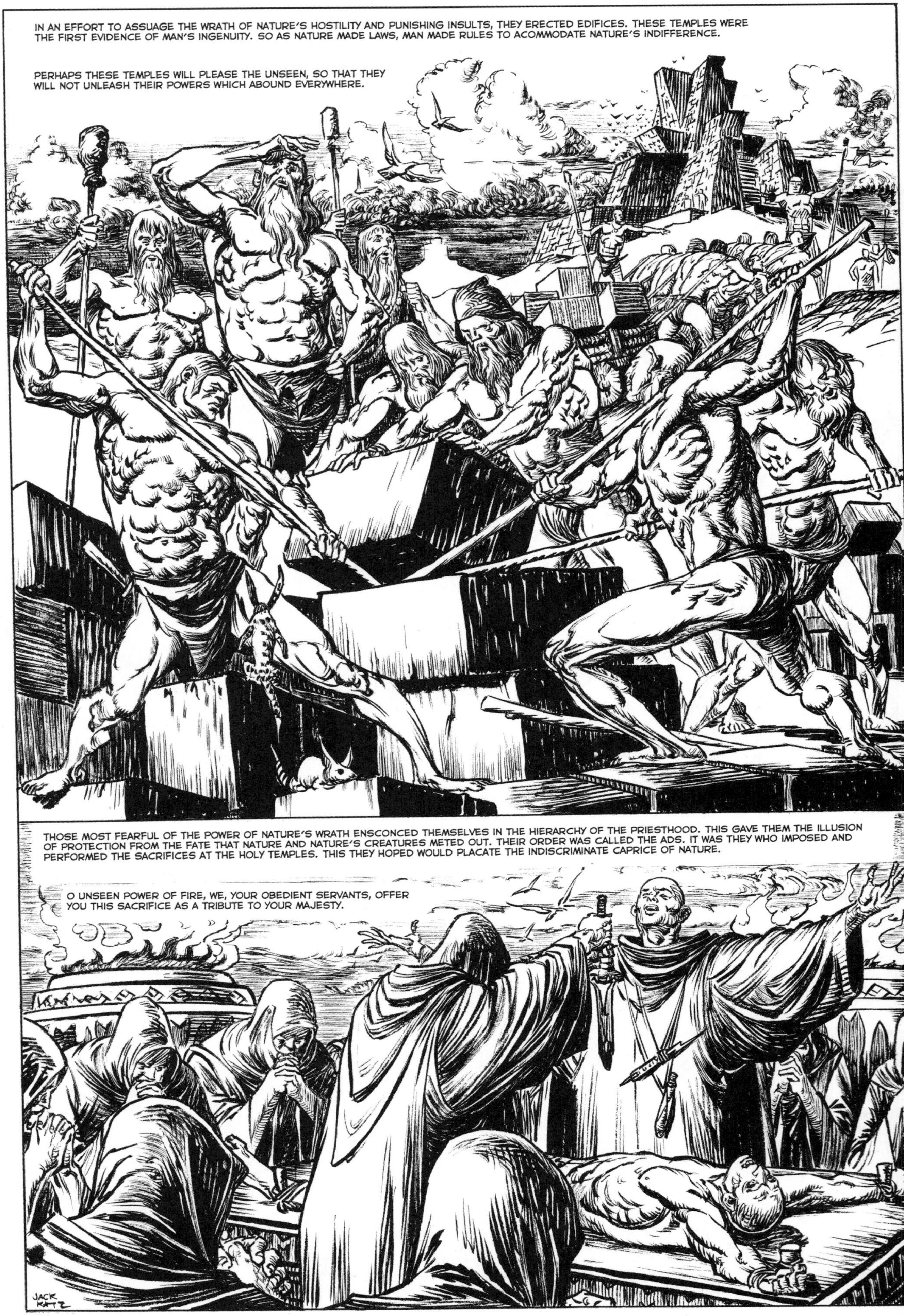

IN AN EFFORT TO ASSUAGE THE WRATH OF NATURE'S HOSTILITY AND PUNISHING INSULTS, THEY ERECTED EDIFICES. THESE TEMPLES WERE THE FIRST EVIDENCE OF MAN'S INGENUITY. SO AS NATURE MADE LAWS, MAN MADE RULES TO ACOMMODATE NATURE'S INDIFFERENCE.
PERHAPS THESE TEMPLES WILL PLEASE THE UNSEEN, SO THAT THEY WILL NOT UNLEASH THEIR POWERS WHICH ABOUND EVERYWHERE.
THOSE MOST FEARFUL OF THE POWER OF NATURE'S WRATH ENSCONCED THEMSELVES IN THE HIERARCHY OF THE PRIESTHOOD. THIS GAVE THEM THE ILLUSION OF PROTECTION FROM THE FATE THAT NATURE AND NATURE'S CREATURES METED OUT. THEIR ORDER WAS CALLED THE ADS. IT WAS THEY WHO IMPOSED AND PERFORMED THE SACRIFICES AT THE HOLY TEMPLES. THIS THEY HOPED WOULD PLACATE THE INDISCRIMINATE CAPRICE OF NATURE.
O UNSEEN POWER OF FIRE, WE, YOUR OBEDIENT SERVANTS, OFFER YOU THIS SACRIFICE AS A TRIBUTE TO YOUR MAJESTY.
JACK KATZ

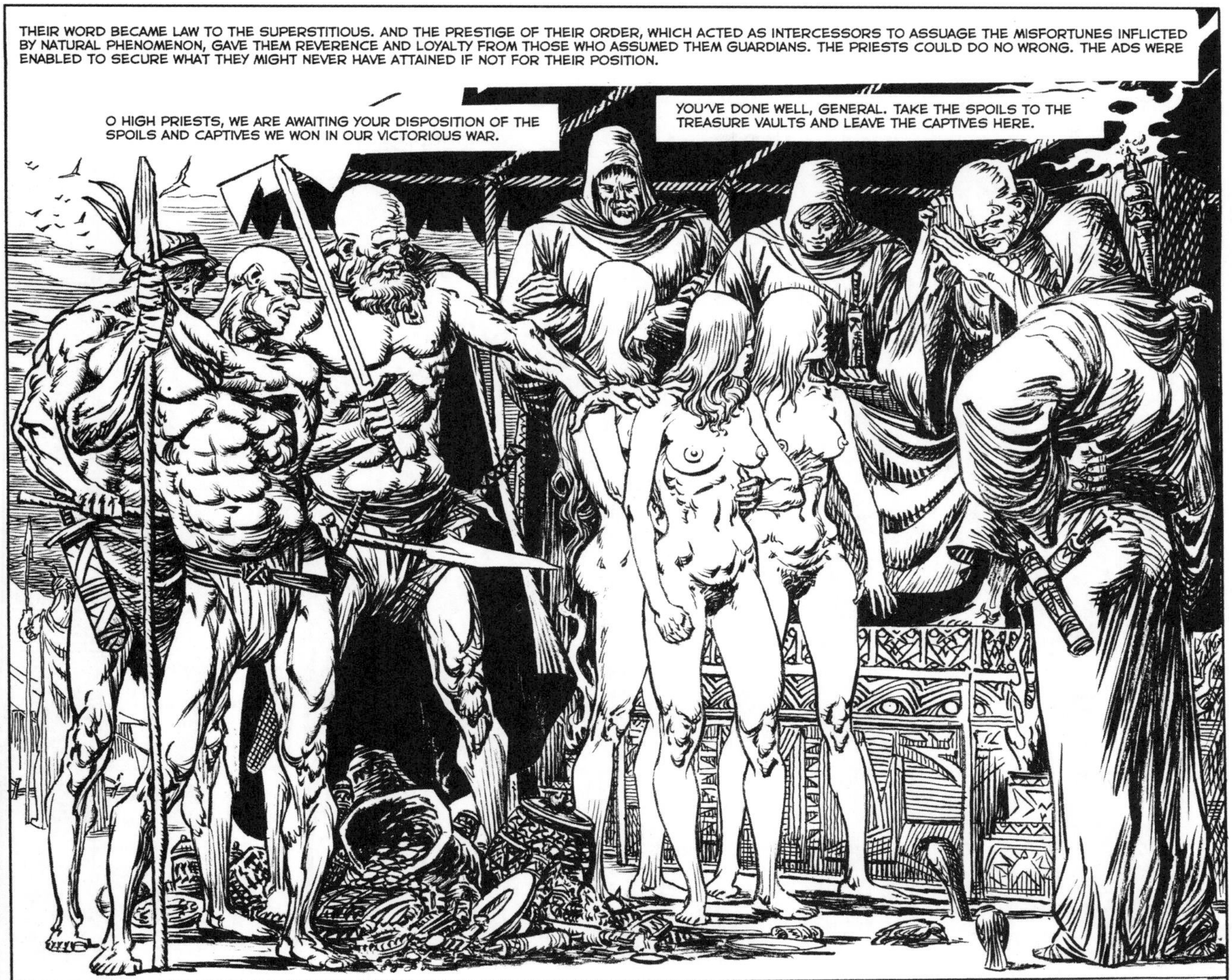
THEIR WORD BECAME LAW TO THE SUPERSTITIOUS. AND THE PRESTIGE OF THEIR ORDER, WHICH ACTED AS INTERCESSORS TO ASSUAGE THE MISFORTUNES INFLICTED BY NATURAL PHENOMENON, GAVE THEM REVERENCE AND LOYALTY FROM THOSE WHO ASSUMED THEM GUARDIANS. THE PRIESTS COULD DO NO WRONG. THE ADS WERE ENABLED TO SECURE WHAT THEY MIGHT NEVER HAVE ATTAINED IF NOT FOR THEIR POSITION.
O HIGH PRIESTS, WE ARE AWAITING YOUR DISPOSITION OF THE SPOILS AND CAPTIVES WE WON IN OUR VICTORIOUS WAR.
YOU'VE DONE WELL, GENERAL. TAKE THE SPOILS TO THE TREASURE VAULTS AND LEAVE THE CAPTIVES HERE.

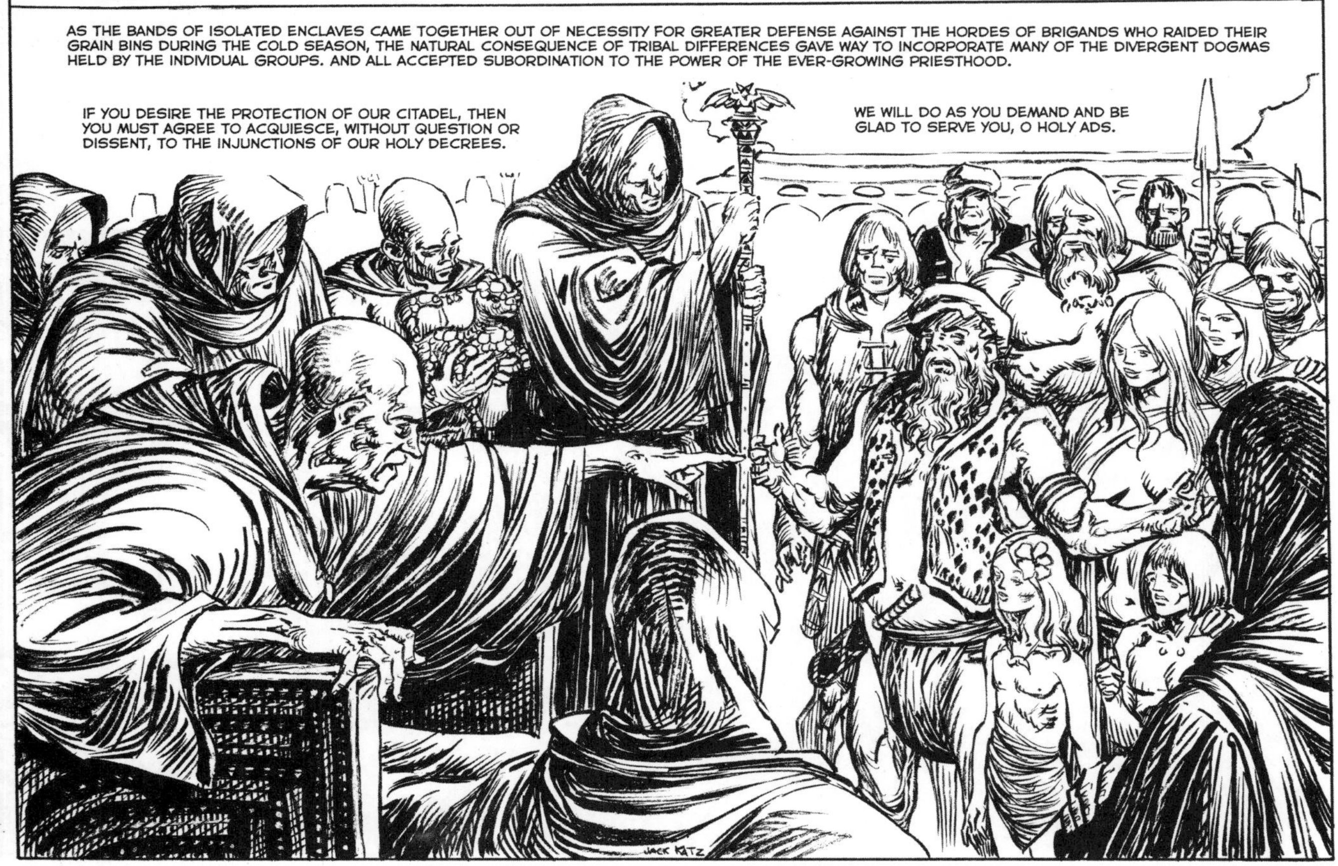
AS THE BANDS OF ISOLATED ENCLAVES CAME TOGETHER OUT OF NECESSITY FOR GREATER DEFENSE AGAINST THE HORDES OF BRIGANDS WHO RAIDED THEIR GRAIN BINS DURING THE COLD SEASON, THE NATURAL CONSEQUENCE OF TRIBAL DIFFERENCES GAVE WAY TO INCORPORATE MANY OF THE DIVERGENT DOGMAS HELD BY THE INDIVIDUAL GROUPS. AND ALL ACCEPTED SUBORDINATION TO THE POWER OF THE EVER-GROWING PRIESTHOOD.
IF YOU DESIRE THE PROTECTION OF OUR CITADEL, THEN YOU MUST AGREE TO ACQUIESCE, WITHOUT QUESTION OR DISSENT, TO THE INJUNCTIONS OF OUR HOLY DECREES.
WE WILL DO AS YOU DEMAND AND BE GLAD TO SERVE YOU, O HOLY ADS.
JACK KATZ

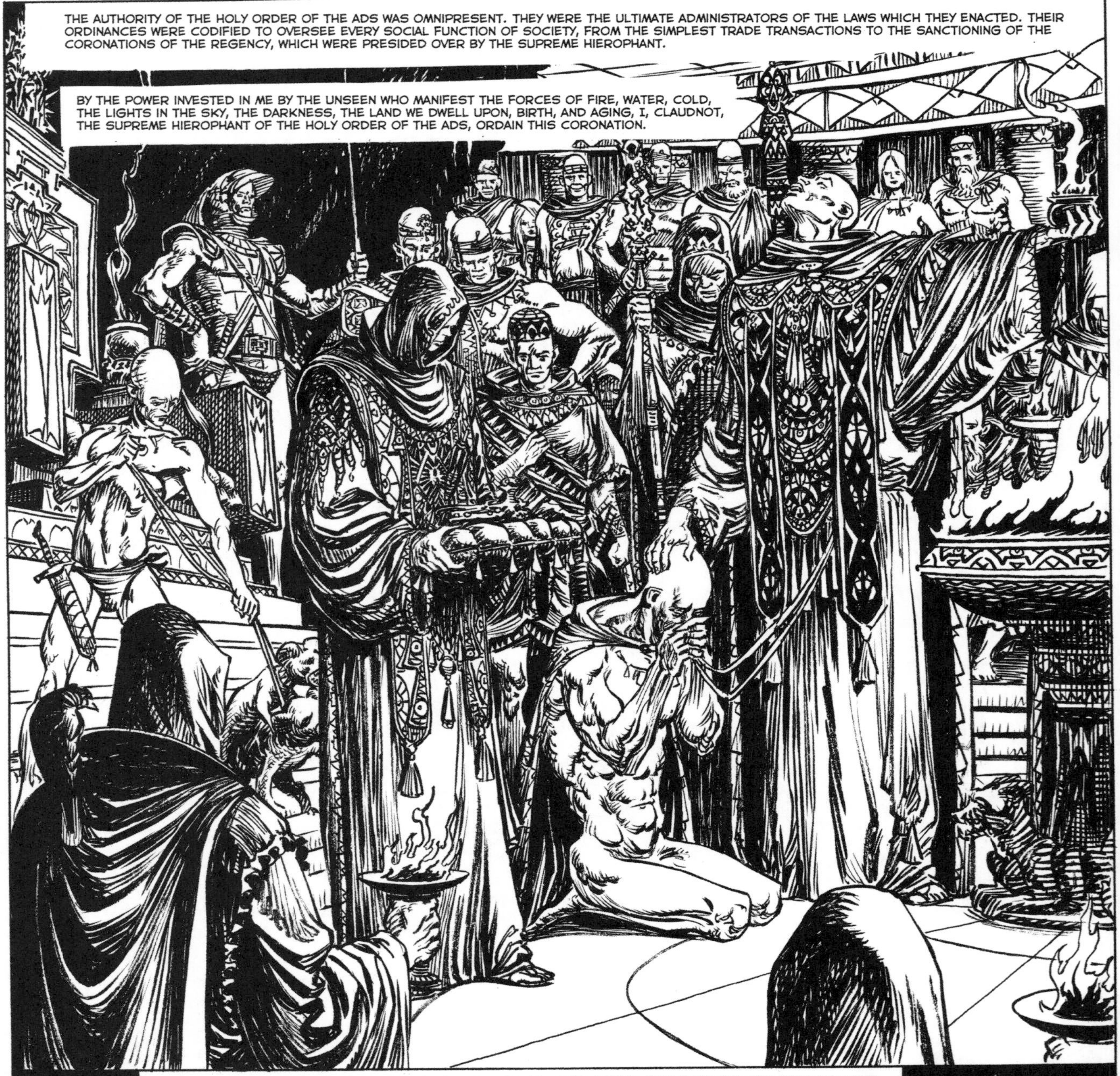
THE AUTHORITY OF THE HOLY ORDER OF THE ADS WAS OMNIPRESENT. THEY WERE THE ULTIMATE ADMINISTRATORS OF THE LAWS WHICH THEY ENACTED. THEIR ORDINANCES WERE CODIFIED TO OVERSEE EVERY SOCIAL FUNCTION OF SOCIETY, FROM THE SIMPLEST TRADE TRANSACTIONS TO THE SANCTIONING OF THE CORONATIONS OF THE REGENCY, WHICH WERE PRESIDED OVER BY THE SUPREME HIEROPHANT.
BY THE POWER INVESTED IN ME BY THE UNSEEN WHO MANIFEST THE FORCES OF FIRE, WATER, COLD, THE LIGHTS IN THE SKY, THE DARKNESS, THE LAND WE DWELL UPON, BIRTH, AND AGING, I, CLAUDNOT, THE SUPREME HIEROPHANT OF THE HOLY ORDER OF THE ADS, ORDAIN THIS CORONATION.

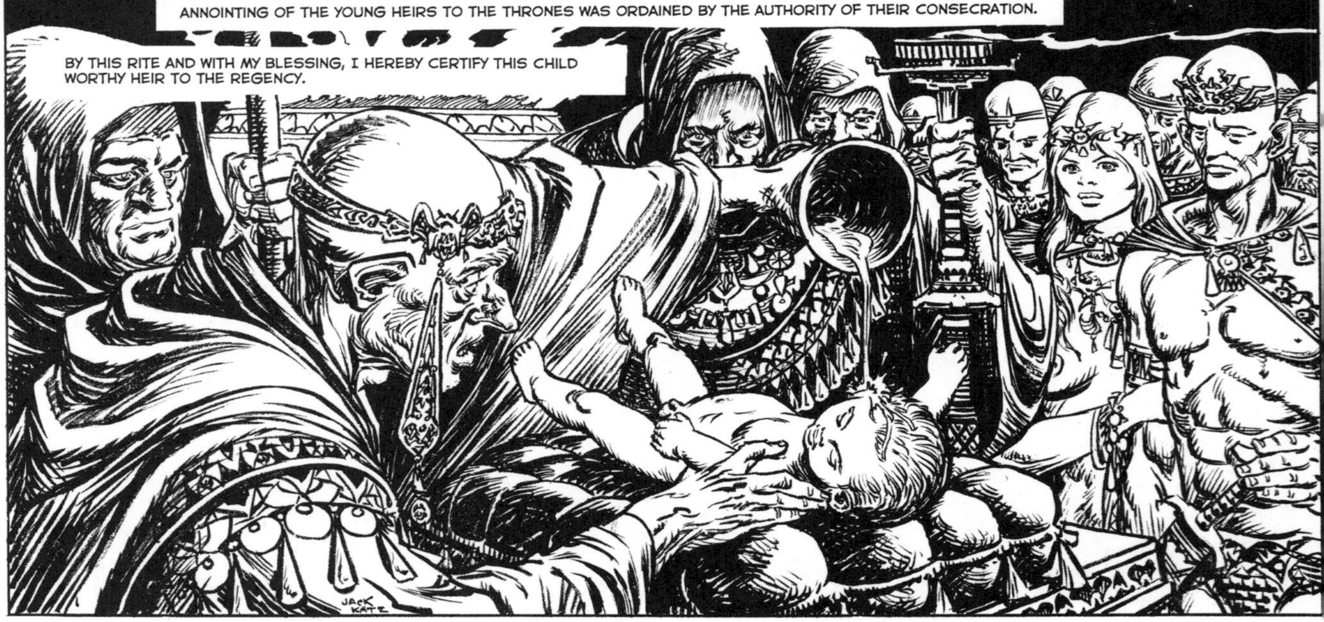
ANNOINTING OF THE YOUNG HEIRS TO THE THRONES WAS ORDAINED BY THE AUTHORITY OF THEIR CONSECRATION.
BY THIS RITE AND WITH MY BLESSING, I HEREBY CERTIFY THIS CHILD WORTHY HEIR TO THE REGENCY.
JACK KATZ

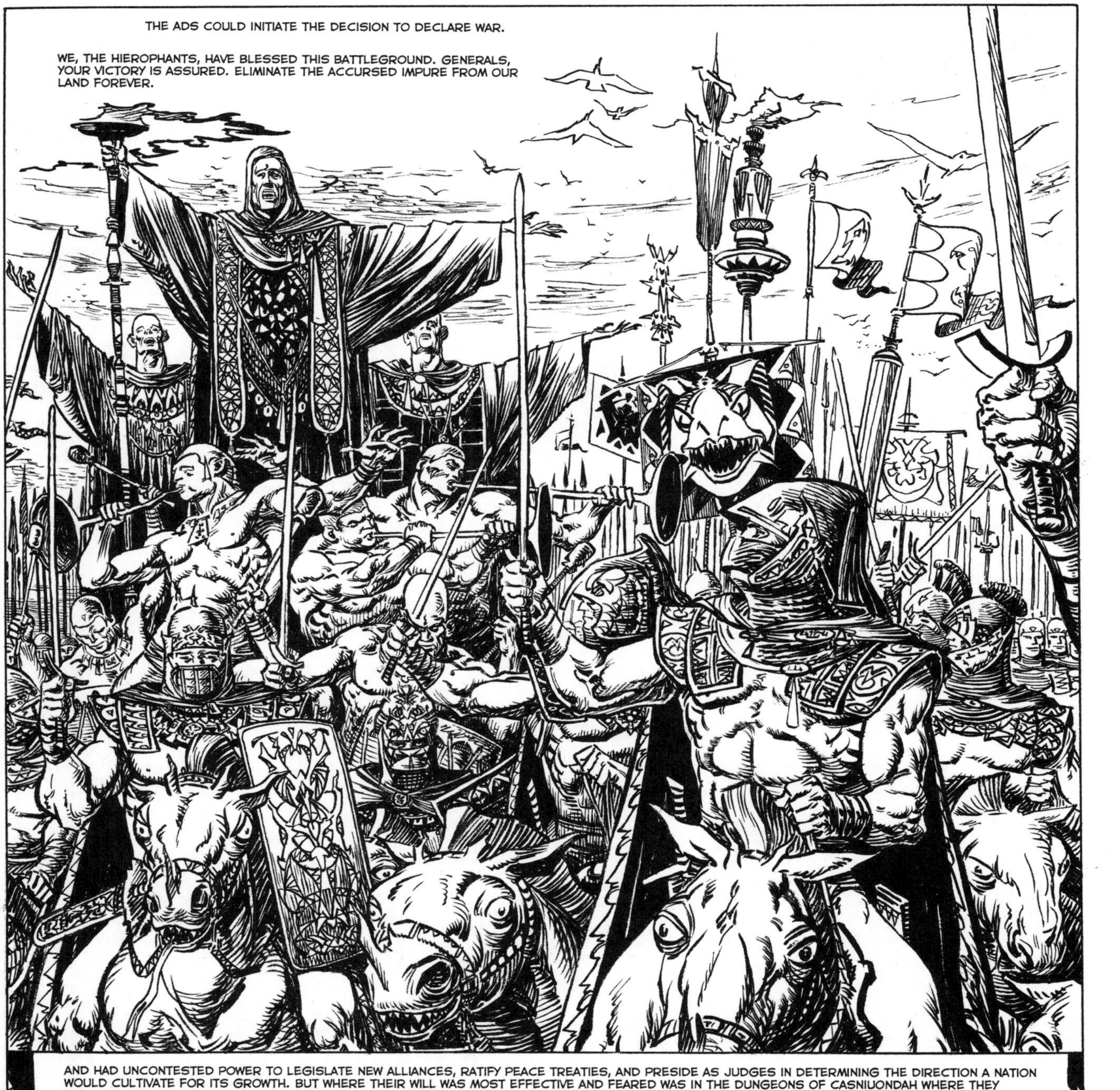
THE ADS COULD INITIATE THE DECISION TO DECLARE WAR.
WE, THE HIEROPHANTS, HAVE BLESSED THIS BATTLEGROUND. GENERALS, YOUR VICTORY IS ASSURED. ELIMINATE THE ACCURSED IMPURE FROM OUR LAND FOREVER.
AND HAD UNCONTESTED POWER TO LEGISLATE NEW ALLIANCES, RATIFY PEACE TREATIES, AND PRESIDE AS JUDGES IN DETERMINING THE DIRECTION A NATION WOULD CULTIVATE FOR ITS GROWTH. BUT WHERE THEIR WILL WAS MOST EFFECTIVE AND FEARED WAS IN THE DUNGEONS OF CASNIUONDAH WHERE THEY INFLICTED UNSPEAKABLE TORTURES ON ANY HERETIC, CAPTURED ENEMY, OR CITIZEN WHO WAS CAUGHT BREAKING THEIR PROSCRIBED EDICTS.

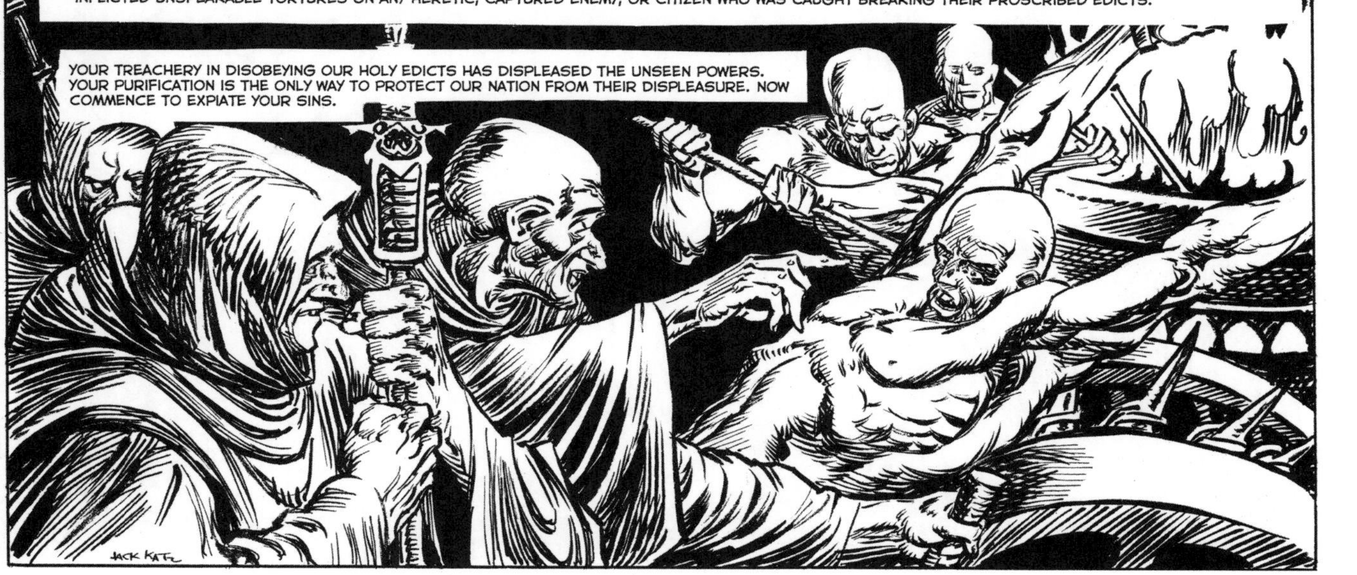
YOUR TREACHERY IN DISOBEYING OUR HOLY EDICTS HAS DISPLEASED THE UNSEEN POWERS. YOUR PURIFICATION IS THE ONLY WAY TO PROTECT OUR NATION FROM THEIR DISPLEASURE. NOW COMMENCE TO EXPIATE YOUR SINS.
JACK KATZ

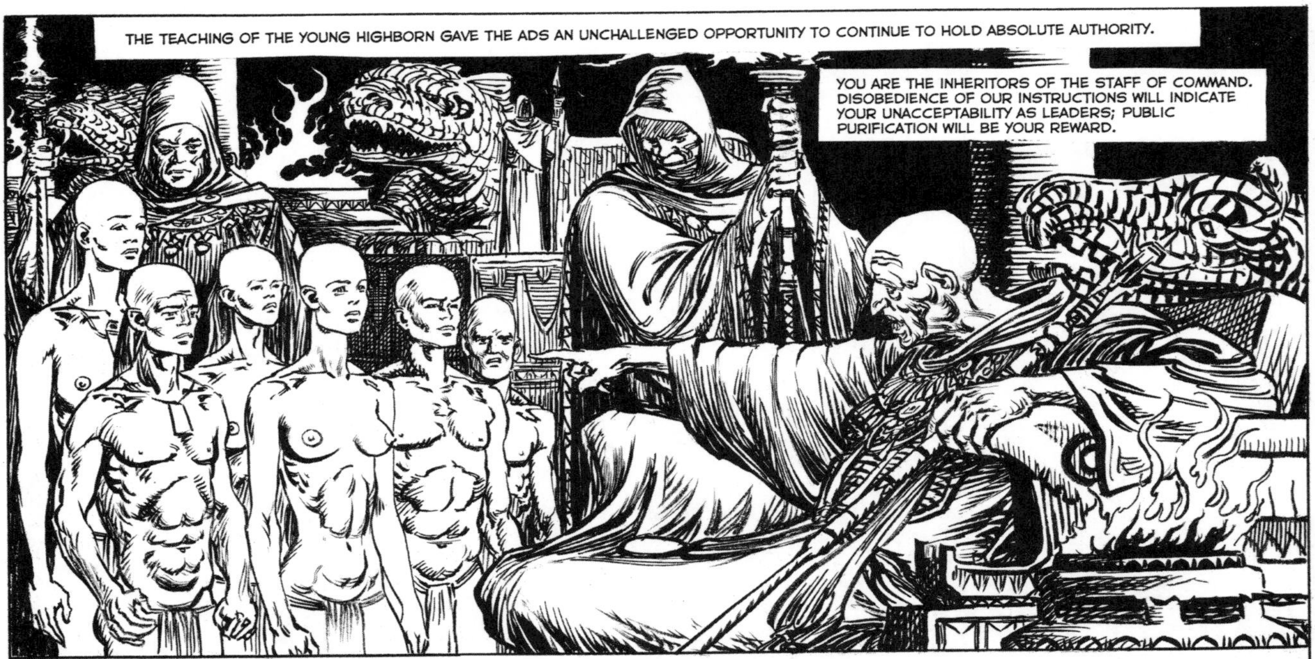
THE TEACHING OF THE YOUNG HIGHBORN GAVE THE ADS AN UNCHALLENGED OPPORTUNITY TO CONTINUE TO HOLD ABSOLUTE AUTHORITY.
YOU ARE THE INHERITORS OF THE STAFF OF COMMAND. DISOBEDIENCE OF OUR INSTRUCTIONS WILL INDICATE YOUR UNACCEPTABILITY AS LEADERS; PUBLIC PURIFICATION WILL BE YOUR REWARD.

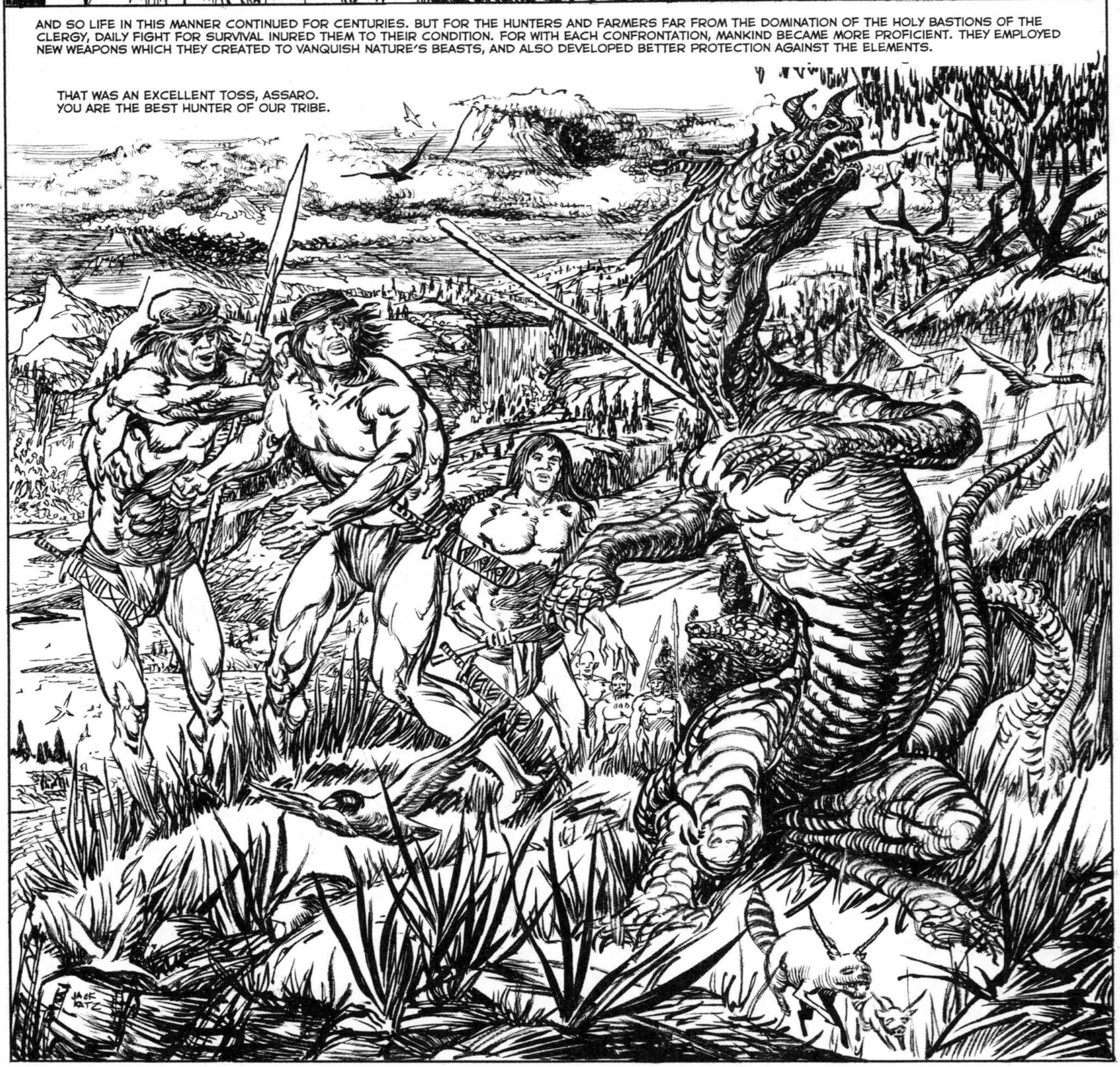
AND SO LIFE IN THIS MANNER CONTINUED FOR CENTURIES. BUT FOR THE HUNTERS AND FARMERS FAR FROM THE DOMINATION OF THE HOLY BASTIONS OF THE CLERGY, DAILY FIGHT FOR SURVIVAL INURED THEM TO THEIR CONDITION. FOR WITH EACH CONFRONTATION, MANKIND BECAME MORE PROFICIENT. THEY EMPLOYED NEW WEAPONS WHICH THEY CREATED TO VANQUISH NATURE'S BEASTS, AND ALSO DEVELOPED BETTER PROTECTION AGAINST THE ELEMENTS.
THAT WAS AN EXCELLENT TOSS, ASSARO. YOU ARE THE BEST HUNTER OF OUR TRIBE.
JACK KATZ

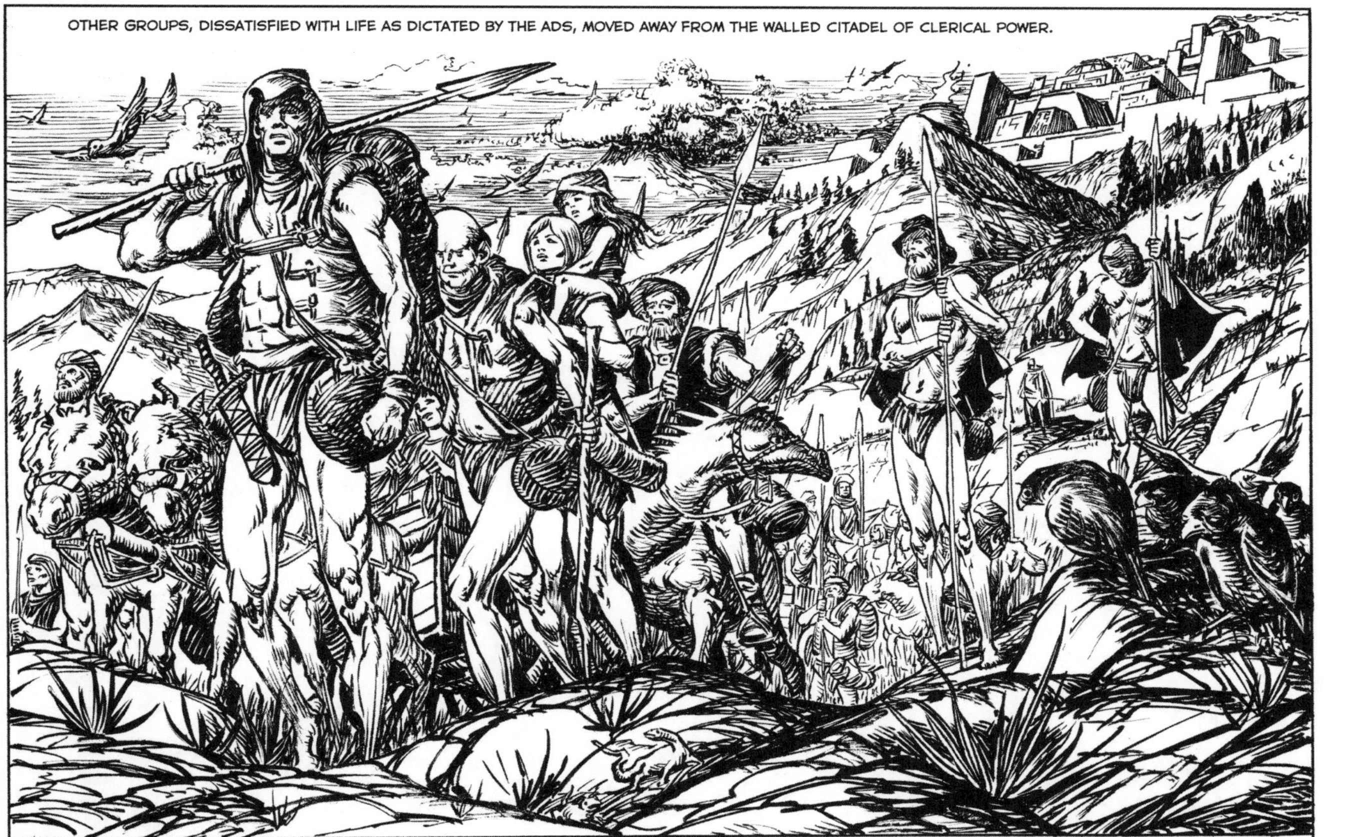
OTHER GROUPS, DISSATISFIED WITH LIFE AS DICTATED BY THE ADS, MOVED AWAY FROM THE WALLED CITADEL OF CLERICAL POWER.

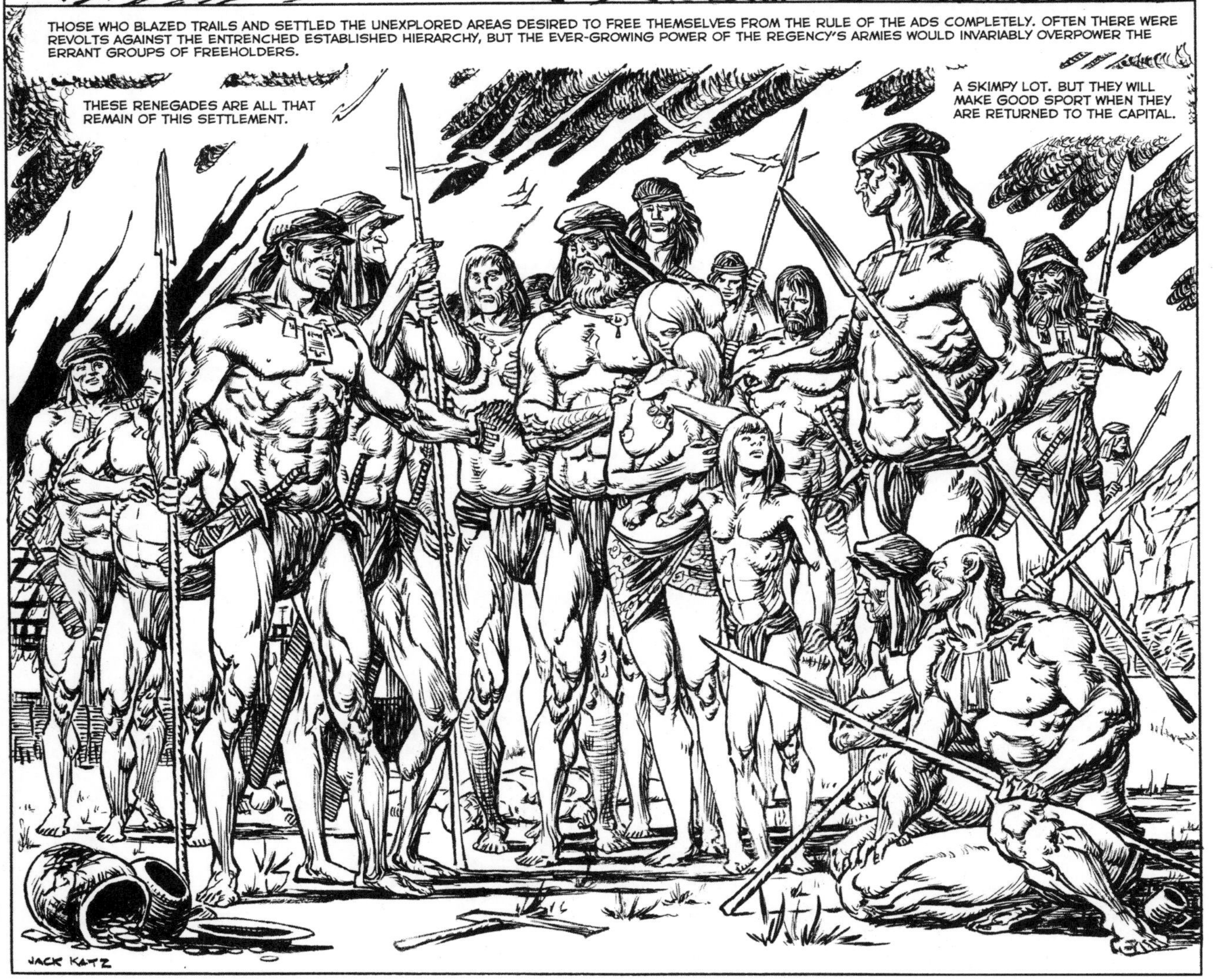
THOSE WHO BLAZED TRAILS AND SETTLED THE UNEXPLORED AREAS DESIRED TO FREE THEMSELVES FROM THE RULE OF THE ADS COMPLETELY. OFTEN THERE WERE REVOLTS AGAINST THE ENTRENCHED ESTABLISHED HIERARCHY, BUT THE EVER-GROWING POWER OF THE REGENCY'S ARMIES WOULD INVARIABLY OVERPOWER THE ERRANT GROUPS OF FREEHOLDERS.
THESE RENEGADES ARE ALL THAT REMAIN OF THIS SETTLEMENT.
A SKIMPY LOT. BUT THEY WILL MAKE GOOD SPORT WHEN THEY ARE RETURNED TO THE CAPITAL.
JACK KATZ

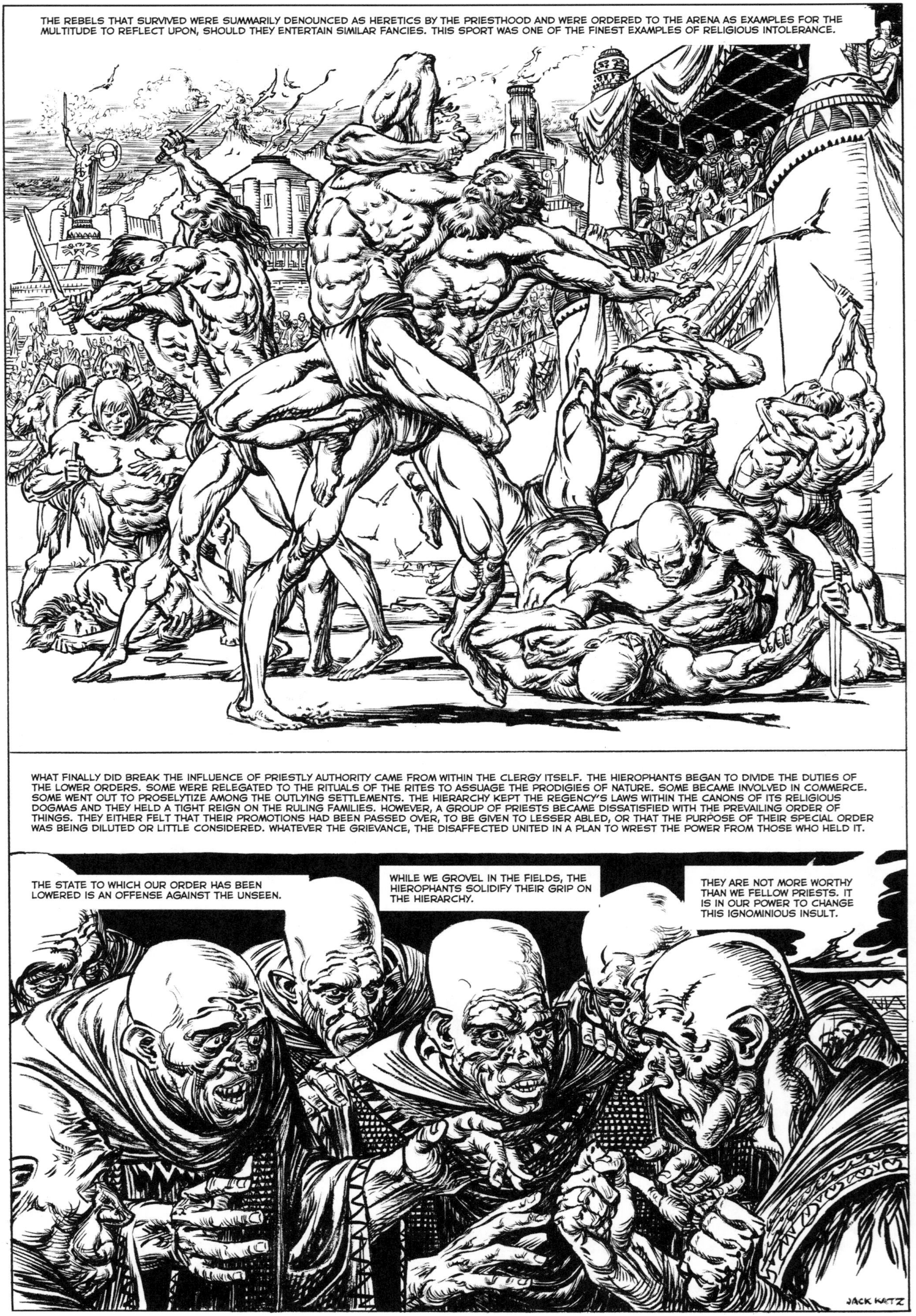
THE REBELS THAT SURVIVED WERE SUMMARILY DENOUNCED AS HERETICS BY THE PRIESTHOOD AND WERE ORDERED TO THE ARENA AS EXAMPLES FOR THE MULTITUDE TO REFLECT UPON, SHOULD THEY ENTERTAIN SIMILAR FANCIES. THIS SPORT WAS ONE OF THE FINEST EXAMPLES OF RELIGIOUS INTOLERANCE.
WHAT FINALLY DID BREAK THE INFLUENCE OF PRIESTLY AUTHORITY CAME FROM WITHIN THE CLERGY ITSELF. THE HIEROPHANTS BEGAN TO DIVIDE THE DUTIES OF THE LOWER ORDERS. SOME WERE RELEGATED TO THE RITUALS OF THE RITES TO ASSUAGE THE PRODIGIES OF NATURE. SOME BECAME INVOLVED IN COMMERCE. SOME WENT OUT TO PROSELYTIZE AMONG THE OUTLYING SETTLEMENTS. THE HIERARCHY KEPT THE REGENCY'S LAWS WITHIN THE CANONS OF ITS RELIGIOUS DOGMAS AND THEY HELD A TIGHT REIGN ON THE RULING FAMILIES. HOWEVER, A GROUP OF PRIESTS BECAME DISSATISFIED WITH THE PREVAILING ORDER OF THINGS. THEY EITHER FELT THAT THEIR PROMOTIONS HAD BEEN PASSED OVER, TO BE GIVEN TO LESSER ABLED, OR THAT THE PURPOSE OF THEIR SPECIAL ORDER WAS BEING DILUTED OR LITTLE CONSIDERED. WHATEVER THE GRIEVANCE, THE DISAFFECTED UNITED IN A PLAN TO WREST THE POWER FROM THOSE WHO HELD IT.
THE STATE TO WHICH OUR ORDER HAS BEEN LOWERED IS AN OFFENSE AGAINST THE UNSEEN.
WHILE WE GROVEL IN THE FIELDS, THE HIEROPHANTS SOLIDIFY THEIR GRIP ON THE HIERARCHY.
THEY ARE NOT MORE WORTHY THAN WE FELLOW PRIESTS. IT IS IN OUR POWER TO CHANGE THIS IGNOMINIOUS INSULT.
JACK KATZ

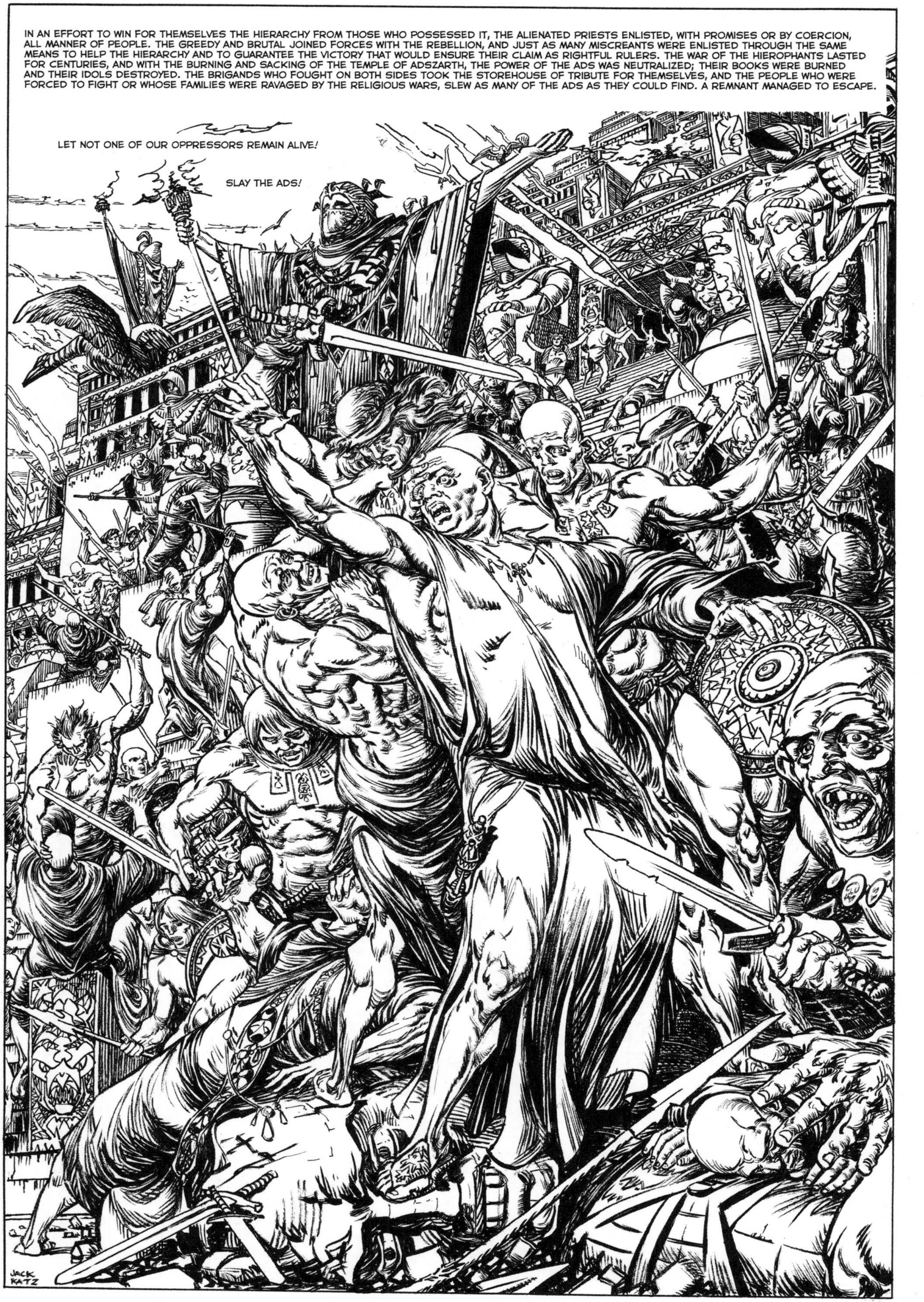
IN AN EFFORT TO WIN FOR THEMSELVES THE HIERARCHY FROM THOSE WHO POSSESSED IT, THE ALIENATED PRIESTS ENLISTED, WITH PROMISES OR BY COERCION, ALL MANNER OF PEOPLE. THE GREEDY AND BRUTAL JOINED FORCES WITH THE REBELLION, AND JUST AS MANY MISCREANTS WERE ENLISTED THROUGH THE SAME MEANS TO HELP THE HIERARCHY AND TO GUARANTEE THE VICTORY THAT WOULD ENSURE THEIR CLAIM AS RIGHTFUL RULERS. THE WAR OF THE HIEROPHANTS LASTED FOR CENTURIES, AND WITH THE BURNING AND SACKING OF THE TEMPLE OF ADSZARTH, THE POWER OF THE ADS WAS NEUTRALIZED; THEIR BOOKS WERE BURNED AND THEIR IDOLS DESTROYED. THE BRIGANDS WHO FOUGHT ON BOTH SIDES TOOK THE STOREHOUSE OF TRIBUTE FOR THEMSELVES, AND THE PEOPLE WHO WERE FORCED TO FIGHT OR WHOSE FAMILIES WERE RAVAGED BY THE RELIGIOUS WARS, SLEW AS MANY OF THE ADS AS THEY COULD FIND. A REMNANT MANAGED TO ESCAPE.
LET NOT ONE OF OUR OPPRESSORS REMAIN ALIVE!
SLAY THE ADS!
JACK KATZ

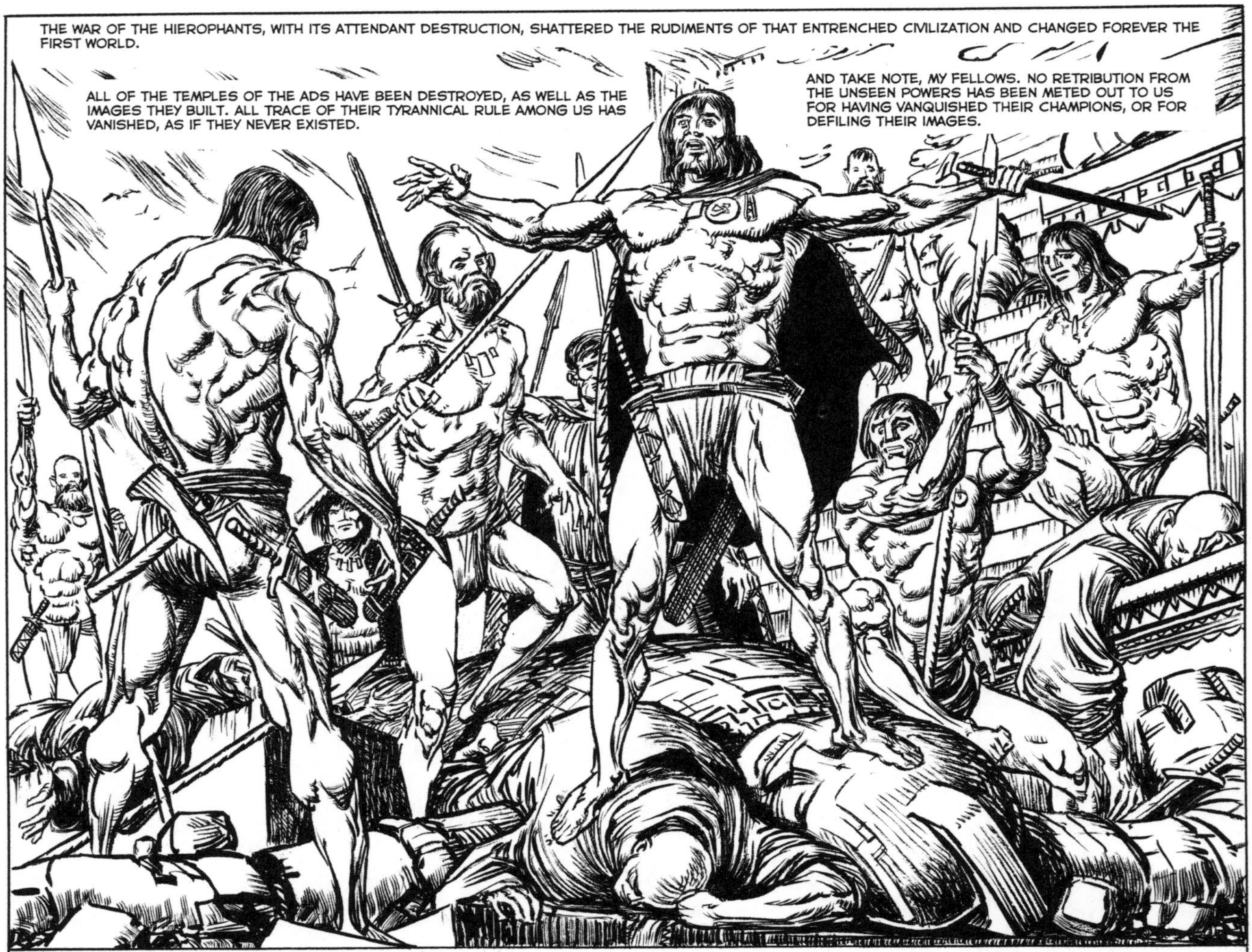
THE WAR OF THE HIEROPHANTS, WITH ITS ATTENDANT DESTRUCTION, SHATTERED THE RUDIMENTS OF THAT ENTRENCHED CIVILIZATION AND CHANGED FOREVER THE FIRST WORLD.
ALL OF THE TEMPLES OF THE ADS HAVE BEEN DESTROYED, AS WELL AS THE IMAGES THEY BUILT. ALL TRACE OF THEIR TYRANNICAL RULE AMONG US HAS VANISHED, AS IF THEY NEVER EXISTED.
AND TAKE NOTE, MY FELLOWS. NO RETRIBUTION FROM THE UNSEEN POWERS HAS BEEN METED OUT TO US FOR HAVING VANQUISHED THEIR CHAMPIONS, OR FOR DEFILING THEIR IMAGES.
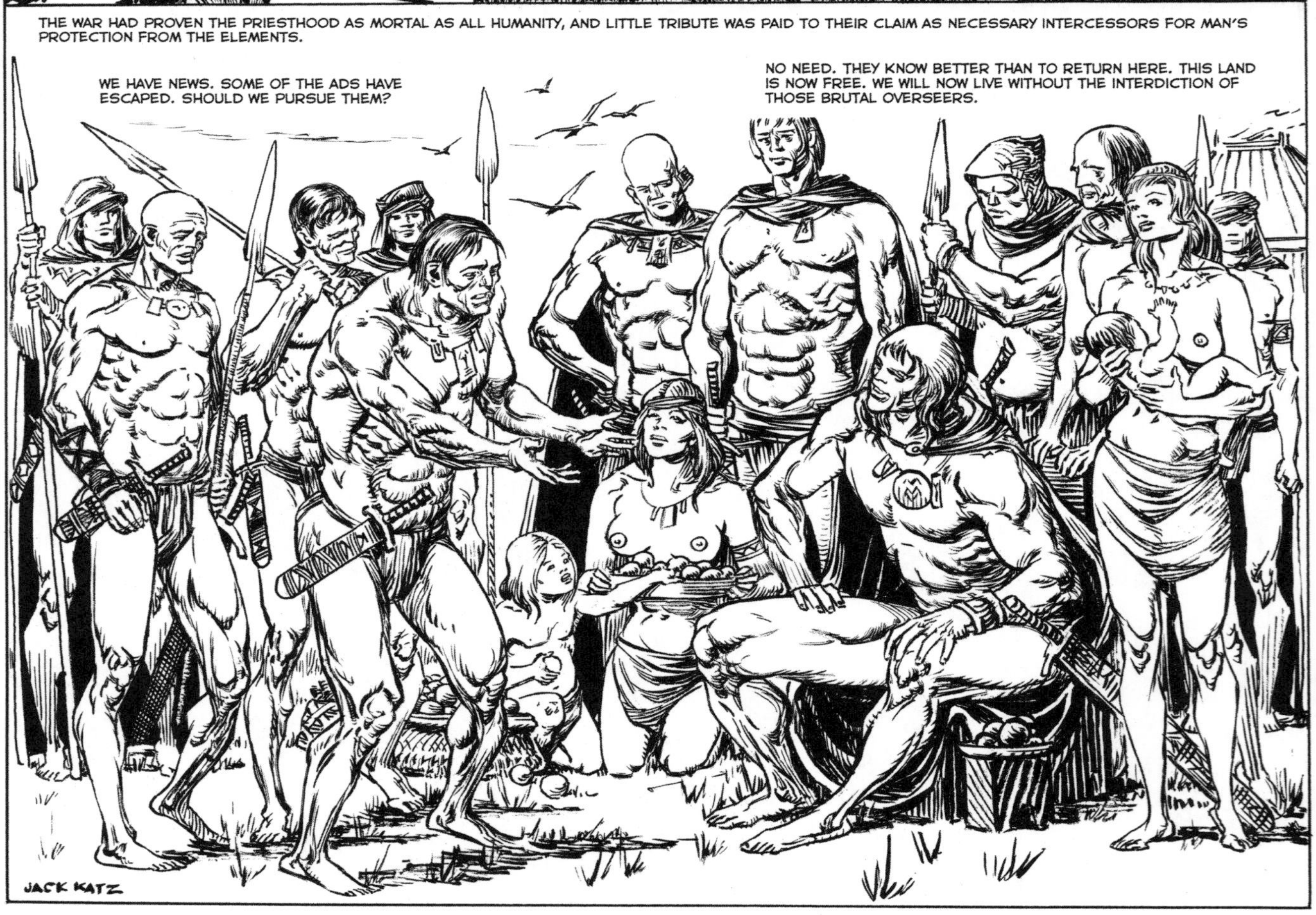
THE WAR HAD PROVEN THE PRIESTHOOD AS MORTAL AS ALL HUMANITY, AND LITTLE TRIBUTE WAS PAID TO THEIR CLAIM AS NECESSARY INTERCESSORS FOR MAN'S PROTECTION FROM THE ELEMENTS.
WE HAVE NEWS. SOME OF THE ADS HAVE ESCAPED. SHOULD WE PURSUE THEM?
NO NEED. THEY KNOW BETTER THAN TO RETURN HERE. THIS LAND IS NOW FREE. WE WILL NOW LIVE WITHOUT THE INTERDICTION OF THOSE BRUTAL OVERSEERS.
JACK KATZ

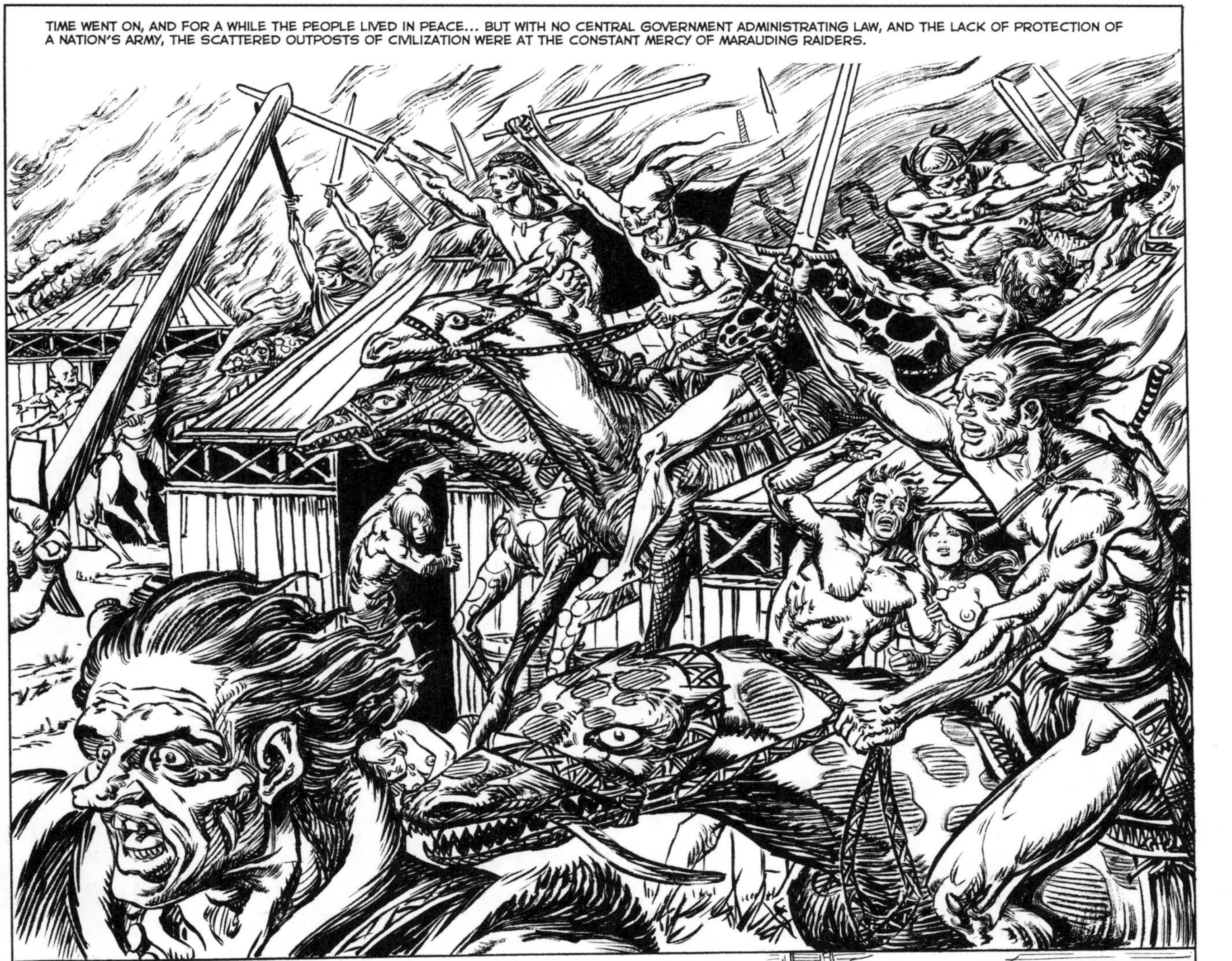
TIME WENT ON, AND FOR A WHILE THE PEOPLE LIVED IN PEACE... BUT WITH NO CENTRAL GOVERNMENT ADMINISTRATING LAW, AND THE LACK OF PROTECTION OF A NATION'S ARMY, THE SCATTERED OUTPOSTS OF CIVILIZATION WERE AT THE CONSTANT MERCY OF MARAUDING RAIDERS.

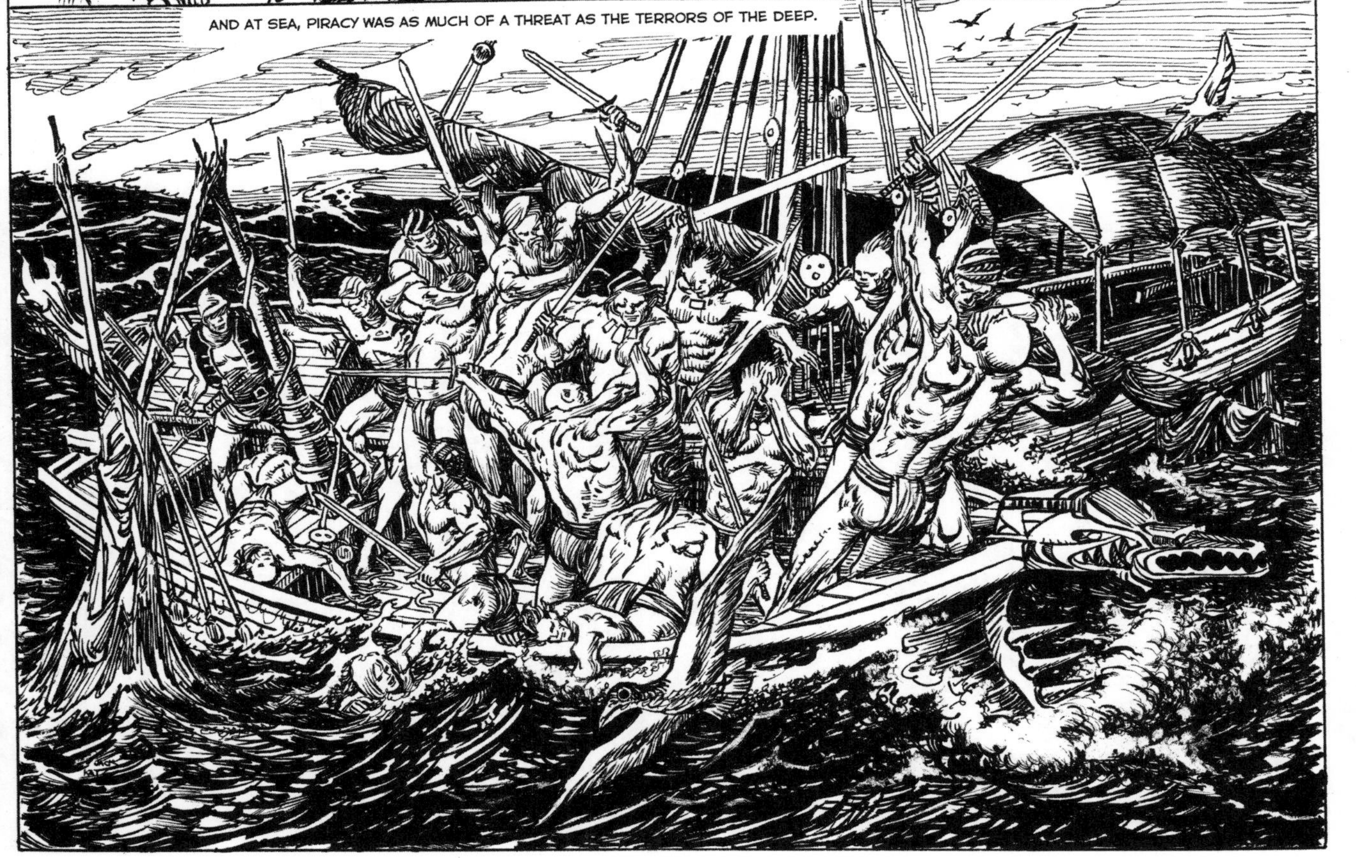
AND AT SEA, PIRACY WAS AS MUCH OF A THREAT AS THE TERRORS OF THE DEEP.

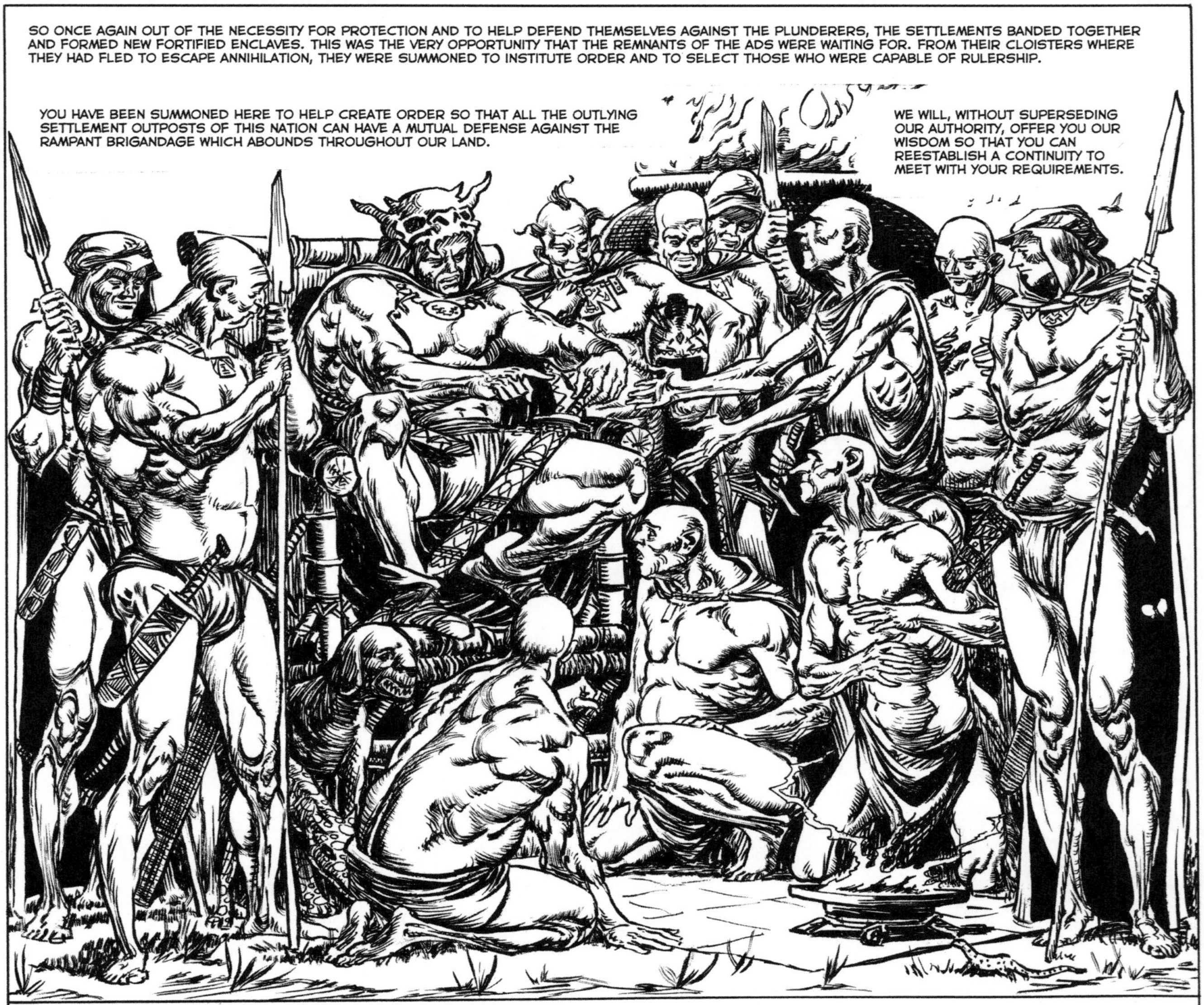
SO ONCE AGAIN OUT OF THE NECESSITY FOR PROTECTION AND TO HELP DEFEND THEMSELVES AGAINST THE PLUNDERERS, THE SETTLEMENTS BANDED TOGETHER AND FORMED NEW FORTIFIED ENCLAVES. THIS WAS THE VERY OPPORTUNITY THAT THE REMNANTS OF THE ADS WERE WAITING FOR. FROM THEIR CLOISTERS WHERE THEY HAD FLED TO ESCAPE ANNIHILATION, THEY WERE SUMMONED TO INSTITUTE ORDER AND TO SELECT THOSE WHO WERE CAPABLE OF RULERSHIP.
YOU HAVE BEEN SUMMONED HERE TO HELP CREATE ORDER SO THAT ALL THE OUTLYING SETTLEMENT OUTPOSTS OF THIS NATION CAN HAVE A MUTUAL DEFENSE AGAINST THE RAMPANT BRIGANDAGE WHICH ABOUNDS THROUGHOUT OUR LAND.
WE WILL, WITHOUT SUPERSEDING OUR AUTHORITY, OFFER YOU OUR WISDOM SO THAT YOU CAN REESTABLISH A CONTINUITY TO MEET WITH YOUR REQUIREMENTS.

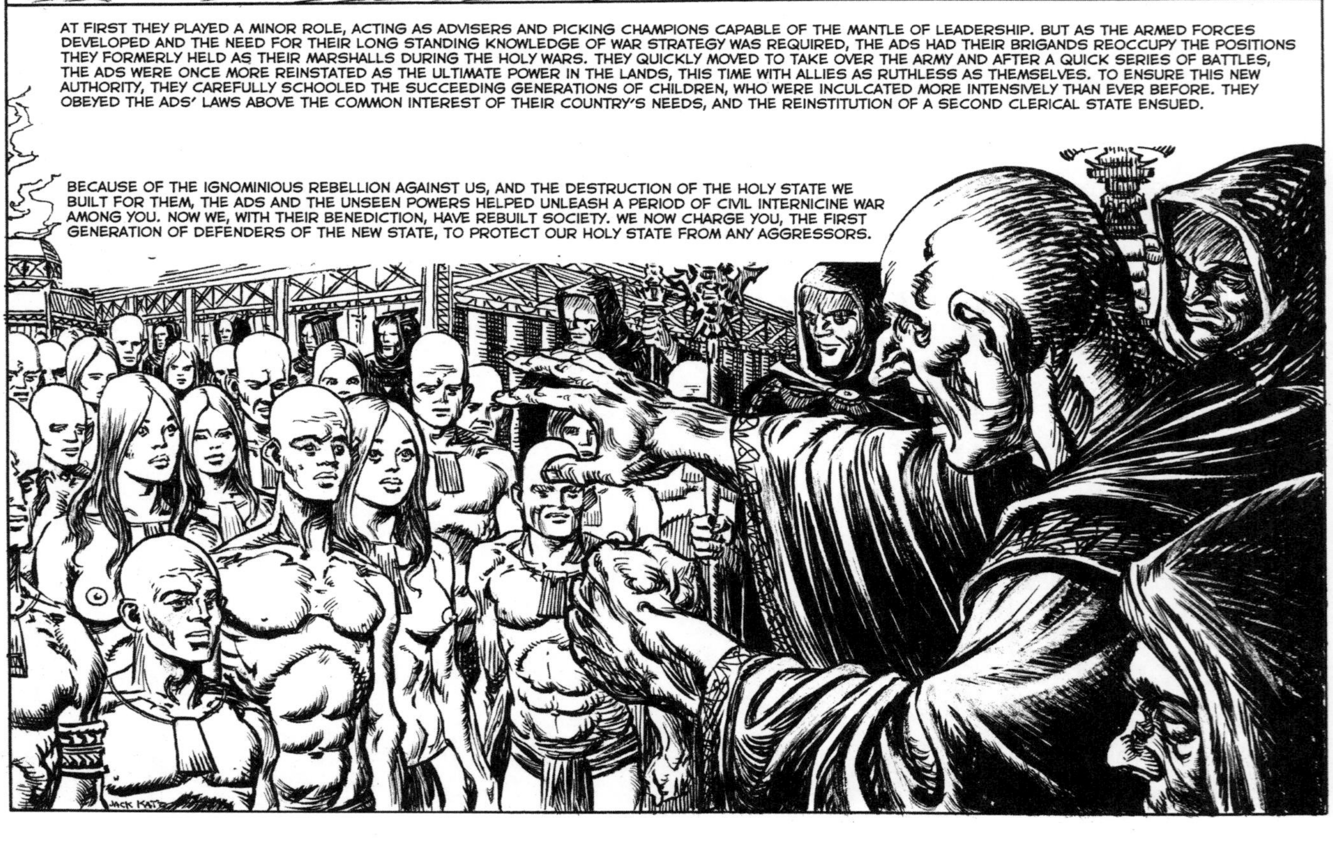
AT FIRST THEY PLAYED A MINOR ROLE, ACTING AS ADVISERS AND PICKING CHAMPIONS CAPABLE OF THE MANTLE OF LEADERSHIP. BUT AS THE ARMED FORCES DEVELOPED AND THE NEED FOR THEIR LONG STANDING KNOWLEDGE OF WAR STRATEGY WAS REQUIRED, THE ADS HAD THEIR BRIGANDS REOCCUPY THE POSITIONS THEY FORMERLY HELD AS THEIR MARSHALLS DURING THE HOLY WARS. THEY QUICKLY MOVED TO TAKE OVER THE ARMY AND AFTER A QUICK SERIES OF BATTLES, THE ADS WERE ONCE MORE REINSTATED AS THE ULTIMATE POWER IN THE LANDS, THIS TIME WITH ALLIES AS RUTHLESS AS THEMSELVES. TO ENSURE THIS NEW AUTHORITY, THEY CAREFULLY SCHOOLED THE SUCCEEDING GENERATIONS OF CHILDREN, WHO WERE INCULCATED MORE INTENSIVELY THAN EVER BEFORE. THEY OBEYED THE ADS' LAWS ABOVE THE COMMON INTEREST OF THEIR COUNTRY'S NEEDS, AND THE REINSTITUTION OF A SECOND CLERICAL STATE ENSUED.
BECAUSE OF THE IGNOMINIOUS REBELLION AGAINST US, AND THE DESTRUCTION OF THE HOLY STATE WE BUILT FOR THEM, THE ADS AND THE UNSEEN POWERS HELPED UNLEASH A PERIOD OF CIVIL INTERNICINE WAR AMONG YOU. NOW WE, WITH THEIR BENEDICTION, HAVE REBUILT SOCIETY. WE NOW CHARGE YOU, THE FIRST GENERATION OF DEFENDERS OF THE NEW STATE, TO PROTECT OUR HOLY STATE FROM ANY AGGRESSORS.
JACK KATZ

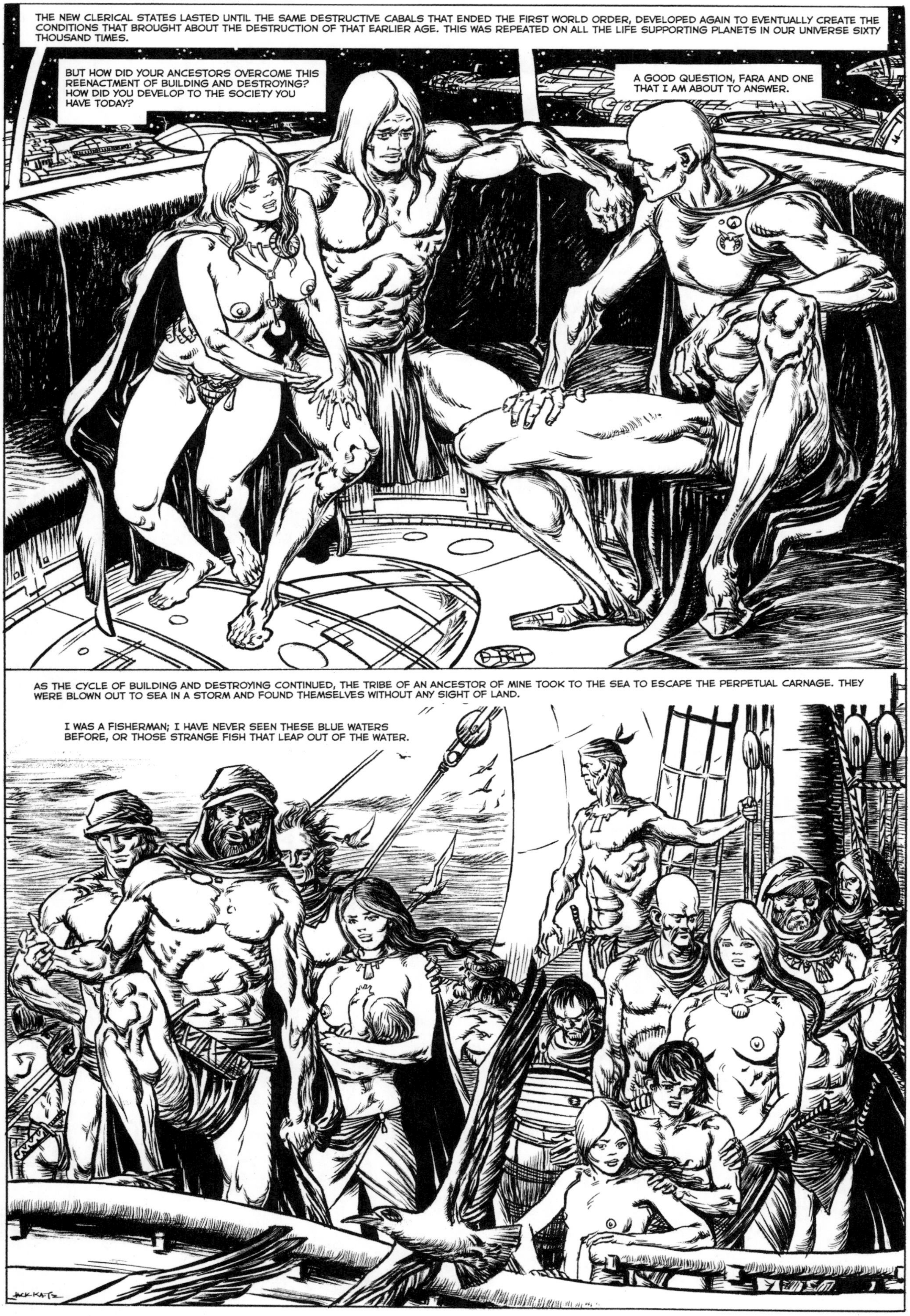
THE NEW CLERICAL STATES LASTED UNTIL THE SAME DESTRUCTIVE CABALS THAT ENDED THE FIRST WORLD ORDER, DEVELOPED AGAIN TO EVENTUALLY CREATE THE CONDITIONS THAT BROUGHT ABOUT THE DESTRUCTION OF THAT EARLIER AGE. THIS WAS REPEATED ON ALL THE LIFE SUPPORTING PLANETS IN OUR UNIVERSE SIXTY THOUSAND TIMES.
BUT HOW DID YOUR ANCESTORS OVERCOME THIS REENACTMENT OF BUILDING AND DESTROYING? HOW DID YOU DEVELOP TO THE SOCIETY YOU HAVE TODAY?
A GOOD QUESTION, FARA AND ONE THAT I AM ABOUT TO ANSWER.
AS THE CYCLE OF BUILDING AND DESTROYING CONTINUED, THE TRIBE OF AN ANCESTOR OF MINE TOOK TO THE SEA TO ESCAPE THE PERPETUAL CARNAGE. THEY WERE BLOWN OUT TO SEA IN A STORM AND FOUND THEMSELVES WITHOUT ANY SIGHT OF LAND.
I WAS A FISHERMAN; I HAVE NEVER SEEN THESE BLUE WATERS BEFORE, OR THOSE STRANGE FISH THAT LEAP OUT OF THE WATER.

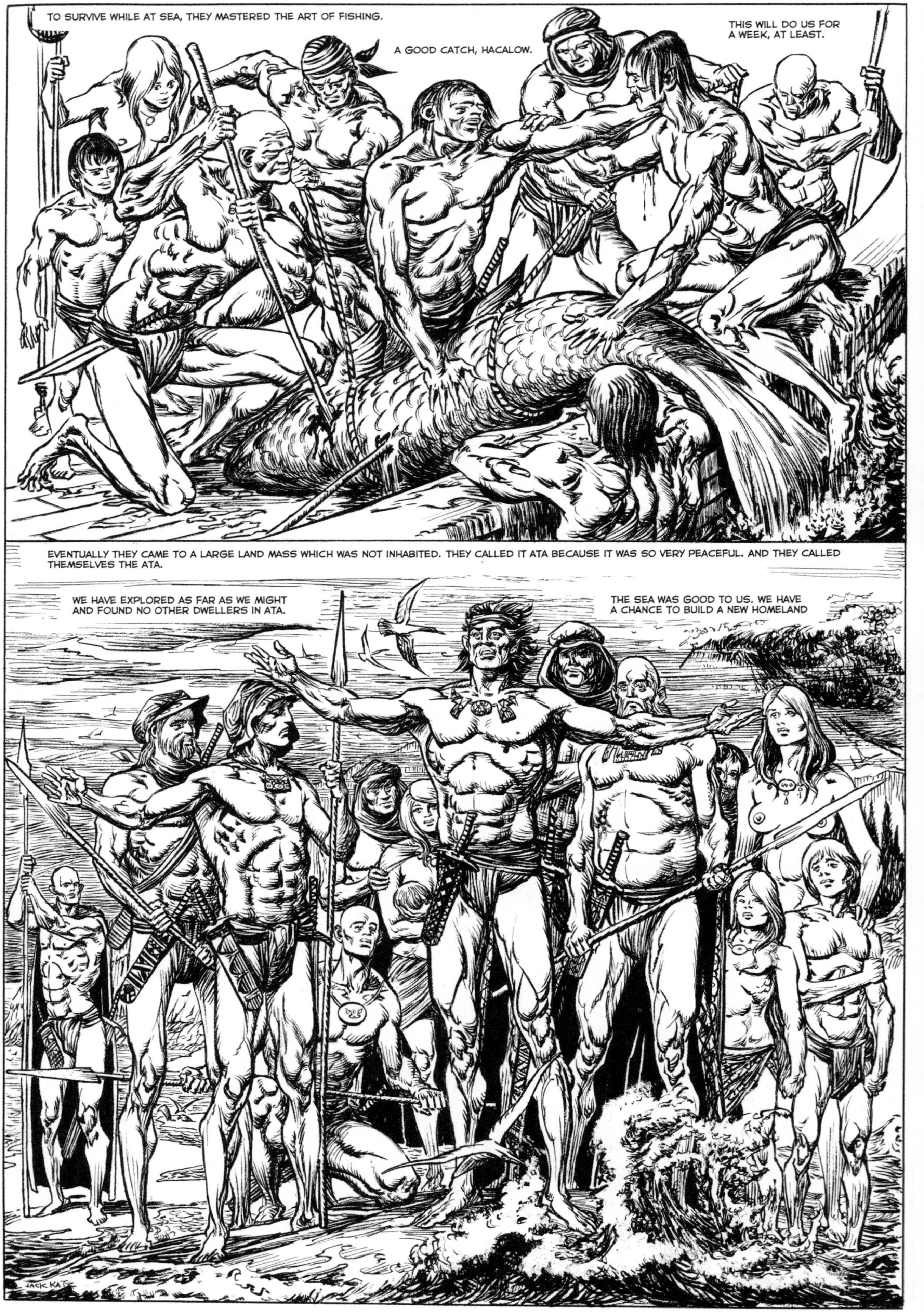
TO SURVIVE WHILE AT SEA, THEY MASTERED THE ART OF FISHING.
A GOOD CATCH, HACALOW.
THIS WILL DO US FOR A WEEK, AT LEAST.
EVENTUALLY THEY CAME TO A LARGE LAND MASS WHICH WAS NOT INHABITED. THEY CALLED IT ATA BECAUSE IT WAS SO VERY PEACEFUL. AND THEY CALLED THEMSELVES THE ATA.
WE HAVE EXPLORED AS FAR AS WE MIGHT AND FOUND NO OTHER DWELLERS IN ATA.
THE SEA WAS GOOD TO US. WE HAVE A CHANCE TO BUILD A NEW HOMELAND

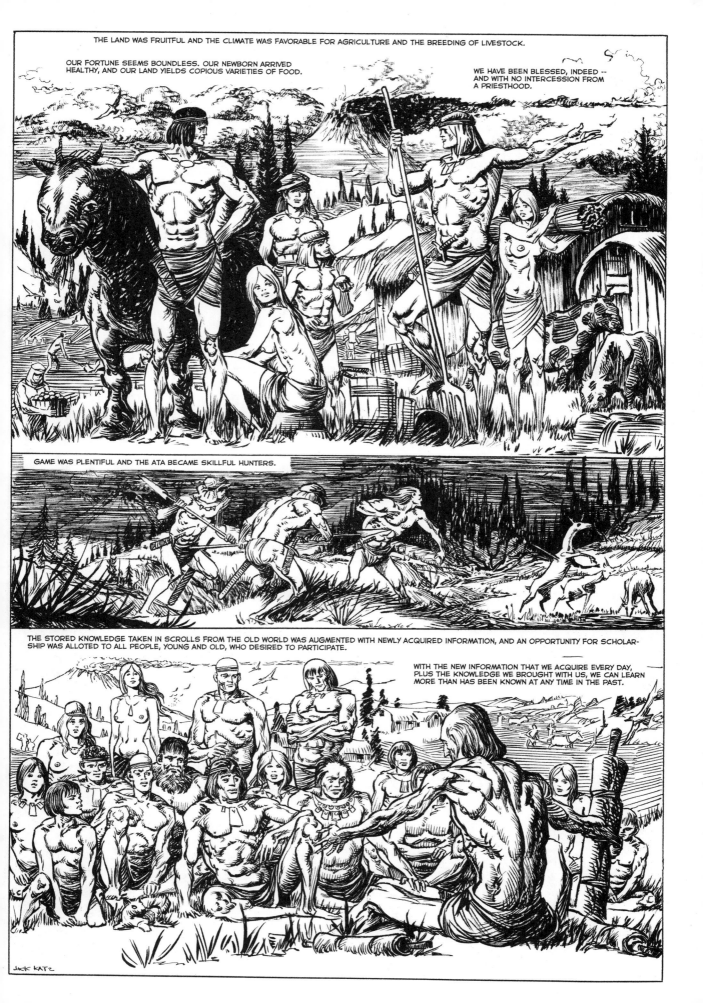

THE LAND WAS FRUITFUL AND THE CLIMATE WAS FAVORABLE FOR AGRICULTURE AND THE BREEDING OF LIVESTOCK.

OUR FORTUNE SEEMS BOUNDLESS. OUR NEWBORN ARRIVED HEALTHY, AND OUR LAND YIELDS COPIOUS VARIETIES OF FOOD.

WE HAVE BEEN BLESSED, INDEED -- AND WITH NO INTERCESSION FROM A PRIESTHOOD.

GAME WAS PLENTIFUL AND THE ATA BECAME SKILLFUL HUNTERS.

THE STORED KNOWLEDGE TAKEN IN SCROLLS FROM THE OLD WORLD WAS AUGMENTED WITH NEWLY ACQUIRED INFORMATION, AND AN OPPORTUNITY FOR SCHOLARSHIP WAS ALLOTED TO ALL PEOPLE, YOUNG AND OLD, WHO DESIRED TO PARTICIPATE.

WITH THE NEW INFORMATION THAT WE ACQUIRE EVERY DAY, PLUS THE KNOWLEDGE WE BROUGHT WITH US, WE CAN LEARN MORE THAN HAS BEEN KNOWN AT ANY TIME IN THE PAST.

JACK KATZ

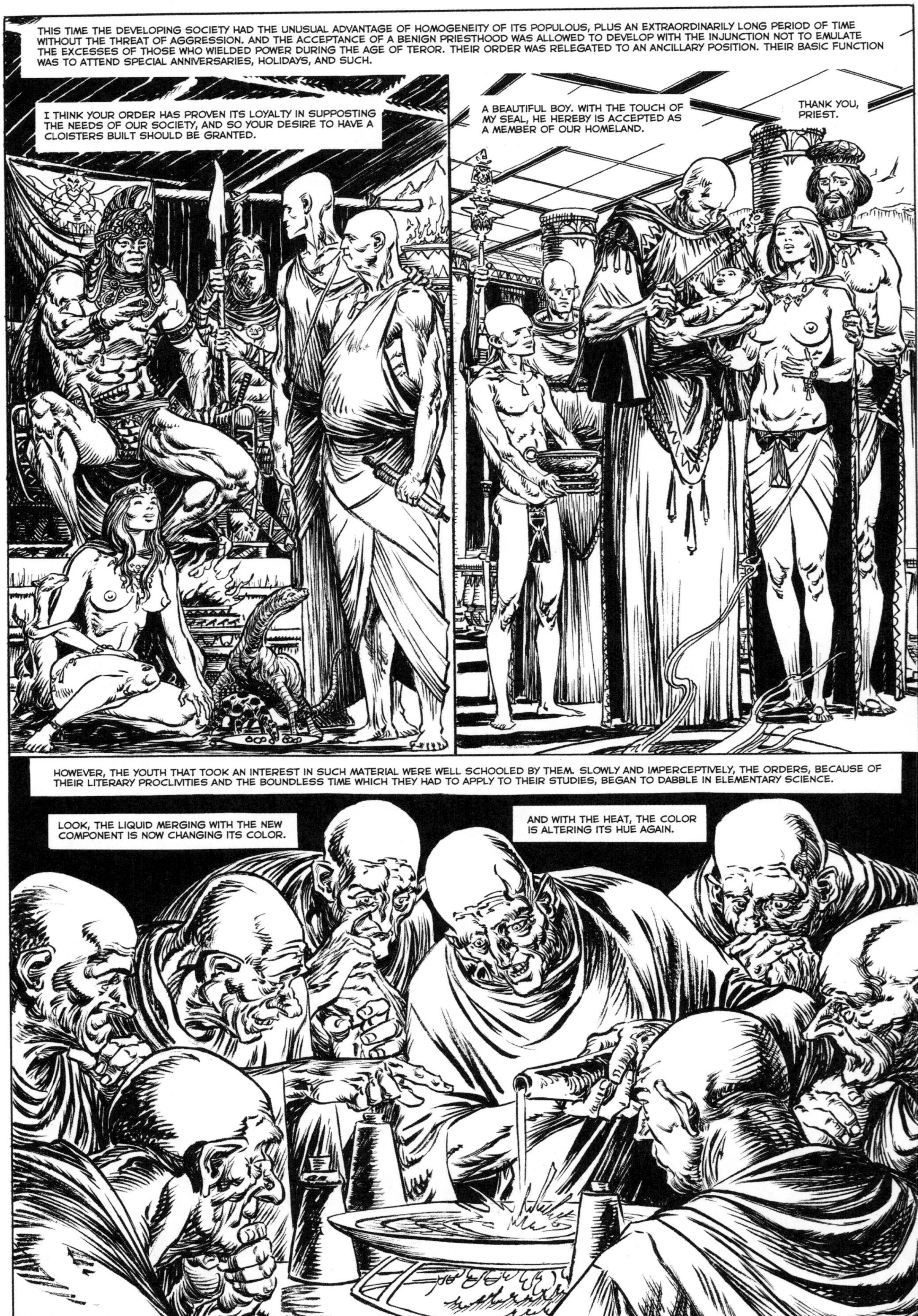
THIS TIME THE DEVELOPING SOCIETY HAD THE UNUSUAL ADVANTAGE OF HOMOGENEITY OF ITS POPULOUS, PLUS AN EXTRAORDINARILY LONG PERIOD OF TIME WITHOUT THE THREAT OF AGGRESSION. AND THE ACCEPTANCE OF A BENIGN PRIESTHOOD WAS ALLOWED TO DEVELOP WITH THE INJUNCTION NOT TO EMULATE THE EXCESSES OF THOSE WHO WIELDED POWER DURING THE AGE OF TEROR. THEIR ORDER WAS RELEGATED TO AN ANCILLARY POSITION. THEIR BASIC FUNCTION WAS TO ATTEND SPECIAL ANNIVERSARIES, HOLIDAYS, AND SUCH.
I THINK YOUR ORDER HAS PROVEN ITS LOYALTY IN SUPPOSTING THE NEEDS OF OUR SOCIETY, AND SO YOUR DESIRE TO HAVE A CLOISTERS BUILT SHOULD BE GRANTED.
A BEAUTIFUL BOY. WITH THE TOUCH OF MY SEAL, HE HEREBY IS ACCEPTED AS A MEMBER OF OUR HOMELAND.
THANK YOU, PRIEST.
HOWEVER, THE YOUTH THAT TOOK AN INTEREST IN SUCH MATERIAL WERE WELL SCHOOLED BY THEM. SLOWLY AND IMPERCEPTIVELY, THE ORDERS, BECAUSE OF THEIR LITERARY PROCLIVITIES AND THE BOUNDLESS TIME WHICH THEY HAD TO APPLY TO THEIR STUDIES, BEGAN TO DABBLE IN ELEMENTARY SCIENCE.
LOOK, THE LIQUID MERGING WITH THE NEW COMPONENT IS NOW CHANGING ITS COLOR.
AND WITH THE HEAT, THE COLOR IS ALTERING ITS HUE AGAIN.
JACK KATZ

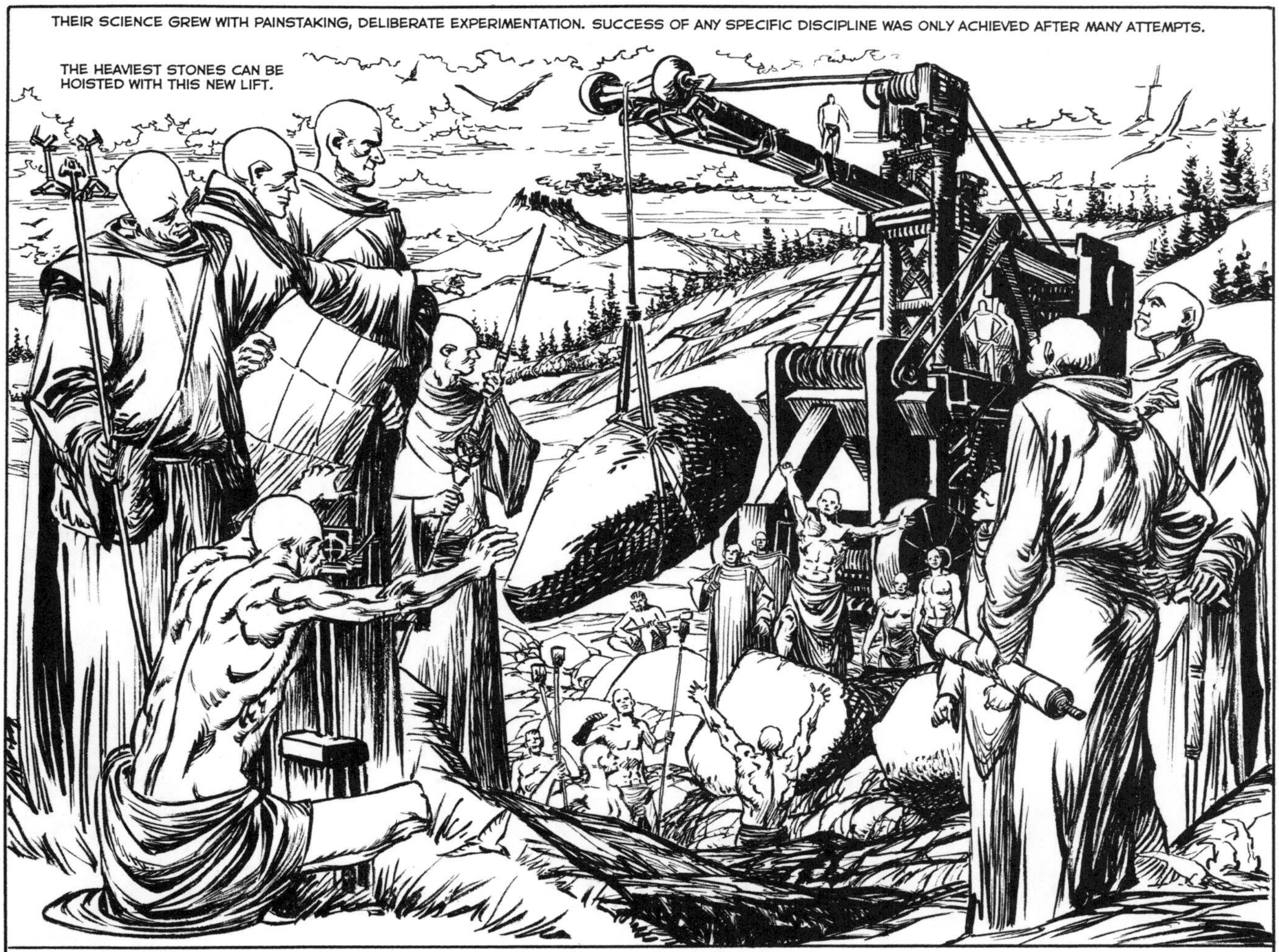
THEIR SCIENCE GREW WITH PAINSTAKING, DELIBERATE EXPERIMENTATION. SUCCESS OF ANY SPECIFIC DISCIPLINE WAS ONLY ACHIEVED AFTER MANY ATTEMPTS.
THE HEAVIEST STONES CAN BE HOISTED WITH THIS NEW LIFT.

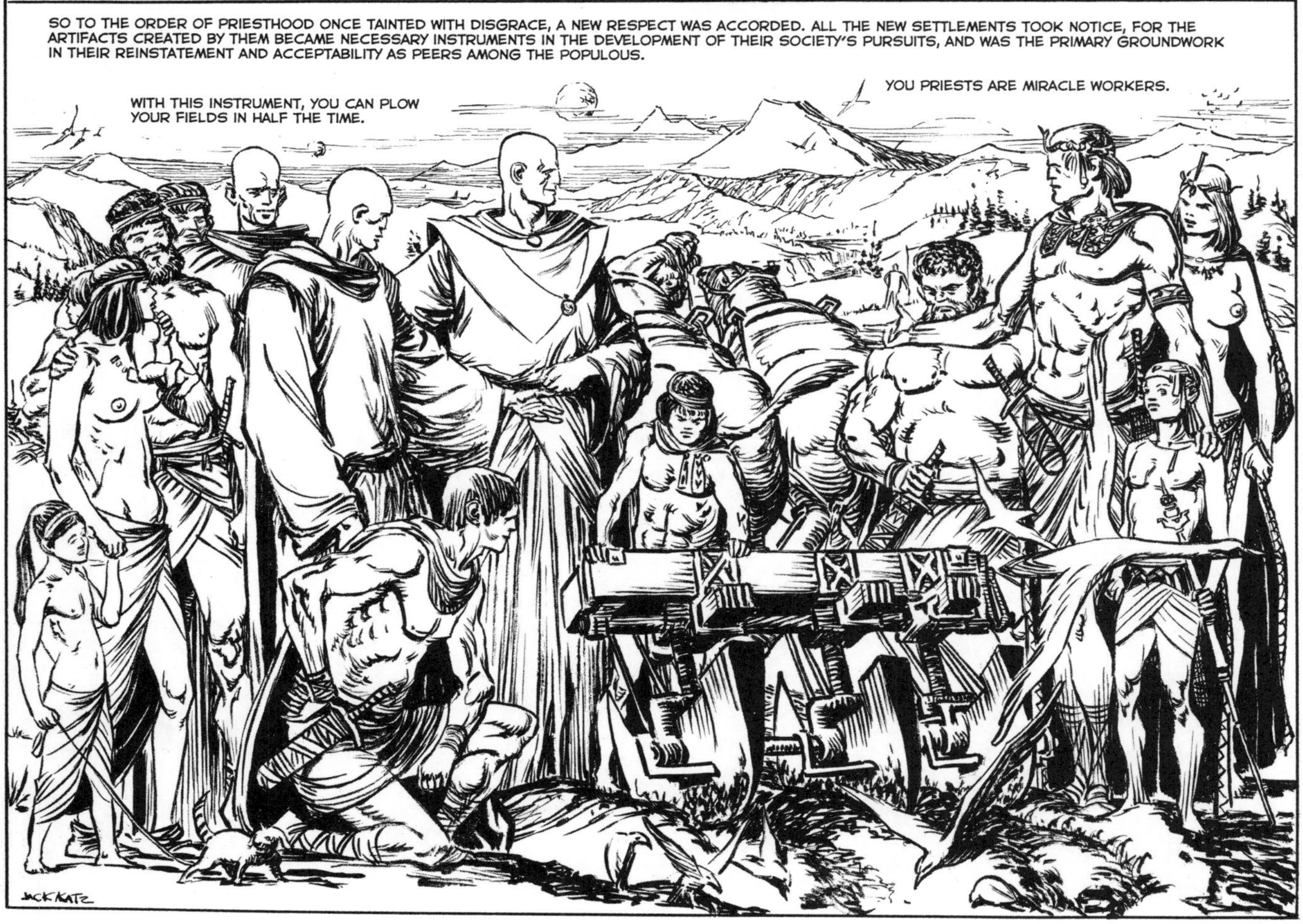
SO TO THE ORDER OF PRIESTHOOD ONCE TAINTED WITH DISGRACE, A NEW RESPECT WAS ACCORDED. ALL THE NEW SETTLEMENTS TOOK NOTICE, FOR THE ARTIFACTS CREATED BY THEM BECAME NECESSARY INSTRUMENTS IN THE DEVELOPMENT OF THEIR SOCIETY'S PURSUITS, AND WAS THE PRIMARY GROUNDWORK IN THEIR REINSTATEMENT AND ACCEPTABILITY AS PEERS AMONG THE POPULOUS.
WITH THIS INSTRUMENT, YOU CAN PLOW YOUR FIELDS IN HALF THE TIME.
YOU PRIESTS ARE MIRACLE WORKERS.
JACK KATZ

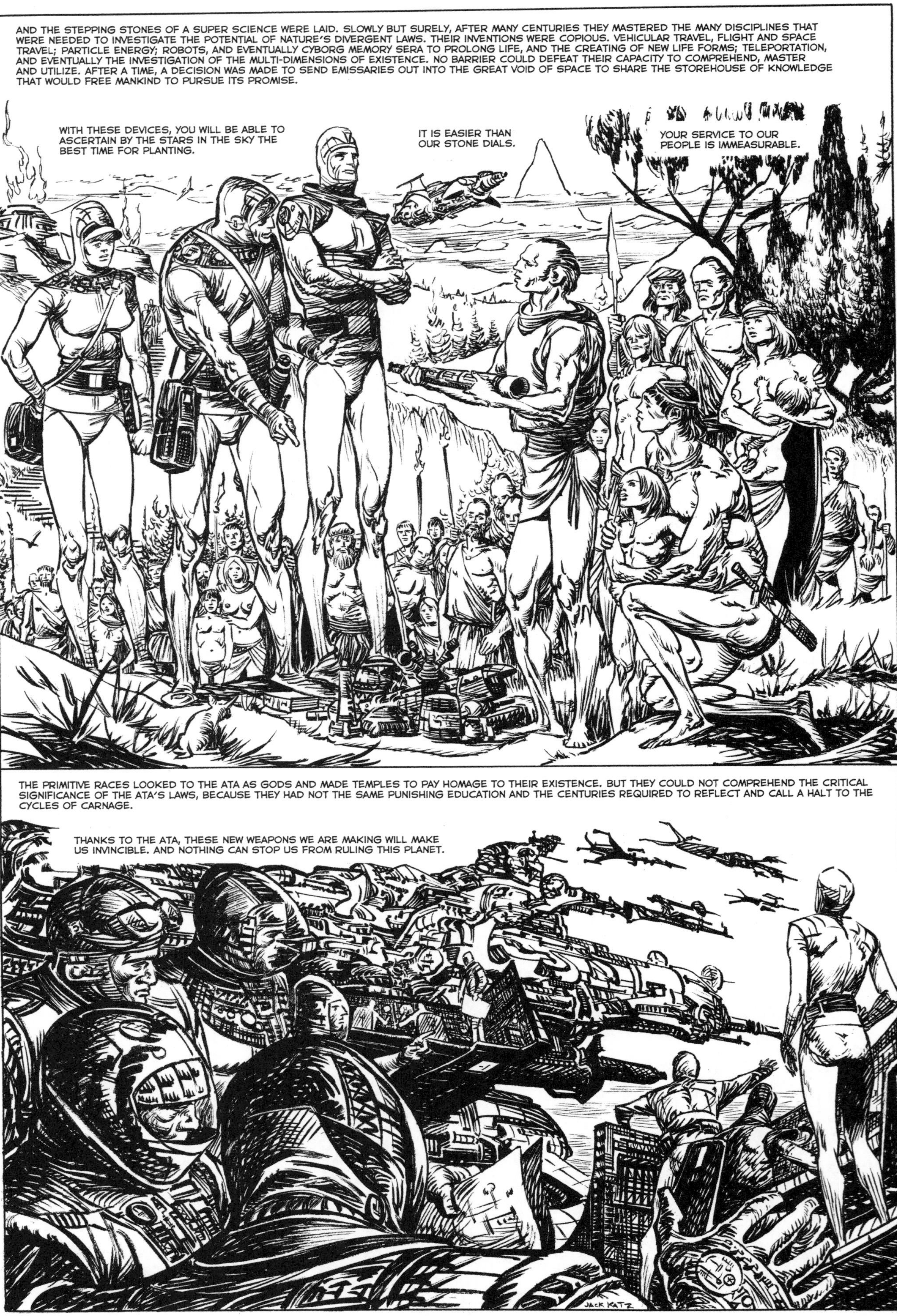
AND THE STEPPING STONES OF A SUPER SCIENCE WERE LAID. SLOWLY BUT SURELY, AFTER MANY CENTURIES THEY MASTERED THE MANY DISCIPLINES THAT WERE NEEDED TO INVESTIGATE THE POTENTIAL OF NATURE'S DIVERGENT LAWS. THEIR INVENTIONS WERE COPIOUS. VEHICULAR TRAVEL, FLIGHT AND SPACE TRAVEL; PARTICLE ENERGY; ROBOTS, AND EVENTUALLY CYBORG MEMORY SERA TO PROLONG LIFE, AND THE CREATING OF NEW LIFE FORMS; TELEPORTATION, AND EVENTUALLY THE INVESTIGATION OF THE MULTI-DIMENSIONS OF EXISTENCE. NO BARRIER COULD DEFEAT THEIR CAPACITY TO COMPREHEND, MASTER AND UTILIZE. AFTER A TIME, A DECISION WAS MADE TO SEND EMISSARIES OUT INTO THE GREAT VOID OF SPACE TO SHARE THE STOREHOUSE OF KNOWLEDGE THAT WOULD FREE MANKIND TO PURSUE ITS PROMISE.
WITH THESE DEVICES, YOU WILL BE ABLE TO ASCERTAIN BY THE STARS IN THE SKY THE BEST TIME FOR PLANTING.
IT IS EASIER THAN OUR STONE DIALS.
YOUR SERVICE TO OUR PEOPLE IS IMMEASURABLE.
THE PRIMITIVE RACES LOOKED TO THE ATA AS GODS AND MADE TEMPLES TO PAY HOMAGE TO THEIR EXISTENCE. BUT THEY COULD NOT COMPREHEND THE CRITICAL SIGNIFICANCE OF THE ATA'S LAWS, BECAUSE THEY HAD NOT THE SAME PUNISHING EDUCATION AND THE CENTURIES REQUIRED TO REFLECT AND CALL A HALT TO THE CYCLES OF CARNAGE.
THANKS TO THE ATA, THESE NEW WEAPONS WE ARE MAKING WILL MAKE US INVINCIBLE. AND NOTHING CAN STOP US FROM RULING THIS PLANET.
JACK KATZ

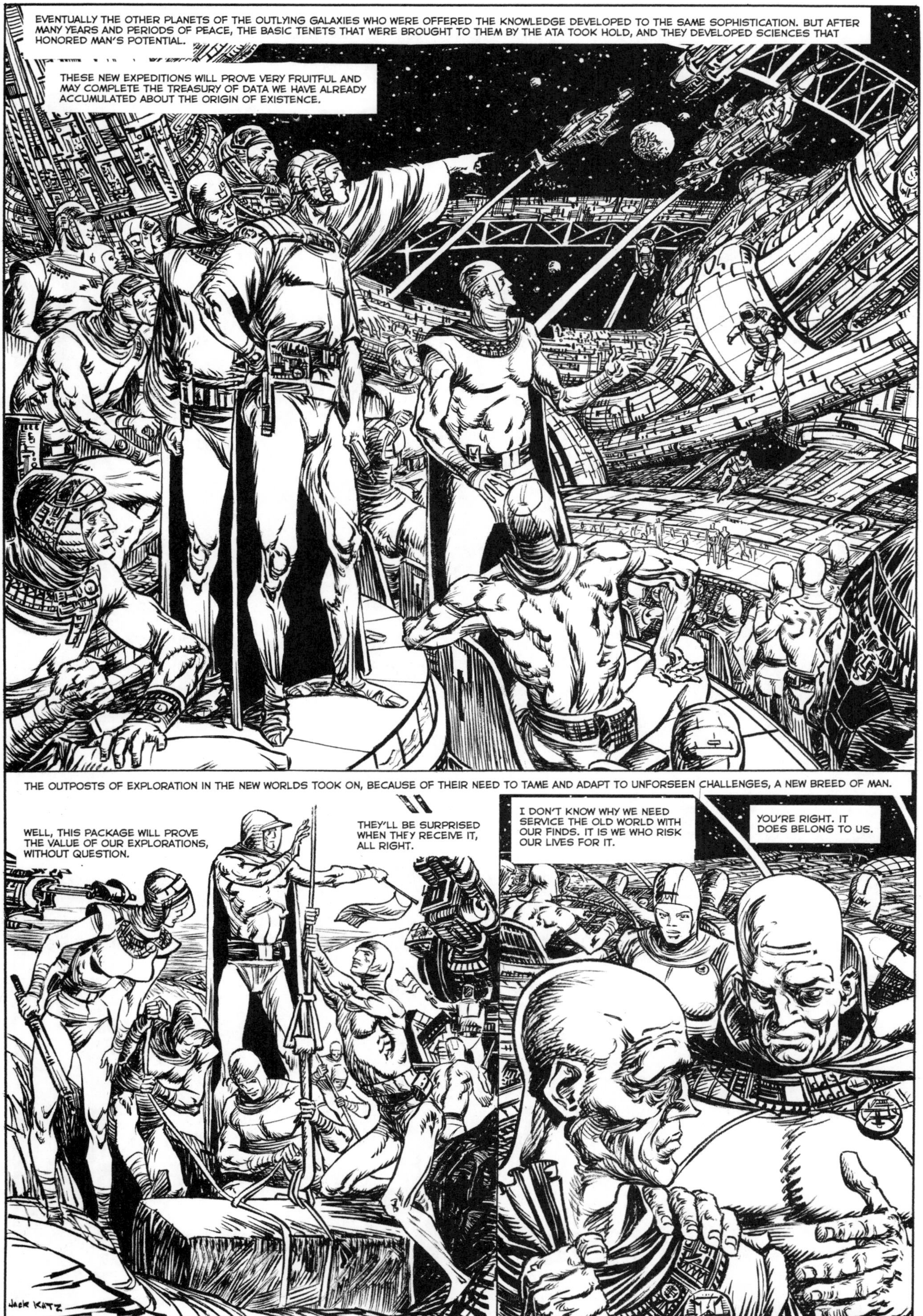
EVENTUALLY THE OTHER PLANETS OF THE OUTLYING GALAXIES WHO WERE OFFERED THE KNOWLEDGE DEVELOPED TO THE SAME SOPHISTICATION. BUT AFTER MANY YEARS AND PERIODS OF PEACE, THE BASIC TENETS THAT WERE BROUGHT TO THEM BY THE ATA TOOK HOLD, AND THEY DEVELOPED SCIENCES THAT HONORED MAN'S POTENTIAL.
THESE NEW EXPEDITIONS WILL PROVE VERY FRUITFUL AND MAY COMPLETE THE TREASURY OF DATA WE HAVE ALREADY ACCUMULATED ABOUT THE ORIGIN OF EXISTENCE.
THE OUTPOSTS OF EXPLORATION IN THE NEW WORLDS TOOK ON, BECAUSE OF THEIR NEED TO TAME AND ADAPT TO UNFORSEEN CHALLENGES, A NEW BREED OF MAN.
WELL, THIS PACKAGE WILL PROVE THE VALUE OF OUR EXPLORATIONS, WITHOUT QUESTION.
THEY'LL BE SURPRISED WHEN THEY RECEIVE IT, ALL RIGHT.
I DON'T KNOW WHY WE NEED SERVICE THE OLD WORLD WITH OUR FINDS. IT IS WE WHO RISK OUR LIVES FOR IT.
YOU'RE RIGHT. IT DOES BELONG TO US.
JACK KATZ

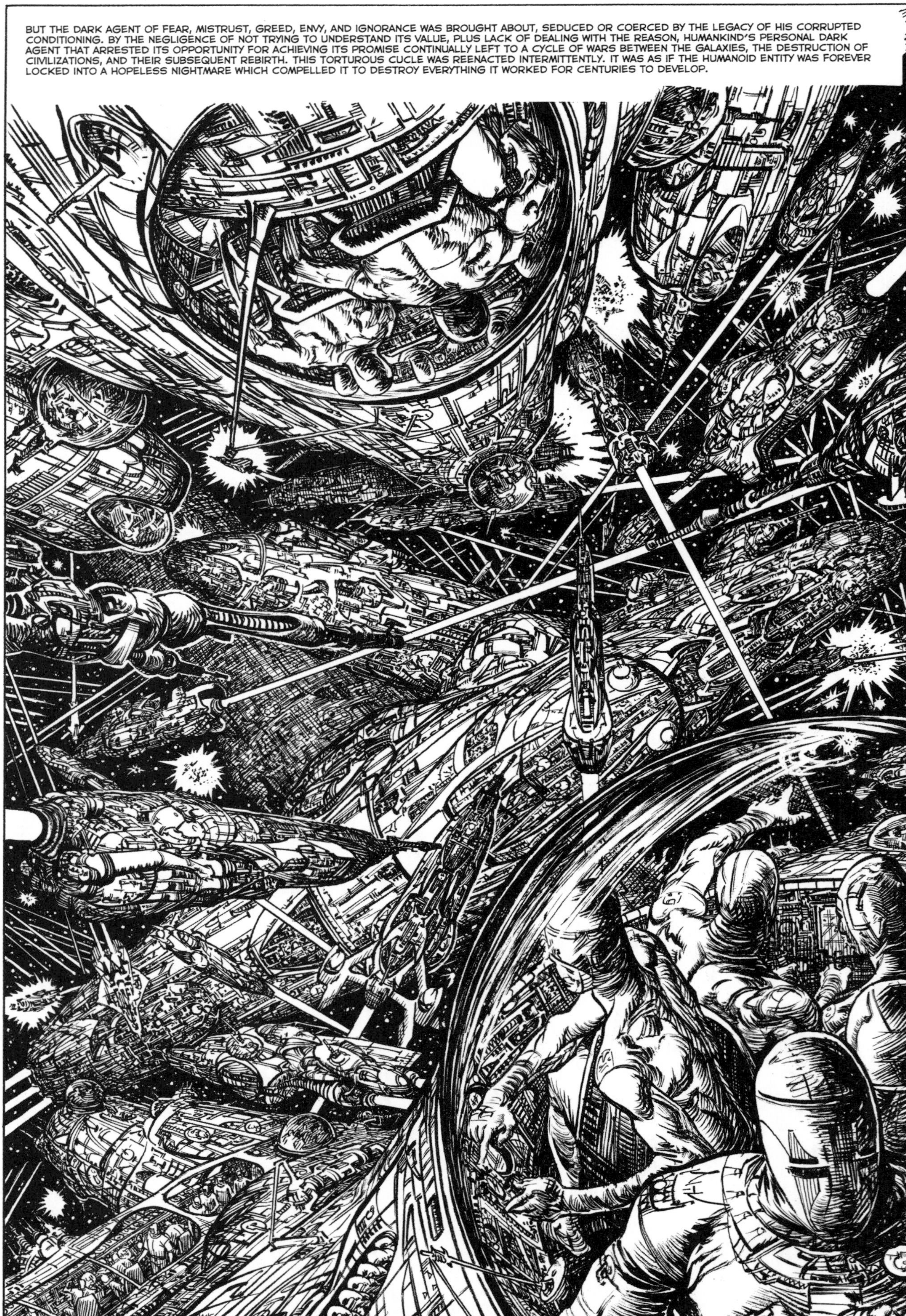
BUT THE DARK AGENT OF FEAR, MISTRUST, GREED, ENVY, AND IGNORANCE WAS BROUGHT ABOUT, SEDUCED OR COERCED BY THE LEGACY OF HIS CORRUPTED CONDITIONING. BY THE NEGLIGENCE OF NOT TRYING TO UNDERSTAND ITS VALUE, PLUS LACK OF DEALING WITH THE REASON, HUMANKIND'S PERSONAL DARK AGENT THAT ARRESTED ITS OPPORTUNITY FOR ACHIEVING ITS PROMISE CONTINUALLY LEFT TO A CYCLE OF WARS BETWEEN THE GALAXIES, THE DESTRUCTION OF CIVILIZATIONS, AND THEIR SUBSEQUENT REBIRTH. THIS TORTUROUS CUCLE WAS REENACTED INTERMITTENTLY. IT WAS AS IF THE HUMANOID ENTITY WAS FOREVER LOCKED INTO A HOPELESS NIGHTMARE WHICH COMPELLED IT TO DESTROY EVERYTHING IT WORKED FOR CENTURIES TO DEVELOP.

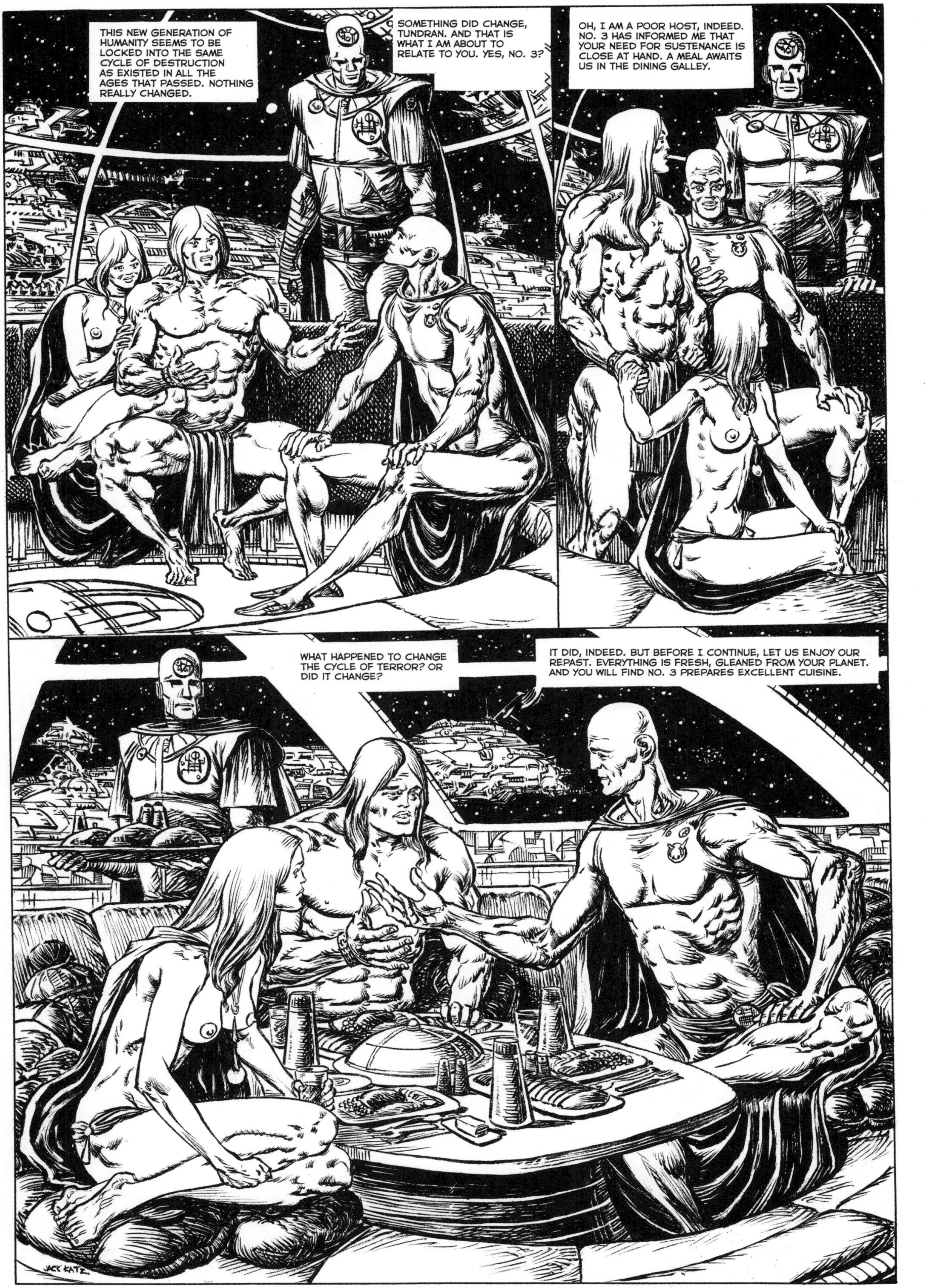
THIS NEW GENERATION OF HUMANITY SEEMS TO BE LOCKED INTO THE SAME CYCLE OF DESTRUCTION AS EXISTED IN ALL THE AGES THAT PASSED. NOTHING REALLY CHANGED.
SOMETHING DID CHANGE, TUNDRAN. AND THAT IS WHAT I AM ABOUT TO RELATE TO YOU. YES, NO. 3?
OH, I AM A POOR HOST, INDEED. NO. 3 HAS INFORMED ME THAT YOUR NEED FOR SUSTENANCE IS CLOSE AT HAND. A MEAL AWAITS US IN THE DINING GALLEY.
WHAT HAPPENED TO CHANGE THE CYCLE OF TERROR? OR DID IT CHANGE?
IT DID, INDEED. BUT BEFORE I CONTINUE, LET US ENJOY OUR REPAST. EVERYTHING IS FRESH, GLEANED FROM YOUR PLANET. AND YOU WILL FIND NO. 3 PREPARES EXCELLENT CUISINE.
JACK KATZ

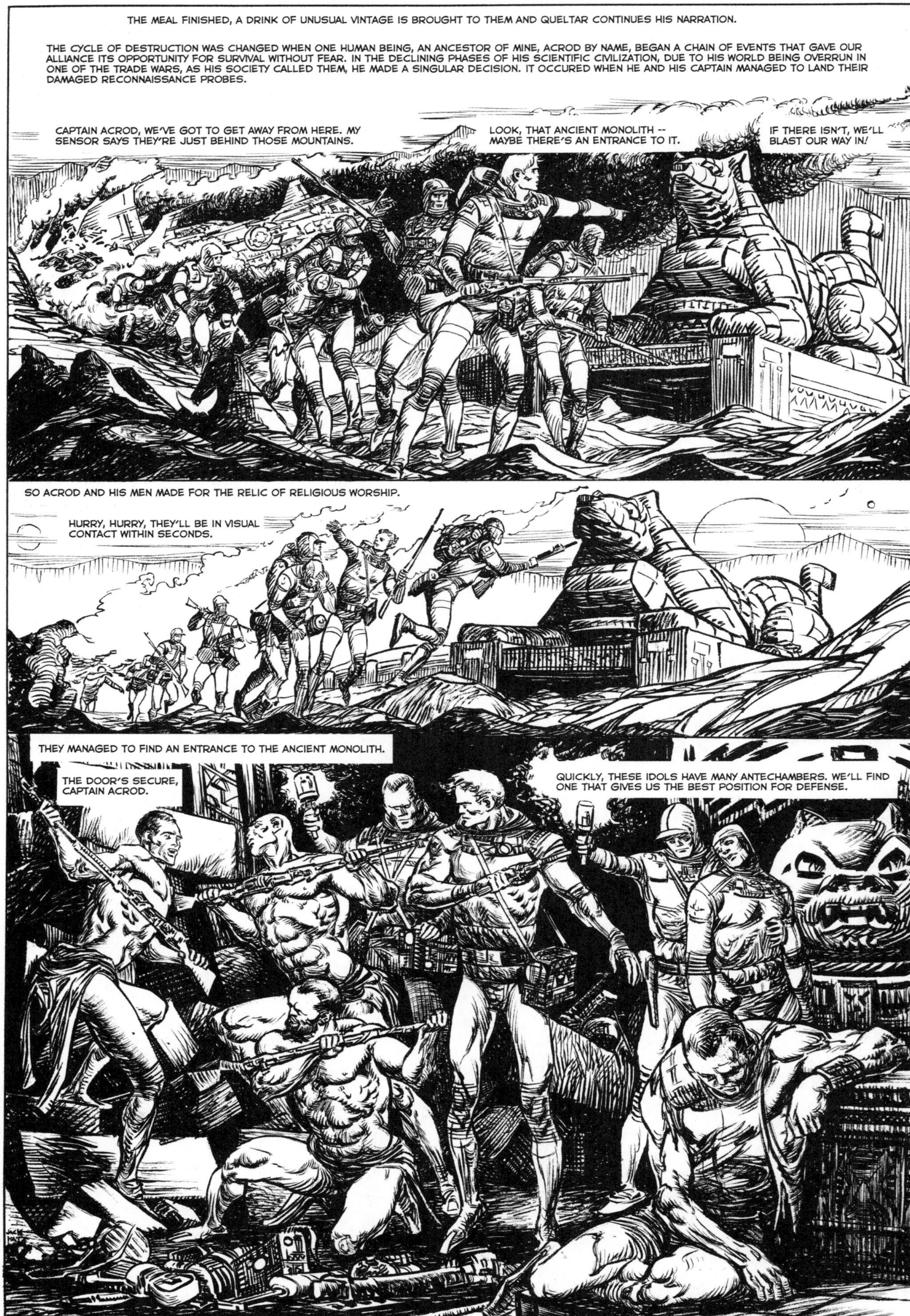
THE MEAL FINISHED, A DRINK OF UNUSUAL VINTAGE IS BROUGHT TO THEM AND QUELTAR CONTINUES HIS NARRATION.
THE CYCLE OF DESTRUCTION WAS CHANGED WHEN ONE HUMAN BEING, AN ANCESTOR OF MINE, ACROD BY NAME, BEGAN A CHAIN OF EVENTS THAT GAVE OUR ALLIANCE ITS OPPORTUNITY FOR SURVIVAL WITHOUT FEAR. IN THE DECLINING PHASES OF HIS SCIENTIFIC CIVILIZATION, DUE TO HIS WORLD BEING OVERRUN IN ONE OF THE TRADE WARS, AS HIS SOCIETY CALLED THEM, HE MADE A SINGULAR DECISION. IT OCCURED WHEN HE AND HIS CAPTAIN MANAGED TO LAND THEIR DAMAGED RECONNAISSANCE PROBES.
CAPTAIN ACROD, WE'VE GOT TO GET AWAY FROM HERE. MY SENSOR SAYS THEY'RE JUST BEHIND THOSE MOUNTAINS.
LOOK, THAT ANCIENT MONOLITH -- MAYBE THERE'S AN ENTRANCE TO IT.
IF THERE ISN'T, WE'LL BLAST OUR WAY IN!
SO ACROD AND HIS MEN MADE FOR THE RELIC OF RELIGIOUS WORSHIP.
HURRY, HURRY, THEY'LL BE IN VISUAL CONTACT WITHIN SECONDS.
THEY MANAGED TO FIND AN ENTRANCE TO THE ANCIENT MONOLITH.
THE DOOR'S SECURE, CAPTAIN ACROD.
QUICKLY, THESE IDOLS HAVE MANY ANTECHAMBERS. WE'LL FIND ONE THAT GIVES US THE BEST POSITION FOR DEFENSE.

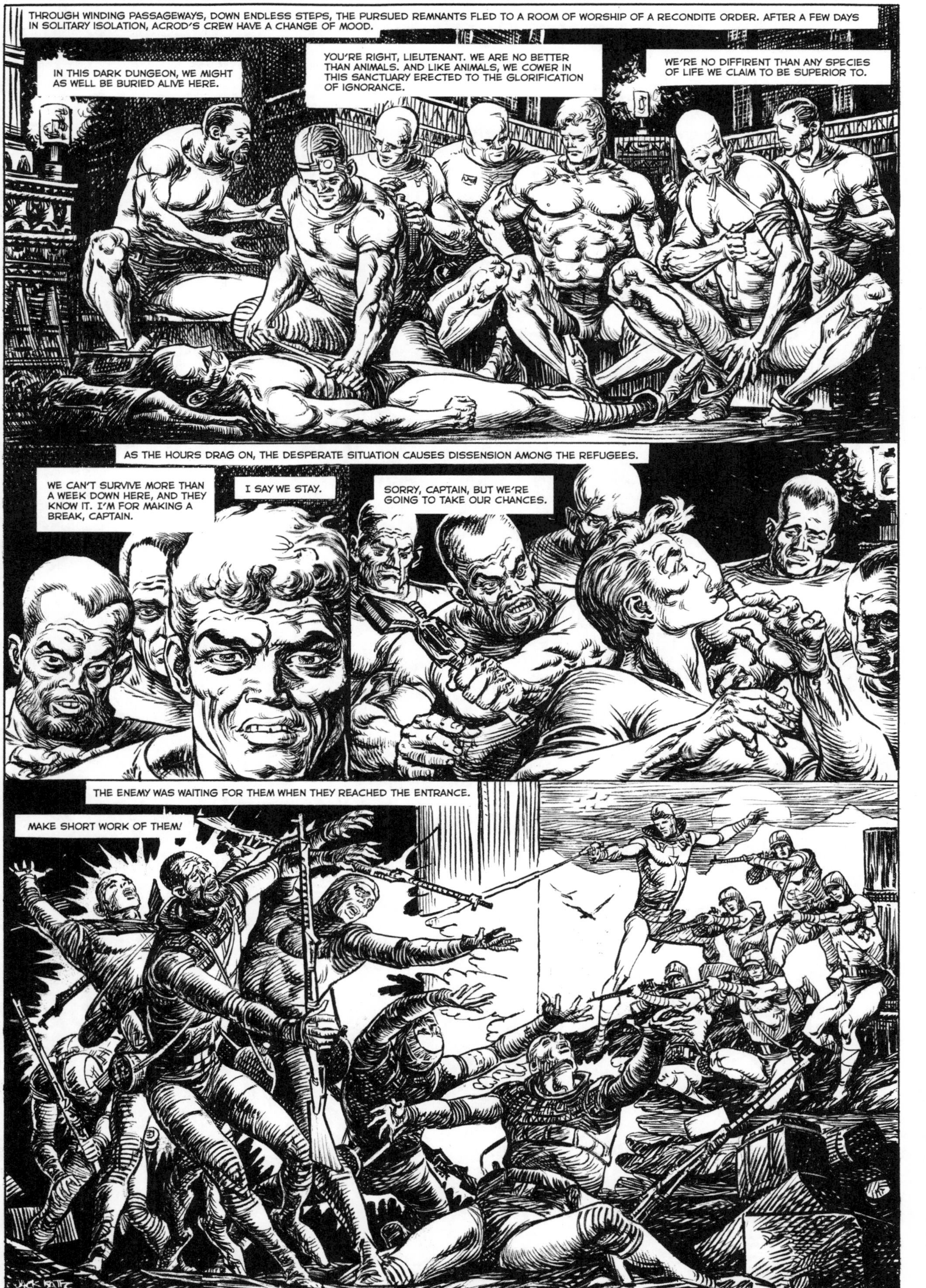
THROUGH WINDING PASSAGEWAYS, DOWN ENDLESS STEPS, THE PURSUED REMNANTS FLED TO A ROOM OF WORSHIP OF A RECONDITE ORDER. AFTER A FEW DAYS IN SOLITARY ISOLATION, ACROD'S CREW HAVE A CHANGE OF MOOD.
IN THIS DARK DUNGEON, WE MIGHT AS WELL BE BURIED ALIVE HERE.
YOU'RE RIGHT, LIEUTENANT. WE ARE NO BETTER THAN ANIMALS. AND LIKE ANIMALS, WE COWER IN THIS SANCTUARY ERECTED TO THE GLORIFICATION OF IGNORANCE.
WE'RE NO DIFFIRENT THAN ANY SPECIES OF LIFE WE CLAIM TO BE SUPERIOR TO.
AS THE HOURS DRAG ON, THE DESPERATE SITUATION CAUSES DISSENSION AMONG THE REFUGEES.
WE CAN'T SURVIVE MORE THAN A WEEK DOWN HERE, AND THEY KNOW IT. I'M FOR MAKING A BREAK, CAPTAIN.
I SAY WE STAY.
SORRY, CAPTAIN, BUT WE'RE GOING TO TAKE OUR CHANCES.
THE ENEMY WAS WAITING FOR THEM WHEN THEY REACHED THE ENTRANCE.
MAKE SHORT WORK OF THEM!
JACK KATZ

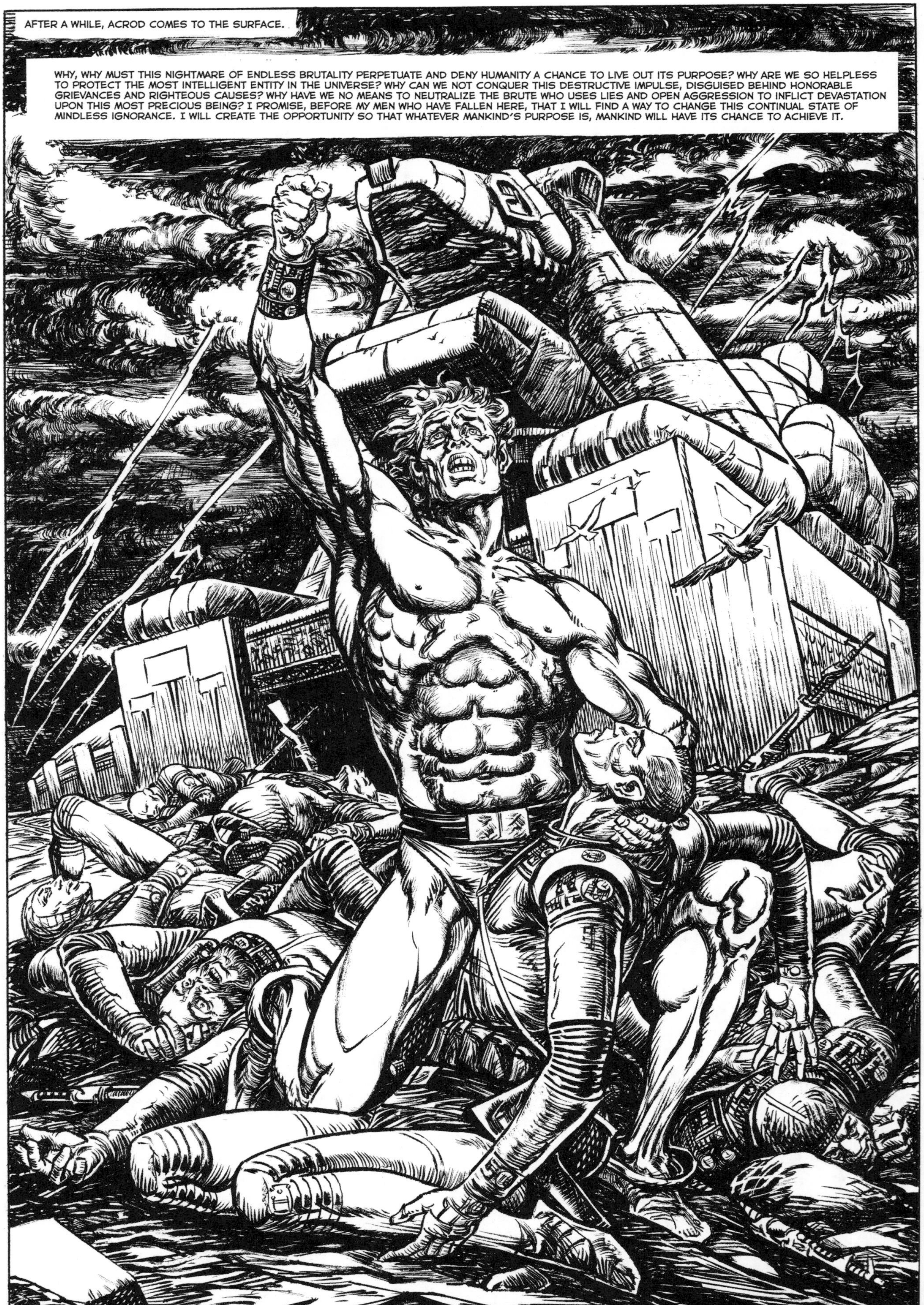
AFTER A WHILE, ACROD COMES TO THE SURFACE.
WHY, WHY MUST THIS NIGHTMARE OF ENDLESS BRUTALITY PERPETUATE AND DENY HUMANITY A CHANCE TO LIVE OUT ITS PURPOSE? WHY ARE WE SO HELPLESS TO PROTECT THE MOST INTELLIGENT ENTITY IN THE UNIVERSE? WHY CAN WE NOT CONQUER THIS DESTRUCTIVE IMPULSE, DISGUISED BEHIND HONORABLE GRIEVANCES AND RIGHTEOUS CAUSES? WHY HAVE WE NO MEANS TO NEUTRALIZE THE BRUTE WHO USES LIES AND OPEN AGGRESSION TO INFLICT DEVASTATION UPON THIS MOST PRECIOUS BEING? I PROMISE, BEFORE MY MEN WHO HAVE FALLEN HERE, THAT I WILL FIND A WAY TO CHANGE THIS CONTINUAL STATE OF MINDLESS IGNORANCE. I WILL CREATE THE OPPORTUNITY SO THAT WHATEVER MANKIND'S PURPOSE IS, MANKIND WILL HAVE ITS CHANCE TO ACHIEVE IT.
JACK KATZ

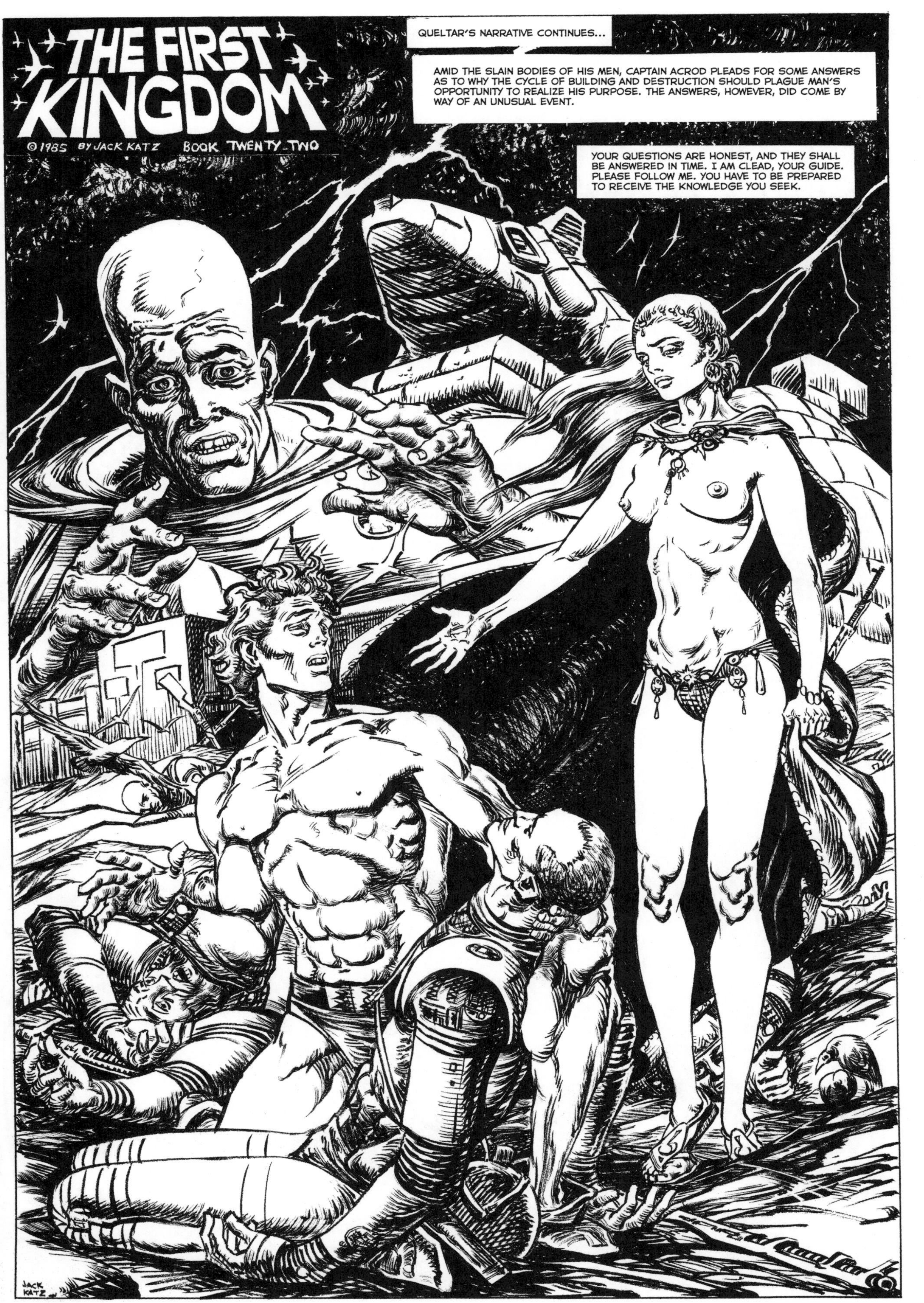
THE FIRST KINGDOM
©1985 BY JACK KATZ BOOK TWENTY-TWO
QUELTAR'S NARRATIVE CONTINUES...
AMID THE SLAIN BODIES OF HIS MEN, CAPTAIN ACROD PLEADS FOR SOME ANSWERS AS TO WHY THE CYCLE OF BUILDING AND DESTRUCTION SHOULD PLAGUE MAN'S OPPORTUNITY TO REALIZE HIS PURPOSE. THE ANSWERS, HOWEVER, DID COME BY WAY OF AN UNUSUAL EVENT.
YOUR QUESTIONS ARE HONEST, AND THEY SHALL BE ANSWERED IN TIME. I AM CLEAD, YOUR GUIDE. PLEASE FOLLOW ME. YOU HAVE TO BE PREPARED TO RECEIVE THE KNOWLEDGE YOU SEEK.
JACK KATZ

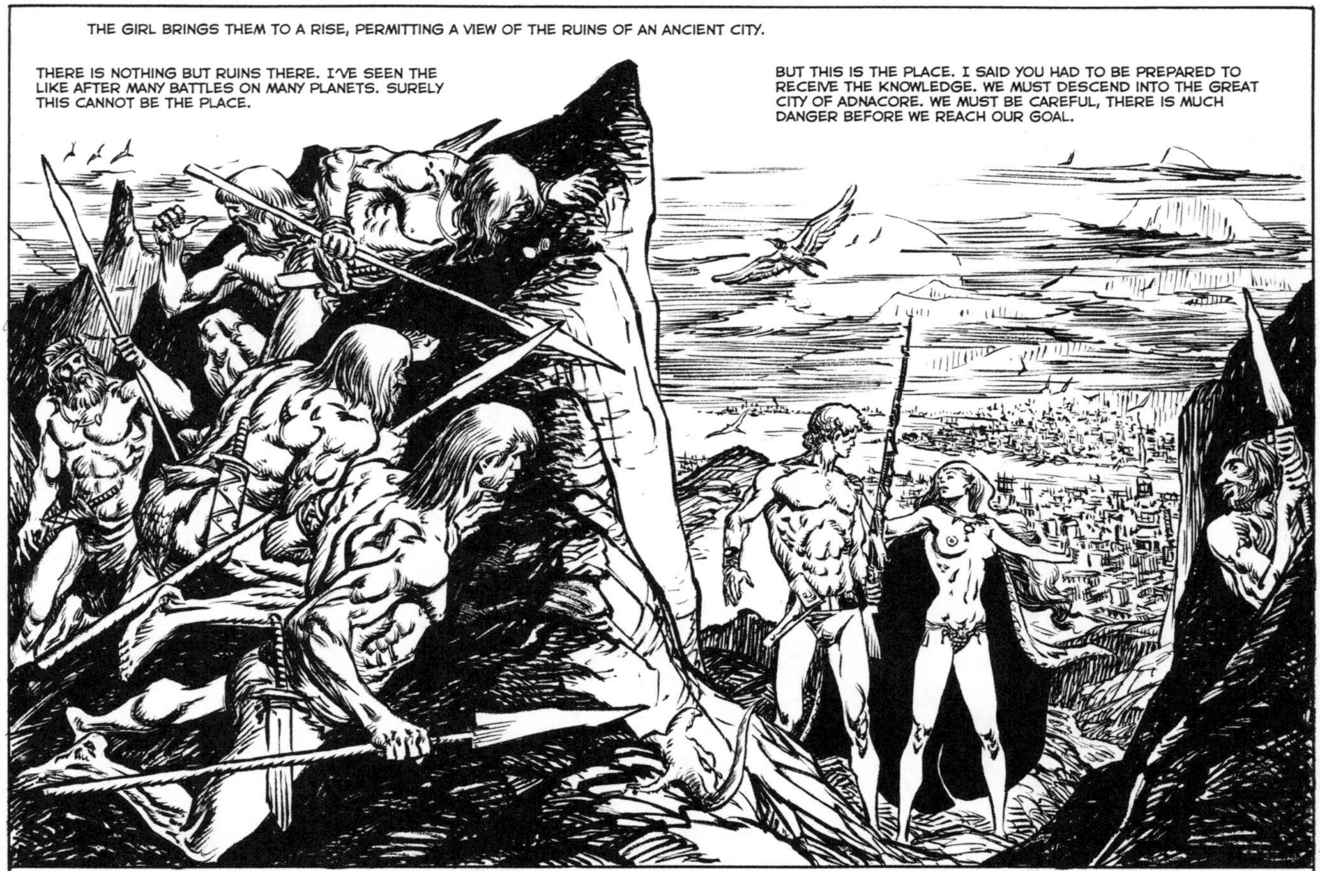
THE GIRL BRINGS THEM TO A RISE, PERMITTING A VIEW OF THE RUINS OF AN ANCIENT CITY.
THERE IS NOTHING BUT RUINS THERE. I'VE SEEN THE LIKE AFTER MANY BATTLES ON MANY PLANETS. SURELY THIS CANNOT BE THE PLACE.
BUT THIS IS THE PLACE. I SAID YOU HAD TO BE PREPARED TO RECEIVE THE KNOWLEDGE. WE MUST DESCEND INTO THE GREAT CITY OF ADNACORE. WE MUST BE CAREFUL, THERE IS MUCH DANGER BEFORE WE REACH OUR GOAL.

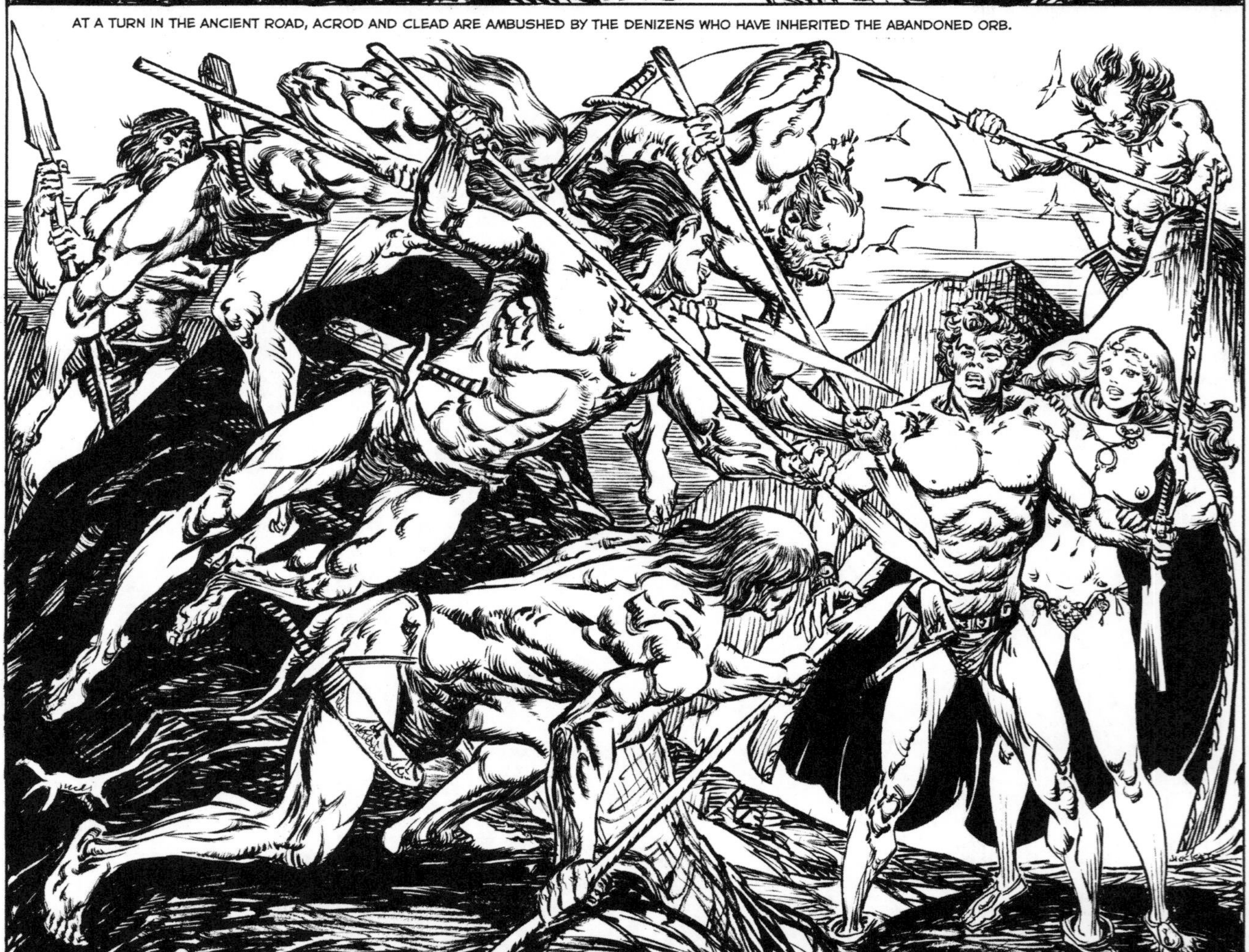
AT A TURN IN THE ANCIENT ROAD, ACROD AND CLEAD ARE AMBUSHED BY THE DENIZENS WHO HAVE INHERITED THE ABANDONED ORB.

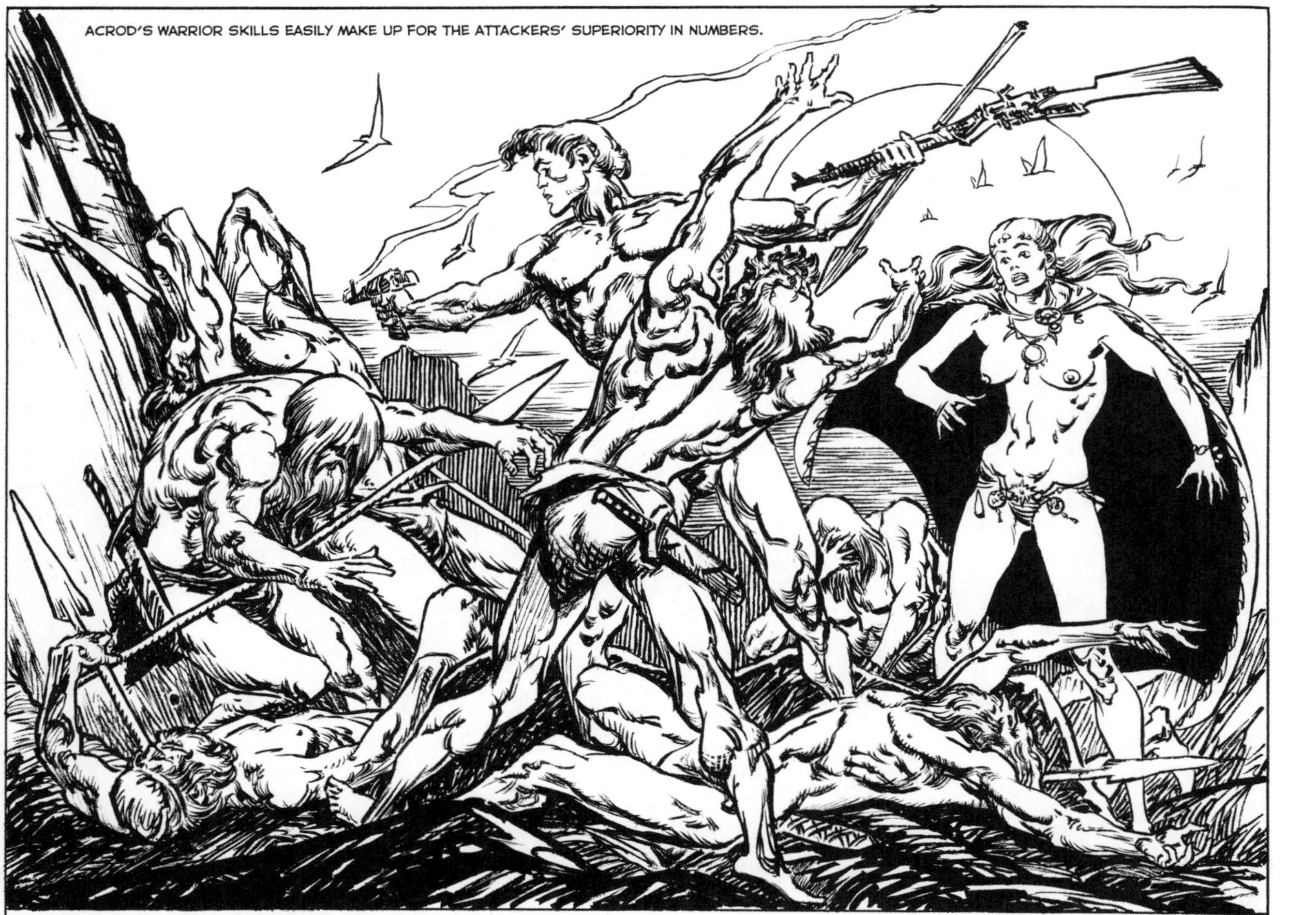
ACROD'S WARRIOR SKILLS EASILY MAKE UP FOR THE ATTACKERS' SUPERIORITY IN NUMBERS.

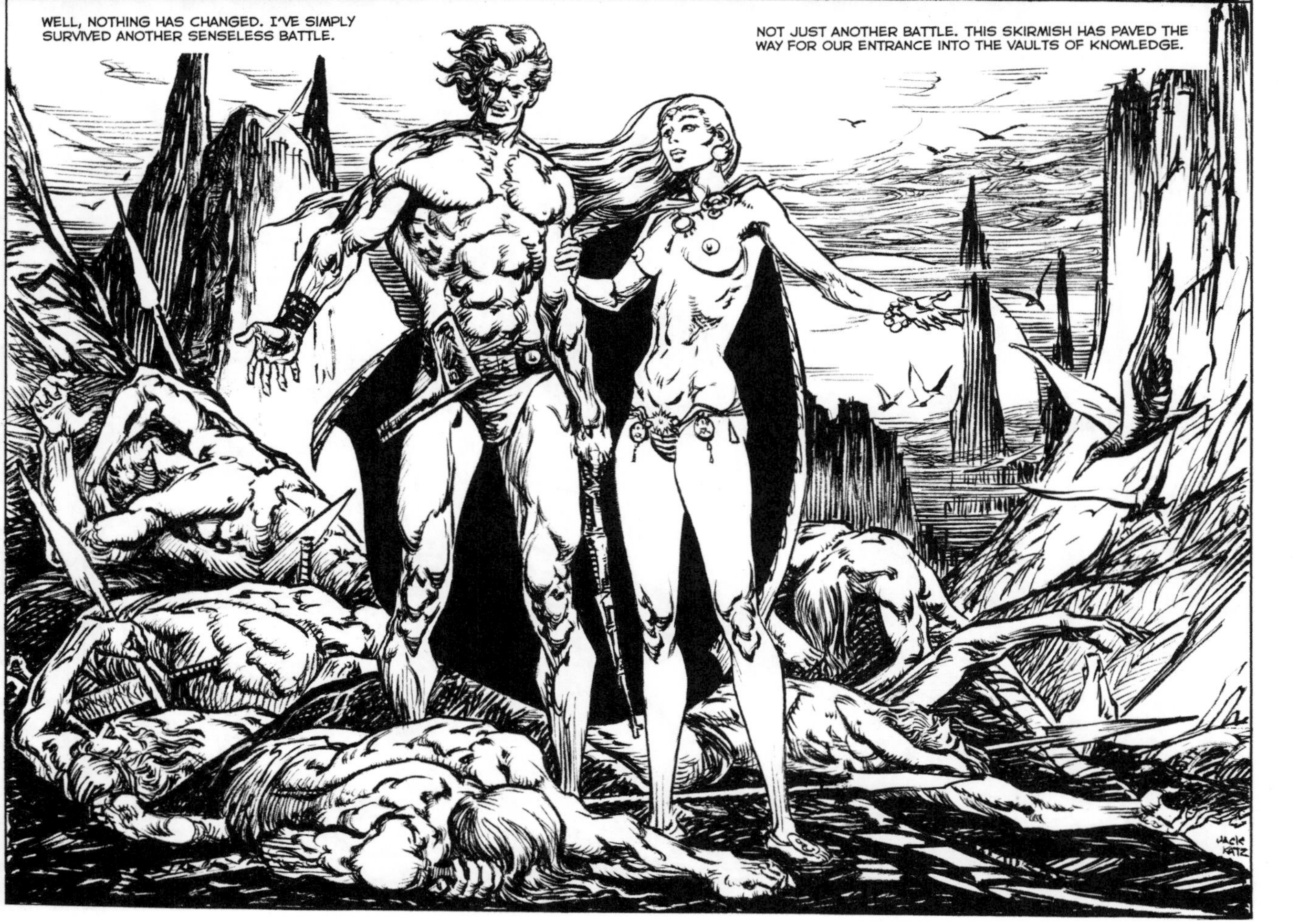
WELL, NOTHING HAS CHANGED. I'VE SIMPLY SURVIVED ANOTHER SENSELESS BATTLE.
NOT JUST ANOTHER BATTLE. THIS SKIRMISH HAS PAVED THE WAY FOR OUR ENTRANCE INTO THE VAULTS OF KNOWLEDGE.
JACK KATZ

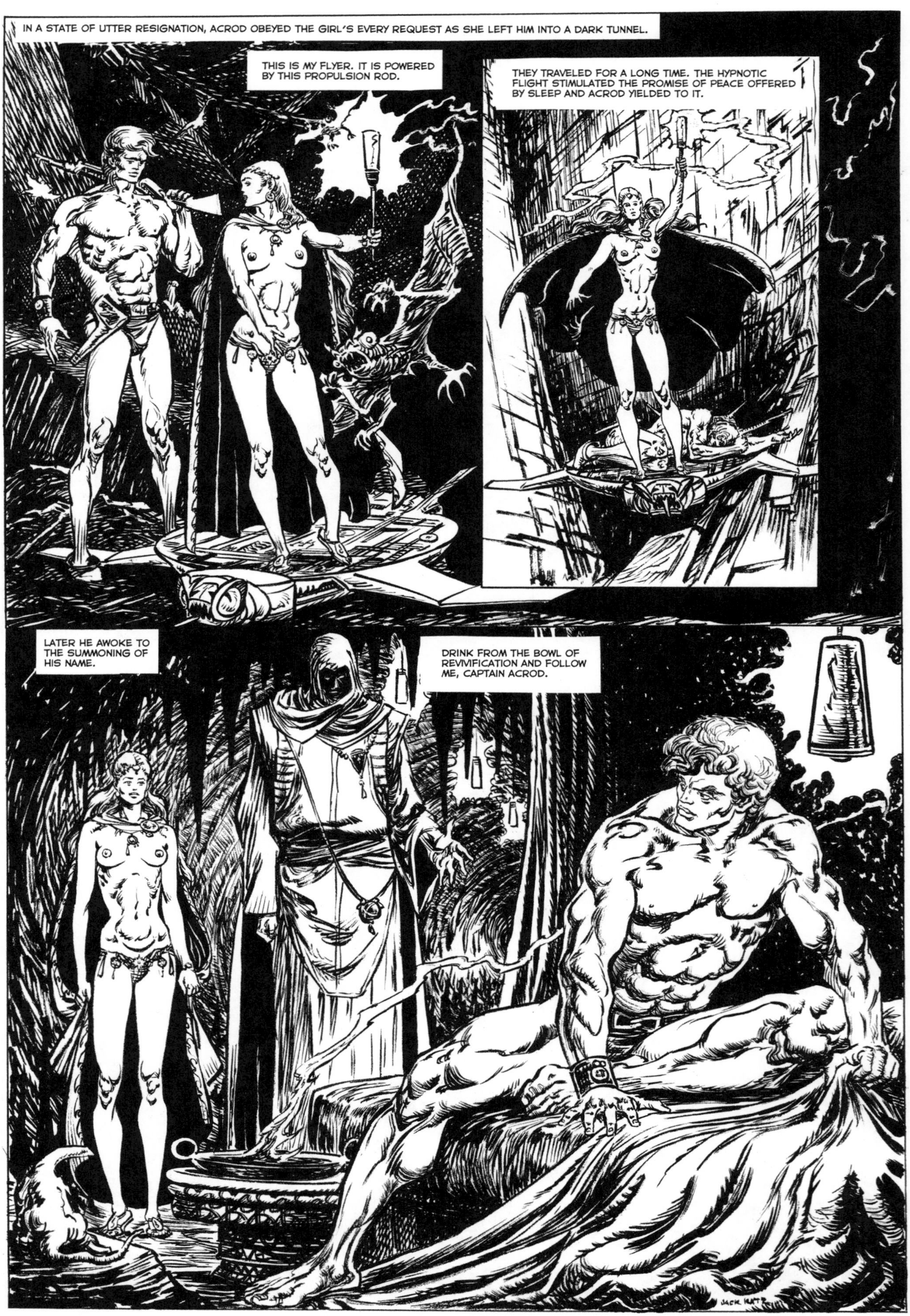
IN A STATE OF UTTER RESIGNATION, ACROD OBEYED THE GIRL'S EVERY REQUEST AS SHE LEFT HIM INTO A DARK TUNNEL.
THIS IS MY FLYER. IT IS POWERED BY THIS PROPULSION ROD.
THEY TRAVELED FOR A LONG TIME. THE HYPNOTIC FLIGHT STIMULATED THE PROMISE OF PEACE OFFERED BY SLEEP AND ACROD YIELDED TO IT.
LATER HE AWOKE TO THE SUMMONING OF HIS NAME.
DRINK FROM THE BOWL OF REVIVIFICATION AND FOLLOW ME, CAPTAIN ACROD.

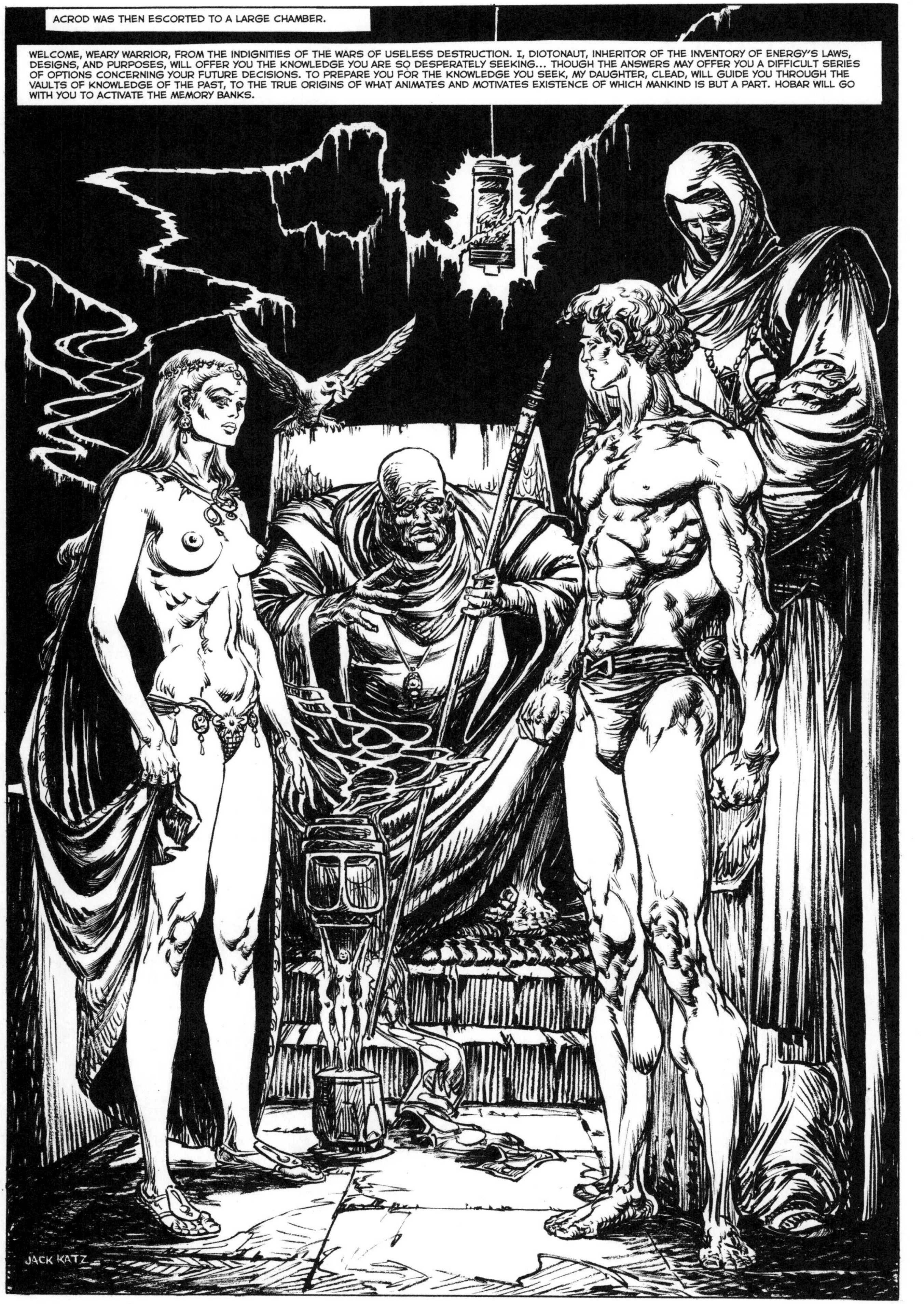

ACROD WAS THEN ESCORTED TO A LARGE CHAMBER.
WELCOME, WEARY WARRIOR, FROM THE INDIGNITIES OF THE WARS OF USELESS DESTRUCTION. I, DIOTONAUT, INHERITOR OF THE INVENTORY OF ENERGY'S LAWS, DESIGNS, AND PURPOSES, WILL OFFER YOU THE KNOWLEDGE YOU ARE SO DESPERATELY SEEKING... THOUGH THE ANSWERS MAY OFFER YOU A DIFFICULT SERIES OF OPTIONS CONCERNING YOUR FUTURE DECISIONS. TO PREPARE YOU FOR THE KNOWLEDGE YOU SEEK, MY DAUGHTER, CLEAD, WILL GUIDE YOU THROUGH THE VAULTS OF KNOWLEDGE OF THE PAST, TO THE TRUE ORIGINS OF WHAT ANIMATES AND MOTIVATES EXISTENCE OF WHICH MANKIND IS BUT A PART. HOBAR WILL GO WITH YOU TO ACTIVATE THE MEMORY BANKS.
JACK KATZ

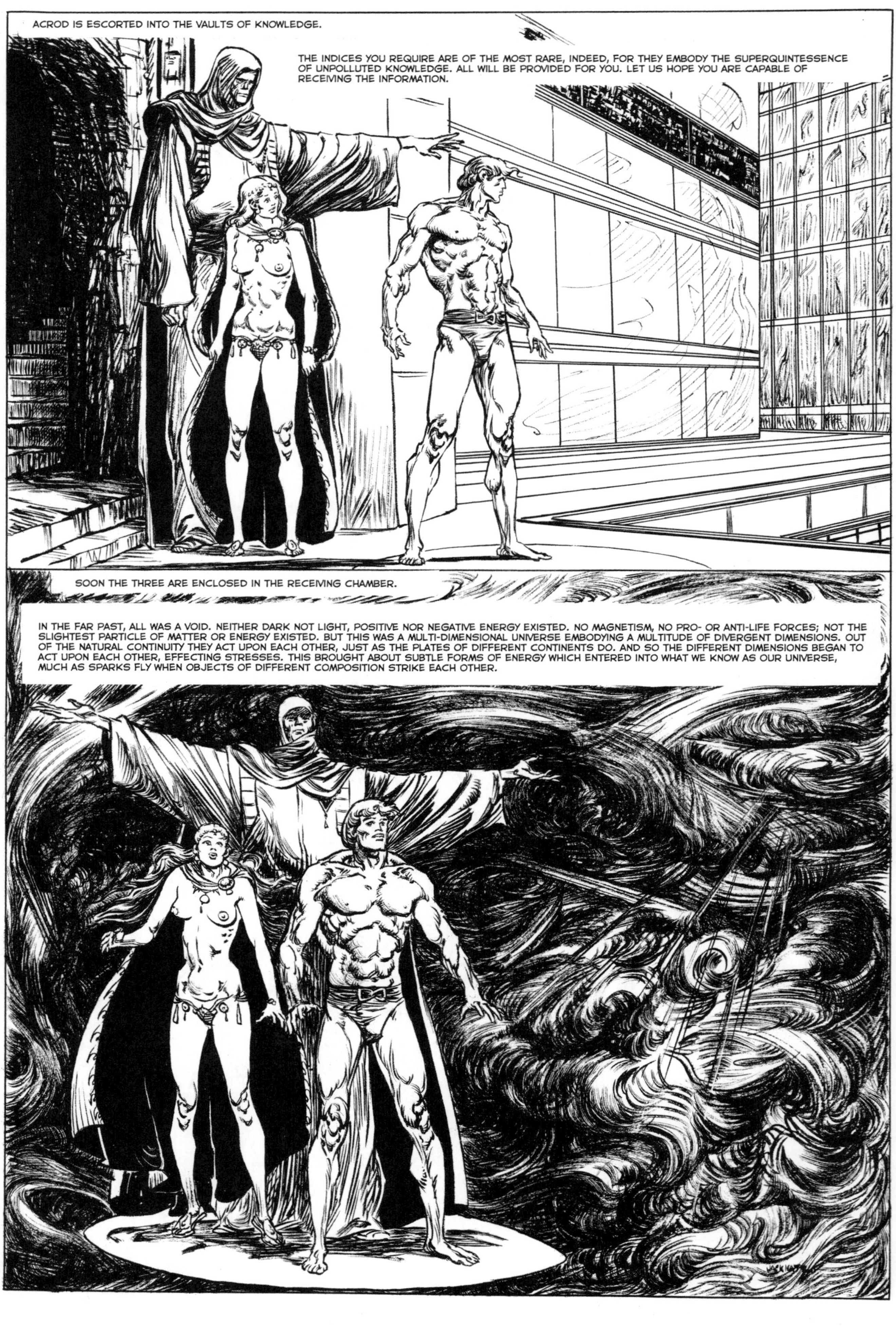
ACROD IS ESCORTED INTO THE VAULTS OF KNOWLEDGE.
THE INDICES YOU REQUIRE ARE OF THE MOST RARE, INDEED, FOR THEY EMBODY THE SUPERQUINTESSENCE OF UNPOLLUTED KNOWLEDGE. ALL WILL BE PROVIDED FOR YOU. LET US HOPE YOU ARE CAPABLE OF RECEIVING THE INFORMATION.
SOON THE THREE ARE ENCLOSED IN THE RECEIVING CHAMBER.
IN THE FAR PAST, ALL WAS A VOID. NEITHER DARK NOT LIGHT, POSITIVE NOR NEGATIVE ENERGY EXISTED. NO MAGNETISM, NO PRO- OR ANTI-LIFE FORCES; NOT THE SLIGHTEST PARTICLE OF MATTER OR ENERGY EXISTED. BUT THIS WAS A MULTI-DIMENSIONAL UNIVERSE EMBODYING A MULTITUDE OF DIVERGENT DIMENSIONS. OUT OF THE NATURAL CONTINUITY THEY ACT UPON EACH OTHER, JUST AS THE PLATES OF DIFFERENT CONTINENTS DO. AND SO THE DIFFERENT DIMENSIONS BEGAN TO ACT UPON EACH OTHER, EFFECTING STRESSES. THIS BROUGHT ABOUT SUBTLE FORMS OF ENERGY WHICH ENTERED INTO WHAT WE KNOW AS OUR UNIVERSE, MUCH AS SPARKS FLY WHEN OBJECTS OF DIFFERENT COMPOSITION STRIKE EACH OTHER.

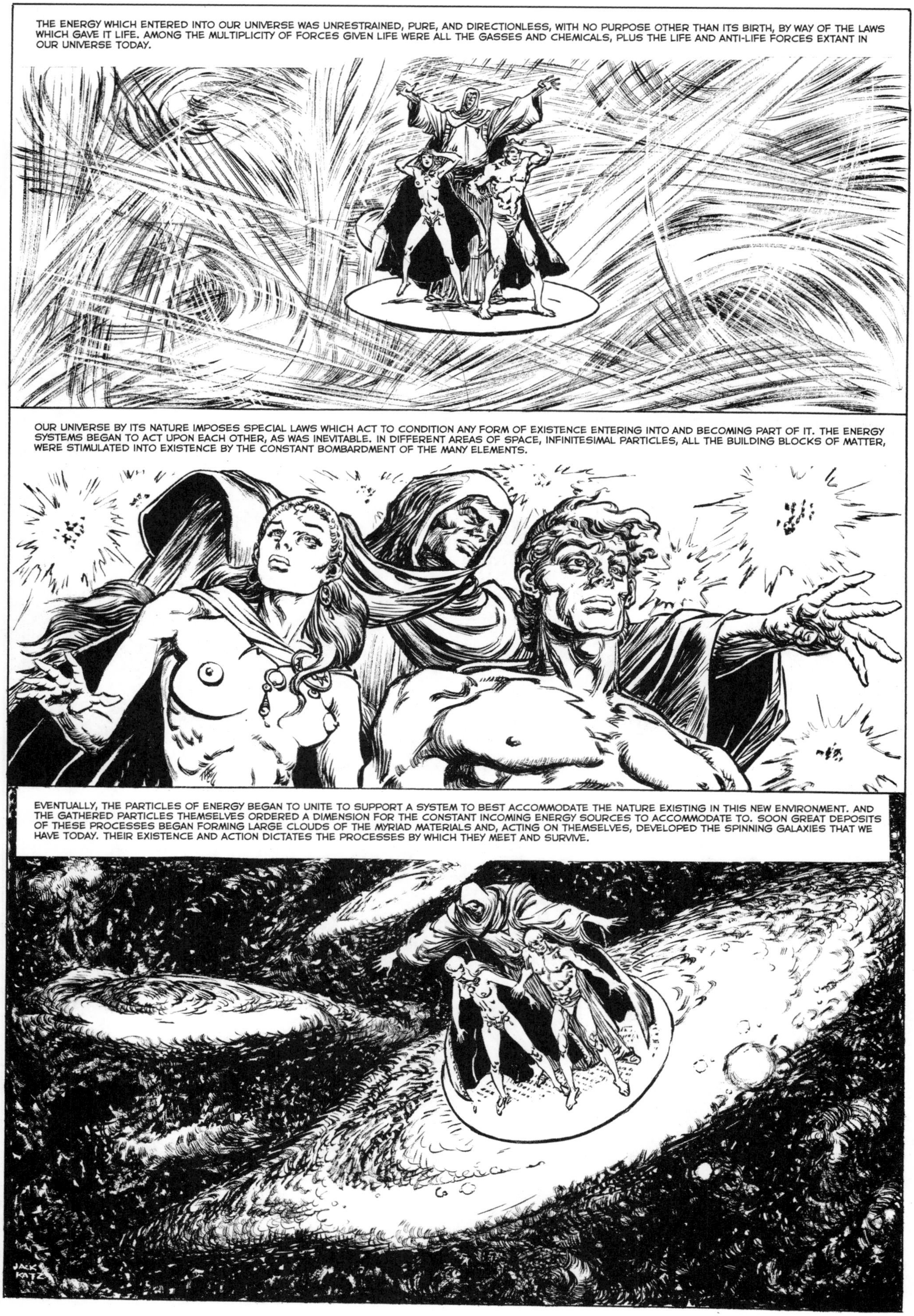
THE ENERGY WHICH ENTERED INTO OUR UNIVERSE WAS UNRESTRAINED, PURE, AND DIRECTIONLESS, WITH NO PURPOSE OTHER THAN ITS BIRTH, BY WAY OF THE LAWS WHICH GAVE IT LIFE. AMONG THE MULTIPLICITY OF FORCES GIVEN LIFE WERE ALL THE GASSES AND CHEMICALS, PLUS THE LIFE AND ANTI-LIFE FORCES EXTANT IN OUR UNIVERSE TODAY.
OUR UNIVERSE BY ITS NATURE IMPOSES SPECIAL LAWS WHICH ACT TO CONDITION ANY FORM OF EXISTENCE ENTERING INTO AND BECOMING PART OF IT. THE ENERGY SYSTEMS BEGAN TO ACT UPON EACH OTHER, AS WAS INEVITABLE. IN DIFFERENT AREAS OF SPACE, INFINITESIMAL PARTICLES, ALL THE BUILDING BLOCKS OF MATTER, WERE STIMULATED INTO EXISTENCE BY THE CONSTANT BOMBARDMENT OF THE MANY ELEMENTS.
EVENTUALLY, THE PARTICLES OF ENERGY BEGAN TO UNITE TO SUPPORT A SYSTEM TO BEST ACCOMMODATE THE NATURE EXISTING IN THIS NEW ENVIRONMENT. AND THE GATHERED PARTICLES THEMSELVES ORDERED A DIMENSION FOR THE CONSTANT INCOMING ENERGY SOURCES TO ACCOMMODATE TO. SOON GREAT DEPOSITS OF THESE PROCESSES BEGAN FORMING LARGE CLOUDS OF THE MYRIAD MATERIALS AND, ACTING ON THEMSELVES, DEVELOPED THE SPINNING GALAXIES THAT WE HAVE TODAY. THEIR EXISTENCE AND ACTION DICTATES THE PROCESSES BY WHICH THEY MEET AND SURVIVE.
JACK KATZ

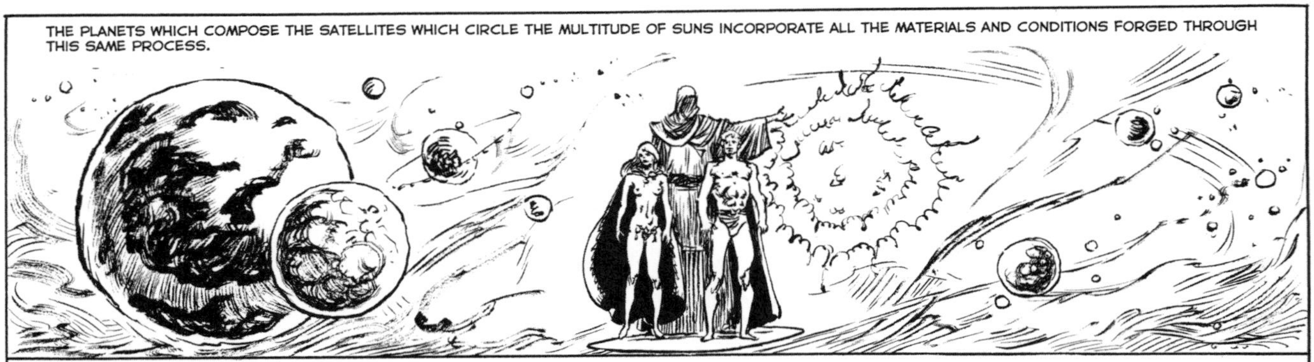
THE PLANETS WHICH COMPOSE THE SATELLITES WHICH CIRCLE THE MULTITUDE OF SUNS INCORPORATE ALL THE MATERIALS AND CONDITIONS FORGED THROUGH THIS SAME PROCESS.

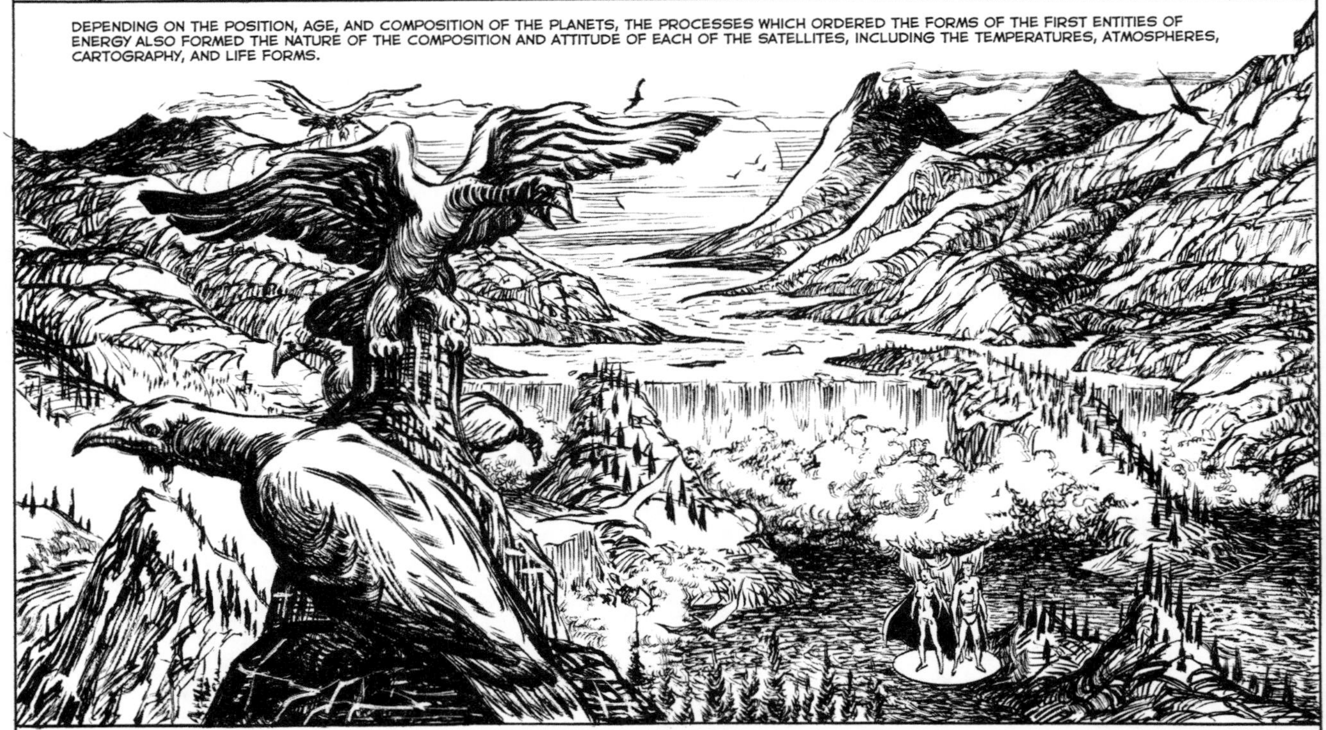
DEPENDING ON THE POSITION, AGE, AND COMPOSITION OF THE PLANETS, THE PROCESSES WHICH ORDERED THE FORMS OF THE FIRST ENTITIES OF ENERGY ALSO FORMED THE NATURE OF THE COMPOSITION AND ATTITUDE OF EACH OF THE SATELLITES, INCLUDING THE TEMPERATURES, ATMOSPHERES, CARTOGRAPHY, AND LIFE FORMS.

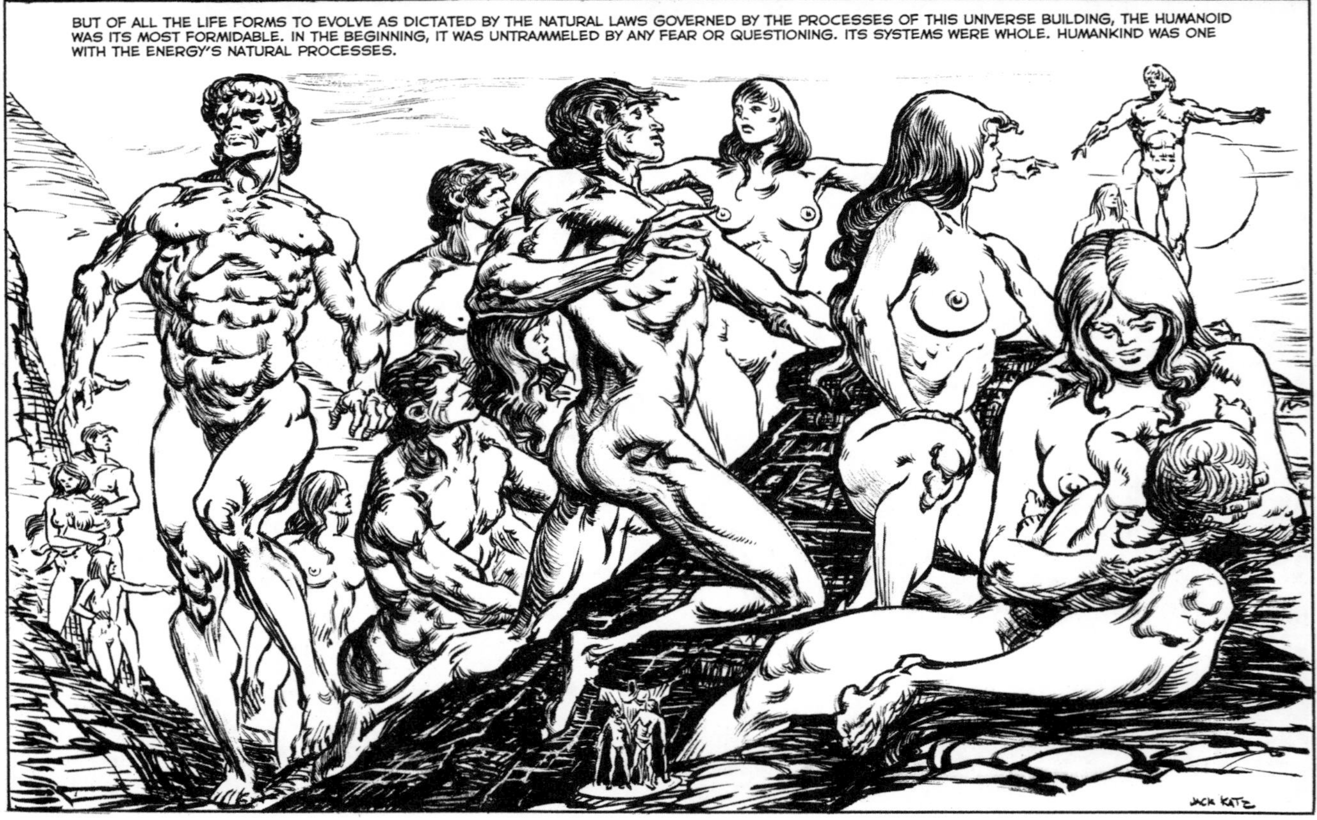
BUT OF ALL THE LIFE FORMS TO EVOLVE AS DICTATED BY THE NATURAL LAWS GOVERNED BY THE PROCESSES OF THIS UNIVERSE BUILDING, THE HUMANOID WAS ITS MOST FORMIDABLE. IN THE BEGINNING, IT WAS UNTRAMMELED BY ANY FEAR OR QUESTIONING. ITS SYSTEMS WERE WHOLE. HUMANKIND WAS ONE WITH THE ENERGY'S NATURAL PROCESSES.
JACK KATZ

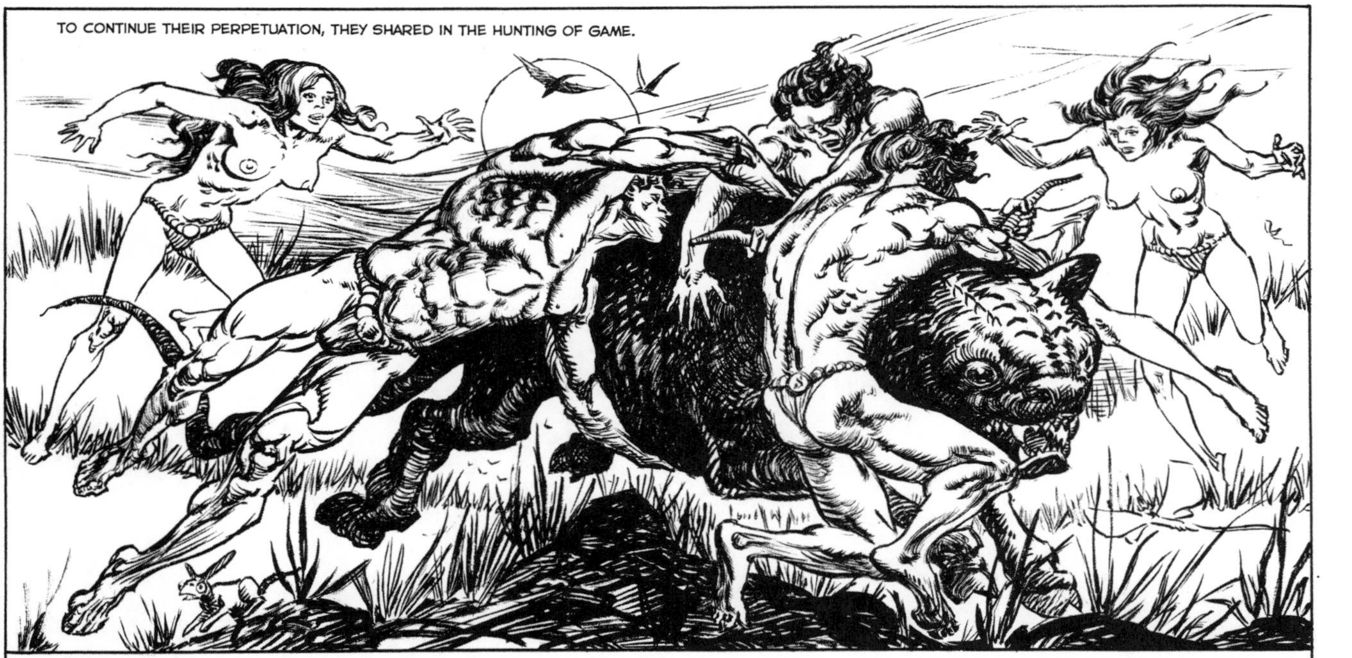
TO CONTINUE THEIR PERPETUATION, THEY SHARED IN THE HUNTING OF GAME.

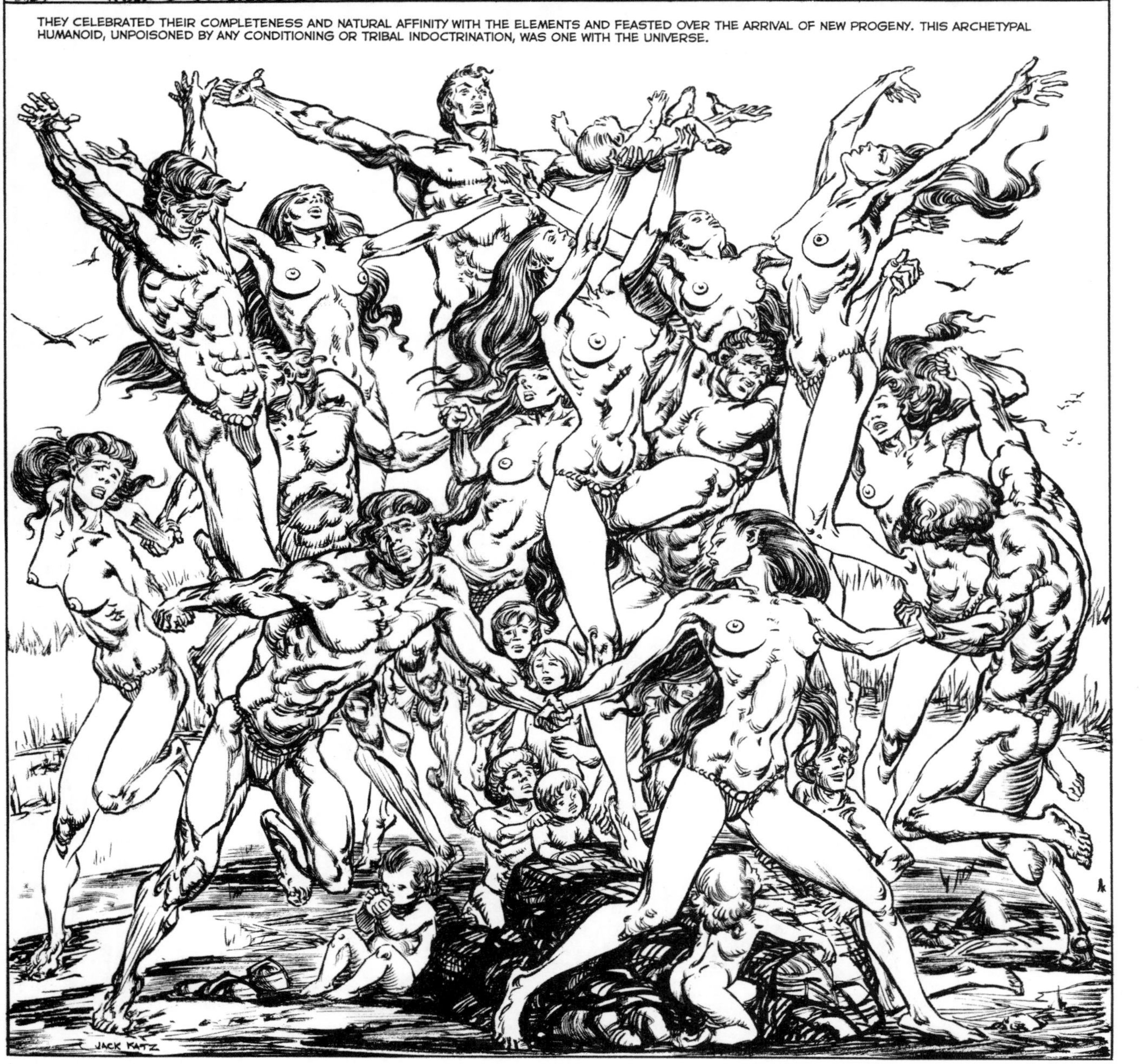
THEY CELEBRATED THEIR COMPLETENESS AND NATURAL AFFINITY WITH THE ELEMENTS AND FEASTED OVER THE ARRIVAL OF NEW PROGENY. THIS ARCHETYPAL HUMANOID, UNPOISONED BY ANY CONDITIONING OR TRIBAL INDOCTRINATION, WAS ONE WITH THE UNIVERSE.
JACK KATZ

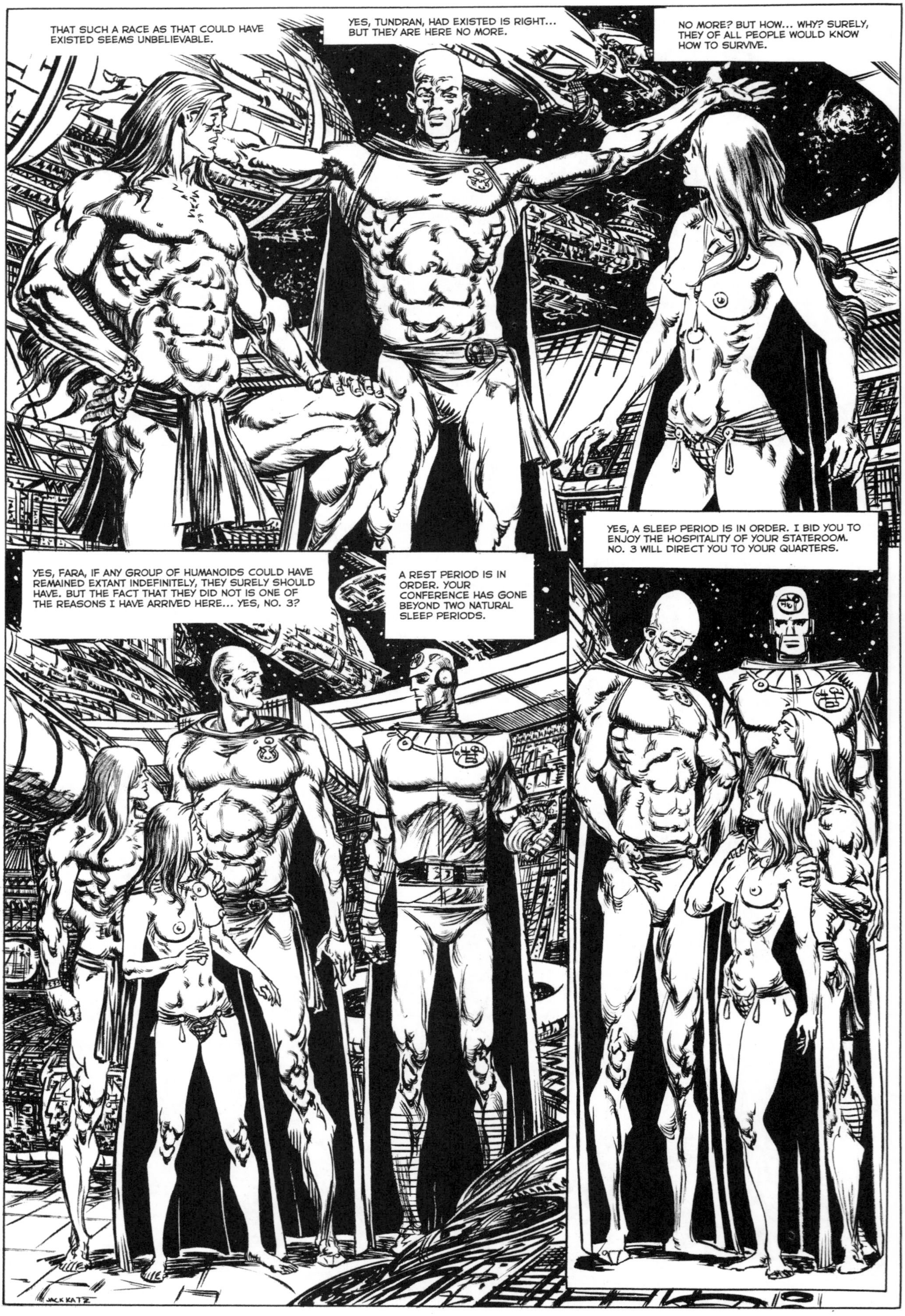

THAT SUCH A RACE AS THAT COULD HAVE EXISTED SEEMS UNBELIEVABLE.
YES, TUNDRAN, HAD EXISTED IS RIGHT... BUT THEY ARE HERE NO MORE.
NO MORE? BUT HOW... WHY? SURELY, THEY OF ALL PEOPLE WOULD KNOW HOW TO SURVIVE.
YES, FARA, IF ANY GROUP OF HUMANOIDS COULD HAVE REMAINED EXTANT INDEFINITELY, THEY SURELY SHOULD HAVE. BUT THE FACT THAT THEY DID NOT IS ONE OF THE REASONS I HAVE ARRIVED HERE... YES, NO. 3?
A REST PERIOD IS IN ORDER. YOUR CONFERENCE HAS GONE BEYOND TWO NATURAL SLEEP PERIODS.
YES, A SLEEP PERIOD IS IN ORDER. I BID YOU TO ENJOY THE HOSPITALITY OF YOUR STATEROOM. NO. 3 WILL DIRECT YOU TO YOUR QUARTERS.
JACK KATZ

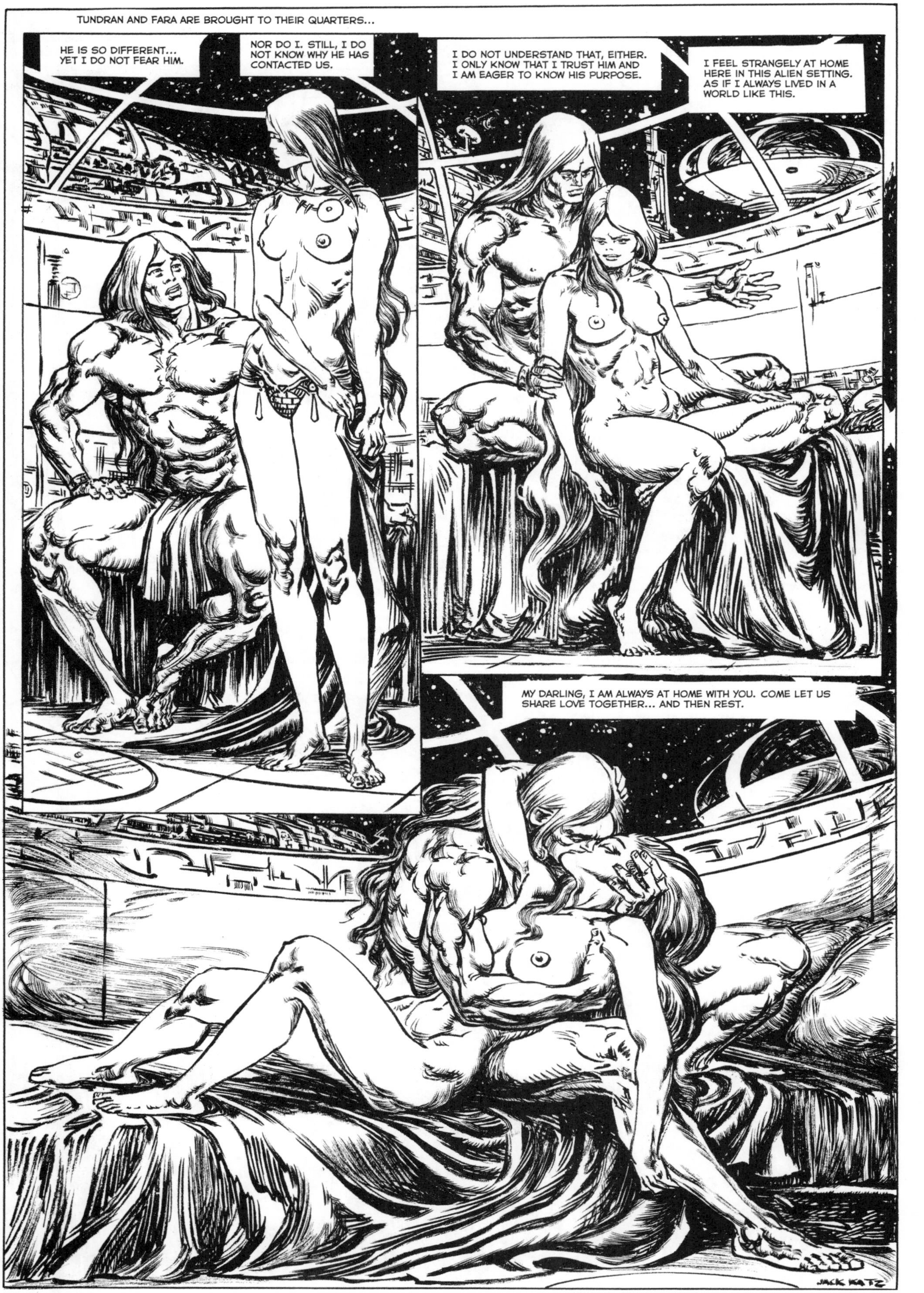
TUNDRAN AND FARA ARE BROUGHT TO THEIR QUARTERS...
HE IS SO DIFFERENT... YET I DO NOT FEAR HIM.
NOR DO I. STILL, I DO NOT KNOW WHY HE HAS CONTACTED US.
I DO NOT UNDERSTAND THAT, EITHER. I ONLY KNOW THAT I TRUST HIM AND I AM EAGER TO KNOW HIS PURPOSE.
I FEEL STRANGELY AT HOME HERE IN THIS ALIEN SETTING. AS IF I ALWAYS LIVED IN A WORLD LIKE THIS.
MY DARLING, I AM ALWAYS AT HOME WITH YOU. COME LET US SHARE LOVE TOGETHER... AND THEN REST.
JACK KATZ

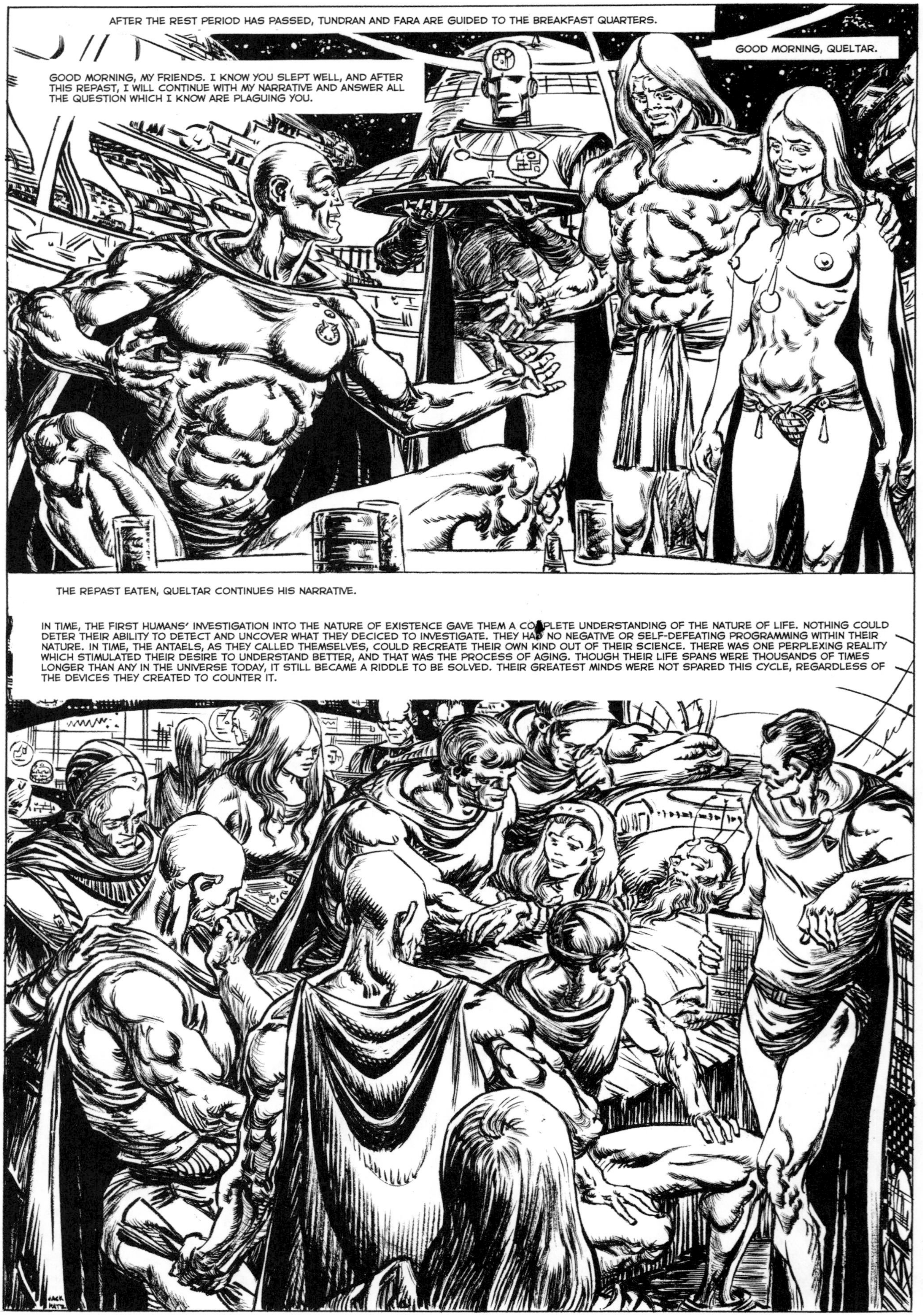
AFTER THE REST PERIOD HAS PASSED, TUNDRAN AND FARA ARE GUIDED TO THE BREAKFAST QUARTERS.
GOOD MORNING, MY FRIENDS. I KNOW YOU SLEPT WELL, AND AFTER THIS REPAST, I WILL CONTINUE WITH MY NARRATIVE AND ANSWER ALL THE QUESTION WHICH I KNOW ARE PLAGUING YOU.
GOOD MORNING, QUELTAR.
THE REPAST EATEN, QUELTAR CONTINUES HIS NARRATIVE.
IN TIME, THE FIRST HUMANS' INVESTIGATION INTO THE NATURE OF EXISTENCE GAVE THEM A COMPLETE UNDERSTANDING OF THE NATURE OF LIFE. NOTHING COULD DETER THEIR ABILITY TO DETECT AND UNCOVER WHAT THEY DECICED TO INVESTIGATE. THEY HAD NO NEGATIVE OR SELF-DEFEATING PROGRAMMING WITHIN THEIR NATURE. IN TIME, THE ANTAELS, AS THEY CALLED THEMSELVES, COULD RECREATE THEIR OWN KIND OUT OF THEIR SCIENCE. THERE WAS ONE PERPLEXING REALITY WHICH STIMULATED THEIR DESIRE TO UNDERSTAND BETTER, AND THAT WAS THE PROCESS OF AGING. THOUGH THEIR LIFE SPANS WERE THOUSANDS OF TIMES LONGER THAN ANY IN THE UNIVERSE TODAY, IT STILL BECAME A RIDDLE TO BE SOLVED. THEIR GREATEST MINDS WERE NOT SPARED THIS CYCLE, REGARDLESS OF THE DEVICES THEY CREATED TO COUNTER IT.
JACK KATZ

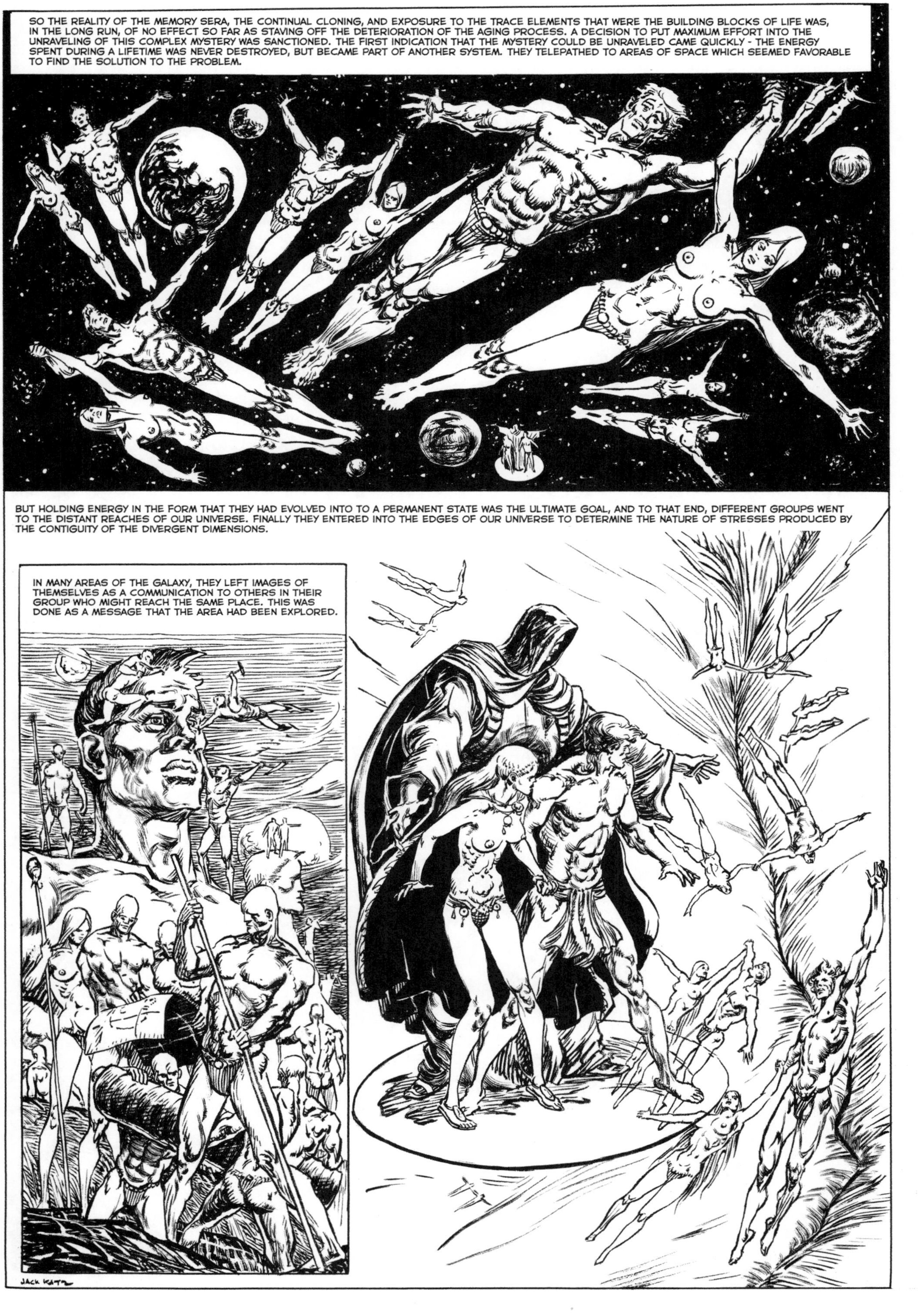
SO THE REALITY OF THE MEMORY SERA, THE CONTINUAL CLONING, AND EXPOSURE TO THE TRACE ELEMENTS THAT WERE THE BUILDING BLOCKS OF LIFE WAS, IN THE LONG RUN, OF NO EFFECT SO FAR AS STAVING OFF THE DETERIORATION OF THE AGING PROCESS. A DECISION TO PUT MAXIMUM EFFORT INTO THE UNRAVELING OF THIS COMPLEX MYSTERY WAS SANCTIONED. THE FIRST INDICATION THAT THE MYSTERY COULD BE UNRAVELED CAME QUICKLY - THE ENERGY SPENT DURING A LIFETIME WAS NEVER DESTROYED, BUT BECAME PART OF ANOTHER SYSTEM. THEY TELEPATHED TO AREAS OF SPACE WHICH SEEMED FAVORABLE TO FIND THE SOLUTION TO THE PROBLEM.
BUT HOLDING ENERGY IN THE FORM THAT THEY HAD EVOLVED INTO TO A PERMANENT STATE WAS THE ULTIMATE GOAL, AND TO THAT END, DIFFERENT GROUPS WENT TO THE DISTANT REACHES OF OUR UNIVERSE. FINALLY THEY ENTERED INTO THE EDGES OF OUR UNIVERSE TO DETERMINE THE NATURE OF STRESSES PRODUCED BY THE CONTIGUITY OF THE DIVERGENT DIMENSIONS.
IN MANY AREAS OF THE GALAXY, THEY LEFT IMAGES OF THEMSELVES AS A COMMUNICATION TO OTHERS IN THEIR GROUP WHO MIGHT REACH THE SAME PLACE. THIS WAS DONE AS A MESSAGE THAT THE AREA HAD BEEN EXPLORED.
JACK KATZ

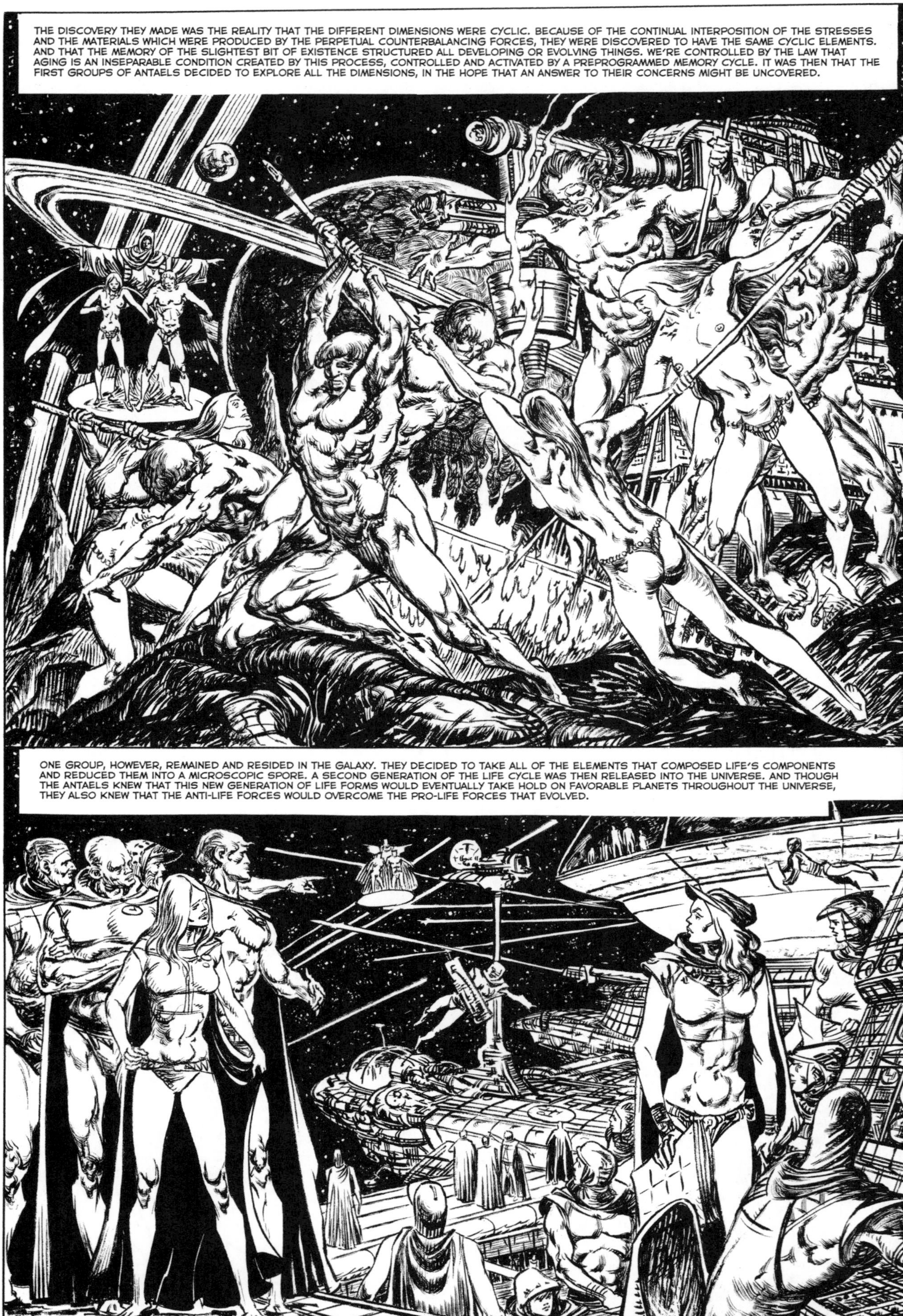
THE DISCOVERY THEY MADE WAS THE REALITY THAT THE DIFFERENT DIMENSIONS WERE CYCLIC. BECAUSE OF THE CONTINUAL INTERPOSITION OF THE STRESSES AND THE MATERIALS WHICH WERE PRODUCED BY THE PERPETUAL COUNTERBALANCING FORCES, THEY WERE DISCOVERED TO HAVE THE SAME CYCLIC ELEMENTS. AND THAT THE MEMORY OF THE SLIGHTEST BIT OF EXISTENCE STRUCTURED ALL DEVELOPING OR EVOLVING THINGS. WE'RE CONTROLLED BY THE LAW THAT AGING IS AN INSEPARABLE CONDITION CREATED BY THIS PROCESS, CONTROLLED AND ACTIVATED BY A PREPROGRAMMED MEMORY CYCLE. IT WAS THEN THAT THE FIRST GROUPS OF ANTAELS DECIDED TO EXPLORE ALL THE DIMENSIONS, IN THE HOPE THAT AN ANSWER TO THEIR CONCERNS MIGHT BE UNCOVERED.
ONE GROUP, HOWEVER, REMAINED AND RESIDED IN THE GALAXY. THEY DECIDED TO TAKE ALL OF THE ELEMENTS THAT COMPOSED LIFE'S COMPONENTS AND REDUCED THEM INTO A MICROSCOPIC SPORE. A SECOND GENERATION OF THE LIFE CYCLE WAS THEN RELEASED INTO THE UNIVERSE. AND THOUGH THE ANTAELS KNEW THAT THIS NEW GENERATION OF LIFE FORMS WOULD EVENTUALLY TAKE HOLD ON FAVORABLE PLANETS THROUGHOUT THE UNIVERSE, THEY ALSO KNEW THAT THE ANTI-LIFE FORCES WOULD OVERCOME THE PRO-LIFE FORCES THAT EVOLVED.
JACK KATZ

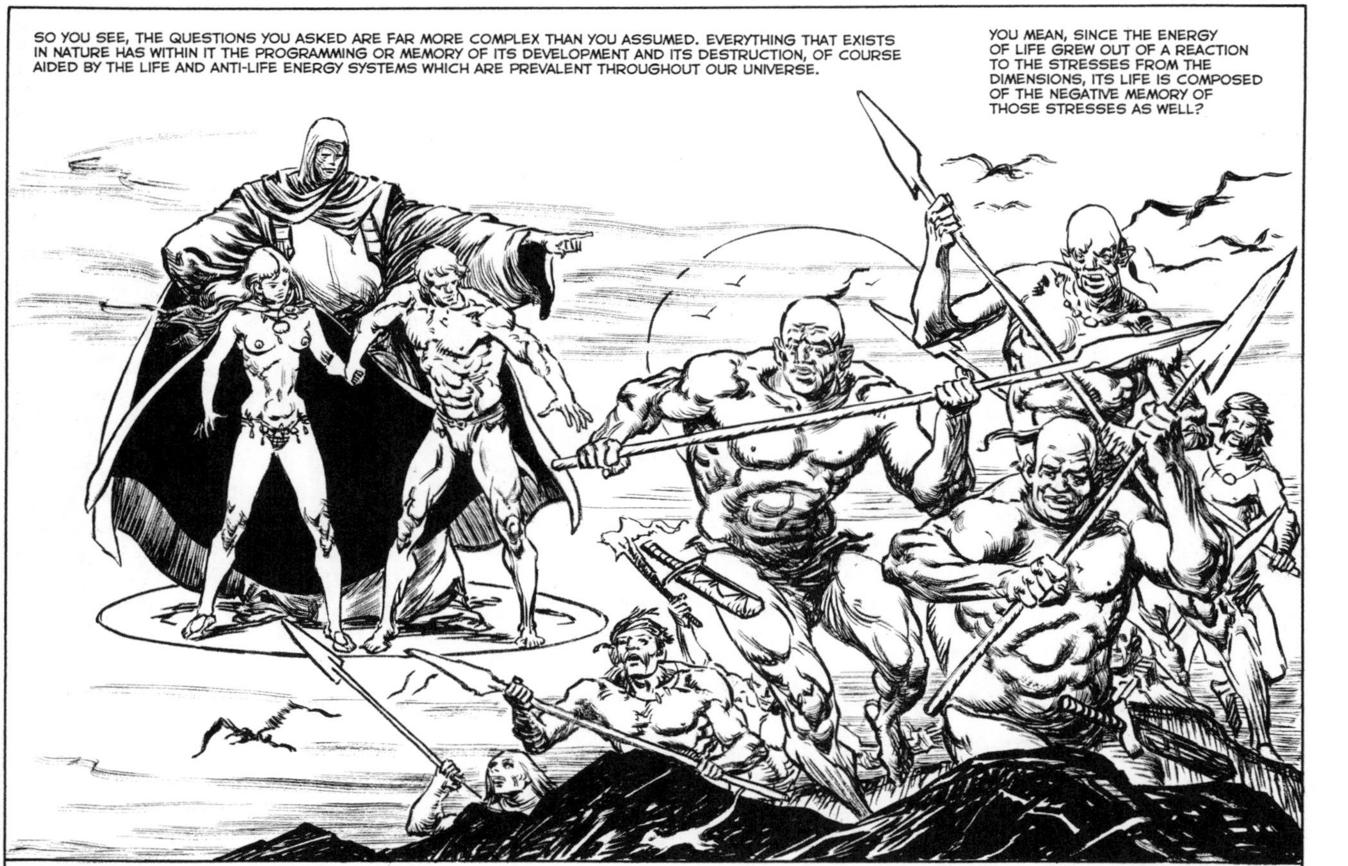
SO YOU SEE, THE QUESTIONS YOU ASKED ARE FAR MORE COMPLEX THAN YOU ASSUMED. EVERYTHING THAT EXISTS IN NATURE HAS WITHIN IT THE PROGRAMMING OR MEMORY OF ITS DEVELOPMENT AND ITS DESTRUCTION, OF COURSE AIDED BY THE LIFE AND ANTI-LIFE ENERGY SYSTEMS WHICH ARE PREVALENT THROUGHOUT OUR UNIVERSE.
YOU MEAN, SINCE THE ENERGY OF LIFE GREW OUT OF A REACTION TO THE STRESSES FROM THE DIMENSIONS, ITS LIFE IS COMPOSED OF THE NEGATIVE MEMORY OF THOSE STRESSES AS WELL?

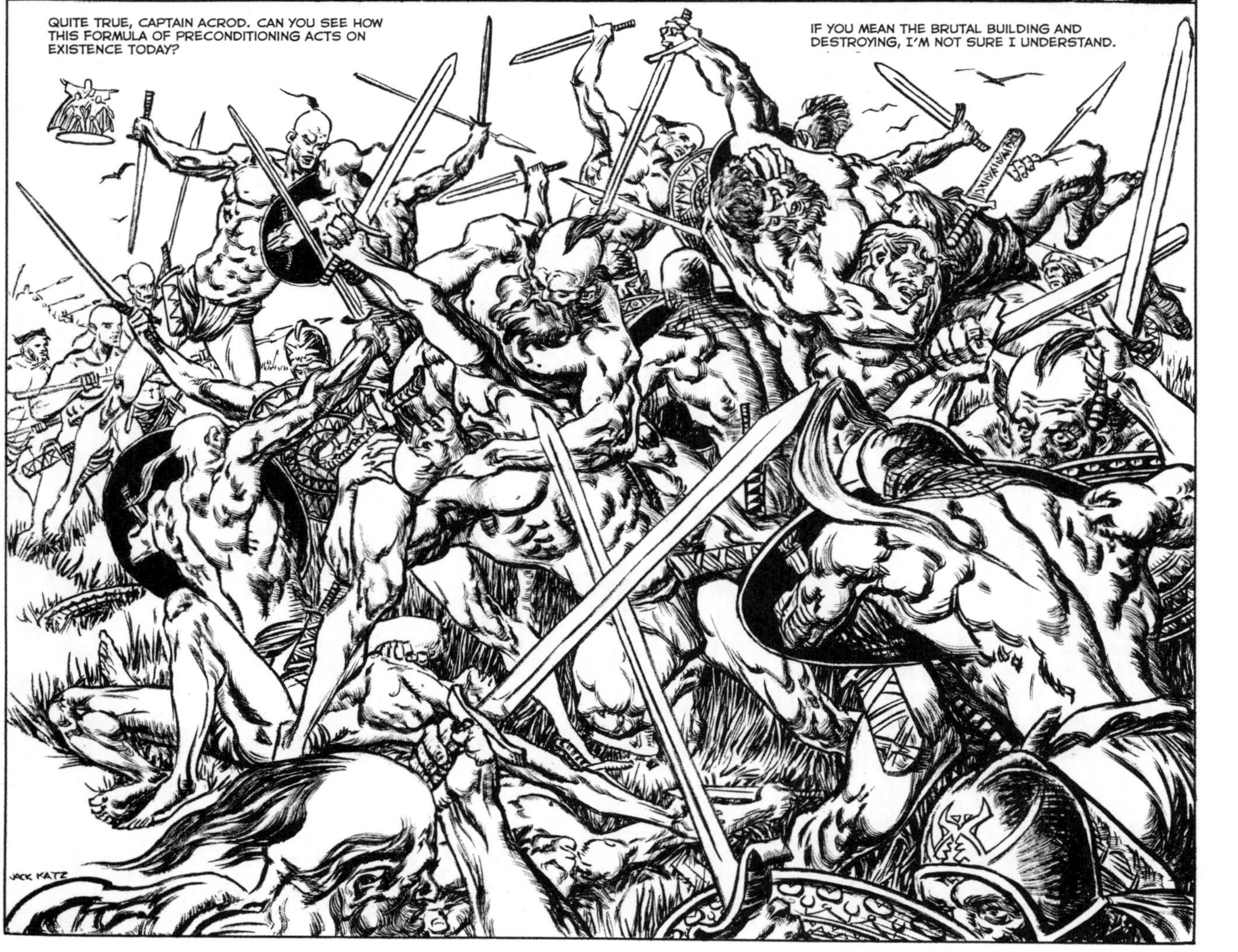
QUITE TRUE, CAPTAIN ACROD. CAN YOU SEE HOW THIS FORMULA OF PRECONDITIONING ACTS ON EXISTENCE TODAY?
IF YOU MEAN THE BRUTAL BUILDING AND DESTROYING, I'M NOT SURE I UNDERSTAND.
JACK KATZ

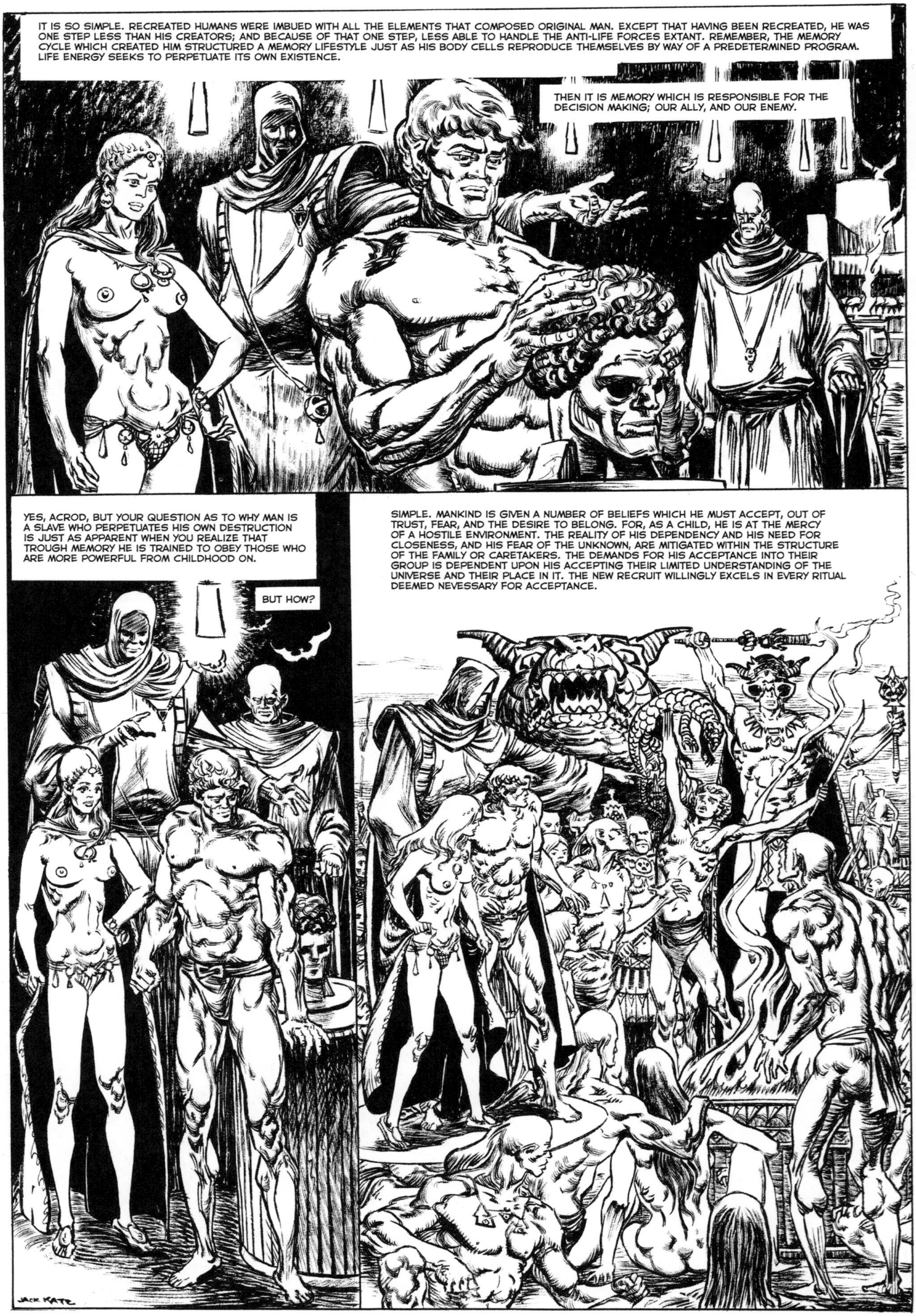
IT IS SO SIMPLE. RECREATED HUMANS WERE IMBUED WITH ALL THE ELEMENTS THAT COMPOSED ORIGINAL MAN. EXCEPT THAT HAVING BEEN RECREATED, HE WAS ONE STEP LESS THAN HIS CREATORS; AND BECAUSE OF THAT ONE STEP, LESS ABLE TO HANDLE THE ANTI-LIFE FORCES EXTANT. REMEMBER, THE MEMORY CYCLE WHICH CREATED HIM STRUCTURED A MEMORY LIFESTYLE JUST AS HIS BODY CELLS REPRODUCE THEMSELVES BY WAY OF A PREDETERMINED PROGRAM. LIFE ENERGY SEEKS TO PERPETUATE ITS OWN EXISTENCE.
THEN IT IS MEMORY WHICH IS RESPONSIBLE FOR THE DECISION MAKING; OUR ALLY, AND OUR ENEMY.
YES, ACROD, BUT YOUR QUESTION AS TO WHY MAN IS A SLAVE WHO PERPETUATES HIS OWN DESTRUCTION IS JUST AS APPARENT WHEN YOU REALIZE THAT TROUGH MEMORY HE IS TRAINED TO OBEY THOSE WHO ARE MORE POWERFUL FROM CHILDHOOD ON.
BUT HOW?
SIMPLE. MANKIND IS GIVEN A NUMBER OF BELIEFS WHICH HE MUST ACCEPT, OUT OF TRUST, FEAR, AND THE DESIRE TO BELONG. FOR, AS A CHILD, HE IS AT THE MERCY OF A HOSTILE ENVIRONMENT. THE REALITY OF HIS DEPENDENCY AND HIS NEED FOR CLOSENESS, AND HIS FEAR OF THE UNKNOWN, ARE MITIGATED WITHIN THE STRUCTURE OF THE FAMILY OR CARETAKERS. THE DEMANDS FOR HIS ACCEPTANCE INTO THEIR GROUP IS DEPENDENT UPON HIS ACCEPTING THEIR LIMITED UNDERSTANDING OF THE UNIVERSE AND THEIR PLACE IN IT. THE NEW RECRUIT WILLINGLY EXCELS IN EVERY RITUAL DEEMED NEVESSARY FOR ACCEPTANCE.
JACK KATZ

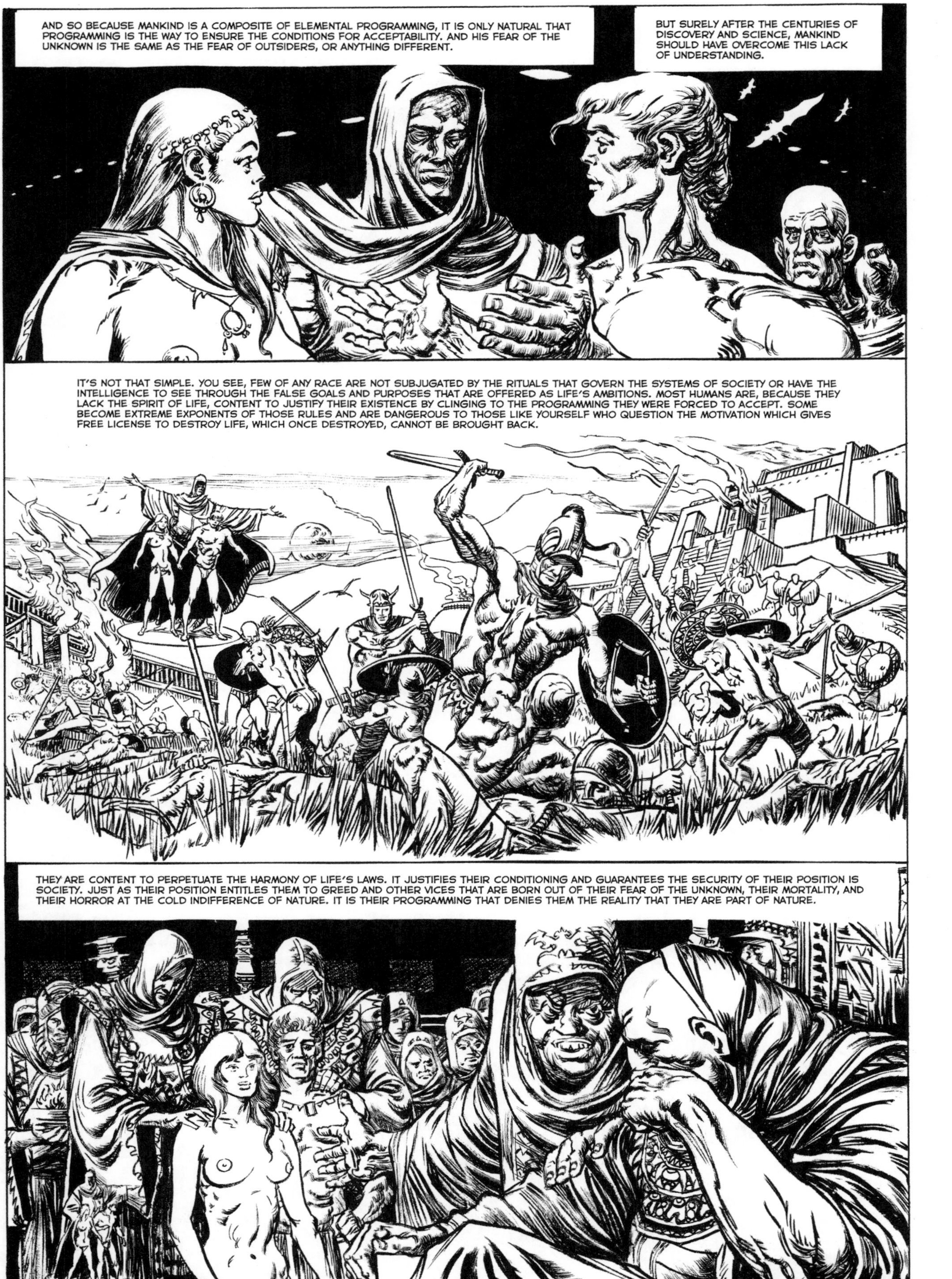
AND SO BECAUSE MANKIND IS A COMPOSITE OF ELEMENTAL PROGRAMMING, IT IS ONLY NATURAL THAT PROGRAMMING IS THE WAY TO ENSURE THE CONDITIONS FOR ACCEPTABILITY. AND HIS FEAR OF THE UNKNOWN IS THE SAME AS THE FEAR OF OUTSIDERS, OR ANYTHING DIFFERENT.
BUT SURELY AFTER THE CENTURIES OF DISCOVERY AND SCIENCE, MANKIND SHOULD HAVE OVERCOME THIS LACK OF UNDERSTANDING.
IT'S NOT THAT SIMPLE. YOU SEE, FEW OF ANY RACE ARE NOT SUBJUGATED BY THE RITUALS THAT GOVERN THE SYSTEMS OF SOCIETY OR HAVE THE INTELLIGENCE TO SEE THROUGH THE FALSE GOALS AND PURPOSES THAT ARE OFFERED AS LIFE'S AMBITIONS. MOST HUMANS ARE, BECAUSE THEY LACK THE SPIRIT OF LIFE, CONTENT TO JUSTIFY THEIR EXISTENCE BY CLINGING TO THE PROGRAMMING THEY WERE FORCED TO ACCEPT. SOME BECOME EXTREME EXPONENTS OF THOSE RULES AND ARE DANGEROUS TO THOSE LIKE YOURSELF WHO QUESTION THE MOTIVATION WHICH GIVES FREE LICENSE TO DESTROY LIFE, WHICH ONCE DESTROYED, CANNOT BE BROUGHT BACK.
THEY ARE CONTENT TO PERPETUATE THE HARMONY OF LIFE'S LAWS. IT JUSTIFIES THEIR CONDITIONING AND GUARANTEES THE SECURITY OF THEIR POSITION IS SOCIETY. JUST AS THEIR POSITION ENTITLES THEM TO GREED AND OTHER VICES THAT ARE BORN OUT OF THEIR FEAR OF THE UNKNOWN, THEIR MORTALITY, AND THEIR HORROR AT THE COLD INDIFFERENCE OF NATURE. IT IS THEIR PROGRAMMING THAT DENIES THEM THE REALITY THAT THEY ARE PART OF NATURE.

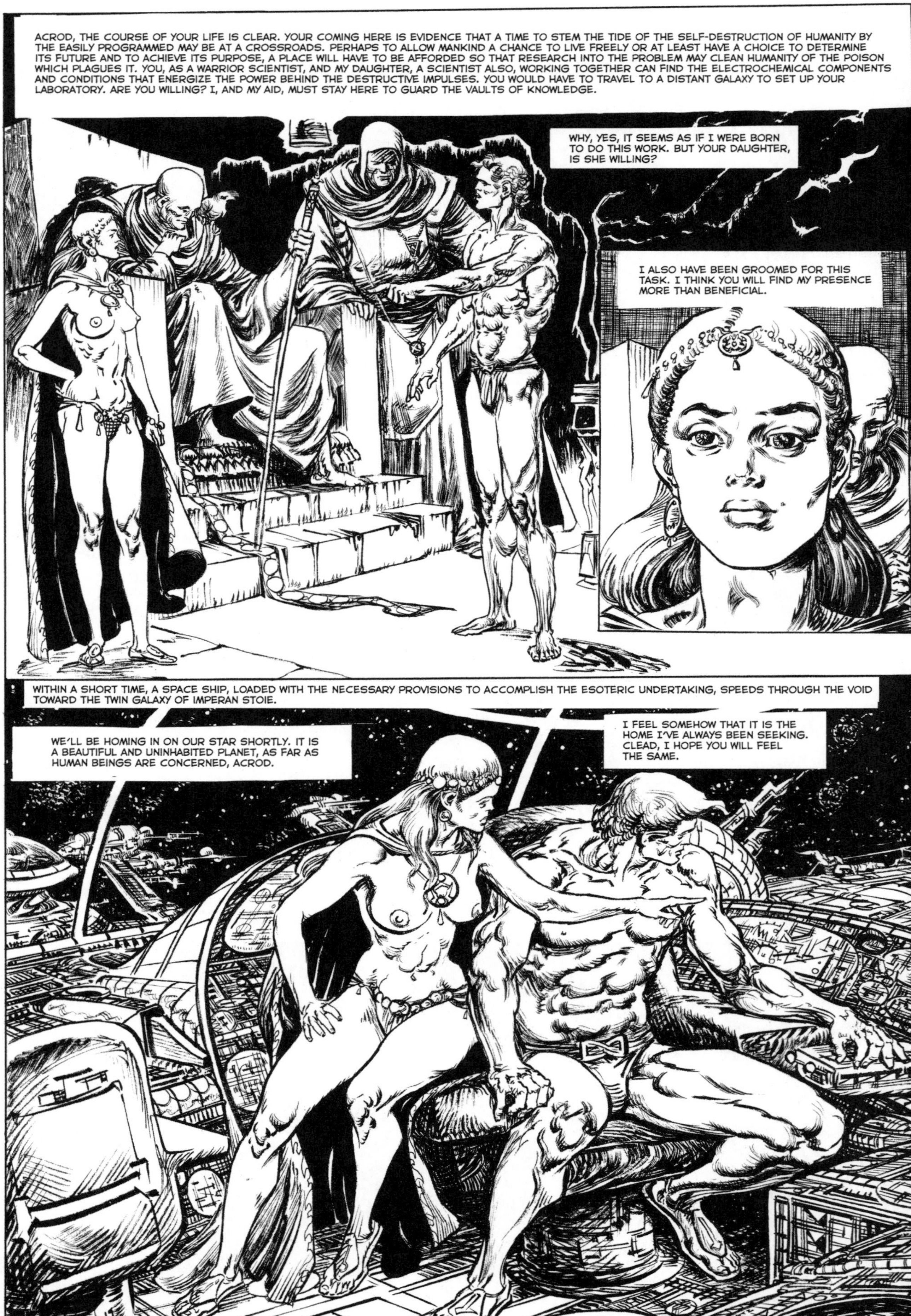
ACROD, THE COURSE OF YOUR LIFE IS CLEAR. YOUR COMING HERE IS EVIDENCE THAT A TIME TO STEM THE TIDE OF THE SELF-DESTRUCTION OF HUMANITY BY THE EASILY PROGRAMMED MAY BE AT A CROSSROADS. PERHAPS TO ALLOW MANKIND A CHANCE TO LIVE FREELY OR AT LEAST HAVE A CHOICE TO DETERMINE ITS FUTURE AND TO ACHIEVE ITS PURPOSE, A PLACE WILL HAVE TO BE AFFORDED SO THAT RESEARCH INTO THE PROBLEM MAY CLEAN HUMANITY OF THE POISON WHICH PLAGUES IT. YOU, AS A WARRIOR SCIENTIST, AND MY DAUGHTER, A SCIENTIST ALSO, WORKING TOGETHER CAN FIND THE ELECTROCHEMICAL COMPONENTS AND CONDITIONS THAT ENERGIZE THE POWER BEHIND THE DESTRUCTIVE IMPULSES. YOU WOULD HAVE TO TRAVEL TO A DISTANT GALAXY TO SET UP YOUR LABORATORY. ARE YOU WILLING? I, AND MY AID, MUST STAY HERE TO GUARD THE VAULTS OF KNOWLEDGE.
WHY, YES, IT SEEMS AS IF I WERE BORN TO DO THIS WORK. BUT YOUR DAUGHTER, IS SHE WILLING?
I ALSO HAVE BEEN GROOMED FOR THIS TASK. I THINK YOU WILL FIND MY PRESENCE MORE THAN BENEFICIAL.
WITHIN A SHORT TIME, A SPACE SHIP, LOADED WITH THE NECESSARY PROVISIONS TO ACCOMPLISH THE ESOTERIC UNDERTAKING, SPEEDS THROUGH THE VOID TOWARD THE TWIN GALAXY OF IMPERAN STOIE.
WE'LL BE HOMING IN ON OUR STAR SHORTLY. IT IS A BEAUTIFUL AND UNINHABITED PLANET, AS FAR AS HUMAN BEINGS ARE CONCERNED, ACROD.
I FEEL SOMEHOW THAT IT IS THE HOME I'VE ALWAYS BEEN SEEKING. CLEAD, I HOPE YOU WILL FEEL THE SAME.

WERE THEY SUCCESSFUL, QUELTAR? DID THEY FIND A CURE FOR HUMANITY'S SUFFERINGS?

I AM GLAD YOU ARE SO TAKEN WITH MY STORY, FARA. COME, LET US TAKE A TOUR ABOUT MY SHIP WHILE I CONTINUE.

BACK ON TAMRA, THE DISAPPEARANCE OF TUNDRAN AND FARA TAKES TOP PRIORITY AMONG THEIR CHIEF AIDS.

WE'VE SEARCHED EVERYWHERE AND WE'VE FOUND NO TRACE OF THEM, ALANDON.

WE MUSTN'T GIVE UP. HE IS OUR KENMOOR. TUNDRAN MUST BE FOUND.

AND WOE BE TO ANY WHO HAVE HARMED THEM.

AT THE SAME TIME, WHILE STROLLING THE MANY BYWAYS OF THE GALACTIC HUNTER, QUELTAR CONTINUES...

THEY ARRIVED AT THE PLANET DESIGNATED BY CLEAD'S FATHER AND SET UP A LABORATORY IN A MOUNTAINOUS REGION FACING A LARGE OCEAN. THE PLANET WAS ALIVE WITH GREAT VARIETIES OF WILD LIFE. ANTICIPATING NO DANGER, ACROD LOCKED AWAY MOST OF THEIR WEAPONS, EXCEPT FOR AN ARCHERY CACHE FOR HUNTING.

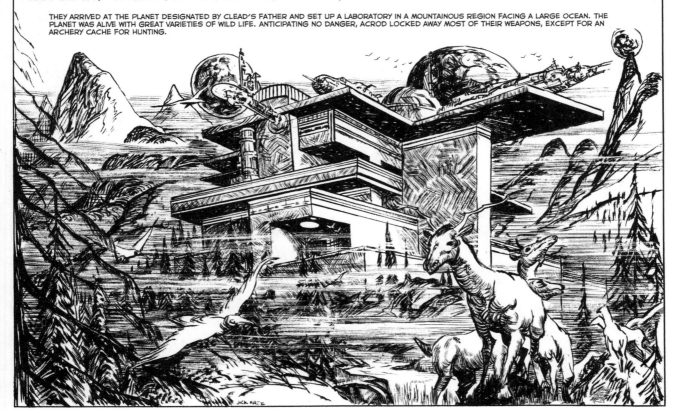

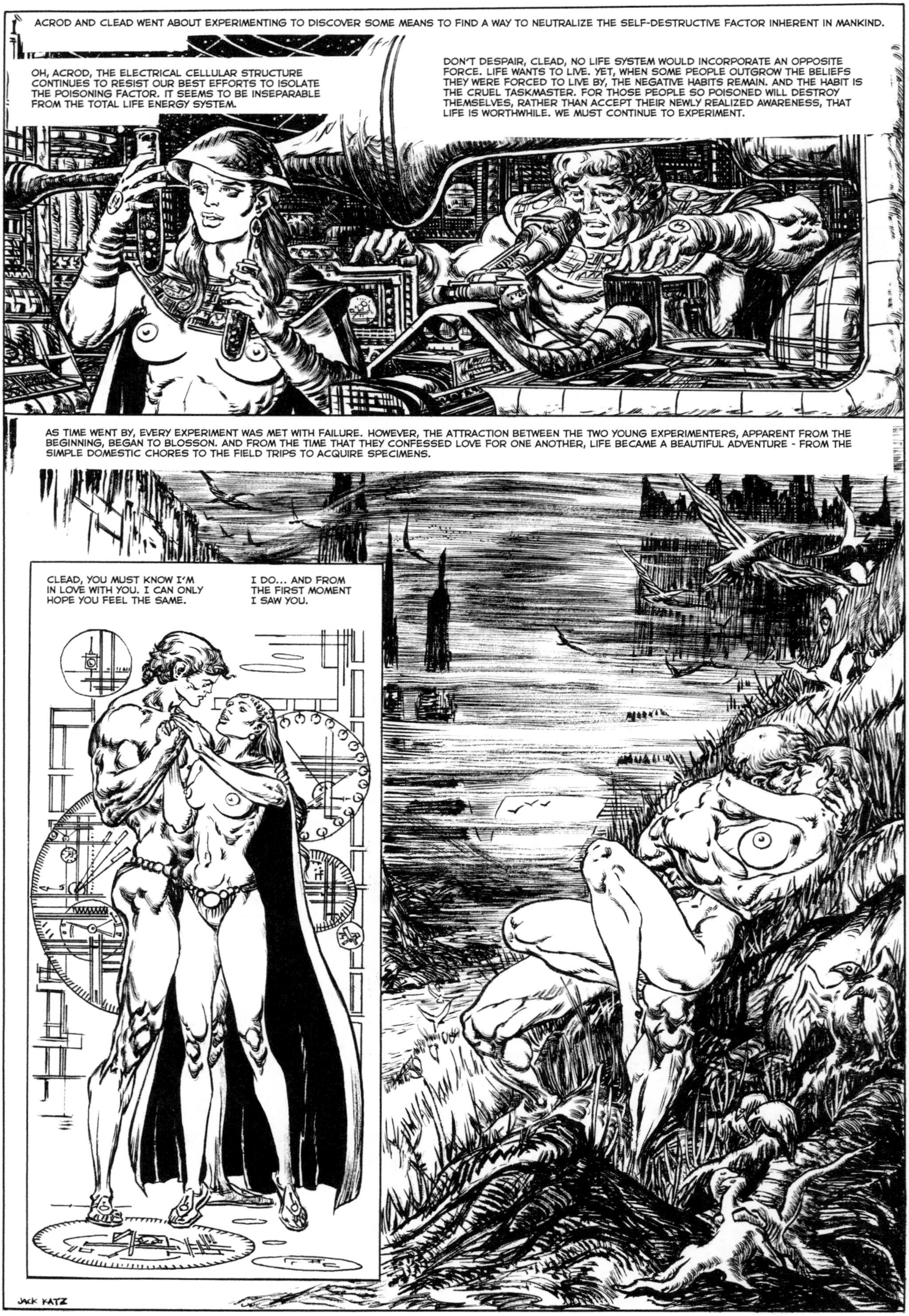
ACROD AND CLEAD WENT ABOUT EXPERIMENTING TO DISCOVER SOME MEANS TO FIND A WAY TO NEUTRALIZE THE SELF-DESTRUCTIVE FACTOR INHERENT IN MANKIND.
OH, ACROD, THE ELECTRICAL CELLULAR STRUCTURE CONTINUES TO RESIST OUR BEST EFFORTS TO ISOLATE THE POISONING FACTOR. IT SEEMS TO BE INSEPARABLE FROM THE TOTAL LIFE ENERGY SYSTEM.
DON'T DESPAIR, CLEAD, NO LIFE SYSTEM WOULD INCORPORATE AN OPPOSITE FORCE. LIFE WANTS TO LIVE. YET, WHEN SOME PEOPLE OUTGROW THE BELIEFS THEY WERE FORCED TO LIVE BY, THE NEGATIVE HABITS REMAIN. AND THE HABIT IS THE CRUEL TASKMASTER. FOR THOSE PEOPLE SO POISONED WILL DESTROY THEMSELVES, RATHER THAN ACCEPT THEIR NEWLY REALIZED AWARENESS, THAT LIFE IS WORTHWHILE. WE MUST CONTINUE TO EXPERIMENT.
AS TIME WENT BY, EVERY EXPERIMENT WAS MET WITH FAILURE. HOWEVER, THE ATTRACTION BETWEEN THE TWO YOUNG EXPERIMENTERS, APPARENT FROM THE BEGINNING, BEGAN TO BLOSSON. AND FROM THE TIME THAT THEY CONFESSED LOVE FOR ONE ANOTHER, LIFE BECAME A BEAUTIFUL ADVENTURE - FROM THE SIMPLE DOMESTIC CHORES TO THE FIELD TRIPS TO ACQUIRE SPECIMENS.
CLEAD, YOU MUST KNOW I'M IN LOVE WITH YOU. I CAN ONLY HOPE YOU FEEL THE SAME.
I DO... AND FROM THE FIRST MOMENT I SAW YOU.
JACK KATZ

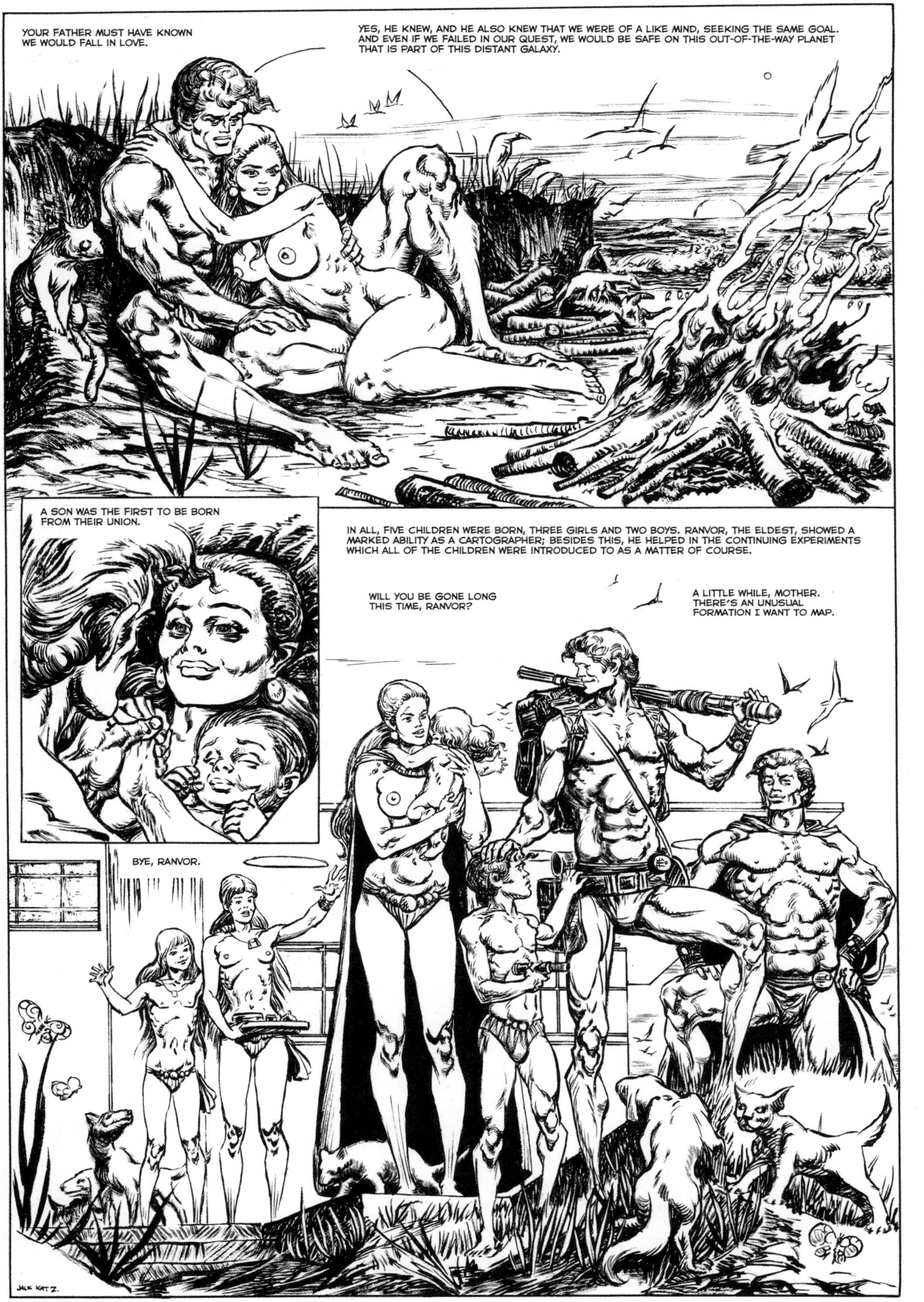
YOUR FATHER MUST HAVE KNOWN WE WOULD FALL IN LOVE.
YES, HE KNEW, AND HE ALSO KNEW THAT WE WERE OF A LIKE MIND, SEEKING THE SAME GOAL. AND EVEN IF WE FAILED IN OUR QUEST, WE WOULD BE SAFE ON THIS OUT-OF-THE-WAY PLANET THAT IS PART OF THIS DISTANT GALAXY.
A SON WAS THE FIRST TO BE BORN FROM THEIR UNION.
IN ALL, FIVE CHILDREN WERE BORN, THREE GIRLS AND TWO BOYS. RANVOR, THE ELDEST, SHOWED A MARKED ABILITY AS A CARTOGRAPHER; BESIDES THIS, HE HELPED IN THE CONTINUING EXPERIMENTS WHICH ALL OF THE CHILDREN WERE INTRODUCED TO AS A MATTER OF COURSE.
WILL YOU BE GONE LONG THIS TIME, RANVOR?
A LITTLE WHILE, MOTHER. THERE'S AN UNUSUAL FORMATION I WANT TO MAP.
BYE, RANVOR.
JACK KATZ.

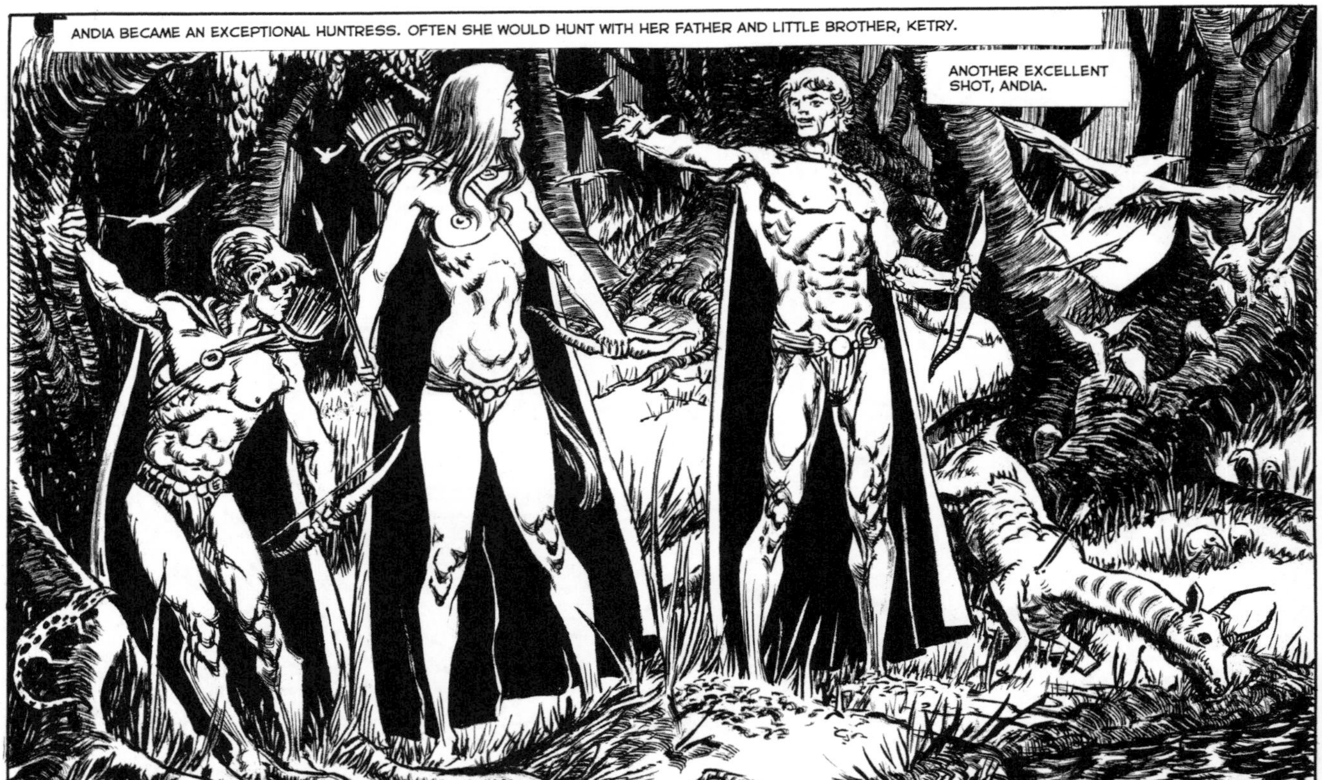
ANDIA BECAME AN EXCEPTIONAL HUNTRESS. OFTEN SHE WOULD HUNT WITH HER FATHER AND LITTLE BROTHER, KETRY.
ANOTHER EXCELLENT SHOT, ANDIA.

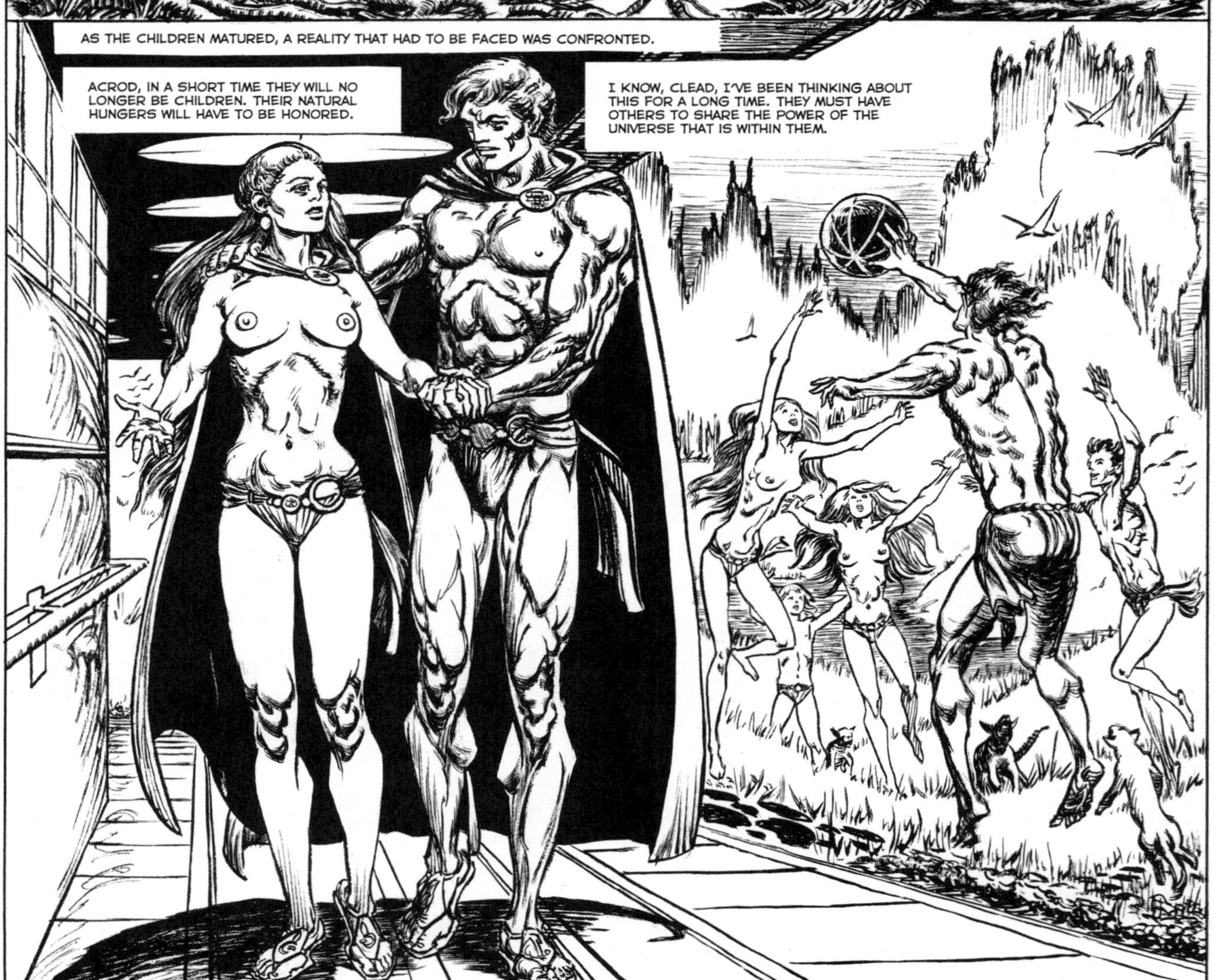
AS THE CHILDREN MATURED, A REALITY THAT HAD TO BE FACED WAS CONFRONTED.
ACROD, IN A SHORT TIME THEY WILL NO LONGER BE CHILDREN. THEIR NATURAL HUNGERS WILL HAVE TO BE HONORED.
I KNOW, CLEAD, I'VE BEEN THINKING ABOUT THIS FOR A LONG TIME. THEY MUST HAVE OTHERS TO SHARE THE POWER OF THE UNIVERSE THAT IS WITHIN THEM.
JACK KATZ

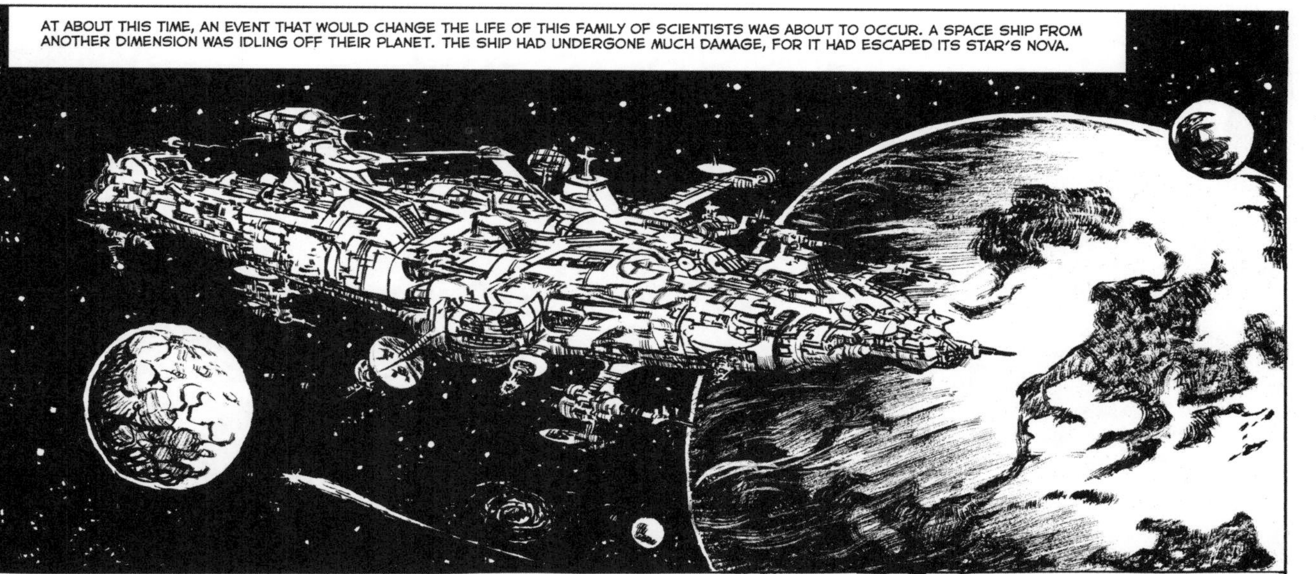
AT ABOUT THIS TIME, AN EVENT THAT WOULD CHANGE THE LIFE OF THIS FAMILY OF SCIENTISTS WAS ABOUT TO OCCUR. A SPACE SHIP FROM ANOTHER DIMENSION WAS IDLING OFF THEIR PLANET. THE SHIP HAD UNDERGONE MUCH DAMAGE, FOR IT HAD ESCAPED ITS STAR'S NOVA.

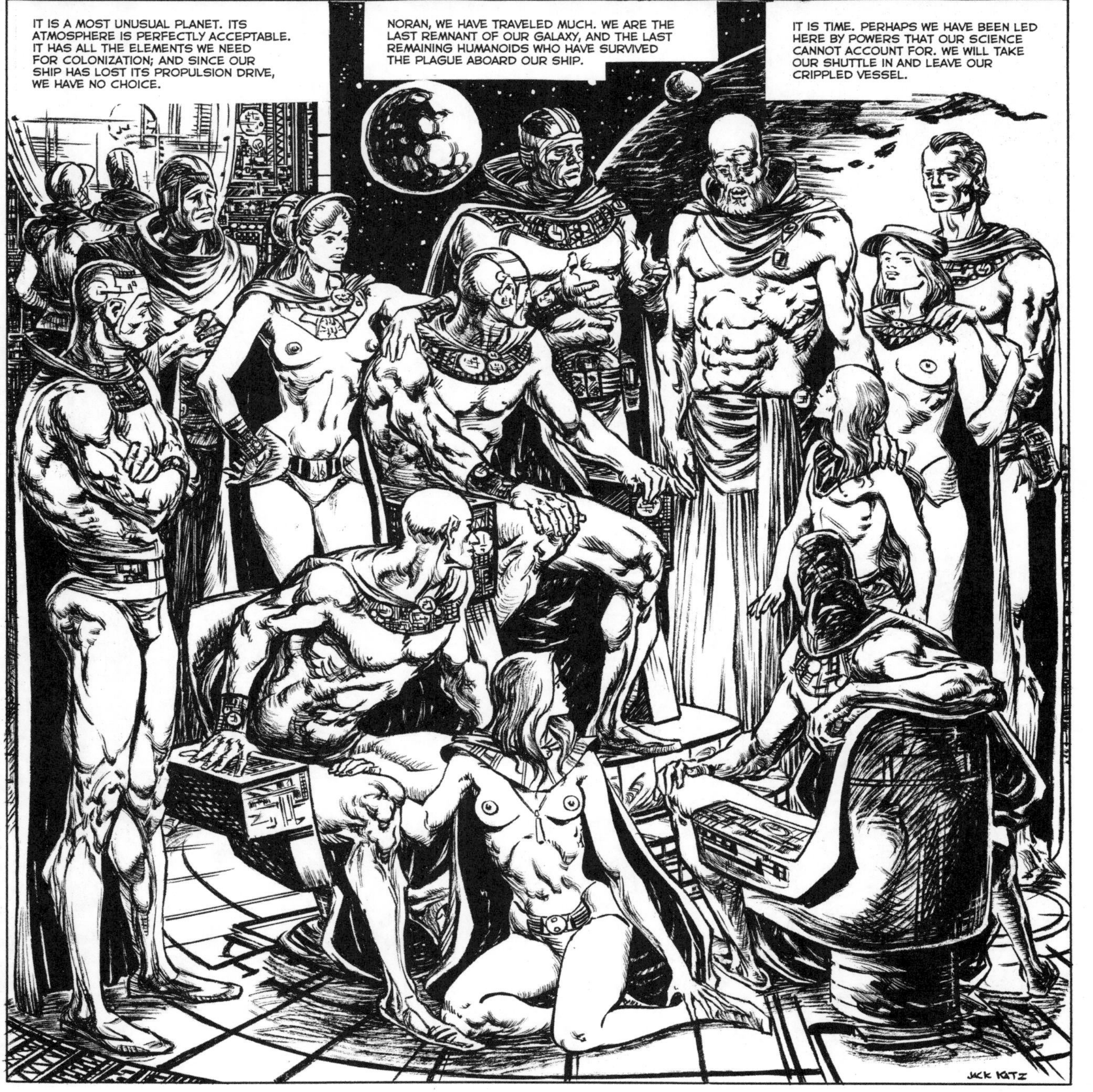
IT IS A MOST UNUSUAL PLANET. ITS ATMOSPHERE IS PERFECTLY ACCEPTABLE. IT HAS ALL THE ELEMENTS WE NEED FOR COLONIZATION; AND SINCE OUR SHIP HAS LOST ITS PROPULSION DRIVE, WE HAVE NO CHOICE.
NORAN, WE HAVE TRAVELED MUCH. WE ARE THE LAST REMNANT OF OUR GALAXY, AND THE LAST REMAINING HUMANOIDS WHO HAVE SURVIVED THE PLAGUE ABOARD OUR SHIP.
IT IS TIME. PERHAPS WE HAVE BEEN LED HERE BY POWERS THAT OUR SCIENCE CANNOT ACCOUNT FOR. WE WILL TAKE OUR SHUTTLE IN AND LEAVE OUR CRIPPLED VESSEL.
JACK KATZ

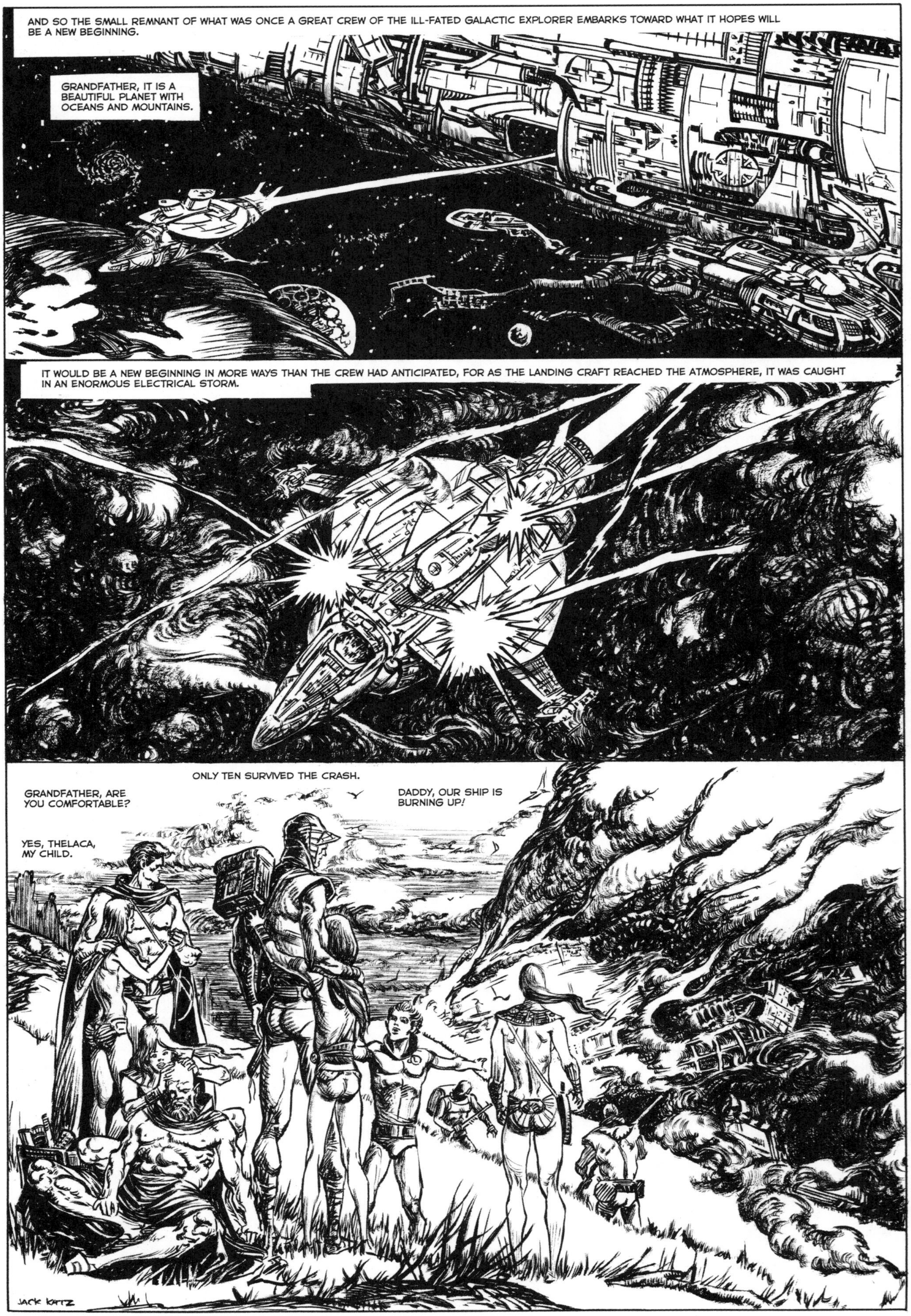
AND SO THE SMALL REMNANT OF WHAT WAS ONCE A GREAT CREW OF THE ILL-FATED GALACTIC EXPLORER EMBARKS TOWARD WHAT IT HOPES WILL BE A NEW BEGINNING.
GRANDFATHER, IT IS A BEAUTIFUL PLANET WITH OCEANS AND MOUNTAINS.
IT WOULD BE A NEW BEGINNING IN MORE WAYS THAN THE CREW HAD ANTICIPATED, FOR AS THE LANDING CRAFT REACHED THE ATMOSPHERE, IT WAS CAUGHT IN AN ENORMOUS ELECTRICAL STORM.
ONLY TEN SURVIVED THE CRASH.
GRANDFATHER, ARE YOU COMFORTABLE?
YES, THELACA, MY CHILD.
DADDY, OUR SHIP IS BURNING UP!
JACK KATZ

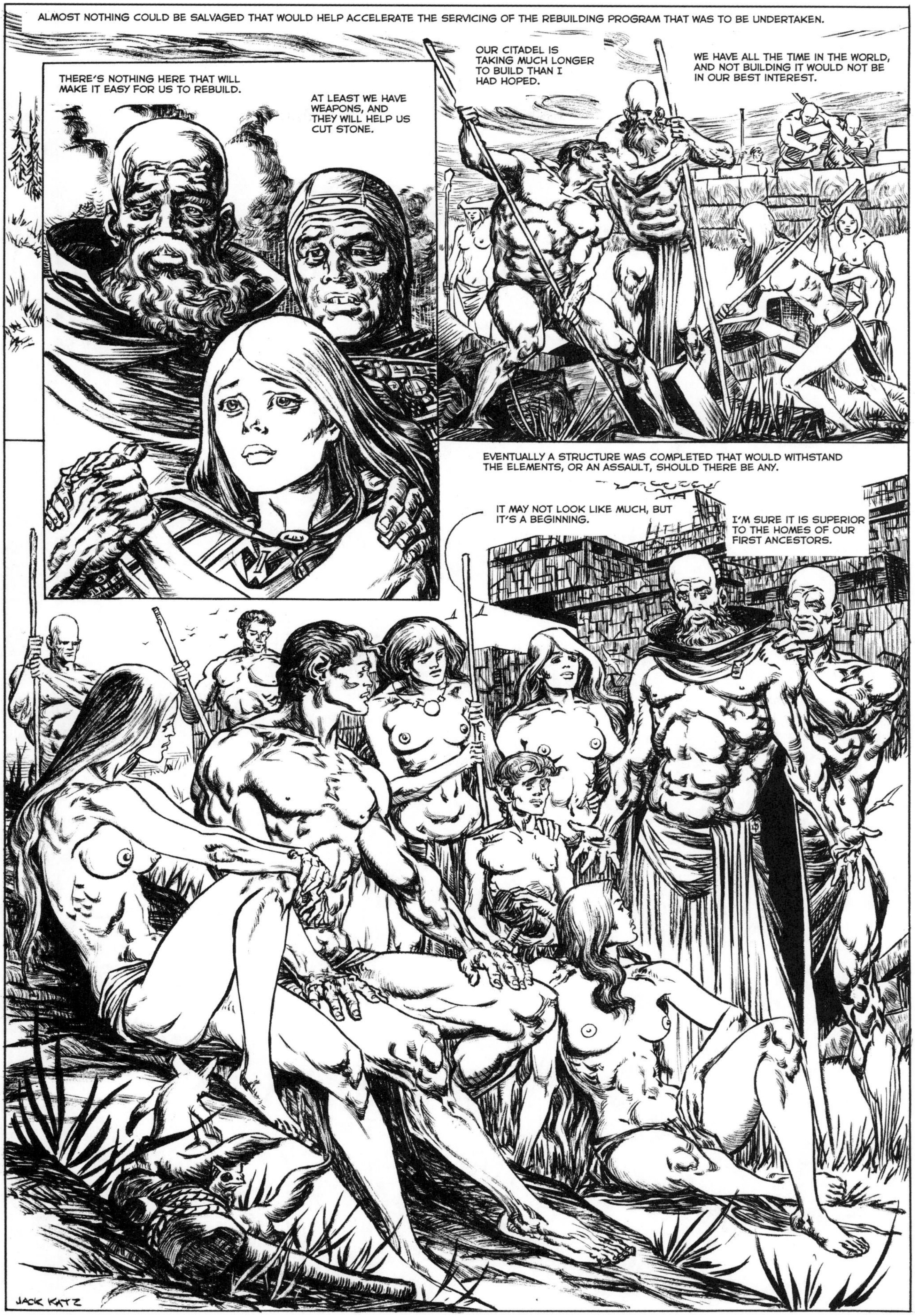
ALMOST NOTHING COULD BE SALVAGED THAT WOULD HELP ACCELERATE THE SERVICING OF THE REBUILDING PROGRAM THAT WAS TO BE UNDERTAKEN.
THERE'S NOTHING HERE THAT WILL MAKE IT EASY FOR US TO REBUILD.
AT LEAST WE HAVE WEAPONS, AND THEY WILL HELP US CUT STONE.
OUR CITADEL IS TAKING MUCH LONGER TO BUILD THAN I HAD HOPED.
WE HAVE ALL THE TIME IN THE WORLD, AND NOT BUILDING IT WOULD NOT BE IN OUR BEST INTEREST.
EVENTUALLY A STRUCTURE WAS COMPLETED THAT WOULD WITHSTAND THE ELEMENTS, OR AN ASSAULT, SHOULD THERE BE ANY.
IT MAY NOT LOOK LIKE MUCH, BUT IT'S A BEGINNING.
I'M SURE IT IS SUPERIOR TO THE HOMES OF OUR FIRST ANCESTORS.
JACK KATZ

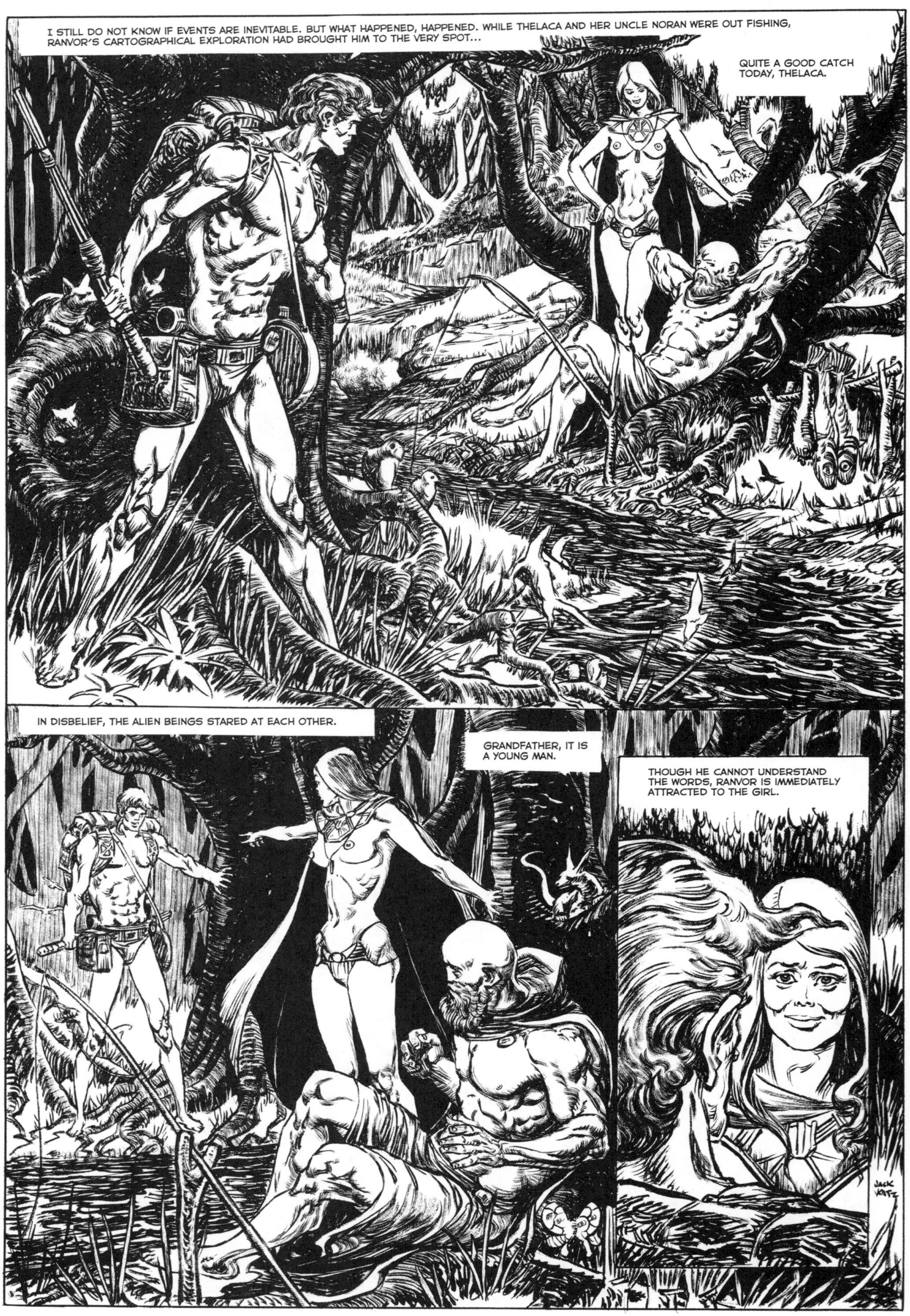
I STILL DO NOT KNOW IF EVENTS ARE INEVITABLE. BUT WHAT HAPPENED, HAPPENED. WHILE THELACA AND HER UNCLE NORAN WERE OUT FISHING, RANVOR'S CARTOGRAPHICAL EXPLORATION HAD BROUGHT HIM TO THE VERY SPOT...
QUITE A GOOD CATCH TODAY, THELACA.
IN DISBELIEF, THE ALIEN BEINGS STARED AT EACH OTHER.
GRANDFATHER, IT IS A YOUNG MAN.
THOUGH HE CANNOT UNDERSTAND THE WORDS, RANVOR IS IMMEDIATELY ATTRACTED TO THE GIRL.
JACK KATZ

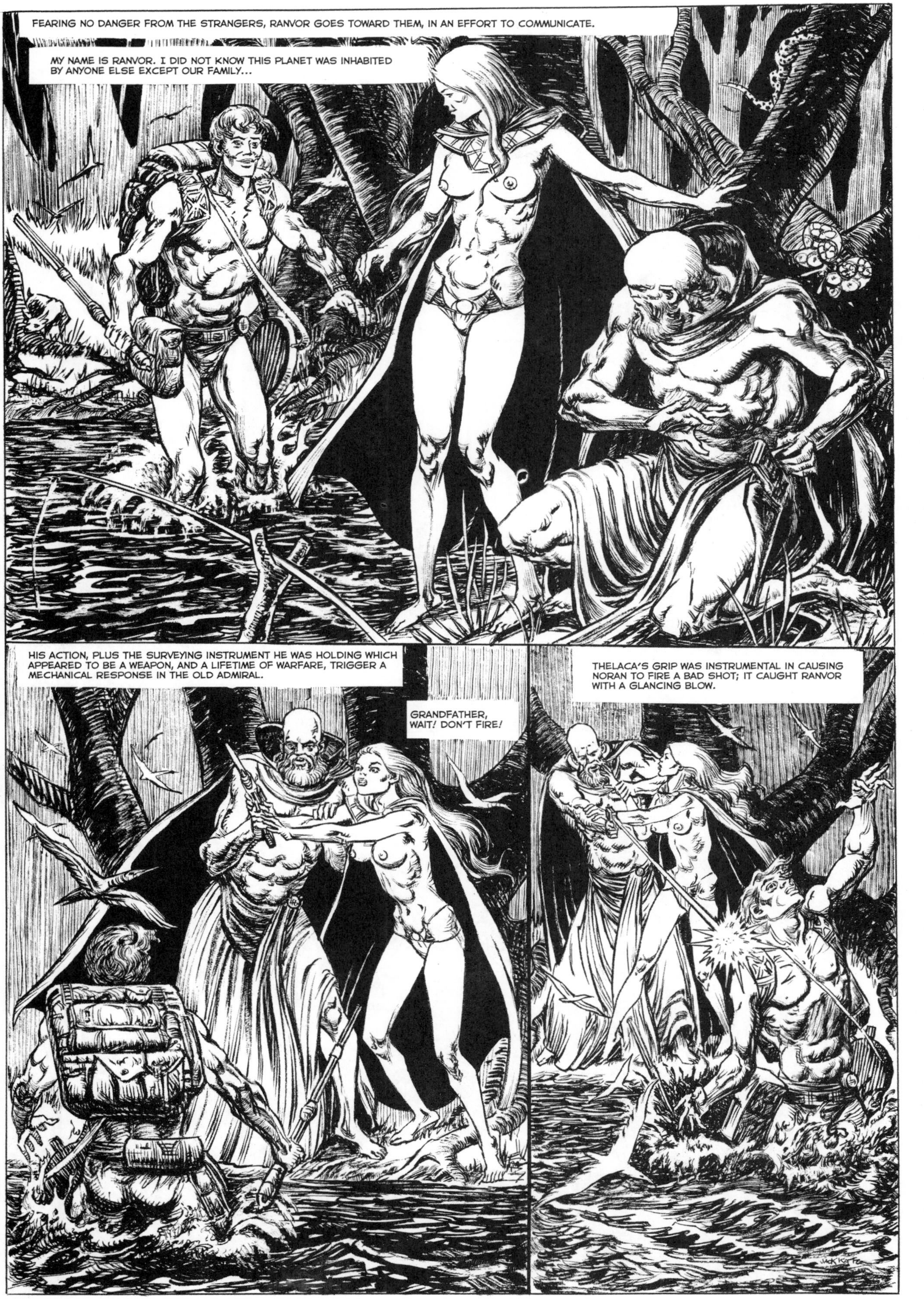
FEARING NO DANGER FROM THE STRANGERS, RANVOR GOES TOWARD THEM, IN AN EFFORT TO COMMUNICATE.
MY NAME IS RANVOR. I DID NOT KNOW THIS PLANET WAS INHABITED BY ANYONE ELSE EXCEPT OUR FAMILY...
HIS ACTION, PLUS THE SURVEYING INSTRUMENT HE WAS HOLDING WHICH APPEARED TO BE A WEAPON, AND A LIFETIME OF WARFARE, TRIGGER A MECHANICAL RESPONSE IN THE OLD ADMIRAL.
GRANDFATHER, WAIT! DON'T FIRE!
THELACA'S GRIP WAS INSTRUMENTAL IN CAUSING NORAN TO FIRE A BAD SHOT; IT CAUGHT RANVOR WITH A GLANCING BLOW.

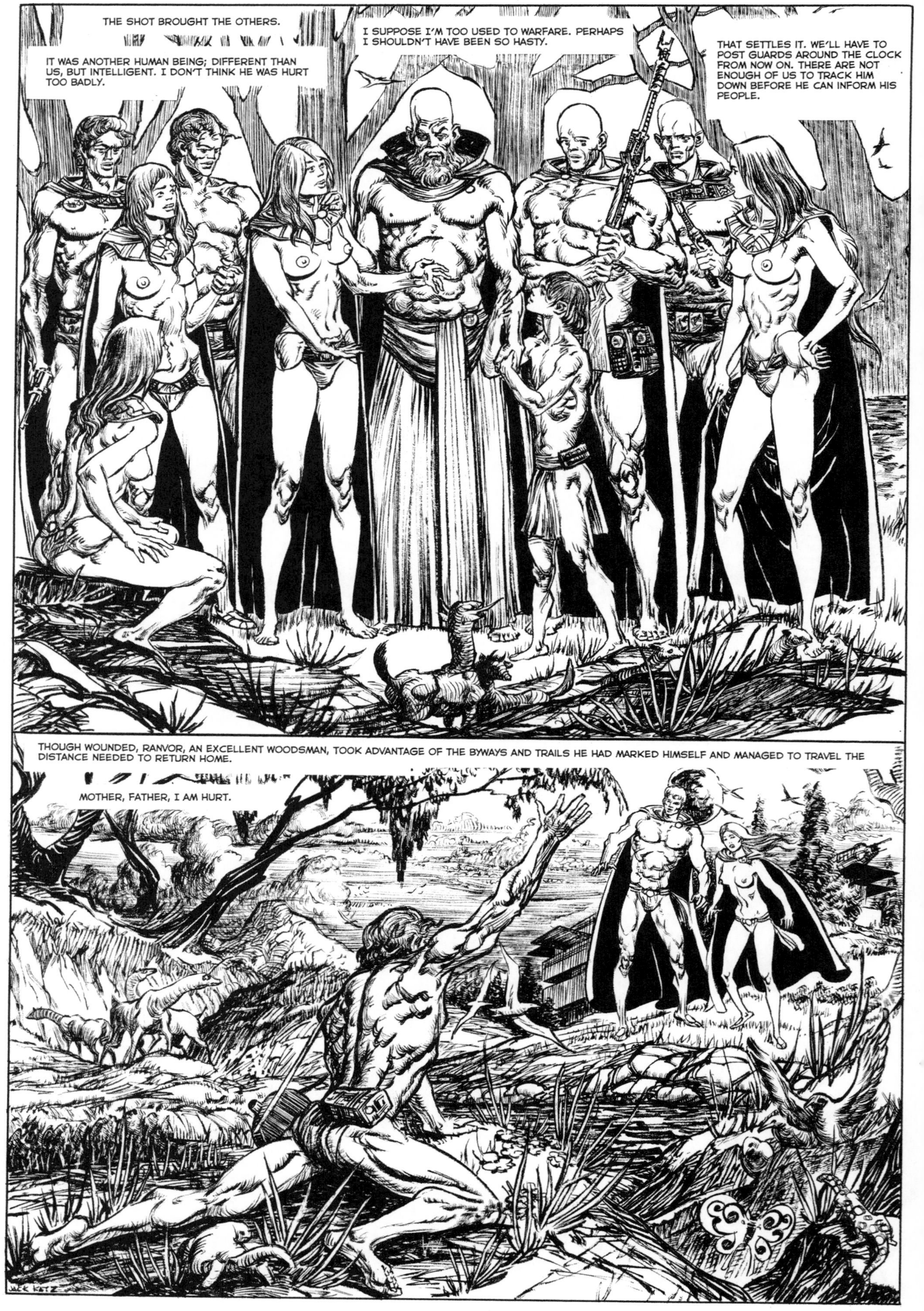
THE SHOT BROUGHT THE OTHERS.
IT WAS ANOTHER HUMAN BEING; DIFFERENT THAN US, BUT INTELLIGENT. I DON'T THINK HE WAS HURT TOO BADLY.
I SUPPOSE I'M TOO USED TO WARFARE. PERHAPS I SHOULDN'T HAVE BEEN SO HASTY.
THAT SETTLES IT. WE'LL HAVE TO POST GUARDS AROUND THE CLOCK FROM NOW ON. THERE ARE NOT ENOUGH OF US TO TRACK HIM DOWN BEFORE HE CAN INFORM HIS PEOPLE.
THOUGH WOUNDED, RANVOR, AN EXCELLENT WOODSMAN, TOOK ADVANTAGE OF THE BYWAYS AND TRAILS HE HAD MARKED HIMSELF AND MANAGED TO TRAVEL THE DISTANCE NEEDED TO RETURN HOME.
MOTHER, FATHER, I AM HURT.

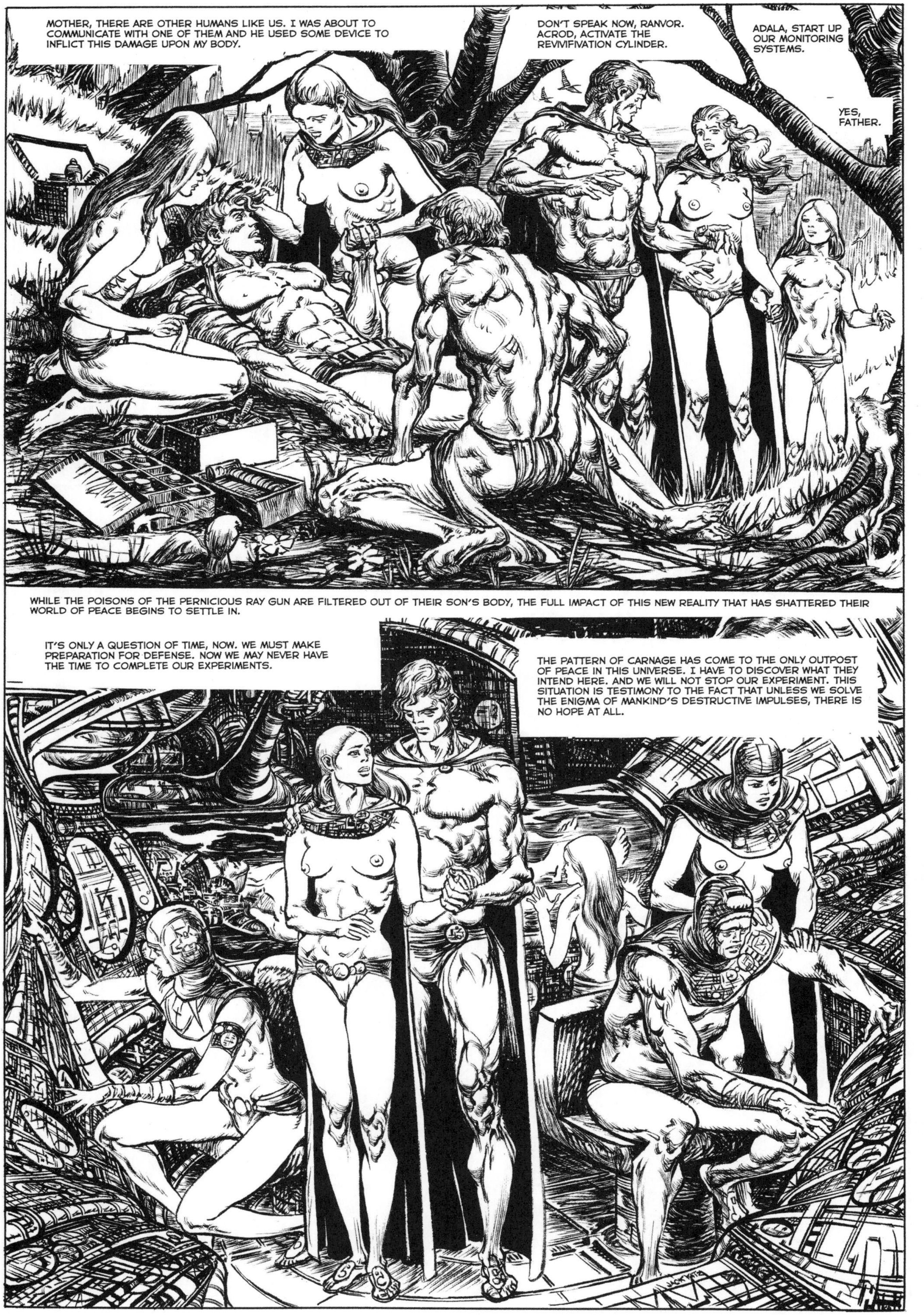
MOTHER, THERE ARE OTHER HUMANS LIKE US. I WAS ABOUT TO COMMUNICATE WITH ONE OF THEM AND HE USED SOME DEVICE TO INFLICT THIS DAMAGE UPON MY BODY.
DON'T SPEAK NOW, RANVOR. ACROD, ACTIVATE THE REVIVIFIVATION CYLINDER.
ADALA, START UP OUR MONITORING SYSTEMS.
YES, FATHER.
WHILE THE POISONS OF THE PERNICIOUS RAY GUN ARE FILTERED OUT OF THEIR SON'S BODY, THE FULL IMPACT OF THIS NEW REALITY THAT HAS SHATTERED THEIR WORLD OF PEACE BEGINS TO SETTLE IN.
IT'S ONLY A QUESTION OF TIME, NOW. WE MUST MAKE PREPARATION FOR DEFENSE. NOW WE MAY NEVER HAVE THE TIME TO COMPLETE OUR EXPERIMENTS.
THE PATTERN OF CARNAGE HAS COME TO THE ONLY OUTPOST OF PEACE IN THIS UNIVERSE. I HAVE TO DISCOVER WHAT THEY INTEND HERE. AND WE WILL NOT STOP OUR EXPERIMENT. THIS SITUATION IS TESTIMONY TO THE FACT THAT UNLESS WE SOLVE THE ENIGMA OF MANKIND'S DESTRUCTIVE IMPULSES, THERE IS NO HOPE AT ALL.

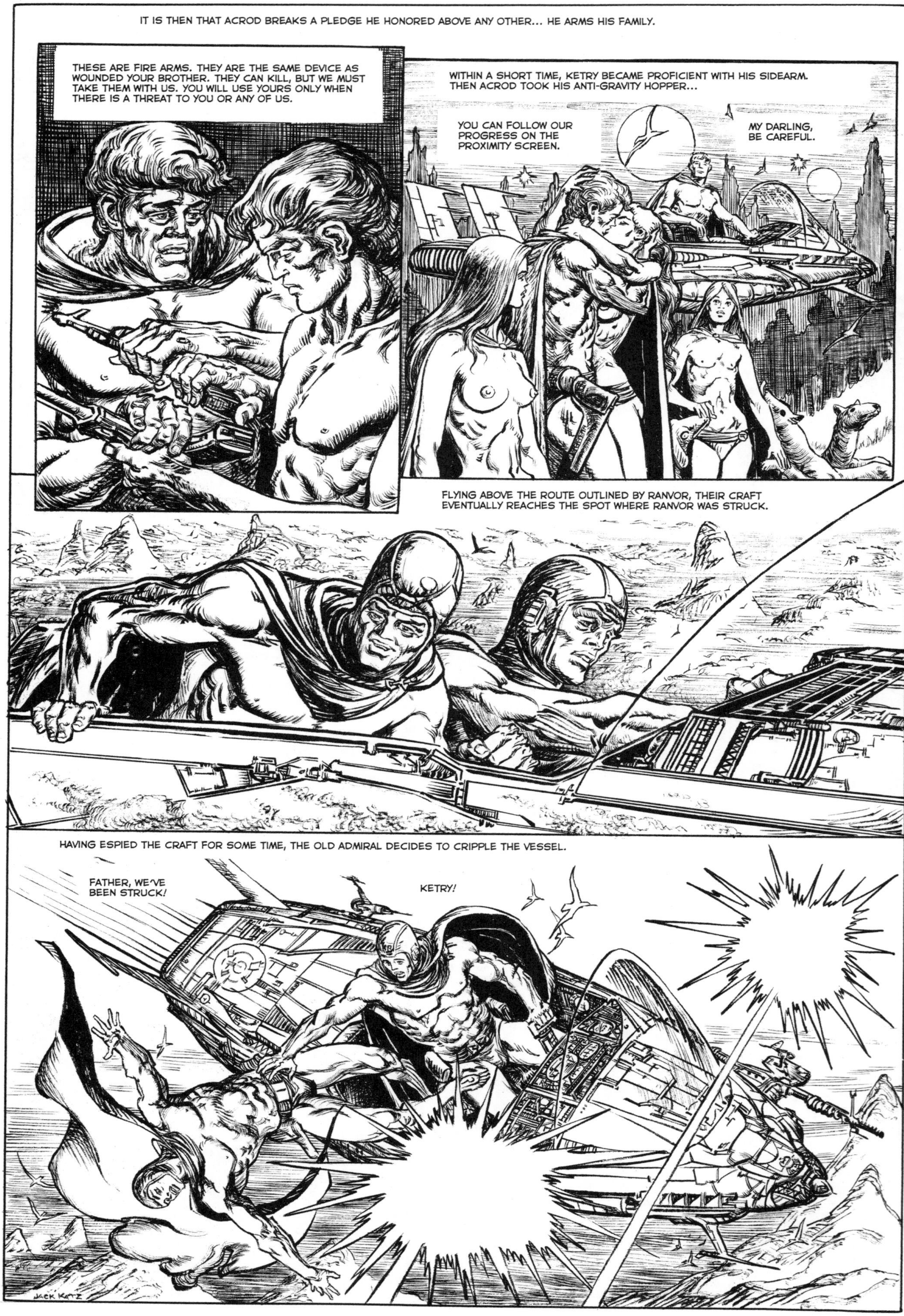
IT IS THEN THAT ACROD BREAKS A PLEDGE HE HONORED ABOVE ANY OTHER... HE ARMS HIS FAMILY.
THESE ARE FIRE ARMS. THEY ARE THE SAME DEVICE AS WOUNDED YOUR BROTHER. THEY CAN KILL, BUT WE MUST TAKE THEM WITH US. YOU WILL USE YOURS ONLY WHEN THERE IS A THREAT TO YOU OR ANY OF US.
WITHIN A SHORT TIME, KETRY BECAME PROFICIENT WITH HIS SIDEARM. THEN ACROD TOOK HIS ANTI-GRAVITY HOPPER...
YOU CAN FOLLOW OUR PROGRESS ON THE PROXIMITY SCREEN.
MY DARLING, BE CAREFUL.
FLYING ABOVE THE ROUTE OUTLINED BY RANVOR, THEIR CRAFT EVENTUALLY REACHES THE SPOT WHERE RANVOR WAS STRUCK.
HAVING ESPIED THE CRAFT FOR SOME TIME, THE OLD ADMIRAL DECIDES TO CRIPPLE THE VESSEL.
FATHER, WE'VE BEEN STRUCK!
KETRY!
JACK KATZ

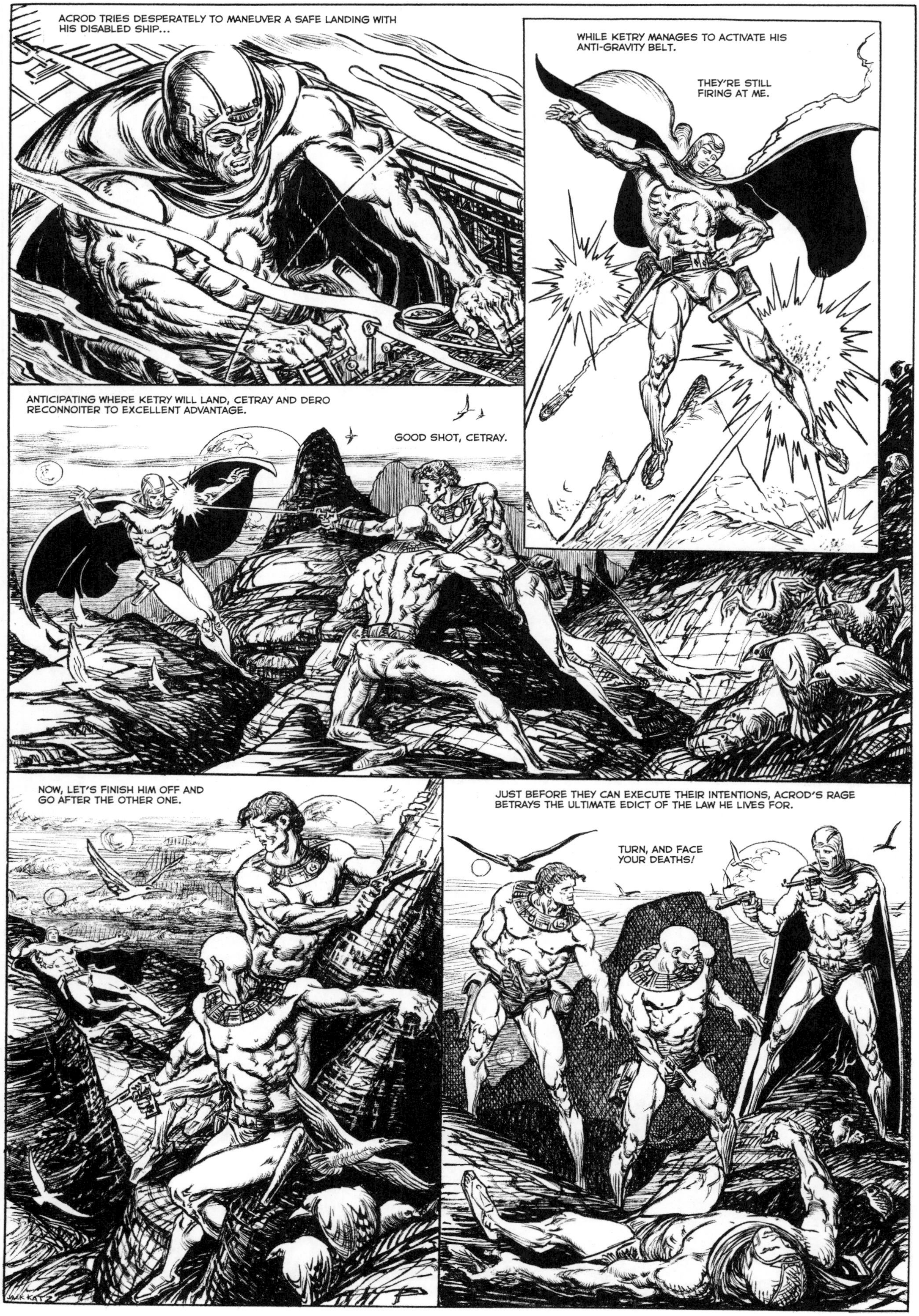
ACROD TRIES DESPERATELY TO MANEUVER A SAFE LANDING WITH HIS DISABLED SHIP...
WHILE KETRY MANAGES TO ACTIVATE HIS ANTI-GRAVITY BELT.
THEY'RE STILL FIRING AT ME.
ANTICIPATING WHERE KETRY WILL LAND, CETRAY AND DERO RECONNOITER TO EXCELLENT ADVANTAGE.
GOOD SHOT, CETRAY.
NOW, LET'S FINISH HIM OFF AND GO AFTER THE OTHER ONE.
JUST BEFORE THEY CAN EXECUTE THEIR INTENTIONS, ACROD'S RAGE BETRAYS THE ULTIMATE EDICT OF THE LAW HE LIVES FOR.
TURN, AND FACE YOUR DEATHS!
JACK KATZ

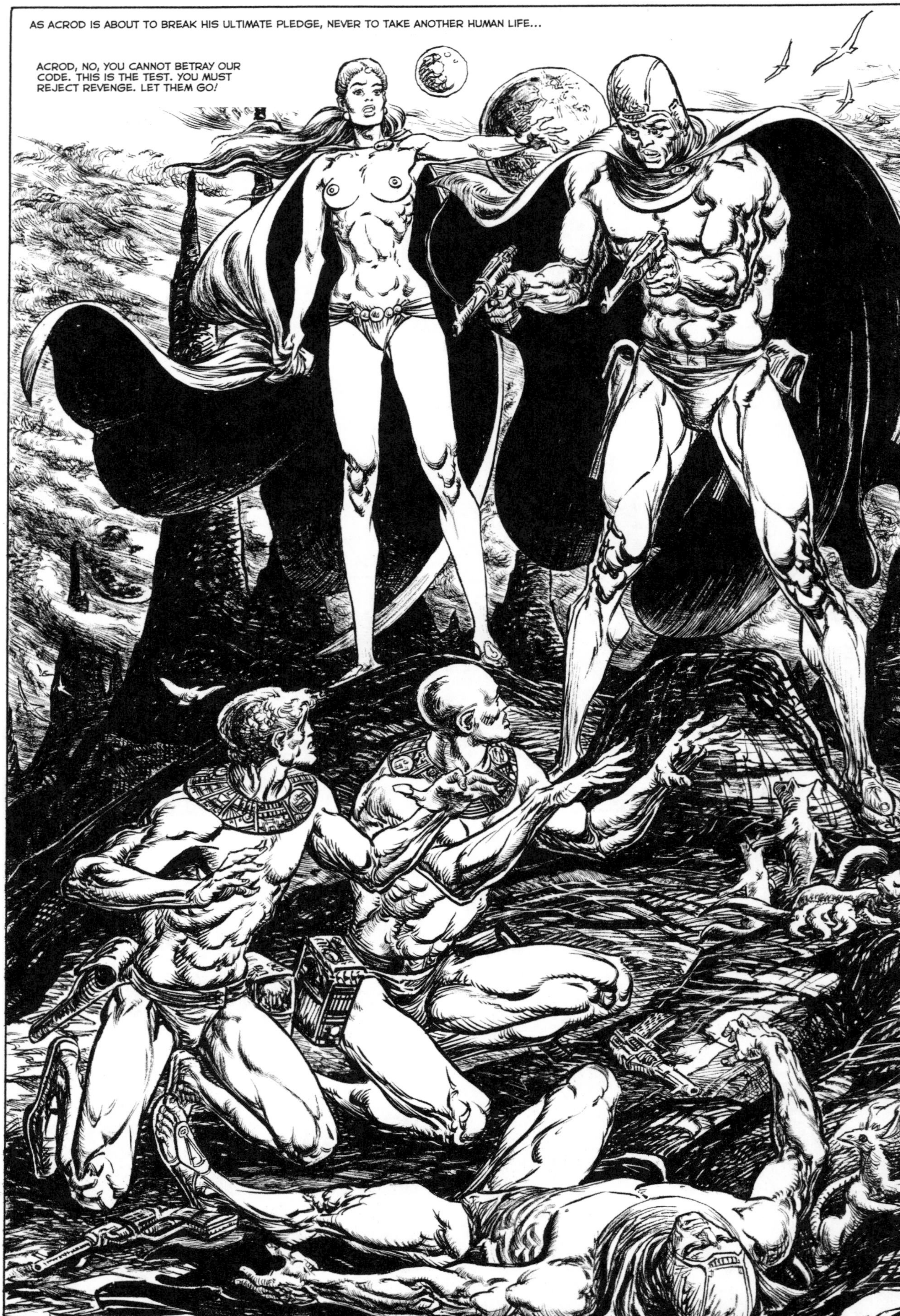

AS ACROD IS ABOUT TO BREAK HIS ULTIMATE PLEDGE, NEVER TO TAKE ANOTHER HUMAN LIFE...
ACROD, NO, YOU CANNOT BETRAY OUR CODE. THIS IS THE TEST. YOU MUST REJECT REVENGE. LET THEM GO!
JACK KATZ

TO BE CONTINUED...

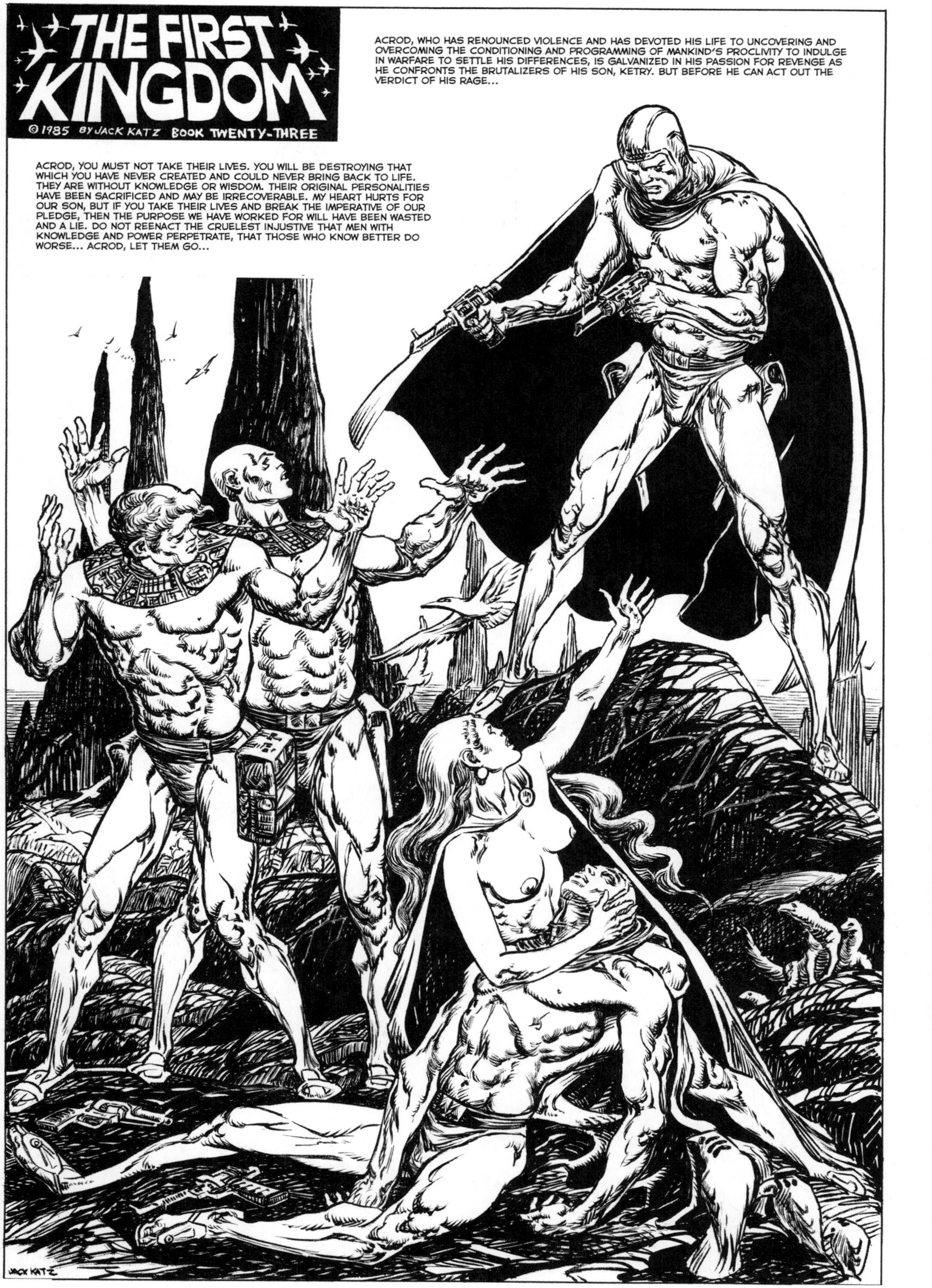
THE FIRST KINGDOM
©1985 BY JACK KATZ BOOK TWENTY-THREE
ACROD, WHO HAS RENOUNCED VIOLENCE AND HAS DEVOTED HIS LIFE TO UNCOVERING AND OVERCOMING THE CONDITIONING AND PROGRAMMING OF MANKIND'S PROCLIVITY TO INDULGE IN WARFARE TO SETTLE HIS DIFFERENCES, IS GALVANIZED IN HIS PASSION FOR REVENGE AS HE CONFRONTS THE BRUTALIZERS OF HIS SON, KETRY. BUT BEFORE HE CAN ACT OUT THE VERDICT OF HIS RAGE...
ACROD, YOU MUST NOT TAKE THEIR LIVES. YOU WILL BE DESTROYING THAT WHICH YOU HAVE NEVER CREATED AND COULD NEVER BRING BACK TO LIFE. THEY ARE WITHOUT KNOWLEDGE OR WISDOM. THEIR ORIGINAL PERSONALITIES HAVE BEEN SACRIFICED AND MAY BE IRRECOVERABLE. MY HEART HURTS FOR OUR SON, BUT IF YOU TAKE THEIR LIVES AND BREAK THE IMPERATIVE OF OUR PLEDGE, THEN THE PURPOSE WE HAVE WORKED FOR WILL HAVE BEEN WASTED AND A LIE. DO NOT REENACT THE CRUELEST INJUSTIVE THAT MEN WITH KNOWLEDGE AND POWER PERPETRATE, THAT THOSE WHO KNOW BETTER DO WORSE... ACROD, LET THEM GO...
JACK KATZ

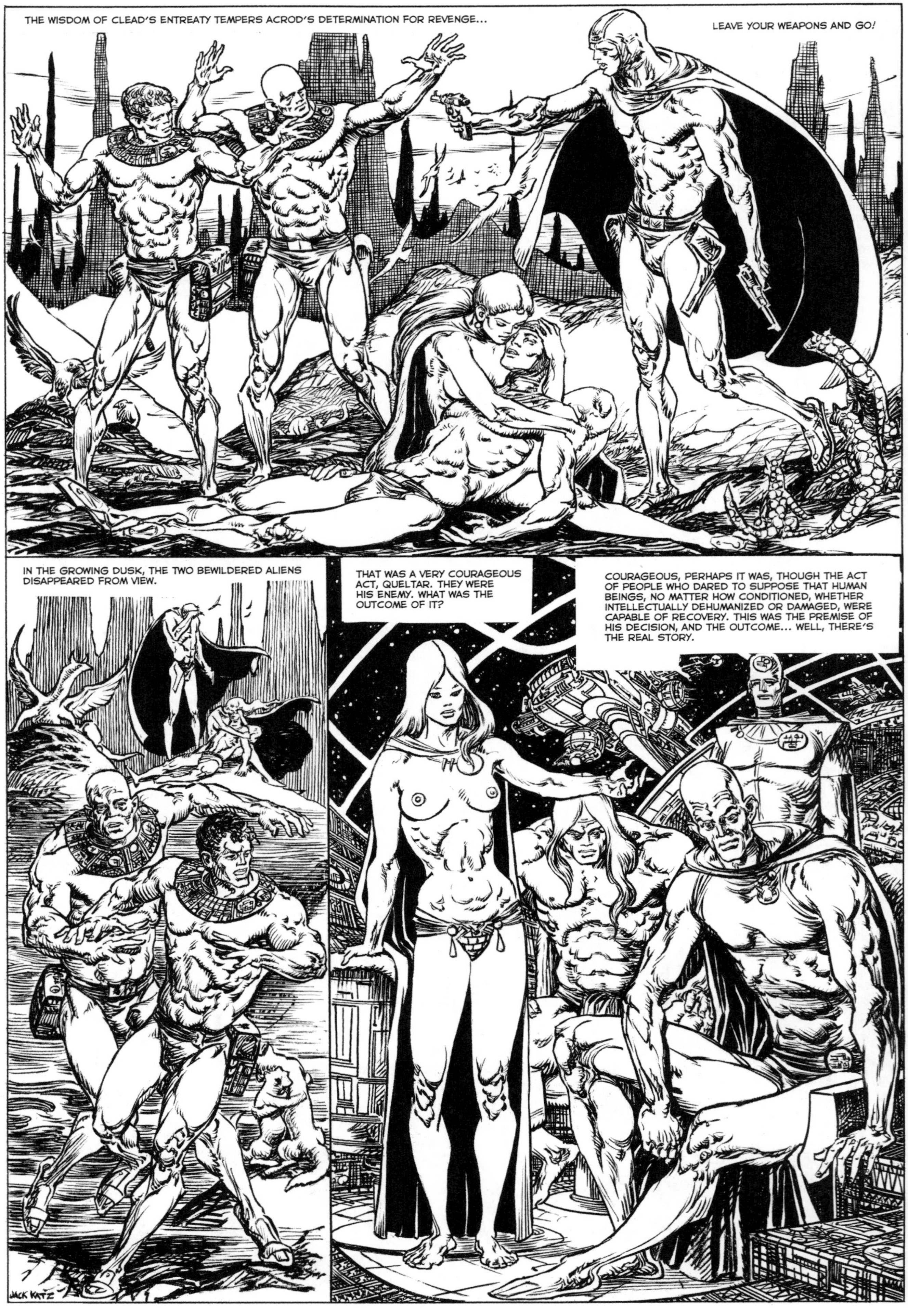
THE WISDOM OF CLEAD'S ENTREATY TEMPERS ACROD'S DETERMINATION FOR REVENGE...
LEAVE YOUR WEAPONS AND GO!
IN THE GROWING DUSK, THE TWO BEWILDERED ALIENS DISAPPEARED FROM VIEW.
JACK KATZ
THAT WAS A VERY COURAGEOUS ACT, QUELTAR. THEY WERE HIS ENEMY. WHAT WAS THE OUTCOME OF IT?
COURAGEOUS, PERHAPS IT WAS, THOUGH THE ACT OF PEOPLE WHO DARED TO SUPPOSE THAT HUMAN BEINGS, NO MATTER HOW CONDITIONED, WHETHER INTELLECTUALLY DEHUMANIZED OR DAMAGED, WERE CAPABLE OF RECOVERY. THIS WAS THE PREMISE OF HIS DECISION, AND THE OUTCOME... WELL, THERE'S THE REAL STORY.

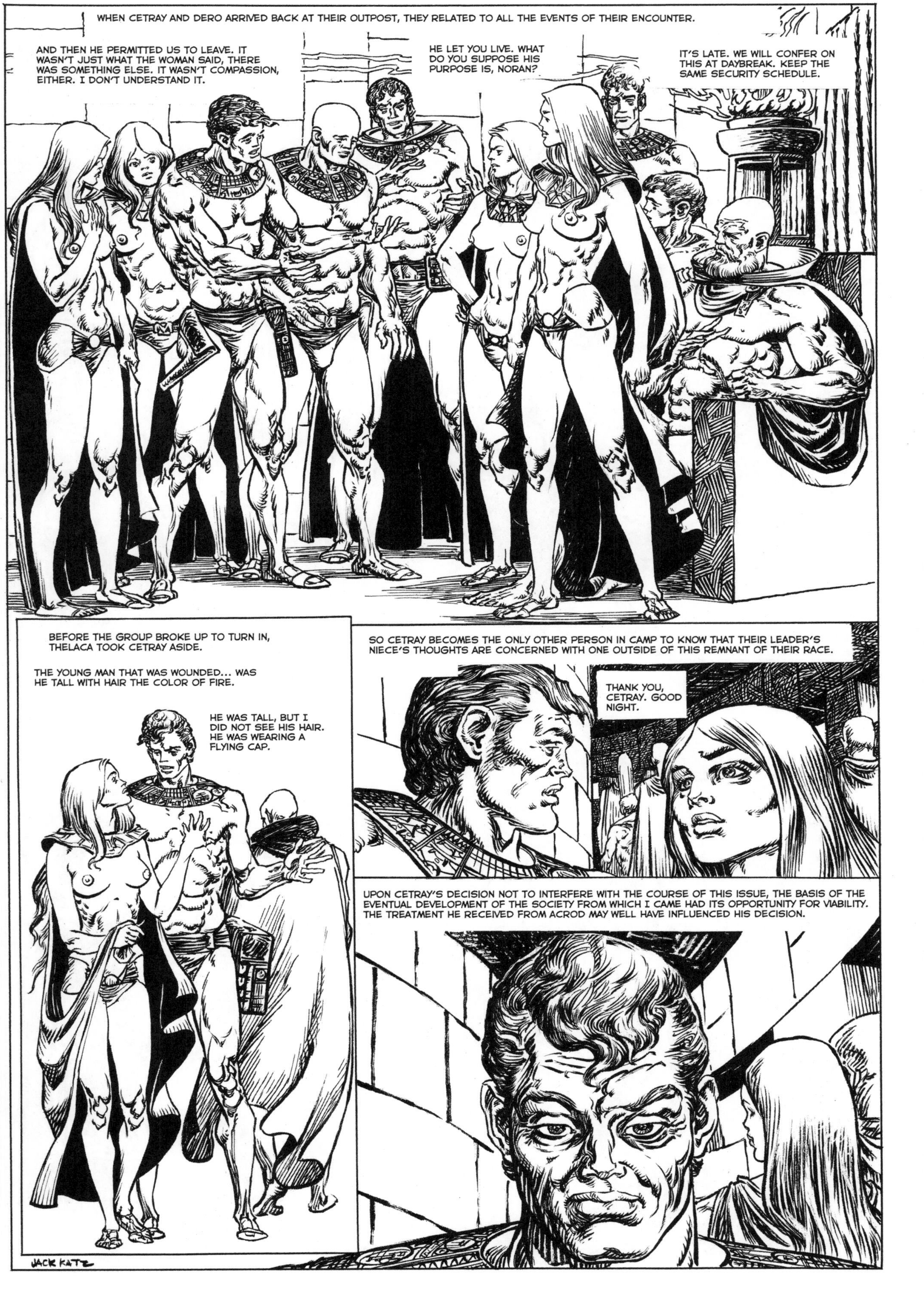
WHEN CETRAY AND DERO ARRIVED BACK AT THEIR OUTPOST, THEY RELATED TO ALL THE EVENTS OF THEIR ENCOUNTER.
AND THEN HE PERMITTED US TO LEAVE. IT WASN'T JUST WHAT THE WOMAN SAID, THERE WAS SOMETHING ELSE. IT WASN'T COMPASSION, EITHER. I DON'T UNDERSTAND IT.
HE LET YOU LIVE. WHAT DO YOU SUPPOSE HIS PURPOSE IS, NORAN?
IT'S LATE. WE WILL CONFER ON THIS AT DAYBREAK. KEEP THE SAME SECURITY SCHEDULE.
BEFORE THE GROUP BROKE UP TO TURN IN, THELACA TOOK CETRAY ASIDE.
THE YOUNG MAN THAT WAS WOUNDED... WAS HE TALL WITH HAIR THE COLOR OF FIRE.
HE WAS TALL, BUT I DID NOT SEE HIS HAIR. HE WAS WEARING A FLYING CAP.
SO CETRAY BECOMES THE ONLY OTHER PERSON IN CAMP TO KNOW THAT THEIR LEADER'S NIECE'S THOUGHTS ARE CONCERNED WITH ONE OUTSIDE OF THIS REMNANT OF THEIR RACE.
THANK YOU, CETRAY. GOOD NIGHT.
UPON CETRAY'S DECISION NOT TO INTERFERE WITH THE COURSE OF THIS ISSUE, THE BASIS OF THE EVENTUAL DEVELOPMENT OF THE SOCIETY FROM WHICH I CAME HAD ITS OPPORTUNITY FOR VIABILITY. THE TREATMENT HE RECEIVED FROM ACROD MAY WELL HAVE INFLUENCED HIS DECISION.
JACK KATZ

UPON RETURNING TO THE LABORATORY, KETRY WAS IMMEDIATELY ENTERED INTO THE REVIVIFICATION UNIT WHERE THE MONITORS INDICATED A GOOD CHANCE FOR THEIR SON'S RECOVERY.

YOU'RE A TELEPORT, CLEAD. THAT'S THE ONLY WAY YOU COULD HAVE COME TO ME AFTER KETRY AND I TRAVELED THAT DISTANCE TO THE ALIEN ENCAMPMENT.

YES, I AM. AND SO ARE YOU, BUT THE POWER REMAINS DORMANT WITHIN YOU. OUR CHILDREN HAVE INHERITED THE POWER AS WELL, THOUGH IT IS NOT NECESSARY TO UTILIZE IT FOR THE RESEARCH WE HAVE EMBARKED UPON. THEY WILL BE TOLD IF THE NECESSITY ARISES.

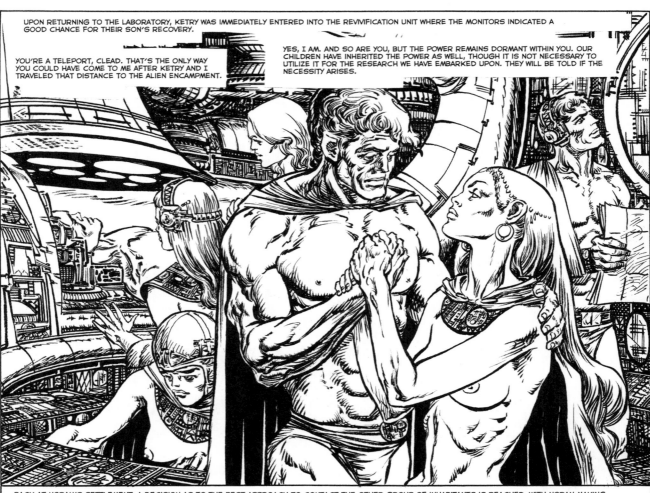

BACK AT NORAN'S SETTLEMENT, A DECISION AS TO THE BEST APPROACH TO CONTACT THE OTHER GROUP OF INHABITANTS IS REACHED, WITH NORAN MAKING AN UNPRECEDENTED ANNOUNCEMENT.

THEN IT IS DECIDED. WE WILL SEEK THEM OUT AND MAKE PEACE WITH THEM.

UNCLE NORAN, PLEASE LET ME GO. IF THERE ARE OTHER YOUNG PEOPLE THERE WITH THEM, THEN MY PRESENCE MAY HELP TO FACILITATE COMMUNICATION.

ALRIGHT, THELACA. ALTHOUGH IT GOES AGAINST EVERY DISCIPLINE OF MY TRAINING, AND THEIR BEHAVIOR HAS NULLIFIED EVERY CONVENTIONAL MEETING BETWEEN TWO ALIEN GROUPS, WE WILL GO TO THEM UNARMED.

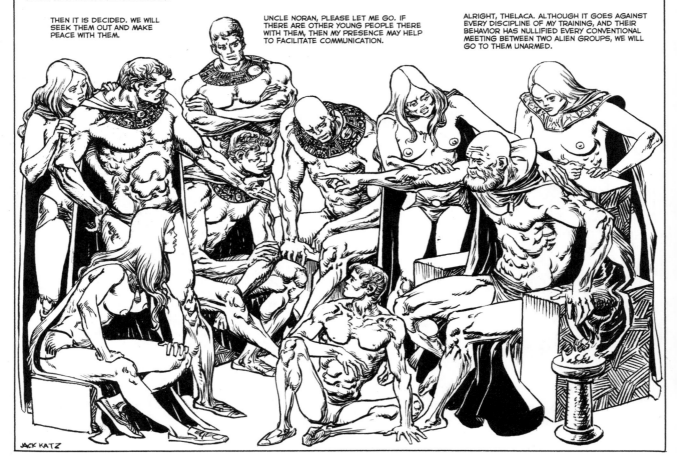

JACK KATZ

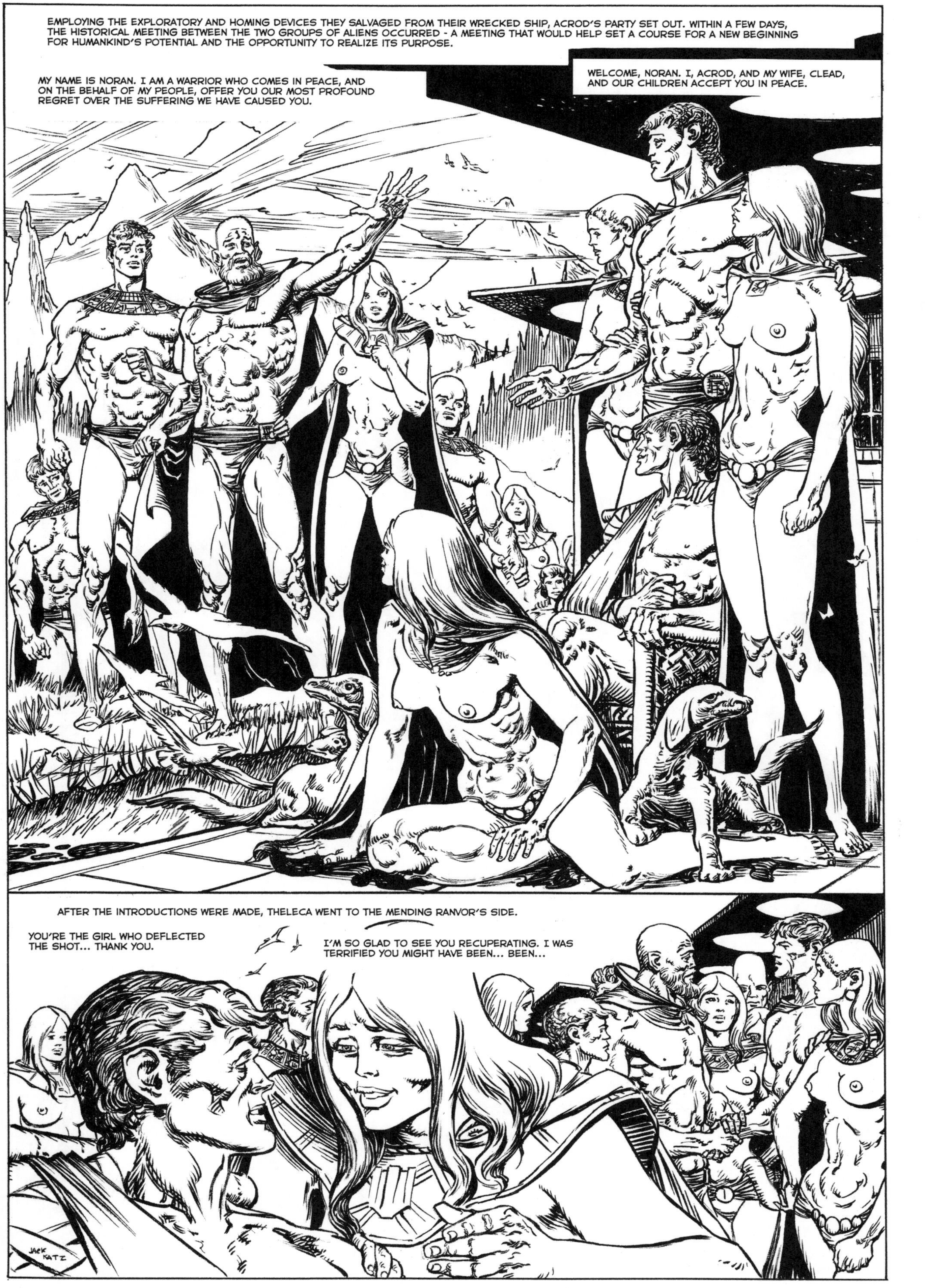
EMPLOYING THE EXPLORATORY AND HOMING DEVICES THEY SALVAGED FROM THEIR WRECKED SHIP, ACROD'S PARTY SET OUT. WITHIN A FEW DAYS, THE HISTORICAL MEETING BETWEEN THE TWO GROUPS OF ALIENS OCCURRED - A MEETING THAT WOULD HELP SET A COURSE FOR A NEW BEGINNING FOR HUMANKIND'S POTENTIAL AND THE OPPORTUNITY TO REALIZE ITS PURPOSE.
MY NAME IS NORAN. I AM A WARRIOR WHO COMES IN PEACE, AND ON THE BEHALF OF MY PEOPLE, OFFER YOU OUR MOST PROFOUND REGRET OVER THE SUFFERING WE HAVE CAUSED YOU.
WELCOME, NORAN. I, ACROD, AND MY WIFE, CLEAD, AND OUR CHILDREN ACCEPT YOU IN PEACE.
AFTER THE INTRODUCTIONS WERE MADE, THELECA WENT TO THE MENDING RANVOR'S SIDE.
YOU'RE THE GIRL WHO DEFLECTED THE SHOT... THANK YOU.
I'M SO GLAD TO SEE YOU RECUPERATING. I WAS TERRIFIED YOU MIGHT HAVE BEEN... BEEN...
JACK KATZ

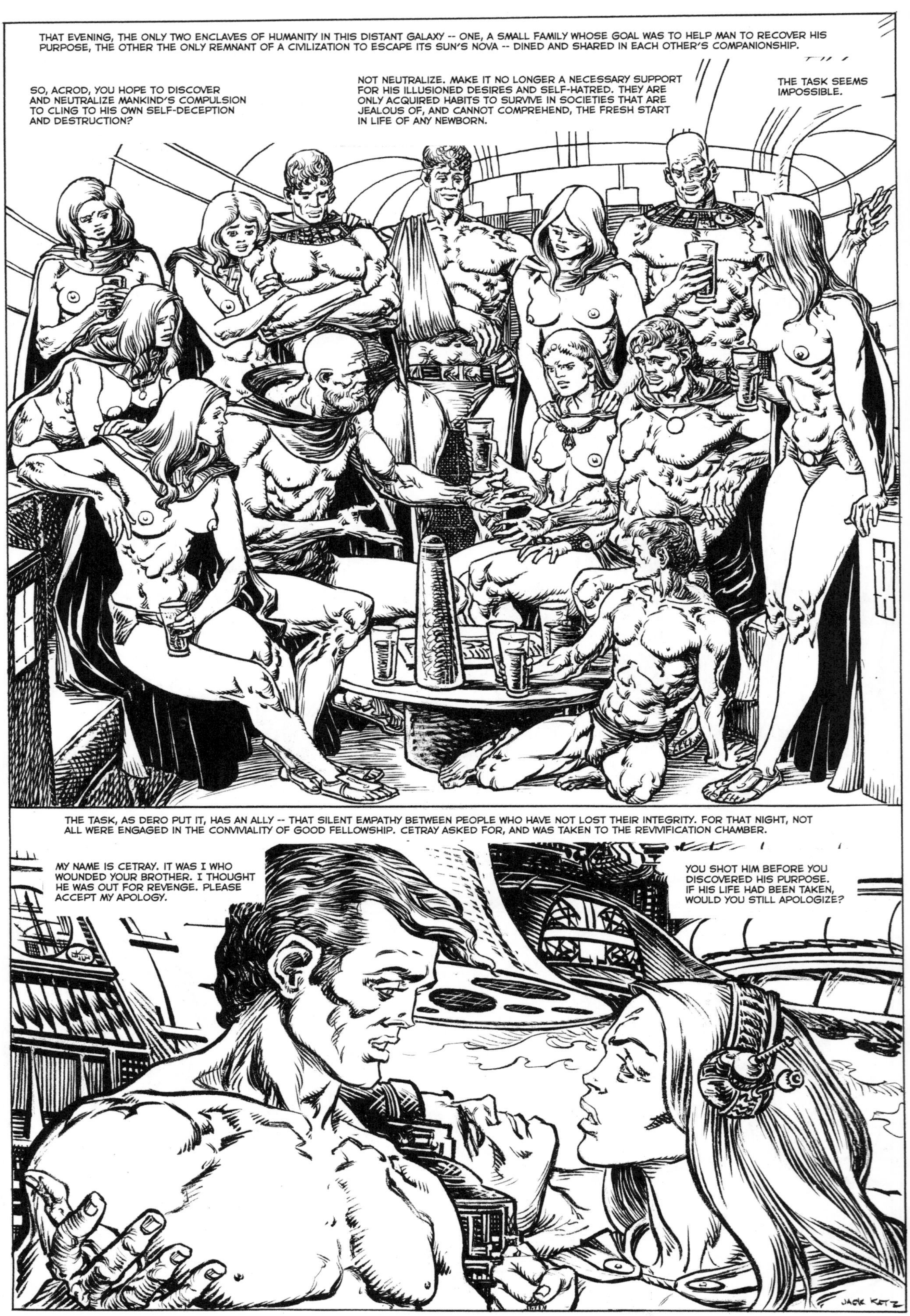
THAT EVENING, THE ONLY TWO ENCLAVES OF HUMANITY IN THIS DISTANT GALAXY -- ONE, A SMALL FAMILY WHOSE GOAL WAS TO HELP MAN TO RECOVER HIS PURPOSE, THE OTHER THE ONLY REMNANT OF A CIVILIZATION TO ESCAPE ITS SUN'S NOVA -- DINED AND SHARED IN EACH OTHER'S COMPANIONSHIP.
SO, ACROD, YOU HOPE TO DISCOVER AND NEUTRALIZE MANKIND'S COMPULSION TO CLING TO HIS OWN SELF-DECEPTION AND DESTRUCTION?
NOT NEUTRALIZE. MAKE IT NO LONGER A NECESSARY SUPPORT FOR HIS ILLUSIONED DESIRES AND SELF-HATRED. THEY ARE ONLY ACQUIRED HABITS TO SURVIVE IN SOCIETIES THAT ARE JEALOUS OF, AND CANNOT COMPREHEND, THE FRESH START IN LIFE OF ANY NEWBORN.
THE TASK SEEMS IMPOSSIBLE.
THE TASK, AS DERO PUT IT, HAS AN ALLY -- THAT SILENT EMPATHY BETWEEN PEOPLE WHO HAVE NOT LOST THEIR INTEGRITY. FOR THAT NIGHT, NOT ALL WERE ENGAGED IN THE CONVIVIALITY OF GOOD FELLOWSHIP. CETRAY ASKED FOR, AND WAS TAKEN TO THE REVIVIFICATION CHAMBER.
MY NAME IS CETRAY. IT WAS I WHO WOUNDED YOUR BROTHER. I THOUGHT HE WAS OUT FOR REVENGE. PLEASE ACCEPT MY APOLOGY.
YOU SHOT HIM BEFORE YOU DISCOVERED HIS PURPOSE. IF HIS LIFE HAD BEEN TAKEN, WOULD YOU STILL APOLOGIZE?
JACK KATZ

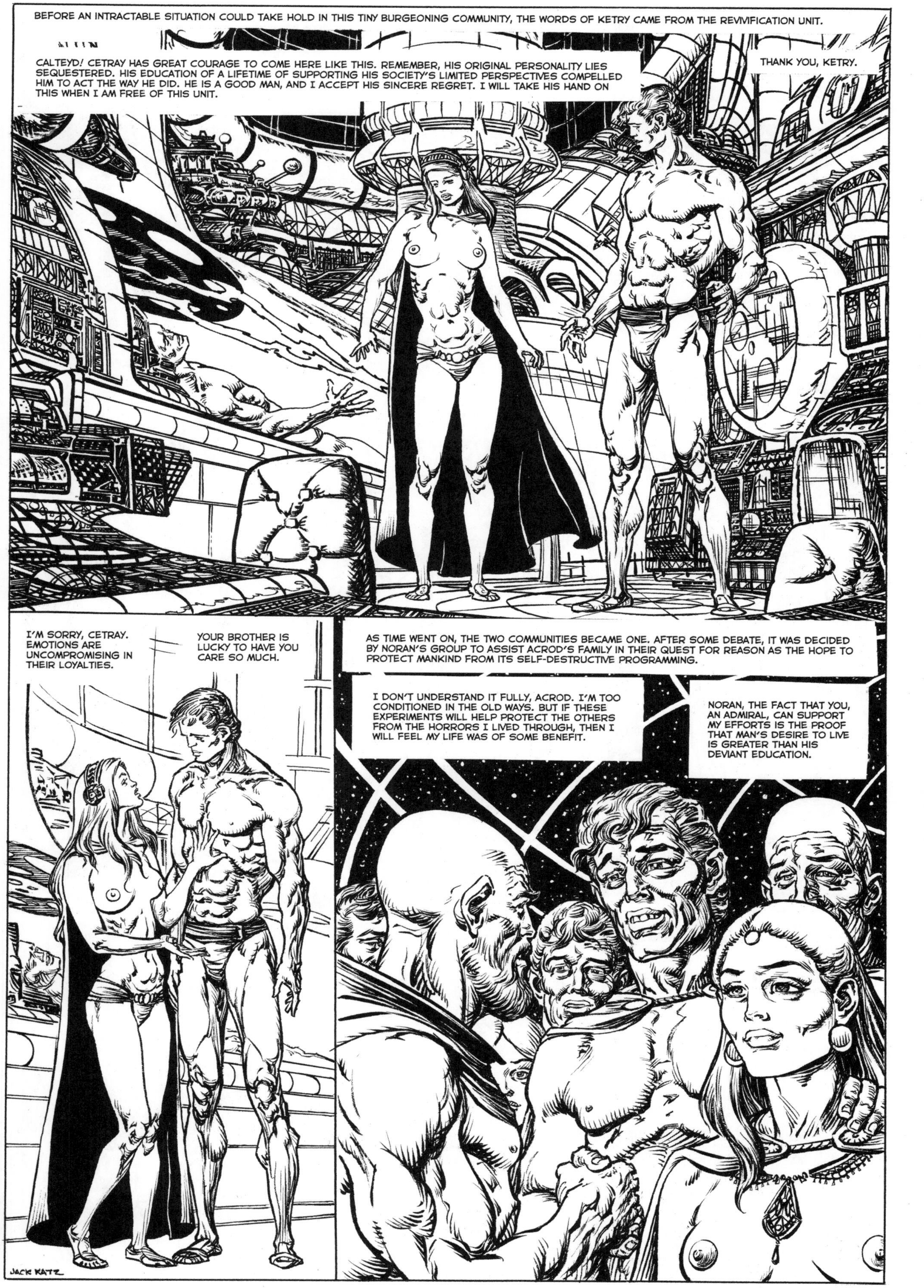
BEFORE AN INTRACTABLE SITUATION COULD TAKE HOLD IN THIS TINY BURGEONING COMMUNITY, THE WORDS OF KETRY CAME FROM THE REVIVIFICATION UNIT.
CALTEYD! CETRAY HAS GREAT COURAGE TO COME HERE LIKE THIS. REMEMBER, HIS ORIGINAL PERSONALITY LIES SEQUESTERED. HIS EDUCATION OF A LIFETIME OF SUPPORTING HIS SOCIETY'S LIMITED PERSPECTIVES COMPELLED HIM TO ACT THE WAY HE DID. HE IS A GOOD MAN, AND I ACCEPT HIS SINCERE REGRET. I WILL TAKE HIS HAND ON THIS WHEN I AM FREE OF THIS UNIT.
THANK YOU, KETRY.
I'M SORRY, CETRAY. EMOTIONS ARE UNCOMPROMISING IN THEIR LOYALTIES.
YOUR BROTHER IS LUCKY TO HAVE YOU CARE SO MUCH.
JACK KATZ
AS TIME WENT ON, THE TWO COMMUNITIES BECAME ONE. AFTER SOME DEBATE, IT WAS DECIDED BY NORAN'S GROUP TO ASSIST ACROD'S FAMILY IN THEIR QUEST FOR REASON AS THE HOPE TO PROTECT MANKIND FROM ITS SELF-DESTRUCTIVE PROGRAMMING.
I DON'T UNDERSTAND IT FULLY, ACROD. I'M TOO CONDITIONED IN THE OLD WAYS. BUT IF THESE EXPERIMENTS WILL HELP PROTECT THE OTHERS FROM THE HORRORS I LIVED THROUGH, THEN I WILL FEEL MY LIFE WAS OF SOME BENEFIT.
NORAN, THE FACT THAT YOU, AN ADMIRAL, CAN SUPPORT MY EFFORTS IS THE PROOF THAT MAN'S DESIRE TO LIVE IS GREATER THAN HIS DEVIANT EDUCATION.

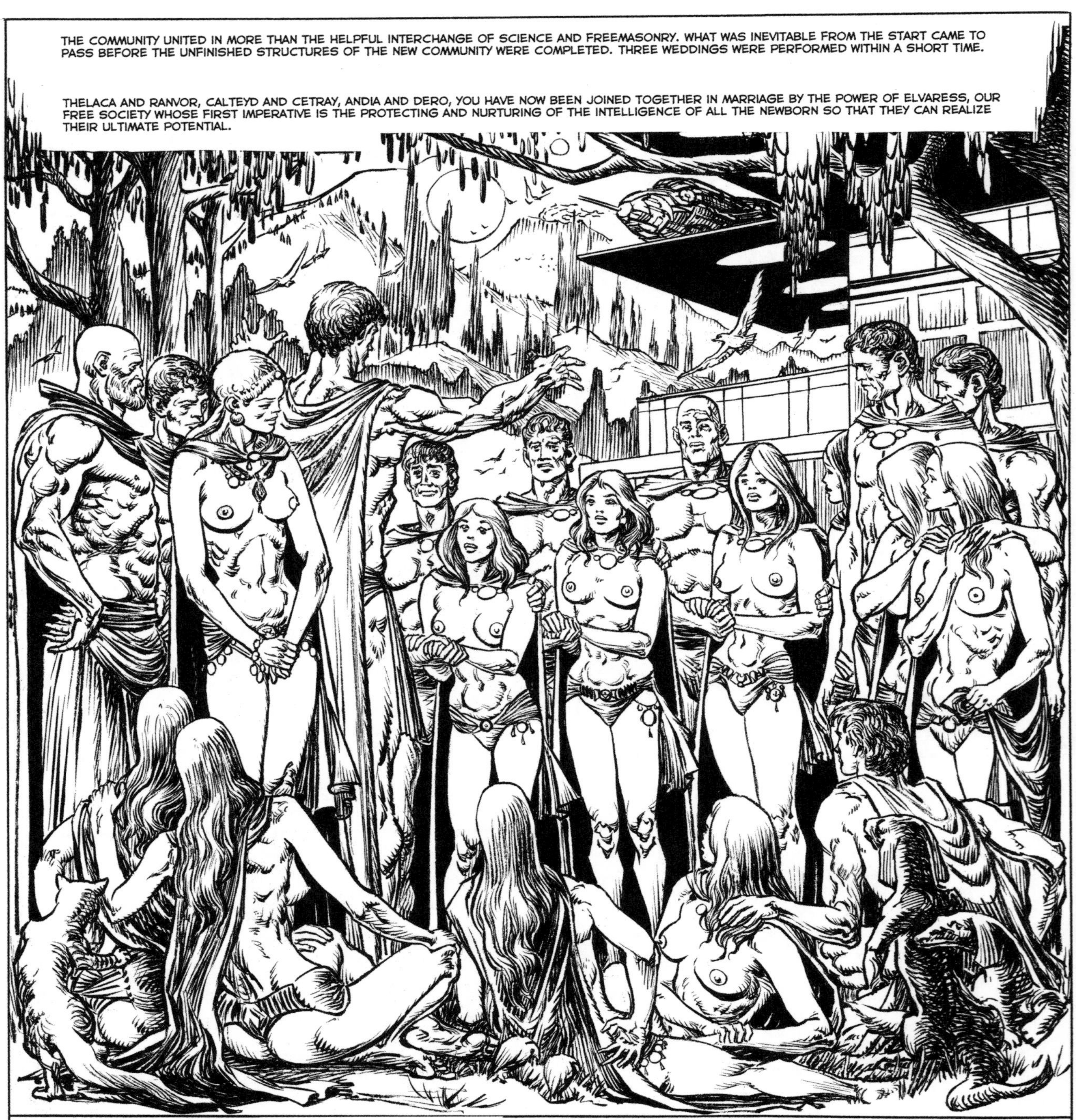
THE COMMUNITY UNITED IN MORE THAN THE HELPFUL INTERCHANGE OF SCIENCE AND FREEMASONRY. WHAT WAS INEVITABLE FROM THE START CAME TO PASS BEFORE THE UNFINISHED STRUCTURES OF THE NEW COMMUNITY WERE COMPLETED. THREE WEDDINGS WERE PERFORMED WITHIN A SHORT TIME.
THELACA AND RANVOR, CALTEYD AND CETRAY, ANDIA AND DERO, YOU HAVE NOW BEEN JOINED TOGETHER IN MARRIAGE BY THE POWER OF ELVARESS, OUR FREE SOCIETY WHOSE FIRST IMPERATIVE IS THE PROTECTING AND NURTURING OF THE INTELLIGENCE OF ALL THE NEWBORN SO THAT THEY CAN REALIZE THEIR ULTIMATE POTENTIAL.

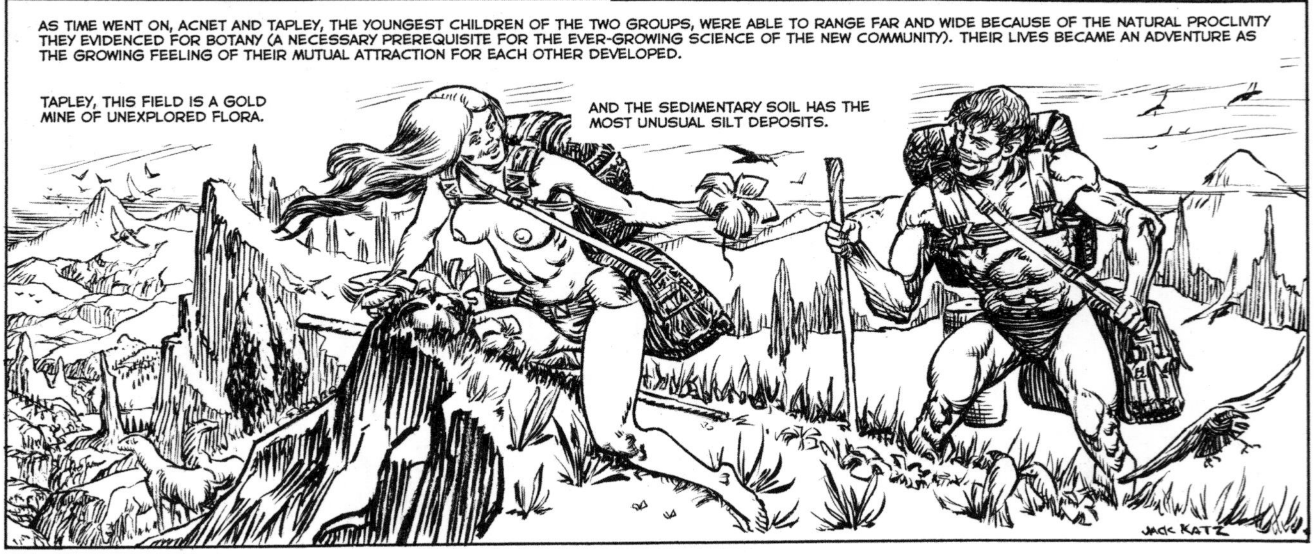
AS TIME WENT ON, ACNET AND TAPLEY, THE YOUNGEST CHILDREN OF THE TWO GROUPS, WERE ABLE TO RANGE FAR AND WIDE BECAUSE OF THE NATURAL PROCLIVITY THEY EVIDENCED FOR BOTANY (A NECESSARY PREREQUISITE FOR THE EVER-GROWING SCIENCE OF THE NEW COMMUNITY). THEIR LIVES BECAME AN ADVENTURE AS THE GROWING FEELING OF THEIR MUTUAL ATTRACTION FOR EACH OTHER DEVELOPED.
TAPLEY, THIS FIELD IS A GOLD MINE OF UNEXPLORED FLORA.
AND THE SEDIMENTARY SOIL HAS THE MOST UNUSUAL SILT DEPOSITS.
JACK KATZ

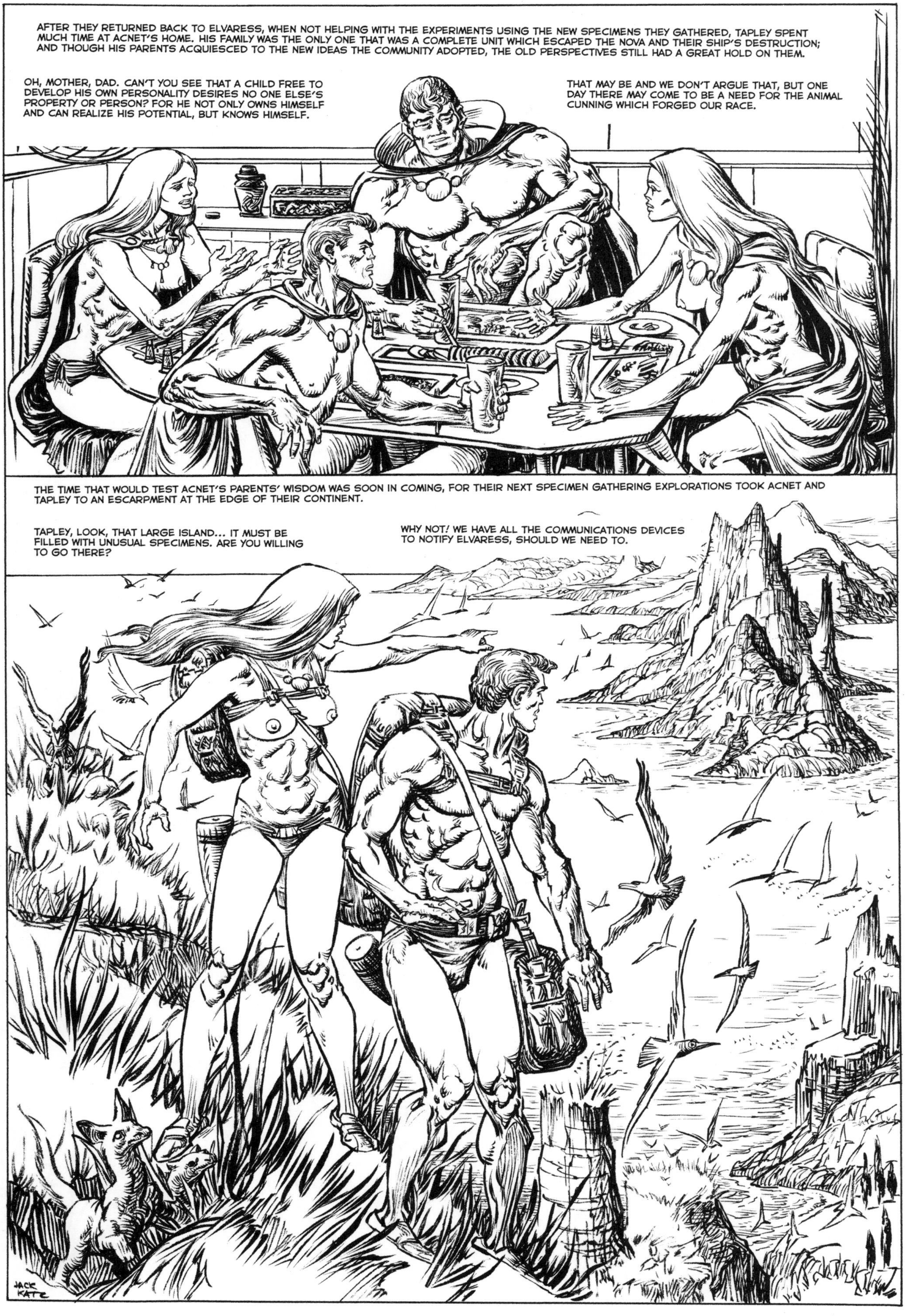
AFTER THEY RETURNED BACK TO ELVARESS, WHEN NOT HELPING WITH THE EXPERIMENTS USING THE NEW SPECIMENS THEY GATHERED, TAPLEY SPENT MUCH TIME AT ACNET'S HOME. HIS FAMILY WAS THE ONLY ONE THAT WAS A COMPLETE UNIT WHICH ESCAPED THE NOVA AND THEIR SHIP'S DESTRUCTION; AND THOUGH HIS PARENTS ACQUIESCED TO THE NEW IDEAS THE COMMUNITY ADOPTED, THE OLD PERSPECTIVES STILL HAD A GREAT HOLD ON THEM.
OH, MOTHER, DAD. CAN'T YOU SEE THAT A CHILD FREE TO DEVELOP HIS OWN PERSONALITY DESIRES NO ONE ELSE'S PROPERTY OR PERSON? FOR HE NOT ONLY OWNS HIMSELF AND CAN REALIZE HIS POTENTIAL, BUT KNOWS HIMSELF.
THAT MAY BE AND WE DON'T ARGUE THAT, BUT ONE DAY THERE MAY COME TO BE A NEED FOR THE ANIMAL CUNNING WHICH FORGED OUR RACE.
THE TIME THAT WOULD TEST ACNET'S PARENTS' WISDOM WAS SOON IN COMING, FOR THEIR NEXT SPECIMEN GATHERING EXPLORATIONS TOOK ACNET AND TAPLEY TO AN ESCARPMENT AT THE EDGE OF THEIR CONTINENT.
TAPLEY, LOOK, THAT LARGE ISLAND... IT MUST BE FILLED WITH UNUSUAL SPECIMENS. ARE YOU WILLING TO GO THERE?
WHY NOT! WE HAVE ALL THE COMMUNICATIONS DEVICES TO NOTIFY ELVARESS, SHOULD WE NEED TO.
JACK KATZ

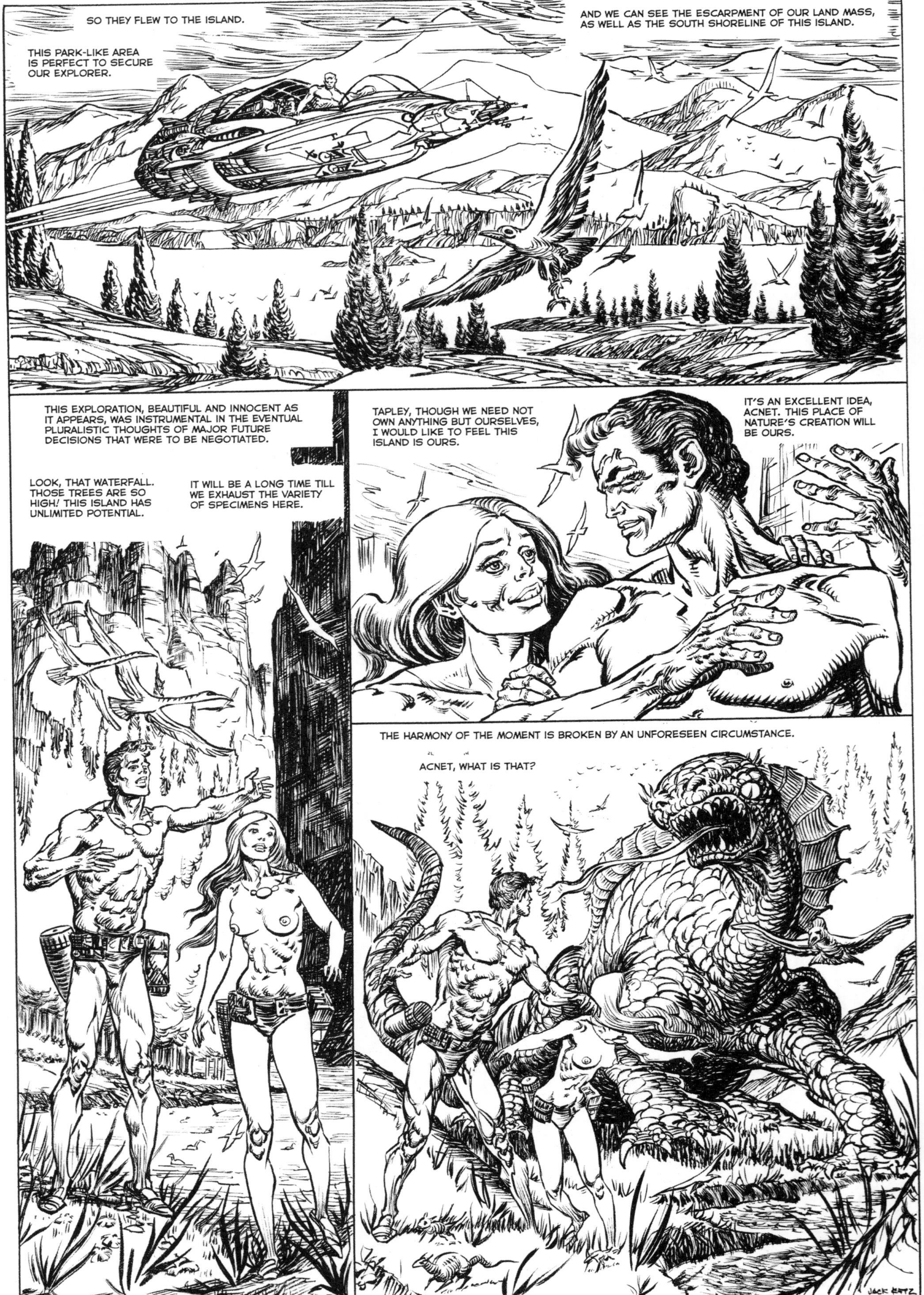
SO THEY FLEW TO THE ISLAND.
THIS PARK-LIKE AREA IS PERFECT TO SECURE OUR EXPLORER.
AND WE CAN SEE THE ESCARPMENT OF OUR LAND MASS, AS WELL AS THE SOUTH SHORELINE OF THIS ISLAND.
THIS EXPLORATION, BEAUTIFUL AND INNOCENT AS IT APPEARS, WAS INSTRUMENTAL IN THE EVENTUAL PLURALISTIC THOUGHTS OF MAJOR FUTURE DECISIONS THAT WERE TO BE NEGOTIATED.
LOOK, THAT WATERFALL. THOSE TREES ARE SO HIGH! THIS ISLAND HAS UNLIMITED POTENTIAL.
IT WILL BE A LONG TIME TILL WE EXHAUST THE VARIETY OF SPECIMENS HERE.
TAPLEY, THOUGH WE NEED NOT OWN ANYTHING BUT OURSELVES, I WOULD LIKE TO FEEL THIS ISLAND IS OURS.
IT'S AN EXCELLENT IDEA, ACNET. THIS PLACE OF NATURE'S CREATION WILL BE OURS.
THE HARMONY OF THE MOMENT IS BROKEN BY AN UNFORESEEN CIRCUMSTANCE.
ACNET, WHAT IS THAT?
JACK KATZ

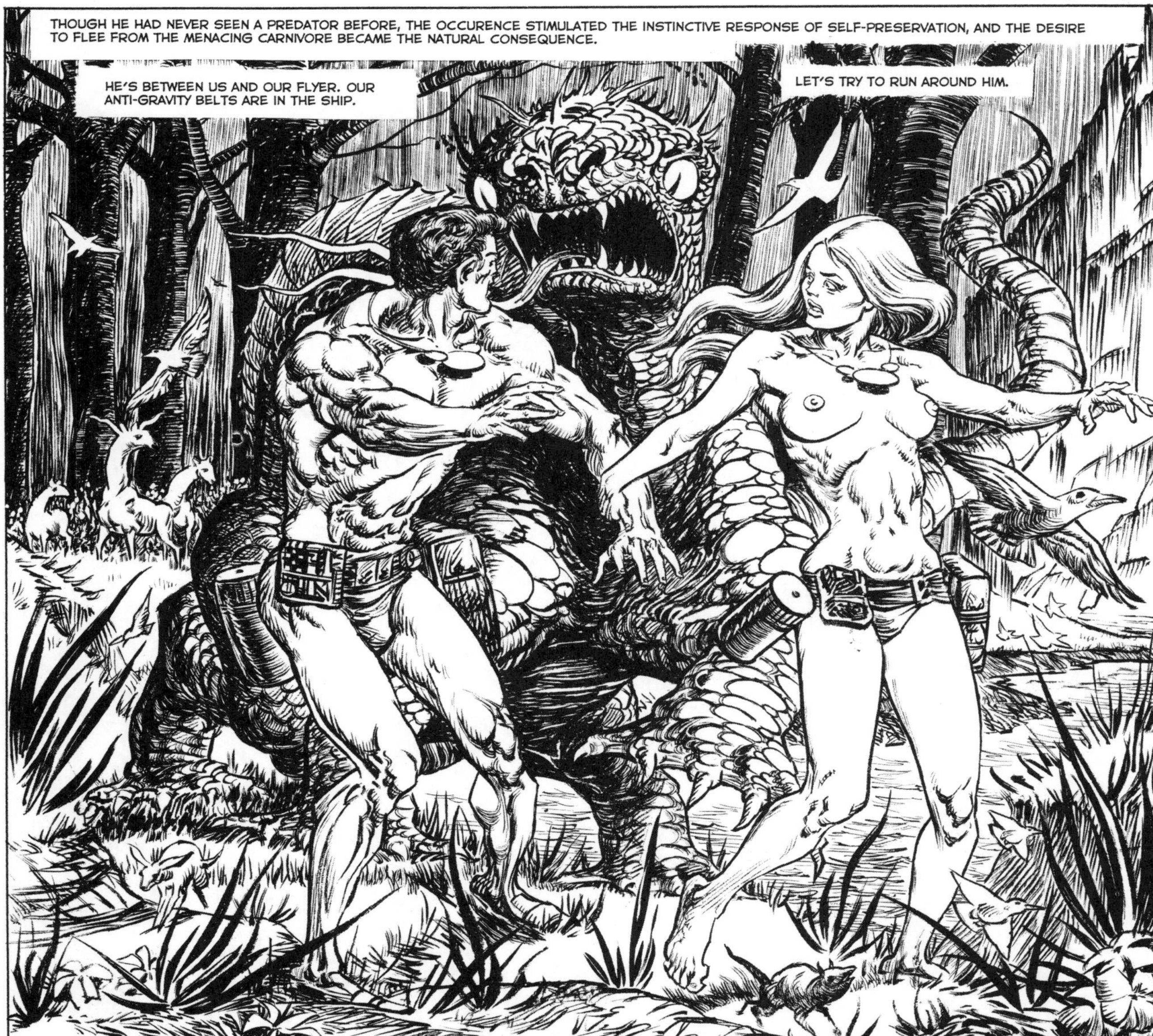
THOUGH HE HAD NEVER SEEN A PREDATOR BEFORE, THE OCCURENCE STIMULATED THE INSTINCTIVE RESPONSE OF SELF-PRESERVATION, AND THE DESIRE TO FLEE FROM THE MENACING CARNIVORE BECAME THE NATURAL CONSEQUENCE.
HE'S BETWEEN US AND OUR FLYER. OUR ANTI-GRAVITY BELTS ARE IN THE SHIP.
LET'S TRY TO RUN AROUND HIM.

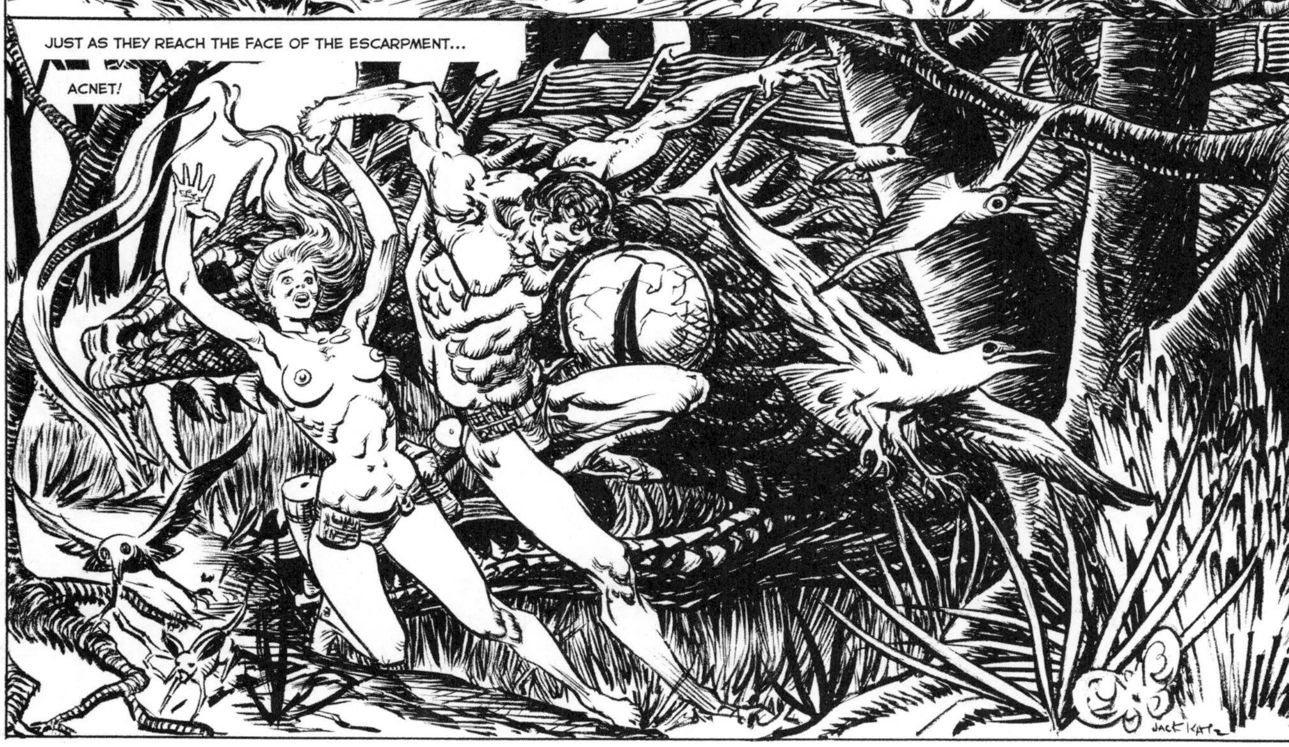
JUST AS THEY REACH THE FACE OF THE ESCARPMENT...
ACNET!
JACK KATZ

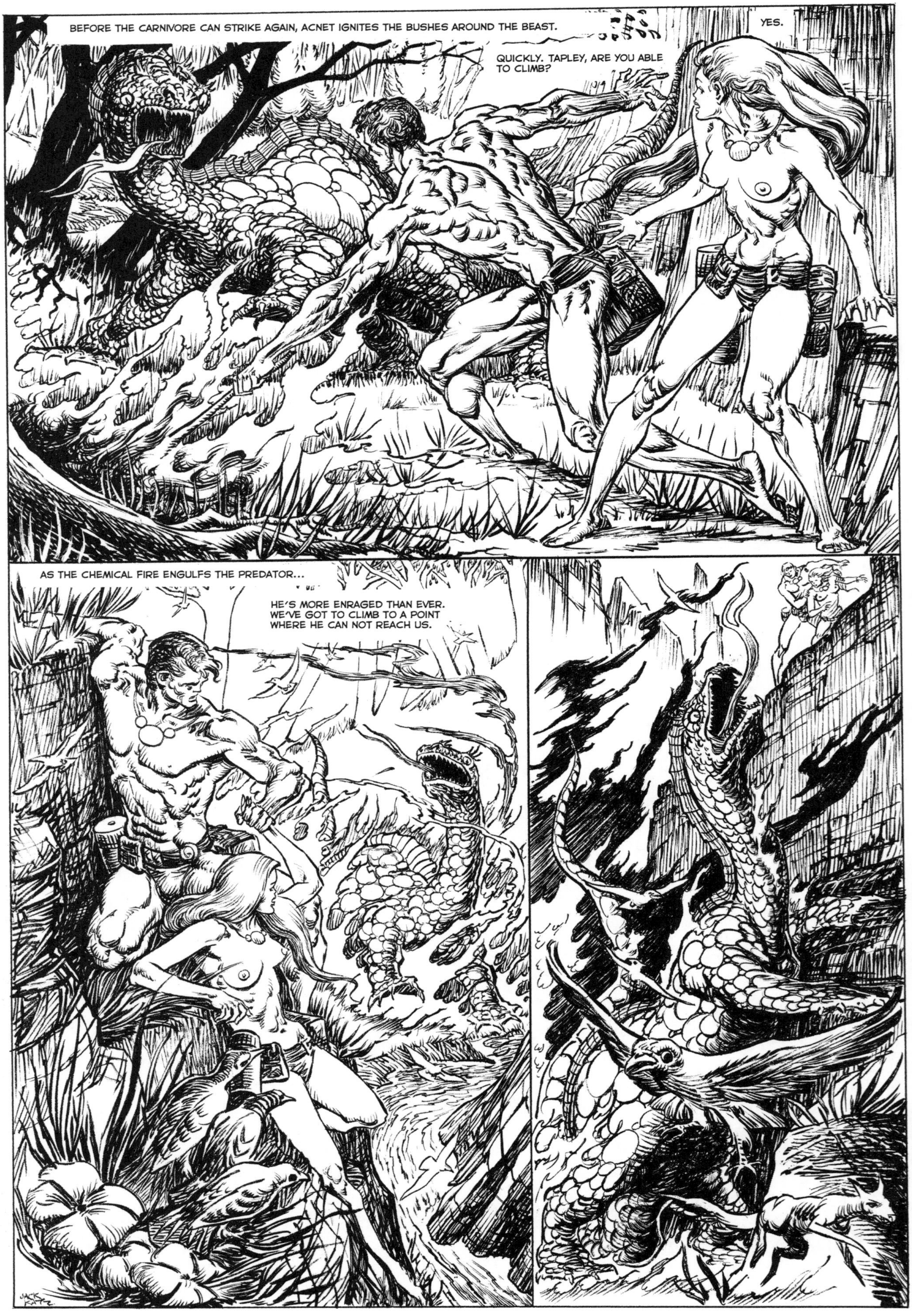
BEFORE THE CARNIVORE CAN STRIKE AGAIN, ACNET IGNITES THE BUSHES AROUND THE BEAST.
QUICKLY. TAPLEY, ARE YOU ABLE TO CLIMB?
YES.
AS THE CHEMICAL FIRE ENGULFS THE PREDATOR...
HE'S MORE ENRAGED THAN EVER. WE'VE GOT TO CLIMB TO A POINT WHERE HE CAN NOT REACH US.
JACK KATZ

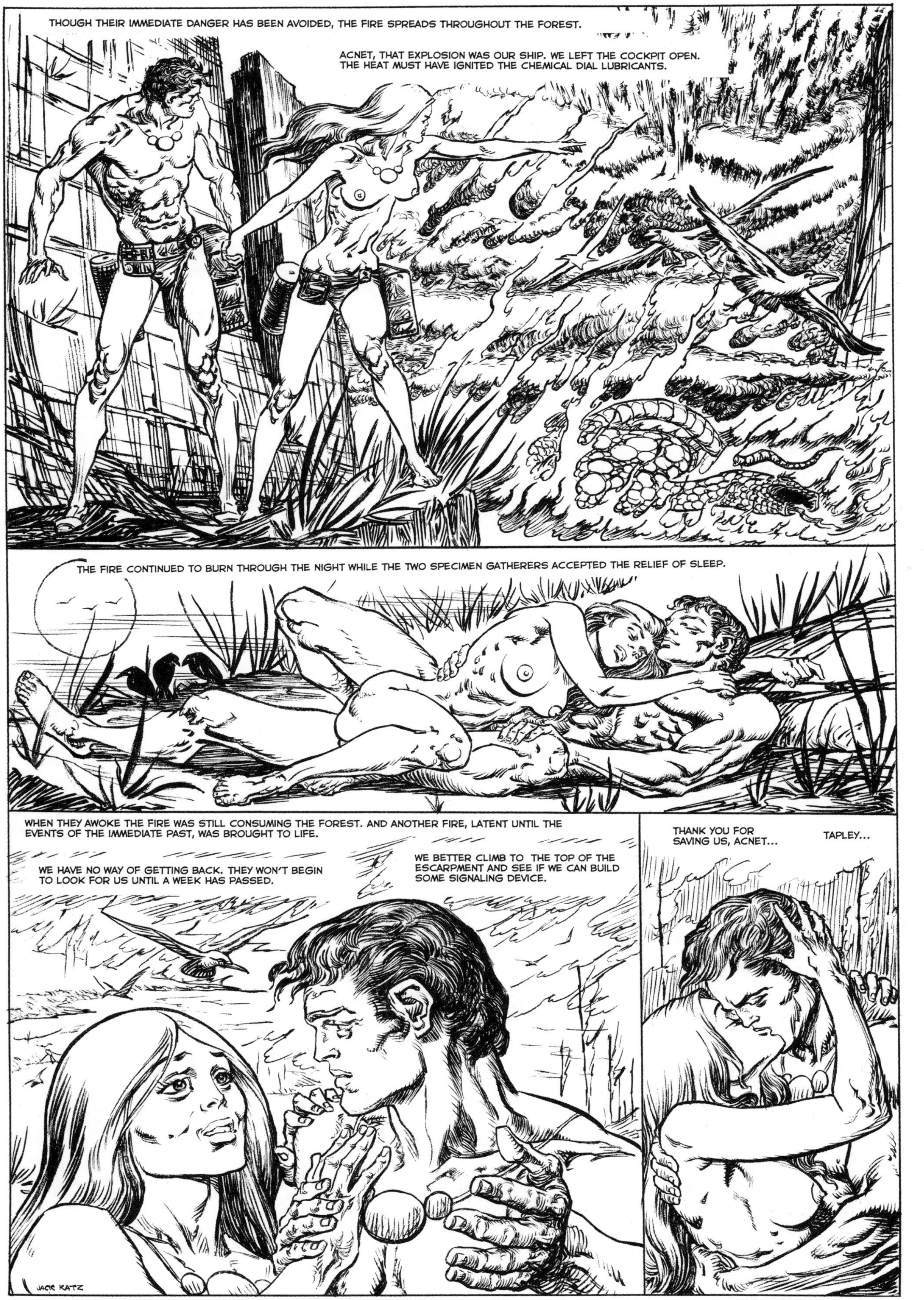
THOUGH THEIR IMMEDIATE DANGER HAS BEEN AVOIDED, THE FIRE SPREADS THROUGHOUT THE FOREST.
ACNET, THAT EXPLOSION WAS OUR SHIP. WE LEFT THE COCKPIT OPEN. THE HEAT MUST HAVE IGNITED THE CHEMICAL DIAL LUBRICANTS.
THE FIRE CONTINUED TO BURN THROUGH THE NIGHT WHILE THE TWO SPECIMEN GATHERERS ACCEPTED THE RELIEF OF SLEEP.
WHEN THEY AWOKE THE FIRE WAS STILL CONSUMING THE FOREST. AND ANOTHER FIRE, LATENT UNTIL THE EVENTS OF THE IMMEDIATE PAST, WAS BROUGHT TO LIFE.
WE HAVE NO WAY OF GETTING BACK. THEY WON'T BEGIN TO LOOK FOR US UNTIL A WEEK HAS PASSED.
WE BETTER CLIMB TO THE TOP OF THE ESCARPMENT AND SEE IF WE CAN BUILD SOME SIGNALING DEVICE.
THANK YOU FOR SAVING US, ACNET...
TAPLEY...
JACK KATZ

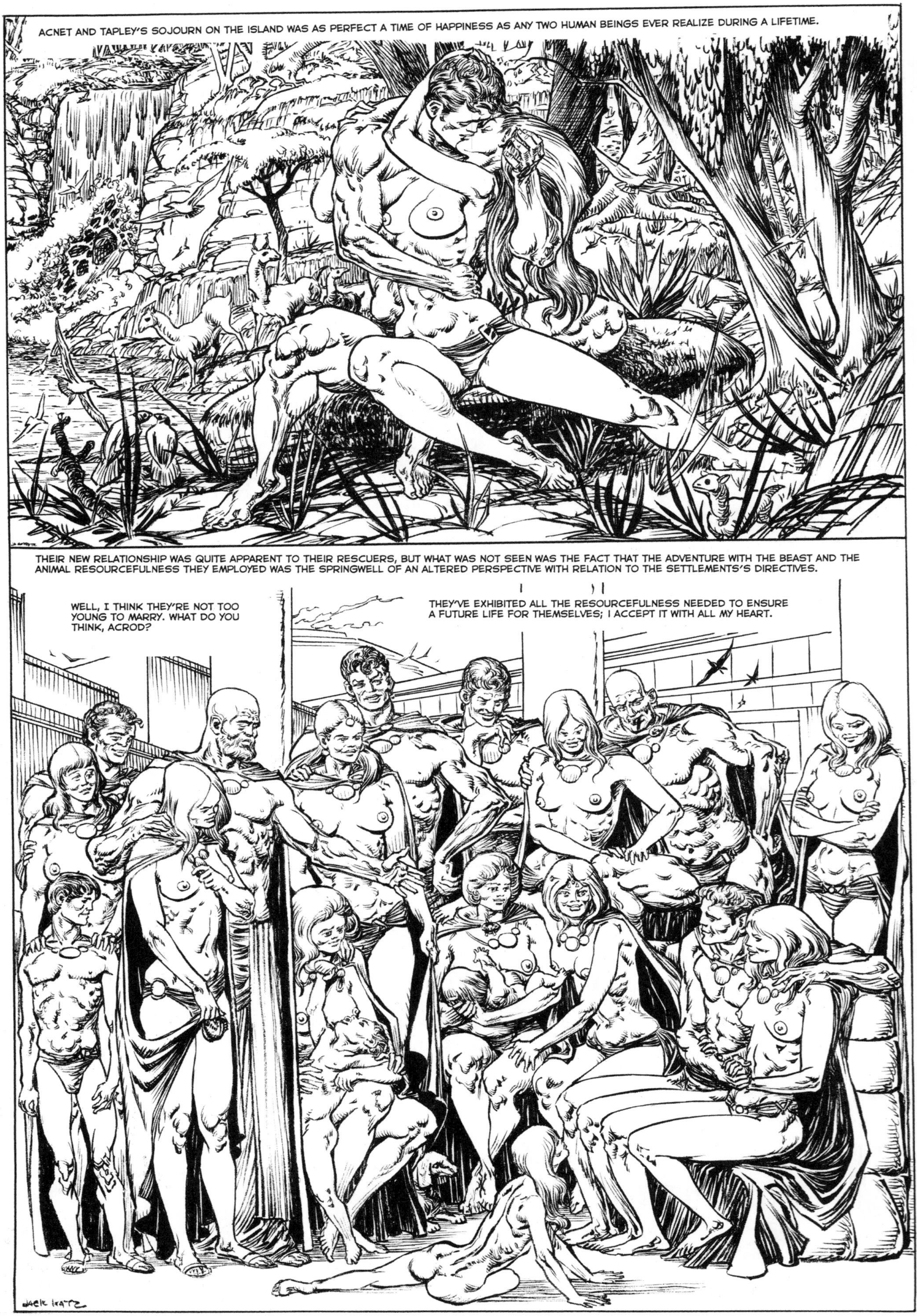
ACNET AND TAPLEY'S SOJOURN ON THE ISLAND WAS AS PERFECT A TIME OF HAPPINESS AS ANY TWO HUMAN BEINGS EVER REALIZE DURING A LIFETIME.
THEIR NEW RELATIONSHIP WAS QUITE APPARENT TO THEIR RESCUERS, BUT WHAT WAS NOT SEEN WAS THE FACT THAT THE ADVENTURE WITH THE BEAST AND THE ANIMAL RESOURCEFULNESS THEY EMPLOYED WAS THE SPRINGWELL OF AN ALTERED PERSPECTIVE WITH RELATION TO THE SETTLEMENTS'S DIRECTIVES.
WELL, I THINK THEY'RE NOT TOO YOUNG TO MARRY. WHAT DO YOU THINK, ACROD?
THEY'VE EXHIBITED ALL THE RESOURCEFULNESS NEEDED TO ENSURE A FUTURE LIFE FOR THEMSELVES; I ACCEPT IT WITH ALL MY HEART.
JACK KATZ

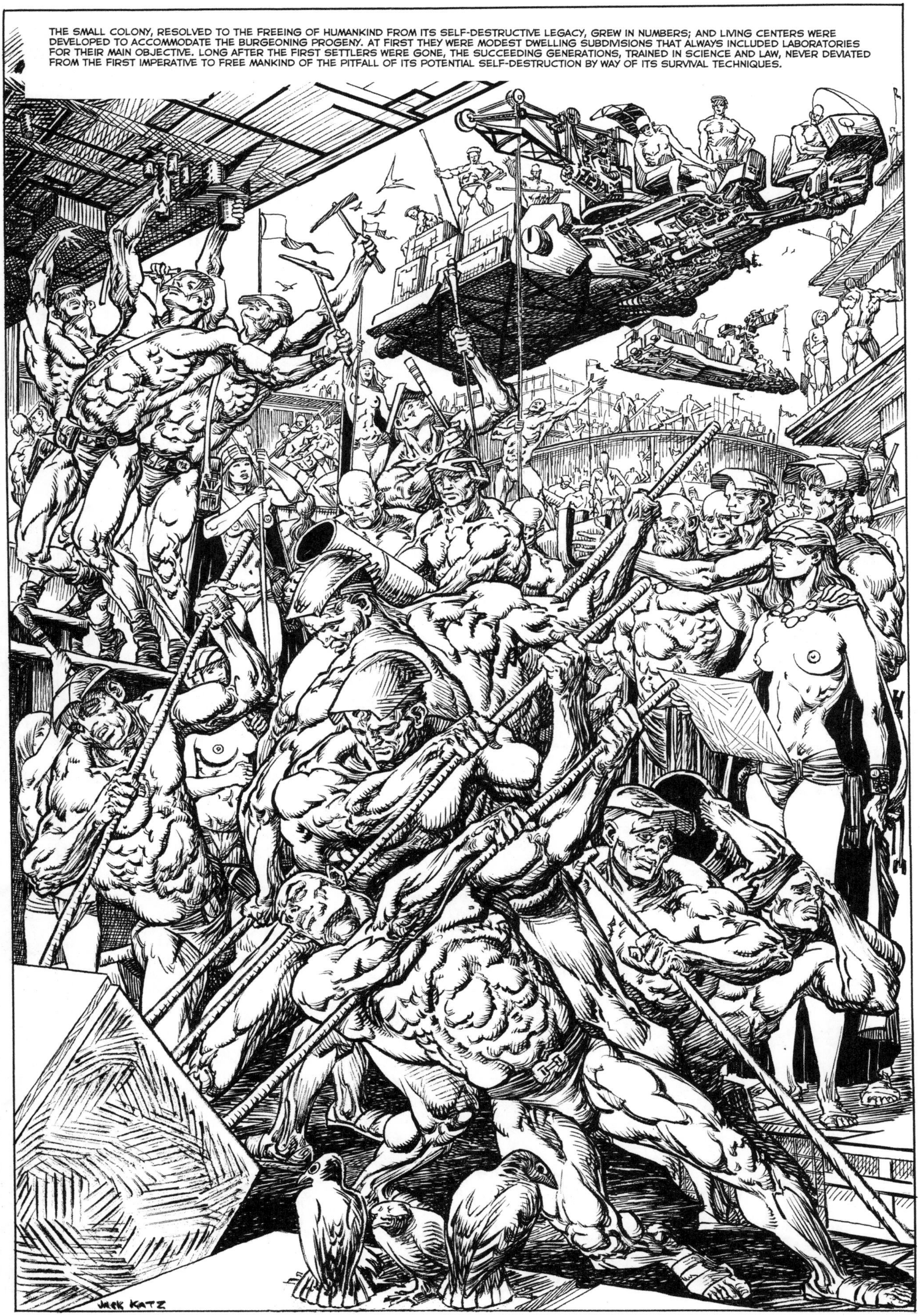
THE SMALL COLONY, RESOLVED TO THE FREEING OF HUMANKIND FROM ITS SELF-DESTRUCTIVE LEGACY, GREW IN NUMBERS; AND LIVING CENTERS WERE DEVELOPED TO ACCOMMODATE THE BURGEONING PROGENY. AT FIRST THEY WERE MODEST DWELLING SUBDIVISIONS THAT ALWAYS INCLUDED LABORATORIES FOR THEIR MAIN OBJECTIVE. LONG AFTER THE FIRST SETTLERS WERE GONE, THE SUCCEEDING GENERATIONS, TRAINED IN SCIENCE AND LAW, NEVER DEVIATED FROM THE FIRST IMPERATIVE TO FREE MANKIND OF THE PITFALL OF ITS POTENTIAL SELF-DESTRUCTION BY WAY OF ITS SURVIVAL TECHNIQUES.
JACK KATZ

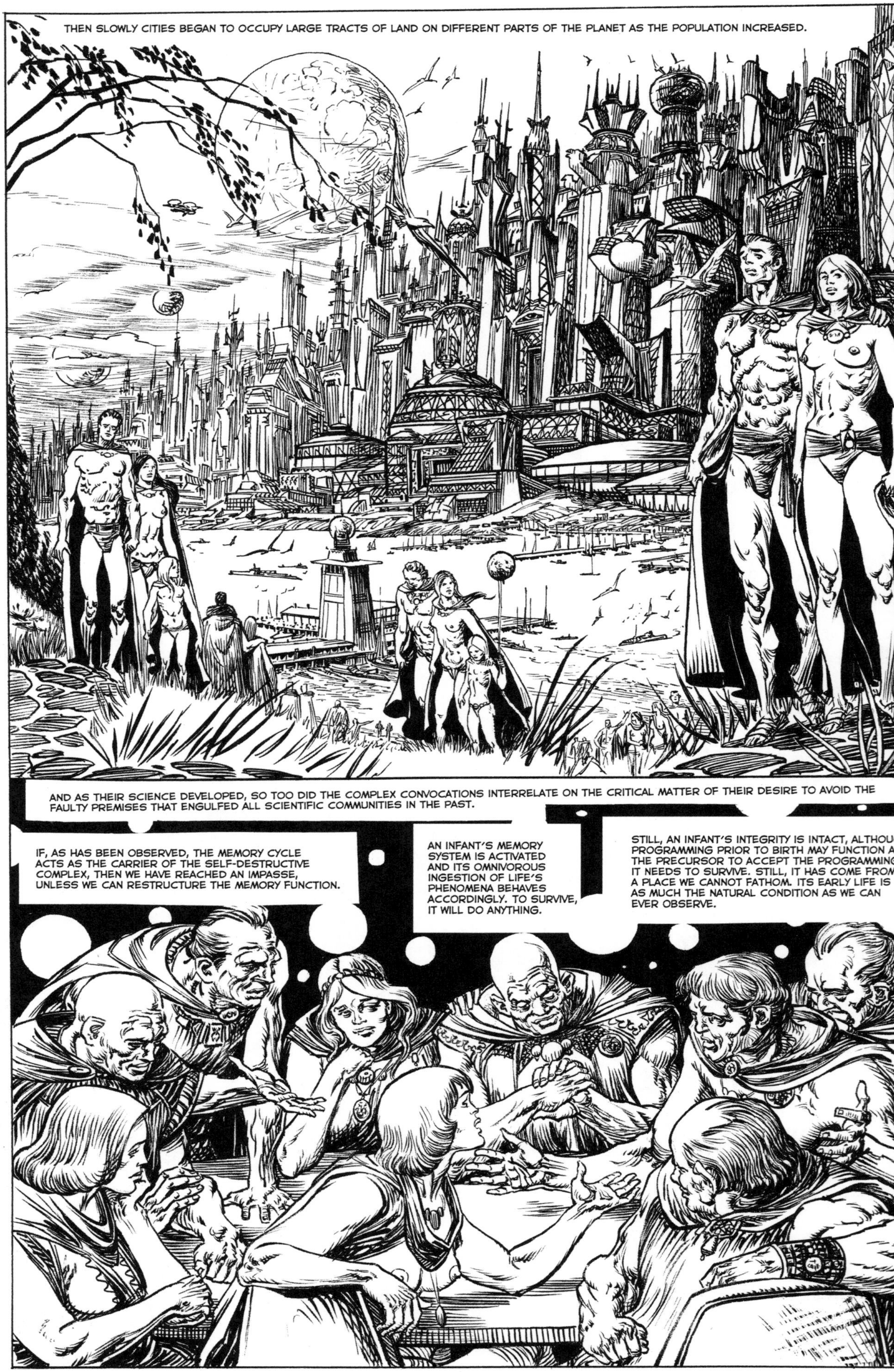
THEN SLOWLY CITIES BEGAN TO OCCUPY LARGE TRACTS OF LAND ON DIFFERENT PARTS OF THE PLANET AS THE POPULATION INCREASED.
AND AS THEIR SCIENCE DEVELOPED, SO TOO DID THE COMPLEX CONVOCATIONS INTERRELATE ON THE CRITICAL MATTER OF THEIR DESIRE TO AVOID THE FAULTY PREMISES THAT ENGULFED ALL SCIENTIFIC COMMUNITIES IN THE PAST.
IF, AS HAS BEEN OBSERVED, THE MEMORY CYCLE ACTS AS THE CARRIER OF THE SELF-DESTRUCTIVE COMPLEX, THEN WE HAVE REACHED AN IMPASSE, UNLESS WE CAN RESTRUCTURE THE MEMORY FUNCTION.
AN INFANT'S MEMORY SYSTEM IS ACTIVATED AND ITS OMNIVOROUS INGESTION OF LIFE'S PHENOMENA BEHAVES ACCORDINGLY. TO SURVIVE, IT WILL DO ANYTHING.
STILL, AN INFANT'S INTEGRITY IS INTACT, ALTHOUGH PROGRAMMING PRIOR TO BIRTH MAY FUNCTION AS THE PRECURSOR TO ACCEPT THE PROGRAMMING IT NEEDS TO SURVIVE. STILL, IT HAS COME FROM A PLACE WE CANNOT FATHOM. ITS EARLY LIFE IS AS MUCH THE NATURAL CONDITION AS WE CAN EVER OBSERVE.

THOUGH ACROD AND CLEAD HAD INSTRUCTED ALL THE GENERATIONS AGAINST FACTIONALISM, AFTER THEIR TIME IS CAME TO PASS - LIKE SO MANY PROGENITORS WHO ARE NOT INTIMATE WITH THE SIGNIFICANCIES OF ANY GIVEN ISSUE. THE ORIGINAL PURPOSE BECAME LOST IN THE DOGMA OF THE SEPARATE PERSPECTIVES HELD BY DIFFERENT SCHOOLS OF THOUGHT. AS THE DEBATES WENT ON, THE QUEST FOR THE ANSWER WAS STILL RESISTANT TO THE MOST EXTRAORDINARY RESEARCH. PHYSICAL MEMORY OF THE BODY'S MEMORY SYSTEMS TO RESTORE ITSELF, VITALIZE ITS FUNCTIONS, AND PERFORM ITS DUTIES WAS INSEPARABLE FROM THE OBJECTIVE AND INTROSPECTIVE MEMORY OF LIFE'S ATTITUDES. THOUGH THE COMMUNITY OF SCHOLARS WAS DIRECTED TO A SINGULAR PURPOSE, TWO FACTIONS DEVELOPED -- THOSE WHO FELT THAT A DEEPER INVESTIGATION INTO PHYSICAL MEMORY WOULD UNRAVEL THE PUZZLE, AND THOSE THAT WOULD STUDY THE CHARACTER OF THE NEWBORN.

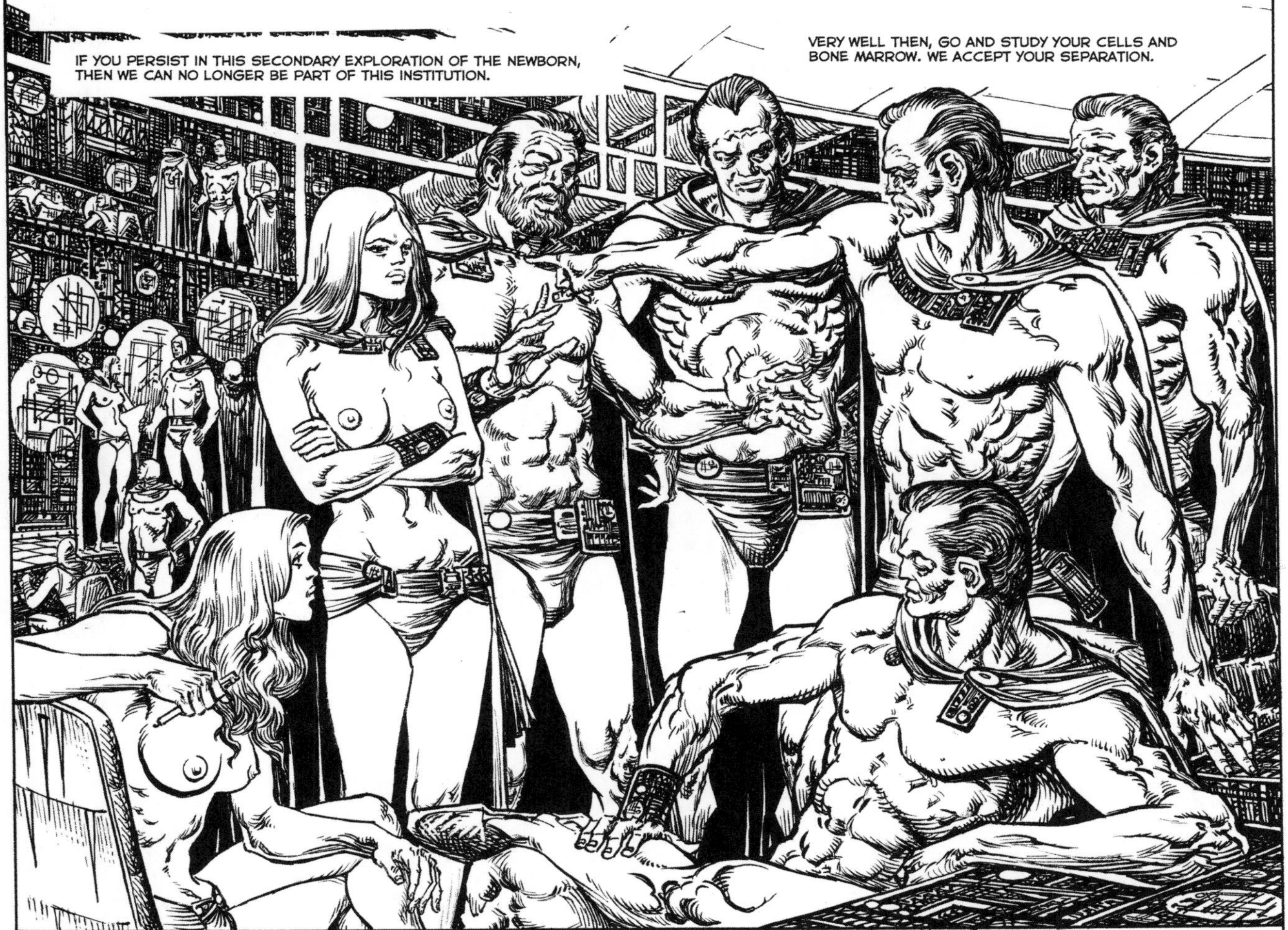
IF YOU PERSIST IN THIS SECONDARY EXPLORATION OF THE NEWBORN, THEN WE CAN NO LONGER BE PART OF THIS INSTITUTION.
VERY WELL THEN, GO AND STUDY YOUR CELLS AND BONE MARROW. WE ACCEPT YOUR SEPARATION.

THOUGH NEITHER GROUP CAME CLOSER TO SOLVING THE PROBLEM, THE FACTIONS BECAME MORE HOSTILE TO EACH OTHER AND A FRACTURE IN THE SCIENTIFIC COMMUNITY DEVELOPED INTO TWO OPPOSING CAMPS. ANGER OVER THE SPIRITING AWAY OF IMPORTANT RESEARCHERS SET BACK CRITICAL EXERIMENTS YEARS. THE RAGE THAT WAS ENGENDERED OVER THE ISSUE CAME TO A HEAD WHEN A BIOCHEMICAL LABORATORY WAS SABOTAGED BY FIRE.

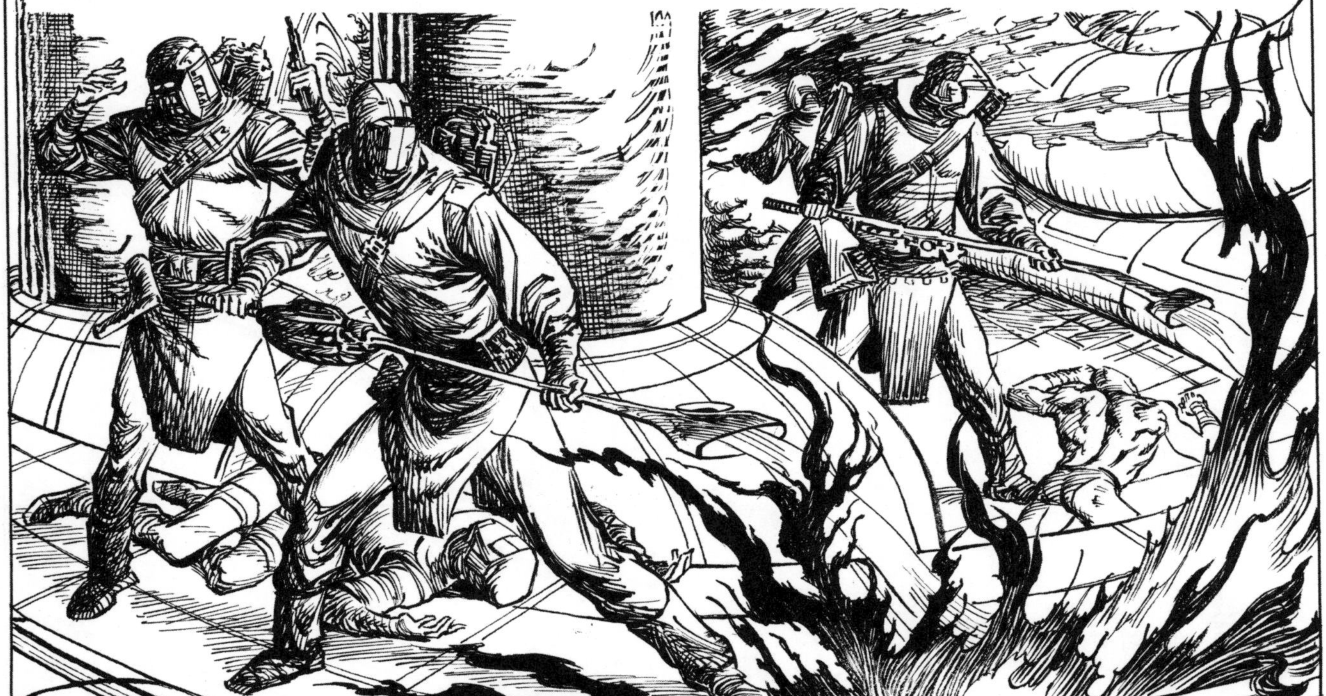
JACK KATZ

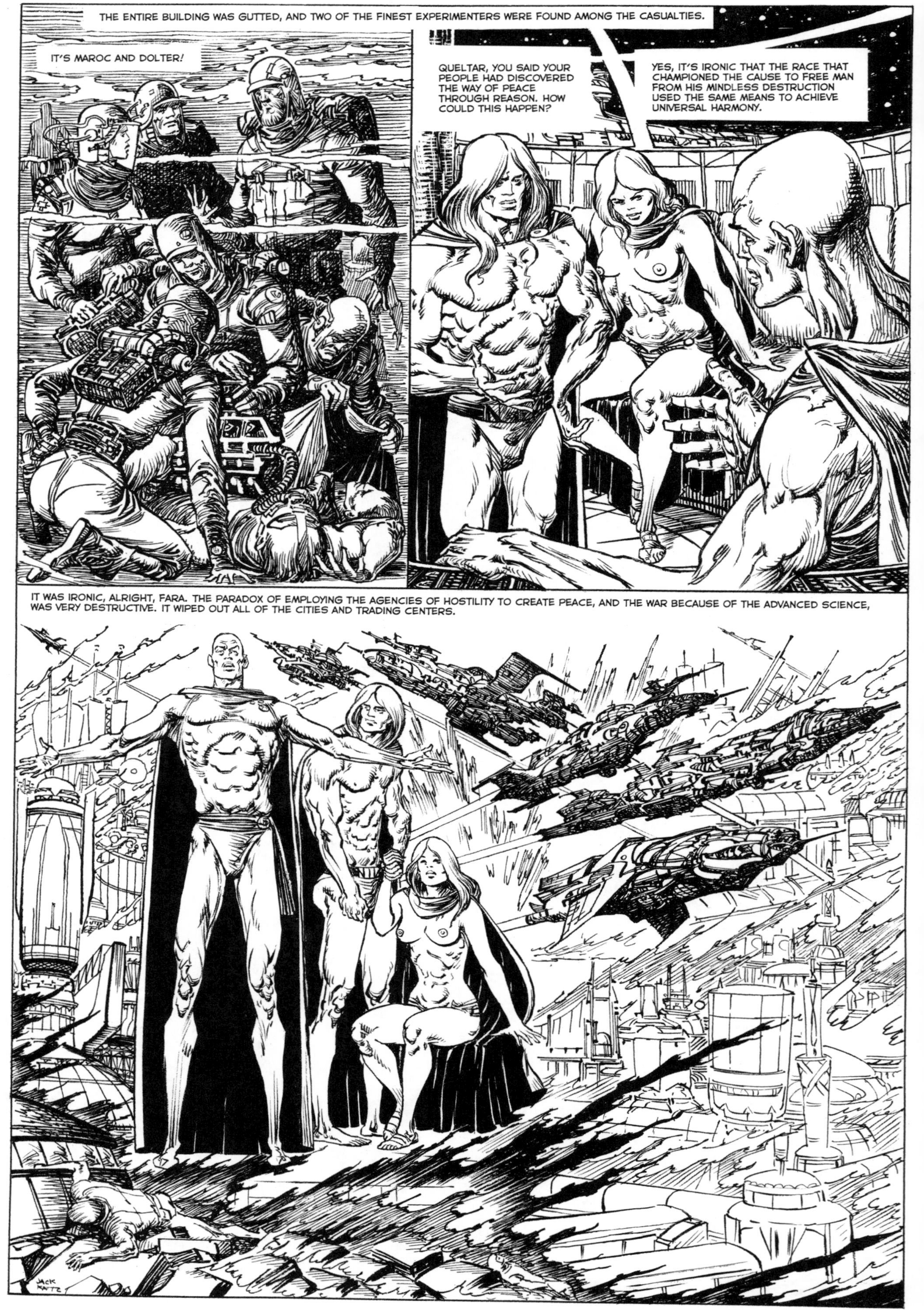
THE ENTIRE BUILDING WAS GUTTED, AND TWO OF THE FINEST EXPERIMENTERS WERE FOUND AMONG THE CASUALTIES.
IT'S MAROC AND DOLTER!
QUELTAR, YOU SAID YOUR PEOPLE HAD DISCOVERED THE WAY OF PEACE THROUGH REASON. HOW COULD THIS HAPPEN?
YES, IT'S IRONIC THAT THE RACE THAT CHAMPIONED THE CAUSE TO FREE MAN FROM HIS MINDLESS DESTRUCTION USED THE SAME MEANS TO ACHIEVE UNIVERSAL HARMONY.
IT WAS IRONIC, ALRIGHT, FARA. THE PARADOX OF EMPLOYING THE AGENCIES OF HOSTILITY TO CREATE PEACE, AND THE WAR BECAUSE OF THE ADVANCED SCIENCE, WAS VERY DESTRUCTIVE. IT WIPED OUT ALL OF THE CITIES AND TRADING CENTERS.
JACK KATZ

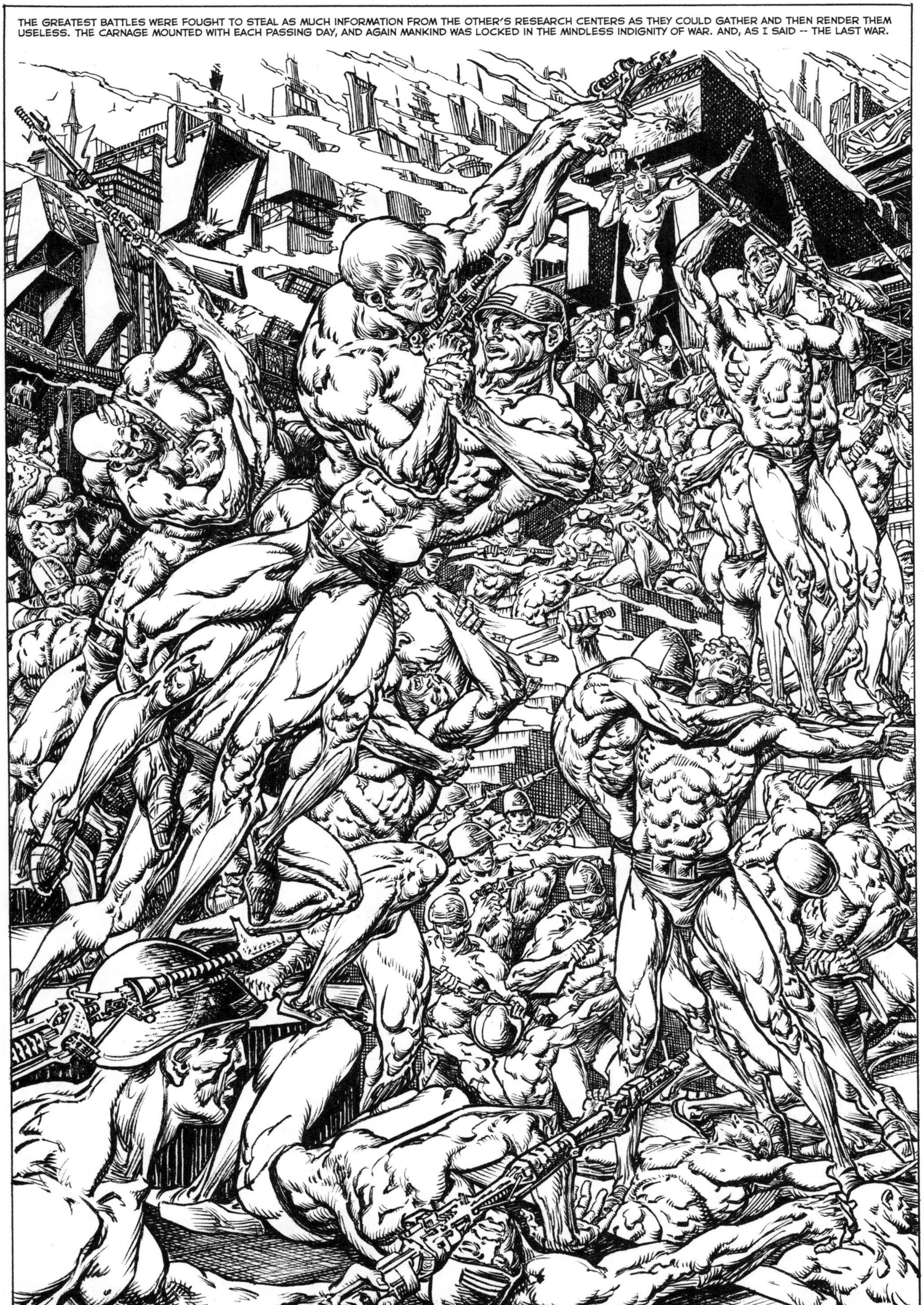
THE GREATEST BATTLES WERE FOUGHT TO STEAL AS MUCH INFORMATION FROM THE OTHER'S RESEARCH CENTERS AS THEY COULD GATHER AND THEN RENDER THEM USELESS. THE CARNAGE MOUNTED WITH EACH PASSING DAY, AND AGAIN MANKIND WAS LOCKED IN THE MINDLESS INDIGNITY OF WAR. AND, AS I SAID -- THE LAST WAR.
JACK KATZ

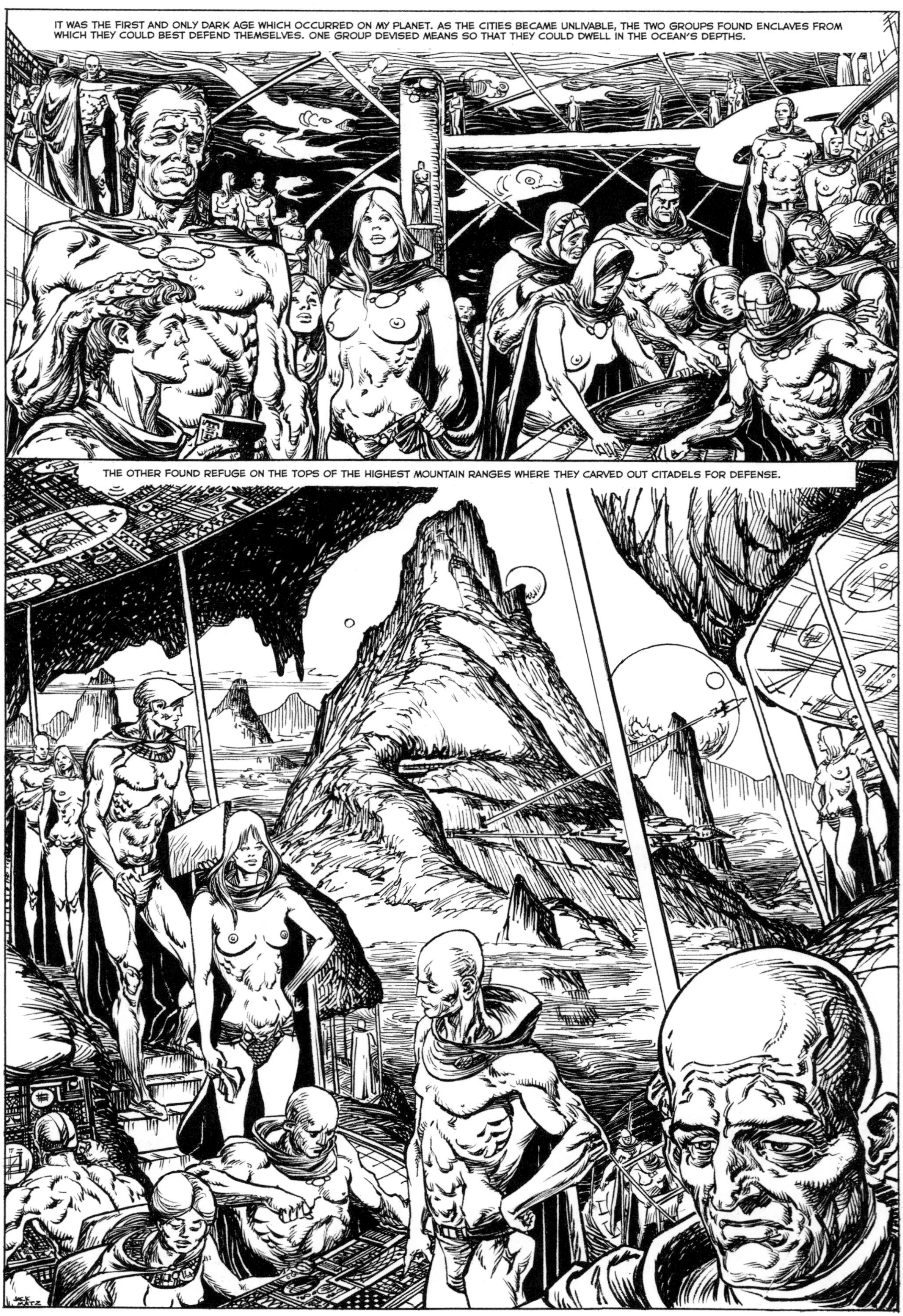
IT WAS THE FIRST AND ONLY DARK AGE WHICH OCCURRED ON MY PLANET. AS THE CITIES BECAME UNLIVABLE, THE TWO GROUPS FOUND ENCLAVES FROM WHICH THEY COULD BEST DEFEND THEMSELVES. ONE GROUP DEVISED MEANS SO THAT THEY COULD DWELL IN THE OCEAN'S DEPTHS.
THE OTHER FOUND REFUGE ON THE TOPS OF THE HIGHEST MOUNTAIN RANGES WHERE THEY CARVED OUT CITADELS FOR DEFENSE.
JACK KATZ

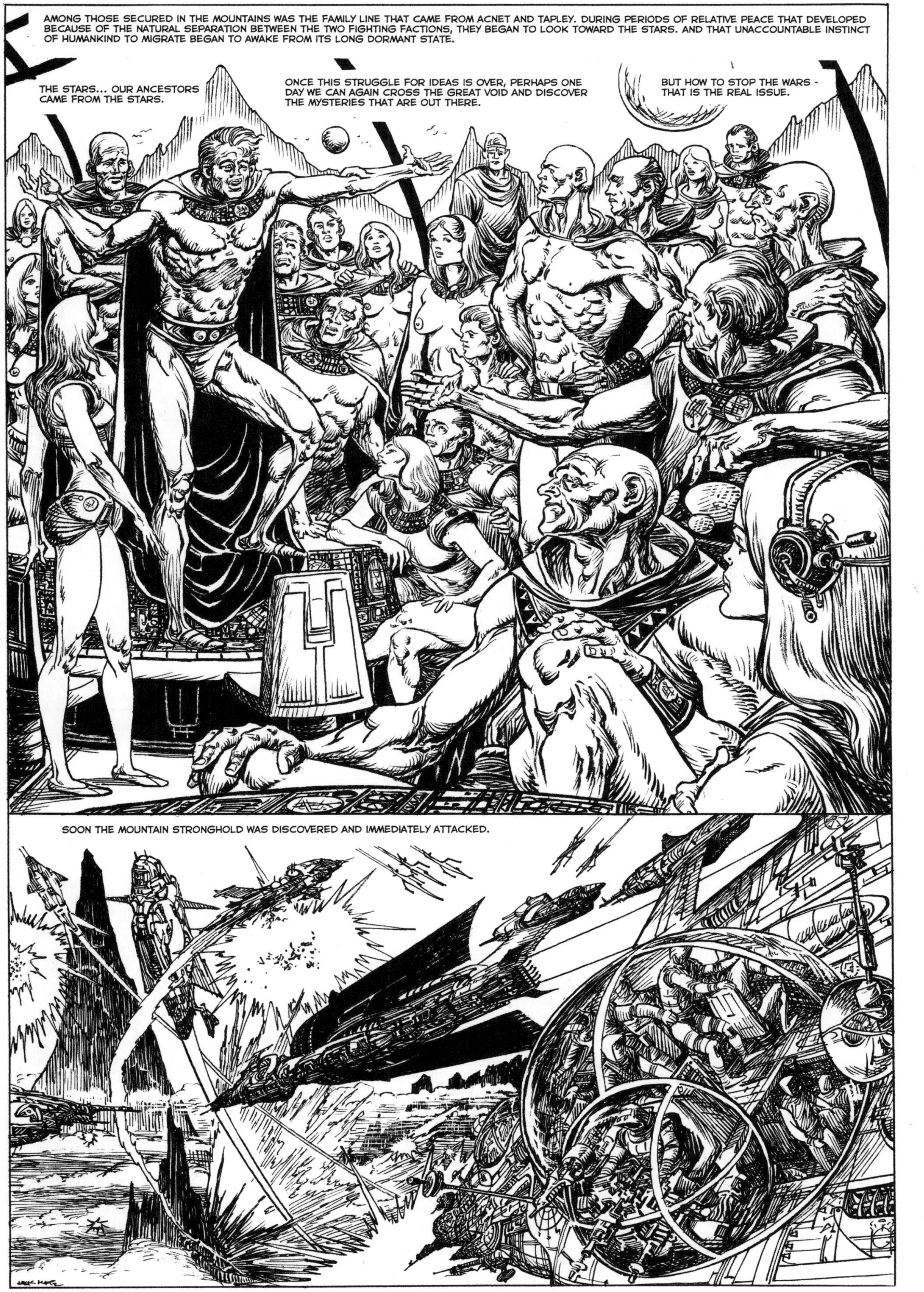
AMONG THOSE SECURED IN THE MOUNTAINS WAS THE FAMILY LINE THAT CAME FROM ACNET AND TAPLEY. DURING PERIODS OF RELATIVE PEACE THAT DEVELOPED BECAUSE OF THE NATURAL SEPARATION BETWEEN THE TWO FIGHTING FACTIONS, THEY BEGAN TO LOOK TOWARD THE STARS. AND THAT UNACCOUNTABLE INSTINCT OF HUMANKIND TO MIGRATE BEGAN TO AWAKE FROM ITS LONG DORMANT STATE.
THE STARS... OUR ANCESTORS CAME FROM THE STARS.
ONCE THIS STRUGGLE FOR IDEAS IS OVER, PERHAPS ONE DAY WE CAN AGAIN CROSS THE GREAT VOID AND DISCOVER THE MYSTERIES THAT ARE OUT THERE.
BUT HOW TO STOP THE WARS - THAT IS THE REAL ISSUE.
SOON THE MOUNTAIN STRONGHOLD WAS DISCOVERED AND IMMEDIATELY ATTACKED.

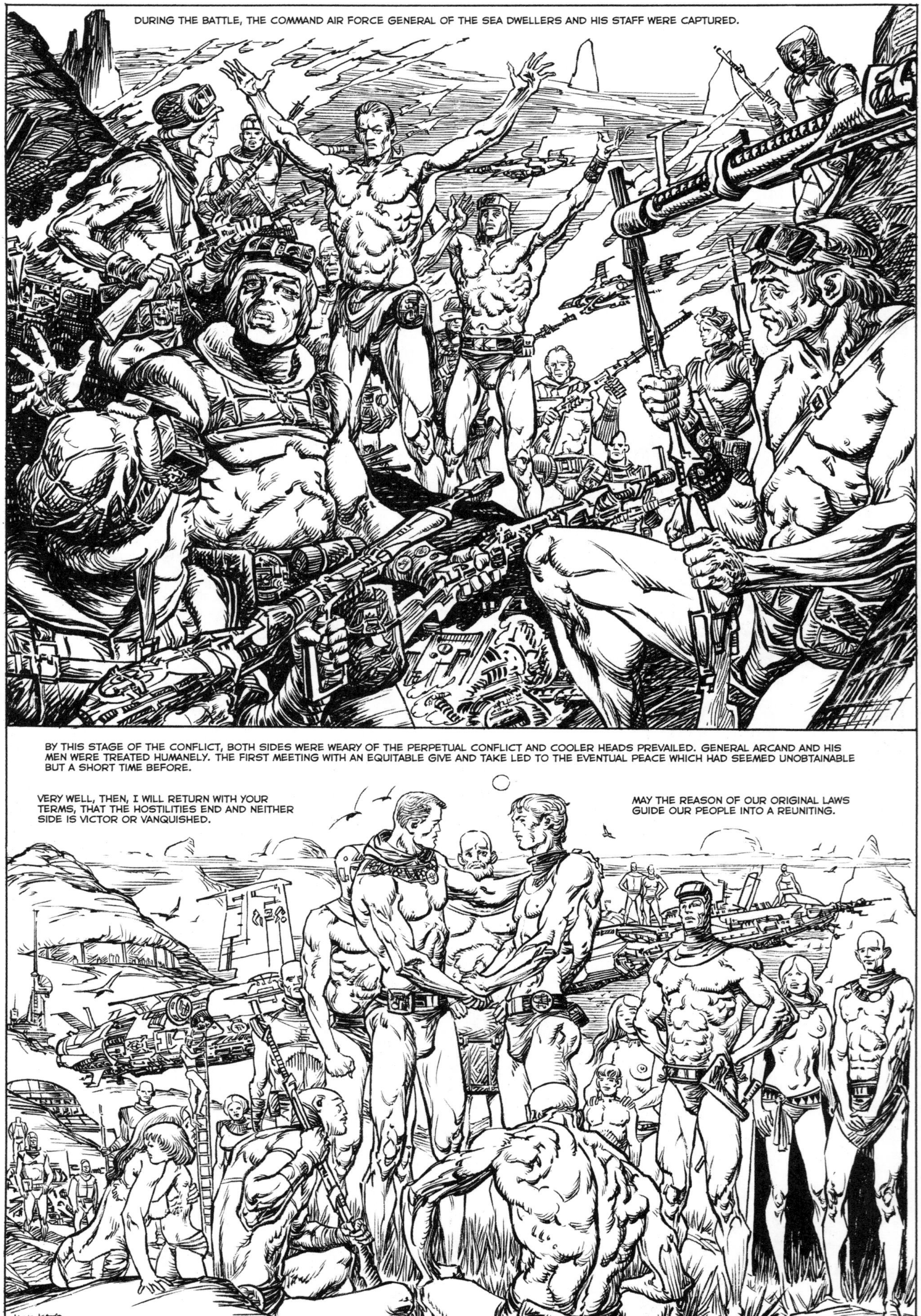
DURING THE BATTLE, THE COMMAND AIR FORCE GENERAL OF THE SEA DWELLERS AND HIS STAFF WERE CAPTURED.
BY THIS STAGE OF THE CONFLICT, BOTH SIDES WERE WEARY OF THE PERPETUAL CONFLICT AND COOLER HEADS PREVAILED. GENERAL ARCAND AND HIS MEN WERE TREATED HUMANELY. THE FIRST MEETING WITH AN EQUITABLE GIVE AND TAKE LED TO THE EVENTUAL PEACE WHICH HAD SEEMED UNOBTAINABLE BUT A SHORT TIME BEFORE.
VERY WELL, THEN, I WILL RETURN WITH YOUR TERMS, THAT THE HOSTILITIES END AND NEITHER SIDE IS VICTOR OR VANQUISHED.
MAY THE REASON OF OUR ORIGINAL LAWS GUIDE OUR PEOPLE INTO A REUNITING.
JACK KATZ

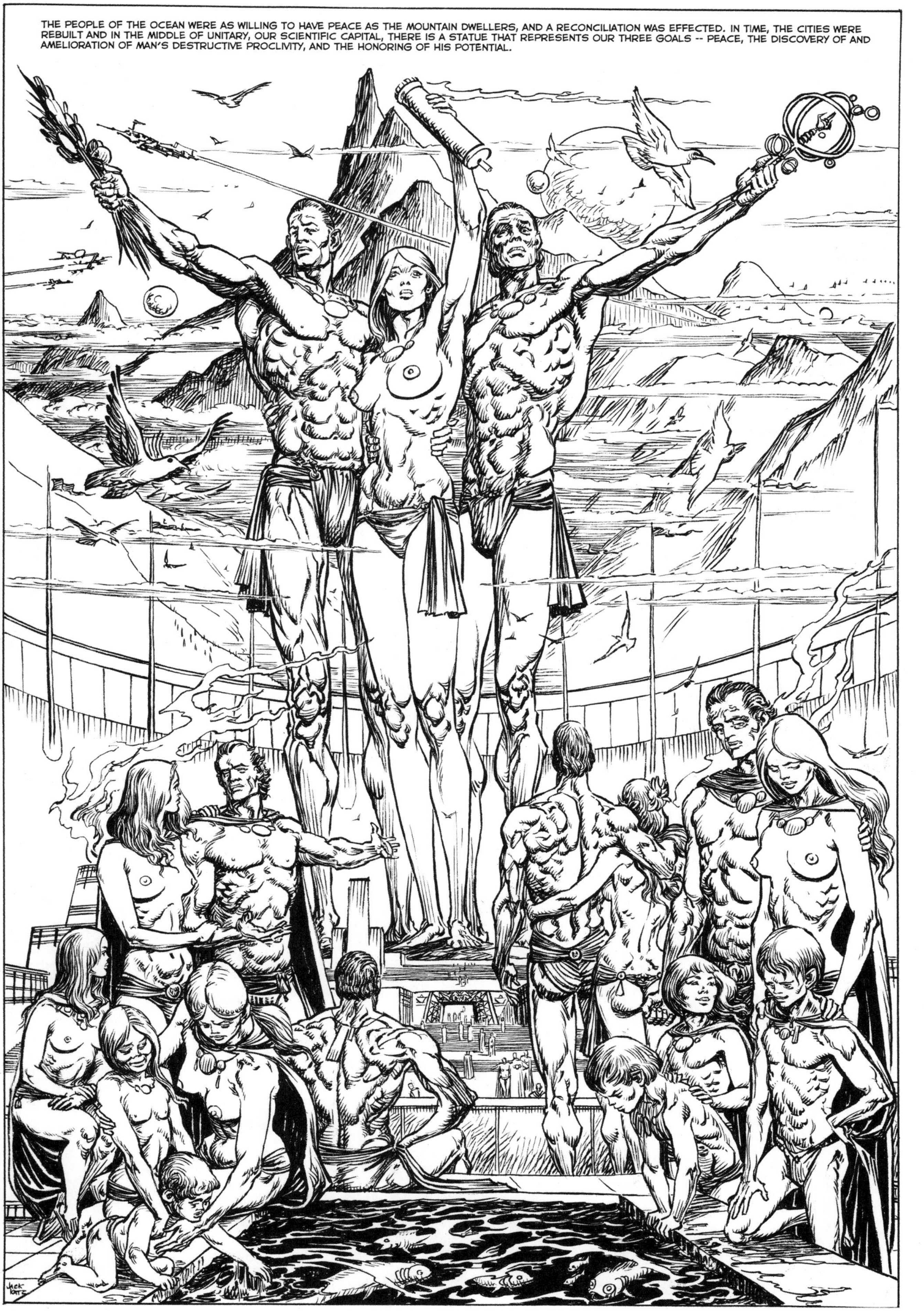
THE PEOPLE OF THE OCEAN WERE AS WILLING TO HAVE PEACE AS THE MOUNTAIN DWELLERS, AND A RECONCILIATION WAS EFFECTED. IN TIME, THE CITIES WERE REBUILT AND IN THE MIDDLE OF UNITARY, OUR SCIENTIFIC CAPITAL, THERE IS A STATUE THAT REPRESENTS OUR THREE GOALS -- PEACE, THE DISCOVERY OF AND AMELIORATION OF MAN'S DESTRUCTIVE PROCLIVITY, AND THE HONORING OF HIS POTENTIAL.
JACK KATZ

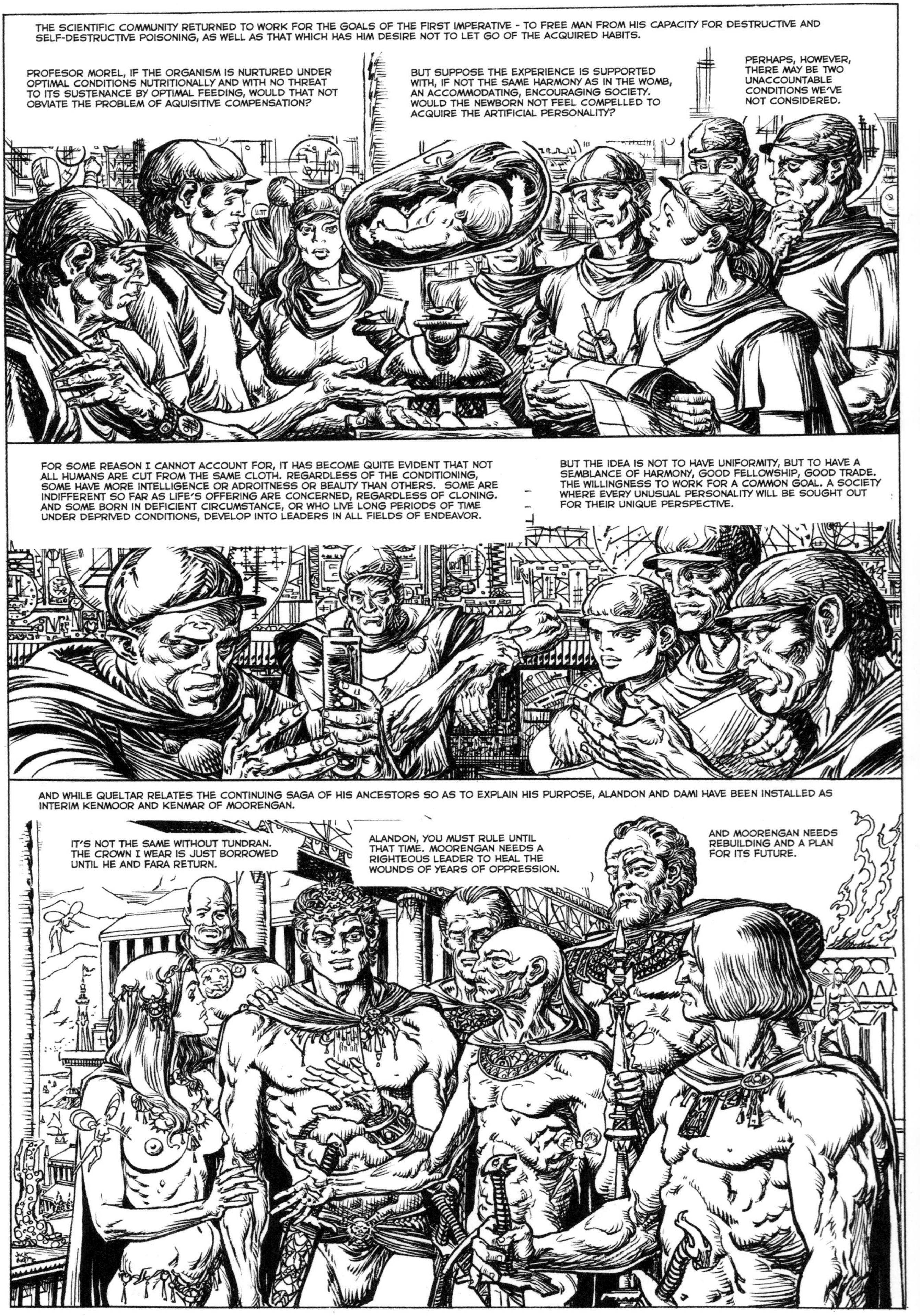
THE SCIENTIFIC COMMUNITY RETURNED TO WORK FOR THE GOALS OF THE FIRST IMPERATIVE - TO FREE MAN FROM HIS CAPACITY FOR DESTRUCTIVE AND SELF-DESTRUCTIVE POISONING, AS WELL AS THAT WHICH HAS HIM DESIRE NOT TO LET GO OF THE ACQUIRED HABITS.
PROFESOR MOREL, IF THE ORGANISM IS NURTURED UNDER OPTIMAL CONDITIONS NUTRITIONALLY AND WITH NO THREAT TO ITS SUSTENANCE BY OPTIMAL FEEDING, WOULD THAT NOT OBVIATE THE PROBLEM OF AQUISITIVE COMPENSATION?
BUT SUPPOSE THE EXPERIENCE IS SUPPORTED WITH, IF NOT THE SAME HARMONY AS IN THE WOMB, AN ACCOMMODATING, ENCOURAGING SOCIETY. WOULD THE NEWBORN NOT FEEL COMPELLED TO ACQUIRE THE ARTIFICIAL PERSONALITY?
PERHAPS, HOWEVER, THERE MAY BE TWO UNACCOUNTABLE CONDITIONS WE'VE NOT CONSIDERED.
FOR SOME REASON I CANNOT ACCOUNT FOR, IT HAS BECOME QUITE EVIDENT THAT NOT ALL HUMANS ARE CUT FROM THE SAME CLOTH. REGARDLESS OF THE CONDITIONING, SOME HAVE MORE INTELLIGENCE OR ADROITNESS OR BEAUTY THAN OTHERS. SOME ARE INDIFFERENT SO FAR AS LIFE'S OFFERING ARE CONCERNED, REGARDLESS OF CLONING. AND SOME BORN IN DEFICIENT CIRCUMSTANCE, OR WHO LIVE LONG PERIODS OF TIME UNDER DEPRIVED CONDITIONS, DEVELOP INTO LEADERS IN ALL FIELDS OF ENDEAVOR.
BUT THE IDEA IS NOT TO HAVE UNIFORMITY, BUT TO HAVE A SEMBLANCE OF HARMONY, GOOD FELLOWSHIP, GOOD TRADE. THE WILLINGNESS TO WORK FOR A COMMON GOAL. A SOCIETY WHERE EVERY UNUSUAL PERSONALITY WILL BE SOUGHT OUT FOR THEIR UNIQUE PERSPECTIVE.
AND WHILE QUELTAR RELATES THE CONTINUING SAGA OF HIS ANCESTORS SO AS TO EXPLAIN HIS PURPOSE, ALANDON AND DAMI HAVE BEEN INSTALLED AS INTERIM KENMOOR AND KENMAR OF MOORENGAN.
IT'S NOT THE SAME WITHOUT TUNDRAN. THE CROWN I WEAR IS JUST BORROWED UNTIL HE AND FARA RETURN.
ALANDON, YOU MUST RULE UNTIL THAT TIME. MOORENGAN NEEDS A RIGHTEOUS LEADER TO HEAL THE WOUNDS OF YEARS OF OPPRESSION.
AND MOORENGAN NEEDS REBUILDING AND A PLAN FOR ITS FUTURE.

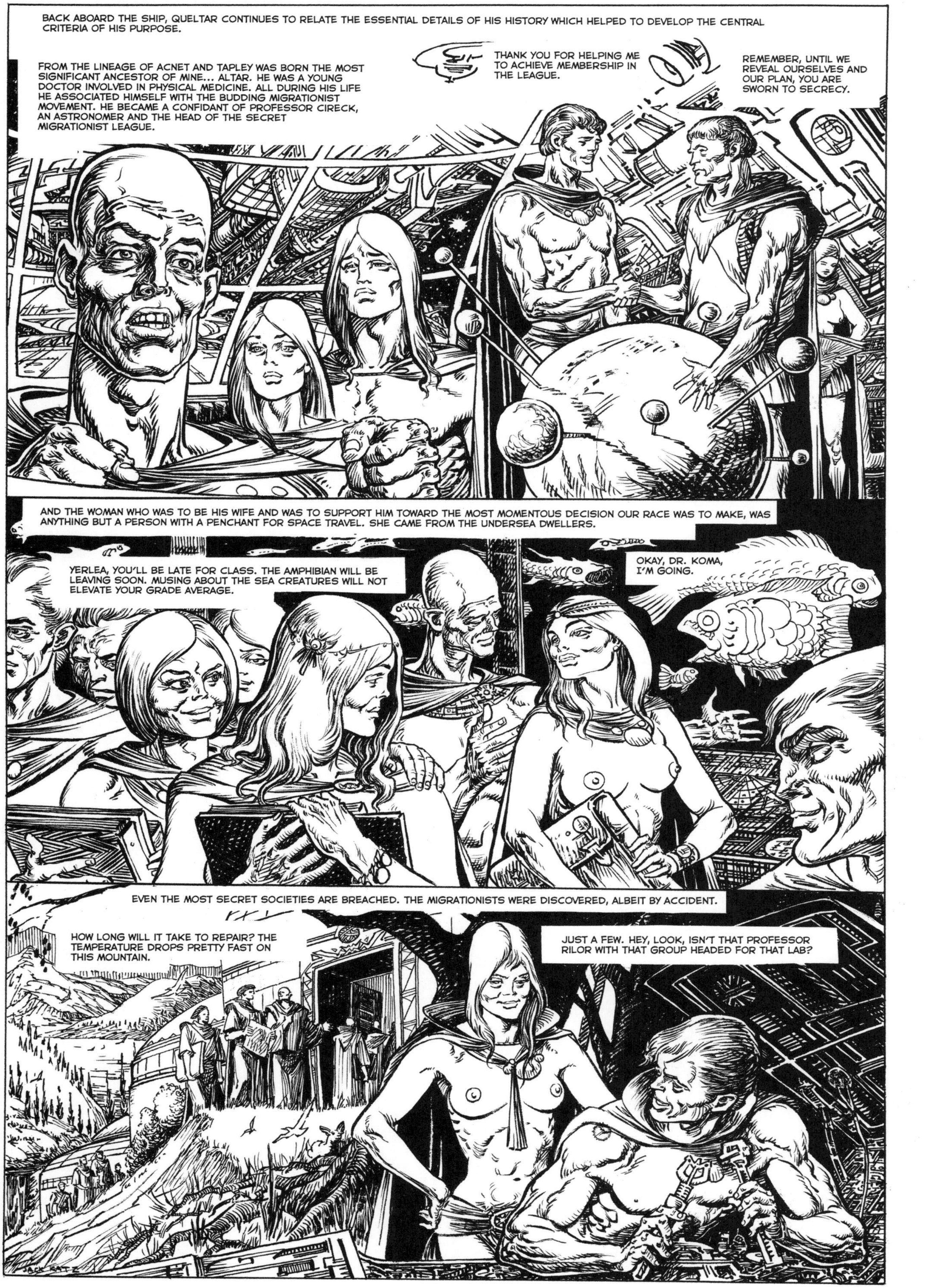
BACK ABOARD THE SHIP, QUELTAR CONTINUES TO RELATE THE ESSENTIAL DETAILS OF HIS HISTORY WHICH HELPED TO DEVELOP THE CENTRAL CRITERIA OF HIS PURPOSE.
FROM THE LINEAGE OF ACNET AND TAPLEY WAS BORN THE MOST SIGNIFICANT ANCESTOR OF MINE... ALTAR. HE WAS A YOUNG DOCTOR INVOLVED IN PHYSICAL MEDICINE. ALL DURING HIS LIFE HE ASSOCIATED HIMSELF WITH THE BUDDING MIGRATIONIST MOVEMENT. HE BECAME A CONFIDANT OF PROFESSOR CIRECK, AN ASTRONOMER AND THE HEAD OF THE SECRET MIGRATIONIST LEAGUE.
THANK YOU FOR HELPING ME TO ACHIEVE MEMBERSHIP IN THE LEAGUE.
REMEMBER, UNTIL WE REVEAL OURSELVES AND OUR PLAN, YOU ARE SWORN TO SECRECY.
AND THE WOMAN WHO WAS TO BE HIS WIFE AND WAS TO SUPPORT HIM TOWARD THE MOST MOMENTOUS DECISION OUR RACE WAS TO MAKE, WAS ANYTHING BUT A PERSON WITH A PENCHANT FOR SPACE TRAVEL. SHE CAME FROM THE UNDERSEA DWELLERS.
YERLEA, YOU'LL BE LATE FOR CLASS. THE AMPHIBIAN WILL BE LEAVING SOON. MUSING ABOUT THE SEA CREATURES WILL NOT ELEVATE YOUR GRADE AVERAGE.
OKAY, DR. KOMA, I'M GOING.
EVEN THE MOST SECRET SOCIETIES ARE BREACHED. THE MIGRATIONISTS WERE DISCOVERED, ALBEIT BY ACCIDENT.
HOW LONG WILL IT TAKE TO REPAIR? THE TEMPERATURE DROPS PRETTY FAST ON THIS MOUNTAIN.
JUST A FEW. HEY, LOOK, ISN'T THAT PROFESSOR RILOR WITH THAT GROUP HEADED FOR THAT LAB?

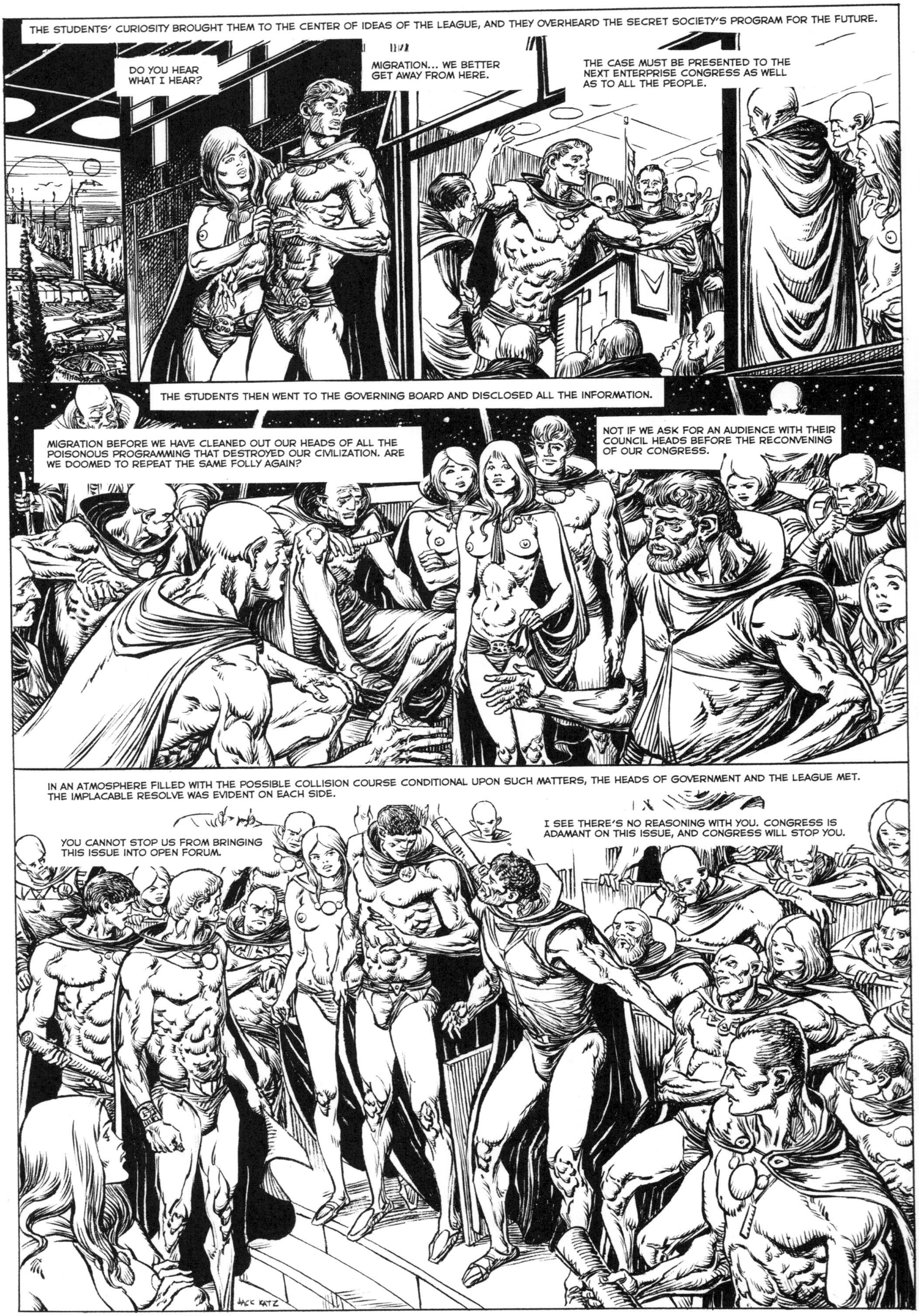
THE STUDENTS' CURIOSITY BROUGHT THEM TO THE CENTER OF IDEAS OF THE LEAGUE, AND THEY OVERHEARD THE SECRET SOCIETY'S PROGRAM FOR THE FUTURE.
DO YOU HEAR WHAT I HEAR?
MIGRATION... WE BETTER GET AWAY FROM HERE.
THE CASE MUST BE PRESENTED TO THE NEXT ENTERPRISE CONGRESS AS WELL AS TO ALL THE PEOPLE.
THE STUDENTS THEN WENT TO THE GOVERNING BOARD AND DISCLOSED ALL THE INFORMATION.
MIGRATION BEFORE WE HAVE CLEANED OUT OUR HEADS OF ALL THE POISONOUS PROGRAMMING THAT DESTROYED OUR CIVILIZATION. ARE WE DOOMED TO REPEAT THE SAME FOLLY AGAIN?
NOT IF WE ASK FOR AN AUDIENCE WITH THEIR COUNCIL HEADS BEFORE THE RECONVENING OF OUR CONGRESS.
IN AN ATMOSPHERE FILLED WITH THE POSSIBLE COLLISION COURSE CONDITIONAL UPON SUCH MATTERS, THE HEADS OF GOVERNMENT AND THE LEAGUE MET. THE IMPLACABLE RESOLVE WAS EVIDENT ON EACH SIDE.
YOU CANNOT STOP US FROM BRINGING THIS ISSUE INTO OPEN FORUM.
I SEE THERE'S NO REASONING WITH YOU. CONGRESS IS ADAMANT ON THIS ISSUE, AND CONGRESS WILL STOP YOU.
JACK KATZ

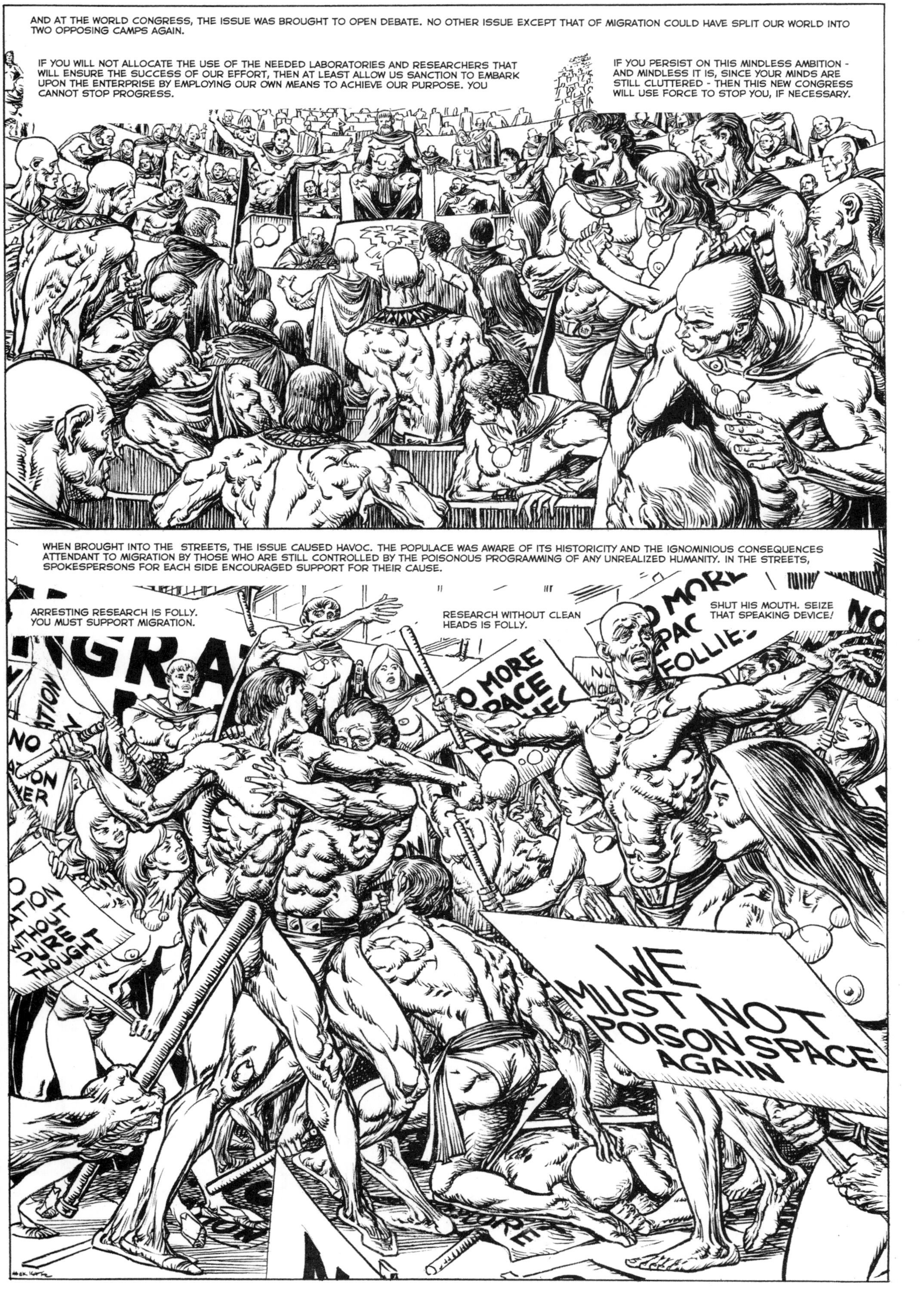
AND AT THE WORLD CONGRESS, THE ISSUE WAS BROUGHT TO OPEN DEBATE. NO OTHER ISSUE EXCEPT THAT OF MIGRATION COULD HAVE SPLIT OUR WORLD INTO TWO OPPOSING CAMPS AGAIN.
IF YOU WILL NOT ALLOCATE THE USE OF THE NEEDED LABORATORIES AND RESEARCHERS THAT WILL ENSURE THE SUCCESS OF OUR EFFORT, THEN AT LEAST ALLOW US SANCTION TO EMBARK UPON THE ENTERPRISE BY EMPLOYING OUR OWN MEANS TO ACHIEVE OUR PURPOSE. YOU CANNOT STOP PROGRESS.
IF YOU PERSIST ON THIS MINDLESS AMBITION - AND MINDLESS IT IS, SINCE YOUR MINDS ARE STILL CLUTTERED - THEN THIS NEW CONGRESS WILL USE FORCE TO STOP YOU, IF NECESSARY.
WHEN BROUGHT INTO THE STREETS, THE ISSUE CAUSED HAVOC. THE POPULACE WAS AWARE OF ITS HISTORICITY AND THE IGNOMINIOUS CONSEQUENCES ATTENDANT TO MIGRATION BY THOSE WHO ARE STILL CONTROLLED BY THE POISONOUS PROGRAMMING OF ANY UNREALIZED HUMANITY. IN THE STREETS, SPOKESPERSONS FOR EACH SIDE ENCOURAGED SUPPORT FOR THEIR CAUSE.
ARRESTING RESEARCH IS FOLLY. YOU MUST SUPPORT MIGRATION.
RESEARCH WITHOUT CLEAN HEADS IS FOLLY.
SHUT HIS MOUTH. SEIZE THAT SPEAKING DEVICE!
WE MUST NOT POISON SPACE AGAIN

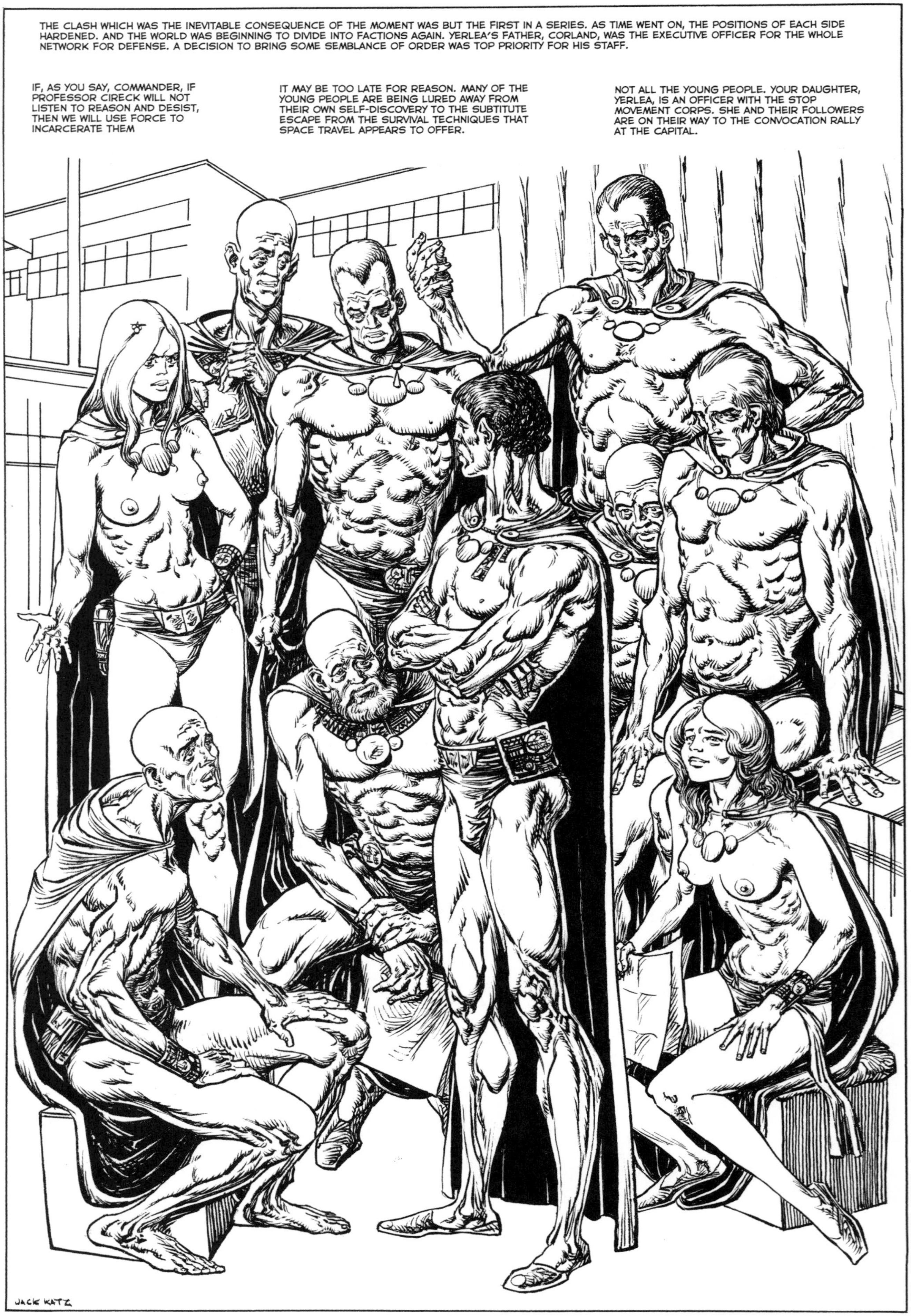
THE CLASH WHICH WAS THE INEVITABLE CONSEQUENCE OF THE MOMENT WAS BUT THE FIRST IN A SERIES. AS TIME WENT ON, THE POSITIONS OF EACH SIDE HARDENED. AND THE WORLD WAS BEGINNING TO DIVIDE INTO FACTIONS AGAIN. YERLEA'S FATHER, CORLAND, WAS THE EXECUTIVE OFFICER FOR THE WHOLE NETWORK FOR DEFENSE. A DECISION TO BRING SOME SEMBLANCE OF ORDER WAS TOP PRIORITY FOR HIS STAFF.
IF, AS YOU SAY, COMMANDER, IF PROFESSOR CIRECK WILL NOT LISTEN TO REASON AND DESIST, THEN WE WILL USE FORCE TO INCARCERATE THEM
IT MAY BE TOO LATE FOR REASON. MANY OF THE YOUNG PEOPLE ARE BEING LURED AWAY FROM THEIR OWN SELF-DISCOVERY TO THE SUBTITUTE ESCAPE FROM THE SURVIVAL TECHNIQUES THAT SPACE TRAVEL APPEARS TO OFFER.
NOT ALL THE YOUNG PEOPLE. YOUR DAUGHTER, YERLEA, IS AN OFFICER WITH THE STOP MOVEMENT CORPS. SHE AND THEIR FOLLOWERS ARE ON THEIR WAY TO THE CONVOCATION RALLY AT THE CAPITAL.
JACK KATZ

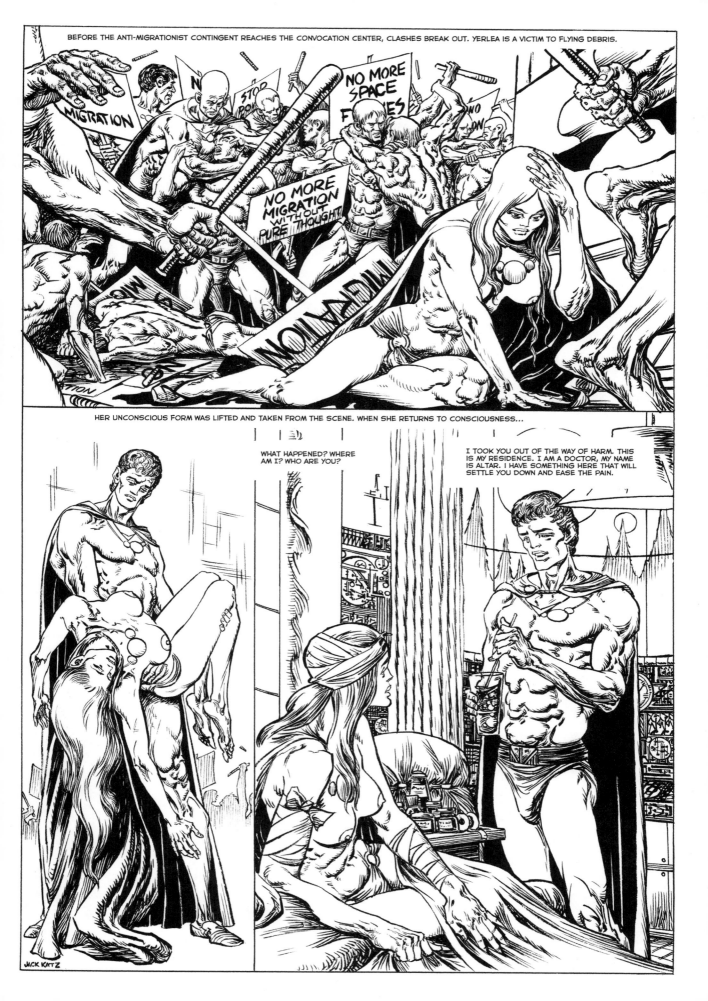

BEFORE THE ANTI-MIGRATIONIST CONTINGENT REACHES THE CONVOCATION CENTER, CLASHES BREAK OUT. YERLEA IS A VICTIM TO FLYING DEBRIS.

NO MORE SPACE FO[...]

NO MORE MIGRATION WITHOUT PURE THOUGHT!

MIGRATION

STOP PO[...]

NO [...] DOW[...]

HER UNCONSCIOUS FORM WAS LIFTED AND TAKEN FROM THE SCENE. WHEN SHE RETURNS TO CONSCIOUSNESS...

WHAT HAPPENED? WHERE AM I? WHO ARE YOU?

I TOOK YOU OUT OF THE WAY OF HARM. THIS IS MY RESIDENCE. I AM A DOCTOR, MY NAME IS ALTAR. I HAVE SOMETHING HERE THAT WILL SETTLE YOU DOWN AND EASE THE PAIN.

JACK KATZ

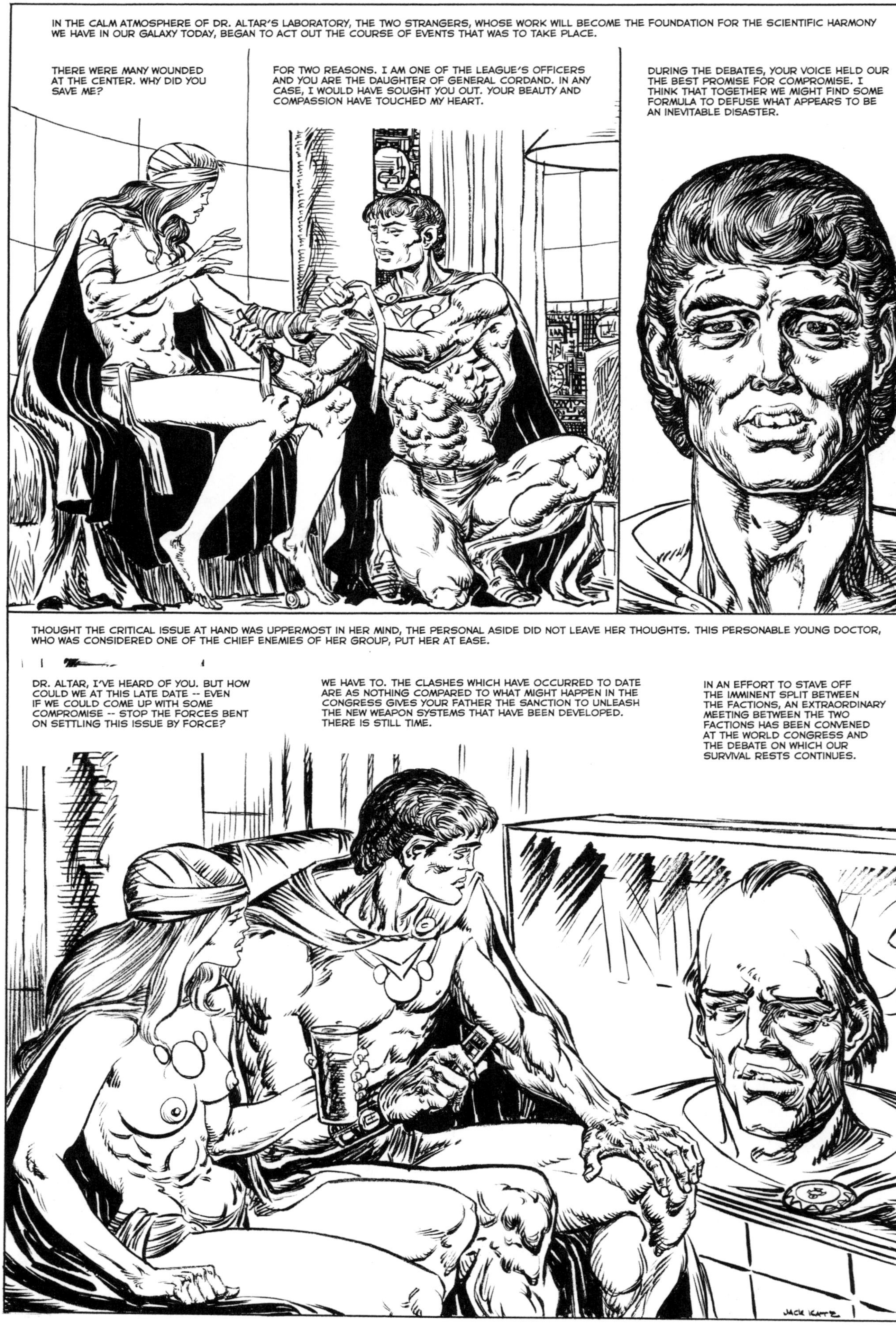
IN THE CALM ATMOSPHERE OF DR. ALTAR'S LABORATORY, THE TWO STRANGERS, WHOSE WORK WILL BECOME THE FOUNDATION FOR THE SCIENTIFIC HARMONY WE HAVE IN OUR GALAXY TODAY, BEGAN TO ACT OUT THE COURSE OF EVENTS THAT WAS TO TAKE PLACE.
THERE WERE MANY WOUNDED AT THE CENTER. WHY DID YOU SAVE ME?
FOR TWO REASONS. I AM ONE OF THE LEAGUE'S OFFICERS AND YOU ARE THE DAUGHTER OF GENERAL CORDAND. IN ANY CASE, I WOULD HAVE SOUGHT YOU OUT. YOUR BEAUTY AND COMPASSION HAVE TOUCHED MY HEART.
DURING THE DEBATES, YOUR VOICE HELD OUR THE BEST PROMISE FOR COMPROMISE. I THINK THAT TOGETHER WE MIGHT FIND SOME FORMULA TO DEFUSE WHAT APPEARS TO BE AN INEVITABLE DISASTER.
THOUGHT THE CRITICAL ISSUE AT HAND WAS UPPERMOST IN HER MIND, THE PERSONAL ASIDE DID NOT LEAVE HER THOUGHTS. THIS PERSONABLE YOUNG DOCTOR, WHO WAS CONSIDERED ONE OF THE CHIEF ENEMIES OF HER GROUP, PUT HER AT EASE.
DR. ALTAR, I'VE HEARD OF YOU. BUT HOW COULD WE AT THIS LATE DATE -- EVEN IF WE COULD COME UP WITH SOME COMPROMISE -- STOP THE FORCES BENT ON SETTLING THIS ISSUE BY FORCE?
WE HAVE TO. THE CLASHES WHICH HAVE OCCURRED TO DATE ARE AS NOTHING COMPARED TO WHAT MIGHT HAPPEN IN THE CONGRESS GIVES YOUR FATHER THE SANCTION TO UNLEASH THE NEW WEAPON SYSTEMS THAT HAVE BEEN DEVELOPED. THERE IS STILL TIME.
IN AN EFFORT TO STAVE OFF THE IMMINENT SPLIT BETWEEN THE FACTIONS, AN EXTRAORDINARY MEETING BETWEEN THE TWO FACTIONS HAS BEEN CONVENED AT THE WORLD CONGRESS AND THE DEBATE ON WHICH OUR SURVIVAL RESTS CONTINUES.
JACK KATZ

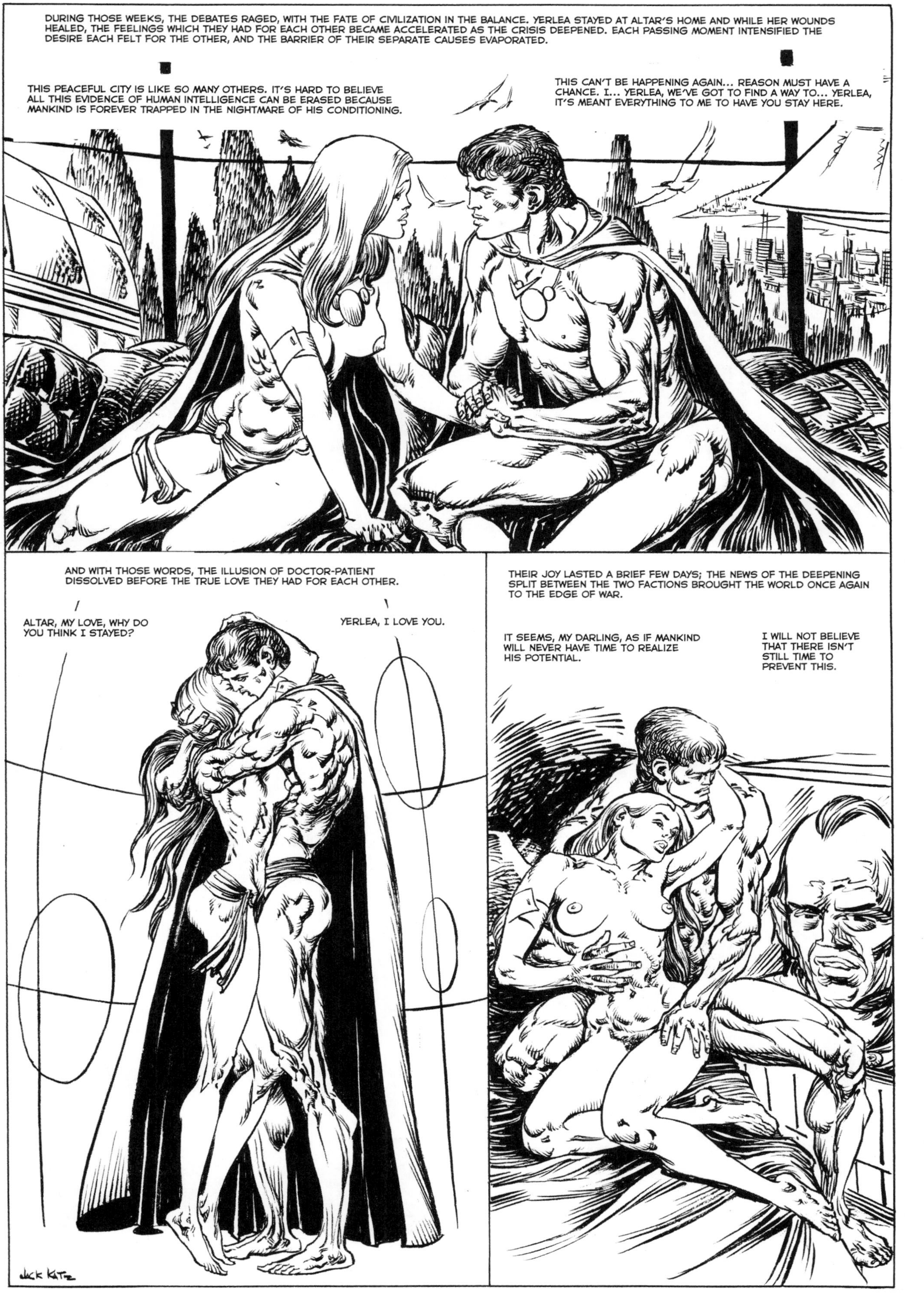
DURING THOSE WEEKS, THE DEBATES RAGED, WITH THE FATE OF CIVILIZATION IN THE BALANCE. YERLEA STAYED AT ALTAR'S HOME AND WHILE HER WOUNDS HEALED, THE FEELINGS WHICH THEY HAD FOR EACH OTHER BECAME ACCELERATED AS THE CRISIS DEEPENED. EACH PASSING MOMENT INTENSIFIED THE DESIRE EACH FELT FOR THE OTHER, AND THE BARRIER OF THEIR SEPARATE CAUSES EVAPORATED.
THIS PEACEFUL CITY IS LIKE SO MANY OTHERS. IT'S HARD TO BELIEVE ALL THIS EVIDENCE OF HUMAN INTELLIGENCE CAN BE ERASED BECAUSE MANKIND IS FOREVER TRAPPED IN THE NIGHTMARE OF HIS CONDITIONING.
THIS CAN'T BE HAPPENING AGAIN... REASON MUST HAVE A CHANCE. I... YERLEA, WE'VE GOT TO FIND A WAY TO... YERLEA, IT'S MEANT EVERYTHING TO ME TO HAVE YOU STAY HERE.
AND WITH THOSE WORDS, THE ILLUSION OF DOCTOR-PATIENT DISSOLVED BEFORE THE TRUE LOVE THEY HAD FOR EACH OTHER.
ALTAR, MY LOVE, WHY DO YOU THINK I STAYED?
YERLEA, I LOVE YOU.
JACK KATZ
THEIR JOY LASTED A BRIEF FEW DAYS; THE NEWS OF THE DEEPENING SPLIT BETWEEN THE TWO FACTIONS BROUGHT THE WORLD ONCE AGAIN TO THE EDGE OF WAR.
IT SEEMS, MY DARLING, AS IF MANKIND WILL NEVER HAVE TIME TO REALIZE HIS POTENTIAL.
I WILL NOT BELIEVE THAT THERE ISN'T STILL TIME TO PREVENT THIS.

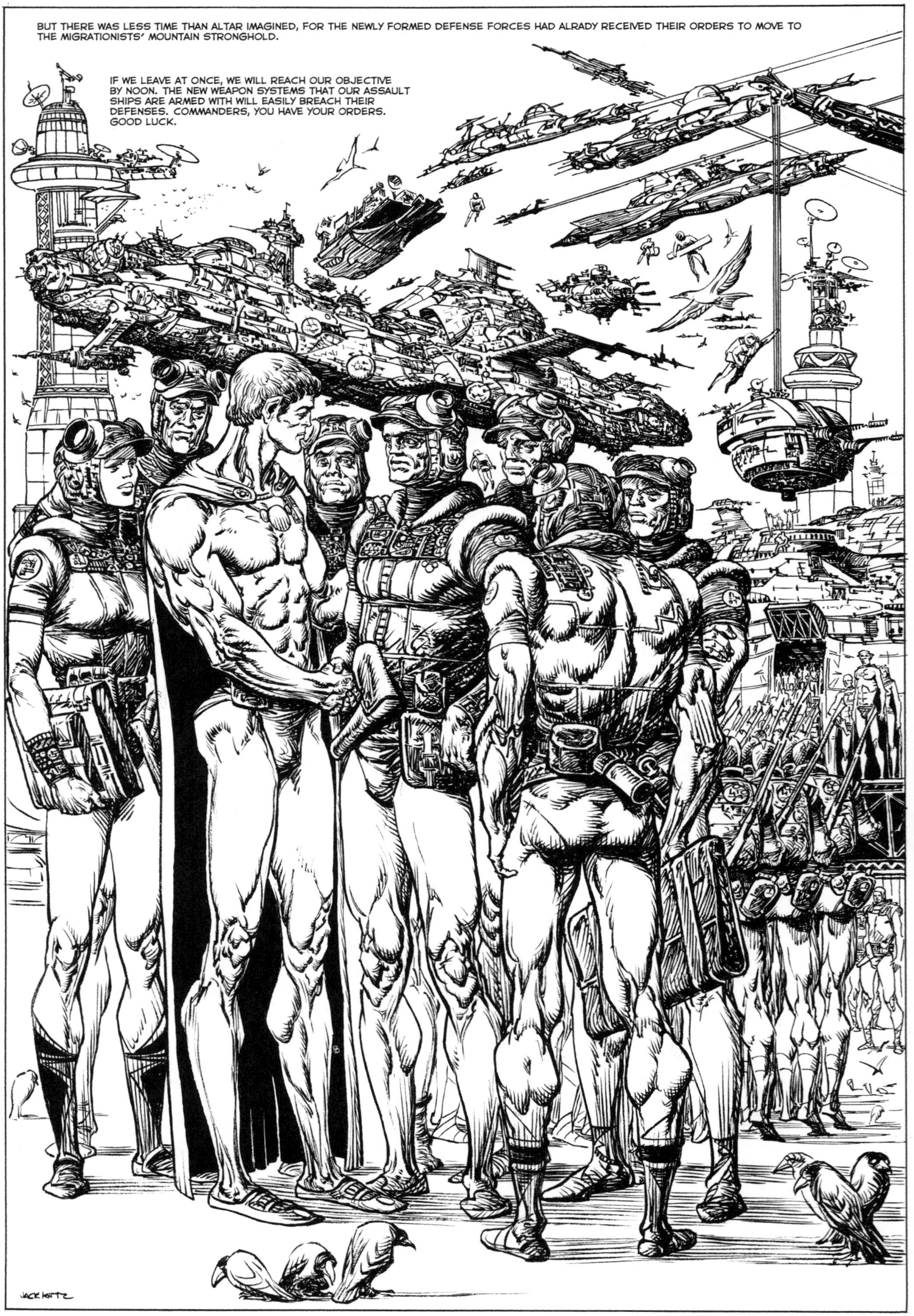
BUT THERE WAS LESS TIME THAN ALTAR IMAGINED, FOR THE NEWLY FORMED DEFENSE FORCES HAD ALRADY RECEIVED THEIR ORDERS TO MOVE TO THE MIGRATIONISTS' MOUNTAIN STRONGHOLD.
IF WE LEAVE AT ONCE, WE WILL REACH OUR OBJECTIVE BY NOON. THE NEW WEAPON SYSTEMS THAT OUR ASSAULT SHIPS ARE ARMED WITH WILL EASILY BREACH THEIR DEFENSES. COMMANDERS, YOU HAVE YOUR ORDERS. GOOD LUCK.
JACK KATZ

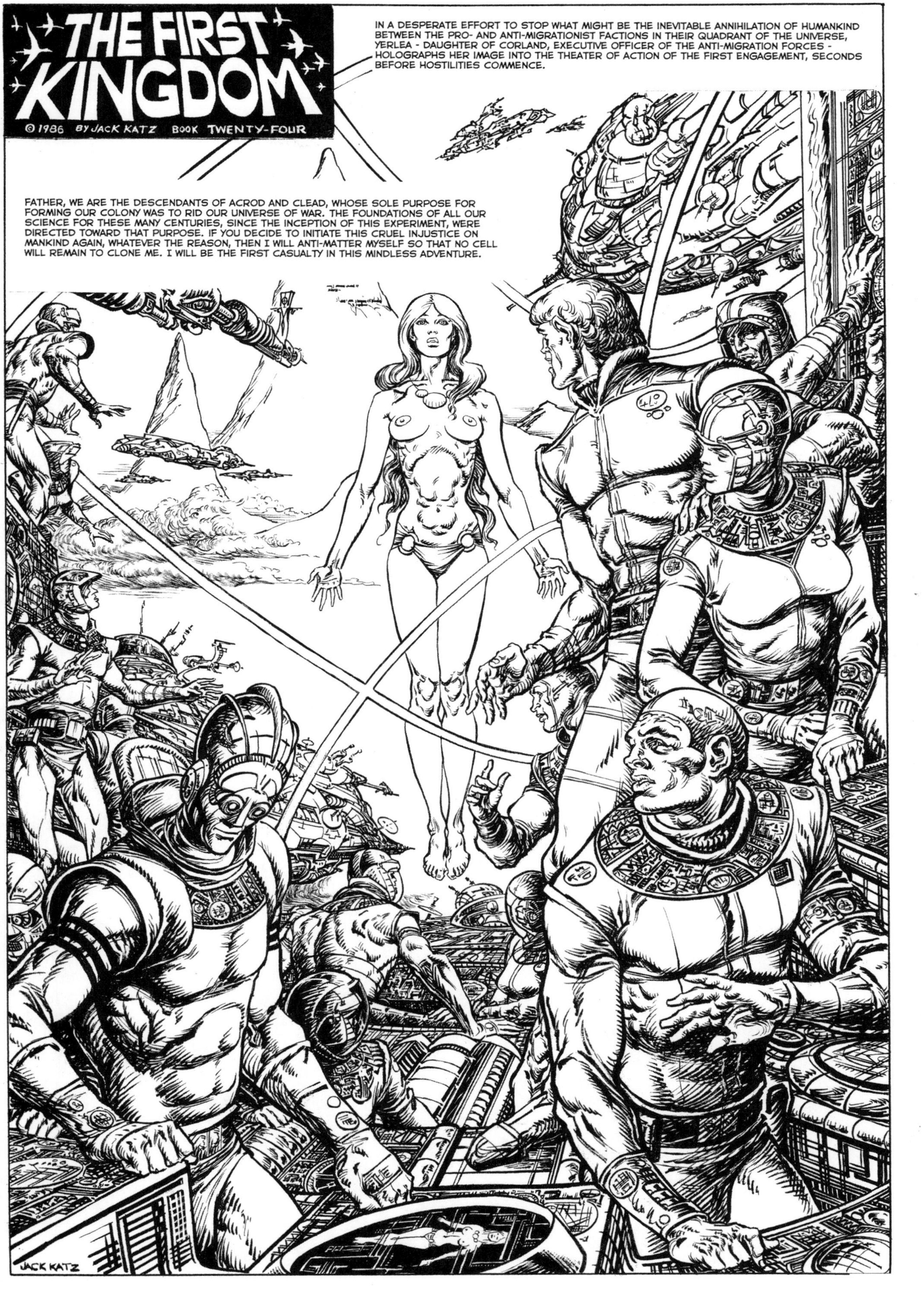
THE FIRST KINGDOM
©1986 BY JACK KATZ BOOK TWENTY-FOUR
IN A DESPERATE EFFORT TO STOP WHAT MIGHT BE THE INEVITABLE ANNIHILATION OF HUMANKIND BETWEEN THE PRO- AND ANTI-MIGRATIONIST FACTIONS IN THEIR QUADRANT OF THE UNIVERSE, YERLEA - DAUGHTER OF CORLAND, EXECUTIVE OFFICER OF THE ANTI-MIGRATION FORCES - HOLOGRAPHS HER IMAGE INTO THE THEATER OF ACTION OF THE FIRST ENGAGEMENT, SECONDS BEFORE HOSTILITIES COMMENCE.
FATHER, WE ARE THE DESCENDANTS OF ACROD AND CLEAD, WHOSE SOLE PURPOSE FOR FORMING OUR COLONY WAS TO RID OUR UNIVERSE OF WAR. THE FOUNDATIONS OF ALL OUR SCIENCE FOR THESE MANY CENTURIES, SINCE THE INCEPTION OF THIS EXPERIMENT, WERE DIRECTED TOWARD THAT PURPOSE. IF YOU DECIDE TO INITIATE THIS CRUEL INJUSTICE ON MANKIND AGAIN, WHATEVER THE REASON, THEN I WILL ANTI-MATTER MYSELF SO THAT NO CELL WILL REMAIN TO CLONE ME. I WILL BE THE FIRST CASUALTY IN THIS MINDLESS ADVENTURE.
JACK KATZ

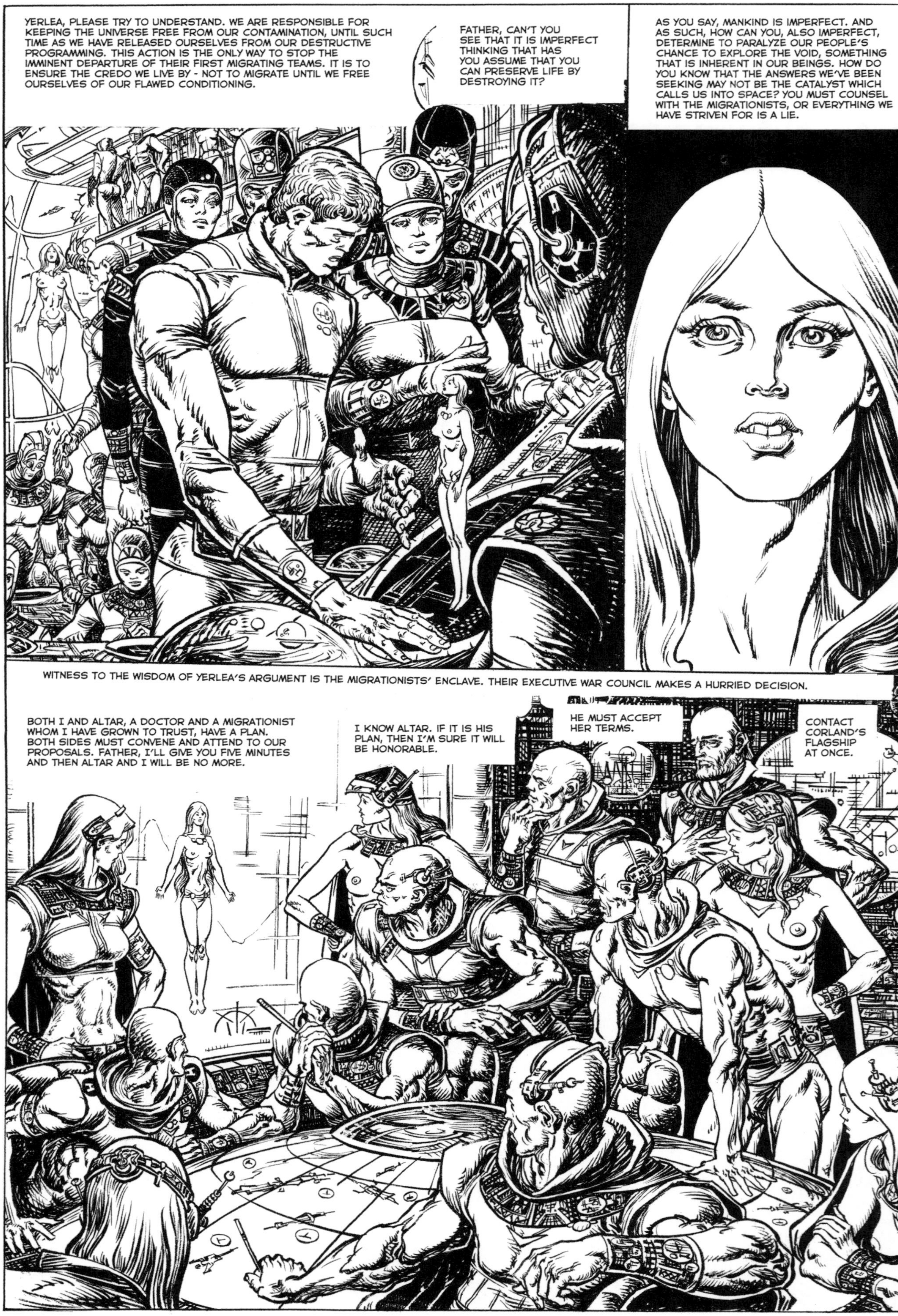
YERLEA, PLEASE TRY TO UNDERSTAND. WE ARE RESPONSIBLE FOR KEEPING THE UNIVERSE FREE FROM OUR CONTAMINATION, UNTIL SUCH TIME AS WE HAVE RELEASED OURSELVES FROM OUR DESTRUCTIVE PROGRAMMING. THIS ACTION IS THE ONLY WAY TO STOP THE IMMINENT DEPARTURE OF THEIR FIRST MIGRATING TEAMS. IT IS TO ENSURE THE CREDO WE LIVE BY - NOT TO MIGRATE UNTIL WE FREE OURSELVES OF OUR FLAWED CONDITIONING.
FATHER, CAN'T YOU SEE THAT IT IS IMPERFECT THINKING THAT HAS YOU ASSUME THAT YOU CAN PRESERVE LIFE BY DESTROYING IT?
AS YOU SAY, MANKIND IS IMPERFECT. AND AS SUCH, HOW CAN YOU, ALSO IMPERFECT, DETERMINE TO PARALYZE OUR PEOPLE'S CHANCE TO EXPLORE THE VOID, SOMETHING THAT IS INHERENT IN OUR BEINGS. HOW DO YOU KNOW THAT THE ANSWERS WE'VE BEEN SEEKING MAY NOT BE THE CATALYST WHICH CALLS US INTO SPACE? YOU MUST COUNSEL WITH THE MIGRATIONISTS, OR EVERYTHING WE HAVE STRIVEN FOR IS A LIE.
WITNESS TO THE WISDOM OF YERLEA'S ARGUMENT IS THE MIGRATIONISTS' ENCLAVE. THEIR EXECUTIVE WAR COUNCIL MAKES A HURRIED DECISION.
BOTH I AND ALTAR, A DOCTOR AND A MIGRATIONIST WHOM I HAVE GROWN TO TRUST, HAVE A PLAN. BOTH SIDES MUST CONVENE AND ATTEND TO OUR PROPOSALS. FATHER, I'LL GIVE YOU FIVE MINUTES AND THEN ALTAR AND I WILL BE NO MORE.
I KNOW ALTAR. IF IT IS HIS PLAN, THEN I'M SURE IT WILL BE HONORABLE.
HE MUST ACCEPT HER TERMS.
CONTACT CORLAND'S FLAGSHIP AT ONCE.

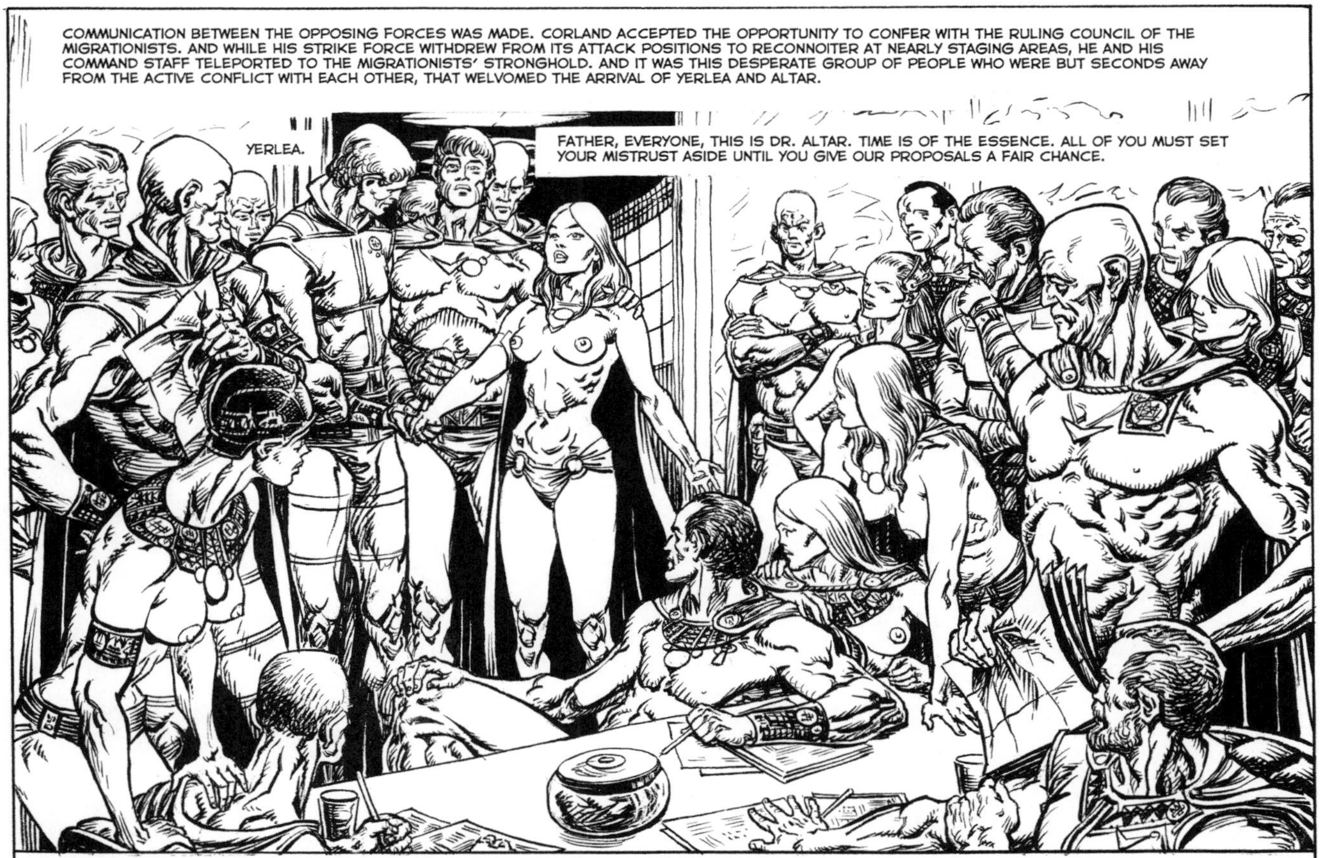
COMMUNICATION BETWEEN THE OPPOSING FORCES WAS MADE. CORLAND ACCEPTED THE OPPORTUNITY TO CONFER WITH THE RULING COUNCIL OF THE MIGRATIONISTS. AND WHILE HIS STRIKE FORCE WITHDREW FROM ITS ATTACK POSITIONS TO RECONNOITER AT NEARLY STAGING AREAS, HE AND HIS COMMAND STAFF TELEPORTED TO THE MIGRATIONISTS' STRONGHOLD. AND IT WAS THIS DESPERATE GROUP OF PEOPLE WHO WERE BUT SECONDS AWAY FROM THE ACTIVE CONFLICT WITH EACH OTHER, THAT WELVOMED THE ARRIVAL OF YERLEA AND ALTAR.
YERLEA.
FATHER, EVERYONE, THIS IS DR. ALTAR. TIME IS OF THE ESSENCE. ALL OF YOU MUST SET YOUR MISTRUST ASIDE UNTIL YOU GIVE OUR PROPOSALS A FAIR CHANCE.

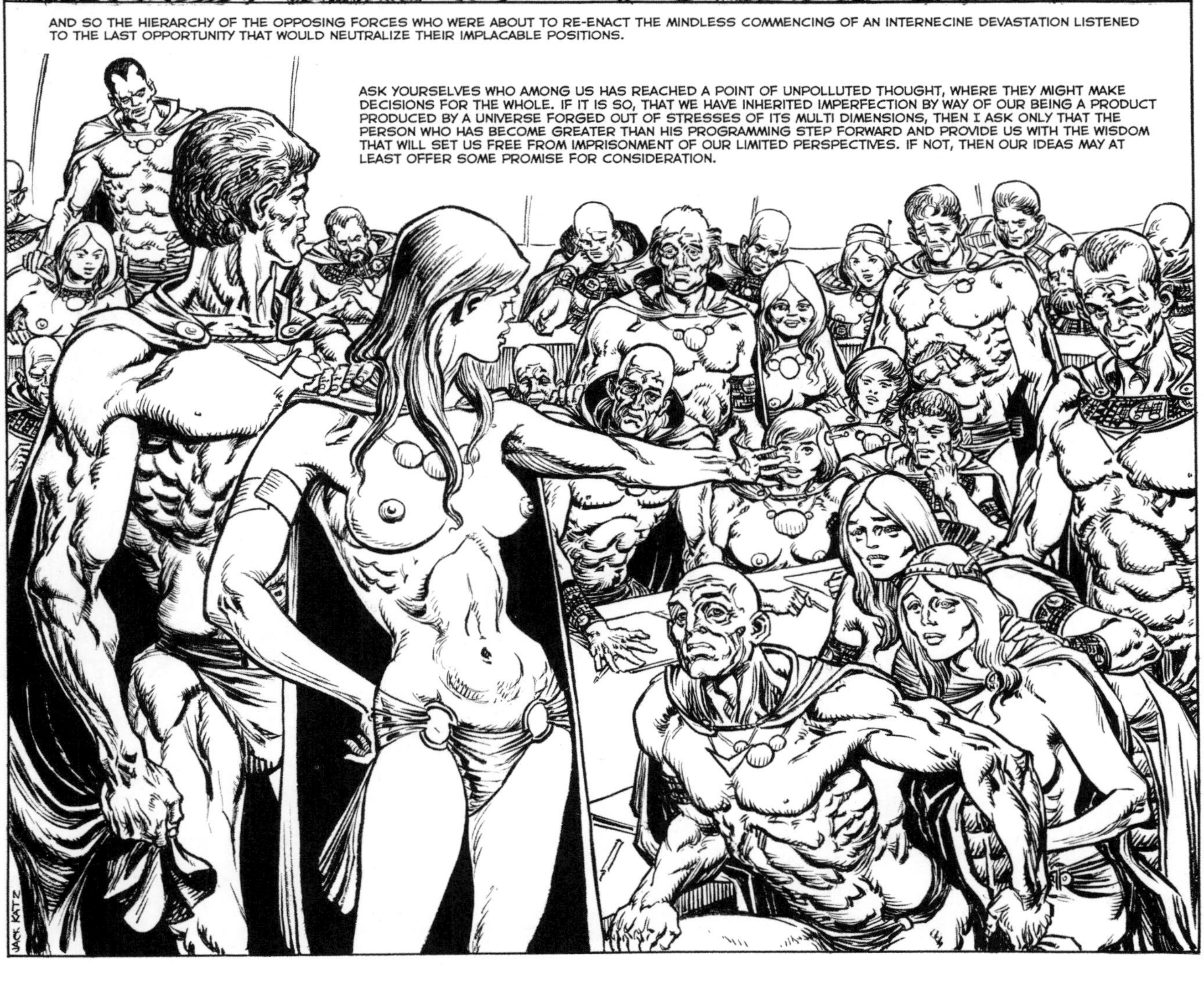
AND SO THE HIERARCHY OF THE OPPOSING FORCES WHO WERE ABOUT TO RE-ENACT THE MINDLESS COMMENCING OF AN INTERNECINE DEVASTATION LISTENED TO THE LAST OPPORTUNITY THAT WOULD NEUTRALIZE THEIR IMPLACABLE POSITIONS.
ASK YOURSELVES WHO AMONG US HAS REACHED A POINT OF UNPOLLUTED THOUGHT, WHERE THEY MIGHT MAKE DECISIONS FOR THE WHOLE. IF IT IS SO, THAT WE HAVE INHERITED IMPERFECTION BY WAY OF OUR BEING A PRODUCT PRODUCED BY A UNIVERSE FORGED OUT OF STRESSES OF ITS MULTI DIMENSIONS, THEN I ASK ONLY THAT THE PERSON WHO HAS BECOME GREATER THAN HIS PROGRAMMING STEP FORWARD AND PROVIDE US WITH THE WISDOM THAT WILL SET US FREE FROM IMPRISONMENT OF OUR LIMITED PERSPECTIVES. IF NOT, THEN OUR IDEAS MAY AT LEAST OFFER SOME PROMISE FOR CONSIDERATION.
JACK KATZ

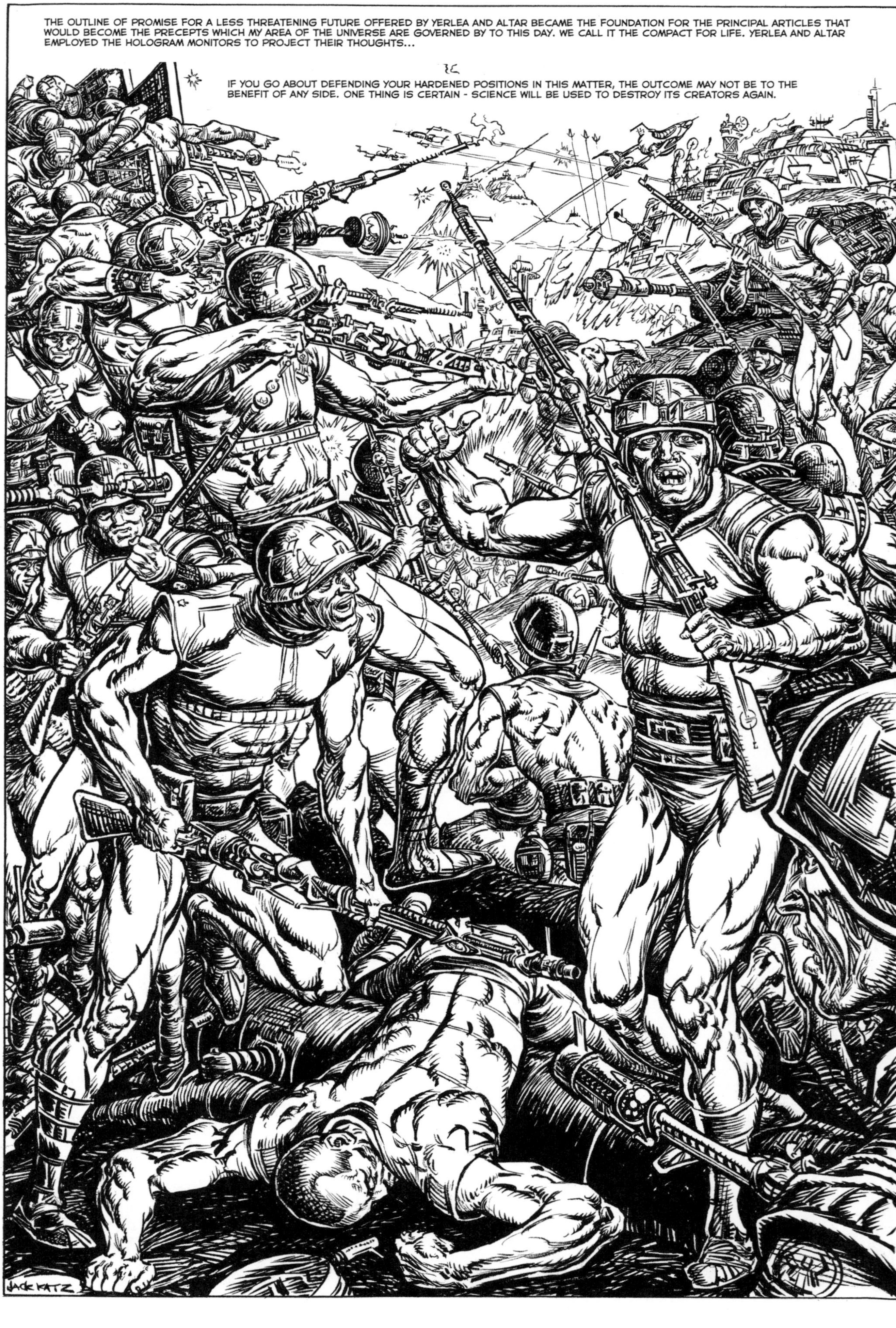
THE OUTLINE OF PROMISE FOR A LESS THREATENING FUTURE OFFERED BY YERLEA AND ALTAR BECAME THE FOUNDATION FOR THE PRINCIPAL ARTICLES THAT WOULD BECOME THE PRECEPTS WHICH MY AREA OF THE UNIVERSE ARE GOVERNED BY TO THIS DAY. WE CALL IT THE COMPACT FOR LIFE. YERLEA AND ALTAR EMPLOYED THE HOLOGRAM MONITORS TO PROJECT THEIR THOUGHTS...
IF YOU GO ABOUT DEFENDING YOUR HARDENED POSITIONS IN THIS MATTER, THE OUTCOME MAY NOT BE TO THE BENEFIT OF ANY SIDE. ONE THING IS CERTAIN - SCIENCE WILL BE USED TO DESTROY ITS CREATORS AGAIN.
JACK KATZ

SHOULD SOME MEASURE OF HUMANITY SURVIVE, THEN POSSESSION FOR THE GAME FIELDS AND WATER RESOURCES WOULD PERPETUATE NEW ROUNDS OF WARFARE - CLASHES BETWEEN BANDS OF BRIGANDS LOCKED IN COMBAT WITH PRIMITIVE WEAPONS, PERHAPS FIGHTING OVER A STRUCTURE OF THE PAST THAT WOULD GIVE THEM A BETTER DEFENSIVE POSITION. OR IF SUPERSTITIOUS RELIGIONS TAKE HOLD, THEY WILL USE THE STRUCTURE AS EVIDENCE OF THE DEITY THEY HAVE INVENTED TO MAKE THE CRUEL DEMANDS OF SURVIVAL PALATABLE.

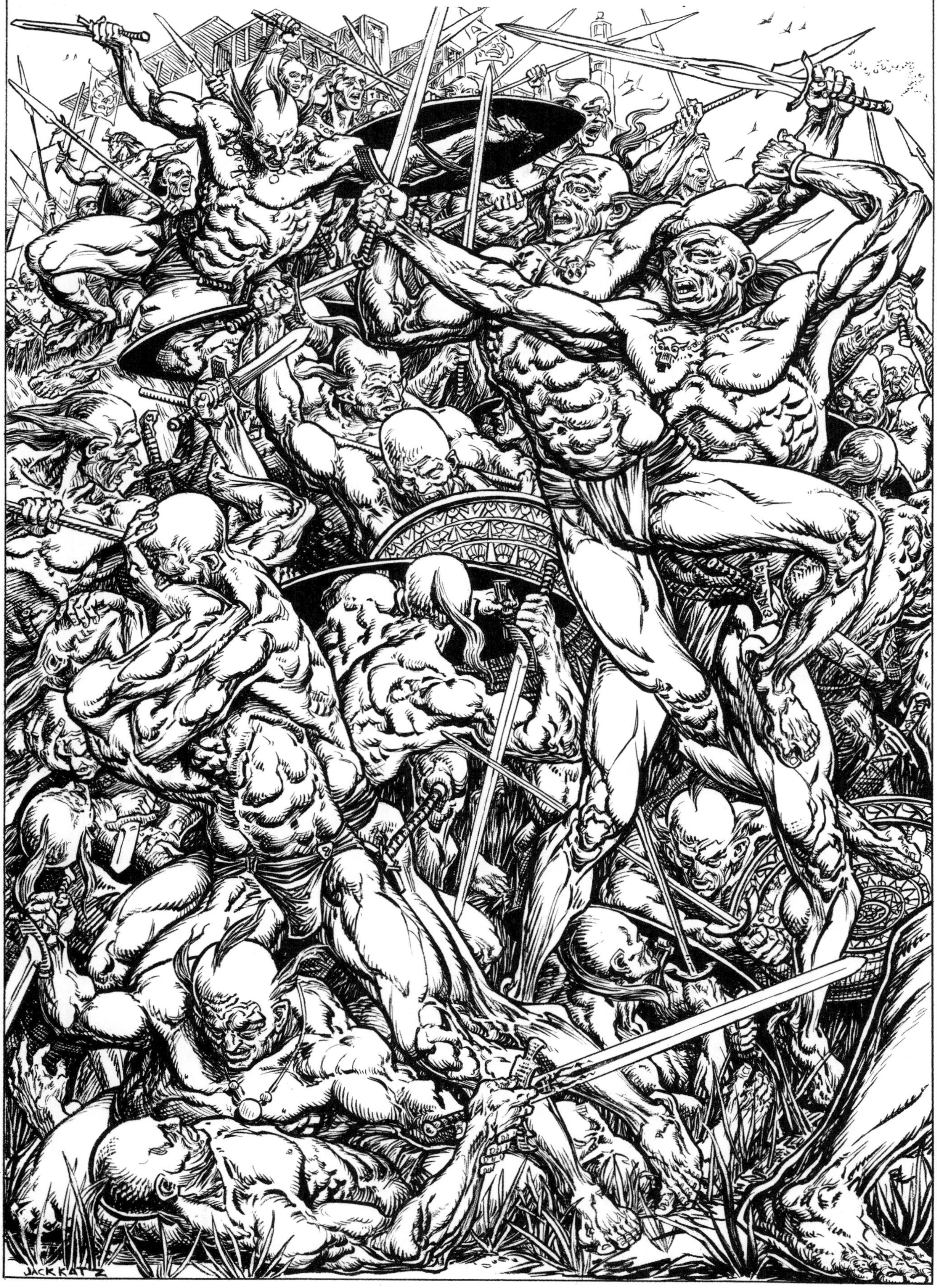
JACK KATZ

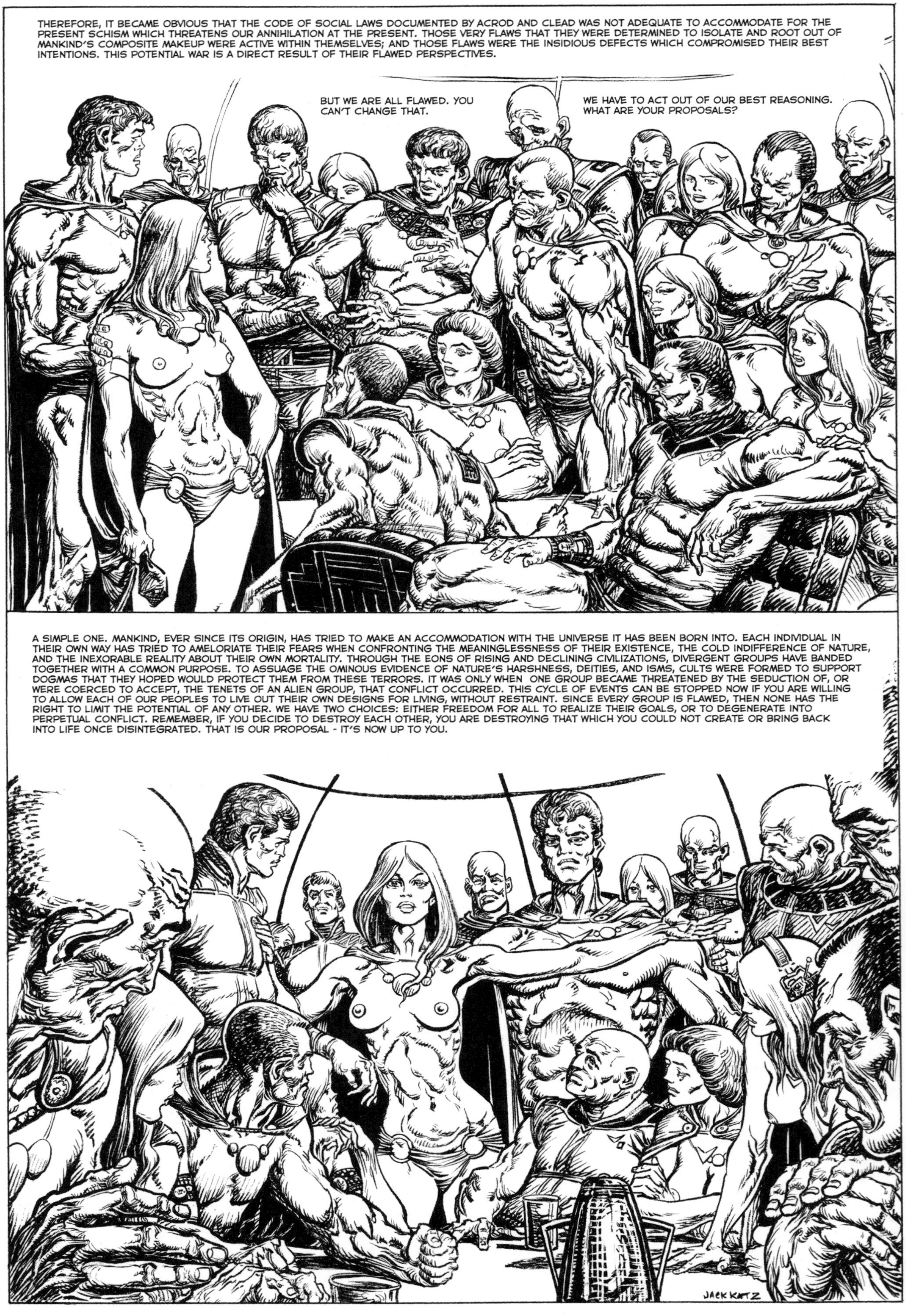
THEREFORE, IT BECAME OBVIOUS THAT THE CODE OF SOCIAL LAWS DOCUMENTED BY ACROD AND CLEAD WAS NOT ADEQUATE TO ACCOMMODATE FOR THE PRESENT SCHISM WHICH THREATENS OUR ANNIHILATION AT THE PRESENT. THOSE VERY FLAWS THAT THEY WERE DETERMINED TO ISOLATE AND ROOT OUT OF MANKIND'S COMPOSITE MAKEUP WERE ACTIVE WITHIN THEMSELVES; AND THOSE FLAWS WERE THE INSIDIOUS DEFECTS WHICH COMPROMISED THEIR BEST INTENTIONS. THIS POTENTIAL WAR IS A DIRECT RESULT OF THEIR FLAWED PERSPECTIVES.
BUT WE ARE ALL FLAWED. YOU CAN'T CHANGE THAT.
WE HAVE TO ACT OUT OF OUR BEST REASONING. WHAT ARE YOUR PROPOSALS?
A SIMPLE ONE. MANKIND, EVER SINCE ITS ORIGIN, HAS TRIED TO MAKE AN ACCOMMODATION WITH THE UNIVERSE IT HAS BEEN BORN INTO. EACH INDIVIDUAL IN THEIR OWN WAY HAS TRIED TO AMELIORATE THEIR FEARS WHEN CONFRONTING THE MEANINGLESSNESS OF THEIR EXISTENCE, THE COLD INDIFFERENCE OF NATURE, AND THE INEXORABLE REALITY ABOUT THEIR OWN MORTALITY. THROUGH THE EONS OF RISING AND DECLINING CIVILIZATIONS, DIVERGENT GROUPS HAVE BANDED TOGETHER WITH A COMMON PURPOSE. TO ASSUAGE THE OMINOUS EVIDENCE OF NATURE'S HARSHNESS, DEITIES, AND ISMS, CULTS WERE FORMED TO SUPPORT DOGMAS THAT THEY HOPED WOULD PROTECT THEM FROM THESE TERRORS. IT WAS ONLY WHEN ONE GROUP BECAME THREATENED BY THE SEDUCTION OF, OR WERE COERCED TO ACCEPT, THE TENETS OF AN ALIEN GROUP, THAT CONFLICT OCCURRED. THIS CYCLE OF EVENTS CAN BE STOPPED NOW IF YOU ARE WILLING TO ALLOW EACH OF OUR PEOPLES TO LIVE OUT THEIR OWN DESIGNS FOR LIVING, WITHOUT RESTRAINT. SINCE EVERY GROUP IS FLAWED, THEN NONE HAS THE RIGHT TO LIMIT THE POTENTIAL OF ANY OTHER. WE HAVE TWO CHOICES: EITHER FREEDOM FOR ALL TO REALIZE THEIR GOALS, OR TO DEGENERATE INTO PERPETUAL CONFLICT. REMEMBER, IF YOU DECIDE TO DESTROY EACH OTHER, YOU ARE DESTROYING THAT WHICH YOU COULD NOT CREATE OR BRING BACK INTO LIFE ONCE DISINTEGRATED. THAT IS OUR PROPOSAL - IT'S NOW UP TO YOU.
JACK KATZ

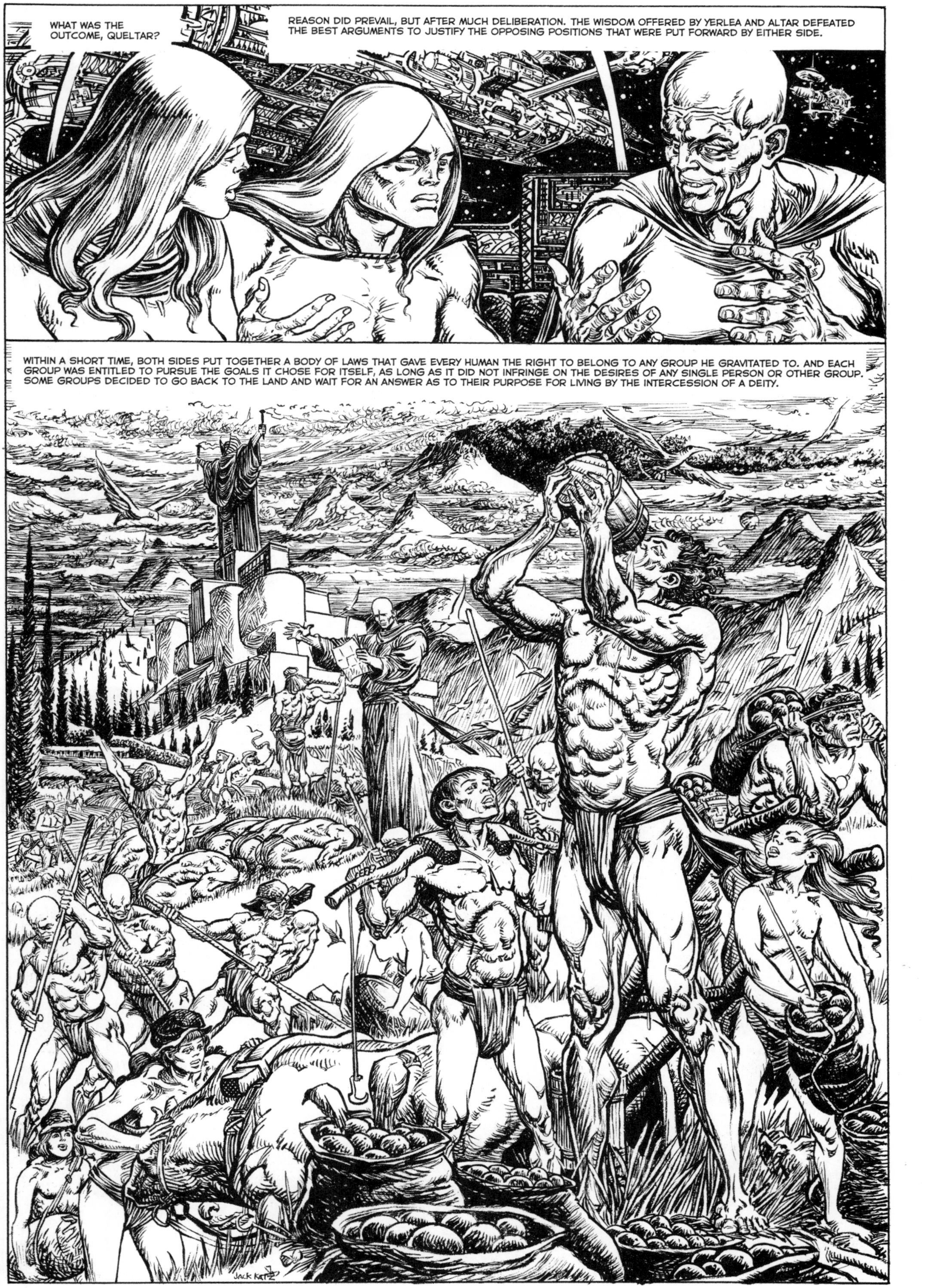
WHAT WAS THE OUTCOME, QUELTAR?
REASON DID PREVAIL, BUT AFTER MUCH DELIBERATION. THE WISDOM OFFERED BY YERLEA AND ALTAR DEFEATED THE BEST ARGUMENTS TO JUSTIFY THE OPPOSING POSITIONS THAT WERE PUT FORWARD BY EITHER SIDE.
WITHIN A SHORT TIME, BOTH SIDES PUT TOGETHER A BODY OF LAWS THAT GAVE EVERY HUMAN THE RIGHT TO BELONG TO ANY GROUP HE GRAVITATED TO. AND EACH GROUP WAS ENTITLED TO PURSUE THE GOALS IT CHOSE FOR ITSELF, AS LONG AS IT DID NOT INFRINGE ON THE DESIRES OF ANY SINGLE PERSON OR OTHER GROUP. SOME GROUPS DECIDED TO GO BACK TO THE LAND AND WAIT FOR AN ANSWER AS TO THEIR PURPOSE FOR LIVING BY THE INTERCESSION OF A DEITY.
JACK KATZ

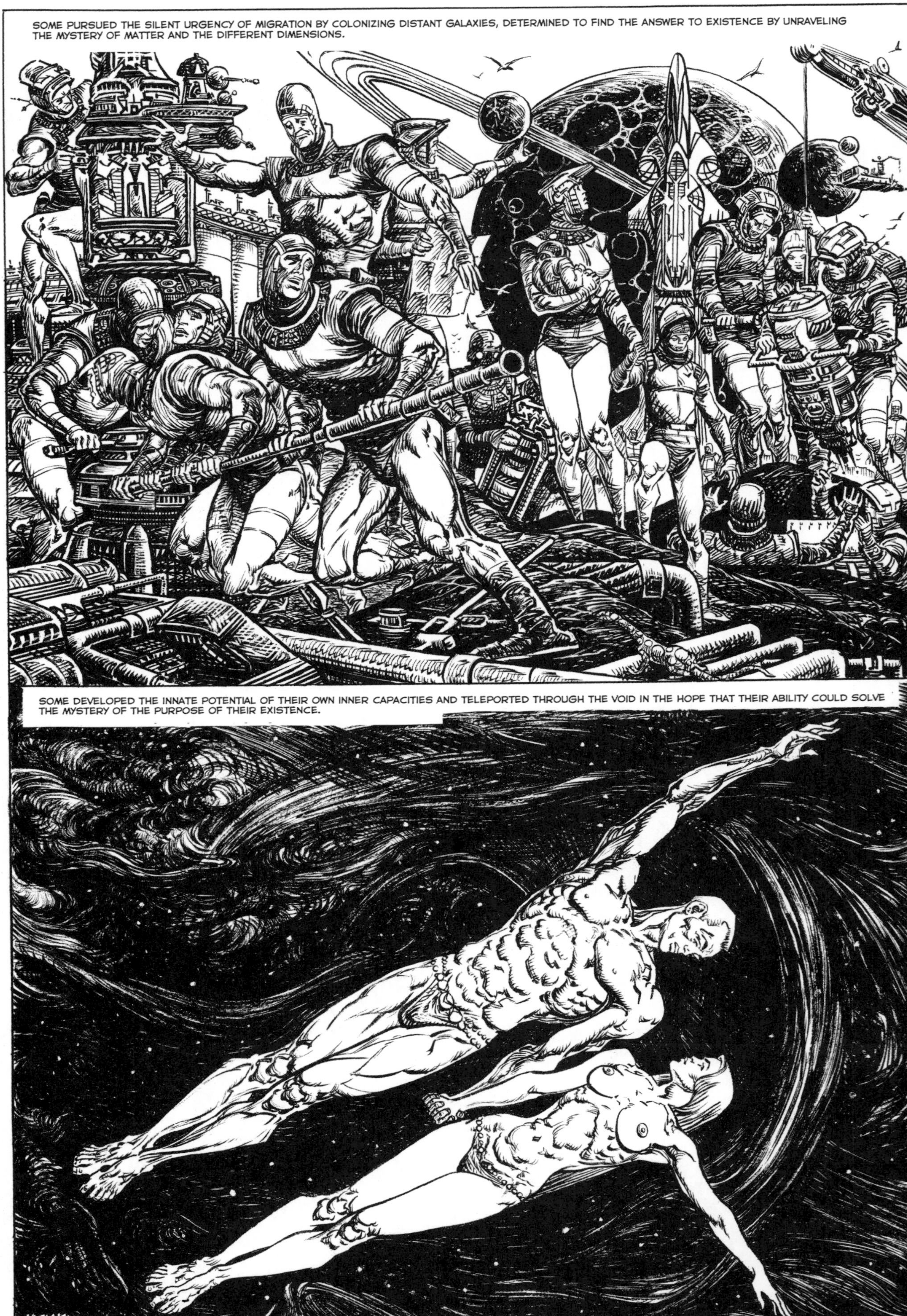
SOME PURSUED THE SILENT URGENCY OF MIGRATION BY COLONIZING DISTANT GALAXIES, DETERMINED TO FIND THE ANSWER TO EXISTENCE BY UNRAVELING THE MYSTERY OF MATTER AND THE DIFFERENT DIMENSIONS.
SOME DEVELOPED THE INNATE POTENTIAL OF THEIR OWN INNER CAPACITIES AND TELEPORTED THROUGH THE VOID IN THE HOPE THAT THEIR ABILITY COULD SOLVE THE MYSTERY OF THE PURPOSE OF THEIR EXISTENCE.
JACK KATZ

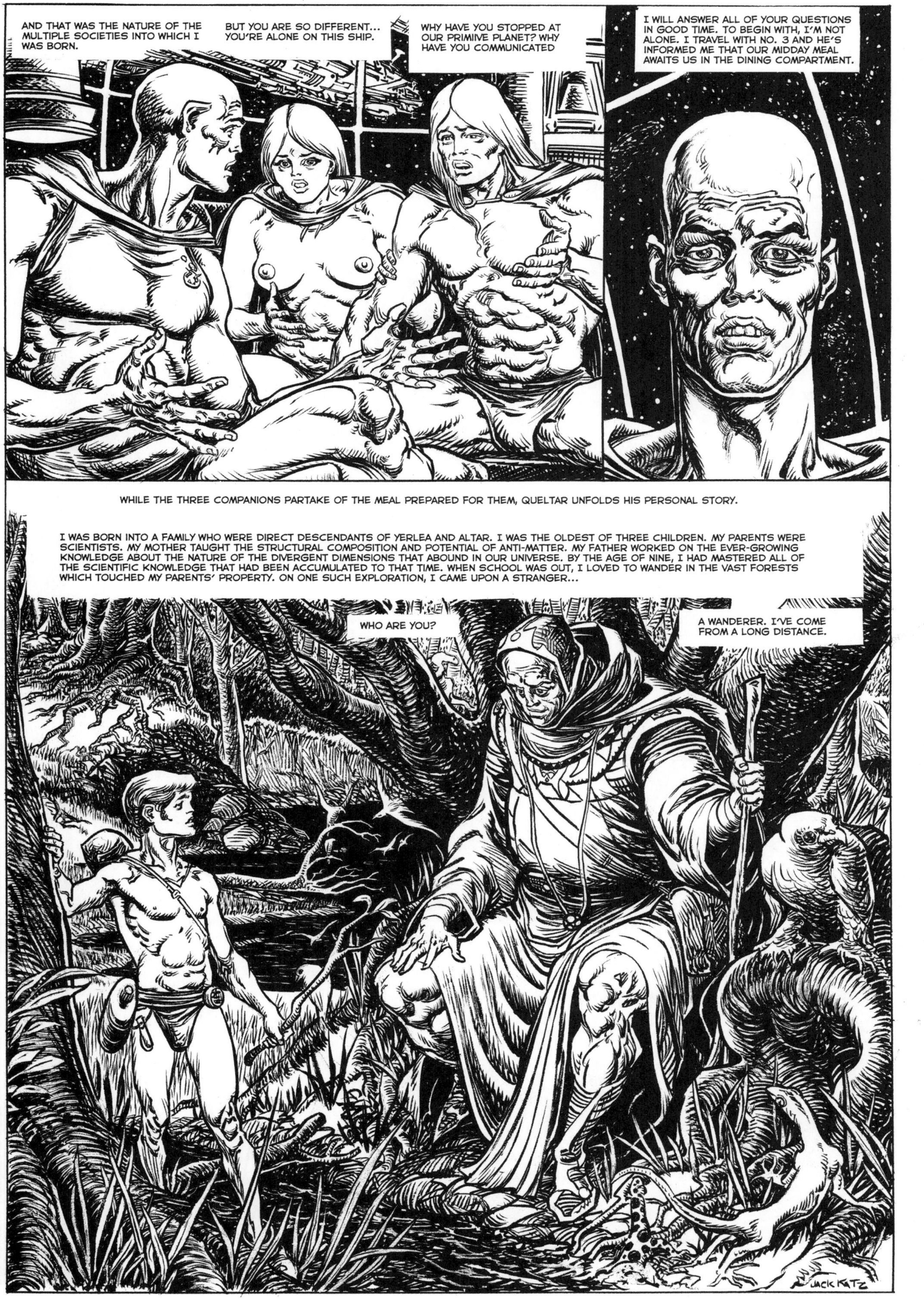
AND THAT WAS THE NATURE OF THE MULTIPLE SOCIETIES INTO WHICH I WAS BORN.
BUT YOU ARE SO DIFFERENT... YOU'RE ALONE ON THIS SHIP.
WHY HAVE YOU STOPPED AT OUR PRIMIIVE PLANET? WHY HAVE YOU COMMUNICATED
I WILL ANSWER ALL OF YOUR QUESTIONS IN GOOD TIME. TO BEGIN WITH, I'M NOT ALONE. I TRAVEL WITH NO. 3 AND HE'S INFORMED ME THAT OUR MIDDAY MEAL AWAITS US IN THE DINING COMPARTMENT.
WHILE THE THREE COMPANIONS PARTAKE OF THE MEAL PREPARED FOR THEM, QUELTAR UNFOLDS HIS PERSONAL STORY.
I WAS BORN INTO A FAMILY WHO WERE DIRECT DESCENDANTS OF YERLEA AND ALTAR. I WAS THE OLDEST OF THREE CHILDREN. MY PARENTS WERE SCIENTISTS. MY MOTHER TAUGHT THE STRUCTURAL COMPOSITION AND POTENTIAL OF ANTI-MATTER. MY FATHER WORKED ON THE EVER-GROWING KNOWLEDGE ABOUT THE NATURE OF THE DIVERGENT DIMENSIONS THAT ABOUND IN OUR UNIVERSE. BY THE AGE OF NINE, I HAD MASTERED ALL OF THE SCIENTIFIC KNOWLEDGE THAT HAD BEEN ACCUMULATED TO THAT TIME. WHEN SCHOOL WAS OUT, I LOVED TO WANDER IN THE VAST FORESTS WHICH TOUCHED MY PARENTS' PROPERTY. ON ONE SUCH EXPLORATION, I CAME UPON A STRANGER...
WHO ARE YOU?
A WANDERER. I'VE COME FROM A LONG DISTANCE.
JACK KATZ

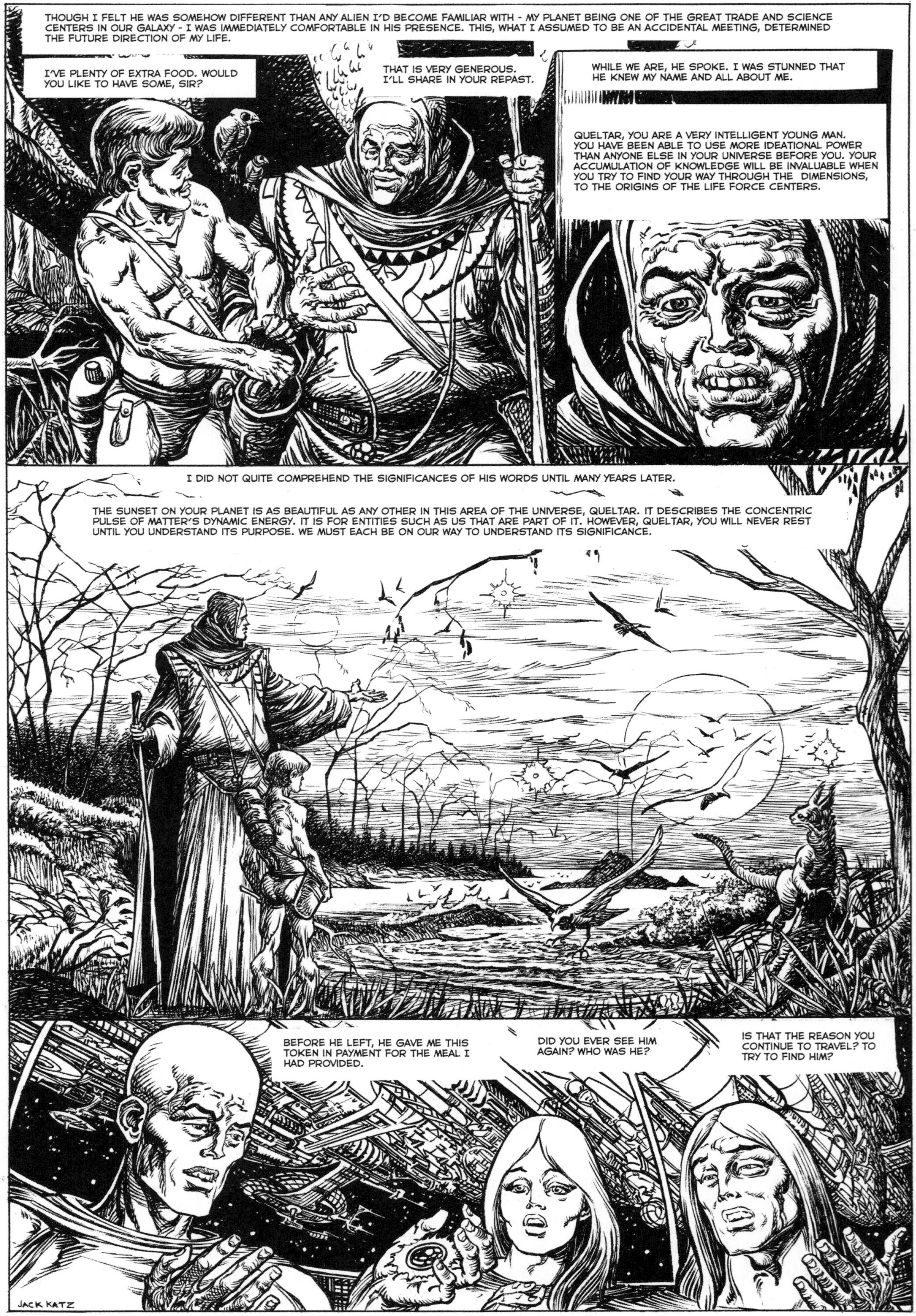
THOUGH I FELT HE WAS SOMEHOW DIFFERENT THAN ANY ALIEN I'D BECOME FAMILIAR WITH - MY PLANET BEING ONE OF THE GREAT TRADE AND SCIENCE CENTERS IN OUR GALAXY - I WAS IMMEDIATELY COMFORTABLE IN HIS PRESENCE. THIS, WHAT I ASSUMED TO BE AN ACCIDENTAL MEETING, DETERMINED THE FUTURE DIRECTION OF MY LIFE.
I'VE PLENTY OF EXTRA FOOD. WOULD YOU LIKE TO HAVE SOME, SIR?
THAT IS VERY GENEROUS. I'LL SHARE IN YOUR REPAST.
WHILE WE ARE, HE SPOKE. I WAS STUNNED THAT HE KNEW MY NAME AND ALL ABOUT ME.
QUELTAR, YOU ARE A VERY INTELLIGENT YOUNG MAN. YOU HAVE BEEN ABLE TO USE MORE IDEATIONAL POWER THAN ANYONE ELSE IN YOUR UNIVERSE BEFORE YOU. YOUR ACCUMULATION OF KNOWLEDGE WILL BE INVALUABLE WHEN YOU TRY TO FIND YOUR WAY THROUGH THE DIMENSIONS, TO THE ORIGINS OF THE LIFE FORCE CENTERS.
I DID NOT QUITE COMPREHEND THE SIGNIFICANCES OF HIS WORDS UNTIL MANY YEARS LATER.
THE SUNSET ON YOUR PLANET IS AS BEAUTIFUL AS ANY OTHER IN THIS AREA OF THE UNIVERSE, QUELTAR. IT DESCRIBES THE CONCENTRIC PULSE OF MATTER'S DYNAMIC ENERGY. IT IS FOR ENTITIES SUCH AS US THAT ARE PART OF IT. HOWEVER, QUELTAR, YOU WILL NEVER REST UNTIL YOU UNDERSTAND ITS PURPOSE. WE MUST EACH BE ON OUR WAY TO UNDERSTAND ITS SIGNIFICANCE.
BEFORE HE LEFT, HE GAVE ME THIS TOKEN IN PAYMENT FOR THE MEAL I HAD PROVIDED.
DID YOU EVER SEE HIM AGAIN? WHO WAS HE?
IS THAT THE REASON YOU CONTINUE TO TRAVEL? TO TRY TO FIND HIM?
JACK KATZ

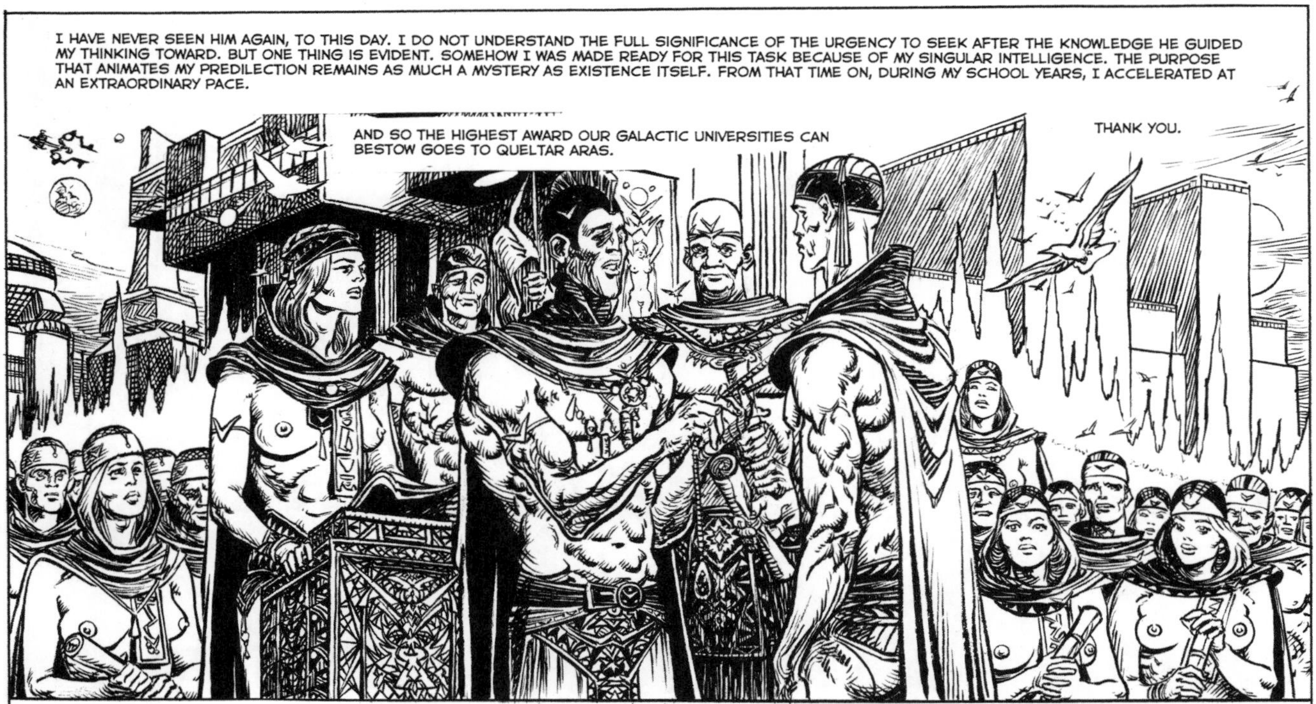
I HAVE NEVER SEEN HIM AGAIN, TO THIS DAY. I DO NOT UNDERSTAND THE FULL SIGNIFICANCE OF THE URGENCY TO SEEK AFTER THE KNOWLEDGE HE GUIDED MY THINKING TOWARD. BUT ONE THING IS EVIDENT. SOMEHOW I WAS MADE READY FOR THIS TASK BECAUSE OF MY SINGULAR INTELLIGENCE. THE PURPOSE THAT ANIMATES MY PREDILECTION REMAINS AS MUCH A MYSTERY AS EXISTENCE ITSELF. FROM THAT TIME ON, DURING MY SCHOOL YEARS, I ACCELERATED AT AN EXTRAORDINARY PACE.
AND SO THE HIGHEST AWARD OUR GALACTIC UNIVERSITIES CAN BESTOW GOES TO QUELTAR ARAS.
THANK YOU.

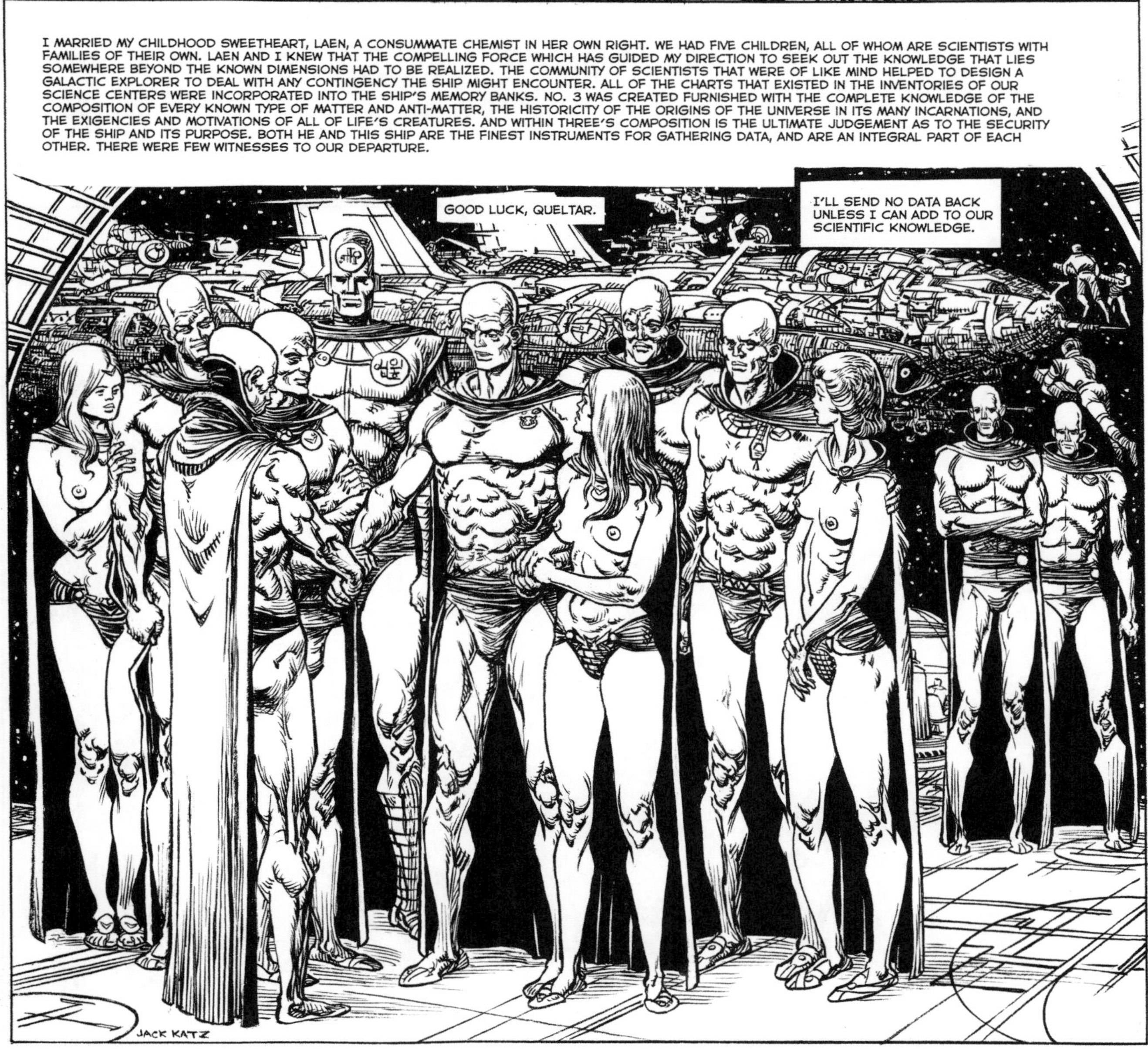
I MARRIED MY CHILDHOOD SWEETHEART, LAEN, A CONSUMMATE CHEMIST IN HER OWN RIGHT. WE HAD FIVE CHILDREN, ALL OF WHOM ARE SCIENTISTS WITH FAMILIES OF THEIR OWN. LAEN AND I KNEW THAT THE COMPELLING FORCE WHICH HAS GUIDED MY DIRECTION TO SEEK OUT THE KNOWLEDGE THAT LIES SOMEWHERE BEYOND THE KNOWN DIMENSIONS HAD TO BE REALIZED. THE COMMUNITY OF SCIENTISTS THAT WERE OF LIKE MIND HELPED TO DESIGN A GALACTIC EXPLORER TO DEAL WITH ANY CONTINGENCY THE SHIP MIGHT ENCOUNTER. ALL OF THE CHARTS THAT EXISTED IN THE INVENTORIES OF OUR SCIENCE CENTERS WERE INCORPORATED INTO THE SHIP'S MEMORY BANKS. NO. 3 WAS CREATED FURNISHED WITH THE COMPLETE KNOWLEDGE OF THE COMPOSITION OF EVERY KNOWN TYPE OF MATTER AND ANTI-MATTER, THE HISTORICITY OF THE ORIGINS OF THE UNIVERSE IN ITS MANY INCARNATIONS, AND THE EXIGENCIES AND MOTIVATIONS OF ALL OF LIFE'S CREATURES. AND WITHIN THREE'S COMPOSITION IS THE ULTIMATE JUDGEMENT AS TO THE SECURITY OF THE SHIP AND ITS PURPOSE. BOTH HE AND THIS SHIP ARE THE FINEST INSTRUMENTS FOR GATHERING DATA, AND ARE AN INTEGRAL PART OF EACH OTHER. THERE WERE FEW WITNESSES TO OUR DEPARTURE.
GOOD LUCK, QUELTAR.
I'LL SEND NO DATA BACK UNLESS I CAN ADD TO OUR SCIENTIFIC KNOWLEDGE.
JACK KATZ

YOUR STORY IS EXTRAORDINARY. BUT WHY HAVE YOU COME HERE AND COMMUNICATED THIS INFORMATION TO US? OUR WORLD IS SO SIMPLE COMPARED TO YOURS.

THAT WHICH YOU ARE COMPOSED OF IS AS COMPLEX AS MYSELF. EXCEPT FOR THE SCIENTIFIC SOPHISTICATION WHICH CAN BE LEARNED EASILY, YOU ARE AS INTELLIGENT AS ANY HUMANS IN THE UNIVERSE. WHICH BRINGS ME TO MY PURPOSE HERE.

YOU SEE, I'M ENLISTING A CREW, AND I'VE DECIDED TO ASK YOU TWO TO SHARE THIS MOST UNPRECEDENTED OF ADVENTURES WITH ME.

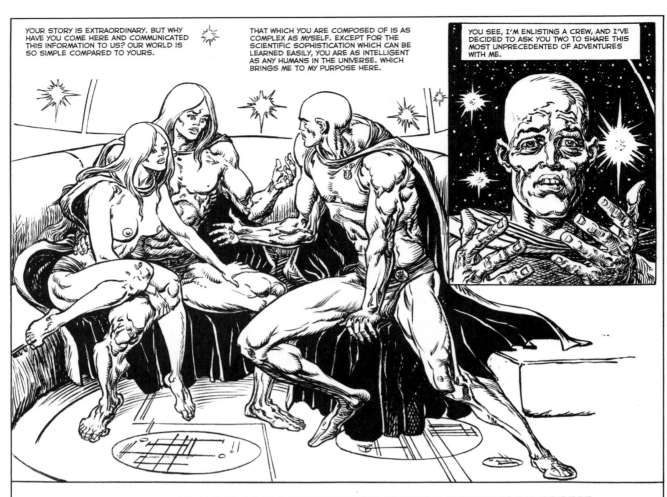

I HAVE TRAVELED FOR EONS, AND IN EVERY AREA OF DEVELOPING HUMANITY, I DISCOVERED NO PERSON OR GROUP THAT MIGHT COMPLEMENT THE REQUIREMENTS THAT I'VE COME TO REALIZE WOULD BE NECESSARY TO COMPLETE ALL OF THE PERSPECTIVES TO ESTIMATE THE SIGNIFICANCE OF NEW PHENOMENA FROM DIFFERENT POINTS OF VIEW. I SAW YOU TWO AT YOUR BIRTHS AND THE EVALUATING INSTRUMENTS REVEALED THAT YOU WERE THE EXACT EXAMPLES OF HUMANITY THAT WOULD FULFILL THAT SERVICE. MOST OF MANKIND NEVER EMERGES GREATER THAN THEIR PROGRAMMING - BUT YOU WERE BORN WITH WHAT IS CALLED SPECIAL POWERS. I SAVED YOUR LIVES MANY TIMES AS YOU GREW UP, AND ONCE IN DISGUISE SPOKE TO YOU, FARA - REMEMBER YONAN, THE GODDESS OF THE HUNT? - AND WATCHED YOUR RESOURCEFULNESS WHEN YOU WERE ABANDONED ON THE TOR OF THE LOST. MOST OF HUMANITY TAKES PART IN THE UNIVERSE - YOU ARE PART OF IT.

JACK KATZ

MY SCIENCE HAS DISCOVERED HOW TO CONTROL WHAT IS THOUGHT OF AS TIME, SO THAT YOUR YOUNG LIVES PASSED BY ME IN THE BLINKING OF AN EYE. NOW YOU CAN, IF YOU WISH, BE RETURNED TO YOUR PEOPLE. IF YOU DO, YOU WOULD REIGN WITH MUCH WISDOM AND COMPASSIN AND BE REVERED FOR MANY CENTURIES.

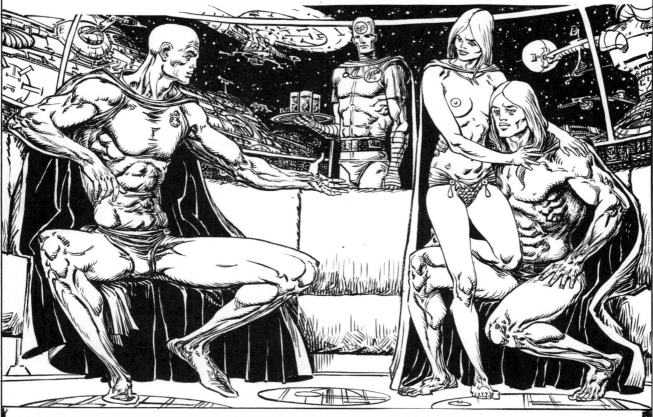

BUT, I ASSURE YOU THIS - EVENTUALLY, PERHAPS IN SIGHT OF STATUES BUILT TO EXALT THE HUMANITY OF YOUR REGENCY - THE OMNIPRESENT LEGACY OF BEING BORN OUT OF THE ENERGY OF STRESS WOULD CORRUPT THOSE WHO PRACTICED THE LAWS YOU INSTITUTED. AND THE MEMORY OF YOUR REIGN WOULD BE USED BY THEM TO MASK THEIR AMBITIOUS DESIGNS TO EFFECT THE SAME CORRUPT PRACTICES THAT HAVE INFESTED ALL OF THE CIVILIZATIONS THAT CAME BEFORE YOU. THE OFFERINGS AT YOUR MONOLITHS WOULD NOT BE TO YOUR LIKING.

JACK KATZ

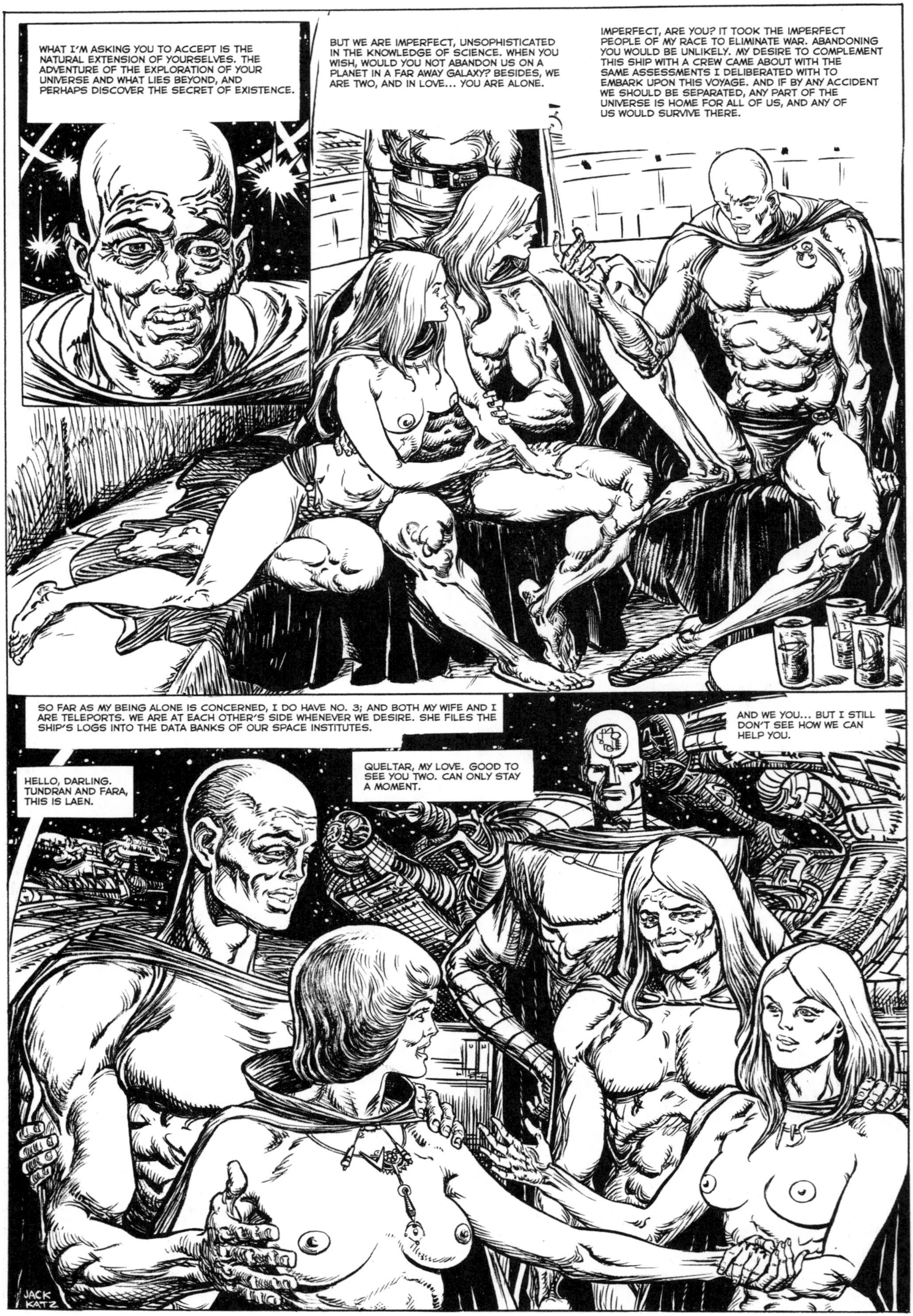
WHAT I'M ASKING YOU TO ACCEPT IS THE NATURAL EXTENSION OF YOURSELVES. THE ADVENTURE OF THE EXPLORATION OF YOUR UNIVERSE AND WHAT LIES BEYOND, AND PERHAPS DISCOVER THE SECRET OF EXISTENCE.
BUT WE ARE IMPERFECT, UNSOPHISTICATED IN THE KNOWLEDGE OF SCIENCE. WHEN YOU WISH, WOULD YOU NOT ABANDON US ON A PLANET IN A FAR AWAY GALAXY? BESIDES, WE ARE TWO, AND IN LOVE... YOU ARE ALONE.
IMPERFECT, ARE YOU? IT TOOK THE IMPERFECT PEOPLE OF MY RACE TO ELIMINATE WAR. ABANDONING YOU WOULD BE UNLIKELY. MY DESIRE TO COMPLEMENT THIS SHIP WITH A CREW CAME ABOUT WITH THE SAME ASSESSMENTS I DELIBERATED WITH TO EMBARK UPON THIS VOYAGE. AND IF BY ANY ACCIDENT WE SHOULD BE SEPARATED, ANY PART OF THE UNIVERSE IS HOME FOR ALL OF US, AND ANY OF US WOULD SURVIVE THERE.
SO FAR AS MY BEING ALONE IS CONCERNED, I DO HAVE NO. 3; AND BOTH MY WIFE AND I ARE TELEPORTS. WE ARE AT EACH OTHER'S SIDE WHENEVER WE DESIRE. SHE FILES THE SHIP'S LOGS INTO THE DATA BANKS OF OUR SPACE INSTITUTES.
HELLO, DARLING. TUNDRAN AND FARA, THIS IS LAEN.
QUELTAR, MY LOVE. GOOD TO SEE YOU TWO. CAN ONLY STAY A MOMENT.
AND WE YOU... BUT I STILL DON'T SEE HOW WE CAN HELP YOU.
JACK KATZ

YOU WILL BE OF GREAT SERVICE. I COULD EASILY ENTER INTO ANY WORLD IN ANY STATE OF DEVELOPMENT WITH THE FORCE FIELD AT MY SERVICE, WITH VERY LITTLE THREAT TO MYSELF. BUT I WOULD BE AN OBVIOUS ALIEN, AND PRIMITIVE RACES WOULD FEAR ME, THOUGHT I MIGHT OFFER THEM MEANS WITH WHICH TO OVERCOME THEIR PREDATORS. BUT YOU WOULD BE MORE EFFECTIVE WITH YOUR WOODCRAFT AND NATURAL AFFILIATION WITH NATURE. YOU WOULD BE LISTENED TO BY VIRTUE OF YOUR HUNTING SKILLS. IF, ON THE OTHER HAND, THE DISPOSITION OF A TYRANT ASSERTS ITSELF IN A MORE SOPHISTICATED SOCIETY, MESMERIZED BY ITS OWN SELF-CONTEMPT FOR ACQUIESCING TO THE ARBITRATY DOGMAS SUSTAINED BY THE LONG LEGACY OF INHERITED POWER, THE ANODYNE THAT WOULD BE NEEDED TO HELP ACCEPT A GENTLER VIEW OF SOCIAL RELATIONSHIP BY PUTTING A HALT TO THE INSULT TO THE INTEGRITY OF THEIR INNER VISION, WOULD BE EFFECTUATED BY MYSELF OR NO. 3, DEPENDING ON THE STATE OF THE ADVANCED SCIENCE THAT WAS EMPLOYED TO SERVICE THEIR SELF-DESTRUCTION.

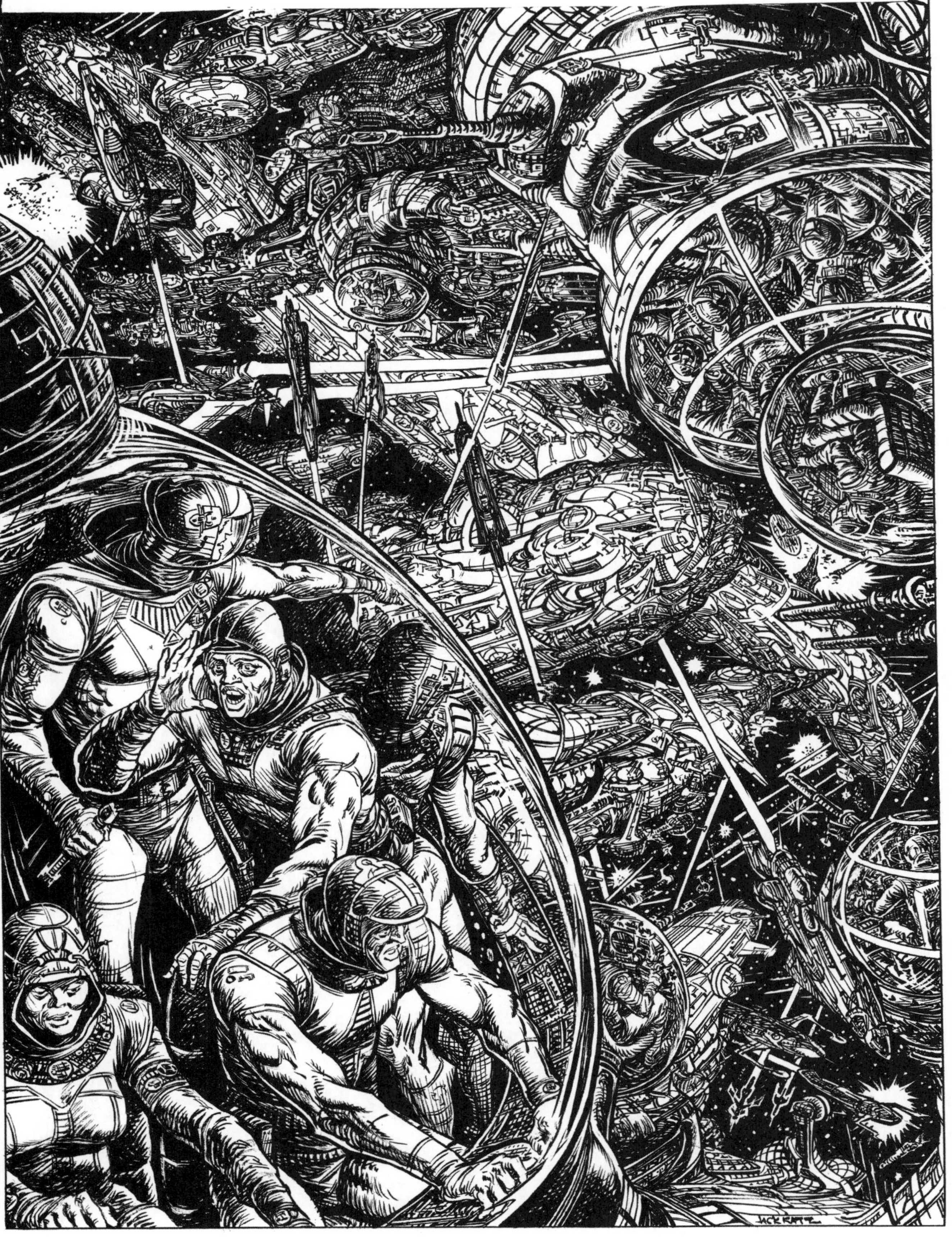
JACK KATZ

OR PERHAPS WE WOULD HAPPEN UPON A SOCIETY SUBJUGATED INTO A SLAVE STATE BY VIRTUE OF A DICTATOR WHOSE CONDITIONING BY THE INELUCTABLE INTRANSIGENCE OF HIS SURVIVAL TECHNIQUES RELENTLESSLY POSSESS HIM. IT SHOULD BE QUITE CLEAR THAT THE HUMANITY WHICH HE RULES OVER WOULD HAVE LONG SINCE BECOME INURED TO THE EXCESSES HE AND THEIR FORMER RULERS WOULD HAVE METED OUT TO THEM. TO CONFRONT SUCH A TYRANT WOULD TAKE A SPECIAL SITUATION THAT COULD BE OBSERVED BY THOSE INFLUENCIAL ENOUGH TO HELP PAVE THE WAY FOR A MORE COMPASSIONATE LEADERSHIP. YOUR SKILLS WOULD BE INDISPENSABLE.

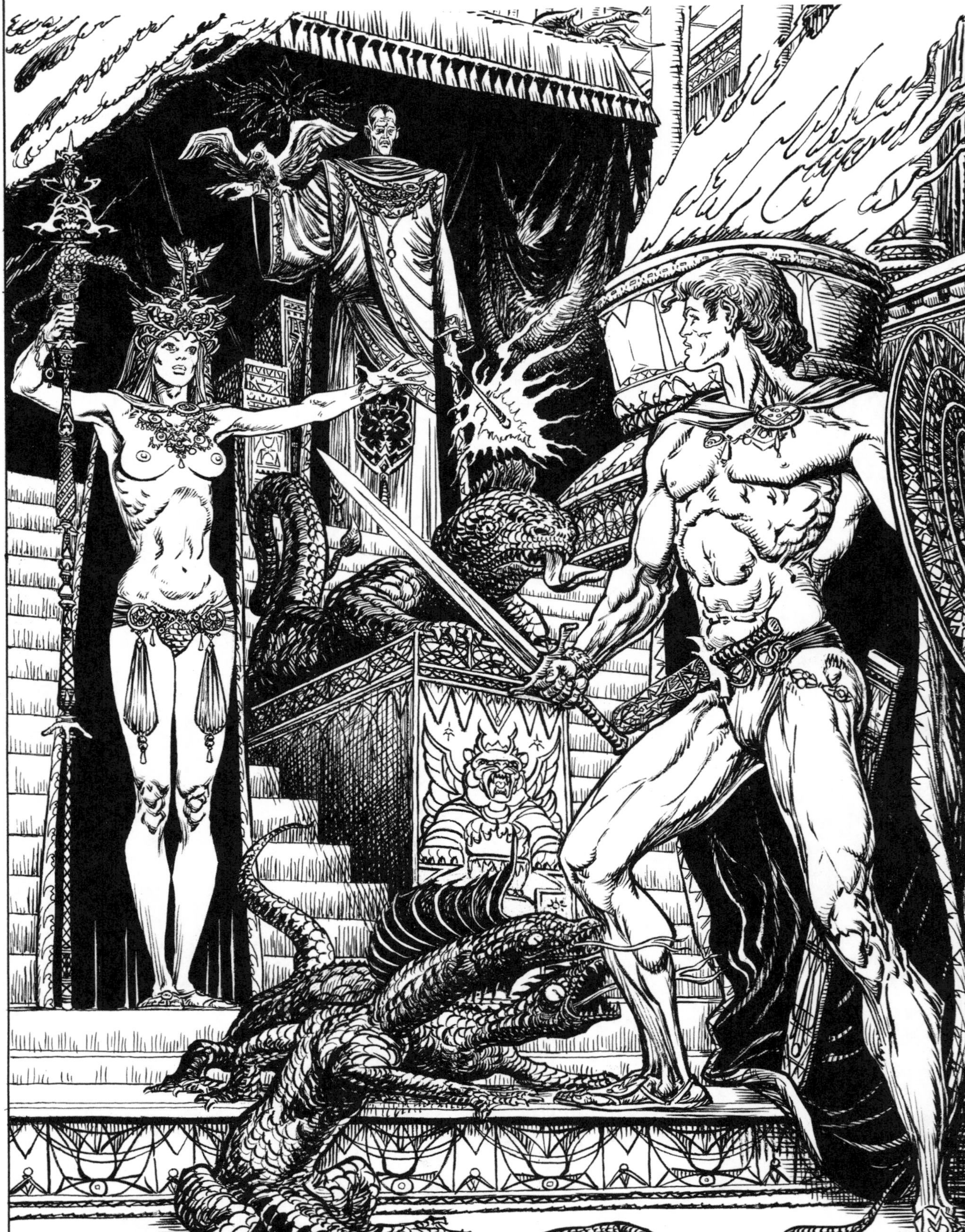
JACK KATZ

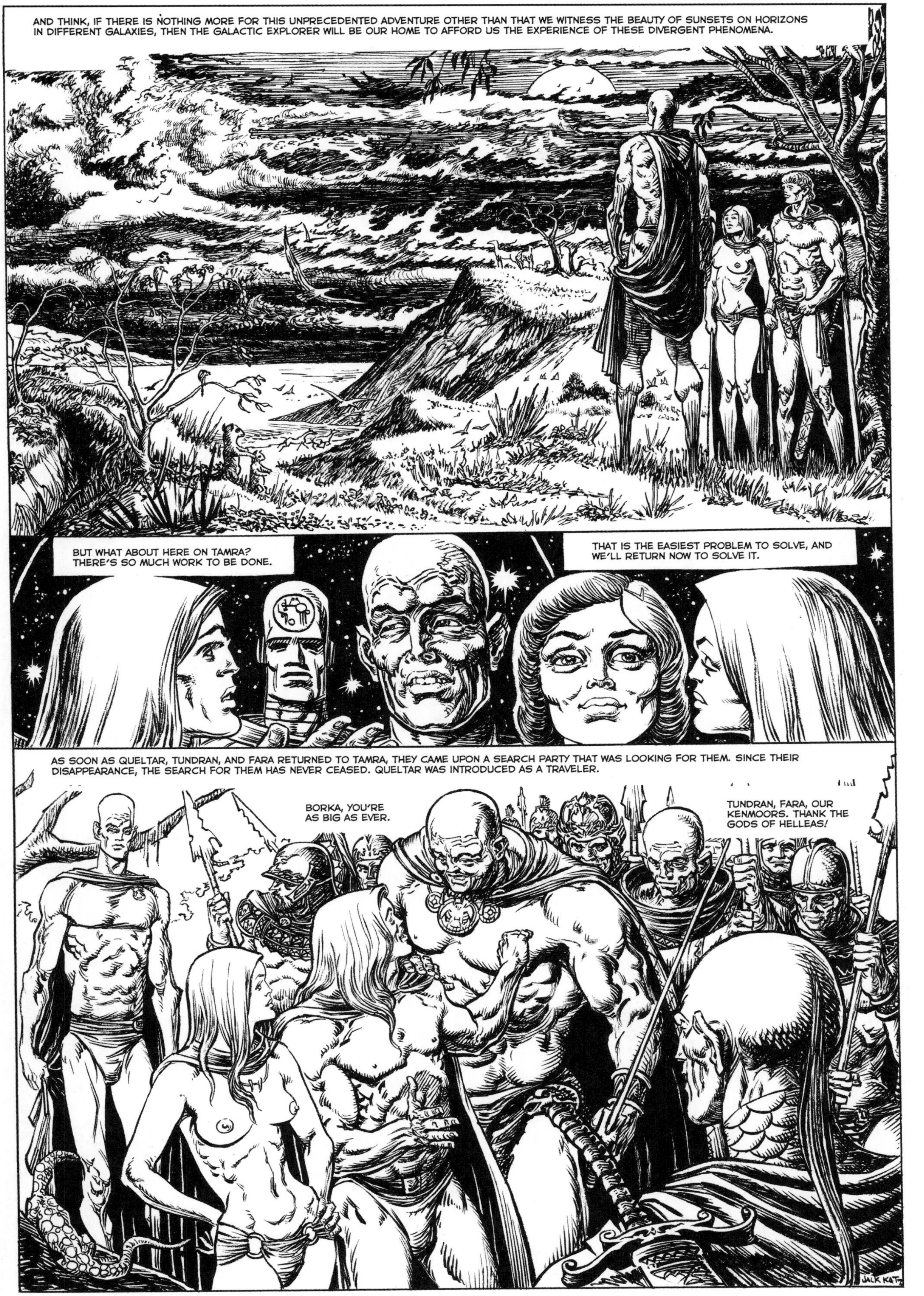
AND THINK, IF THERE IS NOTHING MORE FOR THIS UNPRECEDENTED ADVENTURE OTHER THAN THAT WE WITNESS THE BEAUTY OF SUNSETS ON HORIZONS IN DIFFERENT GALAXIES, THEN THE GALACTIC EXPLORER WILL BE OUR HOME TO AFFORD US THE EXPERIENCE OF THESE DIVERGENT PHENOMENA.
BUT WHAT ABOUT HERE ON TAMRA? THERE'S SO MUCH WORK TO BE DONE.
THAT IS THE EASIEST PROBLEM TO SOLVE, AND WE'LL RETURN NOW TO SOLVE IT.
AS SOON AS QUELTAR, TUNDRAN, AND FARA RETURNED TO TAMRA, THEY CAME UPON A SEARCH PARTY THAT WAS LOOKING FOR THEM. SINCE THEIR DISAPPEARANCE, THE SEARCH FOR THEM HAS NEVER CEASED. QUELTAR WAS INTRODUCED AS A TRAVELER.
BORKA, YOU'RE AS BIG AS EVER.
TUNDRAN, FARA, OUR KENMOORS. THANK THE GODS OF HELLEAS!
JACK KATZ

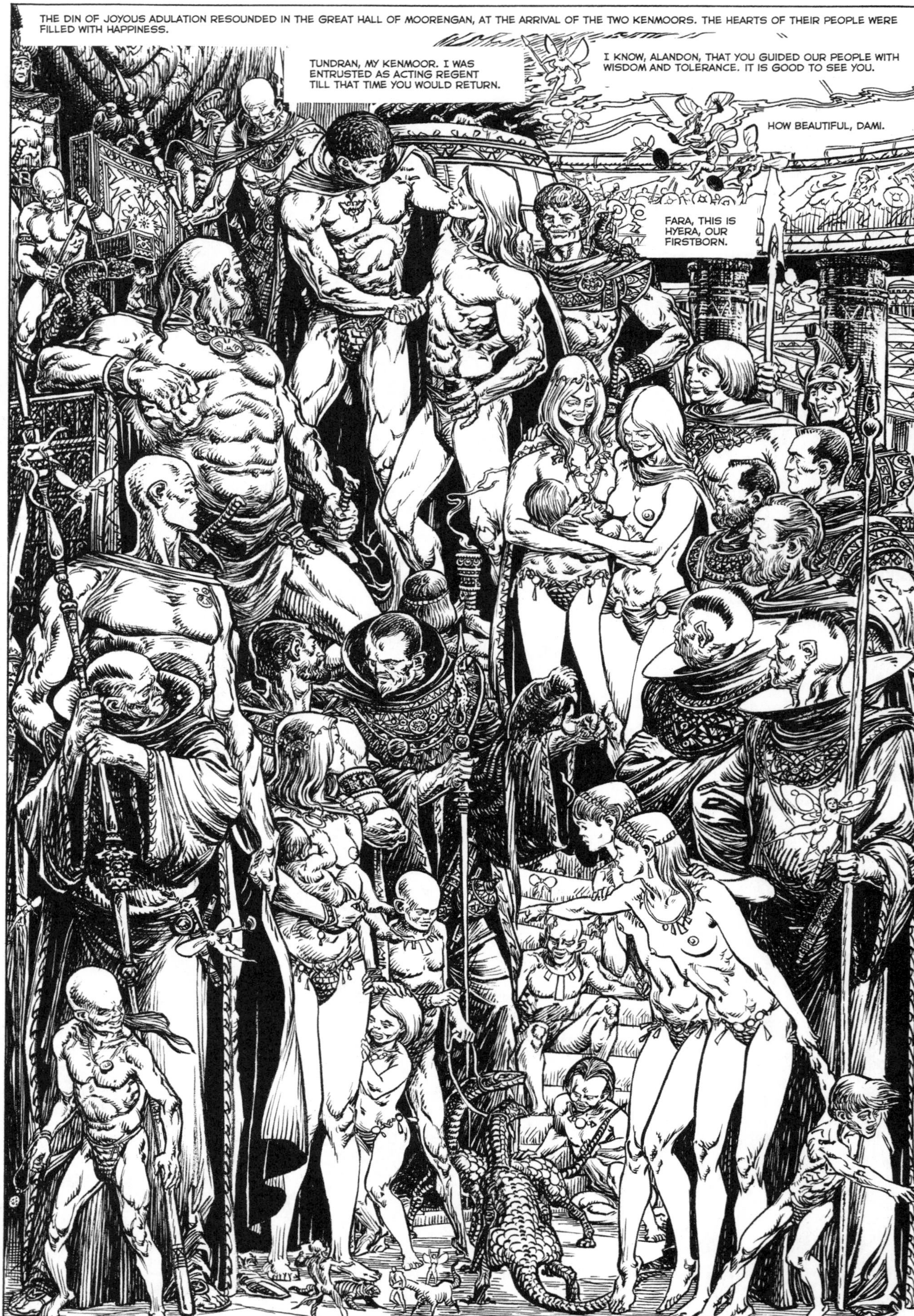
THE DIN OF JOYOUS ADULATION RESOUNDED IN THE GREAT HALL OF MOORENGAN, AT THE ARRIVAL OF THE TWO KENMOORS. THE HEARTS OF THEIR PEOPLE WERE FILLED WITH HAPPINESS.
TUNDRAN, MY KENMOOR. I WAS ENTRUSTED AS ACTING REGENT TILL THAT TIME YOU WOULD RETURN.
I KNOW, ALANDON, THAT YOU GUIDED OUR PEOPLE WITH WISDOM AND TOLERANCE. IT IS GOOD TO SEE YOU.
HOW BEAUTIFUL, DAMI.
FARA, THIS IS HYERA, OUR FIRSTBORN.
JACK KATZ

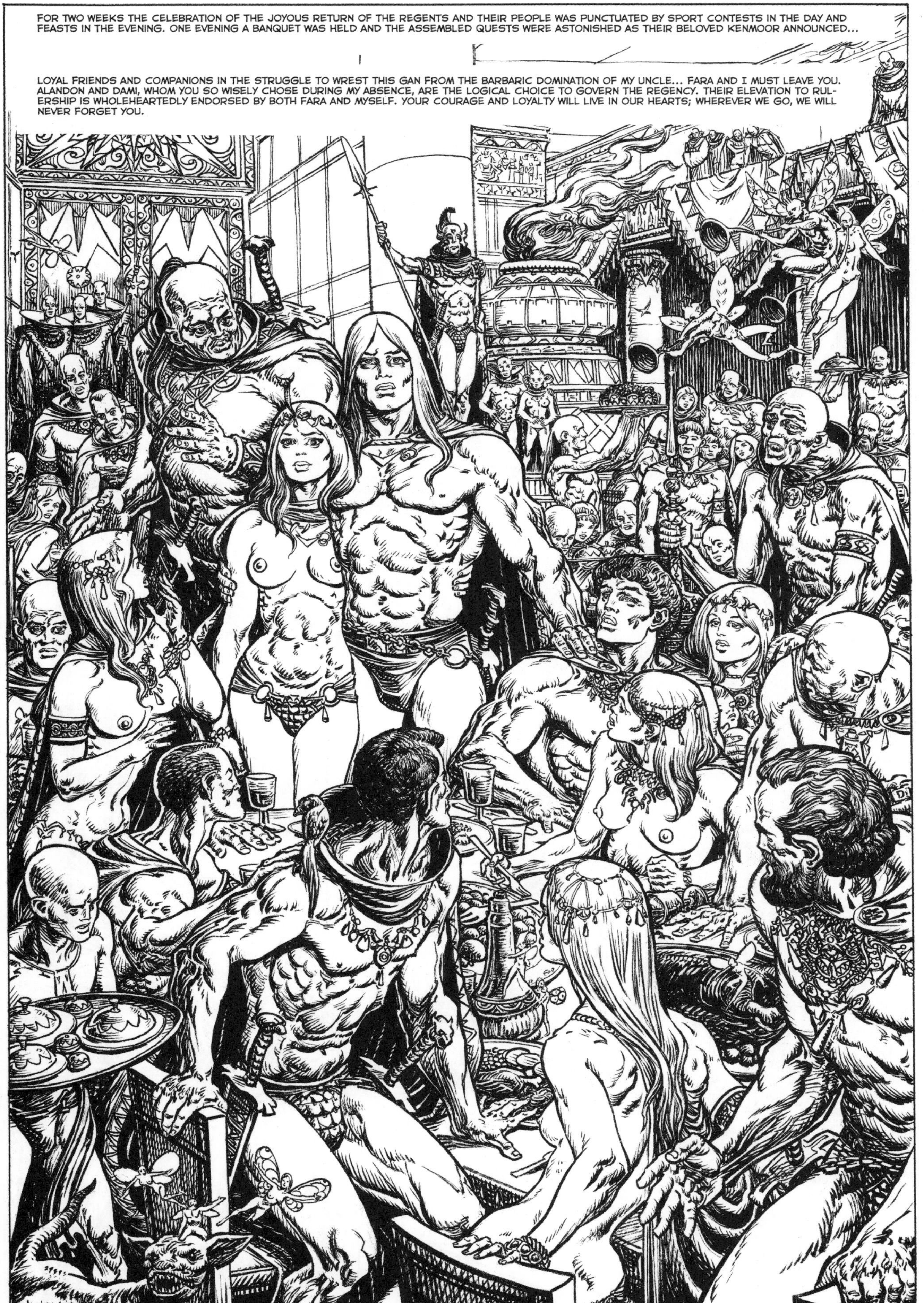
FOR TWO WEEKS THE CELEBRATION OF THE JOYOUS RETURN OF THE REGENTS AND THEIR PEOPLE WAS PUNCTUATED BY SPORT CONTESTS IN THE DAY AND FEASTS IN THE EVENING. ONE EVENING A BANQUET WAS HELD AND THE ASSEMBLED QUESTS WERE ASTONISHED AS THEIR BELOVED KENMOOR ANNOUNCED...
LOYAL FRIENDS AND COMPANIONS IN THE STRUGGLE TO WREST THIS GAN FROM THE BARBARIC DOMINATION OF MY UNCLE... FARA AND I MUST LEAVE YOU. ALANDON AND DAMI, WHOM YOU SO WISELY CHOSE DURING MY ABSENCE, ARE THE LOGICAL CHOICE TO GOVERN THE REGENCY. THEIR ELEVATION TO RULERSHIP IS WHOLEHEARTEDLY ENDORSED BY BOTH FARA AND MYSELF. YOUR COURAGE AND LOYALTY WILL LIVE IN OUR HEARTS; WHEREVER WE GO, WE WILL NEVER FORGET YOU.
JACK KATZ

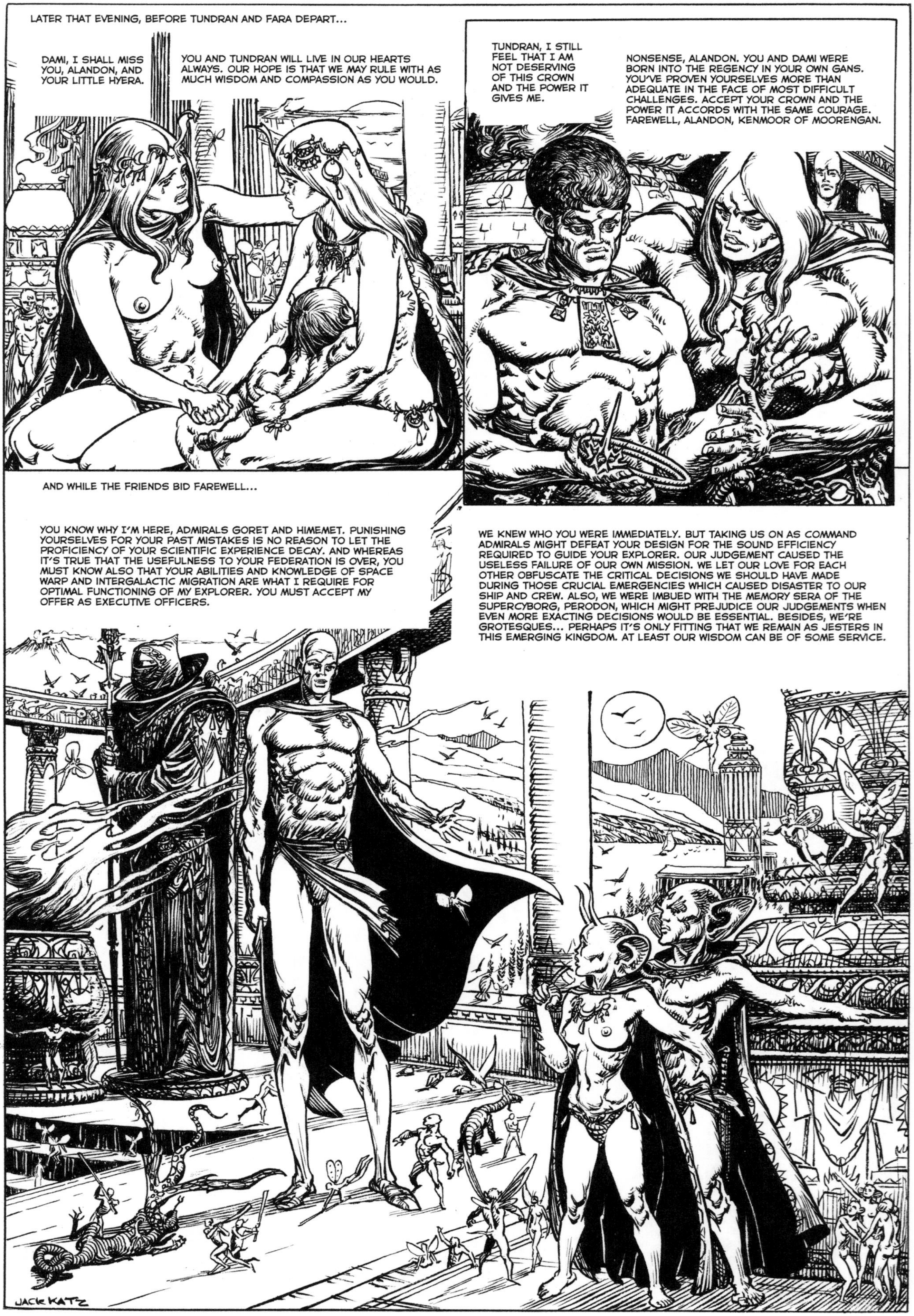
LATER THAT EVENING, BEFORE TUNDRAN AND FARA DEPART...
DAMI, I SHALL MISS YOU, ALANDON, AND YOUR LITTLE HYERA.
YOU AND TUNDRAN WILL LIVE IN OUR HEARTS ALWAYS. OUR HOPE IS THAT WE MAY RULE WITH AS MUCH WISDOM AND COMPASSION AS YOU WOULD.
TUNDRAN, I STILL FEEL THAT I AM NOT DESERVING OF THIS CROWN AND THE POWER IT GIVES ME.
NONSENSE, ALANDON. YOU AND DAMI WERE BORN INTO THE REGENCY IN YOUR OWN GANS. YOU'VE PROVEN YOURSELVES MORE THAN ADEQUATE IN THE FACE OF MOST DIFFICULT CHALLENGES. ACCEPT YOUR CROWN AND THE POWER IT ACCORDS WITH THE SAME COURAGE. FAREWELL, ALANDON, KENMOOR OF MOORENGAN.
AND WHILE THE FRIENDS BID FAREWELL...
YOU KNOW WHY I'M HERE, ADMIRALS GORET AND HIMEMET. PUNISHING YOURSELVES FOR YOUR PAST MISTAKES IS NO REASON TO LET THE PROFICIENCY OF YOUR SCIENTIFIC EXPERIENCE DECAY. AND WHEREAS IT'S TRUE THAT THE USEFULNESS TO YOUR FEDERATION IS OVER, YOU MUST KNOW ALSO THAT YOUR ABILITIES AND KNOWLEDGE OF SPACE WARP AND INTERGALACTIC MIGRATION ARE WHAT I REQUIRE FOR OPTIMAL FUNCTIONING OF MY EXPLORER. YOU MUST ACCEPT MY OFFER AS EXECUTIVE OFFICERS.
WE KNEW WHO YOU WERE IMMEDIATELY. BUT TAKING US ON AS COMMAND ADMIRALS MIGHT DEFEAT YOUR DESIGN FOR THE SOUND EFFICIENCY REQUIRED TO GUIDE YOUR EXPLORER. OUR JUDGEMENT CAUSED THE USELESS FAILURE OF OUR OWN MISSION. WE LET OUR LOVE FOR EACH OTHER OBFUSCATE THE CRITICAL DECISIONS WE SHOULD HAVE MADE DURING THOSE CRUCIAL EMERGENCIES WHICH CAUSED DISASTER TO OUR SHIP AND CREW. ALSO, WE WERE IMBUED WITH THE MEMORY SERA OF THE SUPERCYBORG, PERODON, WHICH MIGHT PREJUDICE OUR JUDGEMENTS WHEN EVEN MORE EXACTING DECISIONS WOULD BE ESSENTIAL. BESIDES, WE'RE GROTESQUES... PERHAPS IT'S ONLY FITTING THAT WE REMAIN AS JESTERS IN THIS EMERGING KINGDOM. AT LEAST OUR WISDOM CAN BE OF SOME SERVICE.
JACK KATZ

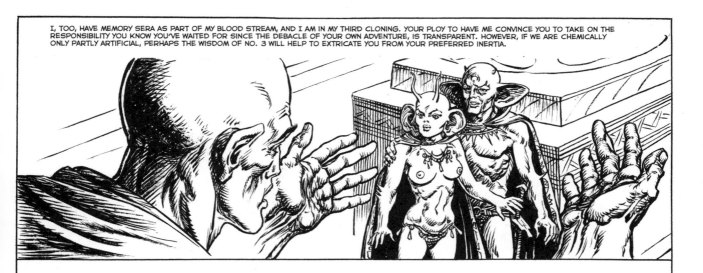

I, TOO, HAVE MEMORY SERA AS PART OF MY BLOOD STREAM, AND I AM IN MY THIRD CLONING. YOUR PLOY TO HAVE ME CONVINCE YOU TO TAKE ON THE RESPONSIBILITY YOU KNOW YOU'VE WAITED FOR SINCE THE DEBACLE OF YOUR OWN ADVENTURE, IS TRANSPARENT. HOWEVER, IF WE ARE CHEMICALLY ONLY PARTLY ARTIFICIAL, PERHAPS THE WISDOM OF NO. 3 WILL HELP TO EXTRICATE YOU FROM YOUR PREFERRED INERTIA.

WHEN NO. 3 FULLY REALIZED THE NATURE OF ITS MECHANICAL COMPOSITION, IT SHUT DOWN ALL ITS CIRCUITS. I WAS ABLE TO REANIMATE IT BY THE SUBTLEST REASON WHICH WOULD ONLY CONJURE A RESPONSE FROM OUR MOST ADVANCED MINDS. AND IT WAS UPON THAT REALITY THAT THREE REACTIVATED ITSELF. BUT THE FACT THAT THREE'S DATA BANKS WERE EQUIPPED WITH ALL THE ACCUMULATED KNOWLEDGE OF THE UNIVERSE WAS NOT SUFFICIENT TO HAVE IT ACCEPT ITS EXISTENCE. IT HAD TO GO BACK TO THE PLANET FROM WHICH I TOOK THE ORES AND MINERALS TO CONSTRUCT IT. THERE, WANDERING THROUGH PRIMAL LIQUID, SEAS OF LIQUID GASSES, AND MOLTEN CHEMICALS, IT CAME TO THE SAME DECISION AS MYSELF - THAT HUMANKIND AND ALL EXISTENCE IS A RESULT OF AN IMPERFECT UNIVERSE; AND THAT THREE'S CREATION WAS AN EXTENSION OF HUMANKIND'S DESIRE TO INVESTIGATE THE MYSTERY OF EXISTENCE. NOT ONLY WAS IT EQUIPPED WITH ALL THE KNOWLEDGE FOR THIS PURPOSE, BUT ALSO BECAUSE MANKIND BUILT THREE, HAD ITS FLAWS. AND ALSO, IT WAS ANIMATED WITH THE SAME COMPELLING DRIVE OF MANKIND TO INVESTIGATE THE UNKNOWN - THIS PROVING THAT NO. 3, DEVELOPED BY HUMANS, HAD THE SAME UNFATHOMABLE FACULTY FOR HUMAN JUDGEMENT AS WELL. ITS DECISION TO CEASE FUNCTIONING PROVED THAT. IT SOJOURNED UPON THE ORB, FINDING THE ELEMENTS THAT COMPOSED ITS SYSTEMS. WHEN IT REALIZED THAT HUMANKIND WAS MADE FROM THE SAME MATERIALS, THREE CHOSE TO EXIST. IT THEN COMMUNICATED WITH THE EXPLORER.

QUELTAR, ELEVATE ME TO OUR SHIP. I WELCOME THE OPPORTUNITY TO SHARE IN THE QUEST TO DISCOVER THE ORIGIN OF EXISTENCE AND OUR FUNCTION IN IT.

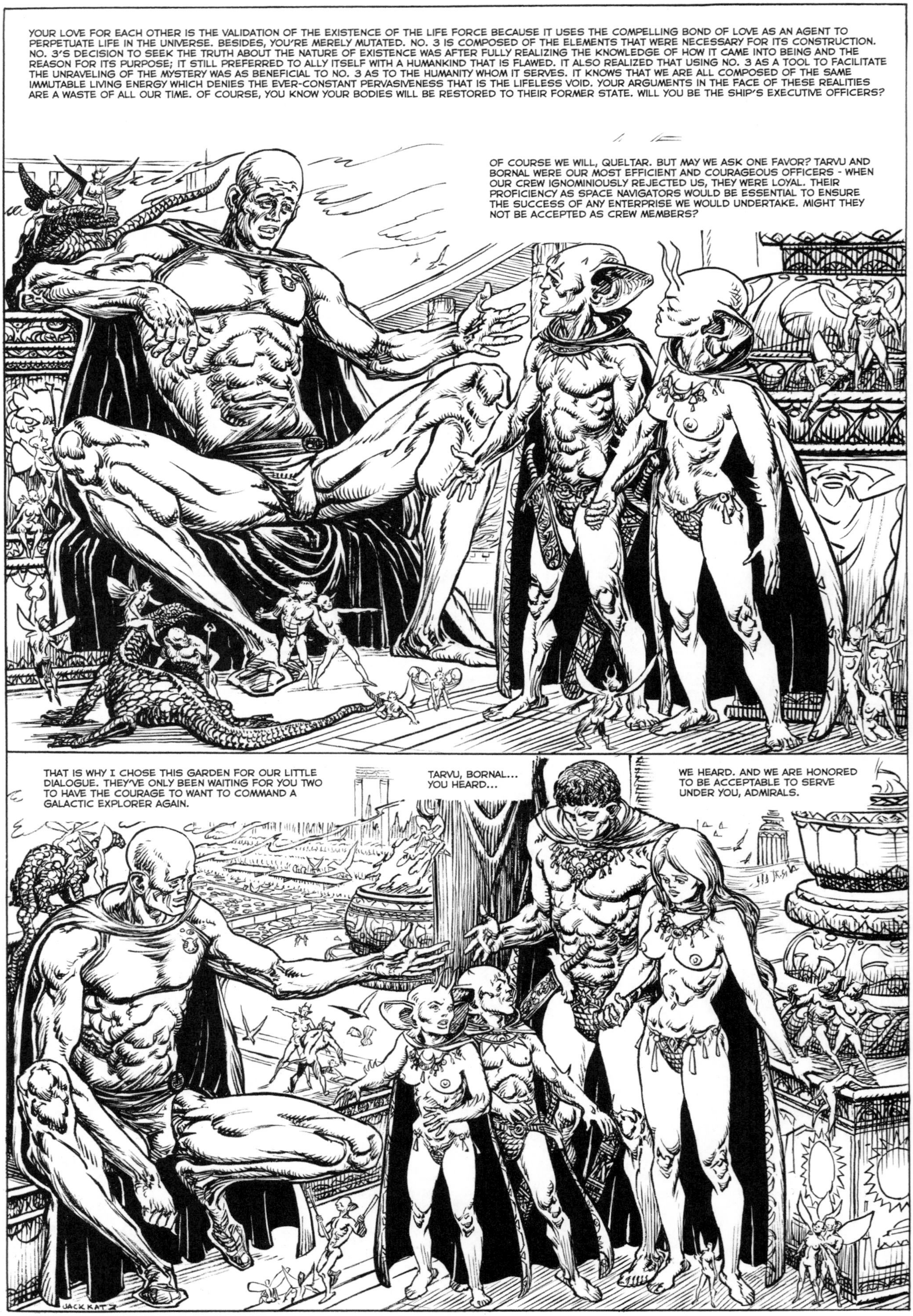
YOUR LOVE FOR EACH OTHER IS THE VALIDATION OF THE EXISTENCE OF THE LIFE FORCE BECAUSE IT USES THE COMPELLING BOND OF LOVE AS AN AGENT TO PERPETUATE LIFE IN THE UNIVERSE. BESIDES, YOU'RE MERELY MUTATED. NO. 3 IS COMPOSED OF THE ELEMENTS THAT WERE NECESSARY FOR ITS CONSTRUCTION. NO. 3'S DECISION TO SEEK THE TRUTH ABOUT THE NATURE OF EXISTENCE WAS AFTER FULLY REALIZING THE KNOWLEDGE OF HOW IT CAME INTO BEING AND THE REASON FOR ITS PURPOSE; IT STILL PREFERRED TO ALLY ITSELF WITH A HUMANKIND THAT IS FLAWED. IT ALSO REALIZED THAT USING NO. 3 AS A TOOL TO FACILITATE THE UNRAVELING OF THE MYSTERY WAS AS BENEFICIAL TO NO. 3 AS TO THE HUMANITY WHOM IT SERVES. IT KNOWS THAT WE ARE ALL COMPOSED OF THE SAME IMMUTABLE LIVING ENERGY WHICH DENIES THE EVER-CONSTANT PERVASIVENESS THAT IS THE LIFELESS VOID. YOUR ARGUMENTS IN THE FACE OF THESE REALITIES ARE A WASTE OF ALL OUR TIME. OF COURSE, YOU KNOW YOUR BODIES WILL BE RESTORED TO THEIR FORMER STATE. WILL YOU BE THE SHIP'S EXECUTIVE OFFICERS?
OF COURSE WE WILL, QUELTAR. BUT MAY WE ASK ONE FAVOR? TARVU AND BORNAL WERE OUR MOST EFFICIENT AND COURAGEOUS OFFICERS - WHEN OUR CREW IGNOMINIOUSLY REJECTED US, THEY WERE LOYAL. THEIR PROFICIENCY AS SPACE NAVIGATORS WOULD BE ESSENTIAL TO ENSURE THE SUCCESS OF ANY ENTERPRISE WE WOULD UNDERTAKE. MIGHT THEY NOT BE ACCEPTED AS CREW MEMBERS?
THAT IS WHY I CHOSE THIS GARDEN FOR OUR LITTLE DIALOGUE. THEY'VE ONLY BEEN WAITING FOR YOU TWO TO HAVE THE COURAGE TO WANT TO COMMAND A GALACTIC EXPLORER AGAIN.
TARVU, BORNAL... YOU HEARD...
WE HEARD. AND WE ARE HONORED TO BE ACCEPTABLE TO SERVE UNDER YOU, ADMIRALS.
JACK KATZ

THERE IS ONE MORE ISSUE WHICH MUST BE ADDRESSED, AND THAT IS THE QUESTION OF TEDRA AND THE FORMER ADMIRAL MANOG. BY NOW THEY'VE MANAGED TO ELEVATE THEMSELVES INTO POSITIONS AS INDISPENSABLE MINISTERS TO THE NEW KENMOOR KARNORE OF NORCAINGIER, ELICITING HIS DEPENDENCY ON THEIR COUNSEL BY A FEW PARLOR TRICKS. MANOG'S DESIRE TO JUSTIFY HIS DESTRUCTIVE ACTIONS, AND TEDRA'S PREJUDICIAL PROGRAMMING ABOUT THE SEPARATION OF THE GODS AND THE MORTALS MUST HAVE AN OUTLET. THEY WILL BE THE DOMINATING INFLUENCE THAT WILL ENCOURAGE KARNORE'S AMBITION TO CONQUER MOORENGAN AND THE TAMRA ITSELF. WITHOUT HIMEMET AND MYSELF, ALANDON MAY BE NO MATCH FOR THEM.

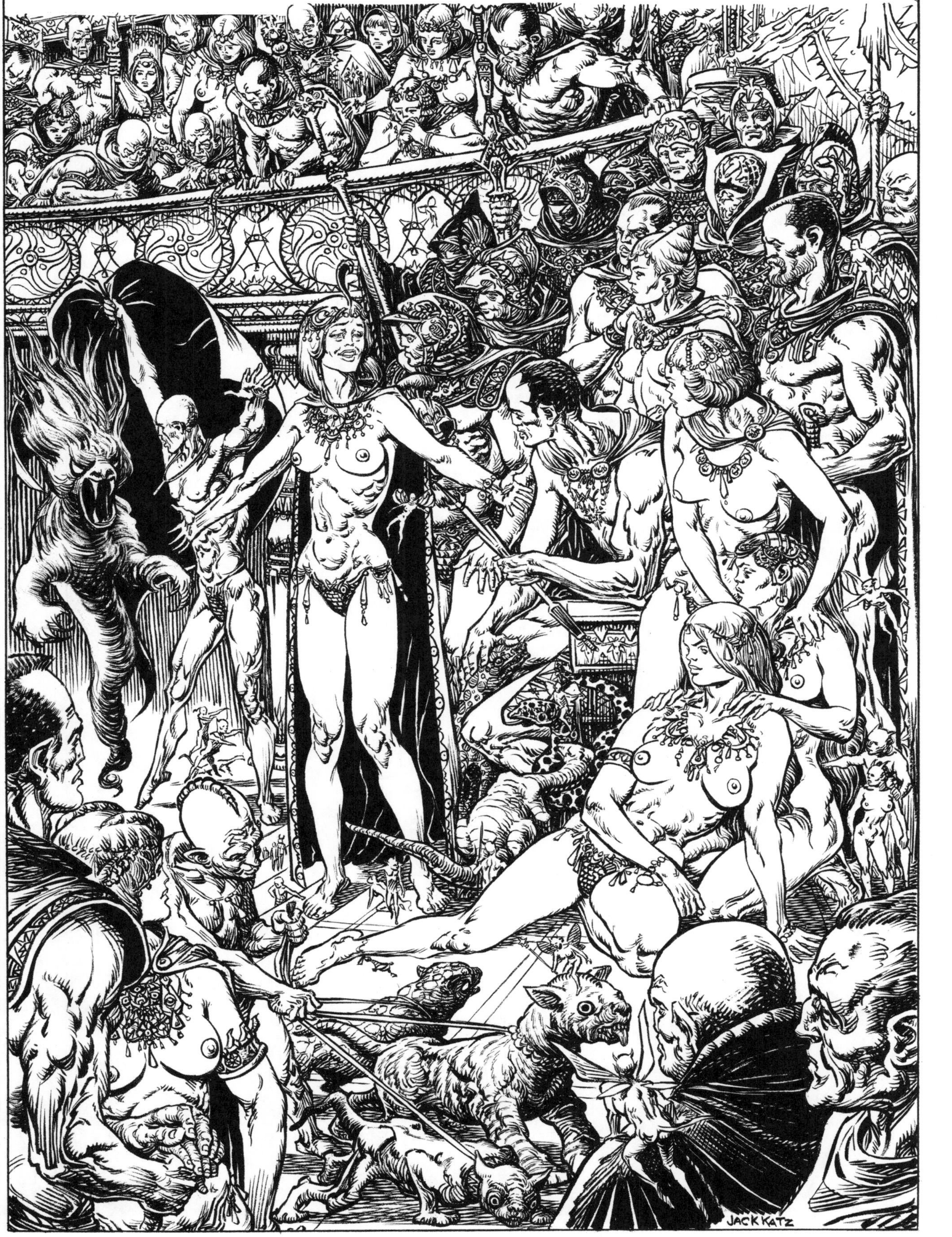
JACK KATZ

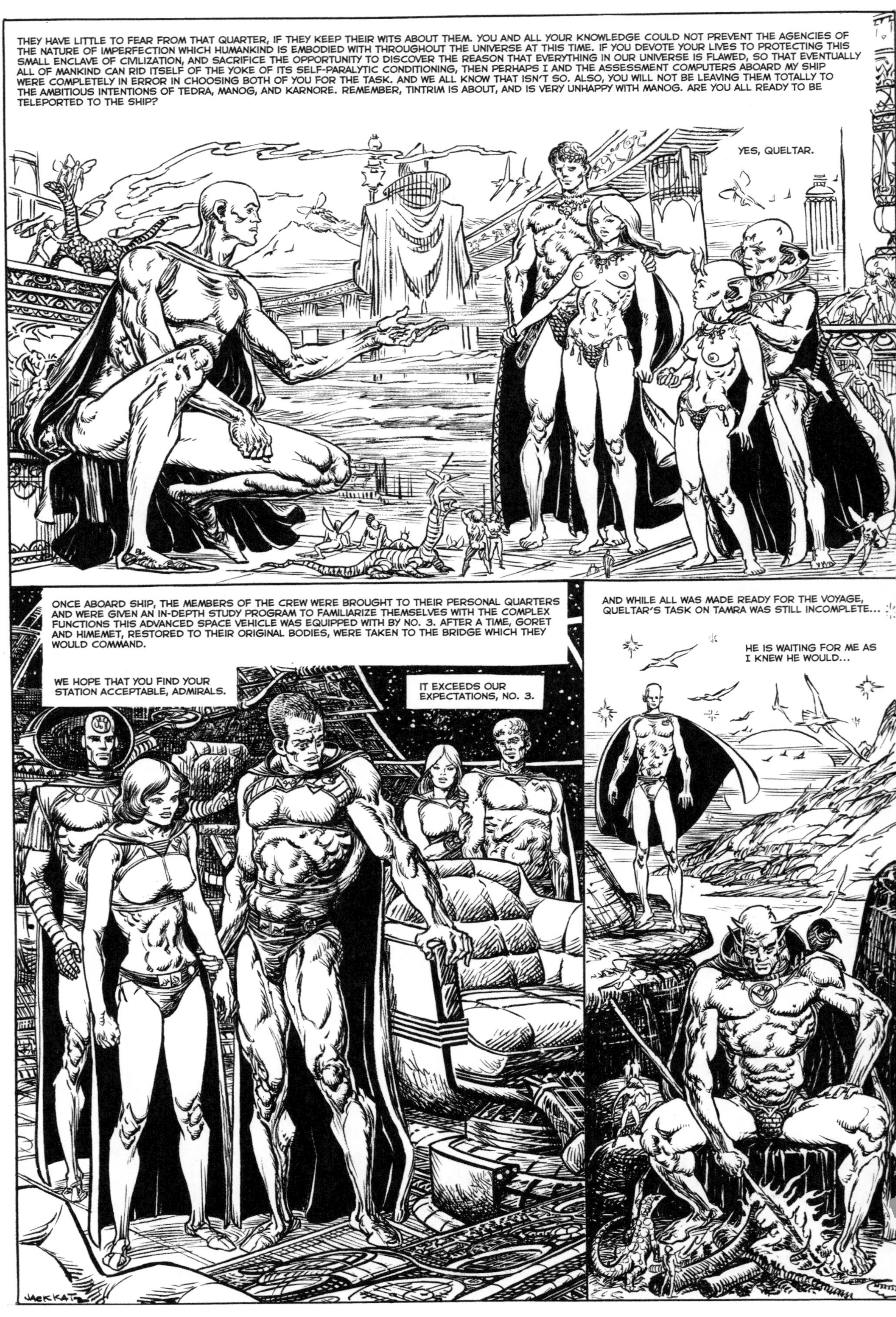
THEY HAVE LITTLE TO FEAR FROM THAT QUARTER, IF THEY KEEP THEIR WITS ABOUT THEM. YOU AND ALL YOUR KNOWLEDGE COULD NOT PREVENT THE AGENCIES OF THE NATURE OF IMPERFECTION WHICH HUMANKIND IS EMBODIED WITH THROUGHOUT THE UNIVERSE AT THIS TIME. IF YOU DEVOTE YOUR LIVES TO PROTECTING THIS SMALL ENCLAVE OF CIVILIZATION, AND SACRIFICE THE OPPORTUNITY TO DISCOVER THE REASON THAT EVERYTHING IN OUR UNIVERSE IS FLAWED, SO THAT EVENTUALLY ALL OF MANKIND CAN RID ITSELF OF THE YOKE OF ITS SELF-PARALYTIC CONDITIONING, THEN PERHAPS I AND THE ASSESSMENT COMPUTERS ABOARD MY SHIP WERE COMPLETELY IN ERROR IN CHOOSING BOTH OF YOU FOR THE TASK. AND WE ALL KNOW THAT ISN'T SO. ALSO, YOU WILL NOT BE LEAVING THEM TOTALLY TO THE AMBITIOUS INTENTIONS OF TEDRA, MANOG, AND KARNORE. REMEMBER, TINTRIM IS ABOUT, AND IS VERY UNHAPPY WITH MANOG. ARE YOU ALL READY TO BE TELEPORTED TO THE SHIP?
YES, QUELTAR.
ONCE ABOARD SHIP, THE MEMBERS OF THE CREW WERE BROUGHT TO THEIR PERSONAL QUARTERS AND WERE GIVEN AN IN-DEPTH STUDY PROGRAM TO FAMILIARIZE THEMSELVES WITH THE COMPLEX FUNCTIONS THIS ADVANCED SPACE VEHICLE WAS EQUIPPED WITH BY NO. 3. AFTER A TIME, GORET AND HIMEMET, RESTORED TO THEIR ORIGINAL BODIES, WERE TAKEN TO THE BRIDGE WHICH THEY WOULD COMMAND.
WE HOPE THAT YOU FIND YOUR STATION ACCEPTABLE, ADMIRALS.
IT EXCEEDS OUR EXPECTATIONS, NO. 3.
JACK KATZ
AND WHILE ALL WAS MADE READY FOR THE VOYAGE, QUELTAR'S TASK ON TAMRA WAS STILL INCOMPLETE...
HE IS WAITING FOR ME AS I KNEW HE WOULD...

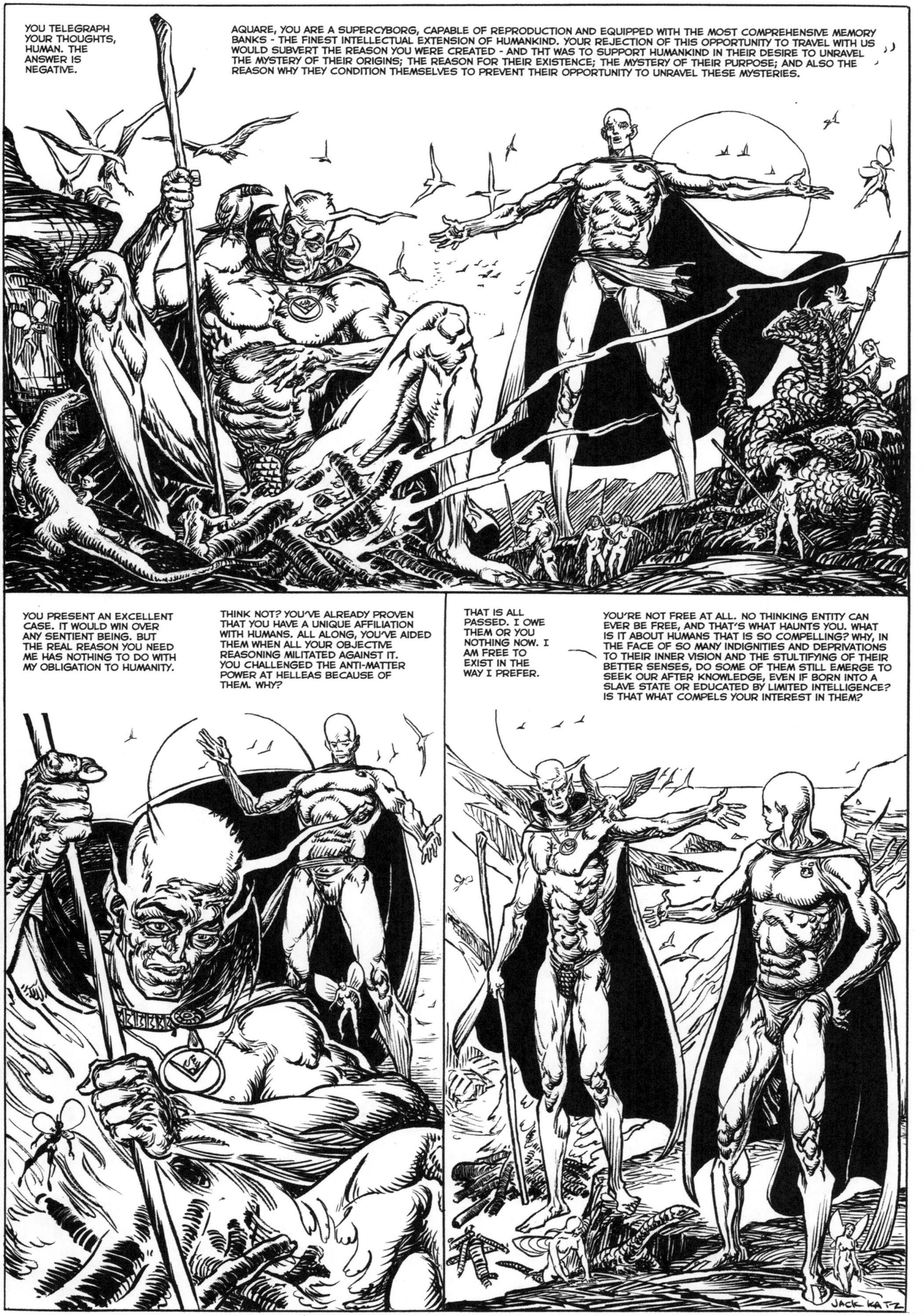
YOU TELEGRAPH YOUR THOUGHTS, HUMAN. THE ANSWER IS NEGATIVE.
AQUARE, YOU ARE A SUPERCYBORG, CAPABLE OF REPRODUCTION AND EQUIPPED WITH THE MOST COMPREHENSIVE MEMORY BANKS - THE FINEST INTELLECTUAL EXTENSION OF HUMANKIND. YOUR REJECTION OF THIS OPPORTUNITY TO TRAVEL WITH US WOULD SUBVERT THE REASON YOU WERE CREATED - AND THT WAS TO SUPPORT HUMANKIND IN THEIR DESIRE TO UNRAVEL THE MYSTERY OF THEIR ORIGINS; THE REASON FOR THEIR EXISTENCE; THE MYSTERY OF THEIR PURPOSE; AND ALSO THE REASON WHY THEY CONDITION THEMSELVES TO PREVENT THEIR OPPORTUNITY TO UNRAVEL THESE MYSTERIES.
YOU PRESENT AN EXCELLENT CASE. IT WOULD WIN OVER ANY SENTIENT BEING. BUT THE REAL REASON YOU NEED ME HAS NOTHING TO DO WITH MY OBLIGATION TO HUMANITY.
THINK NOT? YOU'VE ALREADY PROVEN THAT YOU HAVE A UNIQUE AFFILIATION WITH HUMANS. ALL ALONG, YOU'VE AIDED THEM WHEN ALL YOUR OBJECTIVE REASONING MILITATED AGAINST IT. YOU CHALLENGED THE ANTI-MATTER POWER AT HELLEAS BECAUSE OF THEM. WHY?
THAT IS ALL PASSED. I OWE THEM OR YOU NOTHING NOW. I AM FREE TO EXIST IN THE WAY I PREFER.
YOU'RE NOT FREE AT ALL. NO THINKING ENTITY CAN EVER BE FREE, AND THAT'S WHAT HAUNTS YOU. WHAT IS IT ABOUT HUMANS THAT IS SO COMPELLING? WHY, IN THE FACE OF SO MANY INDIGNITIES AND DEPRIVATIONS TO THEIR INNER VISION AND THE STULTIFYING OF THEIR BETTER SENSES, DO SOME OF THEM STILL EMERGE TO SEEK OUR AFTER KNOWLEDGE, EVEN IF BORN INTO A SLAVE STATE OR EDUCATED BY LIMITED INTELLIGENCE? IS THAT WHAT COMPELS YOUR INTEREST IN THEM?
JACK KATZ

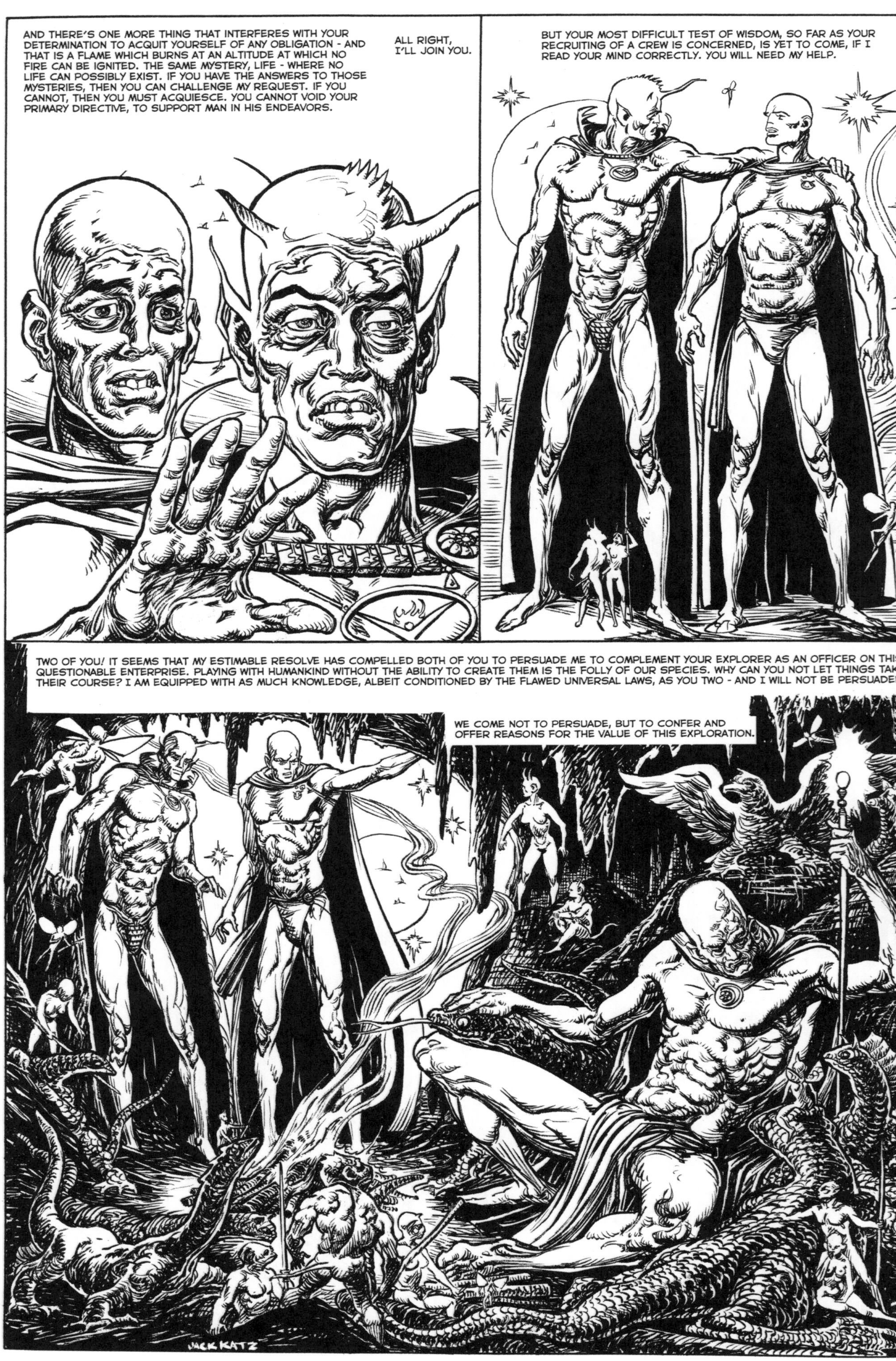
AND THERE'S ONE MORE THING THAT INTERFERES WITH YOUR DETERMINATION TO ACQUIT YOURSELF OF ANY OBLIGATION - AND THAT IS A FLAME WHICH BURNS AT AN ALTITUDE AT WHICH NO FIRE CAN BE IGNITED. THE SAME MYSTERY, LIFE - WHERE NO LIFE CAN POSSIBLY EXIST. IF YOU HAVE THE ANSWERS TO THOSE MYSTERIES, THEN YOU CAN CHALLENGE MY REQUEST. IF YOU CANNOT, THEN YOU MUST ACQUIESCE. YOU CANNOT VOID YOUR PRIMARY DIRECTIVE, TO SUPPORT MAN IN HIS ENDEAVORS.
ALL RIGHT, I'LL JOIN YOU.
BUT YOUR MOST DIFFICULT TEST OF WISDOM, SO FAR AS YOUR RECRUITING OF A CREW IS CONCERNED, IS YET TO COME, IF I READ YOUR MIND CORRECTLY. YOU WILL NEED MY HELP.
TWO OF YOU! IT SEEMS THAT MY ESTIMABLE RESOLVE HAS COMPELLED BOTH OF YOU TO PERSUADE ME TO COMPLEMENT YOUR EXPLORER AS AN OFFICER ON THIS QUESTIONABLE ENTERPRISE. PLAYING WITH HUMANKIND WITHOUT THE ABILITY TO CREATE THEM IS THE FOLLY OF OUR SPECIES. WHY CAN YOU NOT LET THINGS TAKE THEIR COURSE? I AM EQUIPPED WITH AS MUCH KNOWLEDGE, ALBEIT CONDITIONED BY THE FLAWED UNIVERSAL LAWS, AS YOU TWO - AND I WILL NOT BE PERSUADED.
WE COME NOT TO PERSUADE, BUT TO CONFER AND OFFER REASONS FOR THE VALUE OF THIS EXPLORATION.
JACK KATZ

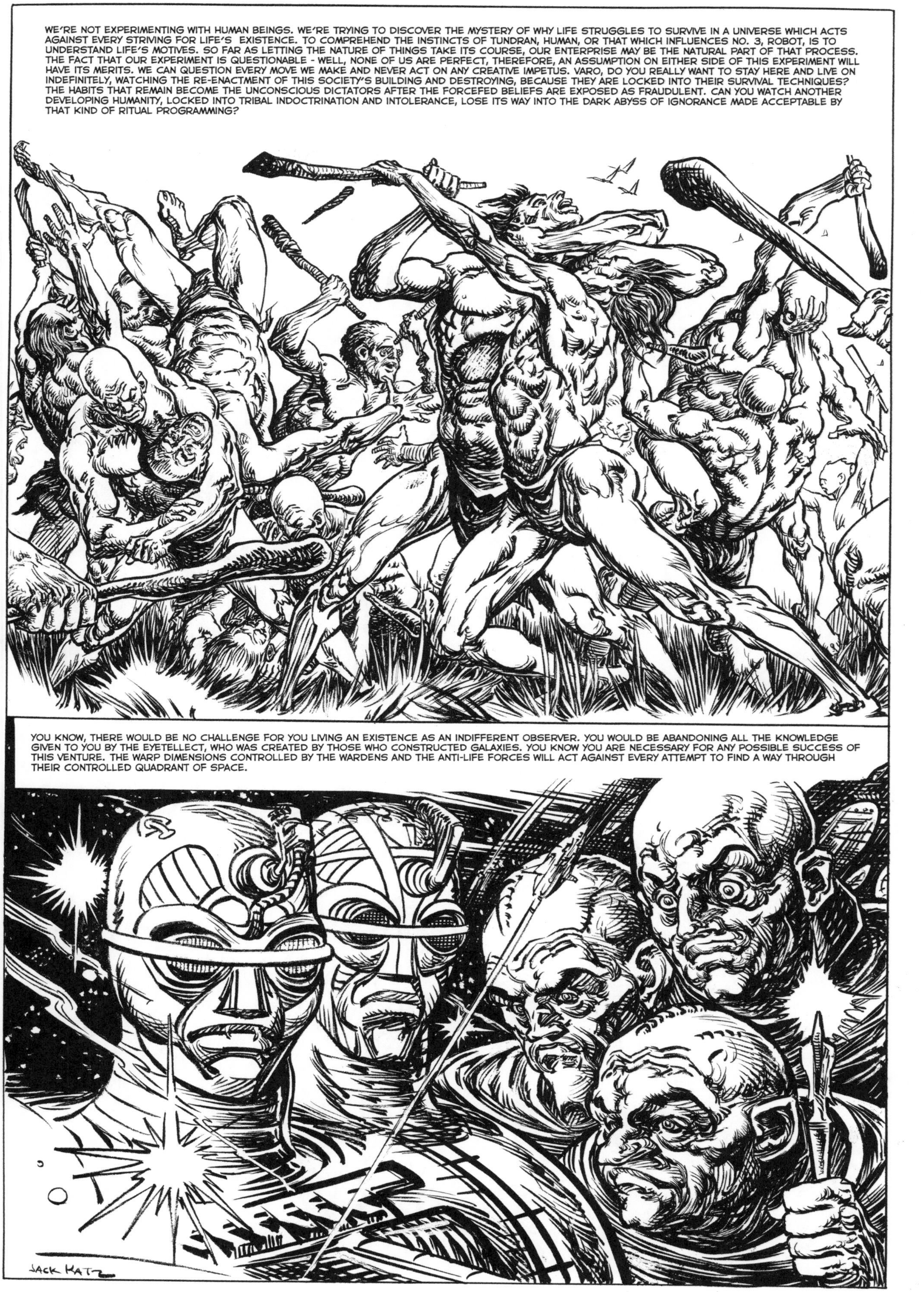
WE'RE NOT EXPERIMENTING WITH HUMAN BEINGS. WE'RE TRYING TO DISCOVER THE MYSTERY OF WHY LIFE STRUGGLES TO SURVIVE IN A UNIVERSE WHICH ACTS AGAINST EVERY STRIVING FOR LIFE'S EXISTENCE. TO COMPREHEND THE INSTINCTS OF TUNDRAN, HUMAN, OR THAT WHICH INFLUENCES NO. 3, ROBOT, IS TO UNDERSTAND LIFE'S MOTIVES. SO FAR AS LETTING THE NATURE OF THINGS TAKE ITS COURSE, OUR ENTERPRISE MAY BE THE NATURAL PART OF THAT PROCESS. THE FACT THAT OUR EXPERIMENT IS QUESTIONABLE - WELL, NONE OF US ARE PERFECT, THEREFORE, AN ASSUMPTION ON EITHER SIDE OF THIS EXPERIMENT WILL HAVE ITS MERITS. WE CAN QUESTION EVERY MOVE WE MAKE AND NEVER ACT ON ANY CREATIVE IMPETUS. VARO, DO YOU REALLY WANT TO STAY HERE AND LIVE ON INDEFINITELY, WATCHING THE RE-ENACTMENT OF THIS SOCIETY'S BUILDING AND DESTROYING, BECAUSE THEY ARE LOCKED INTO THEIR SURVIVAL TECHNIQUES? THE HABITS THAT REMAIN BECOME THE UNCONSCIOUS DICTATORS AFTER THE FORCEFED BELIEFS ARE EXPOSED AS FRAUDULENT. CAN YOU WATCH ANOTHER DEVELOPING HUMANITY, LOCKED INTO TRIBAL INDOCTRINATION AND INTOLERANCE, LOSE ITS WAY INTO THE DARK ABYSS OF IGNORANCE MADE ACCEPTABLE BY THAT KIND OF RITUAL PROGRAMMING?
YOU KNOW, THERE WOULD BE NO CHALLENGE FOR YOU LIVING AN EXISTENCE AS AN INDIFFERENT OBSERVER. YOU WOULD BE ABANDONING ALL THE KNOWLEDGE GIVEN TO YOU BY THE EYETELLECT, WHO WAS CREATED BY THOSE WHO CONSTRUCTED GALAXIES. YOU KNOW YOU ARE NECESSARY FOR ANY POSSIBLE SUCCESS OF THIS VENTURE. THE WARP DIMENSIONS CONTROLLED BY THE WARDENS AND THE ANTI-LIFE FORCES WILL ACT AGAINST EVERY ATTEMPT TO FIND A WAY THROUGH THEIR CONTROLLED QUADRANT OF SPACE.
JACK KATZ

AND THEIR POWER IS DWARFED IN COMPARISON TO THE UNFATHOMABLE POWERS AND SEEMINGLY ENDLESS KNOWLEDGE OF THE SORCERORS OF THE COSMOS, WITH THEIR COLLECTIONS OF GALAXIES WITH WHICH THEY AMUSE THEMSELVES FOR ENTERTAINMENT. THEY HAVE EFFECTIVELY CREATED THE GREATEST BARRIERS FOR FREE PASSAGE BEYONG THE DIMENSIONS. AND IF THAT IS NOT ENOUGH TO CHALLENGE YOUR WISDOM, THEN THE SIMPLE FACT THAT YOU WOULD HOLD YOUR OWN COUNSEL, EQUAL TO MYSELF AND QUELTAR ABOUT ANY ISSUE, SHOULD PERSUADE YOU. THERE IS ONE MORE THING. EVERY LIVING ENTIRY DESIRES TO LIVE. ANY GIVEN VEGETATION SEEKS OUT THE LIFE ENERGIES OF A STAR, THOUGH ITS ROOTS BE HANDICAPPED BY THE IMPOSITION OF A STONE; OR DEFIES THE MISFORTUNE OF SPRINGING TO LIFE IN UNFAVORABLE CLIMATES. AS MANKIND, WITH THE LIABILITY OF THEIR FLAWED PROGRAMMING, STILL DESIRE TO LIVE, TO DARE TO RISK ALL, TO UNDERSTAND THE NATURE OF THAT WHICH PARALYZED THEIR UNLIMITED POTENTIAL TO FULFILL THEIR DESTINY, IS THE EVIDENCE WHICH DEMONSTRATES THAT LIFE IS WORTH LIVING. IF YOU WOULD RATHER WATCH THE UNIVERSE LIVE IN THE PERPETUAL NIGHTMARE OF PLANLESS INDIFFERENCE, THEN STAY HERE AND IMITATE THE SPACE SORCERORS' MINDLESS CAPRICES.

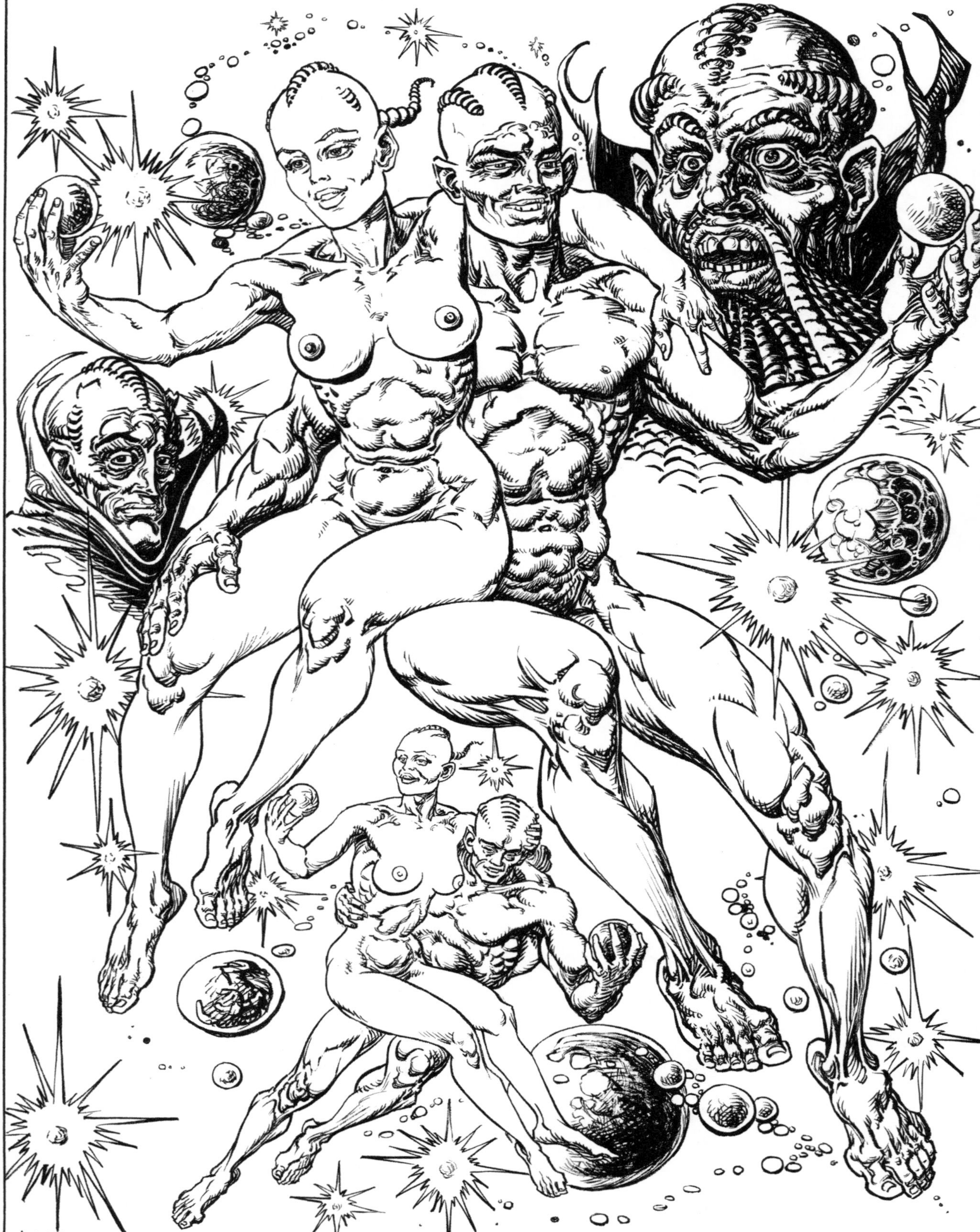
JACK KATZ

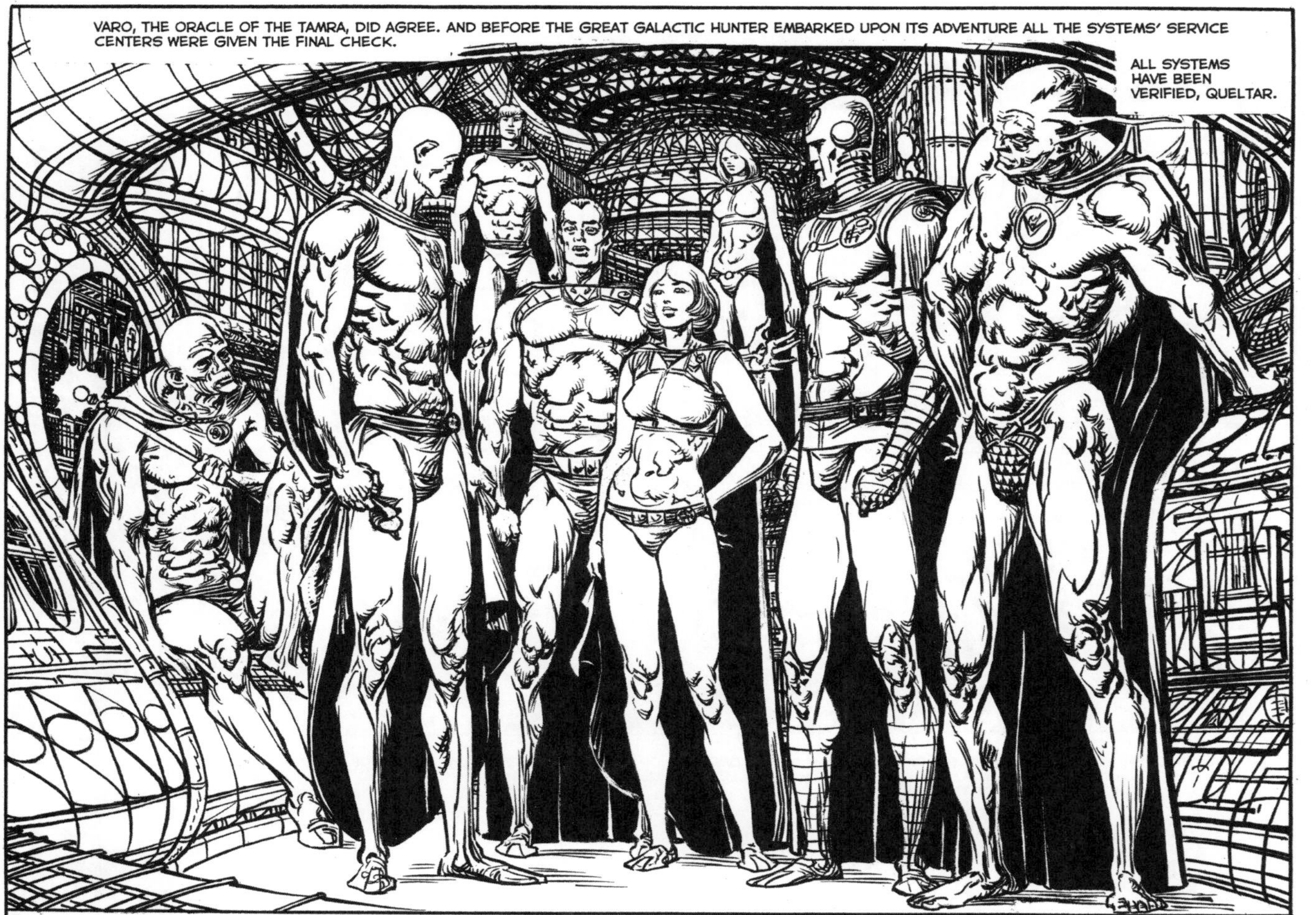
VARO, THE ORACLE OF THE TAMRA, DID AGREE. AND BEFORE THE GREAT GALACTIC HUNTER EMBARKED UPON ITS ADVENTURE ALL THE SYSTEMS' SERVICE CENTERS WERE GIVEN THE FINAL CHECK.
ALL SYSTEMS HAVE BEEN VERIFIED, QUELTAR.

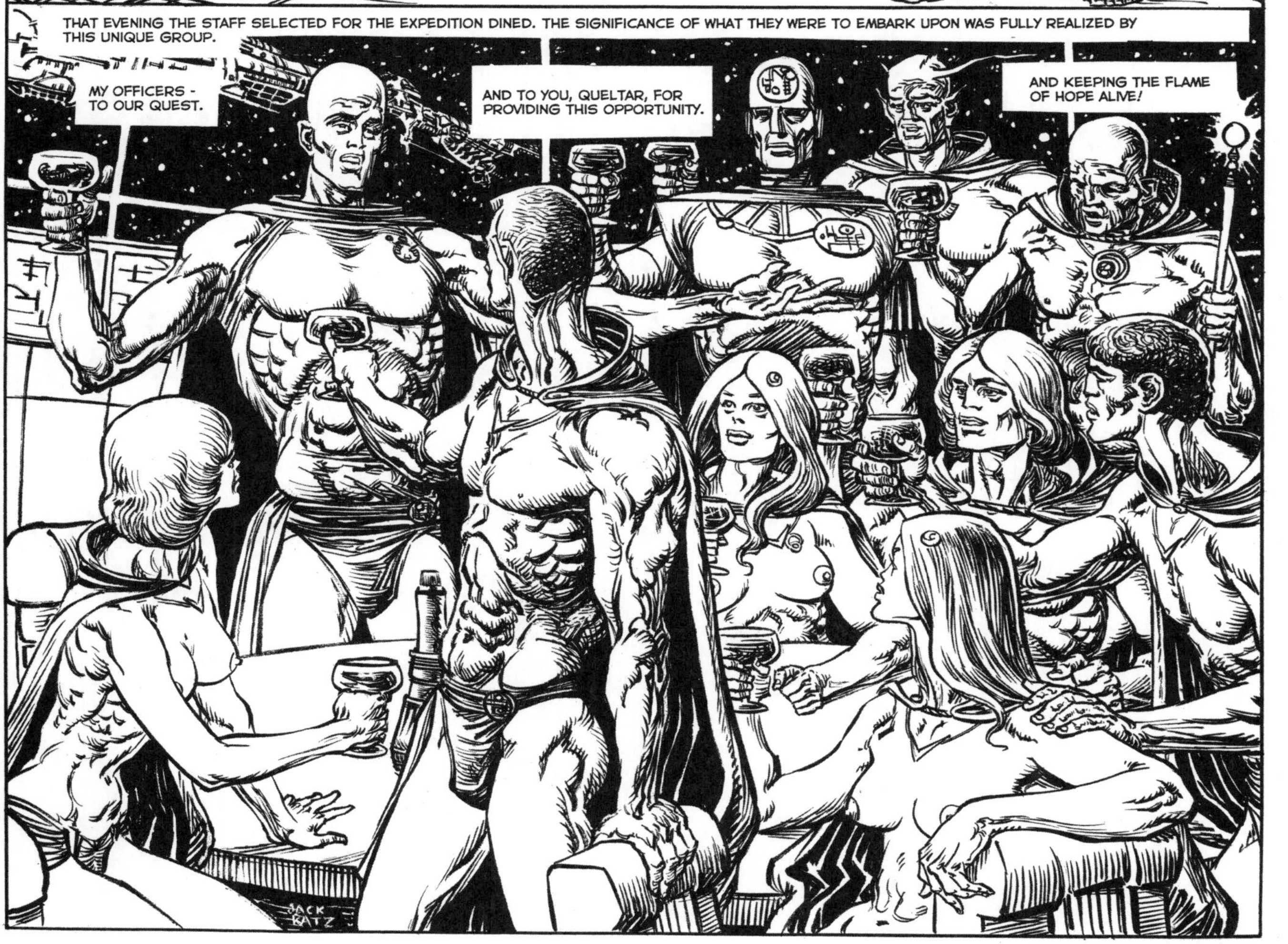
THAT EVENING THE STAFF SELECTED FOR THE EXPEDITION DINED. THE SIGNIFICANCE OF WHAT THEY WERE TO EMBARK UPON WAS FULLY REALIZED BY THIS UNIQUE GROUP.
MY OFFICERS - TO OUR QUEST.
AND TO YOU, QUELTAR, FOR PROVIDING THIS OPPORTUNITY.
AND KEEPING THE FLAME OF HOPE ALIVE!
JACK KATZ

FOR TUNDRAN AND FARA, ADAPTING TO THIS ALIEN MILIEU WAS MITIGATED BY THEIR TOTAL ACCEPTABILITY AS MEMBERS OF THIS EXPLORING TEAM. WHEN THE EVENING RELEGATED FOR FINAL CHECK OF THE SHIP'S STORES AND SYSTEMS BEFORE DEPARTURE ARRIVED, TUNDRAN AND FARA SOUGHT OUT THEIR QUARTERS. AND FOR TWO HUNTER REGENTS, THIS SPACESHIP WOULD BE HOME.

IT IS ALL SO NEW AND EXCITING, AND SOMEHOW IN A STRANGE WAY, NATURAL. ANYWHERE WITH YOU IS HOME, MY LOVE.

IT IS THAT, MY DARLING. LET US MAKE LOVE AND THEN SLEEP IN THIS SMALL UNIVERSE WHICH PROMISES THE GREATEST POTENTIAL FOR DISCOVERY.

AFTER THE SLEEP PERIOD WAS OVER, THE EXTRAORDINARY CREW, COMPOSED OF THE MOST DIVERGENT COLLECTION OF HUMAN AND HUMANOID ENTITIES RESPRESENTING THE UTMOST QUALIFICATIONS FOR THE UNPARALLELED VENTURE, HELD HANDS - AN ACT OF SOLIDARITY THAT SANCTIONED THEIR BOND OF SUPPORT FOR THE PURPOSE OF THEIR ENTERPRISE.

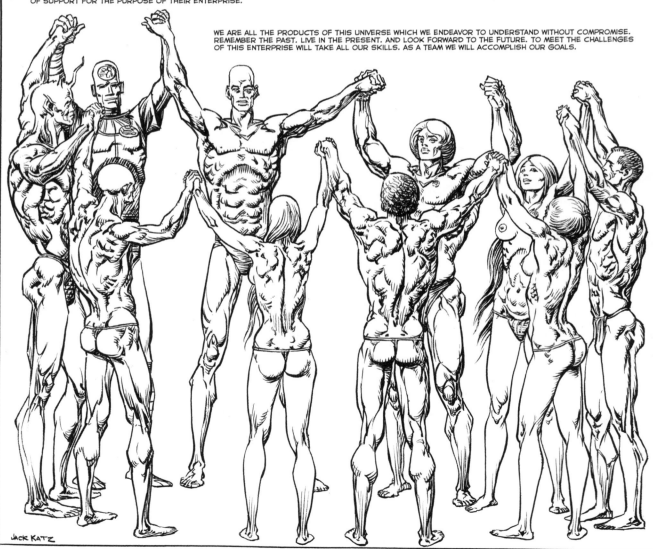

WE ARE ALL THE PRODUCTS OF THIS UNIVERSE WHICH WE ENDEAVOR TO UNDERSTAND WITHOUT COMPROMISE. REMEMBER THE PAST. LIVE IN THE PRESENT. AND LOOK FORWARD TO THE FUTURE. TO MEET THE CHALLENGES OF THIS ENTERPRISE WILL TAKE ALL OUR SKILLS. AS A TEAM WE WILL ACCOMPLISH OUR GOALS.

JACK KATZ

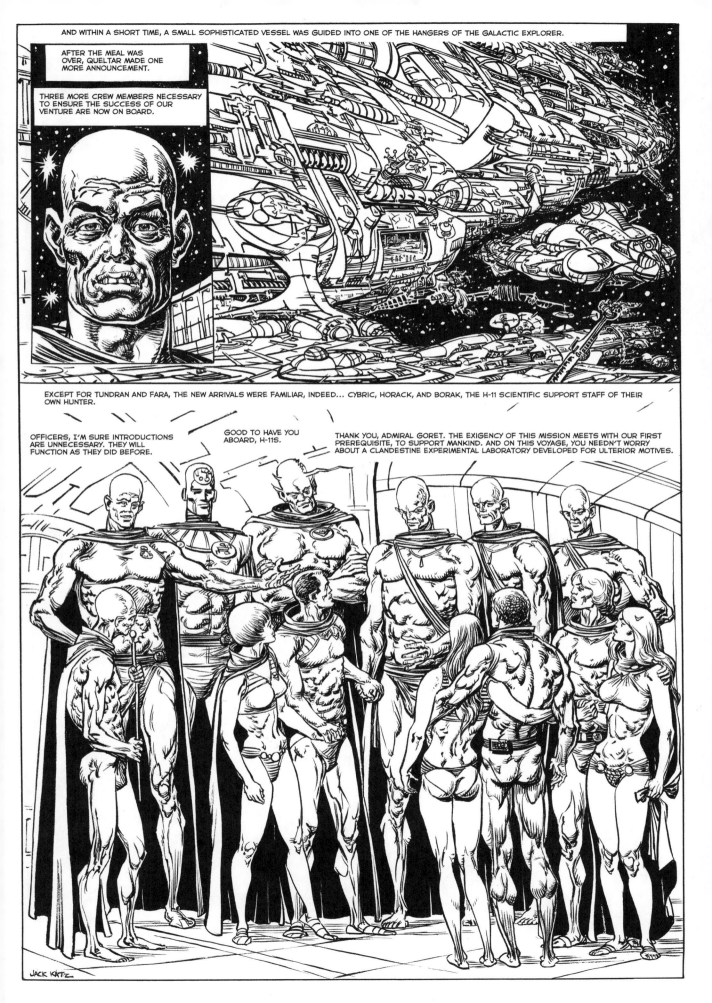

AND WITHIN A SHORT TIME, A SMALL SOPHISTICATED VESSEL WAS GUIDED INTO ONE OF THE HANGERS OF THE GALACTIC EXPLORER.

AFTER THE MEAL WAS OVER, QUELTAR MADE ONE MORE ANNOUNCEMENT.

THREE MORE CREW MEMBERS NECESSARY TO ENSURE THE SUCCESS OF OUR VENTURE ARE NOW ON BOARD.

EXCEPT FOR TUNDRAN AND FARA, THE NEW ARRIVALS WERE FAMILIAR, INDEED... CYBRIC, HORACK, AND BORAK, THE H-11 SCIENTIFIC SUPPORT STAFF OF THEIR OWN HUNTER.

OFFICERS, I'M SURE INTRODUCTIONS ARE UNNECESSARY. THEY WILL FUNCTION AS THEY DID BEFORE.

GOOD TO HAVE YOU ABOARD, H-11S.

THANK YOU, ADMIRAL GORET. THE EXIGENCY OF THIS MISSION MEETS WITH OUR FIRST PREREQUISITE, TO SUPPORT MANKIND. AND ON THIS VOYAGE, YOU NEEDN'T WORRY ABOUT A CLANDESTINE EXPERIMENTAL LABORATORY DEVELOPED FOR ULTERIOR MOTIVES.

JACK KATZ

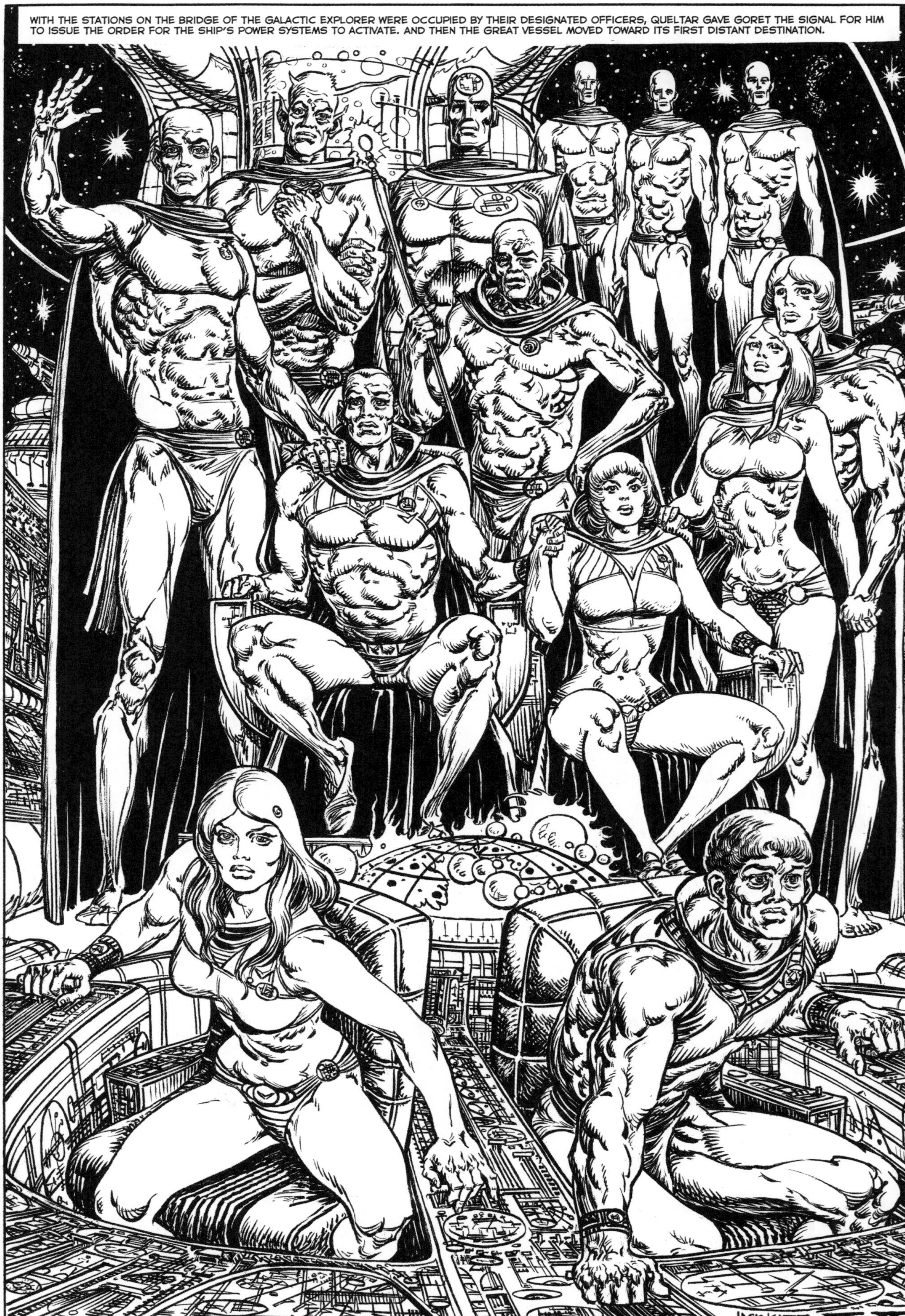
WITH THE STATIONS ON THE BRIDGE OF THE GALACTIC EXPLORER WERE OCCUPIED BY THEIR DESIGNATED OFFICERS, QUELTAR GAVE GORET THE SIGNAL FOR HIM TO ISSUE THE ORDER FOR THE SHIP'S POWER SYSTEMS TO ACTIVATE. AND THEN THE GREAT VESSEL MOVED TOWARD ITS FIRST DISTANT DESTINATION.
JACK KATZ

THE BEGINNING...

THE FIRST KINGDOM
A GLOSSARY

CARADOC

AMPREON: Manifestation with wings, sent to Tamra by the Gods of Helleas Voran

CARADOC: Large beast lizard of the plains

CARNGLIDES: Mutated reptile-like beast

COALTAGS: The hunting tribe of the Plain of Tasreeal where Darkenmoor came from.

CONDORUM: Nadan's citadel, in a high tower on Tamra.

CORAKNOT: Swamp monster that Darkenmoor kills with a spear in the swamp of Indregan.

GAN

CRISTALLI: Chamber of the Hydrodome temple where Adrelar's body is purified before being taken to Deuvean Parganna.

DAVOREEN: The group of islands where Selowan was exiled.

ERETZ: Equivalent of two ounces of gold.

FARA: The sun.

GALACTIC HUNTER: Spaceship specifically built to try to intervene whenever a race threatens the stability of a galaxy because of the sophistication of its weapons.

GAN: City, city-state or country.

GANANOID: Largest reptile of the plains, which Darkenmoor destroys by fire.

GANMAR: Queen.

GANMOOR: King.

GODDESS OF THE SUN: Adoniede, Omrock Oram's wife, whose body metamorphosed into the protective wall of Hyademeya at the destruction of Oram Van.

H-11: The ultimate of efficient cyborgs; incapable of error.

HELLEAS VORAN: The high towers behind the Mountains of Loomeas where the Gods reside.

HIEROLITHS: High priests and priestesses of Oram Van.

HIEROPHANTS: High priests and priestesses of Helleas Voran.

HOLOGLIDES: Flying reptiles used by the Sky Huntsmen.

HORNADON: Guardian of Indregan.

HYADEMEYA: Where Oram Van once stood.

HYDRODOME: The temple where fallen Gods are taken to be prepared for Deuvean Pargamma.

IGON: Tribe of cannibal living in Indregan.

INDREGAN: The swamp region where the dethroned God, Laxton (Nadan's father), rules with his daughter Skyree.

KEN: Empire.

KENMAR: Empress.

KENMOOR: Emperor.

LAW OF SYNTRYON: The transferring of the spirit of a God to an unborn mortal.

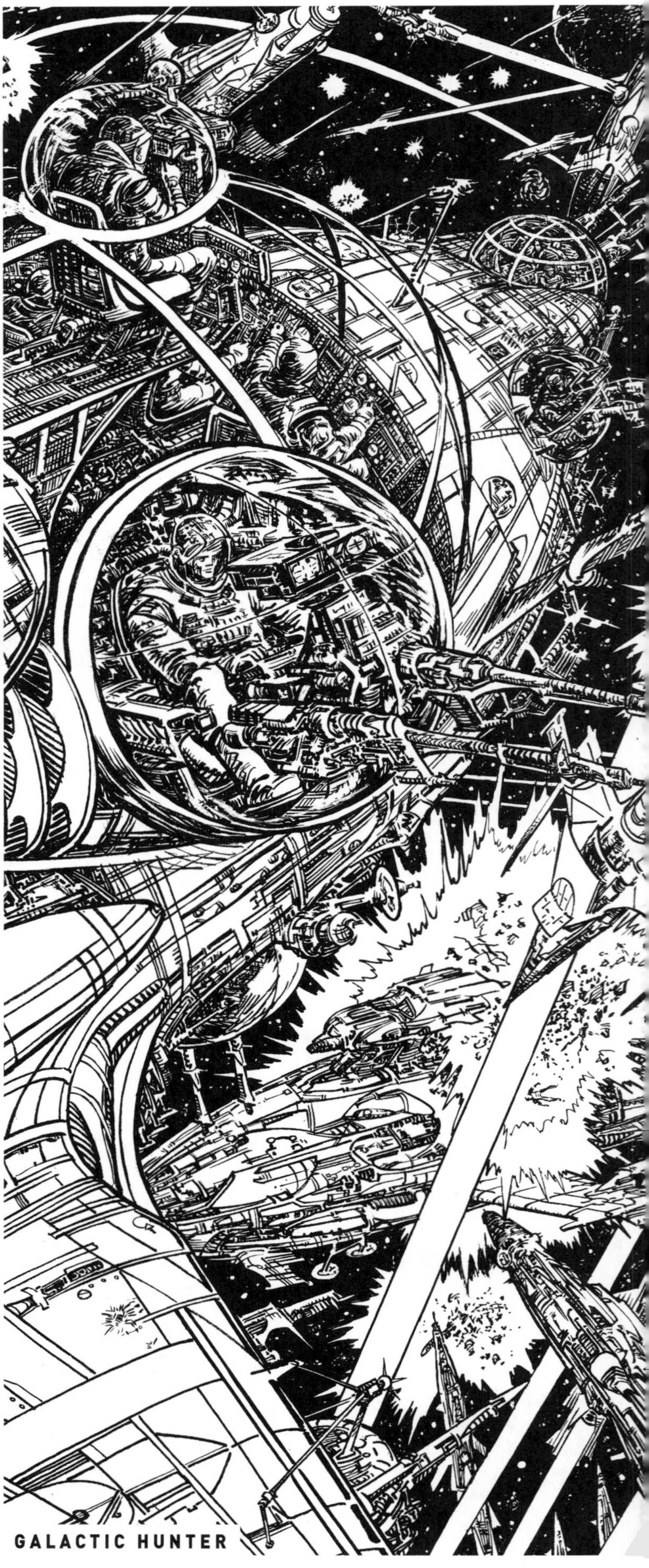

GALACTIC HUNTER

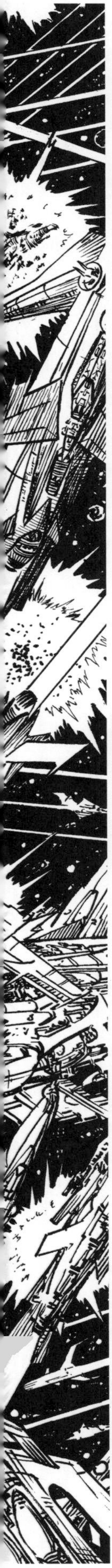

LAW OF UNION: A law of Helleas Voran that forbids the mating of a mortal with a God.

MAGNIVODS: Creature with wings and the body of a man, the head of a beast, and the hands and feet of a lizard.

MERETS: The variety of mutant that abound on Tamra.

MOORENGAN: The First Kingdom, where Drakenmoor is Kenmoor.

MOUNTAINS 0F LOOMEAS: The ranges of mountains beneath the towers of Helleas Voran.

NORCAINGIER: The Evil Kingdom, whose people worship the God Norcaine, the personification of cruelty and brutality.

NOYDE: Crown.

OCEARS: A group of people with scale helmets, who capture Darkenmoor and take him to their ships across the sea of Eivrean.

OGREON: Hunter of man; a giant carnivore.

OMNIHORN: Horn of immortality on the heads of the Gods of Helleas Voran.

OMNI-STONE: The power life stone of Oram Van, derived from the ADIEAUM monolith.

ORAM VAN: The forbidden area; was once the kingdom of Omrock Oram and the Truegods.

ORCIDES: The robot-like assistants of ADIEAUM, Creator of the Gods.

ORDIAM ARENA: Where the tournaments of Helleas Voran are held.

PARGANNA BOAT: Used to take the fallen Gods to Deuvean Parganna.

PLAIN OF TASREEL: The grassy plain where Darkenmoor killed the gananoid and acquired his band of followers.

QUINNITZ: High priests of Norcaingier.

REPTA SAPIENS: Horned, two-legged, violent creatures with short tails that attack Darkenmoor's tribe.

SEA OF EIVREAN: The sea beyond the towers of Helleas Voran, bordering the land of Moorengan.

SKY HUNTSMEN: Tribe of people who ride huge flying reptile called hologlides. Darkenmoor becomes their leader.

TAMRA: The earth after the Cataclysm.

TANGRINS: Chips of bone or sticks, used as in the tossing of coins.

TRANSGODS: Gods with lesser power, coming after the Truegods.

TRUEGODS: Gods with ultimate power, who were the first Gods.

VORANMOOR: The Temple of Moorengan.

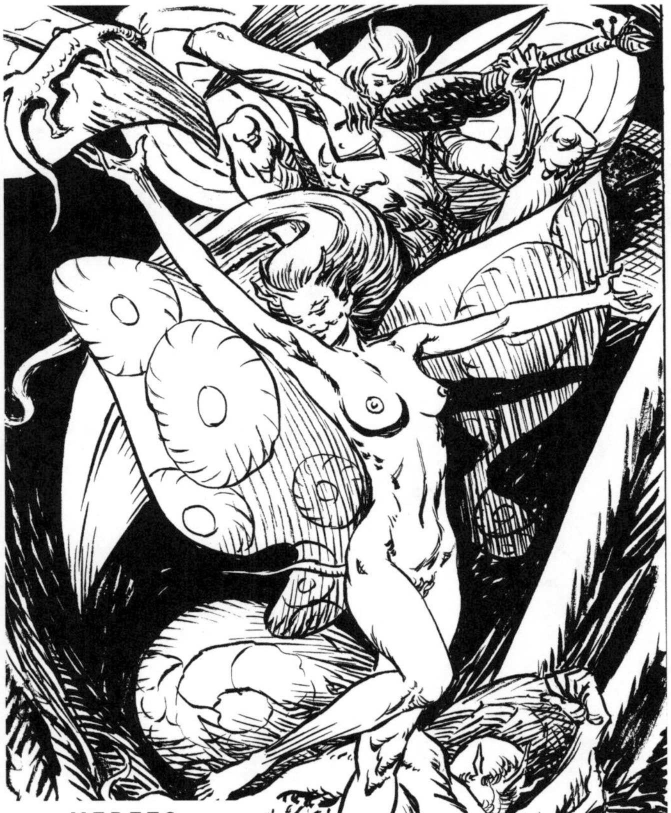

MERETS

SKETCH-BOOK

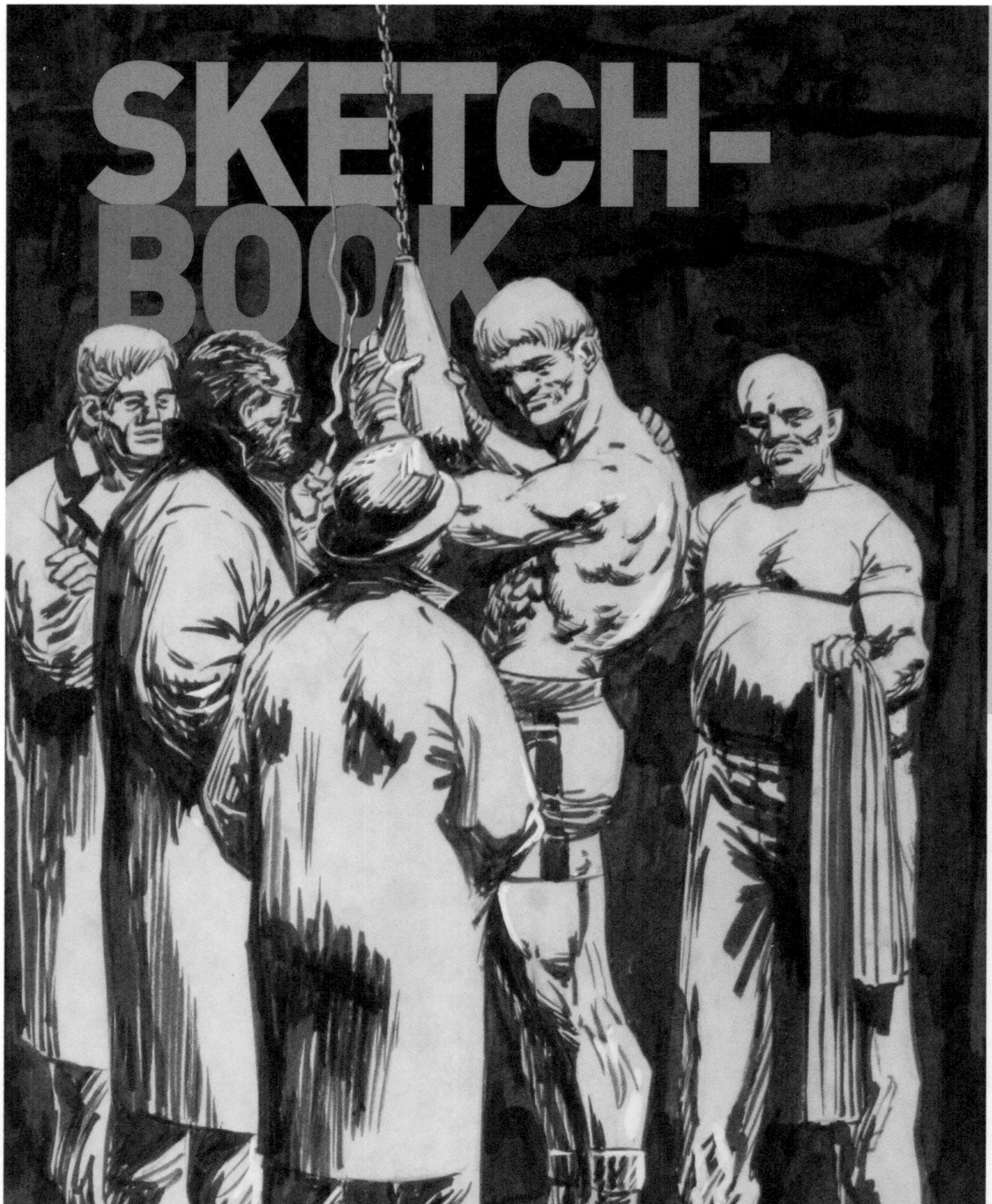

JACK KATZ

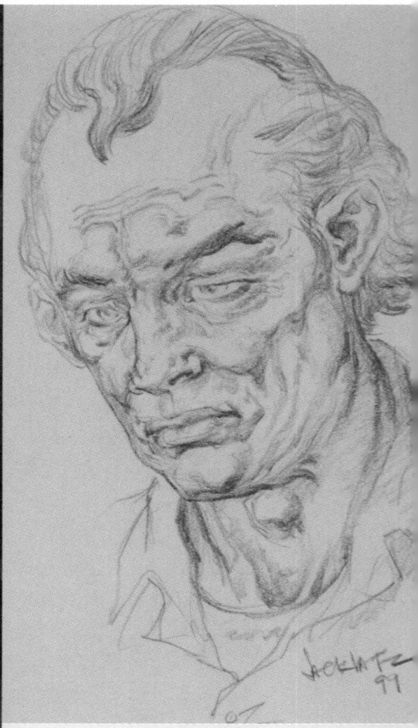

JACK KATZ 99

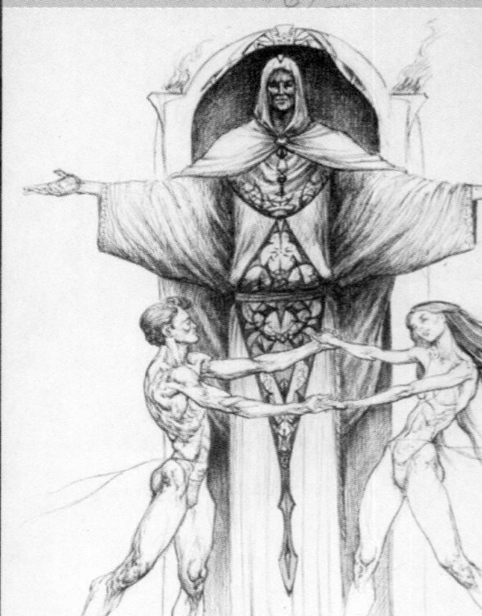

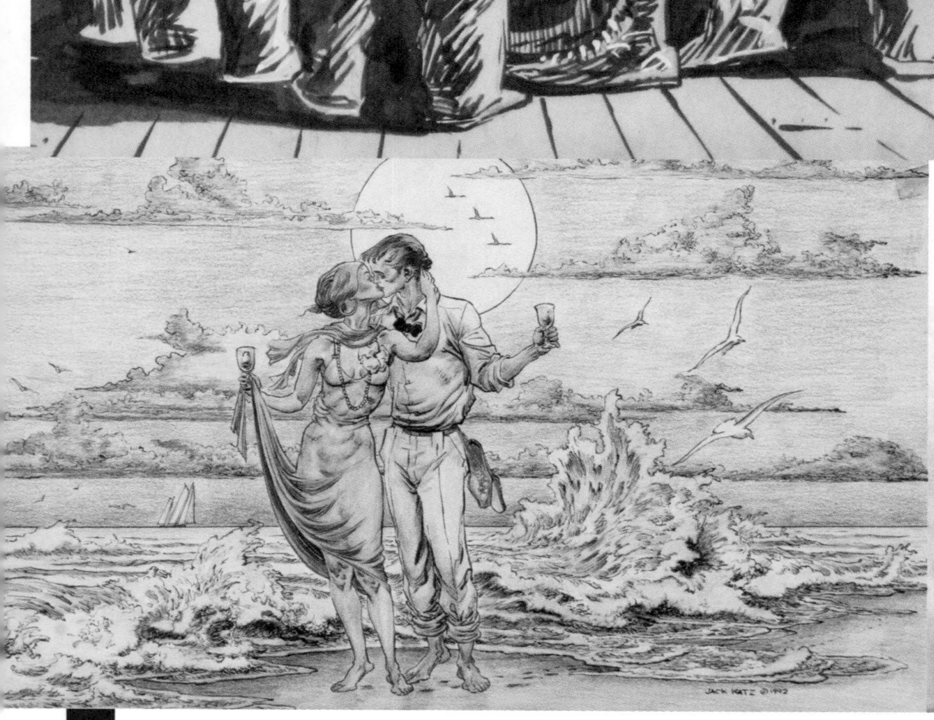

JACK KATZ ©1992

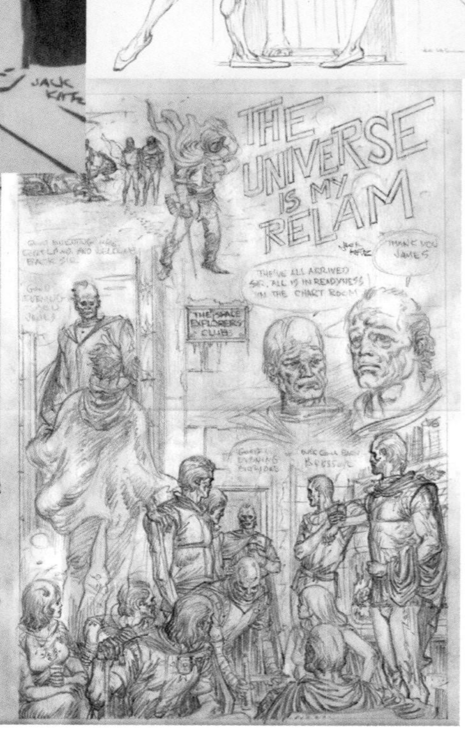

THE UNIVERSE IS MY RELAM
THANK YOU JAMES